Olympic Aspirations

Olympic Aspirations: Realised and Unrealised surveys more than a century of the Olympic Movement's promotion of Olympic ideals internationally. The idea for *Olympic Aspirations* emerged at the world-renowned annual Beijing Academic Forum just months after the city hosted the impressive 2008 Beijing Olympic Games. One section of the Forum was devoted to the impact of the Olympic Movement on China and on China's image in the world. The tone at times was too self-congratulatory for some present. The critical discussion that continued into late 2010 inspired this book.

Olympic Aspirations is a companion volume to the well-received *Olympic Legacies: Intended and Unintended* and draws on expertise from academics in all parts of the world. Both volumes have a similar purpose: to record Olympic ideals achieved but more importantly, to stimulate reflection on those as yet unachieved. Both are constructive in approach, positive in tone and optimistic in attitude. *Olympic Aspirations* offers original and insightful arguments that address the actions the Olympic Movement has taken to improve the Games. It argues that these actions are as yet incomplete. In concert with *Olympic Legacies*, it presents two sides of the same coin minted to advance the purity of the Olympic 'coinage'.

This book was originally published as a special issue of the *International Journal of the History of Sport*.

J.A. Mangan is Emeritus Professor, University of Strathclyde, UK, FRHS, FRAI, D. Litt.(Durham) and Founding Editor of the *International Journal of the History of Sport* and the book series *Sport in the Global Society*. He is editor of *Beijing 2008: Preparing for Glory, Chinese Challenge in the 'Chinese' Century* (with Dong Jinxia) and *Post-Beijing 2008: Geopolitics, Sport and the Pacific Rim* (with Fan Hong) and other publications on the Olympics published by Routledge.

Mark Dyreson is Professor of Kinesiology and History at the Pennsylvania State University, USA, a former president of the North American Society for Sport History, and the author of several books on the history of sport including *Crafting Patriotism for Global Domination: America at the Olympics.*

Olympic Aspirations
Realised and Unrealised

Edited by
J.A. Mangan and Mark Dyreson

Routledge
Taylor & Francis Group

LONDON AND NEW YORK

First published 2012
by Routledge
2 Park Square, Milton Park, Abingdon, Oxfordshire OX14 4RN

Simultaneously published in the USA and Canada
by Routledge
711 Third Avenue, New York, NY 10017

First issued in paperback 2014

Routledge is an imprint of the Taylor and Francis Group, an informa business

© 2012 Taylor & Francis

This book is a reproduction of the *International Journal of the History of Sport*, vol. 27, issue 16-18. The Publisher requests to those authors who may be citing this book to state, also, the bibliographical details of the special issue on which the book was based.

Trademark notice: Product or corporate names may be trademarks or registered trademarks, and are used only for identification and explanation without intent to infringe.

British Library Cataloguing in Publication Data
A catalogue record for this book is available from the British Library

ISBN 978-0-415-52586-2 (hbk)

ISBN 978-1-138-85366-9 (pbk)

Typeset in Times New Roman
by Taylor & Francis Books

Publisher's Note
The publisher would like to make readers aware that the chapters in this book may be referred to as articles as they are identical to the articles published in the special issue. The publisher accepts responsibility for any inconsistencies that may have arisen in the course of preparing this volume for print.

Contents

Future Aspirations

Past Aspirations

Recent Past Aspirations

Coming Aspirations

Mega-Event Global Aspirations

SERIES EDITORS' FOREWORD

On January 1, 2010 *Sport in the Global Society*, created by Professor J.A. Mangan in 1997, was divided into two parts: *Historical Perspectives* and *Contemporary Perspectives.* These new categories involve predominant rather than exclusive emphases. The past is part of the present and the present is part of the past. The Editors of *Historical Perspectives* are Mark Dyreson and Thierry Terret.

The reasons for the division are straightforward. SGS has expanded rapidly since its creation with over one hundred publications in some twelve years. Its editorial teams will now benefit from sectional specialist interests and expertise. *Historical Perspectives* draws on *International Journal of the History of Sport* monograph reviews, themed collections and conference/workshop collections. It is, of course, international in content.

Historical Perspectives continues the tradition established by the original incarnation of *Sport in the Global Society* by promoting the academic study of one of the most significant and dynamic forces in shaping the historical landscapes of human cultures. Sport spans the contemporary globe. It captivates vast audiences. It defines, alters, and reinforces identities for individuals, communities, nations, empires, and the world. Sport organises memories and perceptions, arouses passions and tensions, and reveals harmonies and cleavages. It builds and blurs social boundaries, animating discourses about class, gender, race, and ethnicity. Sport opens new vistas on the history of human cultures, intersecting with politics and economics, ideologies and theologies. It reveals aesthetic tastes and energises consumer markets.

By the end of the twentieth century a critical mass of scholars recognised the importance of sport in their analyses of human experiences and *Sport in the Global Society* emerged to provide an international outlet for the world's leading investigators of the subject. As Professor Mangan contended in the original series foreword: "The story of modern sport is the story of the modern world—in microcosm; a modern global tapestry permanently being woven. Furthermore, nationalist and imperialist, philosopher and politician, radical and conservative have all sought in sport a manifestation of national identity, status and superiority. Finally for countless millions sport is the personal pursuit of ambition, assertion, well-being and enjoyment."

Sport in the Global Society: Historical Perspectives continues the project, building on previous work in the series and excavating new terrain. It remains a consistent and coherent response to the attention the academic community demands for the serious study of sport.

Mark Dyreson
Thierry Terret

SPORT IN THE GLOBAL SOCIETY – HISTORICAL PERSPECTIVES

Series Editors: Mark Dyreson and Thierry Terret

OLYMPIC ASPIRATIONS
Realised and Unrealised

Sport in the Global Society: Historical Perspectives
Series Editors: Mark Dyreson and Thierry Terret

Titles in the Series

Sport in the Global Society
Past SGS publications prior to 2010

Africa, Football and FIFA
Politics, Colonialism and Resistance
Paul Darby

Amateurism in British Sport
'It Matters Not Who Won or Lost'
Edited by Dilwyn Porter and
Stephen Wagg

Amateurism in Sport
An Analysis and Defence
Lincoln Allison

America's Game(s)
A Critical Anthropology of Sport
Edited by Benjamin Eastman,
Sean Brown and Michael Ralph

American Sports
An Evolutionary Approach
Edited by Alan Klein

A Social History of Indian Football
Striving to Score
Kausik Bandyopadhya and
Boria Majumdar

A Social History of Swimming in
England, 1800–1918
Splashing in the Serpentine
Christopher Love

A Sport-Loving Society
Victorian and Edwardian Middle-Class
England at Play
Edited by J.A. Mangan

Athleticism in the Victorian and
Edwardian Public School
The Emergence and Consolidation of an
Educational Ideology, New Edition
J.A. Mangan

Australian Beach Cultures
The History of Sun, Sand and Surf
Douglas Booth

Barbarians, Gentlemen and Players
A Sociological Study of the
Development of Rugby Football,
Second Edition
Eric Dunning and Kenneth Sheard

Beijing 2008: Preparing for Glory
Chinese Challenge in the 'Chinese
Century'
Edited by J.A. Mangan and Dong Jinxia

Body and Mind
Sport in Europe from the Roman Empire
to the Renaissance
John McClelland

British Football and Social Exclusion
Edited by Stephen Wagg

Capoeira
The History of an Afro-Brazilian
Martial Art
Matthias Röhrig Assunção

Crafting Patriotism for Global
Dominance
America at the Olympics
Mark Dyreson

Routledge Online Studies on the Olympic and Paralympic Games Series

Routledge Online Studies on the *Olympic* and *Paralympic Games* (ROSO) is a unique learning resource, publishing scholarly and multidisciplinary research on the Games.

Aimed at academics, researchers, lecturers, students, authors, educators, athletes, coaches, journalists, Olympic and Paralympic centres, policy-makers, professionals and anyone with an interest in the Games, it aims to stimulate the production of new knowledge and facilitate dialogue and connections across disciplines.

ROSO contains over 1000 journal articles and book chapters, including handbooks and major reference works dating back to the 1960s on themes including: the media, education, gender, politics, governance, management, law, business, ethics, legacies, the environment, disability studies, athletic performance and history. ROSO's Managing Editor, Dr Vassil Girginov of Brunel University, UK, has curated the site thematically to enable users to search their areas of interest effortlessly.

Routledge has also commissioned over 40 new journal special issues across disciplines on Olympic and Paralympic Studies that will be unveiled on this innovative platform and published as books.

http://www.routledgeonlinestudies.com/

Titles in the Series

Rule Britannia: Nationalism, Identity and the Modern Olympic Games
Matthew P. Llewellyn

Olympic Aspirations
Realised and Unrealised
Edited by James A. Mangan and Mark Dyreson

Olympic Reform Ten Years Later
Edited by Heather Dichter

Encoding the Olympics
The Beijing Olympic Games and the Communication Impact Worldwide
Edited by Luo Qing and Giuseppe Richeri

The Olympic Movement and the Sport of Peacemaking
Edited by Ramón Spaaij

Olympic Ethics and Philosophy
Edited by Michael J. McNamee and Jim Parry

Prologue: Concerns, Confidence, Caveats

J. A. Mangan

Part One: Concerns

Birth in Beijing

Olympic Aspirations was born in Beijing at the world renowned annual Beijing (Academic) Forum – appropriately in 2008: the year, as the world now knows and will now remember, as the year of the impressive Beijing Olympic Games: vastly expensive, superbly coordinated, splendidly delivered – the successful product of unfettered political support and neatly summarized in significance as follows: 'The 24 months leading up to the opening ceremony were bathed in the warm glow of state controlled positivity: no one was allowed a moments doubt that it would be an absolute triumph: pessimism was banished by government edict. … Don't underestimate the value of a Great Games politically.' [1]

Pertinently one section of the forum was devoted to the Olympic movement. The tone at times was too self-congratulatory for the more objective. This stimulated discussion of Olympic aspirations both realized and unrealized. The tenor of the discussion may be gauged from *Olympic Aspirations*. However the space available in a single publication means that the matters raised can only be touched upon. [2] One point should be made emphatically clear. Where there is criticism of the Olympic movement, it is intended to be constructive to assist the movement in the decades ahead and to help it move closer to the realization of its ideals. *Olympic Legacies: Intended and Unintended*, a companion *International Journal of the History of Sport (IJHS)/Sport in the Global Society* (SGS) publication had a similar purpose with a different approach. Of course, there are, in addition, a good number of other publications of value dealing with the same or similar issues. It is reiterated that this volume, *Olympic Aspirations*, is a contribution to Olympic studies that is intended to record some of the movement's aspirations achieved but also to stimulate the movement's reflection on aspirations as yet unachieved. In conclusion, two reflections:

[is] there a need for the IOC to take on stronger, longer commitment to ensuring that post-Olympic legacies do not tarnish the unquestionable shining, indeed golden, achievements of other aspects of a sports event that, whatever its shortcomings ... brings pleasure, exhilaration and joy to billions? It would be a matter of some regret if the IOC was cast in the role of Tantalus. [3]

For 'legacies' above read 'aspirations'

And:

'Life is a petty thing unless it is moved by the indomitable urge to extend its boundaries.' [4]

Part Two: Confidence

London 2012: Optimism

This short extract holds out an almost celestial prospect for London 2012:

> the island of dreams [The London Olympic Games site] offers the promise of extraordinary experiences. A piece of appallingly polluted, sewage-riddled, semi-derelict land is being transformed into a magical place, full of noble, if sometimes flawed, ideals ... in comparison with the buildings and facilities most towns and cities in Britain enjoy, every project on Olympic Island seems dreamingly glamorous. Every structure here seems as aspirational and representative of a largesse and confidence only possible in a pre-recessionary age – a time when the whole project was conceived and commissioned. So should you book your train tickets and go in 2012? Of course you should. In a post-recession age of hand-wringing and lip-chewing self-analysis, such confident statements seem other-worldly, as if made by different people in a different place, which is exactly what happened. It was even a different government. This genesis affords the Olympic Park an almost overwhelming majesty and ambition. There's a hint that the place will demand standards of excellence in our sports that our athletes have yet to rise to, but there's also a hint of awe-inspiring architecture that we can all rise to. In a new decade of austerity and gloom, there are moments of rare, aching beauty that even Walt Disney would have found difficult to emulate. [5]

The complete article, while at times euphorically sanguine, overall is thoughtfully balanced in approach, although the reference to Walt Disney will both amuse and bemuse some.

Part Three: Caveats

London 2012: Caution

In the 'Health and Socioeconomic Impact of Major Multi-sports Events: Systematic Review (1978–2008)', [6] a measured review of 'sources without restrictions for papers published between 1978 and 2008 – Applied Social Science Index and abstracts

(ASSIA), British Humanities Index (BH). Cochrane database of systematic reviews, Econlit database, Embace, Education Resources Information Center (ERIC) database, Health Management Information Consortium (HMIC) database, International Bibliography of the Social Sciences (IBSS), Medicine, PreMedline, PsycINFO, Sociological Abstracts, Sportdiscus, Web of Knowledge, Worldwide Political Science Abstracts, and the grey literature' [7] – Dr Gerry McCartney and a group of colleagues [8] assessed 'the effects of major multi-sports events on health and socioeconomic determinants of health in the population of the city hosting the event'. [9] The review team remarked in its introduction that a major consideration in the bids for both London 2012 (the Olympics) and Glasgow 2014 (the Commonwealth Games) was the alleged, indeed assumed, potential for these games to generate a wide variety of benefits for the populations of the respective host cities. Collectively referred to as 'legacies' covering improvement in employment levels, the economy, housing, the environment, sports provision and national and local pride, key socioeconomic determinants of health, thus establishing the belief that such investments had the potential to improve health. [10] Indeed, as the review team made clear,

> Detailed outcomes of such an influence associated with these legacies were set out in two respective official assessments. In the case of the London Olympics and Paralympic Games in the Department of Health's 'review of the political physical activity and health legacy', and in the case of Commonwealth Games of 2014 in a legacy consultation document issued by the Scottish Government. [11]

Interestingly, the review team pointed out that both the cost and the likely benefits arising from the London Olympic Games have subsequently been reassessed by the then minister responsible for the initial costing, Tessa Jowell. 'Had we known what we know now,' she has declared, 'would we have bid for the Olympics? Almost certainly not.' [12] Doubtless she was referring in part if not in whole to the soaring costs of the games. Her reassessment was equally sensible with regard to the assumed health benefits, given that the review team came to the unequivocal conclusion that while

> a large amount of research on the impact of major sports events on host populations is available ... this body of research has not been systematically brought together to allow decision makers to make informed judgments on the basis of the known effects and the known areas of uncertainty. The aim of this systematic review was to assess the impact of major sporting events (1978–2008) on the health, and the determinants of health, of the host population. [13]

The review team set down an impressive comprehensive list of criteria for the inclusion of available studies and selection and assessments of their quality, together with data extraction and data synthesis and clear outcomes of review methods:

> *Review methods.* Studies of any design that assessed the health and socioeconomic impact of major multi-sport events on the host population were included. We excluded studies that used exclusively estimated data rather than actual data, that

investigated host population support for an event or media portrayals of host cities, or that described new physical infrastructure. Studies were selected and critically appraised by two independent reviewers. [14]

And the results of the review methods:

Fifty four studies were included. Study quality was poor with 69% of studies using a repeat cross-sectional design and 85% of quantitative studies assessed as being below 2+ on the Health Development Agency appraisal scale, often because of a lack of comparison group. Five studies, each with a high risk of bias, reported health related outcomes, which were suicide, paediatric health service demand, presentations for asthma in children (two studies), and problems related to illicit drug use. Overall, the data did not indicate clear negative or positive health impacts of major multi-sports events on host populations. The most frequently reported outcomes were economic (18 studies). The outcomes used were similar enough to allow us to perform a narrative synthesis, but the overall impact of major multi-sports events on economic growth and employment was unclear. Two-thirds of the economic studies reported increased economic growth or employment immediately after the event, but all these studies used some estimated data in their models, failed to account for opportunity costs, or examined only short term effects. Outcomes for transport were also similar enough to allow synthesis of six of the eight studies, which showed that event related interventions – including restricted car use and public transport promotion – were associated with significant short term reductions in traffic volume, congestion, or pollution in four out of the five cities. [15]

In their discussion, the review team observed that 'there was little evidence that major multi-sports events held between 1978 and 2008 delivered health or socioeconomic benefits for the populations in the host countries' [16] and while 'the available evidence did not refute expectations of a legacy, positive or negative, ... it does establish that very little is known about the impacts of previous large multi-sports events, and therefore, the possible impact of future events'. [17] This finding contrasts starkly 'with official documentation used recently to promote such events'. [18] The review team conceded that the *potential* impacts of their major events are many, embracing changes in health and many social determinants of health but in their inquiry, 'no particular impact had a consistent pattern on outcomes across different events, nor was there evidence of positive impact across a range of options in a single event'. [19] It added, seemingly reprovingly, that various 'opinion articles have suggested other impacts for which we could find no evidence, including commonly regeneration, gentrification and rising inequalities', [20] adding critically that 'these outcomes are not well recorded' [21] and thus no conclusion could be drawn from their review of the material available about whether 'such outcomes are likely to be associated with future events'. [22] The team added further for good measure that with the evidence available varying for events and shifting investigative emphasis, a further limitation on the ability 'to relate the impact of earlier events to contemporary events was [thus] due to the nature of the expected impact appearing to change'. [23] Finally, the review team observed that 'the cost of hosting major multi-sport events such as the Olympic Games and the

Commonwealth Games has increased to such an extent that 'it has become difficult to justify the expenditure on the basis of entertainment or national showcasing alone'. [24] Thus the emphasis regarding returns has become 'the prospect of the generation of a long term positive legacy'. [25] Their summary was starkly succinct:

> **Conclusions** The available evidence is not sufficient to confirm or refute expectations about the health or socioeconomic benefits for the host population of previous major multi-sport events. Future events such as the 2012 Olympic Games and Paralympic Games, or the 2014 Commonwealth Games, cannot be expected to automatically provide benefits. Until decision makers include robust, long term evaluations as part of their design and implementation of events, it is unclear how the costs of major multi-sport events can be justified in terms of benefits to the host population. [26]

And their recommendations are worth quoting in full:

> **Policy implications** Decision makers should consider taking a different approach to the implementation of future events if the cost is to be justified by benefits to the population of the host country. Such approaches might include increasing democratic control of event related spending (for example, channelling funding through existing elected bodies), recasting the events as less costly and simpler sports events, or using impact assessment approaches to optimize the effects of the event 'intervention'.
>
> Knowledge of the impacts of major multi-sport events might improve if evaluations of future events are based on a framework that details a 'theory of change' for the event. Improved reporting of evaluations, use of suitable contemporaneous comparison groups (ideally within longitudinal studies), and inclusion of long term outcomes would all be likely to increase the quality of future evidence. Economic studies in particular would be improved if they used real time data instead of estimates and incorporated opportunity costs in their models. [27]

Is it possible this cautionary inquiry was for some unknown reason or reasons anticipated by Tessa Jowell when she made her volte face mentioned earlier? Did the then Minister for the Olympics have an early premonition that occasioned her *volte face*?

Acknowledgement

Profound thanks are expressed to Professor Dong Jinxia of Peking University who provided the initial stimulus for *Olympic Aspirations* through her inspirational organisation of the Olympics section of the 2008 Beijing Forum to which a number of the contributors to *Olympic Aspirations* were invited.

Notes

[1] Jim White, *Daily Telegraph* (London), 14 July 12010, 23.
[2] Contributions are included in *Olympic Aspirations* that were not presented in Beijing, to add depth and breadth.

[3] Mangan and Dyreson, *Olympic Legacies*, 17.

[4] Jose Ortega y Gasset, in Tripp, *International Thesaurus of Quotations*, 56.

[5] Kevin McCloud, 'Island of Dreams', *Daily Telegraph Weekend Magazine*, 17 July 2010, 29 and 30.

[6] Published in the *British Medical Journal*, 23 May 2010. Consideration of the full inquiry is strongly recommended.

[7] McCartney *et al.*, 'Systematic Review', 1.

[8] The members of the review team were Gerry McCartney, specialist registrar in public health (Medical Research Council Social and Public Health Sciences Unit, Glasgow); Sian Thomas, systematic reviewer (Sandside, Isle of Graemsay, Stromness, Orkney); Hilary Thomson, senior investigator scientist, Medical Research Council Social and Public Health Sciences Unit, Glasgow; John Scott, public health librarian, Public Health Resources Unit, NHS Greater Glasgow and Clyde, Glasgow; Val Hamilton, freelance information scientist (VRH Information Services, Aundorach House, Nethy Bridge, Highlands); Phil Hanlon, professor of public health (Section of Public Health and Health Policy, University of Glasgow); David S Morrison, clinical senior lecturer in cancer epidemiology and director, West of Scotland Cancer Surveillance Unit, University of Glasgow; and Lyndal Bond, professor and associate director, Medical Research Council Social and Public Health Sciences Unit, Glasgow.

[9] McCartney *et al.*, 'Systematic Review', 1.

[10] Ibid., 2.

[11] Ibid.

[12] Ibid.

[13] Ibid.

[14] Ibid.

[15] Ibid., 12.

[16] Ibid., 8.

[17] Ibid., 3.

[18] Ibid., 8.

[19] Ibid.

[20] Ibid., 9.

[21] Ibid.

[22] Ibid.

[23] Ibid., 9–16.

[24] Ibid., 10.

[25] Ibid., 9.

[26] Ibid.

[27] Ibid.

References

Mangan, J.A. and Mark Dyreson. *Olympic Legacies: Intended and Unintended – Political, Cultural, Economic and Educational*. London: Routledge, 2010.

McCartney, Gerry, Hilary Thomson, Val Hamilton, Phil Hanlon, David S Morrison and Lyndal Bond. 'Health and Socioeconomic Impact of Major Multi-sports Events: Systematic Review (1978–2008)'. *British Medical Journal* (20 May 2010): 1–8.

Tripp, Rhoda Thomas. *The International Thesaurus of Quotations*. New York: Thomas Y. Crowell, 1970.

Olympic Challenges

Helmut Digel

The Chinese hosts are not the only people who see the Olympic Games in Beijing as a great success. All active participants experienced the games as unique in many different respects; and apart from a few exceptions they received great appreciation from the participating nations. It is also very significant that the games obviously have had a lasting impact on Chinese society. This becomes evident not only in the infrastructural achievements but first and foremost in the opening up of Chinese society, a process that has been greatly accelerated by the Olympic Games. Changing the perspective and viewing the Chinese games from the angle of the IOC, however, might produce a somewhat different verdict, which could be summed up in the following statement: disaster was close for the IOC – they just made it. The Olympic movement has long been confronted with problems which are frequently not recognized and the solutions to which are, for the most part, not yet in sight. Necessary processes of change are put off again and again. Possible solutions are not vehemently pursued. Some of these problems prove to be of such complexity that – it must be admitted in all fairness – the search for solutions will still be extremely difficult in the future. If we also want Olympic Games to be successful in the future however, these problems need to be openly addressed and discussed and it must be recognized that we are on the way to suitable solutions. In the following, selected problems and challenges will be outlined, as they have become evident during the games in Beijing and afterwards.

The Politicization of the Games

The political character of the Olympic Games became apparent in ancient Greece. With the renewed foundation of the games in 1896 the political character of the event became, in fact, their programme. The objective of fulfilling a peace-enhancing function is appropriate for modern Olympism but the other objectives, as they are laid down in the Olympic Charter, also have a political dimension in a wider sense. Therefore it is not surprising that the Olympic movement is in a constantly changing relationship with the world's political systems. For this reason it is difficult to understand that the International Olympic Committee (IOC) and some of its most important officials are still pursuing the unacceptable ideology of 'non-political sport' and consequently enter into dialogue with political powers rather more passively than actively. The problems arising from such an approach were never more evident than in the time leading up to the Olympic Games in Beijing. For the IOC's part, the discussions about the conflict in Tibet were neither characterized by political awareness nor could any willingness to play a part in addressing such problems be recognized. To some extent this may be based on a lack of experience, on prejudice and insufficient specific competence on the part of leading IOC officials and to some extent also on a lack of awareness of their own duties and objectives. However, it is also apparent that some IOC officials are directly dependent on different political systems. However, it is a matter of fact that the political character of the games is a specific feature of Olympism, which requires competence and care.

The concept of peace during the Olympic Games is awaiting fundamental renewal. While in the past it was both possible and likely to interrupt or stop all wars during the time of the Olympic Games, we have to recognize today that Olympic Games are held and wars occur at the same time, with the warring parties not questioning in the slightest their right to participate in the games. It is therefore necessary to ask the whether the Olympic Games should be cancelled in the event of war at the time in question. As a matter of principle this question needs to be discussed anew.

At the same time there may well be also inappropriate types of politicization or political influence regarding the games. This been evident for some time and in this respect the IOC would be well advised to implement rules for future games that create the necessary distance between the IOC and political systems. Some people within the IOC have rightly pointed out that the presence of political representatives at the games or at the opening ceremony is by no means relevant for the success of a particular Olympic Games. Any attempts to curry favour with political systems has to be a taboo for the IOC and in this context the issue of privileges being granted to politicians visiting the Olympic Games also has to be addressed. The fact that issues of protocol are becoming more important during Olympic Games should lead to a fundamental assessment of the participation of political guests and visitors. The presence of several royal families in Beijing may serve as a positive example, as they humbly joined the ranks of normal visitors; declining all status privileges. Less ideal examples are those ministers and secretaries of various governments who believe that their entire 'entourage' has to be present and at their disposal while visiting a swimming competition or basketball game. If – because a nation's president needs to be put in the limelight for TV – whole seating arrangements in parts of a stadium have to be changed, sports associations will have to be strong enough reject such demands.

Olympic Sports Programme

Each Olympic summer sport assumes a particular quality. Each of the 28 Olympic sports has its own history, with some having undergone interesting processes of change. Some may boast 'heroic achievements and performances' that are remembered beyond their times. Nevertheless, the structures of some of these sports have been fractured in several respects. Each sport should undergo a test to see whether or not it meets the standards required for membership of the Olympic movement. If it can do so, it should continue to belong to the Olympic family.

Already in Atlanta, more so in Sydney or Athens, but especially in Beijing, it became apparent that only few Olympic sports are really 'global' sports. They are practised in only a few regions and in some significant cultural spheres they are hardly known at all. Additionally, the way in which they are presented during the games generates only limited spectator interest. In this context not only traditional Olympic sports such as modern pentathlon need to be critically reviewed, but also supposedly 'modern' and 'young' sports have not passed the test either.

The mountain bike competition in Beijing for example, took place virtually without any public attendance; the race itself could only, if at all, be followed on TV and for spectators at the course it was obviously not interesting. To some extent this is the fault of an inadequate presentation of these sports. Particularly during the Olympic Games, large numbers of spectators without any specific sports-related knowledge are present, with the result that some competitions suffered from a total lack of atmosphere. Only a few sports were in a position to attract a sufficient number of spectators on all competition days. This was achieved by athletics and swimming. In the team sports and almost all others, especially during qualification rounds, the competing teams and their own groups of spectators were present in the arenas but hardly anybody else. There were large gaps with no spectators in the stadiums, which surprisingly, was the case for sports that can rightly be called 'Asian'.

The question of which sports are to be represented at the Olympic Games in the future requires a fair assessment of the current ones as well as an adequate evaluation of those that are possible candidates. In this respect it will be of particular significance if the best athletes will actually compete in these sports. The evident problem concerning the men's football/soccer tournament demands fundamental clarification. The currently existing compromise will not work in the long term, and it would be better to do without the tournament. In another sense the question of the future of Olympic professional sports is hardly relevant at all. The increasing trend towards semi-professionalism or professionalism can only lead to the conclusion that every attractive sport can gain access to the Olympic Games if the sport meets Olympic requirements and its association is willing to adhere to the Olympic rules. Therefore, rugby and golf need to be given their opportunity as well as the different roller or inline skate sports and the martial arts. A further increase of the total programme, however, is by no means an option. Consequently the focus must be on comprehensible and fair evaluation criteria for the selection of Olympic sports.

Olympic Cultural Programme

If the Olympic Games, on the basis of their own Olympic ideal, really claim to be something very special in comparison with world championships, the Olympic cultural programme is indeed of extraordinary importance. In Beijing the cultural programme included all the important areas from the fine arts to literature and from drama to music, with science also being adequately represented. There were numerous events prior to and during the Olympics with cultural events organized in many locations throughout the metropolis. After the games interested visitors were offered an 'after the games programme'. There was, however no obvious connection between the cultural programme and the Olympic Games.

As the sports event schedule contains far too many events, with some days having competitions in more than nine different, simultaneously scheduled, sports, then the Olympic Games are no longer manageable in terms of time if such a comprehensive cultural programme has to be held within the sports event programme. The consequences are readily apparent. The athletes, who should be the focus of attention, are poorly informed about these events and cannot participate in them. The Olympic family is busy dealing with sport events and takes part in the cultural events only in exceptional cases. All other international visitors are so exhausted after watching sports events and visiting tourist attractions that they are not motivated to attend the Olympic cultural programme.

What is more, and what also annoys the hosts, is the fact that it has become common for those nations considering themselves important to meet in their own 'national' houses night after night. 'Casa Italia', 'German House', 'Russian Club', 'Canadian Forum' (or similar) are the names of the meeting places where Germans meet other Germans, praising and boasting their own 'culture', drinking German beer and eating Bavarian sausages or roast pork legs with sauerkraut. Such meetings and those of other national groups can hardly be called intercultural meetings. Night after night the focus is on 'see and be seen' for the really important and the 'wannabe' stars in the respective nations. For this reason an entrance ticket to the German House (or suchlike) has become a very desirable commodity. The slowly but ever-expanding islands in a foreign world contradict starkly the ideas and ideals of Olympism as an international idea.

Beijing as a Special Case

The decision to allocate the Olympic Games to Beijing was both adequate and pioneering at the time it was made. From a post-Olympics perspective this decision has proven to be prudent and responsible. The IOC has rightly opened the door to the Olympic community for the biggest nation, which, at the same time, has the longest cultural traditions, and the National Olympic Committee of China has passed the test with excellence. The unquestionable success of the Beijing games, however, also bears considerable risks, possibly followed by undesirable consequences. This needs to be kept under control as much as possible. The games in Beijing can be neither measure nor model. They are an extraordinary exception, rather than a blueprint for imitation. If the IOC wants to keep the Olympic Games open for the world, then smaller nations must also be in a position to host them in the future. The members of the Olympic movement must therefore be made to recognize that any host of the Olympic Games needs to develop its own identity and that the hosting of a games in a country with 20 million people should be just as possible as in the USA, China, Russia or India.

Neither must the architecture of sports facilities be measured against China. There is no justification whatsoever for an almost completely new construction of sports facilities simply for the purpose of hosting the Olympic Games. The modernization pressure particularly evident in China cannot be the perspective from which future Olympics are planned. Taking sustainability as the measure, this can be clearly achieved much more easily and less problematically in a country with 1.3 billion people than in smaller countries such as Greece or Australia. For this reason alone the IOC is well advised to design the modelling of future Olympic Games in a 'multi-optional' manner. The games must be a house with flexible elements allowing the national hosts to live in them for a longer time afterwards.

Sustainability

In recent times there have been more and more instances of international associations allocating their world championships to cities following the principle of 'scorched earth'. In the bidding contest the associations have exploited the competition between different cities for their own profit, demanding services from the organizing city – which has ultimately led to unjustifiable financial burdens for taxpayers. Examples in the respect are the cycling world championships in Stuttgart or the athletics world championships in Osaka. So far the allocation policy of the IOC has been pleasantly different from such examples. The financial support provided for Olympic Games organizers can indeed serve as a model, and the same is true for the expert counselling in application processes, for the applications themselves and even for the related processes of decision-making. The care taken by the IOC in dealing with a city after the allocation of the games can also truly be called excellent.

Nevertheless, there is the question of sustainability with regard to future Olympic Games and in this context Beijing can hardly serve as a model. The newly-built sport facilities in Beijing will not really be a problem concerning sustainability in a country as large as the continent of Europe with a population of 1.3 billion. Their future use is largely secure, with changes of use being possible at any time. However, looking at the games in Athens or Sydney in this context makes it readily apparent that the question of sustainability will be a key question with regard to future Olympic Games. The IOC will have to address the question of multi-functional architecture and use of spaces in a completely new manner. Sports architecture will have to be seen in the context of different possibilities of use, and the partially sport-specific use of spaces and buildings can no longer have priority in allocation decisions. The size of stadia and the desired number of spectators envisaged by the organizers need to be discussed anew. Getting answers to these questions requires creative competitions with scientific experts and architects who are oriented towards sport-specific urban development questions taking part.

Unrestricted Commercialization

The commercialization of all areas of life including people's private lives can be observed in all societies everywhere in the world. Economic calculation is dominating thinking. Searching for riches and attempts to accumulate individual wealth are straining our private lives, institutions, organizations and whole national entities. For this reason it is not surprising that the phenomenon of unlimited commercialization has corrupted the Olympic movement. The praiseworthy principles of games free from commercial advertising are therefore put to the test and need to be defended with greater determination than ever. Product placement takes place already during the opening ceremony of the games, and large numbers of athletes are subject to commercialism. Violations of the rules prohibiting athletes reporting are constantly to be seen. The Olympic Games are in fact huge investment events tied to substantial economic interests.

The Olympic family itself makes an extraordinary contribution to this doubtful development. Strictly organized according to different privileges, it presents itself to the public as a very special group of people, usually dressed elegantly, driving through the Olympic city in black limousines, hectically moving from one 'privilege' to the next. One reception is chasing the previous one; loaded with gift bags the 'Olympic Family' reaches its own five-star hotel for a brief stopover to get ready for the next big event. Supreme food, wine and champagne are served on all occasions, and at the end of these strenuous days we meet a fair number of Olympic representatives buying additional suitcases in order to be able to carry home all their countless gifts.

Neither can the Olympic sports family be characterized by the ideal of equality, as it is ideologically presented in Olympic rhetoric. Quite the contrary. For some time there has been a conflict between national Olympic committees, members of the IOC and international sports associations, the last of whom regard themselves as the actual upholders of the Olympic Games. It is they who devise the Olympic sport programme, are responsible for the athletes, lay down the rules of their sport and guarantee the organization of the competitions. The Olympic family, however, consists of the national Olympic committees who nominate the Olympic teams of their respective participating nations and who therefore consider themselves entitled to privileges denied to the sport associations. Consequently they enjoy comprehensive accreditations, allowing them access to all sports, while the international sports associations and their responsible representatives are granted access only to those sports which they themselves organize. This kind of class distinction also exists in connection with hotel accommodation and transportation. So it is hardly surprising that during the games there is an ongoing envy debate, usually triggered by the close observation of accreditation symbols on the bodies of members of the Olympic family in order to figure out why who has what privileges and which of them has been made available by what connection structure.

Olympic Education

Since Pierre de Coubertin re-founded Olympism and the Olympic Games at the end of the nineteenth century, it has been one of the important and specific functions of the IOC to convey the ideals that are the foundation of the games to the members of the Olympic movement. The Olympic Academy in Greece has an important function in this respect, and national Olympic committees have been requested to share and contribute to this function with their own academies. The Olympic Museum must play a role in this, just as the globally active and successful 'Olympic Solidarity' organization. The educational programmes should primarily be oriented towards the athletes whose Olympic education needs to be enhanced and improved if Olympism is to be preserved as an effective ideology.

Looking from this perspective at the 10,500 Olympic athletes participating in the Beijing games reveals that Olympic education is, in fact, totally inefficient. Olympic education for Olympic athletes hardly takes place. This became apparent prior to the 2008 Olympic Games when discussing the question of which rules have to be valid for the Olympic Games and what political concept is the basis of Olympic Games. The statements made in response to these questions by athletes, coaches and officials were to a large extent marked by ignorance, lack of information and inexperience. Without any inhibition, the vast majority of athletes talked about their commercial interests in top performance sport with an opportunistic concept of their own participation in the games. Preparation for the games outside Beijing in professionally organized training camps, participation in the games, presentation of their success in the media, fast departure and marketing of their success – these are usually the criteria towards which medal winners are oriented. The whole process is operated and directed by managers and sponsors, and finally everything is directed towards media resonance. There is hardly any room for Olympic education or the conveyance of Olympic values and ideals. Therefore a presumably very large proportion of Olympic athletes contribute to the fact that Olympic Games increasingly acquire the character of an accumulation of world championships, hardly distinguishable from any other world championships. The educational initiatives of the IOC and its NOCs have obviously not reached them. The same is true of spectators and visitors. For many decades materials have been produced for public schools and distributed free of charge without any recognizable effects. The Beijing games have shown once more that the programme of Olympic education needs to stand the test. To continue the programme without some form of validation means wasting time and money.

For this reason a particular challenge for the Olympic movement must be to clarify what is 'Olympic' about the Olympic Games? Never before in the history of Olympism has it become so evident both before and during the games in Beijing that the ideals of Olympism are hardly known – not only among athletes but also among officials and sports journalists.

What distinguishes the Olympic Games from a football world cup, from other big events in sport or from any other part of the entertainment industry is hardly recognizable today. The constitutive features of the Olympic Games, as they are laid down in the Olympic Charter as its foundation, are at best used as a defence against attacks on the idea of Olympism. Only rarely are they an essential part of someone's life.

The Olympic Idea of the Human Being

Questioning the development of man in connection with modern Olympic athletes suggests comparing the winner of the 100m final of the 1896 Olympics with the eight finalists in Beijing. Thomas Burke, a rather slim mid-size American college student, won that first gold medal. His physiognomy reminds us of the winners of youth world championships. The changes in physical features and in body size certainly also have evolutionary explanations. New training possibilities as well as multifarious nutritional alternatives have had an impact globally on the physical development of man. However, the idea of man as represented by the Olympic athletes in Beijing is more than alarming. They show that sport has voluntarily accepted the pressure to optimize human nature, to increase physical and intellectual capabilities and to exploit hitherto unused potentials. The capitalist societies have subjected themselves to the imperative of growth, which now has reached the whole world. Everything is to be optimized: everything needs to be perfect.

Manipulation is the term characterizing human hubris. Consequently it is not surprising that our society is under the spell of doping manipulation and cosmetic surgery, that pharmaceutical manipulation of body size, muscle power, emotional state and memory has long been self-evident. There is pressure starting to build up even before we are born and lasting until we are in the senior citizens' home. This pressure is omnipresent. Nobody can resist it. The Olympic sport associations have subjected themselves to this pressure for a long time, and by their own decisions they contribute to the fact that this pressure is all-inclusive. On the Olympic sporting stage anorexic athletes meet obese heavyweights, muscle-packed monsters and deliberately created dwarves, and in China it was not only the Chinese girls who were suspected of not having reached the age limit of 16 years. Those who watched the gymnastics competitions in Beijing must ask themselves why an international association allows children from the US, Germany, Romania or France to take part in the Olympic Games. The IOC must ask itself why it has not required the Olympic Games to remain an event for adults, as is the case in many Olympic sports.

In associations accepting the former rules concerning age it can be seen how a sport can maintain its quality without giving in to perfection-mania. In this context men's and women's hockey is a good example, as are almost all team sports; and fencing among the individual sports. It is important to point out here that it is no bad reflection on the Olympic Games if superb performances are achieved in youth championships, possibly even better than those of adults. Those who want to stop perfection-mania must ask themselves this question, because the changes in the concept of the human as an Olympic athlete are not presently within any acceptable perspective. Olympic sports that are directly subject to the imperative of increase need rules to limit change. Not everything that is possible can nor should be permitted. Olympic sport has long reached the point where we need to be content with less than perfection. The least we can expect today is that the IOC and the Olympic associations are concerned about this process. Questions regarding the human concept of Olympic athletes have been asked and need to be addressed. Those who are willing to develop an attitude and work to express it will recognize that it is more difficult than sitting at the front of a train that is already moving.

The Fight Against Doping

Aside from unrestricted commercialization, fraud is probably the most dangerous threat to Olympism. Fraud has reached Olympic sport with its full impact. The fact is that this kind of fraud can expand, which means that in practically all Olympic sports instances of positive doping have been exposed in the last few years. However, we must also assume that the existing control system cannot address the actual problem, and this is primarily a result of the sheer size of the Olympic movement and its largely uncontrolled commercialization. The marketing of 'goods' and the usurpation of the Olympic Games by the media have become widespread, which, of course, makes corruption even more likely.

Apart from the fight against increasing corruption in the sport associations and the questionable rise in commercialization, the fight against cheating through doping is of extraordinary significance. The Olympic Games in Beijing have shown that merely increasing controls before and during the games is not sufficient. For some time we have had a situation in which any surprising performance increase and extraordinary achievements are immediately subject to public suspicion. This has increased rather than decreased despite a larger number of controls during training and competition. For this reason it is important that the IOC welcomes control systems as necessary for a credible fight against the dopers, even though they are not sufficient. The member organizations of the IOC therefore must make more effort to cooperate with the judicial systems in their own countries in order to implement sufficient and urgently necessary deterrents for the prevention of cheating through doping. Besides this, active prevention is necessary that is not simply centred on appeals for moral behaviour but which also shows athletes ways of improving performance that will enable them to compete fairly at the highest level. If we want to be more successful in the future, science in the field of doping fraud must be intensified in order to improve both prevention and detection. As long as athletes fall into the 'doping trap' of Olympic sport – and from which there is no escape – there is no way to recognize how doping fraud could be restricted and reduced.

The fascination of Olympic sport is doubtlessly based on its *fortius-citius-altius* imperative. This provided many Olympic sports with a principle that has become the guideline for the actions of athletes. The challenge today is therefore to control this principle. Olympic sport needs sporting competitions that allow participation without cheating. This requires rather more limitations on what is permitted and what is prohibited than we have known so far.

Public Relations Work of the IOC

The question of how the IOC communicates with the world's public has never been as much a focus of attention as during the weeks and months prior to the Olympic Games in Beijing and during the games themselves. Observation of the IOC's communication manner reveals that it is following a strategy previously common in politics and in business.

Commercial agencies are employed in the attempt to present an organization or individual to the world in beautiful colours and with a maximum number of positive stories. The IOC magazines such as the *Olympic Review* and other picture-, text- or sound-based publications may serve as examples in this context, with creativity and aesthetics being of great importance. The objective is to present oneself as modern and up-to-date. Beside this form of communication different types of ritualistic communication are made use of such as, for example, press conferences, statements and exclusive interviews, without recognizing that it is precisely these rituals that cause problems in the presentation of the IOC in the media. Substantial communication on real issues concerning Olympism takes place hardly ever or not at all. The IOC has neither an organ allowing the publication of well-founded reflected essays on Olympism nor a regular systematic and organized reflection in the sense of self-assurance and counselling that takes place either internally or externally. In the face of such poor quality of communication it is not surprising that whenever the IOC comes under pressure and is confronted with attacks it can only 're-act' rather than 'act' positively. There is apparently no active communication policy. Under the leadership of the new IOC president the situation has improved, but the fundamental structures have remained the same. The Tibet conflict has provided evidence of this, as did the public statements made during the Olympic Games. The solution to the problem will certainly not be found in merely changing agencies or people. It will be important and essential to take the content and issues that are to be communicated to the world and to address the questions to which a critical global public is justly awaiting answers.

IOC Membership

The future of the Olympic movement will surely depend on the men and women who will direct Olympic sport in the future. So far fame, power, wealth and political calculation have been the required attributes of anyone tempted into a career in the Olympic movement. In this context fame was originally based on noble birth or Olympic success. The involvement of billionaires, highly-ranked military men, representatives of corporations and politicians have pointed to wealth and power as entry cards, as they have made their way into the IOC with such qualifications. Meanwhile it is more than evident that such qualifications are inadequate selection criteria for competent presence in the IOC.

It is also increasingly inappropriate to try to bring innovation to the IOC through former Olympians. Quite a few of them, it may be assumed, were involved to some degree in the comprehensive doping fraud within the Olympic movement during their active careers. Much more relevant , however, is the fact that many of them have an inadequate education. They often have not done anything else in their lives than understanding the sport they practised at a high level. In the face of the processes of totalization observed in top level sport for quite a while, [1] it is very likely that future Olympic champions will also have such education deficiencies. As during their careers they hardly ever do anything else but dedicate themselves to top-level sport, it is only in exceptional cases that they have academic qualifications or any other specific competences that would be relevant to taking up leading positions in modern sport. Quite frequently foreign-language competence is confused with specific professional or academic competence. Also staff within the Olympic organizations are recruited using criteria that would not be accepted either by the government or the business sector. Not least for this reason there has been for some time an observable intellectual deficit in the committees and commissions of the IOC that is totally unrelated to Pierre de Coubertin's concept of elite selection. The IOC rather too often offers former Olympic athletes pseudo-positions which provide them with large financial returns without ever doing anything substantial in return. Such recruitment is counterproductive to a positive development of the Olympic movement.

The Olympic Movement and its Critical Companions

It is also symptomatic of today's Olympic movement that it has removed virtually all determined critics and replaced them with 'yes-men' who sit on its committees, commissions and advisory boards. Olympic conventions have the character of shows just as sport itself, and speakers are recruited for their 'show qualities'. Thus the (German) TV star Karasek was, for example, a major speaker at the first Olympic convention of the Deutscher Olympischer Sportbund (DOSB). What he said was funny at best, and rarely original. No systematic approach nor any solutions to problems were offered, because a fundamental and stable problem analysis was not undertaken. Therefore the question has to be asked: 'Who shall represent Olympic sport in a world where processes of globalization continuously generate changes?'

Looking at the 'icons' of world sport we recognize that Olympic heroes only play a secondary role. The symbolic power of the of the achievements of Olympic athletes has recently lost so much of its significance that it comes close to an existential threat. In order to prevent this new ideas are needed. Objectives must be clarified, priorities assessed and new ways of communication developed if the Olympic movement wants to prove to be a relevant and modern movement. Future marketing processes will have to be carefully directed. Cases of fraud and corruption must be fought constantly, and usurpation by the media needs to be reduced to a bearable degree. Nether would it be wrong to remember that the actual values, as they are laid down in the Olympic Charter, are still valid today. Nothing seems to be more urgent than for the IOC to have some dialogue with its environment. This requires critical scientific association, with notables from literature, art, architecture and religion as additional advisers; and – last but not least – Olympism needs to find a place as a significant actor in world culture.

Note

[1] Heinilä, 'The Totalization Process'.

Reference

Heinilä, Kalevi. 'The Totalization Process in International Sport'. *Sportwissenschaft* 12, no.3 (1982): 235–54.

How Green Will My (Lea) Valley Be? Olympic Aspirations: Rhetoric or Reality [1]

Peter Horton and Dwight H. Zakus

Much debate surrounds the nature and reality of the legacy left to host cities after they hold an Olympic or a Winter Olympic Games. We argue and provide evidence that the debate is more about sustainability. The sustainability of the International Olympic Committee (IOC) as an organization and of the games that deliver the aspirations and goals of the Olympic movement are central issues in this debate. The IOC identifies its aspirations and goals in the Olympic Charter and within it the philosophy of Olympism. To realize these, the IOC must select a bid submitted by various city, country and national Olympic committee consortia to deliver the games. There are two separate issues here. First, that the host city must meet IOC demands contained in the OC and hosting contracts; that is, that the IOC's aspirations and numerous contractual stipulations are met and that sufficient revenues from operating the games are met. Second, the delivery of the games is to leave a 'legacy' (sustainable outcomes) from delivering the games. Two issues arise about whether host cities can do both – deliver a successful games, within the confines of the agreements, towards achieving IOC aspirations and goals and also deliver sustainable environmental, social and economic outcomes – thereby sustaining the IOC, the Olympic movement, Olympism and the lofty aspirations and goals of the Olympic Charter.

Introduction

The International Olympic Committee (IOC), founded in 1894, entered a space where few sport bodies existed at the national and international level. [2] The IOC was therefore one of the earliest international non-governmental (non-profit) organizations to come into existence. It is one of a few international organizations to exist, or remain sustainable, across three centuries. Temporal changes have significantly impacted all facets of the Olympic Games; however, the ideals of this movement, contained in the organizational philosophy of Olympism, have not varied widely from those established by Pierre de Coubertin in the late nineteenth century. We find these principles expressed in the Olympic Charter (OC) and evident in much of the organizational structure, management and processes of current IOC operations. [3]

The OC contains the aspirations of the Olympic movement. Through its early existence the IOC evolved a set of practices and policies for the global operation of sport. In 1908 the goals and first set of these practices and policies were formalized in the first published OC. [4] Since this first version the charter has undergone enormous change to reflect the IOC's change from a culturally based and driven organization to an economically driven, multinational, non-governmental commercial entity reflecting many of the social forces for change over time. The ideals of Olympism are in essence the ongoing aspirations of the IOC.

The key elements of the charter for this analysis include the following. First, the OC is described as the 'codification of the Fundamental Principles of Olympism, Rules and Bye-Laws adopted by the IOC. It governs the organization, action and operation of the Olympic Movement and sets forth the conditions for the celebration of the Olympic Games.' [5] The second requirement then, is an understanding of Olympism. The OC's first fundamental principle describes this philosophy as

> A philosophy of life, exalting and combining in a balanced whole the qualities of body, will and mind. Blending sport with culture and education, Olympism seeks to create a way of life based on the joy of effort, the educational value of good example and respect for universal fundamental ethical principles. [6]

Finally, the notion of the Olympic movement needs description. Here the OC describes the movement as follows:

> Under the supreme authority of the International Olympic Committee, the Olympic Movement encompasses organisations, athletes and other persons who agree to be guided by the Olympic Charter. The goal of the Olympic Movement is to contribute to building a peaceful and better world by educating youth through sport practised in accordance with Olympism and its values. [7]

This then connects to the fundamental mission of the IOC which is 'to promote Olympism throughout the world and to lead the Olympic Movement' along with their third stated role which, most importantly for the argument here, is 'to ensure the regular celebration of the Olympic Games'. [8]

The need to understand these connections is necessary because the IOC sees its major role in global sport to lead sport to higher and sustainable ideals and aspirations. This role is, at best, an educational one that seeks to strive to improve the world through sport and to improve sport in the world. It can, however, only deliver on these ideals through the regular cycle of Olympic and Winter Olympic Games, [9] which are held in different global locations every two years.

Two key things need emphasizing here: first, the IOC predominantly delivers its aspirations and goals through the Olympic Games where elements of the OC and Olympism become real. Second, the actual holding of the Olympic Games is the responsibility of a city that has its state/regional and national governments' support as well as that of its national Olympic committee (NOC). The catch in all of this is that the host city must ensure that the games meet the IOC's aspirations, goals and requirements for surplus revenues, all within budgetary constraints of governments and the IOC contracts. The host city, it is argued, will derive a benefit or 'legacy' from hosting the games. What this legacy actually is and what it means to the people of the host city remains in debate, as does whether this legacy is a sustainable feature of hosting the games and for the future of the IOC and future games.

Financial matters, unfortunately, are central to this debate, but they must be seen as two separate but concurrent aspects of holding an Olympic Games. A local Olympic Games organizing committee (OGOC) must be established to actually deliver the games. Contracts signed with the IOC stipulate how operational revenues will be shared from holding the games. The main focus of this paper is to identify, discuss and analyse whether the cost of holding an Olympic Games for all involved levels of government is sustainable. As governments must invest or provide billions of dollars to host an Olympic Games, the resulting environmental, social and economic outcomes are a key residue of that hosting activity. Therefore, are the Olympic Games a sustainable use of taxpayers' funds and ultimately what post-Olympic Games benefits derive for the hosts?

With identifiable aspirations driving the IOC, Olympism, the Olympic movement and its games it must be asked whether all of the above actually problematizes the very sustainability of the Olympic movement itself. To make sense of these questions we first provide a discussion of the concept of sustainability. Then a brief analysis of how the IOC qua organization has sustained itself since 1894 is made before looking at four case studies, those of Sydney, Beijing and forward to Vancouver, London and a brief foreword to Rio, to point to the putative legacies and sustainable residues of the movement.

Sustainability, Sustainable Development, Legacy

Often in academic work considerable debate arises around the definition, nature, measurement and application of concepts and theories. The concepts of sustainability, sustainable development and legacy exemplify this debate. The debate around these three concepts is necessary for the discussion that follows, as the conceptual pieces, it is argued, are intertwined with the topic of the sustainability of the Olympic Games and the Winter Olympic Games and by reverse logic that of the IOC and the entire Olympic Movement.

Lexical definitions identify the root word sustain as to 'keep something going over time or continuously'; [10] with sustainable, the adjective, as something is 'able to be sustained' [11] and its derivative, the noun sustainability. Conceptual definitions abound; however, the definition of former Norwegian Prime Minister Gro Harlme Bruntland (in the 1987 report of the World Commission on Environment and Development) is most often cited: 'Development that meets the needs of the present without compromising the ability of future generations to meet their own needs.' [12] We see here that sustainability and sustainable development are conflated. Also, as with the IOC, this United Nations report points to the global level at which sustainability must operate, this again fits nicely with the IOC's aspirations as *the* global organization for sport and as aspiring to permanent membership on the UN.

With hundreds of definitions out there, many organizations have sought to make sense out of this chaos. For instance, The Global Development Research Center offers that 'sustainable development is maintaining a delicate balance between the human need to improve lifestyles and feeling of well-being on one hand, and preserving natural resources and ecosystems, on which we and future generations depend'. [13] In standing committee meetings of the Australian government, they derived the following definition:

> [T]here is no single, universally accepted definition of sustainability or sustainable development and, as evident in this inquiry, any discussion about definition quickly generates debate ... [and others] offer a broader definition of sustainable development that better conveys underpinning ecological, social and economic principles. Sustainable development comprises types of economic and social development that protect and enhance the natural environment and social equity.
> This definition suggests that sustainable development is more a process than an outcome. In fact, one submitter to the Committee's inquiry into sustainable cities stated that the overriding concept of sustainability is ... a journey, not a destination. [14]

Of importance here is firstly that again sustainability is interchangeably used with sustainable development and secondly, that sustainable development is characterized as both a process and an outcome; however contradictory that might seem.

Dale observed that up to 2005 there were 'more than 1,200 definitions of sustainable development'. [15] In the end, however, what is evident from the literature is that humans need to be much more aware of our natural capital/built environment, as well as the human, social and economic aspects of our life on earth. The movement away from a single bottom line of economic, or more specifically financial, sustainability to a triple bottom-line goal that is now mooted has taken much effort, and such thinking has a way to go. A visual representation of community has three concentric circles: the economy exists within society, and both the economy and society exist within the environment (see Figure 1), again as it should be, with the economy being a sub-element of society.

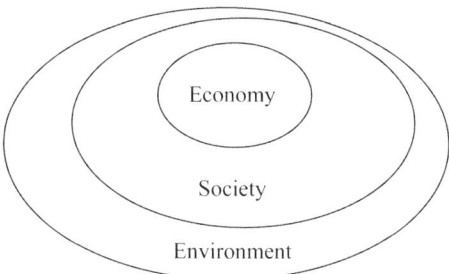

Figure 1 A concentric view of the relationship between the environment, society, and the economy. *Source*: An Introduction to Sustainability. Downloaded from http://www. sustainablemeasures.com on 05 May 2008.

Littig and Griessler added to this discussion stating that 'social sustainability is not only an analytical but is also a normative concept.' [16] They maintain that the concept of social sustainability is

> a quality of societies. It signifies the nature-society relationships, mediated by work [economic aspect], as well as relationships within the society. Social sustainability is given, if work within a society and the related institutional arrangement (a) satisfy a full set of extended set of human needs [and] are shaped in a way that nature and its reproductive capabilities are preserved over a long period of time and the normative claims of social justice, human dignity, and participation are fulfilled. [17]

These values and outcomes are clearly those we hold for sport and for life in communities. To understand sustainability as an element of the Olympic Movement, researchers must actively embrace the above arguments and aspects of the concepts of sustainability and sustainable development.

The final element of the conceptual conundrum surrounds legacy. The full implication of the 'concept', despite the idea of legacy being a primary consideration for the IOC's choice of a host city for an Olympic Games and for the emergence of the Olympic Games Global Impact (OGGI) studies programme, is a moot point. One can suitably ask whether the aspirations, aims, goals and targets of any Olympic Games have ever been fully achieved or, in fact, ever could be achieved.

In his suitably entitled work, *A Bitter-Sweet Awakening: the Legacy of the Sydney 2000 Olympic Games*, Richard Cashman noted that 'the word legacy is elusive, problematic, and even [a] dangerous word for a number of reasons'. [18] Having entered the debate, Cashman also makes reference to Jacques Rogge's comments on the topic: first, he cites Rogge as having 'consistently argued in favour of more modest and sustainable Games' [19] then with a 'more modest and sustainable Games' and finally, in comments at the 2002 legacy conference in Lausanne, that 'an Olympic Games should produce a sustainable legacy that was a long-term benefit to the community of the host city and country'. [20] Here we again see the conflation of legacy with sustainability that we already argue is conflated with sustainable development.

Cashman added to the debate, concluding that the legacy products that emerge from an Olympic Games are not all positive nor were those that turned out to be positive necessarily planned. He also suggests that as a social process 'legacy is dynamic and evolving rather than fixed'. [21] It is suggested that the lasting and most impactful legacies emerging from mega-social events such as an Olympic Games, the biggest of all social events, are often unplanned and often not positive. Interestingly, regarding the Sydney legacy, Horton suggested that perhaps 'the greatest and most profitable feature of the legacy of the Sydney Olympic Games will in fact be the Beijing Games' [22] – an argument explored below.

In recent times several meaningful critiques have emerged on the topic of legacy and the Olympic Games: most noteworthy is the 2008 special collection edited by Mangan and Dyreson, which provocatively opens with a line from Asia's first Nobel laureate Rabindranath Tagore's poem *Stray Birds*: 'If you shut your door to all errors truth will be shut out' [23] – clearly a message from the Emeritus Professor Mangan to those charged with the future integrity, viability and the sustainability of the Olympic Games. Another thought from Tagore's poem may also serve to censure the same fraternity: 'The false can never grow into truth by growing in power.' [24] Mangan and Dyerson's excellent collection contains many more direct censures and suggestions pertinent to the, if not leviathan, then certainly (white) elephantine issue of Olympic legacies. [25] Reflecting upon legacy, what we need to discuss and analyse is how the IOC, through the Olympic Games, is able to aspire to and deliver the ideals of Olympism and of the OC as a form of sustainable development that actually embraces sustainability. [26]

Looking at the delivery of the Olympic Games with an active understanding of sustainability allows us to assess whether or not the aspirations actually eventuate or are possible. Inevitably we need to ask: is the hubris surrounding the products of the Olympic ideals that have colonized 'sustainability' merely rhetoric or is there a tangible functional legacy of Olympism that remains after the games? Initially this analysis will consider the dogma of the Olympic ideals against the aspirations of sustainability from the host cities of some of the most recent festivals, appraising as to whether or not their goals were achieved or not; we will then look to future games. The key question, we feel, is whether the Olympic Games add to the sustainability of the host city and country and if not, should the games as Avery Brundage insisted, go on? [27]

Sustainability of the IOC and the Olympic Games

Despite its historical changes, the IOC remains a club that has provided a model for global sport, one that de Coubertin aggregated from a number of sources [28] but in particular from the British club-based system of amateur leadership, governance and management. [29] From the IOC to the smallest local club, volunteer-based sport organizations (VSOs) provide a base for the sustainability of all sport, at all levels of opportunity and the form of its delivery.

These VSOs are fundamentally based on the altruism and a modernist prowess-based patronage of the volunteers who form these clubs. [30] Loosely speaking, these are forms of *noblesse oblige* or of social responsibility that derive from and largely describe why the human capital involved in the time-honoured practices of sport development and organization continue. That is, of sport's overall sustainability and especially for those volunteers involved in the 'serious leisure' [31] found in organizations such as local sport clubs and as well as the IOC.

In current vernacular of sustainability, four pillars are widely recognized: they are human, social, economic and environmental (both built and natural). [32] Often the human and social are not separated, for good reason. In this first section on the sustainability of the IOC itself we maintain the separation; however, in the analyses of particular games all pillars must be discussed together. OGOCs can, by delivering the sport and cultural festivals that are the Olympic Games, respond to the IOC's human pillar of sustainability.

Finally, the IOC's Agenda 21 propaganda speaks of the environmental and the social (cultural), but not often the economic. It may be asked why the economic aspects are not more prominent in the public discussion of the Olympic Games by the IOC, for the economic rationale for holding mega-sports events, such as an Olympic Games; as Hiller asserts, is one if not the biggest concern for all the major stakeholders in any consortium bidding for an event. [33]

The IOC's Human Pillar

How does sport contribute to humanity and to the celebration of the sustainability of humankind? In terms of the modern games this discussion is based on the writings of Pierre de Coubertin, the *renovateur* and founder of the modern games and the IOC. His adoption of neoclassical philosophical idealism is still apparent in the Olympic principles that operate today. He sought the cultivation of the individual through body, mind and spirit; the development of society (a healthy democracy) as an upshot of the improved social interaction and character development that could be gained through sport; the promotion of peace and international understanding; and the pursuit of human excellence, physically, intellectually and spiritually. [34] All of this achieved through competition in sport.

Both forms of the Olympic Games, as cultural festivals, form the platform for the delivery of these humanistic elements of Olympism. The opening and closing ceremonies and the overall 'party' ambience during the Olympic Games are central to the celebration of world humanity. Most often the human pillar surrounds how to expand sport, often conceptualized as 'sport for all'. In other words, by watching Olympians compete, populations around the world will seek involvement in sport.

While this is a laudable feature of Olympic sport one must ask about the veracity of this ideal and its claims. Numerous studies attempt to answer whether the Olympic Games influence participation in sport. Results were not able to clearly determine an effect, often due to intervening variables, varying data sources, temporal issues, data collection methods and lack of causation being established. Therefore, there is little of empirical or scientific substance on which to ground assertions of this pillar.

As cities and countries continue to bid to host the games despite the extravagant and extensive costs and adjunct cultural events, we argue that sustainability of the human pillar still exists, albeit in an idealistic sense. But are there humanistic legacies sustained after the games end? One would have to argue that humanistic elements do not transfer as widely as hoped for by the IOC. The IOC-developed programmes that seek to sustain sport involvement and sport's humanistic elements incorporate social responsibility programmes (e.g. a Tool for Development, Promotion of Sustainable Development); however, the real success of these programmes is yet to be seen.

The IOC's Social Pillar

The IOC has considerable hegemony over sport and sport organizations globally as they control national Olympic committees (NOCs) and through the international sport federations (ISFs), the sport governing bodies in all aligned countries. [35] The underlying goal of the IOC and its ideological elements is to use sport to enhance human life and build a stronger humanity. This is a noble goal but cannot come from above, whether from the IOC or a national government. It must come from within a country and then the world. There is a serious inversion here.

Simply, the position and locus of control of the IOC and other members of the Olympic family are not conducive to social development, let alone sustainability, in or through sport. While sport is a wonderful vehicle to achieve such goals, achievements are limited to the period leading into an Olympic Games and a few years following. All sorts of educational initiatives arise as do camps, symposia and other opportunities to recruit children and youth into sport participation. The NOCs and national sport federations with their top-down policy initiatives are not readily able to meet the targets necessary for sport and social sustainability. Yet they tend to cream the top without contributing to the athletic input, nor do the IOC's social responsibility programmes noted above. And although Olympism, the Olympic Charter's premises and aspirations and the Olympic Games work to only a limited degree, the Olympic movement continues.

In a theoretical argument on the sustainability and social sustainability of community sport Zakus argued that certain features of human and social capital are necessary to accomplish this goal. [36] The key premise is that community sport is the heart of any sport system and for it to be sustainable certain persons must be present in these organizations. [37] There are many scholars such as these proposing policy and programmes that would help the IOC better achieve its lofty goals.

Writing on an inner-city project in a community near the 2012 games site in London, Mawson spoke of the need for 'social entrepreneurs' [38] who use the existing social capital of community members as assets rather than using a deficit model that blames the victim. [39] The strength of sport is that it has existing networks of these social entrepreneurs within already existing social networks and relationships found in sport organizations. In other words sport volunteers exemplify sound community development practices.

Vail also made this claim in her process for implementing new sport programmes in communities such as those premised in the IOC's Development Tool and Promotion of Sustainable Development programmes. [40] Vail believes that a sustainable sport-based community development initiative requires four key elements. The first relates to community selection, in particular that community's readiness and capacity to change. Second, there is the need for a community catalyst(s)/champion(s) to provide process leadership. Third, there is the need to build a cadre of collaborative group/community partnerships, or community fields from a wide cross-section of people and organizations who share a vision and have the capacity to achieve that vision through true collaboration and true shared decision-making. And finally, there is the need to promote sustainability through community development processes. In all of this we see a mix of agency and structure.

We do not see the IOC or its subsidiaries being able to do such work due to their location and the lack of truly socially sustainable practices and funding; even if, contradictorily, their stated ideology does not support their hegemony in global sport. As will be seen below, this is a key issue in the sustainability of the local delivery of the Olympic Games.

The IOC's Economic Pillar

The viability and sustainability of the IOC, the Olympic Games and the Olympic movement in regard to this pillar took considerable time to evolve. De Coubertin's family inheritance sustained IOC operations up to his death. While the Olympic movement was viable as an ideal, its financial continuity was often under threat. [41] Under Samaranch's presidency the IOC went commercial; [42] in fact, it could be said that it enjoyed an embarrassment of riches, with reputational risk, terrorism and the failure to deliver one games being the key factors that could damage its financial and operational holdings. [43]

That the IOC has substantial financial holdings attests to the commercial revenues it can generate from its own business activities and through proceeds from the operation of the Olympic Games. While the proceeds from the Olympic Games are shared with other elements of the Olympic family through a set formula, the Olympic Games revenues are contractually sorted. It was at the 1984 Los Angeles Olympic Games that the true potential size of these funds was recognized. Every Olympic Games from Rome 1960 forward has earned an operational surplus for the IOC. The size of this surplus in 1984 made it necessary for all future Olympic Games to be bound by contractual entities with the host cities – and as to how the riches would be divided. Clearly the games are sustainable as sport and cultural events in a financial sense as well as more generally.

Still there are risks for the IOC here. First, will cities bid to host the Olympic Games? If the Olympic Games are not held then the financial house of the IOC falls. Second, will the city/country hosting be able to meet its commitment? As noted above, there is reputational risk for the IOC as it chooses the host, but this has not yet happened in Olympic history. And third, will the city/country host receive sustainable outcomes/legacies? We discuss the concomitant nature of these risks in the material below. A more detailed analysis follows in the next section.

Discussion of the future economic legacy, or impact as Toohey describes it, [44] of an Olympic Games or any mega-sports festival tends to polarize public and political opinion, but the corporate sector is rarely ambivalent. Most often this is due to the ultimate profits the private sector garners while the public sector makes the largest investment and so creates large debts. It is the irony of this fact that led to a temporary downturn in cities bidding for the Olympic Games following the 1976 Montreal Olympics.

The now apocryphal outcome of government funding for the Montreal games and the statement by then mayor of Montreal Jean Drapeau is legend. Drapeau boldly stated that the 1976 games could no more have a deficit than a man could have a baby. Nick auf de Mur in his book *Billion Dollar Baby* predicted Drapeau's pregnancy and the Montreal and Quebec governments' financial legacy of debt. [45] As noted, this situation became embedded in the collective memory of Olympic bid aspirants and especially the IOC. [46] Fortunately the lessons were learnt well by all subsequent host cities and, after 2002, with the support of the IOC's Olympic Games Knowledge Services (OGKS), all organizing and candidate cities have access to the collective wisdom of past games with the transfer of knowledge from past organizing committees to those following. [47]

Montreal also transformed the financial mindset of the IOC for if it is, as the Olympic Charter stipulates, 'to ensure the regular celebration of the Olympic Games' [48] both summer and winter Olympic festivals do occur every four years, they are now, as 'the authority of last resort' [49] concerning the Olympic Games, required to assume financial stewardship as the IOC's 'Rights over the Olympic Games and Olympic properties' manifestly demonstrates. [50] The 2004 Athens games caused consternation as the cost overruns and infrastructure delays tested the nerve of the IOC and its resources, financial and human: Might Rio 2016 do the same? The IOC now saves against a games not occurring and has rationalized and patented games operations through its Olympic Games Knowledge Management programme (OGKM). [51]

As previously suggested, the IOC will make an operational profit irrespective of the actual 'bottom line' achieved by the host city and country actually responsible for the considerable costs of infrastructure, transportation, reclamation of land, security, housing and a range of appropriate (state-of-the-art) sport facilities. The history of sport in the Western world, outside the United States of America, is mainly one of Keynesian welfare-state provision. This applies to both the development of sport delivery systems and to sport infrastructure developments (e.g. fields, pools, stadia). As market failure does not hold strong, direct salience in understanding the funding or viability of sport, the intervention of the state nevertheless results as positive externalities and public goods arguments being viable. In fact, positive externalities for the health and social benefits ensuing from sport are clearly part of this rationale. [52] In terms of public goods, there is a wide body of literature on public provision of both public and private sport facilities and tax and other compensation for professional sport franchises in many cities.

The rhetoric, however, continues. Prior to the final presentations by the four 2016 bid cities IOC President Jacques Rogge claimed that 'financial considerations should not drive the decision on which city hosts the 2016 Olympics'. [53] Rogge prevailed upon the bidding cities of Chicago, Madrid, Rio de Janeiro and Tokyo to focus upon technical details in the final closed-door sessions before the announcement of the winner in October 2009. The spectre of the 2007–8 global recession loomed large, so that budgetary plans, financial guarantees and an implicit heightened level of economic scrutiny of all bids prevailed – despite Rogge's assertion that geopolitics should not dominate the process but that what will be best for the athletes should prevail. [54]

Rogge further suggested that a successful bid would not be about 'economics but [about] leaving a sustainable legacy. ... When we leave, we want it to be a bonus for the city, the region and the country.' [55] But sustainable legacies are not cheap to bequeath. As Steven Wilson pointed out, the Chicago bid leader Pat Ryan's major issue at this stage was that his team would talk further about financial guarantees and be able to present a risk-free financial plan, one that 'leaves no white elephants and [that] will foster a lasting urban and sporting legacy'. [56]

The two domains of economics and sustainability are, as illustrated here, irrevocably linked. The sustainability issue of this pillar, to be further analysed below, surrounds the cost of infrastructure and of sport facilities. In this regard, there is a dismal record.

The IOC's Environmental Pillar

In 1999, the IOC eventually adopted its own Agenda 21 that parallels and is adapted from the document developed at the UN Conference on Environment and Development held in Rio de Janeiro in 1992. [57] Thus, the IOC Agenda 21 stands directly beneath the aegis of the UN. The IOC's Agenda 21 focuses on improving socio-economic conditions, conserving and managing resources and strengthening the role of major groups. More recent games and future events (Athens 2004, Turin 2006, Vancouver 2010, London 2012 and Rio 2016) *must* have policies that guide and are examples of best practice, based on principles of stakeholder engagement, long-term planning, accessibility, equity and healthy communities – in other words, sustainable development of the host communities/countries.

It did, however, take nearly a hundred years for the 'penny to drop'. Chappelet provides a rounded historical analysis of the IOC's change in policy on the environment. [58] It took the IOC from the 1992 Rio summit on through to its Centennial Congress in 1994 before it finally adopted its own version of Agenda 21 in 1999. Nonetheless, 'the environment' became the third 'pillar' of the Olympic movement, to stand alongside its two original official pillars of sport and culture.

The mission of the IOC is to sustain the development of global sport and the regular celebration of the Olympic Games through its broad mission of education, Olympism and peace: All of which fit nicely with Samaranch's aspirational goal for the IOC to be a permanent organizational member of the UN and win a Nobel Peace Prize. [59] Again, it is this combination of these relatively varied aspirations through which a host city must deliver the Olympic Games.

The environmental pillar is now entrenched in the Olympic movement as the 2007 charter contains two mission statements that succinctly espouse and embrace the philosophy of sustainability:'

> 13. to encourage and support a responsible concern for environmental issues, to promote sustainable development in sport and to require that the Olympic Games are held accordingly;
> 14. to promote a positive legacy from the Olympic Games to the host cities and host countries. [60]

Whether these are platitudinous or not will be discussed below.

Each games and each host city must be judged against the standards (aspirations) it sets relative to the context of Olympism, the charter and the stringent demands of the IOC's bidding process: there is no one immutable set of standards that can justifiably be adopted to judge, evaluate or compare. Even though the fundamental principles of Olympism found in the Olympic Charter are most specific, each Olympic Games is conducted and characterized by the hosting city, the hosting nation and the hosting culture; each should therefore be unique.

Yet all are linked not just by the laws and regulations of the Olympic Charter or the commands of the IOC but by the spirit of Olympism. Today we still cling to the ideals of Olympism as philosophical justifications for their continuation. The Olympic movement has assumed the role of social change agent as part of its credo with the spirit of Olympism being dedicated to world peace and understanding; equality of opportunity; racial and religious harmony; and the glorification and unification of the youth of the world through sport.

The ideals of Olympism are most laudable; they have a quasi-religiosity and are the only set of ascribed ethical principles that can be applied to the conduct of sport. No other code exists that underpins sport, no other code elevates sport to moral, cultural as well as athletic levels of significance and no other code has the backing of such a powerful vehicle, the Olympic Games. Throughout the history of the Olympic movement, whatever secondary motivations were at work, whether cultural, educational, spiritual and of course political and ideological, the source of the movement's strength came not from the noble underlying ideals but from the fact that they were expressed and channelled through the event, the Olympic Games itself. [61] In the following sections we explore the problematic issue as to whether the expression of the concept of sustainability in regard to the Olympic Games, the delivery of the aspirations and Olympism of the IOC, is indeed in reality achieved or is it mere rhetoric.

The Environmental Pillar and Delivery of the Olympic Games

The IOC's Agenda 21, which sets out environmental issues and presents potential solutions to emerging problems, also seeks to 'to improve socio-economic conditions, conservation and management of resources of sustainable development, and strengthening the role of the main groups'. [62] All pillars of sustainability are typically collapsed into one here, a feature of the remaining discussions. The Vancouver Olympic Organizing Committee (VANOC) states that

> Sustainability is an integral part of our mission, vision, and values. It is present in all our planning and work, including the actions and decision making of our workforce and members of the VANOC Board of Directors. It also includes setting out key policies and charters, posting sustainability procedures on our internal website, and abiding by international standards such as human rights, regulatory compliance, and the spirit of the International Olympic Committee's (IOC's) Agenda 21. [63]

From these key policies VANOC set their own objectives: 'Our sustainability Performance Objectives: Accountability, Environmental Stewardship and Impact Reduction, Social Inclusion and Responsibility, Aboriginal participation and Collaboration, Economic Benefits, Sport for Sustainable Living' [64] – that is, focusing on all four pillars of sustainability. The educational dimension of Olympism is seen as a way for sustainability to flow throughout the local and global sport world.

Sport and its facilities are under the microscope in terms of the environmental aspect. The ecological or carbon footprint of sport facilities, both in terms of credits and debits, certainly since the 2000 summer Olympic Games, has become an issue. The Sydney organizing committee for the Olympic Games made good mileage out of the 'green' aspects of the natural and built capital elements leading up to 2000. It was the release of the *Environmental Guidelines for the Summer Olympic Games* by the Sydney Games Bid Committee that swayed the votes towards Sydney away from Beijing and, as Philippe Furrer, head of the Olympic Games Knowledge Management and Special Projects for the Olympic Games Department since 2007, commented in his provocatively entitled 2002 paper, 'Sustainable Olympic Games: *A dream or reality?*' that 'These guidelines not only served as a great selling argument by convincing many IOC members to choose Sydney as the host city, but also guided much of the Games planning and preparation as well as produced an environmental legacy for all future editions of the Olympic Games'. [65] Motivated by this, the IOC developed its own sustainability policies, particularly regarding the environment; currently all future games organizers must follow the IOC's guidelines, in terms of the construction of facilities and with the delivery of the Olympic Games and emphatically with respect to the Olympic legacy. The significance of the impact of the Sydney Olympics' environmental guidelines was recognized by the United Nations on World Environment Day in 2001, when Sydney was awarded the Global 500 Award for Environmental Excellence. [66] The Sydney 2000 Olympic Games was hailed as being the 'most ecologically responsible in history'. [67] The adoption of environment-friendly strategies, systems and technology and the all-round operational philosophy was in itself an important and enduring legacy.

The Green Games

As noted, Sydney's successful bid for the 2000 Olympic Games, widely heralded as embracing sustainable development, was, as Beyer said, the reason why Beijing was 'supplanted by Sydney' [68] in the 1993 vote. The final catalyst that steeled the IOC into action came just one year after when it added clause 13 to its mission statement in the Olympic Charter (1991 edition). Clause 13 emphatically committed the IOC to environmental sustainability as it links the concept of a 'responsible concern for environmental issues' [69] with the promotion of sustainable sport development.

A tipping point came with the environmental damage caused to the Savoie region during the construction of the Olympic venues for the Albertville games in 1992. Despite the promises of the organizing committee that the Albertville Winter Olympics would offer an 'exemplary games with the lowest possible impact on the environment' [70] the controversial location of the ski jumps and, especially, the bobsleigh/luge run prompted a tremendous backlash from environment protection groups; this was centred on a much-published protest march at the opening ceremony. [71]

The effect on the IOC was profound, particularly after it so recently committed the Olympic movement to the protection of the environment by adding its clause 13, and the legacy of green Olympics advanced, at least notionally, to the top of the selection criteria for the choice of future Olympic hosts. Sydney's environmental aspirations, though tagged as extravagant, [72] facilitated the adoption of a set of environmental guidelines and became the main clarion heralding Sydney's bid. [73] The then president of the IOC, Juan Antonio Samaranch, applauded Sydney's plans to stage a 'green' Olympic Games and was quoted as saying that Sydney 'won partly because of the consideration given to environmental matters'. [74] Sydney's environmental model presented as part of its bid for the 2000 Olympics is by current standards modest yet, as Helen Lenskyj commented, 'It is not surprising that international observers such as Canadian environmentalist David Chernushenko (1994) viewed the

Sydney model as "exemplary" and "revolutionary" based on its 1993 Environmental Guidelines'. [75]

From their conceptualization, dubbed anomalously the 'green games', the Sydney Olympics actually never reached its 'green' aspirations. [76] Criticism of them emerged during and after it closed, because the Sydney organizing committee's 'green' rhetoric far outreached the potential of the entire environmental strategy and the high hopes of all 'green' groups and the public were never fulfilled. [77] The original set of environmental guidelines was later amended and actually weakened by the Olympic Coordination Authority to make them more manageable, which precipitated critical reactions from Green Game Watch 2000 (GGW) and Greenpeace (Australia). [78] However, as unfulfilled as the Sydney Olympic Games' environmental plans may have been in the opinion of critics such as Lenskyj and Booth and Tatz, [79] it is still viewed by the IOC as being a 'significant turning point in the "greening" of the Games'. [80] And this legacy resonates still through the movement.

The Irony of Beijing's Green Olympics

The organizers hoped Beijing's games would satisfy its three mantras: the Green Olympics; the Hi-tech Olympics and, the 'Humanistic (People's) Olympics. [81] Of the three lofty goals set by Beijing Organizing Committee of the Olympic Games (BOCOG), hosting a 'Green Olympics' was widely considered, certainly by cynical Western critics and non-government organizations such as Greenpeace, to be the one that the Chinese would be least likely to achieve, particularly as poor environmental considerations blighted BOCOG's 2000 games bid. The defeat of Beijing's 2000 Olympics bid by Sydney in 1993 was attributed to the fact that Sydney had a viable sustainable development plan and Beijing did not. [82]

BOCOG's enlistment of much of Sydney's Olympic expertise, including SOCOG's environmental strategy, to assist in the preparation of its bid for the 2008 games proved to successful, and Beijing's bid included a comprehensive environmental plan, which helped appease the IOC delegates. [83] The bid did not hide the environmental problems Beijing would face and boldly outlined the existing problems, particularly the city's horrendous air quality, its poor water quality and the environmentally unsound transportation system: evidently the solutions and plans presented impressed the IOC. [84]

Criticism continued as the Olympic Games neared, and considering the smog that was blanketing the city a day before the opening ceremony, it appeared warranted. [85] However, the draconian measures imposed by the central government and the Beijing municipal government proved to be highly successful in reducing, temporarily at least, the polluting haze that normally sits over Beijing in late summer. Much to the chagrin of the sceptics, with almost scripted precision and timing 'the oppressive weather and smog that marked the run-up to the games dissipated quickly, and Beijing enjoyed the best August air quality in many years'. [86] The strategies adopted to address Beijing's infamous atmosphere and to create an energy-efficient, wholesome and aesthetically pleasing environment in and around the Olympic venues and the athletes' village commenced in 2002 when the Beijing Olympic Ecological Environment Protection Plan and the Beijing Olympic Energy Development and Energy Structure Adjustment Specific Plan were established by the Beijing municipal government. [87]

The environmental challenges facing the Chinese were immense and they were all confronted head on: high-polluting factories were moved or shut down; stringent emission controls were instigated; five new lines were added to the city's underground mass-transit system; slums were cleared; water quality was improved; and the Olympic domain and surrounding suburbs were landscaped. Massive influxes of water for irrigation and drainage were re-directed to the capital, not without a level of protest, from outlying regions, in order to sustain the greening of Beijing for the Olympic Games. [88] The country's leaders recognized the significance environmental issues had on the perception of China in the minds of the international community. Environmental issues and the threat of the poor air quality had conveniently subsumed, certainly in the Australian media, some of the more vexatious issues such as human rights and Tibet. [89] Diplomatically it was very sound for the Chinese leadership to 'go with the flow' and be seen to be earnestly committed to this 'lofty' goal.

The efforts made in achieving the environmental initiatives for the Beijing Olympics were largely applauded by Greenpeace in its report, *China after the Olympics: Lessons from Beijing*. [90] Greenpeace complimented the efforts of the authorities to embrace renewable energy production, the amazing improvements in public transportation, including five new subway lines, private car restrictions and the raised emission controls for new vehicles; however, 'The report also identified several missed opportunities that could have ensured a better short- and long-term legacy for the city'. [91] The biggest issue, apart from the lost opportunities in such areas as forestry and water minimization, [92] was the fact that the attempt to host the 'Green Olympics' was marred by the 'limited engagement and minimal third party assessments of its environmental efforts'. [93] A lack of transparency and openness in the management of the programme was noted and the report stressed the lack of access afforded to Greenpeace to pertinent environmental information and verifiable data. [94] However, it was China's centralized system of government that facilitated the Beijing municipal government's use of stringent measures to reduce pollution in the city in the first place. The report congratulated the hosts and suggested that the lessons learned at Beijing would leave an important legacy, saying that their environmental achievements have 'demonstrated the positive impact that the Olympics can have on a city in raising the profile of environmental issues'. [95]

This apparent legacy came at an enormous cost to Chinese industry and all concerned. [96] The massive actions created serious roll-on effects: some plants had to relocate while others were shut down permanently, and of course, workers were not paid throughout these closures: 'greening' Beijing for the Olympic Games was estimated to have cost US$30 billion. [97] The economic consequences of the increase in emission standards for power generators, the shutdown of heavy industries and factories ahead of and during the Olympic Games were, however, accepted as being tolerable in light of the importance of the Olympics to the nation's future; all citizens rallied compliantly to the greater good. [98] But what has happened since the steel mills, petrochemical plants, cement works and brown coal-burning power stations have resumed full operation? Were these efforts, as redoubtable as they appear, merely pragmatic measures to comply with the IOC's demands? A raft of critics insisted Beijing would never deliver a smog-free atmosphere for the 'Green Olympics' but, as we now know, the Chinese duly delivered clear skies for the Olympic Games – but did they deliver a 'green legacy'?

A recently published report from joint US-China study by scientists from Oregon State and Peking universities looking at air pollutants in Beijing during an eight-week period around the Olympics has shown that compared with the three previous summer Olympic Games Beijing's pollution levels were significantly worse: they were twice as bad as in Athens in 2004, 3.5 times worse than Sydney's in 2000 and three times higher than Atlanta's in 1996. [99] The findings of the Oregon-Peking universities' report also suggested that weather conditions, overnight rains and a series of fortuitous wind changes were more responsible than the draconian measures imposed by the Chinese government and the Beijing municipal authority. Climatic factors accounted for 40 per cent of the 'better' air quality during the two weeks of the Olympic Games while the government's pollution control measures were responsible for only 16 per cent. [100]

Was the aspiration of the Chinese to hold a 'Green Olympics' fulfilled? Air quality alone does not holistically represent the 'environment', nor can it said that an environmental legacy has been left, though it is clear the seeds have been sown. Writing shortly after the Beijing games closed Deborah Seligsohn, senior fellow and principal adviser on China's climate and programme director of the Washington-based World Resources Institute's Climate, Energy and Pollution Program in Beijing, asked if there would be a lasting legacy (environmentally) from Beijing's (indeed the whole of China's) Olympian efforts. [101] She pointed out that planning is in place for a five-year plan, to begin in 2011, to achieve more comprehensive air and water quality standards throughout China. [102] The best part of China's attempt to achieve the goal of holding the 'Green Olympics' was that, as Seligsohn pointed out, it was not limited to efforts in Beijing alone; the reforms were made nationwide, [103] which was certainly not the case in Sydney in 2000 or Athens in 2004. Though the Beijing Olympic Games was the perfect showcase to display twenty-first-century China to the world, they were, however, just the preface to the main chapter in the Middle Kingdom's history. Showing that it could develop state-of-the art, clean, attractive and safe cities populated by industrious, attractive and healthy people was part of the plans and aspirations for Beijing 2008. Although China must continue its economic growth, it has shown that it appreciates the need for sustainable development, and its Olympian efforts, as Seligsohn suggested, have 'shown it is indeed possible for China to aggressively pursue economic growth and a cleaner environment at the same time'. [104]

The rhetoric surrounding the legacy to be left following the Beijing 2008 Olympic Games after aspiring to conduct a 'Green Olympics' would, it seems, have been, if not the definitive catalyst, certainly part of the thrust responsible for the laying down of a realistic environmental sustainability policy by China's national government. The draconian measures imposed produced a more acceptable physical environment for the Beijing games; while the success of the nationwide emissions controls and infrastructure developments, particularly transport and electric grid construction ahead of and essentially for the Olympics, demonstrated a 'positive' dimension to authoritarian rule. In January 2009 China's Premier Wen Jiaoboa announced that 'China will be adding greenhouse gas goals in its 12th Five Year Plan, in 2011'. [105]

The World Resources Institute (WRI) fact sheet, 'Energy and Climate Policy Action in China', published in June 2009, posted its evaluation of the related Chinese policy action: the preamble is most supportive of China's efforts: 'In a development little noticed by many in the international community, China is putting numerous domestic energy policies and programs in place that will result in significant progress toward reducing its greenhouse gas output from a business-as-usual scenario.' [106] The report outlined a largely glowing assessment of China's efforts and the headings outlining the report's findings are indicative of this sentiment. [107] The WRI report fact sheet closed with a timely reflection: 'While China and the United States today emit approximately the same amount of greenhouse gases, it is worth noting that China's per capita emissions are only one-fifth of those of the United States.' [108]

The sheer overwhelming size of China's population skews our perception of the impact of its per capita contribution of CO_2 emissions; by 2030 it is projected that it will be producing approximately 7.5 tonnes per capita. Thus, considering that its current population is 1.3 billion and with an anticipated growth in population of 0.4 per cent over the next 21 years, [109] in 2030 China with close to two billion people will be producing 15 billion tons of CO_2 per year. The USA, however, currently produces 18 tonnes per capita each year and with a predicted population of approximately 364 million in 2030 [110] will produce close to 6.6 billion tonnes per year.

So as China aspires to reach the economic development levels of the US it is critical that that it 'decarbonizes' its economy by breaking the nexus between its economic growth and greenhouse gas emissions. [111] The WRI report suggests that China has begun to move in this direction, but it should be said that developed industrial nations such as the US, the EU, Russia, Japan and Australia, as they have higher per capita rates, should also strive to achieve more sustainable levels of carbon emission.

One legacy from the Beijing 2008 Olympic Games is, as Dong and Mangan maintain, 'in the process of construction [which] is compelling to the contemporary world and its concerns – environmental protection'. [112] China is currently taking a major role in global negotiations regarding climate change and the global economic recovery which is indivisibly linked with its industrial production, manufacturing and consumption, [113] with its elevated geopolitical status emerging as a direct flow-on from the adroit manner with which it was able to respond to the global financial crisis of 2008–9.

China's economic power as the world's greatest manufacturer, and thus user of mineral resources, allowed it to ride out the fury of the Global Financial Crisis (GFC), while its massive levels of capital reserves gave it the opening to strengthen its position in offshore assets and despite its exposure to US debt to exert an influential force in the joint efforts of the world's major economies to avert the pending disaster. This was most apparent as it was an undoubted leading player at the G20 summit in London in April 2009. [114] At the United Nations Summit on Climate Change on 22 September 2009, it was the US and China that assumed centre stage and were the subject of the focus of the assembly. [115] So the thread from the 'Green Games' in Sydney to the 'Green Olympics' of Beijing may in a small way lead to Kyoto as well as to London in 2012.

'Towards a One Planet 2012' [116]

The appeal of London was perhaps overwhelming anyway but its almost saturation-bombing-like spin pointedly focused on future legacy, particularly as Taylor suggests on 'two wider issues – the city of London and the overall Olympic movement'. [117] One of the primary aspirations the London 2012 Olympic and Paralympic Games organizers set themselves is 'to stage an inspirational games that capture the imagination of young people around the world and leave a lasting legacy'. [118] The likelihood that they will achieve such a wide-reaching goal, a goal that we feel has never been achieved in Olympic history, with permanency at least, by any Olympic Games. As Cashman said 'legacy' is an elusive word [119] and as an operational concept it is equally as elusive. What are Olympic legacies and what do they really mean?

Gratton and Preuss contend that the idea is itself problematic, for in their opinion the IOC cynically assigns an idiosyncratic and essentially selfish perspective as to what a 'positive' legacy may be:

> One of the main interests of the IOC is a positive 'legacy' of the event. There are three reasons for this. First, a positive legacy avoids the public in the host city/nation blaming the IOC and provides evidence as to why the event has been good for the host city/nation. Second, it justifies the use of scarce public resources for permanent or temporary event infrastructures. Third, a positive legacy motivates other cities/nations to bid for future events. High demand increases the power of the IOC and secures the continuance of the Olympic Games. [120]

They continue their contribution to what they frame as 'a controversial discussion' [121] of the use of investment of 'scarce public resources in mega-sport events such as the Olympic Games' [122] by adding, as they suggest, a 'broader' perspective to the discussion of legacy through their support of the utilization of a three-dimensional gaze, a 'legacy cube', to assess the actual nature and effect of the real legacies that emerge from mega-sport events. [123] As we have commented previously, not all legacies are planned, positive or tangible.

Planning for London 2012 has extravagantly addressed post-Olympic legacies; indeed, the major driving planning philosophy was/is the pursuit of social, environmental and sporting sustainability. These are a major part of London's 'ambitious vision – to use the Olympic and Paralympic Games to make a real change in London, across the UK and globally'. [124] The Olympic Board agreed to the initial Sustainability Plan in 2006 and the current plan outlines its objectives, which are, essentially London's aspirations for the 2012 Olympic Games. The government's final research report, presented in November 2007, [125] was used to formulate the policy decisions for London 2012.

The London 2012 bid team had obviously taken to the task of addressing the IOC framework successfully and the stakeholders involved in the implementation of its vision have certainly and most naturally colonized the nationalistic hubris to promote 'their' own agendas: Labour's values have become 'Olympic values', [126] and not surprisingly the Labour government's Olympic policy arm, the Department of Culture, Media and Sport (DCMS) has morphed the Olympic Legacy into 'Our Promise for 2012' – although some might suggest that the government of the day has appropriated the 2012 games for reasons of own political survival (how could they do anything but?). An Olympic festival is too vast; it contributes too many social, political and economic impacts locally in the host country and globally to *not* be politicized. An analysis of the objectives of *London 2012 Legacy Research Final Report, 2007* provides a suite of legacies that could be suggested are largely driven by social engineering in a very direct response to the demands of the Olympic Legacy framework. [127] As the London games open it will be 101 years from the time Baron de Coubertin reflected upon matters that we now refer to as the Olympic legacy and the issues he expressed concern over. Issues such as the vast spending required, the need to build permanent facilities and the fact that such costs deter(red) small countries from 'putting themselves forward to host the Olympic Games in the future'. [128] The baron's sentiments are even more pertinent today than they were a century ago; indeed, these same 'concerns' are now even less likely to be overcome and as we approach London 2012 similar concerns continue to be raised and viable responses cannot be found.

The waves of criticism are still pounding the London 2012 Olympic Games organizers and the various agencies and stakeholders involved in mounting the festival. Criticism has not only come from established critics of the Olympic movement but from even within the British Olympic fraternity. In July 2009 the chief executive of the British Olympic Association, Andy Hunt, launched a scathing attack on the national government's 'Olympic' department, the DCMS, saying he felt that elite sport was actually being ignored by the government ahead of the Olympics. [129] He further stated that it was his serious belief that the government's plans for sports participation after the Olympic Games would not be met and he believed that elite sport was being marginalized by the Olympic Games Association (OGA). [130]

In response the redoubtable Tessa Jowell, the government minister, who was overseeing the planning and delivery of the 2012 Olympic Games, immediately weighed into the fray saying that 'What won 2012 for London was the scale of our legacy ambition. Not just what the Olympics could do for London but what London could do for the Olympics.' [131] The minister took the opportunity in her 'column' to re-hype some their legacy plans: transforming the heart of east London; making the Olympic Park a sporting, cultural and commercial centre; getting two million more people to become more active; transforming school sport; giving young people five hours of sport a week; and of course not to leave any 'white elephants'. [132]

Both government and opposition seem to be, publicly at least, committed to inspiring the young people of the United Kingdom through sport. With the almost inevitable demise of the Labour government in the UK before 2012 statements made by the Conservative opposition regarding the London Olympics should be considered seriously. The Shadow Minister for Sport and the Olympics, Hugh Robertson, pledged that a Conservative government would arrest the 'disastrous' decline in school sport by reinvigorating it and by turning lottery monies back to towards the original targets. [133] In July 2009 he continued his attack on the government's handling of Olympic Games policy, funding and, particularly, the aspect of legacy. He also attempted to garner the support of elite sporting bodies by promising to restore lottery monies lost to sport at both the elite and community levels. The discourse was, however, restrained; considerable support and recognition of the work of the various Olympic authorities was made in an almost benign manner. Clearly the Conservatives see themselves as being in power (or in a coalition government) in 2012 and thus cannot afford to take a too anti-Olympic stance, fearing the subsequently wrath of the people.

London's bid more than successfully embraced the IOC's 'increased focus on sustainability' [134] and its newly adopted minimum standards for the policies and practices related to the environmental requirements for bidding cities. [135] The official London 2012 Olympic Games website claims that at every stage of the planning sustainability had been built into every aspect of their planning, from recycling construction materials to inspiring a healthy lifestyle, and that it had put sustainability at the heart of its bid for the 2012 games based upon the concept of *Towards a One Planet 2012*. [136]

This discussion will not attempt to critically appraise the plausibility of the London Organising Committee of the Olympic Games Ltd (LOCOG)'s aspirations in the creation of its development legacy; however, an objective examination of the recommendations of the DCMS's final research report and the key commitment areas that emerged elicits, in the authors' minds at least, a deal of scepticism bordering on incredulity: they roll easily off the tongue but are monumental in their substance as they seem to be aimed at influencing (changing) 'wider attitudes and behaviour across the five legacy commitment areas'. [137] The report focused on sporting participation; the regeneration impact; the involvement of young people in community, sporting, cultural and volunteering activities; sustainable environment;

and the promotion of London. [138] Their reflection on the five key commitment areas formed the basis for the final conceptualization of policies, plans and strategies, including the realignment and construction of infrastructure and the Olympic venues and specific sporting facilities.

All of which forms the basis of the Legacy Action Plan for the London 2012 Olympic Games which characterizes London's commitment and obligations to global sustainability. The following five objectives represent London's aspirations for 2012. They are:

- To make the UK a world class-sporting nation, in terms of elite success, mass participation and school sport;
- To transform the heart of east London;
- To inspire a new generation of young people to take part in local volunteering, cultural and physical activity;
- To make the Olympic Park a blueprint for sustainable living;
- To demonstrate that the UK is a creative, inclusive and welcoming place to live in, to visit and for business. [139]

To what extent these aspirations are met cannot be contemplated, except to say, that if the Sustainable Sports Legacy framework with its UK-wide sporting legacy, [140] planned by a prodigious coterie of agencies, can be delivered, then the London Olympics will have achieved a legacy the nature of which no other host city/nation has even approached.

London has planned well and is already putting into action many of its programmes, particularly those aimed sporting and physical activity participation across the age-ranges, such schemes as Play-Sport London [141] and the Inspire-Sport [142] programmes which are flourishing. As Tessa Jowell asserted in the foreword to the 2008 published action plan from the DCMS, *Before, During and After: Making the Most of the London 2012 Games*, as far as the promises made by host cities, 'Too often in the past, governments have expected major events to bring automatic windfall benefits'. [143] London appears to be actually setting the plans into action well ahead.

The scope and detail contained in this 2008 legacy action plan and the associated official London 2012 website publications are replete and unfortunately actually do invoke a slide towards the rhetoric/reality discourse; however, perhaps the critique should shift towards the agency which is, after all, the progenitor of offspring legacies: the IOC. It is the authors' belief that the question should be asked: how real and sustainable are the legacy demands of the IOC? With the selection of Rio de Janeiro as the host city for the 2016 it would appear that the IOC has assumed the role of global social engineer extraordinaire. Reports concerning Rio's domestic social conditions and its logistical problems have suggested a lot will have to be confronted and overcome to create an acceptable environment for the 2016 Olympic Games. [144]

Conclusion

A key psychological aspect of the working concept of sustainability is countering the idea of unlimited growth. Planet Earth and all humans on it cannot expect to see the sort and rate of growth experienced in the last two centuries:

> Rather it is the enhancement of what already exists in the community. A sustainable community is not stagnant; sustainability does not mean things never change. On the contrary, it means always looking for ways to improve a community by strengthening the links between its economy, environment, and society. [145]

This remains a key challenge to the IOC, the Olympic movement and most importantly for the Olympic Games; not to mention its importance for the global community. Change is a constant, but to imagine and live within the limits of that change throws up many challenges.

Although, as Helen Lenskyj suggested a decade ago, the notion of sustainable sport as a concept was new to both sporting and environmentalist lobbies, [146] it was this very dimension of Sydney's bid to host the 2000 Olympics that snatched the millennium games from China's grasp seven years earlier. Sydney's bid manifestly embraced the IOC's soon to be officially adopted environmental mission – that is, the current 13th mission of the Olympic Charter, which aims at encouraging and supporting 'a responsible concern for environmental issues, to promote sustainable development in sport and to require that the Olympic Games are held accordingly'. [147]

The reality of Olympism may well be grounded in humanism, but there has always been an element of contradiction between the ideals and its actual working principles, or the rhetoric and the reality of sport. The early modern Olympic Games (some say *all* Olympic Games!) and the IOC were controlled by what was reminiscent of a Euro-American middle-to upper class 'old boys' club'. It is a gross misconception to believe that the same people regarded sport to be pure, incorruptible and absolutely untarnished by the human frailties of avarice, greed, bigotry and bias. The primary manifestation of the Olympic hegemony at work is the selection and the underlying ideological, political and economic, if not arrant commercial, motives operating and that constrains the cities hosting an Olympic Games.

For sustainability to ensue in sport 'equal attention to the normative, analytical, and political aspects of the concept of sustainability' [148] are required. Dale further argues that the four aspects of sustainability must be 'reconciled' if communities, local or global, are to be sustainable. [149] This is a clear challenge of and for the sustainability of the Olympic Games, the Olympic movement and the IOC. Finally, according to Littig and Griessler, 'if a society is indeed committed to sustainability – the equally legitimate social and cultural needs ought to be taken care of as well. Economic, social, and cultural conditions, efforts, and values are deemed to be resources that also need to be preserved for future generations'. [150] Sport is a major dimension of the culture of most developed/developing societies and has a major role to play in the four pillars of sustainability, as clearly does the IOC.

In the light of the issues facing all future host cities we are of the opinion that the IOC should accept a more active stewardship role over the legacies that it has, essentially, spawned: It should be more involved in ensuring that the legacies are in fact viable; it should oversee them for longer and it should assume a funding and executive role for the implementation programmes for a decade after the Olympic Games. This period of active stewardship of the legacy programmes would incidentally mirror the 11-year cycle of the recent OGGI project. [151]

The IOC would, therefore, be committed to the very legacy of sustainability they approved and instituted in their own enhanced Agenda 21, [152] which they now require of all cities hosting Olympic Games. It would also appear to not be an unreasonable leap to suggest that the IOC's OGKM section could be a very appropriate organizational medium from which the legacy management programmes could be administered.

The IOC has acknowledged that the responsibility for legacy is not solely the responsibility (property) of the hosting city/nation. This acknowledgement was foreshadowed in a statement issued during a symposium jointly organized and held with the IOC Olympic Studies Centre (Autonomous University of Barcelona) in November 2002. The 'Conclusions and Recommendations' of the *Legacy of the Olympic Games: 1984–2000* states that 'It seems clear that the legacy of the Games is not exclusively the property of the former Olympic host cities, rather it should be understood in global and universal terms as the legacy of Olympic Games'. [153] If we look upon 'legacy' as being, like 'sustainability', a journey rather than a destination, [154] who is more competent and more responsible than the IOC to guide and oversee the legacy excursions of future Olympic Games than the IOC? It is after all the Major aspect of the body, and the soul of the trinity: the IOC, the Olympic movement and Olympism that is deliverable.

Notes

[1] This adaptation of the title of Richard Llewellyn's novel may appear to be both obtuse and irreverent. However, the sentiments of this wonderful elegy, which some say is one of the most beautiful novels ever written, and those of this meagre offering are honestly grounded in the hope for the sustainability of humankind and the planet. Reflecting upon his crumbling community, the narrator Huw Morgan looks back to the past and to the future, very much as we are doing so through the Olympic Games.

[2] While many national sport organizations existed by 1896, there were few international sport organizations. These few international sport organizations provided a hegemonic opening for the IOC and the Olympic Movement to enter. See Zakus, 'A Preliminary Examination of the Dialectical Change', ch. 3, especially 42–8.

[3] These factors of the Olympic Charter are more fully described in Zakus, 'The Olympic Charter: A Historical Analysis'.

[4] Zakus, 'The International Olympic Committee'.

[5] IOC, *Olympic Charter* (hereafter OC), 9.

[6] Ibid., 11.

[7] Ibid., 13.

[8] Ibid., 14.

[9] For ease of discussion and writing we refer to both versions of the games through the one term: 'Olympic Games'.

[10] *Concise Oxford Dictionary*.

[11] Ibid.

[12] Cited in Gamble and Hoff, 'Sustainable Community Development'.

[13] Sustainable Development: Definitions, available online at http://www.gdrc.org/sustdev/definitions.html, accessed 6 Sept. 2009.

[14] House of Representatives Standing Committee on Environment and Heritage, *Sustainability for Survival*.

[15] Dale, 'Social Capital and Sustainable Community Development', 15.

[16] Littig and Griessler, 'Social Sustainability', 72.

[17] Ibid.

[18] Cashman, *The Bitter-Sweet Awakening*, 15.

[19] Ibid., 8.

[20] Ibid., 15.

[21] Ibid., 273.

[22] Horton, 'Sport as Public Diplomacy', 857.

[23] Tagore, *Stray Birds*, line 130.

[24] Ibid., line 258.

[25] See Mangan and Dryerson, 'Olympic Legacies', *passim*.

[26] See OC, 15

[27] For a full account of Brundage's Olympic career and of his speech after the terrorist attack in Munich see Guttmann, *The Games Must Go On*.

[28] MacAloon, *This Great Symbol*.

[29] See Allison, *Amateurism in Sport*, 2001.

[30] MacAloon, *This Great Symbol*, *passim*.

[31] Stebbins, 'The Serious Leisure Perspective'.

[32] There is a wide debate on how many pillars of sustainability need to be observed and ensured. Most have three pillars, which apparently lump the human and social together. We speak of these as separate pillars as this is more in keeping with a wider perspective of the concept.

[33] Hiller, 'Assessing the Impact of Mega-Events', 47–9.

[34] Horton, 'Olympism in the Asia-Pacific Region', 173–4.

[35] The IOC has more member nations than the United Nations. An interesting feat.

[36] Zakus, 'Sustainability of Community Sport Organizations'.

[37] See Craig, 'Community Capacity Building'; Lawson, 'Empowering People'; and Vail, 'Community Development and Sports Partcipation'.

[38] Mawson, *The Social Entrepreneur*, 1–14.

[39] We couch this acknowledgement of social entrepreneurs and Mawson's fine community capacity and social capital building while pointing to the inequalities and structural issues of the wider neo-liberal agenda. The underlying issues remain and programmes such as Mawson's are local, limited examples of how to deal with the material inequalities.

[40] Vail, 'Community Development and Sports Participation', 572–9.

[41] See Zakus, 'The International Olympic Committee' for a longer explication of the history of the IOC's financial problems. Also see Barney *et al.*, *Selling the Five Rings*.

[42] Ibid., *passim*.

[43] The IOC holds a wide variety and large volume of financial resources should any of these risks arise. Some of the finances of the IOC can be found on their official website: http://www.olympic.org.

[44] Toohey, 'The Sydney Olympics', 1962–3.

[45] auf der Maur, *The Billion Dollar Game*, passim.

[46] It must be remembered that the Montreal OCOG garnered a surplus; it was the governments of Montreal and Quebec that bore the brunt of Drapeau and his legacy.

[47] See Cashman, *The Bitter-Sweet Awakening*, 129–31.

[48] IOC, 2009b, 14.

[49] Ibid., 19.

[50] OC, 'Rights over the Olympic Games and Olympic properties':
1. The Olympic Games are the exclusive property of the IOC which owns all rights and data relating thereto, in particular, and without limitation, all rights relating to their organisation, exploitation, broadcasting, recording, representation, reproduction, access and dissemination in any form and by any means or mechanism whatsoever, whether now existing or developed in the future. The IOC shall determine the conditions of access to and the conditions of any use of data relating to the Olympic Games and to the competitions and sports performances of the Olympic Games.
2. The Olympic symbol, flag, motto, anthem, identifications (including but not limited to 'Olympic Games' and 'Games of the Olympiad'), designations, emblems, flame and torches, as defined in Rules 8–14 below shall be collectively or individually referred to as 'Olympic properties'. All rights to any and all Olympic properties, as well as all rights to the use thereof, belong exclusively to the IOC, including but not limited to the use for any profit-making, commercial or advertising purposes. The IOC may license all or part of its rights on terms and conditions set forth by the IOC Executive Board.

[51] For an outline of this process in action from the Beijing Games of 2008 to the organizing committee of the London 2012 Olympic Games, see http://www.olympic.org/uk/games/london/full_story_uk.asp?id=2873, accessed 1 Sept. 2009.

[52] See *Towards a One Planet 2012*, 9.

[53] S. Wilson, 'IOC president Jacques Rogge says economic issues shouldn't drive decision on 2016 host city', *Sportsnews*, available online at http://blog.taragana.com/sports/2009/06/16/ioc-president-jacques-rogge-says-economic-issues-shouldnt-drive-decision-on-2016-host-city-4456/, accessed 1 Sept. 2009.

[54] Ibid.

[55] Ibid.

[56] Ibid.

[57] Shipway, 'Sustainable Legacies for the 2012 Olympic Games', 120.

[58] Chappelet, 'Olympic Environmental Concerns as a Legacy of the Winter Games', passim.

[59] For a discussion of the Nobel Prize initiative, see Jennings, *New Lords of the Rings*.

[60] OC, 15.

[61] Horton, '"And the Winner is … Sydney!"', passim.

[62] IOC, 'The Olympic Movement's Agenda 21'.

[63] VANOC, 'Sustainability and Aboriginal Participation'.

[64] Ibid.

[65] Furrer, 'Sustainable Olympic Games', 12.

[66] Ibid., 13.

[67] Ibid., 12.

[68] Beyer, 'The Green Olympic Movement', 423.

[69] OC, 15.

[70] Landry and Yerlè, *One Hundred Years: The Idea, the Presidents, the Achievements*.

[71] Lellouche, 'Albertville and Savoie 1992', 319.

[72] Cashman, *The Bitter-Sweet Awakening*, 192.

[73] Ibid., 192–3.

[74] J-A. Samaranch, quoted in Cashman and Hughes, *The Green Games*, 34, and Cashman, *The Bitter-Sweet Awakening*, 193.

[75] Lenskyj, 'Green Games or Empty Promises?'.

[76] Cashman, *The Bitter-Sweet Awakening*, 213.

[77] Ibid., 215.

[78] Ibid., 202–8.

[79] See Lenskyj, *The Best Olympics Ever?*.

[80] Furrer, 'Sustainable Olympic Games', 12.

[81] 'Goals and Concepts' (2007), Official website of the Beijing 2008 Olympic Games, BOCOG, available at http://en.beijing2008.cn/bocog/concepts/, accessed 2 Sept. 2007. These three themes were chosen by the Chinese very deliberately as they not only indicate an attempt to comply with current dominant international philosophy and policy but are also congruent with the already established *san ge dai bioa* ('The Three Represents') doctrine of: 'most advanced mode of production, most advanced culture and interest of the majority of the people' which, devised by Jiang Zemin in 2000 had been incorporated into constitution in 2003.

[82] Beyer, 'The Green Olympic Movement'.

[83] Ibid.

[84] Ibid.

[85] 'Haze hovers over Beijing day before the opening ceremony', Reuters, 7 Aug. 2008, available online at http://www.reuters.com/article/environmentNews/idUSPEK22736320080807, accessed 8 Aug. 2008.

[86] Seligsohn, 'But Was It the 'Green Olympics?'.

[87] Dong and Mangan, 'Beijing Olympic Legacies', 2032.

[88] Ibid., 2032–3.

[89] See Horton, '"And the Winner is ... Sydney!"', 863.

[90] Greenpeace, 'China after the Olympics'.

[91] Ibid.

[92] Ibid., 'Conclusion – Lessons for future Games and Beijing and Beyond 2008', 42.

[93] Ibid.

[94] Ibid.

[95] Ibid.

[96] The scope of the closures and the strictness of the bans were incredible. Hundreds of mines, steel mills, factories, power stations, cement works, chemical and petrochemical plants were shut down or forced to work at reduced capacities and to reduce emissions. Coke, iron and of course power production was dramatically reduced. These measures were not only imposed on heavy industries in and around Beijing but on coal-burning plants as far afield as Inner Mongolia! (See 'Olympics: Factories and mines shut down to reduce smog', AsiaNewsit.com, 23 July 2008, available at http://www.asianews.it/index.php?l=en&art=12830&size=A, accessed 12 Aug. 2008.

[97] T. Tran, 'Beijing's Air Worse Than at Past Olympics', *US News and Report*, 21 June 2009, available at http://www.usnews.com/articles/science/2009/06/21/study-beijings-air-worse-than-at-past-olympics.html, accessed 20 Sept. 2009.

[98] See Dong and Mangan, 'Beijing Olympic Legacies', 2032–4.

[99] Ibid.

[100] Tran, 'Beijing's Air Worse Than at Past Olympics'.

[101] Seligsohn, 'But Was It the 'Green Olympics?'.

[102] Ibid.

[103] Ibid.

[104] Ibid.

[105] WRI, 'Energy and Climate Policy Action in China'.

[106] Ibid.
[107] See ibid., 1–2:
√ ADOPTED A 20% REDUCTION IN NATIONAL ENERGY INTENSITY BY 2010
Implemented energy efficiency programs.
Raised taxes on petroleum.
Adopted new rural vehicle fuel economy standards.
Put China's energy conservation law into effect.
Required green government procurement
Announced a new program in May 2009 to provide subsides to promote green home appliances
√ PASSED A NATIONAL RENEWABLE ENERGY STANDARD OF 15% BY 2020
Grew its solar industry.
Diversified domestic energy sources.
Implemented coalbed and coalmine methane extraction projects.
√ PROMOTED INFRASTRUCTURE FOR GREEN DEVELOPMENT. ONE-THIRD OF CHINA's STIMULUS PACKAGE IS FOCUSED ON INFRASTRUCTURE THAT WILL PROMOTE ENERGY EFFICIENCY.
The major elements of the stimulus package are:
$90 billion in rail construction in 2009.
$160 billion over two years for electric grid construction.
Made new buildings more energy efficient through clearer regulations and increasing enforcement.
Established a pilot program in 13 cities to subsidize the purchase of hybrids, all electric and hydrogen vehicles for urban government vehicle fleets.
Set goals for energy efficient lighting.
[108] Ibid., 2.
[109] ISEE, 'World Population and GDP Growth'.
[110] US Census Bureau, Population Division.
[111] WRI, 'Energy and Climate Policy Action in China', 2.
[112] Dong and Mangan, 'Beijing Olympic Legacies', 2032.
[113] 'China, US vow urgent action on climate change', *Chinadaily*, 28 Sept. 2009.
[114] B. Malkin, 'G20: Australia lobbies for China to play greater role in IMF', *Daily Telegraph* (London), 23 March 2009, available at http://www.telegraph.co.uk/finance/financetopics/g20-summit/5037981/G20-Australia-lobbies-for-China-to-play-greater-role-in-IMF.htmlst, accessed 5 April 2009.
[115] 'China, US vow urgent action on climate change'.
[116] *Towards a One Planet 2012*, London 2012 Sustainability Plan November 2007.
[117] Taylor and Edmonson, 'Major Sporting Events – Planning for Legacy', 173.
[118] The official London 2012 webpage, cited in ibid.
[119] Cashman, *The Bitter-Sweet Awakening*, 15.
[120] Gratton and Preuss, 'Maximising Olympic Impacts by Building Up Legacies', 1922.
[121] Ibid., *passim*.
[122] Ibid.
[123] Ibid., 1924.
[124] *Towards a One Planet 2012*, 6.
[125] See DCMS, *London 2012 Legacy Research Final Report*.
[126] Tessa Jowell, 'What Social Legacy of 2012?' Speech to the Fabian Fringe, Manchester, 27 Sept. 2007, quoted in Girginov and Hills, 'Sustainable Sports Legacy of the London Olympics', 2101.
[127] IOC, 'Report of the IOC Evaluation Commission for the Games of the XXIX Olympiad in 2008'.

[128] de Coubertin, Olympic Review, April 1911, 59–62, cited in, 'Coubertin on Legacy', *The Olympic Review, 2005*, available at: http://multimedia.olympic.org/pdf/en_report_928.pdf, accessed 20 Sept. 09.

[129] Paul Kelso, 'London 2012: British Olympic Association slams Government's post-Games planning', *Daily Telegraph*, 7 Jul 2009, available at http://www.telegraph.co.uk/sport/othersports/olympics/london2012/5759084/London-2012-British-Olympicassociation-slams-Governments-post-Games-planning.html, accessed 20 Sept. 2009.

[130] Ibid.

[131] Tessa Jowell, 'We are delivering legacy we promised', *Daily Telegraph*, 21 July 2009, available at http://www.telegraph.co.uk/sport/othersports/olympics/london2012/5879054/London-2012-We-are-delivering-legacy-we-promised-says-Tessa-Jowell.html, accessed 20 Sept. 2009.

[132] Ibid.

[133] Richard Bright, 'Conservatives make sporting pledges to wrest Labour decline', *Daily Telegraph*, 25 March 2009, available at www.telegraph.co.uk/sport/.../Conservatives-make-sporting-pledges-to-wrest-Labour-decline.html, accessed 20 Sept. 2009.

[134] Taylor and Edmonson, 'Major Sporting Events – Planning for Legacy', 173.

[135] See IOC, 'Report of the IOC Evaluation Commission for the Games of the XXIX Olympiad in 2008'.

[136] *Towards a One Planet 2012*; DCMS, *London 2012 Legacy Research Final Report*, 3.

[137] The title and fundamental concept for London 2012 Sustainability Plan 2012 was largely derived and inspired by the World Wildlife Fund's BioRegional concept of 'One Planet Living' and its ten guiding principles. See http://www.oneplanetliving.org/index.html, accessed 1 Sept. 2009.

[138] Ibid., 4–5.

[139] Ibid.

[140] Girginov and Hills, 'Sustainable Sports Legacy of the London Olympics', Table 2, 2101.

[141] See http://www.london.gov.uk/playsport/, accessed 1 Sept. 2009.

[142] The Inspire programme of the London 2012 Olympic Games is 'An Olympic and Paralympic first, the Inspire programme officially recognises outstanding non-commercial projects and events inspired by the Games. Sport, culture, education, sustainability, volunteering and business opportunities all feature' (available at http://www.london2012.com/get-involved/inspire-programme/index.php, accessed 3 Oct. 2009).

[143] Tessa Jowell, in DCMS, *Before, During and After*, 2.

[144] A typical comment reported in the Rio newspaper *O Dia* in October 2009, just after Rio won the 2016 Olympic bid was: 'The film director Moacyr Góes confessed he was "haunted by the fear of corruption, the poor use of public money and the electoral use" of the Olympic Games. The Olympics should only take place in Rio, he concluded, "if they are good for those who live … in the areas controlled by drug traffickers or paramilitaries, for education, for those who spend their lives on board a hellish transport system"': Tom Phillips, 'Rio de Janeiro Captures 2016 Olympics – but now the work begins', *The Guardian*, 2 Oct. 2009, available at http://www.guardian.co.uk/sport/2009/oct/02/rio-de-janeiro-2016-olympics/print, accessed 7 Oct. 2009. Phillips goes on to say: 'The aim is also to increase involvement of the local population, improve the socioeconomic and health benefits they derive from it, strengthen international cooperation projects for sustainable development, help combat social exclusion, encourage new consumer habits, promote a sports infrastructure which is even better adapted to social needs, and further improve the integration of development and environment concepts into sports policies. … That may be true. But in Rio de Janeiro, where the roads grow more congested by the day and where there were officially 5,717 homicides last year in the state as a whole, there is much still to be done. Even with a Brazilian God on Rio's side.' Upon reflection these are comparatively minor 'stumbling

blocks' when held up against those the selection of Beijing presented the Olympic fraternity. BBC journalist Paulo Cabral, writing from Deodoro, wrote: 'Rio's victory was received with mixed feelings in the poor and run-down neighbourhood of Deodoro, the second most important site for the 2016 Olympics due. But even in the bars where TV sets were tuned to channels showing the Copenhagen decision, not everybody was paying attention. Unemployed Davidson Costa da Silva complained the government had the wrong priorities. "I don't think this is what we should spend money on now," he said. "Look at our hospitals and our schools and you will know what I mean"' (http://news.bbc.co.uk/2/hi/americas/8288219.stm, accessed 7 Oct. 2009). Such moments, however, are not atypical ahead of most Olympic Games, for example London's and Vancouver's successful bids were greeted with an avalanche of negative comments.

[145] 'An Introduction to Sustainability'.

[146] Lenskyj, *Inside the Olympic Industry*, 155.

[147] OC, 15.

[148] Dale, 'Social Capital and Sustainable Community Development', 15.

[149] Ibid.

[150] Littig and Griessler, 'Social Sustainability', 67.

[151] See Furrer, 'Sustainable Olympic Games', 15–18.

[152] While Agenda 21, which evolved from the Rio Declaration on Environment and Development, the product of the UN Conference held in Rio de Janeiro in June 1992 (the Rio Earth Summit), was exclusively concerned with the environment, the principles of the Olympic Movement's Agenda 21 have a wider remit. (IOC, cited in Furrer, 'Sustainable Olympic Games', 12.)

[153] IOC, 'Conclusion and Recommendations', 4.

[154] Australian House of Representatives Standing Committee on Environment and Heritage, *Sustainability for Survival*.

References

Allison, L. *Amateurism in Sport: An Analysis and a Defence*. London: Frank Cass, 2001.

'An Introduction to Sustainability'. Available online at http://www.sustainablemeasures.com, accessed 5 May 2008.

auf de Maur, N. *The Billion Dollar Game: Jean Drapeau and the 1976 Olympics*. Toronto: James Lorimer, 1976.

Australian House of Representatives Standing Committee on Environment and Heritage. *Sustainability for Survival: Creating a Climate for Change: Inquiry into a Sustainability Charter*, Sept. 2007, available online at http://www.aph.gov.au/House/committee/environ/charter/report/fullreport.pdf, accessed 1 Sept. 2009.

Barney, Robert K., Stephen R. Wenn and Scott G. Martyn. *Selling the Five Rings: The International Olympic Committee and the Rise of Olympic Commercialism*. Salt Lake City, UT: University of Utah Press, 2002.

Beyer, S. 'The Green Olympic Movement: Beijing 2008'. *The Chinese Journal of International Law* 5 (2) (2006): 423–40 [originally published online on 19 May 2006 and available at http://chinesejil.oxfordjournals.org/cgi/content/abstract/5/2/423, accessed 10 Dec. 2008].

Booth D. and Colin Tatz. '"Swimming with the Big Boys": The Politics of Sydney's Olympic Bid'. *Sporting Traditions* 11, no. 1 (Nov. 1994): 3–23.

Booth, D. and Colin Tatz. *One-eyed: A View of Australian Sport*. Sydney: Allen and Unwin, 2000.

Brown, A. and J. Massey. *The Impact of Major Sporting Events: The Sports Development Impact of the Manchester 2002 Commonwealth Games: Initial Baseline Research For UK Sport*. Manchester Institute for Popular Culture, Manchester Metropolitan University, June 2001.

Cashman, R. *The Bitter-Sweet Awakening: The Legacy of the Sydney 2000 Olympic Games*. Sydney: Walla Walla Press, in conjunction with the Centre for Olympic Studies, University of Technology, Sydney, 2006.

Cashman, R. and A. Hughes, A. *The Green Games: A Golden Opportunity*. Sydney: Centre for Olympic Studies, UNSW, 1998.

Chappelet, J.-L. 'Olympic Environmental Concerns as a Legacy of the Winter Games'. *The International Journal of the History of Sport*, 25, no. 14 (2008): 1884–1902.

Concise Oxford Dictionary, 11th edn (CD version). Oxford: Oxford University Press, 2009.

Coubertin, Pierre de. *Olympic Review*, April 1911, 59–62, In *The Olympic Review*, 2005, available online at http://multimedia.olympic.org/pdf/en_report_928.pdf, accessed 20 Sept. 2009.

Craig, G. 'Community Capacity Building: Something Old Something New?' *Critical Social Policy* 27 (2007): 335–59.

Dale, A. 'Social Capital and Sustainable Community Development: Is There a Relationship?' In *A Dynamic Balance: Social Capital and Sustainable Community Development*, edited by A. Dale and J. Onyx. Vancouver: UBC Press, 2005: 13–30.

DCMS (Department of Culture, Media and Sport). *London 2012 Legacy Research Final Report*. London: DCMS, November, 2007.

DCMS. *Before, During and After: Making the Most of the London 2012 Games*. London: DCMS, 2008.

Dong Jinxia and J.A. Mangan. 'Beijing Olympic Legacies: Certain Intentions and Certain and Uncertain Outcomes'. *The International Journal of the History of Sport* 25, no. 14 (Dec. 2008): 1869–2169.

Furrer, P. 2002. 'Sustainable Olympic Games – *A dream or a reality?*' Unpublished discussion paper, available online at http://www.omero.unito.it/web/Furrer%20(eng.).PDF, accessed 17 Sept. 2009.

Gamble D.N. and M.D. Hoff. 'Sustainable Community Development'. In *The Handbook of Community Practice*, edited by M. Weil. Thousand Oaks, CA: Sage, 2005: 169–88.

Girginov, V. and Laura Hills. 'Sustainable Sports Legacy of the London Olympics: Creating a Link between the London Olympics and Sports Participation'. *The International Journal of the History of Sport* 25, no. 14 (Dec. 2008): 2091–116.

Goodland, R. 'Sustainability: Human, Social, Economic, and Environmental'. In *Encyclopaedia of Global Environmental Change*. London: John Wiley and Sons, 2002.

Gratton, C. and Holger Preuss. 'Maximising Olympic Impacts by Building Up Legacies'. *The International Journal of the History of Sport*, 25, no. 14 (2008); 1922–38.

Greenpeace. 'China after the Olympics: Lessons from Beijing, July 28, 2008'. Available online at http://www.greenpeace.org/china/en/press/reports/green, accessed 27 Jan. 2009.

Guttmann, A. *The Games Must Go on: Avery Brundage and the Olympic Movement*. New York: Columbia University Press, 1984.

Hiller, Harry H. 'Assessing the Impact of Mega-Events: A Linkage Model'. *Current Issues in Tourism* 1 (1998): 47–57.

Horton, P.A. 'Olympism in the Asia-Pacific Region: A Question of Naivety or Pragmatism?' *Culture Society, Sport* 1, no. 1 (May 1998): 167–84.

Horton, P.A. 'Sport as Public Diplomacy and Public Disquiet: Australia's Ambivalent Embrace of the Beijing Olympics'. *The International Journal of the History of Sport*, 25, no. 7 (Jan. 2007): 851–75.

Horton, P.A. '"And the Winner is … Sydney!" Olympic Engagement as Public Diplomacy'. In *Collection of Papers and Abstracts, Beijing Forum 2008, The Harmony of Civilizations and prosperity for All: The Universal Value and the Development Trend of Civilization* ('Olympic Spirit and World Harmony' panel), 7–9 November. Beijing: Beijing Forum Organizing Committee, 2008: 348–70.

IOC (International Olympic Committee). 'Report of the IOC Evaluation Commission for the Games of the XXIX Olympiad 2008'. Available at: http://www.olympic.org/common/asp/ download_report.asp?.file=en_report_299.pdf&id=299, accessed 17 April 2009.

IOC (International Olympic Committee). 'Conclusion and Recommendations', International Symposium on Legacy of the Olympic Games, 1984–2000, Joint Symposium, IOC Olympic Studies Centre Olympic Studies Centre (Autonomous University of Barcelona), November 2002.

IOC. *Olympic Charter: In Force as from the 7 July 2007*. Available at http://www.olympic.org/uk/ olympic_charter, accessed 30 Aug. 2009.

IOC. 'Manual for Candidate Cities for the Games of the XXIX Olympiad 2008'. Available at http:// multimedia.olympic.org/pdf/en_report_296.pdf, accessed 17 April 2009.

IOC. 'The Olympic Movement's Agenda 21, 2009'. Available at http://www.olympic.org/uk/ organization/mission/environment/agenda_uk.asp, accessed 17 April 2009.

ISEE (International Sustainable Energy Exchange). 'World Population and GDP Growth'. Available at http://www.hart-see.com/index.php?pagex=world-population-gdp-growth#PopFacts, accessed 26 Sept. 2009.

Jennings, A. *New Lords of the Rings: Olympic Corruption and How to Buy Gold Medals*. London: Pocket Books, 1996.

Landry, Ferdnand and Yerlè. *One Hundred Years: The Idea, the Presidents, the Achievements, Vol. III: The Presidencies of Lord Killanin and Juan Antonio Samaranch*. Lausanne: International Olympic Committee, 1996.

Lellouche, Lawson, H. 'Empowering People, Facilitating Community Development, and Contributing to Sustainable Development: The Social Work of Sport, Exercise, and Psysical Education Programs'. *Sport, Education and Society*, 10, no. 1 (2005): 135–60.

Lellouche, Michele. 'Albertville and Savoie 1992'. In *Historical Dictionary of the Modern Olympic Movement*, edited by John E. Findling and Kimberly D. Pelle. Westport: CT: Greenwood Press, 1996: 318–25.

Lenskyj, H.J. *Inside the Olympic Industry: Power, Politics and Activism*. Albany, NY: State University of New York Press: 2000.

Lenskyj, H.J. *The Best Olympics Ever? Social Impacts of Sydney 2000*. Albany, NY: State University of New York Press, 2002.

Lenskyj, H.J. 'Green Games or Empty Promises? Environmental Issues and Sydney2000'. In *Fourth International Symposium for Olympic Research – 'Global and Cultural Critique: Problematizing the Olympic Games' Proceedings, Fourth International Symposium for Olympic Research* (October 1998), edited by Robert K. Barney, Kevin B. Wamsley, Scott G. Martyn and Gordon H. MacDonald. London, ON: The University of Western Ontario, 1998: 173–80.

Littig, B. and E. Griessler. 'Social Sustainability: A Catchword Between Political Pragmatism and Social Theory'. *International Journal of Sustainable Development* 8, no. 1–2 (2005): 65–79.

MacAloon, J. *This Great Symbol: Pierre de Coubertin and the Origins of the Modern Olympic Games*. Chicago: University of Chicago Press, 1981.

Mangan. J.A. and M. Dyerson, M., eds. 'Olympic Legacies: Intended and Unintended – Political, Cultural, Economic, Educational'. Special edition, *The International Journal of the History of Sport* 25, no. 14 (Dec. 2008).

Mawson, A. *The Social Entrepreneur: Making Communities Work*. London: Atlantic Books, 2008.

Seligsohn, D. 'But Was It the 'Green Olympics?' Blog available at www.greenbiz.com/blog/2008/08/ 26/but-was-it-green-olympics, accessed 5 Jan. 2009.

Shipway, R. 'Sustainable Legacies for the 2012 Olympic Games'. *Journal of the Royal Society for the Promotion of Health* 127, no. 3 (May 2007): 119–24. Available at http://www.soci.ucalgary.ca/ seriousleisure/MainPages/BasicConcepts.htm, accessed 29/ May 2009.

Stebbins, R. 'The Serious Leisure Perspective: Basic Concepts'. University of Calgary, 2009. Available at http://www.soci.ucalgary.ca/seriousleisure/MainPages/BasicConcepts.htm, accessed 29 May 2009.

Tagore, Rabindranath. *Stray Birds*. Minneapolis, MN: Filiquarian Publishing LLC, 2007.

Taylor, M. and I. Edmonson. 'Major Sporting Events – Planning for Legacy'. *Proceedings of the Institution of Civil Engineers, Municipal Engineer* 160, issue ME4 (Dec. 2007): 171–6.

Toohey, K. 'The Sydney Olympics: Striving for Legacies – Overcoming Short-Term Disappointments and Long-Term Deficiencies'. *The International Journal of the History of Sport* 25, no. 14 (2008): 1953–72.

Towards a One Planet 2012 (London 2012 Sustainability Plan, November 2007). Available at http://www.london2012.com/documents/locog-publications/london-2012-sustainability-plan.pdf. Accessed 31 July 2009.

US Census Bureau, Population Division. Interim State Projections, 2005, Table A: 'Interim of Total Population for the United States and States: April 1, 2000 to July 1, 2030'. Release date 21 April 2005, available at http://www.census.gov/population/projections/SummaryTabA1.pdf, accessed 26 Sept. 2009.

Vail, S. 'Community Development and Sports Participation'. *Journal of Sport Management* 21 (2007): 571–96.

VANOC (Vancouver Olympic Games Organizing Committee). (2009). 'Sustainability and Aboriginal Participation'. Available at http://www.vancouver2010.com/en/sustainabiltyand-abooriginalpart/, accessed 17 April 2009.

WRI (World Resources Institute). 'Energy and Climate Policy Action in China', fact sheet,2009. Available at http://pdf.wri.org/factsheets/factsheet_china_policy.pdf, accessed 25 Sept. 2009.

Zakus, D.H. 'A Preliminary Examination of the Dialectical Change in "Modern" Sport and the Intervention of the Canadian State in Sport Between 1968 and 1988'. Unpublished doctoral dissertation, University of Alberta, 1988.

Zakus, D.H. 'The International Olympic Committee'. In *Encyclopaedia of the Modern Olympic Movement*, edited by J. Findling and K. Pelle. Westport, CT: Greenwood, 2004: 439–52.

Zakus, D.H. 'The Olympic Charter: A Historical Analysis of a Hegemonic Document for Global Sport'. In *Beyond the Torch – Olympics and the Australian Culture*, edited by N. Guoth, D. Adair and B. Coe. Melbourne: ASSH, 2005: 5–14.

Zakus, D.H. 'The Philosophy of Olympism'. Keynote address to the Singapore Olympic Academy, Singapore, July 2005.

Zakus, D.H. 'Sustainability of Community Sport Organizations'. Distinguished speaker presentation, IV Gijón Economics of Sports Congress ('Social Responsibility and Sustainability in Sports'), 8–9 May 2009.

Manly Displays: Exhibitions and the Revival of the Olympic Games

Lia Paradis

This article explores the shift from international exhibitions to the Modern Olympic Games as the preferred site for the public performance of manly character. As fin-de-siecle European and American societies increasingly grew concerned about the waning vitality of men and the individual's marginalization in a mechanized world, they sought out a new form of mass spectacle. National tensions grew that would eventually lead to WWI, and citizenry previously enraptured by the displays of state-directed competition at the international exhibitions were attracted to a venue in which the performance and effort of the individual was the central focus. The Games, particularly in the emergence of the marathon as the showcase event, became the preferred location for the performance of active masculinity that did not involve aggression but, instead, individual excellence achieved through discipline and the adherence to rules.

Introduction

The great exhibitions of the nineteenth century were where modernity was on display. Engaged in an escalating nationalist discourse that took many forms, nations flaunted their bureaucratic sophistication and the maturity of their civic institutions just as much as their industrial and cultural accomplishments, through the planning and execution of these fairs. The Crystal Palace Exhibition, organized by Prince Albert, established these events of civic display as de rigueur for any nation wishing to assert its modernity. It drew more than six million visitors, and the popularity of such events continued to grow: the 1889 and 1900 *expositions universelles* in Paris drew 32 and 50 million visitors, respectively. [1] Why, then, did the Olympics emerge as a popular new form of civic spectacle during the 1890s and 1900s, eventually rivalling the exhibitions in the public imagination? Why was Pierre de Coubertin successful at re-inventing the Olympic Games when the exhibitions still seemed to provide such a satisfying display?

In fact, in the West such exhibitions were increasingly unsatisfying by the end of the nineteenth century. Through their success, they had become synonymous with the modern nation state and so, as concern grew about the deleterious effects that modernity was having on men, the display of modernity (and masculinity) at exhibitions became a target for people's anxieties. Men had tamed the nation by legislating reform and establishing effective institutions of governance, but this meant that the public sphere was increasingly seen as a domesticated and, therefore, feminized space. [2] The diffuse, bureaucratic power of modernity was effective in direct proportion to the invisibility of its coercive elements and so there were fewer opportunities for political force on the domestic front. [3] By the 1880s, the growing rivalry between nations, particularly through their imperial efforts, had many worried that middle-class European and American men no longer possessed the aggressive, action-oriented masculinity that might soon be required. [4] At the same time, the sporting tradition in Britain's elite schools was becoming widely accepted as *the* method for moulding middle-class men who valued fair play, self-sacrifice and collective effort. Other countries either attempted to replicate this model or formulated nationally their own specific methods of athletic pedagogy. What was not really up for debate was the fundamental connection between sports, appropriate masculinity and the continuing health of the nation and the empire. Of course, much of this sporting activity was happening behind the walls of elite institutions; usually private schools or military clubs. [5] Meanwhile, newer forms of sport that were captivating the public imagination were feared to be further manifestations of a vulgarized public space popularized by the expanding influence of mass society.

De Coubertin asserted a direct line of descent from physical education pedagogy to the revival of the Olympic Games. [6] It will be argued here, however, that the exhibitions movement was as much a source of the Olympic movement as athletic culture. Sporting culture focused on the inculcation of certain values and a sense of unity, but emphasized the 'doing' rather than the 'displaying'. The original Olympics in ancient Athens were intended first and foremost as spectacles for the expression and promotion of civic ideals, and the proponents of exhibitions had the nation (and the world, for that matter) in their sights as the target audience for similar lessons. By the 1890s, growing concerns about the connection between modernity and declining virility brought into question the efficacy of both sports and the exhibitions at instilling masculine ideals. The Olympics were successfully revived because over time they proved to be a better medium for the public display and promotion of active heroic masculinity as nationalist and imperialist pressures grew more urgent at the turn of the century. The Olympics combined the values attached to both amateur athletics and the major public exhibitions in a new civic spectacle that welcomed the public spectatorship of the exhibitions, but emphasized the sporting culture's focus on action and individual achievement.

The Exhibitions and Sports

The 26-year-old Baron Pierre de Coubertin addressed the *concours des exercises physiques* at the 1889 Universal Exhibition on the importance of physical education to the reform of the French school system. He, and many others, still stinging from the nationalist shame of the Franco-Prussian War, were interested in finding ways to *rebronzer la France*, as he put it. A major idea he had towards that end was that the ancient Olympic Games should be revived. [7] His suggestion was met, he later said, with 'total, absolute incomprehension'. [8] So what views did his contemporaries have on the roles of exhibitions and sports that could explain why, at a meeting filled with fellow sporting enthusiasts, held in the midst of the largest and most popular civic display ever mounted, de Coubertin's suggestion for something that would amalgamate the two concepts, should fall on such deaf ears?

Both de Coubertin and the commissioner of the 1889 Exposition, Edouard Lockroy, understood the relationship between civil society and the mode of spectacle each was championing. At the time, Lockroy wrote: 'The great fairs followed the [ancient] Olympic Games. The Expositions followed the great fairs; I do not know what will follow the Expositions, but one can assume that it will once again be the same thing.' [9] In the narrative put forward by Lockroy, there was a traceable genealogy of civic displays that started with the Olympic Games in their ancient form. As societies developed, so did their spectacles. The exhibitions were the most recent opportunity for a community to celebrate its connectedness. [10] The nineteenth-century liberal agenda to which Lockroy and de Coubertin both subscribed sought to encourage that collective identification and regulate it in order to utilize it in the service of national progress. [11]

Since the Crystal Palace Exhibition in London in 1851, exhibitions had been privileged locations of discourse on both the present and future condition of nations. [12] One can appreciate what place exhibitions held in the contemporary imagination by examining two exhibitions mounted during the years of de Coubertin's campaign for the Olympics that are considered classics of the model: Paris 1889 and Chicago 1893. Organizers took the 1889 Exposition as an opportunity to represent, as much to their own people as to the rest of the world, the virility and dynamism of republican France. The thematic content was obvious, as the exposition was to occur in the centennial year of the French Revolution. [13] It was conceived as a monument to rationalism, progress and the secular religion of France but by 1889, the virulent chauvinist movement of General Boulanger almost brought down the very republic that the exhibition was intended to celebrate. [14]

The 1889 Exhibition was a carefully orchestrated model of reality. Unprecedented in its size and scope, it was attended over the course of almost six months by more than 32 million people. The *Palais des Machines* and the Eiffel Tower declared in iron the strength and virility of the French Republic. The individual was represented through his association with other individuals in the cooperative project of nation-building. One message was undoubtedly the impossibility of achieving anything on so large a scale as that presented at the expo without an effort that was both coordinated and nationwide. 'Through the provision of object lessons in power – the power to command and arrange things and bodies for public display' – the exhibitions enabled the public to see the process by which they were constituted as a single unit: a society.

[15] Naming this phenomenon the 'exhibitionary complex', Tony Bennett describes how this form of spectacle fulfils the civic role that Lockroy implied, rendering 'the forces and principles of order visible to the populace' so that, in their awareness of themselves as part of that ordering, the public 'was transformed … into a people, a citizenry'. [16] Organizers categorized and homogenized the 'contents' of the nation in order to define it; and the audience simultaneously observed both the process and the fact that they were sharing it with others.

The first great American 'world's fair' was held in Chicago in 1893. Not discouraged after his first efforts at the 1889 meeting, de Coubertin made Chicago a specific destination on his 1893 US tour as he promoted an Olympic revival at the congress on athletics, one of many intended, as in Paris, to gather 'intellectuals, labour leaders, and social reformers to debate significant political and philosophical issues of the age'. [17] The 'World Columbian Exhibition' also commemorated an anniversary, in this case the 400th anniversary of the landing of Columbus (financial difficulties had postponed the fair for a year). Again, organizers put forward a story of progress: this new (post-Civil War) nation 'where the rights of one citizen only ends where the rights of another begins' was an improvement on the old European model, 'Peopled by … the most enlightened and most progressive of the human race … dedicated to the highest civilizing links of humanity, liberty, justice and equality'. The fair's promoters focused on the achievements of civilization and the speed with which America had acquired them. It was taking place in a 'metropolis, around which is rapidly crystallizing the trade and commerce of the world'. So rapidly, in fact, that 'no artist, however great, could paint [it], for, while he was preparing his sketches … Chicago would have outgrown the picture'. [18]

Following the model already established in Europe, a key element to the fair was its ability to transform space and create an environment where the population was seeing a display of civic harmony and achievement. In Paris, the exposition was superimposed on the unregimented street plan of an old city; Chicago's fair sprang up on land that had yet to be taken over by the city. In both cases, the exhibition was symbolic of the task each nation was asserting that it had achieved: either the modernization of an ancient nation or the establishment in the wilderness of a new one. Also in both cases, the content emphasized inclusivity, focusing on *collective efforts* in education, industry, medicine and conquest, even as its values were unarguably middle-class.

And it was always a display; there was always an audience. One of the most important audiences for France's display of industrial might in 1889 was not even present. When Guy de Maupassant said that the exhibition had 'shown the world … the strength, the vigour … of France', the 'world' for whom that message was intended was Germany. [19] The symbols of the revolution centenary were deployed to champion the Third Republic as its legitimate heir, in stark contrast to the crypto-absolutism of Bismarck's Germany. Chicago also had a double audience: those at home – for whom the exhibitionary complex would, in its full measure, help to consolidate a national identity, and for many of whom the western US and its cities were still not quite legitimately civilized – and those in Europe, for whom the exhibition was intended to provide incontrovertible proof that the United States had arrived. In Paris, Chicago and every other exhibition and world's fair during this period, we see these central concepts of audience, and *active participation* through observation.

The sporting model was different. Neither democratic inclusivity nor public spectacle had figured in what were considered legitimate sporting models up until this point. J.A. Mangan and others have detailed the dominant construction of sporting culture as one in which a private project created public leaders. In the most elite traditional field sports, an audience was barely imagined, and even in the newer team sports models, the only opportunity for 'spectacle' was for 'pupils at school and students at university to display their unquestionable masculinity to their respectively admiring peers'. The value placed on 'fair play' in the elite educational institutions of Great Britain, and those hoping to recreate that model on the continent (including de Coubertin) and in the United States, only served to emphasize that the usefulness of athleticism was believed to be in the doing, not in the watching. [20]

Mangan points out that the English public-school sports culture admired by de Coubertin was developed in the mid-Victorian period primarily at schools whose elite status was not firmly established. Innovators such as Thomas Arnold promoted their schools by touting the benefits of their methods (both to the boy and the greater nation). The cultivation of athletic and corporate-minded middle-class men was treated as a natural process of development rather than a particular scheme of gender and class indoctrination, but their benefits were sold most forcefully to a newly-arriving class of families who needed reassuring that, through this process, their sons would be made into *useful gentlemen* – both attributes equally important. [21] Arnold and the others intended that these boys should learn to exercise self-control and cooperation within the cohort of their own class and gender. Such an education delineated them as men of exceptional character, separated from the rest of society.

The exhibitions displayed and espoused this mid-Victorian model of masculinity but also asserted that all citizens were intertwined *equally* in a web of democratic obligation. Through sport the middle-class boy was taught differently – he was specially equipped, both by nature and by training. The weight of the nation and the empire (or the republic) was put on his shoulders. [22] However, all of this was done within a private or semi-private setting; either the school or the university. The majority of the men who listened to de Coubertin's exhortations at the 1889 exhibition would, therefore, have struggled to understand how a public athletics display would aid in his intended purpose of inculcating civic virility and social harmony. Among the aristocracy of Europe, military culture (shooting, fencing) and the life of the country squire (hunting) were not sporting models that lent themselves to display. On the continent various forms of gymnastics – neither competitive nor spectator sport – were very popular among the growing middle classes and were overtly touted as methods for inculcating national pride, identity and masculine virility. [23] So it is likely that when de Coubertin spoke to the *concours*, examples of the sports that everyone would watch at these new Olympics did not spring readily to mind.

There were other popular sports during the same period in nations that also were fond of mounting elaborate exhibitions. They just weren't the kind that de Coubertin's audience was either familiar or comfortable with. Team sports were increasingly popular in Great Britain and its settler colonies, as well as the United States. In most cases, however, they were sources of division, not unification, within nations because they reinforced class differences. Some, like cricket, rugby and football, began as markers of elite culture and status because they were identified with elite school and university athletics. However, by the end of the century only cricket and one form of rugby retained that identity because the working classes had claimed both football and a version of rugby as their own with team members who couldn't afford to play without pay. [24] In America, on the other hand, some sports never had a purely amateur existence. The growing popularity of baseball, for example, did not fit the amateur athletics ethos cherished by a new indigenous American elite, still suffering from an inferiority complex regarding their European cousins. The particular American enthusiasm for the Olympics, which will be discussed further below, was perhaps in part because it was seen as a way to combat baseball and the professionalization of other sports.

For de Coubertin's audience at the 1889 *concours* and those who attended with him the athletics congress at the Chicago World's Fair, athletic amateurism was a very important class marker. Public sporting events in France, such as free equestrian exhibitions where members of the aristocracy displayed their skills, were tellingly segregated so that the wealthy and the working classes did not attend on the same day. They were not therefore seen as an opportunity, like the fairs, where every citizen could imagine their shared community. [25] Cycling was the one new sport in France that was quickly becoming a spectator phenomenon across classes, even prompting the first newspaper sports column in the country. It is interesting to note, however, that the combination of spectatorship for both exhibitions and sporting events, and the accompanying anxieties about what kind of active masculinity the nation wanted to promote, found a transatlantic connection in the creation of the first indoor velodrome in France, in 1894. Known as the *Vélodrome de Buffalo*, it was built on the site of Buffalo Bill's 1889 Wild West show. Meanwhile, even as cycling was becoming the first mass spectator sport in France, at the Chicago fair in 1893, Bill Cody had been denied permission to mount his show in the city during the fair, and had been forced to set up (with great success) just outside the city boundaries. The organizers of the fair did not find the Wild West show a suitable addition to their message of civilization. [26] On both sides of the Atlantic, there were anxieties about what kinds of public displays of masculine action – whether sports or a staging of 'frontier' skills – should or should not be encouraged.

At the moment that de Coubertin suggested joining these two cultural phenomena there were firmly entrenched ideas of what both exhibitions and sport were intended to achieve and how. In 1889, an event such as de Coubertin was describing suggested professional athletes who, it would have been assumed, could never instil any sense of honour or self-sacrifice in observers because the participants were being paid for their efforts. His suggestion came just as a nagging uncertainty was taking hold about the social structures that the exhibitions were intended to celebrate, as well as the educational model that produced the men who created them. It also came on the cusp of a wave of interest in new sporting models, as well as an acceleration in nationalist competition. De Coubertin and others found a much more receptive audience during the following five years until, sooner than most may have imagined, the Athens Olympics gained enough support for a planning committee to be created in 1894.

Degeneracy and Action

A lot changed between 1889 and 1894. Concerns about the degenerative effects of modern life gathered momentum during these years, making the exhibitions major occasions for the voicing of these concerns. Not unrelated was the fact that at that time various nations were also putting more and more emphasis on their respective indigenous sporting models as markers of nationally specific masculine character. This greatly helped de Coubertin and the newly-formed Olympic Committee to build support for the games, and to sustain that support even when the first few Olympiads had been far from triumphant. What carried them through was the emphasis on the efforts of the individual, but within the framework of an international competition. International tensions grew, imperial ambitions spawned diplomatic and military incidents, and both governments and the man in the street worried about keeping up and catching up.

There has been much scholarly work on the heightened public concerns about degeneracy during the period examined here. Deborah Silverman has argued that the celebrations of art, culture and social harmony on display at the exhibitions were becoming increasingly associated in the popular imagination with the declining virility of modern men. [27] In 1889, the thematic focus on machines that reduced the need for men to toil was not wholly triumphant. M.G. Valbert, writing about the 'Age of Machines' during an exhibition of which the central architectural achievements were the Eiffel Tower and the Palace of Machines, summarized the melancholy assessment of many of his peers when he said that 'the age of machines had a greater tendency than any other to exalt the individual but that, without realizing it, and with the best intentions, the age in fact worked to diminish him'. [28]

Popular magazines were also fascinated with *les jeunes parisiens*. Accompanying a series of sketches of extremely thin, effete young Parisiens, *Punch* described in detail the faults of the 'Parisian lounger', who had been reduced by modern life to a passive existence. [29] The young men's behaviour seemed to echo the passive and voluptuary characteristics often associated in contemporary writing with the males of the increasingly popular ethnographic displays – particularly oriental males. De Coubertin commented, matter-of-factly, on the 'natural indolence of the oriental'.

[30] Passivity, it was feared, was becoming a characteristic of the modern male *and* the colonial subject he was supposed to rule.

In 1893, coverage and criticism of the Chicago Fair was also focused on appropriate manifestations of civilization and progress, which had ramifications for the state of masculinity. As previously mentioned, Buffalo Bill was denied space for his show within the grounds of the Midway Plaisance, even though other entertainments involving 'barbarous' or 'savage' people – from the Philippines, Dahomey etc. – were included. Buffalo Bill's show was about the American frontier, not a foreign one. They were a source of both pride and potential embarrassment for Americans who were eager to assert that modern America had arrived because the frontier no longer existed, even as they congratulated themselves on having produced the brave men who tamed it. One way that these two positions were reconciled in the press was by celebrating that America (unlike Europe, it was implied) was a place where such men could test their mettle. Additionally, the structures of the fair received criticism for rejecting what was worthy of celebration about American culture and civilization in favour of a less dynamic European tradition. The architect Louis Sullivan, whose firm designed the only exhibition building not in the neoclassical style, decried the planning committee's adoption of a 'European' architectural style for the fair because he felt it should have been the occasion to promote and celebrate a new, indigenous and virile American architecture. [31]

With the exhibitions becoming so full of anxieties regarding the state of the nation and of the race, measured in culture and aesthetics, it is perhaps, not surprising that there was an explosion in the popularity of spectator sports during the same period; nor is it surprising that sport became another proxy in the escalation of belligerent nationalism that was steadily growing. Assumptions about national affinity for one sport or another became standard fare in the new journalistic field of sports writing. Walt Whitman famously held up baseball as a defining characteristic of Americanism, telling Horace Traubel that it had 'the snap, go fling, of the American atmosphere: – [it] belongs', he argued, 'as much to our institutions, fits into them as significantly, as our constitution [and] laws'. This 'boosterism' of national sports was not always so positively articulated. In *Punch*, for example, a series of articles lampooned French attempts to play English sports. In one, a list of reasons why each member of a French cricket side had to withdraw from a match include one player's pince-nez being shattered in an attempt to catch the ball and another having a 'shivering fit' at the mere contemplation of the force of a bowl. [32] The Nordic Games in Scandinavia, and gymnastics competitions in Germany, were proposed as 'national' alternatives to the Olympics when de Coubertin was trying to drum up support. As one commentator put it, 'Strong is the bond of nationality, strong are the ties of commerce, but stronger than either is the "union of hearts" which comes from devotion to the same forms of recreation'. [33] Consequently, the suggestion of an international sports competition might have seemed to many to be both pointless and impossible.

Nevertheless, during those years that de Coubertin continued to travel, write and lecture, he was not alone in believing that international sporting events could be beneficial. In 1891, in Great Britain, J. Astley Cooper, began to promote his idea for the Pan-Britannic Festival, which he imagined to be a means by which the ties between the colonies and the motherland could be strengthened through a celebration of shared economic and cultural bonds. What made this festival different from the exhibitions was his suggestion that sports should be one of the main attractions. 'Athletic exercises', wrote Cooper, 'should have a place [at the festival], for before we are a political, or even a commercial and military people, we are a race of keen sportsmen.' The sports component very soon became the central focus of media coverage of his proposal. Cooper was suggesting the need for such a festival – intended to strengthen the ties between Great Britain, its colonies and settler dominions – precisely because of the drastic increase in European imperial competition during the previous decade. Neither the popular press nor the public at large paid much attention to the part of the festival proposal that fitted the exhibitionary model, and instead voiced their collective enthusiasm for an inter-empire sporting event. However, the festival never got off the ground. One problem may well have been that sporting competition between 'cousins' would have created a hierarchy of winners and losers, which would have done little to promote unity. What was even more to be feared was that the metropole may not have emerged victorious, nor might white members of the empire be assured victory over the darker 'subject' peoples. In any case, Cooper later derided the Olympics as 'a hybrid, babel gathering'. He truly saw the empire as a single unit, making the festival sports competitions a domestic affair reinforcing unity rather than an international one celebrating difference. [34]

John Tosh argues that, at least in Britain, late-nineteenth-century sensibilities were less focused on the *character* of the individual, instead placing more emphasis on the group through the idea of *duty* 'to an over-riding imperial loyalty and identification with a set of collective imperial values'. He concludes that 'teamwork subordinated the individual'. [35] However, in the era of high imperialism and emergent mass society, there was also a competing strain of hero worship stemming from the fear of being 'diminished', as Valbert had put it, and the lack of obvious opportunity to test one's character in modern society. Concurrent with the development of team sports leagues that contributed to a collective identity among the working classes, and the deep internalization of the colonial mission by the middle and upper-middle classes, there was also a sustained interest in the individual soldier hero of empire – not only in Europe, but in the United States as well – for what were the heroes of the frontier west but models of the imperial soldier?

Whether the figure was Bill Hickok, Pierre Savourgnan de Brazza or General Gordon, there was an explosion of popular imaginings of what an individual man of character was capable of if stripped of the limiting social constraints of the metropole (or the eastern seaboard.) John Tosh argues that a 'flight from domesticity' occurred during this period, both literally and figuratively. The fantasies of the imperial hero reinforced the growing conviction that at home, all space had been pacified, regulated, domesticated, feminized. Empire, or the western frontier, were therefore the only remaining realms of the masculine. The fictional soldier-hero was an astonishingly popular archetype for both young boys and adults. He was an individual man of character. Even though the frontier at this late date offered little scope for adventure of the order of General Gordon, the promise was still there for men to prove that they could 'draw on moral resources to prevail over adversity', particularly when social and cultural reinforcements were far away. [36]

It is also interesting to note that success seemed to be beside the point. This might seem odd in a climate of hysteria about the decline of the nation due to ineffectual, emasculated men. But part of the attraction of the frontier was finding out whether one had the character to face defeat honourably. The iconic painting of Gordon standing at the top of the stairs of the palace in Khartoum, awaiting his inevitable fate with courage, encapsulated the fantasy of flight from the domesticated metropole into the homo-social realm of action promised on the frontiers of European power. Over the next decade, ideas of empire and national strength were still displayed at exhibitions, but how could exhibitions display the spectacle of 'character' and 'honour'? Imperial success demanded the kind of masculinity that could only be displayed in action. The traditional image of the ancient Olympic Games was, in fact, the perfect sporting metaphor for the soldier hero of empire. Stripped of everything, the lone, naked Olympian was, like other soldier-heroes, 'extrovert, self-reliant [and] achieving'. [37]

The Modern Olympic Games

De Coubertin made his successful second bid for the revival of the Olympic Games in 1894. There had been a proposal by others to create an international athletics association and de Coubertin invited representatives from sporting organizations to Paris for a congress on the international athletics movement. When in June of 1894, 2,000 people gathered in an amphitheatre of the Sorbonne to discuss the future of international athletics, many would have also read an article de Coubertin had written entitled 'Le retablissement des jeux olympiques', that appeared in the *Revue de Paris*. He also had the programme for the congress printed with the title 'Congress for the Reestablishment of the Olympic Games'. A year earlier, antique poems had been unearthed in Athens. One, 'The Hymn to Apollo', had been set to music and de Coubertin commissioned a performance of it at the congress. His hard sell approach worked. By the end of the sessions, the International Olympic Committee (IOC), dedicated to the mounting of an Olympic Games in Athens in 1896, had been formed. [38]

However, the first Olympiad could have also been the last – nothing more than an exercise in nostalgia – if the social and political conditions that drove their proposed revival had not become more entrenched. The first five Olympiads had the good fortune to coincide with the escalating preoccupation with degeneracy, national competition and racial strength – sufficiently to allow the potential benefits of the

Games to overcome their disastrous showing in Paris in 1900 and in St Louis in 1904. By the time the 1908 Games were held during the Franco-British Exhibition in London, however, Western nations had settled on specific shared concerns that perfectly suited the Olympic model. As war loomed, the soldier-hero, fictitious though he was, was caught in a double bind that resonated throughout Western society. The culture of militarism, the glorification of violence and domination that was de rigueur at the *fin de siècle* was in constant tension with the story of civilization and Christian virtue that was popular with the same class of men at the same time. The London and Stockholm Games were the perfect venues in which these two competing ideals could be reconciled in an international civic fantasy of pacifist competition.

It has been pointed out that the generic ideals of Hellenism were probably the only set of ideals at this combative moment among Western nations that could have achieved universal support. [39] The imagery and symbolism of the Athens Games fitted perfectly with the convergence of ideals seen as vital by the various participating countries, organizations and individuals in championing amateurism, combating degeneracy, asserting the continued superiority of European civilization and reinventing civic spectacle so that the active individual was central. Nevertheless, the first modern Olympics was confusing to many precisely because of this mix and the Games had to be explained to people. De Coubertin cautioned: 'We must establish the tradition that each competitor shall in his bearing and conduct as a man of honour and a gentleman endeavour to prove in what respect he holds the Games and what an honour he feels to participate in them.' Honourable participation was the goal. The evocation of an ancient tradition and the simplicity of athletic rather than material competition created the opportunity for different kinds of victories from those lauded at the exhibitions.

De Coubertin stated unequivocally 'the true Olympic hero ... is the adult male individual athlete'. But organizers were not revolutionaries. They wanted the Olympics to seem, from the start, as part of a continuum. In his report on the first Olympiad, de Coubertin repeatedly invokes the motif of continuity and progress. In speaking of the site of the original games and the renovation of the Stadion, he asserted that 'the Games had burned with so bright a lustre in the past of the Greeks that they could not but have their revival at heart'. [40] But the 'they' here is Europe, claiming a direct line of descent from the Olympic athletes of the Athenian city-state. The image of the Games in the Stadion was potent because it seemed to answer anxieties already discussed. Here was the continuity of the Olympic Games within the logic of civic display as laid out by Lockroy years earlier. The Games were not a revival but rather a continuation of European civilization and its spectacles; implying its inevitably continuity for another 2,500 years.

At the Athens Olympics, the marriage of individual achievement and civic pride was embodied in the running of the marathon, which, of all the events, quickly became the epitome of the Olympic ideal, even though many thought it too dangerous. It had never been tried before and had not been part of the original games. However, the myth of the self-sacrificing messenger was too good a story and provided exactly the spectacle that the new games needed. Greek youths had been training for a year for the event. Greek women lit votive candles and prayed that the winner would be one of their own. Their prayers were answered. So overcome were they with national pride that Prince George and Crown Prince Constantine rushed down from the royal enclosure and ran with Spiridon Loues for the final lap of the Stadion, cheered on by an estimated 120,000 spectators. Afterwards, it was 'discovered' that Loues was a shepherd from a remote village who had never run an organized race before. At least that was the myth that developed around the man. [41] In this single race, de Coubertin was given the appropriate symbol of the Olympic ideal. The strength of character of an individual amateur athlete had resulted in a personal victory and reflected honourably on the nation he represented.

Unfortunately, the story of Spiridon Loues was really the only event that captured the public imagination outside of Greece, and the international press treated the Olympics as a single, nostalgic, exhibitionary spectacle. The Olympics were not yet understood as a unique form and in 1900 they were again paired with another exhibition, with the outcome that the two events reinforced each other's weaknesses. For commentators, both had more than a faint whiff of femininity and elitism. The 1889 Exhibition was focused on machinery, iron and the inescapable phallic presence of the Eiffel Tower. By contrast the art nouveau aesthetic chosen by the 1900 exhibition organizers was far too feminine for the tastes of many proud Frenchmen. The reality of the escalating arms race in Europe meant that each of the great powers were vying more for industrial and military superiority than ever before. The failure of French industry to achieve the level of its German and British counterparts was seen as being directly tied to the new 'feminine' aesthetic of art nouveau that permeated the exhibition. [42] This time, Germany was in residence at the fair. Chemical and metallurgical developments were displayed along with Zeppelin's incredible dirigibles, while the French seemed incapable of changing their own culture to ensure their survival in a Darwinian world of ruthless competition. One observer noted with chagrin that France 'exercises its fantasies on fabrics and jewellery, on furniture, glassware, and ceramics', while 'it is still painfully searching for its identity and its laws', let alone, it was implied, its spine. [43]

The Games in 1900 were not even given the title 'Olympic'. They were called *Les concours internationaux d'exercices physiques*, and many of the participants stated later that, at the time, they were completely unaware that it was an Olympic competition. Continuing the preoccupation with the first Olympiad, the marathon was the only event given reasonable coverage in the press and in keeping with the dismal showing of the exhibition, the story that came out of it involved cheating. Although it could not be proven (and he kept his first place finish), the Frenchman Michel Theato was accused of having used his intimate knowledge of the back streets of Paris to take a short cut to the finish line. [44] The Olympic Games in Paris were, in many ways, a repudiation of the pedagogic ideals that gave the Olympics mass appeal in 1896. Not only were many of the events in Paris obscure in their origins, but also in their observability. An institutional emphasis on amateurism barred most working-class athletes from participating and many of the events were culled from the sporting traditions or even just fashionable crazes of the upper classes (from pigeon shooting to ballooning). The universal and democratic nature of the Olympics as far as many of its original organizers were concerned (including de Coubertin), lay in the goal of having the working classes observe the spectacle in order to imbibe the lessons of honourable, manly competition from their betters. But even this was discouraged as the city refused to permit a purpose-built stadium, instead insisting that the Olympic organization hosting the events should use already available facilities and outdoor venues, such as the Bois de Boulogne. This resulted in such bizarre situations as javelin throwers having to avoid hitting trees as they competed. Spectatorship was further discouraged by the holding of events over five months, throughout the exhibition. [45] Even so, if the games had been mounted along the same lines as 1896, the homo-social symbolism could have been used as a rejection of the degenerative effects of modern, domesticated life. Instead, the issue of amateurism and a general lack of comprehension on the part of officials hindered the creation of a viable public spectacle that could rival the exhibitions.

Meanwhile, throughout the West, some began to question whether continued overseas aggression could be considered 'civilized', as the world castigated Britain for its savagery and hypocrisy during a series of colonial crises. In 1892, the government was forced to investigate allegations that the Indian government was subsidizing itself by trafficking in opium. The question of Irish Home Rule was also under debate throughout the decade, and the convergence of the Boer War from 1899 to 1902 and the Boxer Rebellion of 1900 further destabilized Britain's self-identification. Morality and civilization could no longer be seen as the untroubled manifestations of directed civic action abroad.

Britain's self-characterization as the benevolent imperial power had been an extremely successful propaganda campaign, both at home and abroad. While its colonial holdings were a source of resentment and nervousness for other nations such as Germany and France, the success of its project was understood to be in direct relation to its level of civilized development. As a result of these two crises, most particularly the Boer War, the relationship between manliness and action was troubled. It was felt that some kind of qualifier needed to be put on manifestations of virile patriotism for fear they might be taken out of the sphere of manliness and into the realm of savagery.

The 1904 Olympics were held in St Louis in conjunction with the World's Fair. After the debacle of the Boer War (including the rejection by the British Army of two out of every five recruits) and the news that Russia had lost a war to the Japanese, the fate of nations and empires rested even more emphatically on racial strength as measured by appropriate masculine action. However, Caucasian solidarity in the face of external threats was not to be. The exhibitions in Chicago and St Louis were both intended as measures of the extent of American progress and civilization, but European members of the International Olympics Committee (IOC), and even de Coubertin himself, who had visited Chicago in 1893, did not bother to attend the

1904 games. The international component was almost non-existent. Faced with the prospect of the imagined wilderness frontier of St Louis, as well as the effort and expense required to get there, most Europeans stayed away. Of the 554 athletes, 432 were American, which reduced the possibility for rivalries between men of European descent. Instead, there were events at the exhibitions expressly intended to provide a comparison between civilized, grown-up America and more primitive peoples.

The local organizers of the fair and the games felt that the spectatorship of both would benefit from a series of Anthropology Days, at which 'savages' from the pseudo-educational 'ethnographic' sideshows, particularly the 47-acre Philippine 'Reserve' (marking the United States' recent acquisition of the islands), were made to play versions of their indigenous games as well as Western team sports, at the latter of which, of course, they made a very poor showing in comparison to the Olympic teams – undoubtedly the idea. [46] This did however highlight one of the great quandaries with which the Olympics had to contend. The 'notion of using primitive bodies to advance civilized ideals enjoyed widespread popularity', both in the United States and in Europe; but in America, the primitive continued to be, for some, a little too readily available.

America's claim to national legitimacy on the world stage was still tenuous. [47] The Anthropology Days, as well as the ethnographic displays at the fair, can be explained within this context. They placed Americans closer to their European counterparts in the symbolic order of civilized nations by casting in sharp relief the vast distance between white American society in its great gateway city and 'savage' peoples. But the primitiveness from which America had so recently been claimed was not only across oceans but right there. Ironically, if the Olympics were attractive precisely because they could display the character of European men stripped of their cultural trappings, the racist preoccupations at the St Louis Games showed how highly valued those trappings remained.

In St. Louis, the marathon was again the one event that was sure to be mentioned in the European press. It was won by a brass worker named Thomas Hicks, who declared exuberantly that he 'would rather have won this than be President of the United States'. [48] Of course, the fact that he was English-born meant that he couldn't be president but the British press was able to point out how a British émigré, a man from the working classes, still held on to the (British) values of amateur sportsmanship. Emigration was seen as a key way in which British culture and civilization could continue to expand and renew itself overseas. In numerical terms, emigration vastly outstripped opportunities for imperial soldiering by the turn of the century. Meanwhile their American counterparts made much of the fact that what made America great was that someone *like* Hicks, a brass worker with the strength of character to win a marathon, *could* be president.

The survival of the Olympic Games is quite possibly due to the fact that at the fourth and fifth Olympiads, organizers finally married sporting ideals and exhibitionary concept in an effective and coherent manner. In 1908, for the last time, the Olympics were held in concert with an exhibition, but this time with one with a pointedly propagandist purpose that precisely matched Olympic rhetoric. Framed as a celebration of the *entente cordiale*, the exhibition was really about the primacy and transparency of rules – friendly rivalry versus unwarranted aggression, either on the sports field or in international relations. Where once the exhibitions were about allowing the public to see themselves as part of a web of mutual obligation and accomplishment within the nation, now both the Olympics and the Franco-British Exhibition touted those same virtues on an international scale. 'The Exhibition marks the development of the great Anglo-French understanding that is to-day the key stone of the European political situation, and the most powerful instrument working for the maintenance of the world's peace,' organizers explained. [49]

Rules, transparency and the obligation for all countries to approach the arena of competition equally were at the crux of the controversies that emerged at these games. The British Olympic Council set out very specific measurements, restrictions and distances for all of the events that are still used today, including the odd length of the marathon, which is the distance from Windsor Castle to the finish line in Shepherd's Bush. Protests by the American team that British officials were biased also brought about international, rather than host-nation, judging. As a result, equality, honest performance and the rule of law became the rhetorical backdrop as well as literal framework for the games. [50] Even in this, the games stood as a metaphor for the escalating tensions in the West, caused in part by the varying approaches of old monarchies, new republics and all models of government in between towards international agreements and obligations. As nations moved closer to the battlefield, one of the few reassurances left was that once there, the individual man called into action could bring his character and honour to bear in a straightforward manner. At these games, the American contingent was large and well-prepared. Just as de Coubertin and the IOC had dreamed, the United States treated the games as a serious opportunity to further national prestige, and others followed. The Americans' reverence for the rules provided an appropriate counterpoint to the exhibition's subtext of Germany's unwarranted aggression. [51]

Coming into the 70,000-seater, purpose-built stadium, it was an Italian, Dorando Pietri, who led the field in the marathon, which once again provided the signature story. According to press coverage, the standing-room-only crowd cheered him on. The finish line was almost an entire lap away in front of the royal box from where the Queen looked on. Then, just metres away from the tape, Pietri collapsed. Some of the members of the audience knew that if they went forward to help him he would be automatically disqualified but others, more worried that he might actually die in the presence of the Queen, did so and helped him to his feet. By all accounts, what followed had definite operatic elements. To the deafening cheers of the crowd he stumbled forward, then fell again – and yet again. Finally, not able to stand it any more, an official picked Pietri up in his arms and carried him across the finishing line. Although he was, of course, disqualified, 'Dorando' was hailed in the popular press and given a special trophy by the Queen. Irving Berlin even wrote a song about him. [52]

The moment offered a spontaneous performance of the idealized death of the imperial soldier-hero for consumption by a metropolitan audience. What captured the public imagination was that after the first intervention the runner knew he was disqualified but insisted on finishing the race. The US team protested about Dorando's victory when they thought that his performance would be seen as a legitimate one, and were criticized in the press for their churlishness. However, as has been pointed out by John MacKenzie, among others, the ultimate test of the soldier-hero's character, and therefore his victory, is how he meets death. In the context of the Olympic spectacle, Dorando's loss was the equivalent of Gordon standing and waiting to meet the Mahdi's army. [53] The strict adherence to the rules, reinforced by the fact that he was not awarded a medal, was of course necessary in this narrative, in order to give value to the games as an institution and to the effort of the individual who submitted to the rules – no matter what.

Through the success of the London games and the further entrenchment of the rules of conduct in Stockholm in 1912, the Olympics became the site for the performance of individual competition in the name of national glory but tempered by a code of conduct. De Coubertin had stated years earlier that his vision that the games would be a 'potent ... factor in securing world peace'. [54] Now the subtext of both spectacles was not peace, but *appropriate* forms of competition and, regrettably, warfare. In 1912, the Olympic Games did not accompany an exhibition. They were *the* event. Held over a few short weeks, there was a coherence to the presentation that signalled the games had reached a certain maturity. They no longer had to be explained to their audience. Nations from all five continents competed for the first time and the rules were so firmly established that they were voluntarily held to. This was apparent in the extremely unfortunate story of Jim Thorpe, the Native American runner, who won the brand new all-round athletic event, the pentathlon. The United States returned his medals when it was discovered that he had previously been paid to participate in a sporting event. Race is a complicating factor here, of course. Some Europeans had already protested over the participation of a non-white, and Thorpe's breach of amateurism was, quite possibly, taken as a marker of racial difference. Certainly the US authorities seemed unwilling to champion Thorpe as a true exemplar of amateur ideals, but the US team did put the Olympic rules above national interest.

Echoing the earlier description of the function of exhibitions, European men in that moment, with those concerns, were able to present a story of themselves to themselves. The spectacle of the Olympics was masculine action, voluntarily subjected to rules of conduct, whether for the soldier-hero, far from the metropole, or for the athlete, performing alone in the stadium. The exhibitions had articulated a reasoned explanation of how nations and their citizens had arrived at legitimacy but the public's interest (and anxiety) had moved on to focus on the future. While they hoped that the actions of athletes were illustrative of the fundamental civility of European society, they also understood that Europe was moving towards a moment when actions could speed out of control. In such a climate, the Olympic Games were reassuring.

It was therefore the convergence of certain social, cultural and political preoccupations during two-and-a-half decades that had rendered the Olympics a more efficacious venue for displaying appropriate masculine behaviour than the exhibitions. Firstly, the exhibitions had become synonymous with modernity at a time when it was feared that it was weakening rather than strengthening the male polis by concentrating too much on collective accomplishments and cooperation to the neglect of the individual. Secondly, the sporting and athletic traditions of the mid-nineteenth century were no longer sufficiently inclusive and public to be a useful tool for socialization in an age of mass society. Thirdly, the overwhelming success of reform and governmental intervention in the metropole had fed a psychological fascination with the archetype of the soldier-hero and established the frontier as the only place where real masculinity could be tested.

The Olympic Games provided a metaphorical frontier in the metropole, where the individual male could prove his character while stripped of the accoutrements of his culture and society. This combined the elements of action and character-building from the athletics tradition, and the elements of civic display and international competition from the exhibitionary tradition. The result was that by 1912, on the cusp of war and perhaps because of it, the Olympics had become firmly entrenched in the public imagination. In 1889, the normative spectacle for the modern nation state was the exhibition; so much so that *Punch*'s correspondent wrote that, upon arrival 'in the Great Exhibition ... your first impression is that the Government have annexed a large slice of Paris'. [55] By 1912, de Coubertin could claim, albeit with a certain biased enthusiasm, that 'the whole of Stockholm was impregnated with ... Olympism ... so that Hellenism and progress seemed to have joined forces to act as hosts together'. [56] MacAloon points out that, in Athens, the Olympics were literally an indescribable spectacle. Commentators had struggled to find language for this combination of sports, national civic display and international congress, because the cultural vocabulary for such an event did not then exist. Now, Hellenism and progress could coexist in the public imagination. [57] The Olympics suggested that men could compete honourably even if their nations could not. Through the shared experience of watching the spectacle of the 'lone, male athlete', the audience could imagine the fate of their community in the hands of the individual soldier-hero, rather than the diffuse authority of the modern nation state.

Notes

[1] General information on the exhibitions and world's fairs is drawn from Finding, *Encyclopedia of World's Fairs and Expositions*; Smithsonian Institution Libraries, *The Books of the Fairs*; and Allwood, *The Great Exhibitions*.

[2] Tosh, 'Domesticity and Manliness', in *Manful Assertions*, 65–8.

[3] Horne, 'The Age of Nation-States', 28.

[4] Holt, 'Contrasting Nationalisms', 40; Mangan, and McKenzie, 'The Other Side of the Coin', in particular 76–7; but also various other examples in Mangan, *Making European Masculinities*; Tosh, *Manliness and Masculinities*, 194.

[5] I would argue that the class tension surrounding field sports detailed in Mangan and McKenzie, 'The Other Side of the Coin', supports this assertion.

[6] All references to de Coubertin's attitudes and strategies, unless otherwise noted, come from de Coubertin, *Memoires Olympiques*.

[7] Krüger, 'Buying Victories', note 25.

[8] De Coubertin, *Memoires Olympiques*, 9.

[9] Lockroy, 'Preface', *L'Exposition Universelle de 1889*, vol. 1, xxxi.

[10] Nord, *The Republican Moment*, 7.

[11] Rydell, 'The Literature of International Expositions', 9.

[12] Sieburth writes that the exhibitions were thought of as 'utopias of transparency and equality … (inasmuch as [they] project both an archaic fantasy of the classless prehistory of society and a wish-symbol of the future):'Introduction', ix.

[13] Details of the organization and planning of the 1889 *Exposition Universelle* can be found in Monod, *Exposition Universelle*, vol. 1.

[14] Silverman, 'The 1889 Exhibition', 73, and *Art Nouveau*, 43.

[15] Giedion, *Space, Time and Architecture*, 270.

[16] Bennett, 'The Exhibitionary Complex'.

[17] Rydell, 'A Cultural Frankenstein?', 143.

[18] Jones, *World's Fair: Chicago, 1893*, 110.

[19] Guy de Maupassant, quoted in Silverman, 'The 1889 Exhibition', 78.

[20] Mangan and McKenzie, 'The Other Side of the Coin',76–7.

[21] Mangan, *Athleticism*, 36–42; John Tosh references this same phenomenon when he discusses the evolving cultural designations of 'gentlemanly' and 'manly' through the second half of the nineteenth century: Tosh, *Manful Assertions*, 65–8.

[22] Mangan, *Athleticism*, 202. Mangan quotes Welldon explicitly deriding working-class lack of appreciation for the importance of 'pulling together' or 'playing the game' that he designates as 'public school' values.

[23] For a variety of examples, see Mangan, *Tribal Identities*.

[24] Baker, 'Making of a Working Class Football Culture', 244.

[25] For American attitudes towards sports, see MacAloon, *This Great Symbol*, 113–128, where he details de Coubertin's 1889 trip to the US; for de Coubertin's ideas about what sports were supposed to stave off, see Weber, 'Pierre de Coubertin and the Introduction of Organised Sport in France', 16: 'Industrial civilization stood for the four Sancho Panzas of the Apocalypse: greater comfort, specialization, exaggerated nationalism, and the triumph of democracy'.

[26] MacAloon, *This Great Symbol*, 155.

[27] Silverman, *Art Nouveau*, 75–106.

[28] Valbert, *L'age de Machines*, quoted in Silverman, *Art Nouveau*, 44.

[29] *Le revue des deux mondes*, 1 June 1889; *Punch*, 29 June 1889.

[30] De Coubertin, 'The Olympic Games of 1896'.

[31] Rydell, 'A Cultural Frankenstein?', *passim*.

[32] Whitman, quoted in Traubel, *With Walt Whitman in Camden*, vol. 4, 508; *Punch*, 8 June 1889.

[33] The 'union of hearts' quote is from an anonymous contributor to the *St James Gazette*, quoted in Moore, '"Love of Fair Play"', 73.

[34] Cooper on 'race of sportsmen', *Greater Britain*, 15 July 1891, quoted in ibid.; for details of the Pan-Britannic effort, see ibid., 72–3; for Cooper quote on 'babel gathering' see MacAloon, *This Great Symbol*, 168.

[35] Tosh, *Manliness and Masculinities*, 197.

[36] Dawson, *Soldier Heroes, passim*. Tosh proposes the 'flight from domesticity' in 'Domesticity and Manliness' in *Manful Assertions*; and Dawson explores in 'The Blond Bedouin' that the public substantially redirected its gaze towards empire in the search for opportunities to exhibit and witness examples of appropriate masculinity both prior to and immediately after the First World War. Both are found in Roper and Tosh, *Manful Assertions*. The specific quote is from Tosh, *Manliness and Masculinities*, 197.

[37] Tosh, *Manliness and Masculinities*, 207.

[38] Mandell, *The First Modern Olympics*, 85–9.

[39] MacAloon, *This Great Symbol*, 174.

[40] De Coubertin, 'The Olympic Games of 1896', 115.

[41] etails of the first Modern Olympiad are taken from: de Coubertin, 'The Olympic Games of 1896'; Walechinsky, *The Complete Book of the Olympics*, 47; and MacAloon, *This Great Symbol*, 226–36.

[42] Silverman, *Art Nouveau*, 53; Mandell, *Paris, 1900*, 113.

[43] *Le Rire*, 15 Dec. 1900.

[44] Guttmann, *The Olympics*. 22–4.

[45] Details of these games come from Walechinsky, *The Complete Book of the Olympics*, xxi, and 48; and Large, *Nazi Games*, 17.

[46] All of the details of the St Louis Games, come from Guttmann, *The Olympics*, 25–6.

[47] Putney, *Muscular Christianity*, 6.

[48] Hicks quoted in Guttmann, *The Olympics*, 49.

[49] *Illustrated London News*, 18 May 1908.

[50] Details of the London Games come from Walechinsky, *The Complete Book of the Olympics*.

[51] From the level of training and number of participants, it is apparent that the United States took the Olympics seriously as a nationalistic pursuit earlier than other countries. For a detailed examination of how quickly the two are combined elsewhere, see Krüger, "Buying Victories is Positively Degrading," in Mangan, ed. *Tribal Identities.*.

[52] Olympic/Exhibition supplement to *Illustrated London News*, 1 Aug. 1908, as well as 18 and 25 July editions.

[53] MacKenzie, 'Heroic Myths of Empire', 134.

[54] MacAloon, *This Great Symbol*, 261.

[55] *Punch*, 29 June 1889.

[56] De Coubertin quoted in Mallon and Widlund, *The 1912 Olympic Games*, 27.

[57] MacAloon, *This Great Symbol*, 271.

References

Allwood, J. *The Great Exhibitions*. London: Studio Vista, 1977.

Baker, William J. 'Making of a Working Class Football Culture'. *Journal of Social History*, 13, no. 2 (1979): 241–51.

Bennett, T. 'The Exhibitionary Complex'. *New Formations* 4 (1988): 73–102.

Colls, R. and P. Dodd, eds. *Englishness: Politics and Culture, 1880–1920*. London: Croom Helm Ltd., 1986.

Cook, Theodore Andrea, ed. *The Fourth Olympiad; Being the Official Report of the Olympic Games of 1908*. London: British Olympic Association, 1909.

Coubertin, P. de. 'The Olympic Games of 1896'. *The Century Magazine* LIII, no. 1 (Nov. 1896): 39–55.

Coubertin, P. de. *Memoires Olympiques*. Lausanne: Bureau International de Pedagogie Sportive, 1931.

Dawson, Graham. *Soldier Heroes: British Adventure, Empire, and the Imagining of Masculinities*. London: Routledge, 1994.

Finding, John E. and Kimberley D. Pelle, eds. *Encyclopedia of World's Fairs and Expositions*. Jefferson, NC: McFarland and Co., 2008.

Giedion, Sigfried. *Space, Time and Architecture: The Growth of a New Tradition*. Cambridge, MA: Harvard University Press, 1967.

Graham, P.J. and H. Ueberhorst. *The Modern Olympics*. Cornwall, NY: Leisure Press, 1976.

Guttmann, Alan. *The Olympics: A History of the Modern Games*. Champaign, IL: University of Illinois Press, 1992.

Hamon, P. *Expositions: Literature and Architecture in Nineteenth Century France*. Trans. K. Sainson-Frank and L. Maguire. Berkeley, CA: University of California Press, 1992.

Holt, Richard. 'Contrasting Nationalisms'. In *Tribal Identities: Nationalism, Europe, Sport*, edited by J.A. Mangan. London and Portland, OR: Frank Cass, 1996.

Horne, John 'The Age of Nation-States'. In *Masculinities in Politics and War: Gendering Modern History*, edited by Stefan Dudink, Karen Hagemann and John Tosh. Manchester: Manchester University Press, 2004.

Jones, John, ed. *World's Fair: Chicago, 1893, Illustrated*. Chicago: Anabogue Publishing Co., 1892.

Krüger, Arndt 'Buying Victories is Positively Degrading'. In *Tribal Identities: Nationalism, Europe, Sport*, edited by J.A. Mangan. London and Portland, OR: Frank Cass, 1996.

Large, David Clay. *Nazi Games: The Olympics of 1936*. New York, NY: W. W. Norton and Co., 2007.

Le Rider, J. *Modernity and Crises of Identity: Culture and Society in Fin-De-Siecle Vienna*. Trans. R. Morris. New York: Continuum Pub., 1993.

Lockroy, Edouard. 'Preface'. In *L'Exposition Universelle de 1889: Grand Ouvrage illustré historique, encyclopédique descriptif*. Paris: E. Dentu, Librarie de la Société des gens de lettres, 1890.

MacAloon, J.J. *This Great Symbol: Pierre de Coubertin and the Origins of the Modern Olympic Games*. Chicago: University of Chicago Press, 1981.

MacKenzie, John M. 'Heroic Myths of Empire'. In *Popular Imperialism and the Military*, edited by John M. MacKenzie. Manchester: Manchester University Press, 1992.

Mallon, Bill and Ture Widlund. *The 1912 Olympic Games: Results for All Competitors in All Events, with Commentary*. Jefferson, NC: McFarland and Co., 2002.

Mandell, R.D. *Paris, 1900: The Great World's Fair*. Toronto: University of Toronto Press, 1967.

Mandell, R.D. *The First Modern Olympics*. Berkeley, CA: University of California Press, 1976.

Mangan, J.A. *Athleticism in the Victorian and Edwardian Public School*. London and Portland, OR: Frank Cass, 2000.

Mangan, J.A., ed. *Tribal Identities: Nationalism, Europe, Sport*. London and Portland, OR: Frank Cass, 1996.

Mangan, J.A., ed. *Making European Masculinities: Sport, Europe, Gender (European Sports History Review 2)*. London and Portland, OR: Frank Cass, 2000.

Mangan, J.A. and John M. McKenzie. 'The Other Side of the Coin'. In *Tribal Identities: Nationalism, Europe, Sport*, edited by J.A. Mangan. London and Portland, OR: Frank Cass, 1996.

Monod, É. *L'Exposition Universelle de 1889: grand ouvrage illustré historique, encyclopédique descriptif*. Paris: E. Dentu, Librarie de la Société des gens de lettres, 1890.

Moore, K. '"Love of Fair Play"'. In *Contemporary Studies in the National Olympic Games Movement*, edited by Roland Naul. New York: Peter Lang, 1997.

Nord, P. *The Republican Moment: Struggles for Democracy in Nineteenth Century France*. Cambridge, MA: Harvard University Press, 1995.

Nye, R.A. *Crime, Madness and Politics in Modern France: The Medical Concept of National Decline*. Princeton, NJ: Princeton University Press, 1984.

Putney, Clifford. *Muscular Christianity: Manhood and Sports in Protestant America, 1880–1920.* Cambridge, MA: Harvard University Press, 2001.

Richards, T. *The Commodity Culture of Victorian England: Advertising and Spectacle, 1851–1914.* Stanford, CA: Stanford University Press, 1990.

Roper, Michael and John Tosh, eds. *Manful Assertions: Masculinities in Britain since 1800.* New York: Routledge, 1991.

Rydell, Robert W. 'The Literature of International Expositions'. In Smithsonian Institution Libraries, *The Books of the Fairs, Materials about the World's Fairs, 1834–1916.* Chicago and London: American Library Association, 1992.

Rydell, Robert W. 'A Cultural Frankenstein?' In *Grand Illusions: Chicago's World's Fair of 1893,* edited by Neil Harris, Wim de Wit, James Gilbert and Robert W. Rydell. Chicago: Chicago Historical Society, 1993.

Sieburth, Richard 'Introduction'. In *Expositions: Literature and Architecture in Nineteenth Century France,* by P. Hamon. Berkeley, CA: University of California Press, 1992.

Silverman, D. 'The 1889 Exhibition: Crisis of Bourgeois Individualism'. *Oppositions* 8 (1977): 71–91.

Silverman, D. *Art Nouveau in Fin-De-Siecle France: Politics Psychology and Style.* Berkeley, CA: University of California Press, 1989.

Smithsonian Institution Libraries. *The Books of the Fairs: Materials about the World's Fairs, 1834–1916.* Chicago and London: American Library Association, 1992.

Tosh, John. *Manliness and Masculinities in Nineteenth Century Britain: Essays on Gender, Family, and Empire.* London: Pearson Longman, 2005.

Traubel, Horace, *With Walt Whitman in Camden,* vol 4. Walt Whitman Archives, available online at http://www.whitmanarchive.org/criticism/disciples/traubel/WWWiC/4/med.0000, accessed 14 July 2009.

Walechinsky, D. *The Complete Book of the Olympics.* New York: Penguin Books, 1984.

Weber, Eugen. 'Pierre de Coubertin and the Introduction of Organised Sport in France'. *Journal of Contemporary History* 5, no. 2 (1970): 3–26.

Young, D.C. *The Modern Olympics: A Struggle for Survival.* Baltimore, MD: Johns Hopkins University Press, 1996.

Planning and Reconversion of Olympic Heritages: The Montreal Olympic Stadium

Romain Roult and Sylvain Lefebvre

For hosting cities, the summer Olympic Games (OG) has become an extremely expensive and complex urban project, partly used for urban regeneration. We can also observe that the Olympic stadium's problematic of reconversion is recurring as this infrastructure, the most significant of the Olympic park, needs colossal financing for its construction and its management. However, despite a few planning measures, we notice that after the OG a considerably low percentage of these stadiums are actually utilized. Through an in-depth study and historiography of the planning and reconversion phases of the 1976 Montreal Olympics' heritage, this article aims to demonstrate how such a facility, central to the hosting of the OG, has become a model of post-Olympic failure. Within a few years, although it was initially planned in a modest way and as a means to regenerate the entire neighbourhood, this facility had become a 'white elephant', costing triple what was originally planned, while we still wonder to this day what we should or could do with this mega-infrastructure.

Introduction

Several recent studies indicate that the Olympic Games can partly be used to regenerate and convert complete urban neighbourhoods. [1] Within the analytic frame of the Summer Games in which we are interested [2] We observe that since the professionalization of the event (Munich 1972), its impacts on hosting territories has increased significantly. This is partly related to the increasing organizational requirements of the International Olympic Committee (IOC), the international federations (IFs) and the international media. These multiple organizational requirements induce the municipal authorities in charge to plan these urban projects in the long term (ten to 30 years), trying to make them profitable or at least to reconvert them successfully as it sometimes happens (Barcelona 1992). As the organization of summer Olympics now requires about $10 to $20 billion, this international sporting event reaches the level of an extremely complex and expensive urban project for hosting cities, given that this project has a very deep impact on the urban framework. [3]

Following the structural, architectural and financial extravagances of the last Games in Beijing (2008), and despite the difficult conversion of the Olympic equipments of the Athens games (2004), it seems relevant to understand how the hosting infrastructures, and particularly the Olympic stadium itself, are planned and re-used within an urban environment that is rarely staged. Despite certain planning measures, put into place and justified by authorities to manage and legitimize the subsequent use of such mega projects, it is interesting to note that a very low percentage of these stadiums are actually utilized after the games with a few avoid turning into 'white elephants'. [4] In order to understand therefore how the planning process of the Olympic stadium and the management of its post-Olympic phase influenced its conversion, it is proposed to analyse the case of the 1976 Montreal Olympic Games, which is considered amongst the scientific community to be the perfect model of post-Olympic failure. [5] The exhaustive study of this atypical case will enable the identification of factors that allowed a financial deception as well as the catastrophic conversion of the stadium. In order to uncover these analytical results, it is necessary to examine both pre and post-Olympic phases – by means of precise research questioning. Firstly, how was the Montreal Olympic stadium planned, within the overall preparation of the OG and for the post-Games and secondly, how was its post-Olympic conversion managed after 1976? Finally, more than 30 years after the Games, why are the conversion and utilization of this infrastructure still causing so much trouble?

This research is divided in three sections. First it will look at the principal writings concerning this urban Olympic problem, with a particular focus on the stadium. Secondly, the working methodology will be exposed by specifying documentary sources; and thirdly, the research results on the Montreal case will be presented, considering the analysis of 'pre' and 'post' Games phases specified earlier.

Conceptual and Methodological Aspects

Olympic Games and Urban Revitalization

The summer Olympics developed into true international sports manifestations; as the associated organizational and architectural requirements became so important and expensive they are now bracketed alongside more global urban development projects. [6] To talk about Olympic Games nowadays does not simply mean an analysis of this phenomenon as a sport or an event, but to understand how, as considerable as it is, it assimilates globalized urban logics. [7] The scope of the event causes numerous authors to state that the summer Olympics cannot be interpreted as other simple urban projects but more as great urban projects. This is because their economic and socio-spatial impacts are major. [8] These approaches force us to consider the place that sport is taking in our society and, more precisely, in the urban spaces. In fact, now that the Olympics are increasingly utilizing market logics, focussing on the image and the prestige of hosting cities, they are becoming part of modern culture treads as structuring elements of cities. [9] as their utilization and their presence contribute to the development and to the affirmation of certain territories. As Coaffee puts it,

> in recent years, the relationship between sport and strategic urban regeneration has gripped the imagination of policy-makers. This is largely due to the perceived economic and social benefits of hosting major sporting events and developing sport infrastructure, which offer perceptions that have increasingly permeated policy-making agendas linked, inter alia, to economic revitalization and the development of sustainable communities. [10]

Therefore, the Olympic Games are not only referring to political and economic domains, but to urbanism. To become an Olympic city does not simply imply a need to fulfil the IOC requirements, but to consider a city in the long term, according to new urban objectives. [11] In Hiller's perspective, too much attention was given to the economic and tourism spin-offs of the Games, causing the authorities to overlook infrastructural aspects of the project (urban revitalization, the role of the sports facilities, the subsequent conversion of the Olympic village's etc.), which are much more important for the future of the metropolis. Some authors also mention that the immaterial impacts of the Olympics (the hosting city's international image, its notoriety and visibility) are being prioritised and used by those in charge of such projects in order to legitimize the use of public funds to the local population. [12] Often the urban, financial and technical considerations related to the planning of Olympic facilities are either overlooked or 'glossed over' as they are thought to be the weakest points of the project. The organizational extravagance of the Games, supported by the Olympic authorities, justifies the construction of gigantic installa-tions that are detached from urban realities and the local hosting communities. Because being part of wider urban development strategies, the organization of Games is no longer the only finality for Olympic cities, it is necessary to plan these urban elements during the pre-Olympic phase in order to keep them attractive in the post-Olympic phase. [13] One does not go without the other. [14] To plan for the post-Olympics use is one thing, but it is most important to recognize whether the measures taken to do so are adequate or whether they are simply 'deceptions' put into place by the creators of the project.

The Stadium as an Urban Structuring Element

Although there are some differences between North American and European stadia when it goes to financial and planning models, the majority of the infrastructures built during the last 20 years were part of a revitalization plan for the hosting communities. According to Paramio et al., in an exhaustive research on European football stadiums, the difference lies mainly within the conception and the commercialization of the stadiums. After three generations of modern stadiums (end of the 19th century to 1920; 1920 to 1950; 1950 to 1990) we entered the post-modern era, in which stadia are not only configured to host sports events. [15] They are now dedicated to host a range of sporting and cultural events but they also offer facilities including businesses, corporate hosting, restaurants, bars and children spaces, etc.

The stadium has become an element of urban marketing, [16] and should not simply be regarded as a place for hosting sports competitions, but as an urban marker, taking part in an overall urban branding process. The logics governing the establishment of a stadium are essential to understanding the urban regeneration strategies that underlie the phenomenon. 'Three possible scenarios can be identified concerning the location of a new stadium – city centre, edge city and deprived neighbourhood – with different implications.' [17] The downtown location offers the possibility of reinforcing the tourist sector as well as the entertaining image of the city as it expands the already existing hosting amenities. The establishment of the stadium within the peripheral zone can, on the other hand, become the catalyst for the development of an entire commercial and economic zone, which would improve the image, the transportation infrastructure as well as the real property value of this area. Finally, the construction of a stadium within deprived areas can be used as an agent of change for both the image as well as the functional orientation of this territory, especially if the planning is connected to other urban interventions (commercial implantation, office spaces, etc.).

Within the context of the Olympic Games, the stadium has become the event's jewel-case. [18] The architectural audacity, the building's technical features as well as the renown of its designer are becoming just as significant as the organization of the event itself. If this stadium is coupled with an urban regeneration project, its significance will be further enhanced. However, to build a new stadium for the Games is one thing, but to design it for the post-Olympic period is something else. [19] This phase is the most critical of the entire project and its success depends on long term planning. What stands out from the several researches existing about this problematic feature is that there are two central issues to keep in mind when considering the conversion of the Olympic stadium. First, there is the pre-Olympic phase that requires the implementation of actions that will determine the long term success of the project. Secondly, there is the post-Olympic phase, where those earlier preparations need to be followed up, maintained or adjusted in order to provide for a different context than that for which the project was initially planned. Subsequent metropolitan development objectives are not necessarily centred on the original 'Olympic purpose and will based upon a possible diminution of investment, financial spin-offs, media visibility and the sport and other activities within these facilities in the post-games period). [20] The conversion and re-utilization of the

Olympic stadium need constant effort that will continuously be renewed according to urban, economic and social logics, which will also be subject to constant change. [21]

Methodological Considerations

This research is based on a qualitative method, following an inductive and interpretative approach. It also respects the methodological indications given by Gratton and Jones in their publication concerning sports studies and especially the section about literature review through documentary research. [22] Therefore, this article is built as an historical study of the event, based on archive study and using the clear distinction between the 'pre' and 'post' elements of Olympic Games. The case study of Montreal was analysed by means of an examination of different documentary sources including the city's candidacy form, the official reports of the Organizing Committee for the Olympic Games (OCOG), the Olympics equipments' planning and management reports for the pre and post phases, issued by both the Ministries in charge of the projects (the Ministries of Finance, of Municipal Affairs and of Heritage and Sports for both Canada and Quebec respectively) and the municipal authorities of the time. Moreover, different archives from the Olympic Movement, the Olympics Installations Board (RIO) and the management authority of Montreal Olympic Park were consulted as well as the press release concerning this problem. Finally, research material from several universities was examined in order to complement an exhaustive scientific corpus on the case of Montreal's Olympic Games.

Montreal 1976, a Heavy Heritage

1970–6, from Modest Games to Extravagance

'In Montreal, the Olympic Games are guaranteed to keep a human grandeur imprinted with nobility and marked with simplicity'. [23] Partly because of the Olympic Games, Montreal succeeded in becoming a beacon for sport and enter-tainment, but it ended up costing three times more than was initially planned (more than $1.2 billion instead of the original $400 million). This colossal additional cost, which was contracted for the Olympic Games and paid for about 30 years afterwards, created important management and reconversion problems for these Olympic installations and tarnished the reputation of the city.

   After missing out in the race to hold the 1972 Olympics, the Mayor of the city, Jean Drapeau, achieved his goal in 1970 in Amsterdam, when Montreal was awarded the 1976 Games. Betting on the popular and media success of the 1967 Universal Exposition (despite the fact that the organizational costs doubled, passing from $167 to $430 billion), on the economic and cultural attractiveness of the city, as well as on strong dynamism and conviction, Drapeau was able to attract the entire Olympic family to his city. [24] However, he was able to convince the Olympic authorities of the soundness and the seriousness of Montreal's candidacy through its intention to plan modest Games (initially estimated to $24 millions in 1970) that would be more centralized than Los Angeles' but less so than Moscow's [25] and therefore, going back to the roots of the Olympic spirit as well as to amateurism. [27]

This Olympics designation was due to a more global metropolitan sport politic, initiated at the start of the 1960s, which had as a principal objective to reinforce the basis of professional sport in Montreal. This sporting and economic strategy was initially based on the intention of bringing back a major baseball franchise to Montreal. This ambition was realized in 1968 when the Major League Baseball (MLB) announced an expansion phase of the league towards Montreal and San Diego. However, the creation of this team, called the Expos (referring to the 1967 Universal Exposition), raised the problem of the hosting infrastructure. At the time, Montreal did not possess a stadium with more than the 35,000 seats required by the MLB. The eventual hosting of the 1976 Olympics was therefore perceived as a way of meeting this requirement, whilst at the same time reinforcing Montreal's international recreational and tourist appeal. However, the MLB requirements, for an indoor stadium based on the model of Houston's Astrodome, contrasted with the necessity for an open-air stadium for the Olympic competitions. Hence, this undermined from the start the planning of this infrastructure while revealing the weak preparation and management of the municipal authorities regarding these multiple and complex issues.

As Morin reminds us, 'the accession to power of a new government in Quebec, the municipal electoral preparations and the tense political situation that led to the October crises [27] make us think that the Olympic matter was not considered a priority before 1971'. [28] This relatively unstable political situation combined with an organizational process directed solely by Mayor Drapeau weakened the 1976 Olympic Games Organizing Committee. [29] The Mayor's contesting of the choice of architect in charge of the construction of the Olympic park simply amplified the problem. Drapeau preferred the French architect Roger Taillibert and disappointed the Quebec Architects' Order which, from 1972, denounced the mayor's partisan decision not to follow the regulation requiring such work to be put out to tender. This regulation required the immediate organization of an international competition for the stadium project. Since the recommendation was followed, the nomination of Taillibert was very poorly received and added to the already substantial list of interventionist actions adopted by the Mayor (choice of the competitions sites, new equipments and Olympic village's constructions).

At the same level than Sydney's Opera House or Yamoussoukro's Notre-Dame-de-la-Paix, the great urban project of Montreal's Olympic stadium was never referred to any market, needs or beneficial-costs analyses. It was erected as a monument, to the glory of a people or, as the architect Jean-Claude Marsan is now suggesting, to the sole credit of a Mayor [30] In fact, since he was never able to achieve his 1967 project for an inclined tower ('Tour Paris-Montreal') during the Universal exposition, the mayor saw Taillibert's proposal for a retractable dome stadium maintained by an inclined tower instead of an indoor stadium as a way of satisfying his ambition to give Montreal a unique globally significant architectural symbol and to leave a mark of his stay as the head of the city. [31] The choice of the site for the Olympic park was also decided using electoral logic as it was situated in the electoral region of Hochelaga-Maisonneuve where Drapeau was elected. This choice also created financial reinforcing strategies for the east of Montreal. With the construction of the Olympic Park and the Olympic Village in the Maisonneuve area, the Mayor wanted to regenerate this declining area by giving a boost to its services and transportation offers as well as to its tourist appeal. The development of this site was partly imitating the strategy employed in preparation for the Munich Games where most of the sport sites were localized in one area closely connected to the Olympic village. [32] Beyond the construction of a cycle stadium, a swimming pool, an arena, a new pyramidal residential complex (the Olympic Village) situated on a 46 hectares' site, the project included the re-designing of multiple neighbouring green spaces, the extension of the metro (20 km), the erection of a new airport (Mirabel) as well as a range of hosting amenities. Despite all these plans, the major element remained the construction of a stadium with 70,000 places, which followed extremely innovative architectural principles.

Despite the idea of reproducing a more imposing version of Paris' Parc des Princes, Roger Taillibert undoubtedly complicated the planning of this colossal building by multiplying the architectural complexities, overlooking the realities of Montreal's climate and failing to allow for the area's urban tissue. Also, he did not take into account the architectural tendencies of North American stadiums of his time. Actually, despite the fact that he knew, from 1971, what types of sporting use the post-Olympics' stadium would be put to (American football and baseball), Taillibert persisted in creating a majestic infrastructure dedicated to athletics, while sacrificing the architectural intimacy necessary for North American professional sport. According to Kidd:

> preparations were complicated by the ambitious design Drapeau had encouraged French architect Roger Taillibert to devise for the main facilities in Olympic Park. Olympic Stadium was to include a fifty-story tower and a retractable roof. ... Construction was frequently disrupted by Taillibert's penchant for last-minute changes, the incompetence of contractors hired for political connections, and strikes and stoppages, in the context of continuing federalist-separatist and English-French tensions, and rapid inflation. [33]

The foundations of the stadium were only begun in August 1974, principally because Montreal's municipality and the OCOG had difficulties in guaranteeing the financial basis for this Olympic project as well as in justifying the specific and unique concept of a 'stadium-dome-mast' to the provincial authorities. Indeed, this architectural feature was jeopardized in January 1973 when the University of Stuttgart published a technical report from the research project *'Wide-Span Lightweight Structures'*. This project demonstrated that it would be problematic to build a retractable dome in the context of a rough climate such as that of Canada. [34] Therefore, the construction of this gigantic stadium commenced only 23 months before the opening of the Olympic Games. The construction process was harmed again during the autumn of 1974, when multiple strikes caused a four-month delay on the planned schedule, thus highlighting some irregularities in the management of the project. [35] These irregularities served to reinforce doubts as to the ability of the municipality to manage and conclude this project within the proposed financial and time constraints as well as on its ability to prevent eventual frauds and other corruption. These delays in the construction of the Olympic stadium caused the director of the OCOG, M. Roger Rousseau, to propose another solution for this project in the eventuality that it would not be ready for the Games in January 1975. [36] He submitted two main ideas, supported by different engineering and architecture firms, proposing the utilization of the existing auto-stadium situated in Montreal's southeast downtown, which was also used for American football. His first proposition was to increase it's the hosting capacity of this stadium from 33,000 to 55,000 places (22 000 less than Taillibert's stadium) via temporary structures. Rousseau also proposed to dismantle the auto-stadium and rebuild it within the Olympic Park, increasing the number of seats, for a total cost of $100 million ($60 million less than the estimate for Taillibert's stadium). The Mayor saw these propositions as a way of questioning his authority as well as what he saw as 'his Olympic project' and he strongly opposed them. Quebec's parliamentarians also declined these suggestions, principally because they were poorly justified in terms of architecture and techniques. Despite these refusals, as Pinard puts it:

> M. Rousseau achieved his objective: if the stadium was not completed in July 1976 or if it cost more than what was planned in January 1975, the parliamentarians would only have themselves to blame as they were the ones to agree, with the Mayor, that Taillibert's project remained the best emergency solution. [37]

In 1975, the chaotic construction process coupled with weak support given to the project caused the Quebec government to take charge of the preparation for these games by creating *La Régie des installations olympiques* (RIO, The Olympic Installations Board). [38] This public corporation carried the mandate to manage the construction of the Olympic installations until the Games (with a total fee that exceeded the original one by $800 million), adopting a very tight schedule as well as multiples interventionist measures. For example, they forbade the architect Taillibert to enter the building site. Using these tactics, the RIO was able to maintain a high level of productivity, which enabled the completion of the Olympic Park on time for the opening ceremony (17 July 1976) but with a stadium that did not have either a mast or a dome.

Moreover, it can be pointed out that the organization of Montreal's Olympic Games took place within a relatively morose political context. The stock market inflation and the petrol crises that affected most of the occidental countries during the first half of the 1970s strongly influenced the budget given to this project and, at the same time, seriously increased the Olympic debts (the governmental financial support ranged from 30 to 50%) [39]. Globally, the difficult political and economic context critically harmed the post-Olympic planning of these installations.

1976–2006, a Fallen Cathedral

Only two days after the closing ceremony of the 1976 Olympic Games the OCOG gave the keys to the Olympic Park back to the RIO so that they could finalize the construction of its installations (including the mast and the dome of the stadium, completed in November 1987). The RIO also needed to put into place a viable exploitation and commercialization process for the site. The election of the *Parti Québécois* (the separatists political party) as the new provincial government of Quebec in November 1976 transformed the relationship between Montreal's town hall and the provincial government with regard to the future of the Olympic facilities into a virtual 'cold war'. [40] In 1977, Quebec's Minister of Sports and Entertainment (*sports et loisirs*) and responsible for the RIO, Claude Charron, put the architect Jean-Claude Marsan at the head of a reflection committee with a mandate to study several development scenarios for these facilities. In October 1977, apart from the recommendation to transform the Olympic village into a locative residential complex, this committee reached multiple conclusions concerning the difficulties of the stadium's conversion. Two fundamental elements stand out from this work. On one hand, there was an urgency to complete the stadium's mast and its dome so that its playing surface could be used all year long, thereby reinforcing the sportive and ludic re-utilization of the infrastructure. However, on the other hand, according to this committee, this process needed to be completed within the context of a better integration of the facility to its urban framework, by de-compartmentalizing the concrete structure and by creating relations with the local population. In February 1978, the government of Quebec committed to itself following these recommendations, but also imposed a one-year moratorium (which actually ended in 1984) to consider the technical and financial feasibility of Taillibert's plans for the mast and the dome of the stadium. These different development strategies were widely implemented during the 1980s and the 1990s, but never reached the desired configuration. This can partly be explained by the succession of technical problems that harmed the image of the stadium [41] and by the departure in 2004 of the Expos, the professional baseball team. [42] At the same time, the nature of the stadium itself when compared to Montreal's true needs, as well the non-attractiveness of the local area, which had few transportation and services facilities to link the stadium to the city's downtown area or to create a major tourist centre, also serve to explain the failure of the project. [43]

In 1977, when it was realized that several of the project's records contained management irregularities, the Quebec government instituted an Investigation Board to look through the finances of this 21st Olympiad. In June 1980, this Commission, directed by Judge Albert H. Malouf, filed a report that was very disturbing for those who took part in the Games' organization. Malouf's report presented several conclusions explaining the exponential increase of the cost of the Games, which reached more than $1.2 billion rather than the $400 millions originally planned. According to this commission, this huge increase was due to the organisation and surveillance of the defective building operations, the administrative irresponsibility, the rapid shift from a modest to an extravagant Games, the absence of a pre-established overall budget and project direction, the acquisition of superfluous and luxurious installations, as well as the decision to choose a completely new and unique architectural concept. The report also put into context the real needs of a medium-sized city in terms of recreational and tourist matters while openly blaming Montreal's authorities, the OCOG, the architect Taillibert, the trade unions and the entrepreneurial milieus, the Canadian Olympic Association as well as the International Federations for their bad management and planning of the Games. This report also allowed several scientists to verify Montreal as a model of post-Olympic failure. [44]

This $1.2 billion Olympic deficit first enforced the provincial authorities to sanction Montreal City, requiring the reimbursement of $214 million for the construction of the facilities. However, from 1976, the RIO, for which two principal sources of revenues were created and reinforced, finally had to assume most of this deficit. As a way to help cover these costs, the Canadian Government first permitted the extension of the Olympic Lottery until December 1979 but from May 1976, it was mainly the levying of a new provincial tax on tobacco that serviced the reimbursement of this debt. Then again, as Morin puts it, 'from 1979, the government eroded, little by little, the percentage taken for the Olympic debt from tobacco taxes'. [45] In fact, the reimbursements of this debt fell from $119 to $10,3 millions per year between 1988 and 1994, which made the hypothetical balance increase by roughly 15% during the 1990s. These fluctuating reimbursement levels never permitted the RIO to profit from the Olympic Park or from the stadium in particular. It also exposed the strong financial and decision-making dependency of this institution on subsidized public authorities. Moreover, this administration was never related to a particular ministry but supervised by diverse ministerial authorities (Economic Development Ministry, Tourism Ministry, the *Conseil du trésor*, etc.) This complex administrative situation complicated decision-making, made the stadium's re-conversion strategic plan more complex in the long term, and it penalized the efficient marketing, following principles of public-private partnership, of this facility.

According to Taillibert's expectation, this Olympic debt should have been reimbursed by 1985. However, it was not repaid until 30 years after the Games (November 2006) and ended up costing three times more than the Olympic Park itself. The completion of this reimbursement also raised some questions regarding the post-debt future of the site and its stadium. Because of the absence of a long-term strategic vision, this structure, which has an everyday management cost of over $40 million per year, was actually never profitable for the city. [46] In fact, although planning and management reports on the Olympic installations were published after the Games, no true data or other recommendations were mentioned with regard to the long-term future of these facilities and in particular of the stadium:

> If Barcelona is to be considered as the best example of an Olympic city benefiting from a strong urban planning tradition, Montreal 1976 was city planning's worst nightmare. It is not so much that the city planning process was ill-adapted (as in the case of Moscow), too centrally-decided (as in Seoul) or purely elite-oriented (Atlanta), rather that it simply did not exist. [47]

Therefore, within a context of emergency that existed both before and after the Olympic Games, it is comprehensible and logical that no concrete post-Olympic planning was put into place for this stadium or more widely for the Olympic Park.

2006–2010, New Ambitions for the Stadium

Since the last stripping of the stadium's dome in 1999, during the Montreal international motor show, the playing surface is unused from November to March every year. This therefore reduces the possibilities of the stadium being used to only eight months per year. On the 5 May 2008, whilst considering these observations, the president of the RIO, M. André Gourd, publicly announced in the Quebec media that the Olympic Stadium would soon be clothed with a new dome, thereby increasing the building's exploitation. According to Gourd, this new $100 million dome would allow year long utilization of the playing surface and 'instead of losing $25 million for 20 events, we will be able to decrease the costs to $5 million and host 40 events". [48] However, this financial forecast is not as promising as it sounds, especially if we consider the activities undertaken before the stripping of the dome by the RIO in 1999.

Between 1995 and 1998, while the playing surface was accessible all year long, the stadium hosted about 37 events from January to December. However, if the Expos' baseball games, which were still taking place at the time, are subtracted from this the average decreases to 22 events per year. This appears to differ quite considerably from the figures suggested by the RIO. [49] As the economic, recreational and tourist impacts of this new dome diminished, it should also be highlighted that new events spaces, directly competing with the stadium, appeared or were redesigned in Montreal since 1999. The *Palais des congrès* (The Congress Palace), the Bell centre, the Bonaventure square, the *Quartier des spectacles* (The Spectacles' Quarter) all directly affected the traditional tourist appeal of the Olympic infrastructure. The Olympic stadium's future is no longer guaranteed, especially if we consider that a host of events, which traditionally took place in the stadium (the motor show, concerts) or could be organized there (shows and exhibitions), are now taking place elsewhere. Generally, organizers prefer more central locations that are less expensive and better equipped for the logistics of hosting (Figure 1).

We can easily imagine that the dome replacement alone will not be sufficient to boost the stadium, as it will not necessarily guarantee the organization of 40 the

Figure 1 Montreal Olympic Stadium. *Source:* Sylvain Lefebvre/GREF photographs bank (April 2009)

events per year that RIO expects. If re-designing is an incontestable preamble to the revitalization of this efacility, the dome replacement alone can certainly not support the stadium's entire development. [50] The presence of the Biodome (the Olympic Velodrome converted into a nature museum), the insectariums, the botanic garden, a 10-room theatre complex, the new 13,000 seater football stadium for the *Impact* professional football team (inaugurated in May 2008), two metro stations, more than 4,000 parking places and the upcoming opening of a planetarium in and around the Olympic Park expose the recreational and tourism attractiveness of this site as well as its important development capacity, particularly when it comes to the stadium. If this immense concrete quadrilateral remains partly functional, it remains cold and disconnected from the existing urban framework. Moreover, amongst the population it is not considered as a place where it's nice to hang out or as a 'must see' sight, welcoming and attractive. The challenge is important and makes sense. However, it requires a certain brand of town-planning and political audacity. It requires a fine, progressive and flexible strategy in order to create social consensus for the future of the stadium and its Olympic Park.

Since the reimbursement of the Olympic debts, the RIO apparently desires to invest in the global revitalization of the Olympic Park by further reinforcing recreational and tourist development strategies. However, although the stadium appears to be an important urban marker for the local collective imagination, there is an incontestable 'love-hate' relationship between public opinion (population and media) and this sports theatre. This complex relationship is based on both good moves and well-known disappointments. [51] Thus, one the fundamental challenge for the Olympic park and the stadium's development logics is to change the image of the site as well as the way in which it is perceived by the Quebec population, significant local figures and the media. Despite seeking the population's approbation for the transformation of the Park, what seems necessary is a vision of re-design, based upon sustainable development practices and in which the environmental element would be at the centre of the perspective. If we consider international experiences, such as those of Munich (1972), Barcelona (1992) or Sydney (2000), the option of designing a great integrated and prestigious urban park as a development vector for the stadium seems a most judicious strategy in order to integrate the population and help it to accept the process of urban transformation. Moreover, local participation, the branding and revitalization of the site also needs repositioning in terms of its recreational and tourist potential following international examples in such matters. [52] Thus, social and educational activities, engaging the local population and following sporting and cultural trends could also be combined with commercial, profitable and visible events, organized for a local, national and international clientele.

Conclusion

Montreal's post-Olympic financial downfall is now considered to be a unique tale within Olympic Games' history. It is the subject of frustration for an entire city and province that transformed the stadium into both a symbol and a scapegoat. Montreal's experience demonstrates the controversial attitude of an interventionist municipal organization, which did not consider local expectations and needs. While the municipality stubbornly limited itself to building majestic infrastructures without taking into account the impact of the building upon its urban surroundings, Montreal became the typical case of post-Olympic failure. Without denigrating the heritage of the 1976 Games a symbolic gesture needs to be made in order to reinvigorate the pride of these Olympic installations. The site and its stadium should be renowned and turned towards the future, re-calling positive connotations and underlying important changes. If the construction of the new dome is to take about two to three years, it would seems proper to simultaneously conduct diverse planning and marketing operations of the entire site. At this crucial stage of the stadium's history, it is time to invest and to reinforce the collective pride towards the entire site and its sports facilities. A new prestigious and integrated urban park, connected to the rebirth of this great stadium, could truly become the catalyst of a future entertaining and sporting Montreal.

Acknowledgements

The authors would like to thank the members of the GREF (Research Group on Entertaining Spaces) for their significant help with this research as well as the Olympic International Committee and the International Centre for Sport Studies, for its support within the context of archive consultations. The authors also thank Montreal's Archives Centre as well as the *Régie des installations olympiques* (RIO) for authorizing us to go through its archives.

Notes

[1] Pitts and Liao, *Sustainable Olympic Design and Urban Development*; Gold and Gold, *Olympic Cities, City Agendas*; Horne and Manzenreiter, *Sports Mega-events*.

[2] It is necessary to make the distinction between the summer and the winter Olympic Games since they do not generate the same impacts on the hosting territories. The number of participating athletes and disciplines as well as the necessary infrastructure is different. The summer games generally host about 300 events for more than 10,000 athletes, while the winter games hold 80 events for a little more than 4,000 participants. From an urban point of view, we also note a difference as the summer OG are organized, since 1972 in particular, within multi-billionaire metropolises while the winter games' physical conditions as well as its infrastructure specificities need to take place within medium-size cities (500,000 to 2 million inhabitants).

[3] Maguire *et al.*, 'Olympic Legacies'.

[4] Gold and Gold, *Olympic Cities, City Agendas*.

[5] Preuss, *The Economics of Staging the Olympics*; Essex and Chalkley, 'Urban Development Through Hosting International Events'.

[6] Andranovich *et al.*, 'Olympic Cities: Lessons Learned'.

[7] Gold and Gold, 'Olympic Cities: Regeneration, City Rebranding and Changing Urban Agendas'.

[8] Horne and Manzenreiter, *Sports Mega-events*.

[9] Zukin, *The Cultures of Cities*.

[10] Coaffee, 'Urban Regeneration and Renewal', 150.

[11] Hiller, 'Post-event Outcomes and the Post-modern Turn'.

[12] Gold and Gold, 'Olympic Cities: Regeneration, City Rebranding and Changing Urban Agendas'.

[13] Essex and Chalkley, 'Urban Development Through Hosting International Events'.

[14] Searle, 'Uncertain Legacy'; Essex and Chalkley, 'Urban Development Through Hosting International Events'.

[15] Paramio *et al.*, 'From Modern to Postmodern'.

[16] Thornley, 'Urban Regeneration and Sports Stadia'.

[17] Ibid., 815.

[18] Garcia, 'Sydney 2000'.

[19] Pitts and Liao, *Sustainable Olympic Design and Urban Development*.

[20] Hiller, 'Post-event Outcomes and the Post-modern Turn'.

[21] Wilson, 'What is an Olympic City?'

[22] Gratton and Jones, *Research Methods for Sport Studies*.

[23] Unless otherwise noted, all translations are our own. 'A Montréal, les Jeux Olympiques sont assurés de conserver une grandeur humaine empreinte de noblesse et marquée de simplicité': Drapeau, *Lettre de candidature pour les Jeux de la XXIe Olympiade*, 1969: 1.

[24] Howell, *The Montreal Olympics*.

[25] Other applicant cities for the 1976 OG.

[26] Latouche, 'Montreal 1976'; Morin, *La cathédrale inachevée*, 1997.

[27] The 'October crises' refers to series of separatists' social and political events, which took place in October 1970 in Quebec.

[28] '[L]' accession au pouvoir d'un nouveau gouvernement au Québec, les préparatifs électoraux municipaux et la situation politique tendue qui conduisit à la crise d'octobre donnent à penser que le dossier olympique ne fut pas considéré comme prioritaire avant le début de 1971': Morin, *La cathédrale inachevée*, 81.

[29] Latouche, 'Montreal 1976'.

[30] Marsan, *Montréal en évolution*.

[31] Gignac, *Le maire qui rêvait sa ville*.

[32] Howell, *The Montreal Olympics*.

[33] Kidd, 'The Culture Wars of the Montreal Olympics', 154

[34] Morin, *La cathédrale inachevée*, 110.

[35] Auf der Maur, *The Billion Dollar Game*, 114.

[36] Howell, *The Montreal Olympics*.

[37] 'M. Rousseau a atteint son objectif: si, en juillet 1976, le stade n'est pas terminé ou s'il a coûté beaucoup plus cher que prévu qu'en janvier 1975, les parlementaires n'auront qu'eux-mêmes à blâmer, puisque ce sont eux qui ont convenu, comme le maire Jean Drapeau, que la meilleure solution d'urgence se trouvait encore dans le projet Taillibert': G. Pinard, 'Rousseau voulait que Québec choisisse lui-même le type de stade désiré', *La Presse*, 11 Feb. 1975, Montreal edition, Actuality section, 1.

[38] Kidd, 'The Culture Wars of the Montreal Olympics'.

[39] Auf der Maur, *The Billion Dollar Game*, 125.

[40] Morin, *La cathédrale inachevée*, 1997.

[41] Multiple cracks and other concrete drops on the stadium's structure were accumulated during the 1980s and 1990s. Since 1987 and the decision to install a fixed dome on the stadium, multiple tears happened, the most important being in 1999 when the playing surface closed from November to March every year. This remains until today.

[42] Lefebvre and Latouche, *L'impact socio-culturel d'un nouveau stade de baseball*.

[43] Lefebvre and Roult, 'L'après-JO'.

[44] Gold and Gold, *Olympic Cities, City Agendas*; Essex and Chalkley, 'Urban Development Through Hosting International Events'.

[45] 'Le pourcentage prélevé à même la taxe sur le tabac pour payer la dette olympique fut érodé, petit à petit, par le gouvernement à partir de 1979': Morin, *La cathédrale inachevée*, 166.

[46] Lefebvre and Roult, 'L'après-JO'.

[47] Latouche, 'Montreal 1976', 210.

[48] 'Au lieu de perdre 25 millions de dollars en tenant 20 événements, on pourra peut-être réduire cela à 5 millions en tenant 40 événements': S. Rodrigue, 'Rénovations majeures et nouveau toit', *La Presse*, 6 May 2008, Montreal edition, Actuality section, 12.

[49] S. Lefebvre and R. Roult, 'Un nouveau toit pour le stade olympique; vecteur de développement ou fausse lueur d'espoir', *Le Devoir*, 9 June 2008, Montreal edition, Actuality section.

[50] Roult and Lefebvre, *Réflexion sur le positionnement stratégique*.

[51] Ibid.

[52] Ibid.

References

Andranovich, M.J., Burbank, G.A. and C.H. Heying. 'Olympic Cities: Lessons Learned from Mega-Event Politics'. *Journal of Urban Affairs* 23, no. 2 (2001): 113–31.

Auf der Maur, N. *The Billion Dollar Game*. Toronto: Lorimier, 1975.

Coaffee, J. 'Urban Regeneration and Renewal'. In *Olympic Cities, City Agendas, Planning and the World's Games, 1896–2012,* edited by J. Gold and M. Gold. New York: Routledge, 2007: 150–62.

Drapeau, J. *Lettre de candidature pour les Jeux de la XXIe Olympiade*. Montréal: Ville de Montréal, 1969.

Essex, S. and B. Chalkley. 'Urban Development Through Hosting International Events: A History of the Olympic Games'. *Planning perspectives* 14 (1999): 369–394.

Garcia, B. 'Sydney 2000'. In *Olympic Cities, City Agendas, Planning and the World's Games, 1896–2012*, edited by J. Gold and M. Gold. New York: Routledge: 237–64.

Gignac, B. *Le maire qui rêvait sa ville*. Montréal: Éditions La Presse, 2009.

Gold, J. and M. Gold, eds. *Olympic Cities, City Agendas, Planning and the World's Games, 1896–2012*. New York: Routledge, 2007.

Gold, J. and M. Gold. 'Olympic Cities: Regeneration, City Rebranding and Changing Urban Agendas'. *Geography Compass* 2, no. 1 (2008): 300–18.

Gratton, C. and I. Jones. *Research Methods for Sport Studies*. New York: Routledge, 2006.

Hiller, H. 'Post-event Outcomes and the Post-modern Turn: The Olympics and Urban Transformations'. *European Sport Management Quarterly* 6, no. 4 (2006): 317–32.

Horne, J. and W. Manzenreiter, eds. *Sports Mega-events, Social Scientific Analyses of a Global Phenomenon*. Oxford: Blackwell Publishing, 2006.

Howell, P.C. *The Montreal Olympics. An Insider's View of Organizing a Self-financing Games*. Montreal: McGill-Queen's University Press, 2009.

Kidd, B. 'The Culture Wars of the Montreal Olympics'. *International Review for the Sociology of Sport* 27, no. 2 (1992): 151–162.

Latouche, D. 'Montreal 1976'. In *Olympic Cities, City Agendas, Planning and the World's Games, 1896–2012*, edited by J. Gold and M. Gold. New York: Routledge, 2007: 197–217.

Lefebvre, S. and D. Latouche. *L'impact socio-culturel d'un nouveau stade de baseball pour les Expos de Montréal*. Montréal: Rapport Final, Collection Culture et Ville, 1997.

Lefebvre, S. and R. Roult. 'L'après-JO: Reconversion et réutilisation des équipements olympiques'. *Revue Espaces* 263 (2008): 30–42.

Maguire, J., S. Barnard, K. Butler and P. Golding. 'Olympic Legacies in the IOC's "Celebrate Humanity" Campaign: Ancient or Modern?'. *International Journal of the History of Sport* 25, no. 14 (2008): 2041–59.

Mangan, J.A. 'Prologue: Guarantees of Global Goodwill: Post-Olympic Legacies – Too Many Limping White Elephants?'. *International Journal of the History of Sport* 25, no. 14 (2008): 1869–83.

Marsan, J.C. *Montréal en évolution – Historique du développement de l'architecture et de l'environnement urbain montréalais*. Montreal: Éditions Méridien/Architecture, 1994.

Morin, G.R. *La cathédrale inachevée*. Montréal: XYZ Éditeur, 1997.

Paramio, J.L., B. Buraimo and C. Campos. 'From Modern to Postmodern: The Development of Football Stadia in Europe'. *Sport in Society* 11, no. 5 (2008): 517–p34.

Pitts, A. and H. Liao. *Sustainable Olympic Design and Urban Development*. London: Routledge, 2009.

Preuss, H. *The Economics of Staging the Olympics*. Cheltenham: Edward Elgar Publishing, 2004.

Québec. Comité consultatif. *Rapport consultatif chargé d'étudier l'avenir des installations olympiques*. Québec: Publications Gouvernementales, 1977.

Québec. Commission d'enquête. *Rapport de la commission d'enquête sur le coût de la 21e olympiade* (Rapport Malouf). Québec: Publications Gouvernementales, 1980.

Roult, R. and S. Lefebvre. *Réflexion sur le positionnement stratégique et les balises d'un plan d'affaires pour l'avenir du Parc olympique de Montréal*. Montréal: GREF/Régie des Installations Olympiques, 2009.

Searle, G. 'Uncertain Legacy: Sydney's Olympic Stadiums'. *European Planning Studies* 10, no. 7 (2002): 845–60.

Thornley, A. 'Urban Regeneration and Sports Stadia'. *European Planning Studies* 10, no. 7, (2002): 813–18.

Wilson, H. 'What is an Olympic City? Visions of Sydney 2000'. *Media, Culture & Society* 18 (1996): 603–18.

Zukin, S. *The Cultures of Cities.* Oxford, Blackwell, 1995.

Mexico City 1968: Oscillating Aspirations

Keith Brewster

Mexico City's staging of the Olympic Games in 1968 provided a unique opportunity; a moment when a nation at ease with itself and its place in the world, played proud host to a global celebration of youthful vigour. This study argues, however, that while the cosmopolitan members of the Organising Committee deeply resented international scepticism of Mexico's ability to stage the Games, they shared a fear that with the eyes of the world upon them, their compatriots would reveal Mexico's aspirations to first world status to be a fraud. Constantly having to defend its actions against hostile international scrutiny, this domestic dilemma led to the confused international posture that Mexico assumed during the Games. While seemingly eager to sustain an image of modernity and progression, Mexico simultaneously took shelter in its role as a leader of the Third World. Mexico's oscillation between polarities of economic development was natural, in that it merely mirrored, and arguably continues to mirror, a Mexican society in which both exist.

Introduction

When members of the International Olympic Committee (IOC) awarded the 1968 summer Olympics to Mexico City, the host nation erupted in a burst of uncontrollable joy and pride. [1] For those behind the bid to host the games, the IOC's decision appeared to endorse their portrayal of their country as modern, dynamic and on the threshold of achieving first-world status. For the Olympic movement itself, the decision was no less historic. This was the first time that the games had been awarded to a host city beyond the first world. Moreover, it was the first time that the games would be held in a Spanish-speaking country and the first time that it would be held in Latin America. For a variety of different reasons, the 1968 Olympic Games represented a watershed, an event heavily laden with opportunity and symbolic value. Yet as soon as the result of the Baden-Baden vote was announced, it stimulated a wave of international criticism. Officials from international federations, coaches, journalists and athletes all expressed grave misgivings about competing at altitude, while many commentators questioned the wisdom of bestowing the games on a country that many perceived to be too poor to stage a successful event. The contrast between Mexican aspirations and international misgivings could not have been more stark. There was an obvious mismatch between these two camps, but why had those behind the project possessed the confidence to propose staging the games, and why did their critics find it difficult to share this confidence?

That there should be contrasting views between how a nation sees itself and how it is viewed by others is not rare. Yet international opinions of Mexico were only partially based upon a rational assessment of its true stage of social and economic development. They were also laced by decades, if not centuries, of negative assumptions about the Mexican character that worked to undermine any actual advances Mexico had achieved. Simultaneously, patriotism sustained the impetus of the Mexican elite's bid to host the games: the games would provide an opportunity to set the record straight. National pride made them less receptive, however, to the argument that the games was a luxury that a developing nation could not afford. By exploring the origins and nature of foreign stereotypes, and contrasting these with the state of Mexican economic and social development in the years preceding the games, it becomes easier to appreciate the true nature of the contrasting perceptions of Mexico '68.

Having laid out the context behind reactions to Mexico City's successful bid, this contribution assesses the ways in which this affected preparations for the games and influenced foreign perceptions of Mexico. What becomes clear is that the weight of criticism and concern voiced about Mexico placed the organizing committee on the defensive. Rather than being able to maintain a primarily confident front, the committee was constantly forced to defend its actions and offer reassurance. Furthermore, by reviewing foreign comments expressed during and immediately after the Olympics, it is clear that even though most officials, competitors and spectators believed the games to have succeeded beyond their expectations, this was insufficient to erode deep-seated prejudices. In turn, this raises the question of the degree to which any Olympic Games truly has the potential to redeem or drastically alter the international image of the host country. The case of Mexico suggests that any such potential is, at best, short-lived and is quickly overshadowed by more fundamental influences that determine a nation's reputation on the stage of world opinion.

'Typical Mexicans': The Perception and the Reality

A dominant stereotype that popular culture has ascribed to Mexicans is the vaguely paternalistic image of poncho-clad peasants with large sombreros and even larger moustaches, dozing beneath the shade of a cactus. While this infers a lazy, perhaps docile, persona, it is possible to argue that there is no malign intent in this enduring image. Yet even the most cursory glance at how this image has been articulated produces a harsher edge to the foreign gaze on Mexicans. Consider the following two observations, one made at the beginning of the twentieth century and the other on the eve of the Olympic Games. When travelling through the country in 1909, British travel writers, Arnold Channing and Frederick Tabor Frost gave vent to their thoughts on the nature of the Mexican people. Having derided both the Spanish and 'Indian' groups, they rounded upon the remainder of the population: 'The mestizos – near half the population – have all the worst features of their Spanish and Indian parents. Turbulent, born criminals, treacherous, idle, dissolute, and cruel, they have the Spanish lust and the Indian natural cynicism, the Spanish luxury of temperament with the Indian improvidence.' [2]

It might seem convenient to explain such derogatory remarks as a product of their time. In an age when politicians and intellectuals lent credence to social Darwinism, the authors were probably addressing a readership that shared an assumed superiority of the Anglo-Saxon race. What is less easy to dismiss, however, were comments made in early 1968 by Siegfried Kogelfranz in the German newspaper, *Der Spiegel*. Kogelfranz argued that, due to their mixed race, Mexicans did not have the capacity to organize the games, still less an ability to win any medals. While Mexican officials swiftly dismissed the remarks as having been penned by one of the dwindling remnants of Germany's Nazi past, they nonetheless caused great indignation within Mexico. [3]

While the above cases were undoubtedly extreme, the fact that such sentiments endured throughout the twentieth century is significant because it suggests a corrosive element within the composition of foreign perceptions of Mexico that undermined more positive impressions. Although the stereotype of the sleeping peasant may have been one that opportunistic street-traders in Mexico were happy to replicate in kitsch merchandise sold to tourists, the disarming, less racist portrayal nonetheless perpetuated underlying assumptions of subordination, limited ambitions, laziness and a propensity to prevaricate: all vital characteristics of those who inhabited the 'land of *mañana*'.

The other persistent stereotype attributed to Mexicans, and indeed to all Latin Americans, was the role that violence played in political and everyday life. The idea that 'life is cheap' in Mexico is something that foreign visitors and commentators perpetuated. It helped to explain the perception that arguments between two drunks in a canteen or, for that matter, between two opposing political leaders was likely to be resolved through violence. Contributing towards this attitude was the fact that throughout Latin America's turbulent postcolonial history, violent coups, military dictators and civil war had marred the region's economic and political development. Indeed, the chances of Buenos Aires winning the bid to host the 1968 games were dealt a severe blow by the fact that even as its delegates sought to persuade IOC members of the hospitable welcome that awaited them, Argentina's military generals were engaged in a series of coups bent on wresting political power from their opponents. Civil wars in Colombia, Central America and the Cuban Revolution merely added weight to the conviction overseas that much of Latin America was ungovernable (and that many Latin Americans were incapable of embracing Western-style democracy).

The frustration of those attempting to sustain Mexico's international reputation was that they believed their country to be undeserving of this violent 'Latino' trait. True, the Mexican Revolution (1910–17) had been a devastating civil war that, no doubt, contributed to the stereotypical Hollywood depiction of Mexico as a land maligned by marauding 'desperados'. Yet the fact was that in 1968 Mexico had experienced four decades of stable, civilian government. While the quality of its democracy and freedom of speech could be questioned, the basic facts demonstrated an adherence to constitutional politics and a succession of peaceful transitions of power from one administration to the next. Sporadic, low-level state repression did much to curb major challenges to the political order without creating the impression of a uniformly authoritarian state.

In terms of Mexico's economic standing in the world, there is no denying that it was seen, at best, as one of those developing countries that showed potential. Yet this was another source of frustration for the country's political and economic leaders, who believed Mexico to be on the verge of first-world status. In assessing exactly how onlookers viewed Mexico's economy as it prepared for the Olympic Games, it is important not to judge it on the basis of economic crises that were yet to befall it. Rather, a true measure of the expectations and/or concerns with Mexico's economic position in 1960s is best found by analysing what academics and economists were saying about the robustness of the national economy at the time.

In 1970, Clark Reynolds provided a detailed assessment of Mexico's economic performance in the twentieth century – see Table 1. Reynolds's overview of gross domestic product (GDP) is particularly enlightening in that whereas earlier periods showed moderate to modest growth rates, between 1940 and 1965 there was dramatic growth. This was the so-called 'miracle years' of economic development. Reynolds placed the beginning of this recovery down to the policies of President Manuel Avila Camacho (1940–6) who agreed to indemnify former owners of Mexico's nationalized petroleum industry, to settle defaulted Mexican bonds, and to encourage new foreign direct investment, particularly in manufacturing and commerce. [4] Import substitution policies had the effect of cementing Avila Camacho's positive economic policies in the 1950s. Foreign companies were encouraged to invest in capital goods

Table 1 Income levels in the Mexican economy

Year	GDP (million pesos at 1950 value)
1900	8,540
1910	11,825
1925	17,081
1935	17,820
1940	21,658
1965	99,700

Source: Reynolds, *The Mexican Economy*, 16.

and, as a consequence, Mexico saw the arrival of more efficient machinery and equipment to replace its obsolete stock. Simultaneously, protective tariffs deterred the importation of foreign consumer goods. A rising domestic demand for consumables would be satisfied by the growth of a domestic manufacturing sector, largely equipped by this new foreign machinery. Government investment in infrastructure further attracted foreign investment while concurrently offering ostentatious examples for a domestic audience that Mexico was, indeed, experiencing miracle years.

As far as foreign economic analysts such as Reynolds were concerned, the one cloud on the economic horizon was the fact that Mexico's flow of foreign capital was severely undermined by the rising share of borrowing for refinancing and the growing costs of debt service. [5] However, the full implications of these concerns would not be apparent for many more years and cannot be taken as a significant factor in foreign perceptions of Mexico on the eve of the 1968 Olympics. Within the global economic sector, Mexico was a good place in which to do business and many multinationals unhesitatingly sought to do just that.

The domestic implications of the miracle growth that Reynolds charts are particularly relevant to preparations for the Olympic Games. Another study, published in 1970 by Timothy King, comprised a synopsis of Mexico's economic policies in the previous three decades for the Organisation for Economic Cooperation and Development (OECD). What is clear is that a wartime policy of boosting the manufacturing sector at the expense of the country's traditional agricultural base grew apace in the decades that followed. As a result, the latter sector became increasingly inefficient and in relative decline compared to urban economic development. Statistics relating to family income distribution in the very year that Mexico City won the vote at Baden-Baden offer a revealing picture of the consequences of this dislocation in economic development (Table 2).

This Bank of Mexico survey can be analysed in many ways, but the social and demographic aspects are particular relevant. It is clear that the underlying trend often

Table 2 Family income distribution, by principal occupation, 1963

Monthly income, pesos	% of total families	% of families in agriculture	% of families in industry	% of families in service
0–300	18.4	28.9	7.3	12.3
301–600	25.1	34.9	20.5	16.3
601–1,000	21.6	17.7	28	22.6
1,001–1,500	10.9	5	18.6	13.4
1,501–3,000	15	9.5	15.1	21.4
3,001–4,500	4.5	2.1	5.8	6.7
4,500–6,000	1.9	0.9	2.3	2.9
6,001–10,000	1.6	0.7	0.9	3.1
Over 10,000	0.9	0.2	1.6	1.3

Source: Bank of Mexico, household inquiry data, cited in King, *Mexico*, 29.

associated with developing nations, that of unequal income distribution, was experienced in Mexico. Although the figures confirm the growth of a middle class linked to manufacturing and service industries, the stark contrast between the minority elite and impoverished majority remained a salient factor. Another important observation to draw from the survey is the chronic degree of rural poverty. By far the majority of the poorest families lived in the countryside while urban economic development appeared to offer the possibility of increasing a family's chance of a better life.

The socio-demographic consequences of these underlying economic factors are, perhaps, predictable in that they followed the trends of other countries that were trying to manage the transition from an agricultural to manufacturing-based economy. Whereas in 1930, only one-third of Mexico's population lived in urban areas, by 1960 the figure had risen to 50.7 per cent. For the first time in Mexico's history, the urban population outnumbered those who lived in rural areas. [6] Migration away from the countryside to urban conurbations, particularly Mexico City, created real pressure on urban housing, jobs and social cohesion. While investment in Mexico City was able to reflect the relatively healthy economy through the construction of houses and schools, and in services and manufacturing initiatives, it could not totally absorb the ever-increasing demands of internal migration. As a result, the appearance of informal settlements, both on the peripheries and on vacant land within the capital, became a common phenomenon. Dwellings made of cardboard or wood offered an uncomfortable juxtaposition with the skyscrapers that were proclaiming the Mexican miracle. A proliferation of street stalls and hawkers bore witness to the growth of an informal economy that was totally divorced from the world in which middle-income and elite Mexicans lived.

The fact was that, on the eve of the Mexico Olympics, the country's social, economic and political complexion was full of contradictions and contrasts. Many of its political and business leaders were aware of, and indeed were central to, the rapid transformation of Mexico's economic growth. They bristled with confidence and took shelter in the modern skyscrapers in Mexico City that were the physical manifestation of that confidence. At the same time, there could be no denying that significant sectors of the population had been left behind; either in the increasingly desolate countryside, or the equally dismal urban slums and shanty towns that sprang up on the outskirts of Mexico's major cities. Mexican society in the 1960s was in a state of flux and the consequences of unequal wealth distribution provoked as many problems at it resolved.

Similarly, foreign perceptions of Mexico and its people were contradictory and, in some important respects, outdated. It is clear that many international financiers and businesses had well-established relationships with their Mexican counterparts and continued to see Mexico as a good place in which to do business. For such individuals, the image of the poncho-clad Mexican peasant may have seemed quaintly anachronistic in an economy that was rapidly losing its rural roots. Many more foreigners, without first-hand experience and reliant upon second-hand stereotypes, would continue to see Mexico in a less positive light. For them, Mexico continued to be a poor country in which dishevelled peasants scratched a living from the dusty soil and took succour from periodic swigs from a tequila bottle.

Furthermore, it is probable that the psyche of foreign attitudes towards Mexico were yet more complex in that each extreme could impinge on the other. Those with business operations in Mexico might oscillate in their views towards Mexicans, willing to give them the benefit of the doubt until an obstacle arose to prompt their reversion to more hapless images of the 'typical Mexican'. Conversely, from the point of view of the Mexico Olympics, the 'land of *mañana*' depiction that many foreigners had of Mexico might dampen expectations and enable the host nation to earn disproportionate praise when things were conducted in an efficient manner. In many respects, the extent to which the Mexican organizers of the 1968 games would achieve their ambitions of re-inventing their nation's international image depending on wresting control of the processes by which foreign opinion might be swayed. Attention needed to be diverted away from the poor housing, their impoverished inhabitants and the less savoury aspects of Mexican life. Rather, the foreign gaze needed to be directed towards the forward-looking, entrepreneurial Mexico that was confident of its place in the world.

In May 1968, the organizing committee's public relations director, Roberto Casellas, addressed those gathered for the annual dinner of the British/Mexican Society:

> On this occasion [the Olympic Games] Mexico wishes to show its true image to the world. We want to do away with the picture of the Indian sleeping his eternal 'siesta' and with the dramatic representation of a country plagued by revolutions. While both of these images may have been representative of Mexico's past, they are no longer true in the present. We want to make known our progress in the fields of science and technology. We want to show the inspired works of our artists, the charm of our cities, the great natural beauty show of our countryside and our achievements in modern architecture. [7]

This was the mission that the organizing committee had set out to achieve. It remained to be seen whether they had sufficient skills to convince a highly sceptical overseas audience.

Combating the Stereotypes

When the results of the Baden Baden vote became public, a jubilant President López Mateos was in no doubt why Mexico City had been chosen:

> It is a worldwide acknowledgement of the strength of the Mexican people in maintaining and raising their international standing in the world of sport, and also of their economic and political stability, which is undoubtedly based on their unswerving doctrine of pacifism and friendship towards all peoples of the world. [8]

The Mexican press was equally triumphant. Representative of sentiments expressed in many papers, *El Universal* assessed the significance of the vote in the following manner:

> Mexico managed to win ... not because it is a great sporting power, but because our nation has clearly been able to demonstrate that it is a progressive nation enjoying a totally stable political situation. For this reason, the triumph does not belong exclusively to Mexican sport: it belongs to all the active forces in Mexico, beginning with the President, who in addition to having always supported sporting initiatives, has been singled out for the outstanding nature of his domestic and international policies, which encourages friendship among all peoples of the world, respect for self-determination, and a resolute search for world peace. [9]

The euphoria at having gained such a prestigious international honour was presented as a vote of confidence in the Mexican nation, in its system of government, and in its economic progress. In this respect, it represented a degree of continuity with the arguments and visions shared by the three men who had been the driving force in obtaining the games. President López Mateos and the two Mexican members of the International Olympic Committee, José de Clark Flores and Marte I. Gómez, were all from a sector of society that believed in the capacity of Mexico to deliver when placed under extreme international scrutiny. They were cosmopolitan in outlook; they possessed a vision of their country that went beyond national boundaries and, as reflected in *El Universal*'s column, they believed that Mexico was able and willing to make a mark in the world.

Another significant theme within this burst of euphoria, however, was the emphasis on Mexico's calm diplomacy amidst a global context of heightened international tension: Mexico as a promoter of peace and self-determination. In many respects, this was the international facet of a rising degree of self-confidence among Mexico's elite. No longer was it sufficient to uphold Mexico's dignity abroad; by grasping the nettle and portraying itself as a forerunner in the search for peace, it was showing the world that it was capable of assuming a leading role. Indeed, an increasingly prominent message emerging from the Olympic preparations was that of positing Mexico as a leader of Latin America and other developing countries of the world. A dominant theme in the official rhetoric was that this was Latin America's Olympic Games; the Olympic Games of the Spanish-speaking world. By staging a successful event, Mexico was not only serving its own purposes, but enhancing the much maligned international image of its neighbours. Inherent within this portrayal was the fact that Mexico, above all other nations, was in the strongest position to assume such a role. The same economic and political development that instilled such confidence among its elite placed it in an ideal position to vocalize the interests of those countries that, like Mexico in the past, were currently ignored by the rest of the world.

If, however, there was any risk of this wave of self-congratulations turning into complacency, the international reaction to the Baden-Baden vote would have acted as a timely corrective. Avery Brundage's immediate communication with Clark Flores offered a hint of the rising incredulity within the international community: 'I must say that there are many who are still stunned ... at the success of Mexico.' [10] Brundage may, of course, have been alluding to the size of Mexico City's majority in the first round of voting. Mexico had received sufficient votes not to make a second round necessary. He may, however, have been reflecting an element of shock and surprise that the generally conservative members of the IOC had taken such a chance on a host from the developing world.

For an overview of the concerns relating to Mexico City's hosting of the 1968 games, one needs to look no further than the Mexican Olympic Committee's own annual report after the games had ended. [11] It lists all the criticisms levelled at Mexico prior to the games:

1. Mexico was not a mature country.
2. The installations would not be ready.
3. The expenses would be too much for the country to afford.
4. The organization would be a disaster and it would be better for Mexico to give up the responsibility of hosting the games to avoid the inevitable bad publicity.
5. Mexican athletes would be ridiculed in front of the sporting world's crème de la crème.
6. The high altitude of Mexico City would cause death and/or permanent damage to the athletes. [12]

As the report made clear, it was not only a sensationalist international press that lodged such charges against the Mexicans. In key aspects of the organization, international sports administrators had stoked the fires with periodic press releases and complaints to the IOC regarding different aspects of Mexico City's preparations.

Of the various concerns outline above, the only one that did not link specifically to negative perceptions of the host nation was the question of altitude. The possible adverse effects on athletes performing at 7,400 feet was raised early and often by international sporting bodies. Indeed, Mexico City's bid team had anticipated such concerns and offered full cooperation in any investigations that might be needed to allay such fears. Even when the IOC laid out a set of scientifically-backed recommendations that were designed to ensure the safety of competitors, foreign bodies and press still feared the worse. Most dramatically, although by no means unrepresentative, in July 1966 a New Zealand newspaper issued a passionate appeal: 'Change the site of the Olympic Games! We are in danger of dying.' [13] Almost in exasperation, Avery Brundage had to remind competing nations that 'the Olympic Games belong to the world – North and South, East and West, hot and cold, dry and humid, high and low, and Mexico will be the first Latin American country and the first Spanish speaking country to have the honour of staging the Games'. [14] In the event, no one died; although it is true to say that athletes from countries who routinely trained at high altitude enjoyed a definite advantage in endurance sports.

Conversely, recognized athletes in explosive sports, such as the sprints, high-jump and long jump, relished conditions that helped them to new world records.

While the issue of altitude was beyond the control of the organizing committee, the persistent fears expressed overseas contributed towards the negative aura surrounding the Mexico games. In order to gain control of the process that informed international opinion, the organizing committee's task was to combat the stereotypes of poverty, inefficiency and inexperience outlined above by emphasizing modernity, sophistication and ingenuity.

Ingenuity was essential to balance the imperative of recognizing Mexico's economic limitations with its desire to be a generous host. One of the easiest lines of criticism against Mexico hosting the Olympic Games was the accusation that the consequent expense would draw investment away from much-needed social and welfare projects. Both domestic and international critics dwelt on the more obvious examples of an unequal economy that could construct impressive office tower blocks while within the same district people lived in flimsy houses with no electricity or sanitation. Pedro Ramírez Vázquez, the chairman of the organizing committee, became accustomed to offering a solid defence. As an architect of world repute he was, perhaps, well placed to talk with confidence about Mexico's social commitment. He pointed out to critics that they should never lose sight of the fact that 'every hour another classroom is built and that in last 30 years we have managed to provide irrigation for an area the size of France'. [15] In his first annual report after the Olympics, President Gustavo Díaz Ordaz emphasized that the overwhelming majority of the 2.2 billion Mexican pesos of government investment in the games had been spent within Mexico and, hence, ploughed back into the domestic economy for the benefit of all citizens. [16]

Criticisms of this nature did have the effect of maintaining a large degree of social responsibility on the organizing committee's deliberations. Long before it was fashionable, the committee was talking about the Olympic legacy and the need to maximize the long-term benefits of hosting the games. As such, wherever possible, existing facilities were refurbished and used for Olympic competition. The Olympic Stadium in the new National University campus had already been built, as had the Estadio Azteca, in which the football tournament was held. The Olympic villages were constructed using private money and the committee merely rented the apartments for the duration of the games before they were then sold on the open market. Where new stadiums were required, the committee resisted the temptation of concentrating them in one area. While this would have eased transport considerations for competitors and visitors, the committee wanted to ensure that after the games had finished, various areas of Mexico City would be left with a sporting complex available for public use. In this respect, the Mexico City games could boast a large measure of success. To the present day, the velodrome, gymnastics hall, swimming pool and rowing lanes continue to be valuable, well-used public facilities.

While such frugality may have quietened some critics and, indeed, won many international plaudits, the Olympic project had to do more than that. It was insufficient to prove that Mexico could be responsible by not spending beyond its means. It needed to convince the world to share its optimism, its self-confidence and its ambition. The new Olympic installations provided the perfect vessels for sending this highly symbolic message overseas, and Ramírez Vázquez was richly qualified to accomplish the task. The emphasis of the new designs was economy, innovation and modernity. Using the limited resources available, the result was a truly stunning array of buildings that raised the bar in terms of what could be created with concrete and steel.

Simultaneous with the construction projects, the organizing committee put together a year-long series of events that comprised the Cultural Olympiad. On a hitherto unprecedented scale (and one never to be repeated), the organizing committee invited all competing nations to contribute aspects of their cultures that might enrich human understanding. Why the committee decided to embrace this additional range of organizational burdens is open to various interpretations. Elsewhere, I have argued that a degree of national self-interest was a stake. [16] As the Mexican Olympic Committee's annual report following the games testifies, before the games there were many who feared that the host nation's athletes would be humiliated in front to a world audience. The one thing that all Mexicans could agree upon, however, was that they lived in a country that was rich in culture. While the official documentation expressly ruled out any suggestions of this being a competitive Cultural Olympiad, the fact that the Mexicans could hold their own in this aspect of the games must have had widespread national appeal.

There is, however, a less cynical interpretation of the cultural initiative. The altruistic foreign diplomacy that the Mexican government sought to follow in its dealings with the rest of the world lends a large degree of credence to Ramírez Vázquez's stated intentions for resurrecting the Cultural Olympiad. Alluding to the fact that the 1968 Olympics would be the first to which many of the newly-formed African nations would send competitors, Ramírez Vázquez maintained that poorer training facilities made it less likely for these athletes to win medals. However, he argued that every competing region, no matter how disadvantaged, could make a valuable contribution through offering an example of its unique cultural heritage. [18] By doing so, it could leave Mexico feeling that its national dignity not only remained intact, but had been enhanced by the experience of having an appreciative global audience. By mirroring the altruism of his own government, Ramírez Vázquez's promotion of a Cultural Olympiad offered opportunities to send out various coded messages to the world. The Mexican hosts recognized their commitment not only to the more affluent nations of the world, but to all those nations struggling to raise a team to compete at the games. They sent a message to every nation: that Mexico valued their culture and wished to honour it by providing a global stage upon which it could be celebrated. The Cultural Olympiad also suggested that the host nation was above brash displays of nationalistic pride; rather it was a cultured country that recognized the value of returning to the ethos of the ancient games. Certainly, it was a country that took scientific and technological advances seriously, and various exhibitions within the Cultural Olympiad would ably demonstrate this. However, the true mark of a civilized society was its appreciation of high and popular culture, and in this respect the cultural programme could do much to counter the less positive stereotypes of Mexico that pervaded the international psyche.

A Host of Contrasts

Considering the many siren voices predicting a disastrous Olympic Games, in the event, the Mexican Organizing Committee could justifiably feel proud with the end result. In an address to members of the IOC immediately prior to the opening ceremony, Avery Brundage expressed his own assessment by referring directly to previous negative stereotypes:

> Mexico is well equipped to be the Capital of the World of Sport. Visitors for the first time are discovering that Mexico City is a great, cosmopolitan metropolis with all the facilities of any important capital. Mexico is no longer the land of 'mañana'; you get out of the way or you'll get run over. So far as bandits are concerned, they exist today only in the films. [19]

The installations were ready on time; there were no major technical hitches that impaired the smooth running of the games and there were no significant incidents that directly affected competitors or visitors. Yet rather than rely on the predictably upbeat pronouncements of IOC officials, a better measure of Mexico City's success as host can be gleaned from a survey of the notoriously difficult to please international press. As ever, perhaps, the results were mixed. One Spanish publication refuted all the previous criticisms of Mexico in turn. Most significantly, the article argued that despite many fears that were voiced concerning Mexico's ability to stage the event, the organization had been excellent and not one sporting event had been delayed due to any lapse in administration. [20] J.L. Manning of the *Daily Mail* was equally encouraging, suggesting that 'the Games overcame unprecedented problems of size, numbers, organization and competition. They defeated continuous political onslaught and withstood cruel defamation. That must be considered a remarkable success for Mexico and the movement.' [21]

Signs that foreign observers were less easily convinced were not hard to find. Peter Wilson of the *Daily Mirror*, questioned aspects of the organization and reflected that 'Mexico, despite colour and exuberance and a determination to prove that it had truly come of age, was not properly geared up to staging this modern unwieldy extravaganza of sport'. [22] Similarly, an article in *The Honolulu Star* on 22 October 1968 drew specific attention to the fact the economic disparity between the hi-tech facilities for the athletes and the dirt tracks and decrepit transport that most Mexicans had to endure: 'It appears as though there is no link between everyday lives and the Olympics. The Mexicans are out of their depth – disorganization at all levels shows weakness in preparation and execution.' [23] For such foreign observers, there was an enduring suspicion that the Olympic project had merely erected a façade of civility and sophistication behind which lay a reality that confirmed their negative perceptions of the country and its people.

Criticisms of this nature went to the heart of Mexico's complex and disparate society. While the organizers appear to have covered all angles within the controlled environment of the sporting arenas, an equally formidable task faced them in preparing the immediate environments for the influx of overseas visitors. It should be remembered that Mexico City in the 1960s was undergoing a process of constant change. Ambitious building projects, not all of which were connected to the Olympic Games, underlined the country's economic growth. Simultaneously, less auspicious constructs provided scant shelter for the influx of migrants forced to eke out a subsistence existence in the informal economy. Bearing in mind the negative preconceptions of Mexican society that many of the arriving foreign visitors possessed, the organizing committee's need to emphasize the positive aspects was all the more imperative.

In common with all hosts of major international events, the Mexican organizers engaged in considerable window dressing. As a correspondent for the *Seattle Post Intelligencer* noted five months before the games began, 'Apart from the Olympic sites, Mexico City itself, always impressive, has been remarkably spiffed up and polished in preparation for the Games. New fountains and plazas have been built, baroque palaces and churches have been restored.' [24] Considerable efforts were also made to mask the less palatable aspects of society from foreign eyes. Vagrants and street sellers were cleared away from any areas of the city where visitors might be. While such measures represented tacit acknowledgement that the high ideals of Mexico's leaders did not quite match the harsh realities of Mexican life, the level of embarrassment that this might cause was reduced by short-term cosmetic measures.

It is a matter of considerable irony that the one event that threatened to undermine all the Olympic preparations was beyond the organizing committee's power to control. Like their counterparts in many parts of the globe, throughout the summer of 1968, Mexican students had taken to the streets of the capital city with a series of demands ranging from the freedom of political prisoners to the autonomy of higher education. While it is clear that the protesters were capitalizing on the heightened international profile of the Olympic year to voice their demands, there is little evidence to suggest that the majority intended to jeopardize the actual event. [25]

On 2 October, just ten days before the opening ceremony, Mexican security forces opened fire on a crowd after a student rally at a square in Tlatelolco, a residential suburb of Mexico City. While official reports claimed that there were 30 deaths, estimates from eyewitnesses put the number of dead as over 400. There were immediate calls for the IOC to cancel the games and Avery Brundage was under considerable pressure to make some sort of official response. When it came, his statement was designed to reassure the world that the games were not in jeopardy:

Mexico City is a huge metropolis of more than six million people and none of the demonstrations or violence here have, at any time, been directed against the Olympic Games. We have conferred with the Mexican authorities and we have been assured that nothing will interfere with the peaceful entrance of the Olympic Flame into the stadium on October 12, nor with the competitions which follow. [26]

The idea that the massacre of students was a purely Mexican affair may have been true, but did little to deflect the impression that Latin American politics was characterized by violence. Ironically, the measures that the Mexican officials took to ensure the safety of competitors and visitors only contributed to this idea. The British athlete Mary Peters voiced her unease at the military presence on the streets:

You saw these soldiers ... not many of them, mostly unarmed. I suppose they took us by a quiet route. But you suddenly started to think about the troubles and you felt a bit scared. It suddenly hit you what you were doing. But once you were in the stadium, all these feelings disappeared. [27]

A heavy military presence, characterized by lines of armed troops guarding installations and transportation routes, was obviously intended to offer reassurance, but the message that such a scene sent out was diametrically opposed to the image of peaceful hospitality.

The Olympic Legacy

Referring again to the 1969 annual report of the Mexican Olympic Committee, the tone of measured euphoria reflected the fact that none of the dire predictions regarding Mexico's ability to host the Olympic Games were realized. The report concluded that 'the demonstration before the world of our organizational capacity has projected an image of Mexico that will erase forever, the erroneous image that many have of our country as apathetic, lazy and backward'. [28] While such triumphalism was understandable, things were not quite as simple as this statement would suggest. When considering such intangible elements as national prestige and international reputation, it is hard to measure the extent to which any one event can make a lasting change.

At its most basic, a disastrous Olympic Games can do much to tarnish a country's reputation and, in the case of countries such as Mexico that already had a questionable reputation, it could act as yet another nail in the coffin. Yet it is rarely the case that the reverse is true. Certainly an underlying assumption of those who sponsored the Olympic campaign was that a good Olympics would act as a medium through which Mexicans could transmit its message of professionalism in commerce, trade, technology and politics. Yet the overall success of the Mexico City Games did not automatically dissolve decades of negative stereotypes. In considering this issue, it is again useful briefly to reflect on quantitative and qualitative factors.

During the 1970s, events appeared to be moving in Mexico's favour. Rising oil prices coincided with the discovery of oil reserves in the Gulf of Mexico. Foreign earnings from the Mexican petroleum industry increased from half a billion US dollars in 1976 to six billion by 1980. On the strength of projected future earnings, the Mexican government borrowed heavily from the international market to fund major investments in infrastructure and social welfare projects. In one respect, such initiatives could be taken as a sign of the political elite's recognition that it must do something to mollify the conditions of poverty for those Mexicans not swept up in the Mexican 'miracle' or the later oil boom. To the nation's great misfortune, the subsequent plummet in world oil prices during the early 1980s not only curtailed such projects but left the nation with crippling foreign debts that it struggled to pay. That Mexico did not sink fully into the Latin American quagmire of inflation and defaulting on debts was due to the harsh domestic measures designed to cut public spending. While the nation just about rescued its international reputation it did so at the cost of measures that sought to remedy the fundamental inequalities within Mexican society. Only in the 1990s, when Mexico signed a trade agreement with Canada and the United States (the North Atlantic Free Trade Agreement) did Mexico's rehabilitation within the international economic arena demonstrably appear to be complete.

It is much more difficult to assess whether or not the Olympic Games erased any 'erroneous images' of Mexico. In part this relates to the nature of public attitudes towards the Olympic Games as a phenomenon; it is also due to the obstinate nature of national stereotypes. Attitudes towards any hosts are rarely complex and frequently short-lived: they often move from intense scrutiny to benign indifference. While, for example, Beijing 2008 fostered considerable debates prior to the games regarding human rights issues, these quickly subsided after the games had begun. With almost indecent haste, once the closing ceremony of one games is over the attention of athletes, the media and the public quickly turns to the next. In one respect this tendency may have benefited Mexico more than it detracted from its success. As far as the world beyond was concerned, the Mexico '68 games were little more than a fleeting episode. Although there may have been some international outcry when the students were killed at Tlatelolco, as soon as the games began – and even more so once they had finished – the world took its eye off the students' plight. Prolonged international condemnation of the Mexican government's actions was never a realistic prospect.

One way in which Mexico's international reputation did undergo a significant change in the decades that followed the Olympics was its image as a tourist destination. Prior to the games, the majority of international tourists had come from the United States. While there had always been a measure of appreciation for Mexico's cultural heritage, the vast majority of these tourists were interested in sun, sea and tequila. A priority of the organizing committee's public relations section was to redeem Mexico's reputation by persuading tourists not to see it purely in terms of a hedonistic playground and tacky souvenirs. Considerable energy and money was invested in drawing tourists towards the architectural gems of many colonial towns. Similarly, the development of, and greater accessibility to, the country's archaeological sites was designed to underline the cultural richness that Mexico possessed. While Cancun, a latter-day version of 1950s Acapulco, signifies that resort attractions are still important to the tourist sector, a growing appreciation of other aspects of what Mexico has to offer is now firmly entrenched within the tourist's vision. This more popular appreciation of pre-Columbian and colonial culture began to take hold during the 1960s and must, at least in part, have been connected with the hosting of the Olympics.

Fundamentally, however, the deeper significance of hosting a successful Olympic Games is appreciated by a relatively small group of international onlookers. It was clear that the Mexico '68 games did confound many who believed the hosts to be incapable of efficient organization. Within the small world of international sports bodies, the idea that Mexico could put on a good show probably did take hold. Success in 1968 was consolidated two years later when, in the eyes of many experts, Mexico staged one of the most memorable FIFA (Fédération Internationale de Football Association) World Cup tournaments in the competition's history. When plans to hold the 1986 World Cup in Colombia floundered, FIFA showed little hesitation in accepting Mexico's offer to step in at short notice. In many respects, therefore, Mexico's ability to organize world sports events was proven in 1968 and became consolidated in the years that followed.

Importantly, Mexico's image on the international arena can only partly be judged by the way in which foreigners view the country. The other crucial factor is how Mexicans perceive themselves. In *The Labyrinth of Solitude* Nobel Prize-winning author Octavio Paz offered reflections on the character of his fellow Mexicans. Perceptively, he drew attention to the latent sense of inferiority that Mexicans often show in their relationships with developed countries. The need to prove itself on the international arena weighed heavily upon Mexico. This imperative certainly bore down on those who staged the 1968 Olympic Games, but the transitional state of the country acted to weaken the strength of its message. As often as the Mexicans issued messages of reassurance, international critics pointed out organizational deficiencies. Mexico's bold claims to first-world status were undermined by the poverty on the capital city's streets. The degree to which it portrayed itself as a developed nation rather than a leader of the Third World acted as a barometer of self-confidence. Oscillation from one to the other suggests a lack of conviction that foreigners were predisposed to share.

Notes

[1] The IOC vote took place during the IOC session in Baden-Baden 16–20 Oct. 1963.
[2] Channing and Tabor Frost. 'The Rule of Porfirio Diaz, 1909'.
[3] 'Continúan las Censuras al Hitlerista que Injurió a México en "Der Spiegal"', *El Nacional*, 3 March 1968; Leopoldo Zea, 'Golpe Racista a México', *Novedades*, 3 March 1968.

[4] Reynolds, *The Mexican Economy*, 37.

[5] Ibid., 40.

[6] Mexico, *1966. Facts, Figures and Trends* (México: Banco Nacional, 1968), 32 cited in Meyer *et al.*, *The Course of Mexican History*, 629.

[7] Archivo General de la Nación (hereafter AGN), COJO, Box 403, 154, tomo IV, 14 May 1968.

[8] Campos Bravo, 'Reconocen el Esfuerzo del Pueblo Mexicano', *El Nacional*, 19 Oct. 1963.

[9] See *El Universal*, 19 Oct. 1963.

[10] Zolov, 'Showcasing the 'Land of Tomorrow', 164.

[11] AGN, COJO, Box 401, report dated 28 April 1969.

[12] AGN, COJO, Box 401, See the committee's annual report to the assembly dated 28 April 1969.

[13] AGN, COJO, Box 300. Memo from José Rogelio Alvárez to Lic. Manuel Noriega de la Concha dated 2 October 1967.

[14] Frederick J. Ruegsegger Papers, 1928–1978, Folder 22: Sept.–Dec.1967. See drafts of speech by made by Brundage at his birthday party.

[15] AGN, COJO, Box 300, 40. Co-presidencia 15 Nov. 1967: Ramírez Vázquez, speech to an audience of architects at the National Polytechnic Institute.

[16] *Diario de los Debates*, 1 Sept. 1969. Presidential informe.

[17] Brewster and Brewster, 'Mexico City's Hosting of the 1968 Olympic Games', 841–6.

[18] Keith Brewster, interview with Pedro Ramírez Vázquez, Mexico City, 26 April 2001.

[19] Archive of the International Olympic Committee, Lausanne, (hereafter IOC/HA): Avery Brundage, 67th IOC session, Mexico City, 7 Oct. 1968, 4–5.

[20] IOC/Juegos Olímpicos, Articles de Presse 1968–68 Notice no. 0105829: 'Una sorpresa para muchos: la perfecta organización'.

[21] The comments were highlighted by an unidentified US newspaper. IOC/HA: Brundage Microfilm Collection, reel 102, box 177: US Press Clippings.

[22] The comments of both reporters were highlighted by an unidentified US newspaper. IOC/HA: Brundage Microfilm Collection, reel 102, box 177: US Press Clippings.

[23] AGN, COJO, Box 403, 154, v. 5 Relaciones Públicas – copy of article dated 22 Octo. 1968.

[24] Ron Butler, 'Mexico Awaits Starting Gun', *Seattle Post Intelligencer*, 7 April 1968.

[25] For a fuller discussion of the relationship between the student movement and the Olympics, see Brewster and Brewster, 'The Mexican Student Movement of 1968', 814–39.

[26] IOC/HA: file CE/CNO – Mexico, 3–11 Oct. 1968: meeting of the Executive Board, 1.

[27] Mary Peters quoted in John Samuel, 'The Ceremony of Relief', *The Guardian*, 14 Oct. 1968, 17.

[28] AGN, COJO, Box 401, report dated 28 April 1969.

References

Brewster, Keith and Claire Brewster. 'Mexico City's Hosting of the 1968 Olympic Games'. In *Representing the Nation: Sport, Control, Contestation, and the Mexican Olympics.* Special monograph issue of *The International Journal of the History of Sport* 26, no. 6 (May 2009): 840–865.

Brewster, Keith and Claire Brewster. 'The Mexican Student Movement of 1968'. In *Representing the Nation: Sport, Control, Contestation, and the Mexican Olympics.* Special monograph issue of *The International Journal of the History of Sport* 26, no. 6 (May 2009): 814–39.

Channing Arnold and Frederick J. Tabor Frost: 'The Rule of Porfirio Diaz, 1909'. In *The World's Story: A History of the World in Story, Song and Art*, vol. XI: *Canada, South America, Central America, Mexico, and the West Indies,* edited by Eva March Tappan. Boston, MA: Houghton Mifflin, 1914: 526–34.

King, Timothy. *Mexico: Industrialization and Trade Policies since 1940*. London: Oxford University Press, 1970.

Meyer, Michael, William Sherman and Susan M. Deeds. *The Course of Mexican History*. Oxford: Oxford University Press, 2003.

Reynolds, Clark W. *The Mexican Economy: Twentieth-century Structure and Growth*. New Haven, CT and London: Yale University Press, 1970.

Zolov, Eric. 'Showcasing the "Land of Tomorrow": Mexico and the 1968 Olympics'. *The Americas* 61, no. 2 (2004): 164.

Post-Sydney 2000 Australia: A Potential Clash of Aspirations Between Recreational and Elite Sport

Kristine Toohey

The extent to which the Australia government values elite sport following the euphoria of the Sydney 2000 Olympic Games is demonstrated through its policy and funding commitments. However, this forms only part of its overall responsibility to sport in a nation with a sport ethic that values success. As a relatively small country it has to balance the struggle to match the increasing budgets of its more successful international competitor nations, such as Great Britain, while confronting the problem of an increasingly unfit population which is more interested in watching than participating in sport.

In the last hundred years the history of elite sport in Australia has followed a path through a maze of contradictions evidenced by early periods of high achievement gained with little or no funding to more recent times of unprecedented levels of funding marked by fluctuating success rates but high expectations. Perhaps the only thing to remain constant in terms of elite sport in Australia throughout this period is the centrality of sport, and especially Olympic sport, to the Australian psyche. However, the importance of sport extends well beyond this aspect. According to the Australian Bureau of Statistics (ABS), during 2004–5 sports generated A$8.8 billion and 10.5 million (65.9 per cent) Australians 15 years and over participated in physical activities for recreation, exercise and sport. Of these, 4.4 million (42.1 per cent) were involved in organized sports and physical recreation. Conversely, direct health care costs attributable to physical inactivity in Australia have been estimated at upwards of A$370 million per annum. [1] The need to improve the health of the Australian population through sport is becoming an imperative: physical fitness is declining and obesity levels are rising.

Australia is currently challenging the US for the 'title' of the world's fattest country. This is clearly not a title to aspire to. At the same time, elite sport is undergoing its own crisis of sorts. Australia was placed sixth in the Beijing gold medal count. While this could justifiably be considered an enviable achievement, considering the population of Australia is only 21 million, the result is two places below the results of the country at the Sydney and Athens Olympics. Although ostensibly this in itself is not a major setback, the fact that the nation was overtaken by Great Britain (considered for much of Australia's white history to be 'the mother country' and a major sport rival) was seen to be a blight on Australia's sports record.

This contribution will examine to what extent the national government is repositioning its sports identity following the euphoria of the Sydney 2000 Olympic Games as it struggles to match the increasing budgets of its more successful international competitor nations, such as Great Britain, and confronts the problem of an increasingly unfit population which is more interested in watching than participating in sport.

Background

In the 1950s Australia's international sport record was one to envy. Without any significant federal government support, individual effort produced a raft of champions. Percy Cerruty and Franz Stampfl coached world-champion track and field athletes, the former through the force of his charisma and the latter by employing the latest scientific methods of the time. Concurrently, Harry Hopman's charges dominated the tennis world and the success of the stable of swimmers trained by Forbes Carlile was attracting international attention. During this purple patch the sport dominance of the country (which made many of its achievements in other areas of endeavour seem ordinary) meant that the Australian public began to expect success as its due. The Olympic Games were one of a collection of sport arenas that provided the nation with sufficient victories to satisfy its increasing appetite for sport domination. At the 1956 Melbourne Olympics, the first mega-sport event held in the nation, Australian athletes stepped up on the victory dais often enough to sate the public's expectations: they won 36 medals, 13 of which were gold. The success of the Australian Olympic athletes and the national pride generated by hosting the games meant that the Melbourne Olympic influence extended further than victory per se. As a relatively insignificant player in world politics, sport had become a potent vehicle for the nation to gain international exposure. After the games, the Liberal Party leader, Australian Prime Minister Robert Menzies, not known for supporting sport financially (although he was a passionate cricket follower), somewhat ironically and perhaps not accurately declared to the International Olympic Committee president, Avery Brundage, that the 1956 Olympics were the most important event in the history of Australia. [2]

The Australian Olympic success in Melbourne had been achieved despite a paucity of federal funding to athletes or indeed to the organization of the games themselves. At that time, and since 1941, the very small pool of available federal sport funding had been channelled principally to recreational sport, through the passage of the

National Fitness Act, which had been passed by the United Australia Party government. This was the only piece of Australian federal legislation related to sport development until 1982. [3]

However, despite the lack of financial and policy support, there was some high-level political awareness of the place that sport held for the Australian public, as evidenced in the 1962 federal Department of the Interior document entitled 'Sport: A Reference Paper'. It was a discrete product in that it was the only official statement from federal authorities that dealt with elite sport policy prior to the Labor government of Gough Whitlam. It was the Whitlam Labor government which, soon after its election victory in 1972, created the first Australian federal sport department, known as the Department of Tourism and Recreation. However, in 1962, ten years before this, the view of the Menzies Liberal government to elite or even recreational sport was one of complacency. It stated that:

> Australia can be expected to go on producing sportsmen and sportswomen able to take their place with confidence among the sporting cream of the world – confident that Australia's cream will battle it out with the best because Australia's cream has come to the top of an enormous amount of milk. [4]

Over time the cream soured and Australian elite athletes eventually paid the price for this governmental laissez-faire attitude. While in the 1960s there was a total of 19 gold medals won by Australians at the three Olympic Games held in Rome, Tokyo and Mexico City, they were becoming increasingly difficult to win. Other countries had begun selecting and training their athletes more scientifically (sometimes with the very systemic aid of drugs), and greater government financial backing, especially in the Eastern bloc countries, was reaping great dividends. At the 1976 Montreal Olympic Games the Australian team won no gold medals. Athletes, sports officials and the public demanded to know why the country had fallen from its earlier high-ranking position to one near the bottom of the Olympic pile. Angry citizens claimed that Australia was now composed of sport also-rans. Indeed one article published in *The Australian* was entitled 'Requiem for a Sporting Super Race'. [5] As a result of the dearth of medals, an ugly aspect of the Australian psyche was exposed: the public identified passionately with winners but was intolerant of sport failures. Years of sport success had not equipped them to accept the possibility of such a complete turnaround of fortunes.

The onus of blame was laid squarely at the feet of government (now once again in the hands of the Liberal Party), regardless of the fact that in 1972 the Labor Government of Gough Whitlam had created the Department of Tourism and Recreation, and sport had maintained a portfolio in the new regime of the Liberal government when it was elected in 1975. Back in 1972 one of the first administrative responsibilities of the new department had been to determine the amount of financial assistance to be channelled towards the development of elite sport; the other was the provision of leisure activities for the general population. Furthermore, two review groups, the first led by John Bloomfield (1973) and the second led by Allan Coles

(1975), were commissioned to provide reports to government about the place of elite sport: the former through its report on 'The role, scope and development of recreation in Australia' (1973) and the second through its 'Report of the Australian Sports Institute Study Group' (1975). The latter noted that:

> There still exists a considerable degree of mindless polarity on the issue of 'sport for all or sport for the elite?' Such an issue should not exist at all, since mass participation and excellence in sport are not mutually exclusive. While not all sport participants will necessarily receive an equal share of the tax dollar, the opportunity for increasing the quality of life through meaningful sports participation at any level can and ought to be provided for any attempt to further define and meet the sporting needs of Australia. [6]

While the Australian Sports Institute Study Group may have naively considered that there should not be an issue about whether federal funding for sport was directed to elite or recreational sport, their thinking was not shared by all or, it appears, even many, either before or since. It is still a contentious issue.

In the aftermath of the Montreal gold-medal drought, the public stridently demanded increased government funding of elite sport to allow it to return to the halcyon days of the 1950s and 1960s. Thus winning international sport events was of unquestionable desirability to the Australian sports follower. Long-standing amateur ideals inherited from Great Britain were becoming less important than victory, given that other nations were overtly or covertly paying their sport stars. Perhaps this attitude had always been the case, but until now it had never really been put to the test. [7] Significantly, both the federal government, through the Bailey Task Force on Coordination in Health and Welfare, and the Australian Olympic Federation (AOF), later to become the Australian Olympic Committee (AOC), undertook evaluations of the poor 1976 performance, with a view to restoring Australia to what was considered to be its rightful place in the top echelon of Olympic nations.

The AOF's review concluded that the primary causes of 'failure' in Montreal were: the lack of substantial and ongoing support at levels equivalent to those of the successful nations; insufficient international competition for Australian athletes; and a shortage of basic facilities which were taken for granted in other developed countries. As all these factors had been present during the zenith of Australia's sport triumphs in the 1950s and 60s, it indicates that the progress that had occurred internationally in sport structures had not been mirrored to the same extent in Australia. [8] One of the most tangible and enduring aspects of Australia's poor performance in Montreal was the establishment of the Australian Institute of Sport (AIS) in 1980, following the recommendations of the 1975 study. Interestingly, the government issued its official announcement about the AIS's establishment during a campaign it was conducting to deter Australian athletes from competing in the 1980 Moscow Olympic Games. Since this untimely inception the AIS has continued to improve in quality and continues to expand its sphere of influence. Currently it has 35 sport programmes in 26 sports.

The AIS also appears to have become the magnet that continues to reinvigorate debates about the direction of federal sport policy and philosophy – where funding should be directed, to the elite or recreation levels. The debate gained further impetus with the IOC's 1993 decision to award the 2000 Olympic Games to Sydney. This decision affected the balance and direction of federal sport policy and funding, tipping it firmly in the direction of the elite as the nation prepared for making the most of its home-town advantage. [9]

The Sydney 2000 Olympic Games

According to Magdalinski, part of the myth of Australian passion for sport has relied on the construction of close ties between Australia and the modern Olympic Games. As an example she suggests that

> the 2000 Sydney Olympic Games provided a potent occasion for exploration of Australian identity and nostalgic remembering in a climate of economic restructuring and social turmoil. ... The Olympic Games provided a useful cultural focal point around which images of the Australian nation could be generated. In particular, Australia's sporting past assumed a primary position in the process of provoking a cohesive national identity. [10]

However, heroic images from Australia's Olympic sport past would have been useless and even counterproductive to any national identity formation in the early years of the twenty-first century without significant Australian athletic success at the Sydney Olympic Games. Building towards this goal, federal funding firmly swung the way of elite sport, specifically through the creation of a A$418 million, six-year elite development programme which included a specific Olympic Athlete Programme (OAP) component. As part of the OAP, Australia's first national talent identification programme was introduced. This was an extensive and truly national initiative, involving a range of organizations at all levels of the nation's sport development pyramid, from local clubs and schools to regional and state academies and institutes, all the way to the AIS. The OAP also resulted in the appointment of 14 new national head coaches in Olympic sports, and another 20 specialist coaches appointed to the AIS. Additionally, ten designated sports received additional subsidies. [11]

While the federal government contributed greatly to funding the training of athletes, its relationship with the organization of the games was one of less direct involvement and some tension. Federal involvement was originally predicated on arrangements negotiated during the development and presentation of the Olympic bid. According to the *Sydney 2000 Olympic Games Official Report*:

> SOCOG's [Sydney Organising Committee for the Olympic Games] initial requests for additional support from the Federal Government were piecemeal and did not always take into account the Government's established policy positions or regulatory arrangements. The change of Federal Government in March 1996 resulted in significant changes to the operating environment. SOCOG had relied on

strong but informally expressed commitments made by the former government in the Bid and early development phase. In mid 1997, the Federal Government determined that, as a general principle, wherever practicable, user charging/cost-recovery arrangements were to be put in place and charges should reflect full cost. [12]

Due to growing tensions between SOCOG and the federal government, in February 1998 'the Federal Government established a whole-of-government policy position and supporting structure and created the Sydney 2000 Games Coordination Task Force, located in the Department of Prime Minister & Cabinet. This provided a single point for high-level negotiations, which allowed the matters under consideration to progress.' [13] It did not eliminate all political discord.

There were still tensions between various governments (federal, state and local) and Olympic organizers, although the new arrangement allowed for greater cooperation between the Liberal federal government and the Labor New South Wales state government, the chief financial provider to the games. Ultimately the federal government directly contributed A$30.79 million to the Sydney Organising Committee for the Olympic Games with the stipulation that these funds be used only by SOCOG for services and facilities which could be provided by either federal agencies or other organizations. [14] Despite this limited funding towards the organization of the games by the federal government, the *Sydney 2000 Olympic Games Official Report*, a document overseen by the NSW government, noted that federal involvement in games organization was valuable:

> The support of the Federal Government in key areas was crucial to the success of the Games and came in a variety of forms. Legislation was passed by the Federal Parliament to stop ambush marketing and the Federal Government also underwrote the cost of taking the Olympic Torch Relay to the nations of Oceania in the Olympic region. The Federal Government also provided funding for the aquatic and athletic centres built at Sydney Olympic Park, Homebush Bay, during the bid period and agreed to the sale of the Newington site land to the NSW Government for the construction of the Olympic Village. Finally, a number of Federal Government agencies struck purely commercial arrangements with SOCOG. Telstra, a Government owned telecommunications company, became a Team Millennium sponsor. The Royal Australian Mint conducted the Olympic Coin Program under license from SOCOG. [15]

The perspective of Pru Goward, the Australian Commonwealth spokesperson for the Sydney 2000 games indicated that the federal government had contributed to the games' organization to an even greater extent. She also highlighted the importance of federal contributions to other bodies that played a role in the success of the Australian team:

> Since Sydney won that bid in 1993, the Commonwealth has allocated another $520 million to the staging of the Games. Another $100 million has been absorbed by Commonwealth agencies such as the Australian Defence Force to ensure a safe and

successful Games. ... More than 1500 national squad athletes have received support services. In total, sports funding from the Federal Government will have reached almost $300 million over those six years. ... It is estimated that the support from the Commonwealth – combined with the Australian Olympic Committee and State Government support – totals $1.2 million each week for Olympic sports this year. ... The Australian Sports Commission can boast that the vast majority of Australian athletes forming the nation's largest ever Olympic team will have benefited from some Commonwealth involvement in Sport. [16]

Over 10,000 athletes from 199 nations took part in the Sydney Olympic Games, including the largest ever contingent from Australia. Since Sydney had been elected to host the games in 1993, Australia's expectations had been high that its team's results would be one of its most successful Olympic efforts. The Australian team, which competed in all of the 28 sports on the programme, comprised 632 athletes (349 men and 283 women). The results justified the expectations: Australian athletes won 58 medals (16 gold, 25 silver and 17 bronze) to finish fourth in the medal table behind the United States, Russia and China. [17] Athletes who had trained at the AIS contributed greatly to this success: 315 current and former AIS athletes competed for Australia in 19 sports. They won 31 medals – seven gold, 11 silver and 13 bronze. [18]

Given the federal government's investment in the games, there were also expectations that recreational sport would be a beneficiary of the legacy that the games would provide. One prospect was that the nation's recreational sport participation would increase.

Recreational Sport

Once Sydney had won the right to host the 2000 games, Australian sports officials, especially those from the peak federal government sport organization, the Australian Sports Commission (ASC), were eager to promote the possibility of an association between the games and increased participation in sport. While the ASC, which had a vested interest in the administration of recreational sport, advanced the notion of the trickle-down effect (i.e. a successful performance by elite athletes would result in greater participation at the sport-for-all level), it also cautioned that this would not occur without suitable planning and additional funding. [19] The ASC cautioned that 'We need to make sure that when the Games are over this motivation is harnessed and captured by all those groups that provide sport and recreation programs to the community'. [20] Studies have shown that this did not occur. Research by Veal, Toohey and Frawley noted that it was impossible to conclude that the 2000 games left a legacy for recreational sport. [21] Other studies resulted in similar findings, all suggesting there was very insignificant change to sport participation numbers at the recreational level, with the exception of a short-term spike after 2000. [22]

Even government figures showed similar patterns. Australian Bureau of Statistics (ABS) figures noted that in the 12 months to April 2001, an estimated 4.1 million people (27.1 per cent of all people aged 15 years and over) were involved in organized sport and physical activity. This included both players and others involved in non-playing roles. These figures indicate that this was a smaller percentage of the population than was physically active in pre-games years. For example, during 1998 and 1999, ABS data indicated that 28.9 per cent of the population participated in organized sport or physical activity. [23] In fact, it has been claimed that passive involvement, such as live and television spectating, was the most significant recreational sport-related impact of the Sydney 2000 Olympic Games. [24]

The success of Australian Olympic athletes combined with disappointing participation outcomes for recreational sport suggests that the federal government would now have a legitimate case if it wanted to switch the focus of its funding from the elite to the recreational sector, if not immediately after the games, then certainly when the results of the above studies and surveys were known. In the aftermath of the games the debate about the future direction of federal sport policy and funding was reinvigorated; however, debate does not necessarily result in action.

Post-Sydney 2000

After the Sydney games there was some unease in sport that some or much of its federal budget might be redirected to government agendas other than sport. Some proponents of recreational sport were more optimistic and thought that it was finally to be their day in the sun. Their optimism was not rewarded. In 2001 the federal government's next sport policy statement, covering the period to 2005, was outlined in the document *Backing Australia's Sporting Ability* (BASA). In this federal policy direction and funding continued to favour elite sport. From 2001 to 2005 an additional A$161.6 million was allocated to sport, bringing the total funding for sport to a record level of A$547 million. Of this, elite sport was allocated A$408 million (approximately 75 per cent). Because of this Green suggested that this indicates that the federal government was seeking outcomes other than increased physical activity from its investment. [25]

This may well be the case, as a study by Stewart, Nicholson, Smith and Westerbeek suggested that 'the BASA policy and the TSPG programmes represent a strategic move towards the implementation of activities and programmes that can be evaluated more easily and effectively' [26] than recreational ones. It also reveals Australia's continuing preoccupation with elite athlete development even when presented with confirmation that the benefits of success do not 'trickle down' to recreational sport, combined with growing evidence of Australia's obesity crisis.

This policy has continued:

> It is very clear from a federal government media release in May 2006 that there is to be no rescinding of the government's aim to deliver sporting excellence and to 'help the Institute [AIS] retain its position as a world-leader in elite athlete development'. Thus participation activities will receive just over half the amount awarded for the development of the country's elite performers during 2006–07. In other words, it

appears that in Australia the quest for sustained excellence at the international level is difficult to forgo once established. [27]

It can be argued that one of the greatest indirect beneficiaries of this policy are Olympic athletes and the AOC. This organization, responsible for Olympic-related matters in Australia, has a vested interest in ensuring funding to elite sport continues so that the Australian Olympic team will not suffer a repeat of the ignominy of its 1976 Montreal results. It has been an active lobbyist to government for elite sport support. John Coates, the AOC president, outlined the AOC's strategy for preparing for the 2012 London Olympic Games. He announced in his presidential speech at the 2009 AOC Annual General meeting that

> I have been involved in a number of submissions now with the AOC to Government. The first one was when we got the additional $10 million ... back in the mid 80s, from Senator Richardson. Then we did the Gold Medal Plan in 1993, which resulted in an additional $135 million ... for the six years leading into Sydney. Then we did another plan to take to Prime Minister Howard at the end of the Sydney Games, which resulted in a continuation of the earlier funding and some additional.
>
> But this ... is by far the most comprehensive plan that we have ever put together. ... We have a document here that was not easy to put together, in fact it is easier to find out the funding for sports in Great Britain than it is here in Australia – a little more transparent over there. You will know we have been able to not only work out on a consistent basis what you need ... to succeed at the next few Games, but also to look at the funding that our major competitors are receiving and therefore point out to Government how far behind we are in that area. ... The Australian Government does firmly believe that sport has a fundamental and important role to play in our community. We recognise that sport is a positive and integral part of our nation and as the Prime Minister has indicated previously, we are committed to remaining a strong financial partner of sport and working in partnership with you to ensure that Australian sport remains strong and thriving. [28]

Thus, from a financial perspective, it appears that in 2009 support and funding for elite sport is relatively secure. However, the continuing vexed issue of decreasing recreational sport engagement and level of funding is less promising. Yet, the need to increase participation in physical activity remains an important issue for all Australians. Rates of overweight (41 per cent of males and 25 per cent of females) and obesity (18 per cent of males and 17 per cent of females) have doubled in the past two decades. A direct link to this increase in weight is suggested by data collected in 1997, 1999 and 2000 indicating physical activity participation by Australians has decreased and remains relatively low. [29] Later work by Bowles, Rissel and Bauman (2006) found that almost half the population of Australia is insufficiently active to achieve recommended levels of physical activity. They noted that there is still a naive belief in the potential for the hosting of mega-sport events, such as the Olympic Games, to positively influence community interest in physical activity. However, similar to earlier studies, Bowles, Rissel and Bauman's results indicated that with the passing of five years there was still no evidence to demonstrate that the 2000 Sydney Olympics had a positive effect on physical activity prevalence. [30]

Despite these results, as noted, potential event host cities, governments and sport governing bodies continue to claim that increased recreational sport participation is an anticipated legacy of the Olympic Games. While this may be part of the campaign to muster public support and to justify expenditure of public funds on the event, this furphy should be exposed to rigorous testing. This can only be done by ensuring that measures of sport participation are available before and after the hosting of sport events. For example, a recent IOC initiative, the Olympic Games Global Impact (OGGI), requires organizing committees to collect annually a range of data from the time of the announcement of the successful bid until two years after the event. Among this data is 'participation rates in sport'. [31] In terms of Australia it is probably of little consequence in terms of the Olympics as it is unlikely that the nation will stage another games in the short term. However, its ambitions are still high: the nation is seeking to host a 2018 or 2022 FIFA Football World Cup.

The Current Situation

Since the 2000 Olympics the nation's political landscape has changed. After a long time in opposition, a Labor government, under the leadership of Kevin Rudd, was elected by Australian voters in 2007. One obvious portent for change in sport policy direction is that responsibility for sport now lies with the Australian government Department of Health and Ageing which has clearly signalled that sports policy will play a central role in a preventative health agenda. [32]

While the mainstream Australian media mostly continue to glorify the nation's international sport successes, the new government has recently commissioned a review (the Crawford Review) to determine its future sport policy. One of the outcomes of great interest is whether the new funding model will continue to concentrate on support for elite athletes or focus more on funding recreational sport. At the same time as this review is in progress, the Rudd government's 2009–10 federal budget has made both contributions and cutbacks to the sport and recreation sectors. For example, the ASC received approximately A$240 million in the 2008 budget, as well as another A$30 million left over from 2007's appropriation of A$279 million. Additionally, A$160 million was allocated for the development of elite athletes. [33] Both elite and recreational sport officials were encouraged when the Australian government Department of Health and Ageing announced that

> Reform of the Australian sports system – both at elite and community level – can be put off no longer. Over the past decade there have been many reports into sport … and yet very few of the recommendations have been acted upon. It is clear that we need new directions in sport to meet the emerging challenges and to maintain our status as one of the world's greatest sporting nations.

If we are to act responsibly and safeguard the future of Australian sport, we must now embrace reform. And it must range from the very highest levels of elite sport, right down to the grassroots. The Rudd Government believes we need new direction in two key areas: the way we support elite sport; and the manner which we use sport to boost participation and physical activity to help build a healthier nation.

We need to put the necessary reforms in place now to resume Australia's innovative approach to elite sport or risk jeopardising our place as a leading sporting nation. [34]

Nonetheless, one worrying feature of upcoming Department of Health and Ageing sports policy lies in a statement combining the naivety of the Australian Sports Institute Study Group of 1975 and the fallacy of the trickle-down effect. The department stated that

The Federal Government believes rather than debating the merits of elite sports versus community sport, we should embrace and recognize the vital interconnections between the two. The reality is that our elite sport system only prospers when we have a strong talent base on which to draw. Equally, having successful and high performing role models in sport is integral to encouraging children to take up sport and aspire to reach their own dreams. [35]

Conclusion

Nine years on from the euphoria of the Sydney Olympics it seems the battle for federal government resources and recognition between elite and recreational sport continues in Australia. In the lead-up to the Sydney games, understandably elite sport came to the fore. However, since then little has changed, despite the nation's increasing sedentary lifestyle and associated obesity problems. The Olympic aspirations of elite sport have been realized; those of recreational sport remain unrealized. While many Australians continue to measure our international standing by our sport successes, the well-being of the Australian community is not determined solely at the elite level, but also at localized levels. Our nation's obsession with sport is not necessarily reflected by a similar preoccupation in participating in sport. Striking the right balance between recognition and funding of recreational sport and elite sport continues to be a major challenge for the federal government, especially when powerful sport organizations such as the AOC continue to lobby it to advance their agendas.

A dynamic outcome will only be found if measuring the value of sport goes beyond tallying victories. Federal sports policy should be based on and reflect the benefits of sport to economic, social, and cultural sectors. This will not lessen our Olympic outcomes. It will clearly demonstrate that the Australian government has advanced its sports agenda from the early days of neglect of the entire sector and then a latter imbalance towards privileging the 'cream'. The question remains: should and can it suitably value and support all of sports strata?

Notes

[1] Bauman *et al.*, *Trends in Population Levels*.
[2] Toohey, 'The Politics of Australian Elite Sport', 14, 54.
[3] Ibid.
[4] Australia, Department of the Interior, 'Sport: A Reference Paper', 92.
[5] Toohey, 'The Politics of Australian Elite Sport', 14.
[6] Australia, Department of Tourism and Recreation, *Report of the Australian Sports Institute Study Group*, xxvi
[7] Toohey, 'The Politics of Australian Elite Sport', 15.
[8] Ibid., 173.
[9] Green, 'Olympic Glory or Grassroots Development?'.
[10] Magdalinski, 'The Reinvention of Australia', 308–9.
[11] Green, 'Olympic Glory or Grassroots Development?'.
[12] Toohey, *Official Report of the XXVII Olympiad*, 346.
[13] Ibid, 344. See also www.gamesinfo.com.au/postgames/en/pg002076.htm, accessed 30 Sept. 2008.
[14] Ibid.
[15] Ibid., 346.
[16] Goward, Speech to National Press Club, Canberra, 12 April 2000. Available at: http://fulltext.ausport.gov.au/fulltext/2000/npc20000412.pdf
[17] Australian Olympic Committee and Australian Paralympic Committee, *National High Performance Plan*.
[18] Australian Sports Commission, 'Australian Institute of Sport Timeline'.
[19] Toohey, 'The Sydney Olympics: Striving for Legacies'.
[20] Australian Sports Commission, 'Developing an Olympic Legacy for Community Sport'. Available at: http://fulltext.ausport.gov.au/fulltext/2000/ascmedia/20000627.html, accessed 28 Feb. 2009.
[21] Veal *et al.*, '"Sport for All" and the Legacy of the Sydney 2000 Olympic Games'; Toohey and Veal, 'the (Sporting) Legacy of the Sydney 2000 Olympic Games'.
[22] See National Centre for Culture and Recreation Statistics, *The Impact of the Olympics on Participation in Australia*, 2001; Australian Sports Commission, 'Impact of Hosting the Sydney 2000 Olympic and Paralympic Games; Toohey and Veal, 'The (Sporting) Legacy of the Sydney 2000 Olympic Games'.
[23] Australian Bureau of Statistics, 'Involvement in Organised Sports and Physical Activities'.
[24] Veal *et al.*, '"Sport for All" and the Legacy of the Sydney 2000 Olympic Games'.
[25] Green, 'Olympic Glory or Grassroots Development?'.
[26] Stewart *et al.*, *Australian Sport – Better by Design?*.
[27] Green, 'Olympic Glory or Grassroots Development?'
[28] Coates, 'President's Address to the Australian Olympic Committee Annual General Meeting'. Available at: http://corporate.olympics.com.au/files/79/AGM_09_President_Address_with_HPP_2_.pdf
[29] Bauman *et al.*, *Trends in Population Levels*; Bauman, 'Updating the Evidence' .
[30] Bowles *et al.*, 'Mass Community Cycling Events'.
[31] Toohey and Veal, *The Olympic Games: A Social Science Perspective*, 74.
[32] Australia, Department of Health and Ageing, *Australian Sport: Emerging Challenges, New Directions*, 10.
[33] Australia, Department of Health and Ageing, *Sport*.
[34] Ibid.
[35] Ibid., 10.

References

Australian Bureau of Statistics. 'Involvement in Organised Sports and Physical Activities', available online at http://www.abs.gov.au/Ausstats/abs%40.nsf/46d1bc47ac9d0c7bca256c470025ff87/ea4ba506f23871f4ca256cae0010851a!OpenDocument, accessed 30 Sept. 2008.

Australia, Department of Health and Ageing. *Australian Sport: Emerging Challenges, New Directions.* Available at http://www.health.gov.au/internet/main/publishing.nsf/Content/sport-australian-sport#reform 2008, accessed 30 Sept. 2008.

Australia, Department of Health and Ageing. *Sport.* Available at http://www.health.gov.au/internet/main/publishing.nsf/Content/sport, 29 May, 2009, accessed 30 Sept. 2008.

Australia, Department of the Interior. 'Sport: A Reference Paper.' In *Sport in Australia: Selected Readings in Physical Activity,* edited by T.D. Jaques and J.R. Pavia. Sydney: McGraw Hill, 1976.

Australia, Department of Tourism and Recreation. *Report of the Australian Sports Institute Study Group.* Canberra: Australia Government Publishing Service, 1975.

Australia, Department of Tourism and Recreation. *The Role, Scope and Development of Recreation in Australia.* Canberra: Australia Government Publishing Service, 1973.

Australian Olympic Committee and Australian Paralympic Committee. *National High Performance Plan for Olympic and Paralympic Sport in Australia.* Available at http://corporate.olympics.com.au/, accessed 28 Feb. 2009.

Australian Sport Commission. 'Impact of hosting the Sydney 20000 Olympic and Paralympic Games on Participation and Volunteering in Sport and Physical Activity in Australia'. Unpublished paper, Sport Development Unit, Australian Sport Commission, Canberra, 2001.

Australian Sports Commission. 'Australian Institute of Sport Timeline'. available at http://corporate.olympics.com.au/, accessed 28 Feb. 2009.

Australian Sport Commission. 'Impact of hosting the Sydney 20000 Olympic and Paralympic Games on Participation and Volunteering in Sport and Physical Activity in Australia'. Unpublished paper, Sport Development Unit, Australian Sport Commission, Canberra, 2001.

Australian Sports Commission. 'Australian Institute of Sport Timeline'. available at http://www.ausport.gov.au/ais/history/timeline, accessed 30 Sept. 2008.

Bauman A., I. Ford and T. Armstrong. *Trends in Population Levels of Reported Physical Activity in Australia, 1997, 1999 and 2000.* Canberra: Australian Sports Commission, 2001.

Bauman Adrian. 'Updating the Evidence That Physical Activity is Good for Health: An Epidemiological Review 2000– 2003'. *Journal of Science and Medicine in Sport* 7, no. 1 (2004): 6–19.

Bowles, Heather R., Chris Rissel and Adrian Bauman. 'Mass Community Cycling Events: Who Participates and Is Their Behaviour Influenced by Participation?' *International Journal of Behavioral Nutrition and Physical Activity* 3 (2006): 39.

Green, Mick. 'Olympic Glory or Grassroots Development?: Sport Policy Priorities in Australia, Canada and the United Kingdom, 1960–2006'. *The International Journal of the History of Sport* 24, no. 7 (2007): 921–53.

Jaques, T.D. and G.R. Pavia. *Sport in Australia: Selected Readings in Physical Activity.* Sydney: McGraw-Hill, 1976.

Magdalinski, Tara. 'The Reinvention of Australia for the Sydney 2000 Olympic Games'. *The International Journal of the History of Sport* 17, no. 2 (2000): 305–22.

National Centre for Culture and Recreation Statistics. *The Impact of the Olympics on Participation in Australia: Trickle Down Effect, Discouragement Effect or No Effect?* Adelaide: Australian Bureau of Statistics, 2001.

Stewart, Bob, Matthew Nicholson, Aaron Smith and Hans Westerbeek. *Australian Sport – Better by Design?: The Evolution of Australian Sport Policy.* London: Routledge, 2004.

Toohey, Kristine. 'The Politics of Australian Elite Sport: 1949–1983'. PhD diss., Pennsylvania State University, 1990.

Toohey, Kristine. *Official Report of the XXVII Olympiad.* Sydney: SOCOG, 2001.

Toohey, Kristine. 'The Sydney Olympics: Striving for Legacies – Overcoming Short-Term Disappointments and Long-Term Deficiencies'. *The International Journal of the History of Sport* 25, no. 14 (2008): 1953–71.

Toohey, Kristine and A.J. Veal. *The Olympic Games: A Social Science Perspective,* 2nd edn. Wallingford: CABI Publishing, 2007.

Toohey, K. and A.J. Veal. 'The (Sporting) Legacy of the Sydney 2000 Olympic Games: Some Observations'. Paper given at 'Beyond the Torch – Olympics and the Australian Culture', Australian Society for Sports History (ACT Chapter) Conference, Canberra, April 2004.

Veal, A.J., K. Toohey and S. Frawley. '"Sport for All" and the Legacy of the Sydney 2000 Olympic Games'. Paper given at 13th Commonwealth International Sport Conference, Melbourne, Australia, March 2006.

Athens' Post-Olympic Aspirations and the Extent of their Realization

Penelope Kissoudi

As host to the world's largest sporting event, Athens hoped to revise its image in the eyes of the world by securing the social, economic, environmental, cultural and sporting recognition appropriate to a modern metropolis. This was not to be. Some hopes remained unfulfilled aspirations. The post-Olympic era was characterized by missed opportunities that mainly concerned the utilization of the Olympic venues, which, hampered by bureaucracy and lack of long-term planning, remained unexploited having been abandoned after the games. Nonetheless, Athens saw some of its aspirations realized: it acquired a modern transport infrastructure which reduced air pollution, an urban regeneration programme which resulted in a renovated city centre, selective upgrading of the outlying Attica districts and a boost to economic investment which increased tourism. Athenians also benefited from significant cultural events in the post-games period. However, these benefits failed to eradicate the negative impressions of Athens held by the wider world and the disappointments of unrealized aspirations as a consequence of missed opportunities.

Introduction

Nowadays large cities frequently seek a solution to their urban degradation, transport and environmental problems by bidding for important sporting and commercial events. The Olympic Games, a positive global force, stimulates the creation of modern facilities, urban regeneration and improvements in transport and tourism infrastructure as well as measures for the protection of the environment and other improvements. More importantly, successful organization of the games provides the host country with the opportunity to improve international relations at regional and international level and to promote its history, traditions and culture. As a consequence, the aspirations of the host country in general and the host city in particular are high, encompassing social, economic, cultural, sporting and environmental factors. [1] Since the impact of the games outlives the narrow chronological span of the athletic event itself, great opportunities for economic development and a wide rage of transformative possibilities are offered. Although the economic benefits may not be immediately evident, the host country usually experiences an increase in tourism, improves its global prestige, enjoys the goodwill of the world and reinforces its political influence at both regional and international level. [2]

In particular, by bidding for the Olympics the host city aspires to boost its economy by promoting itself in the global tourism market, upgrading urban areas and transport infrastructure and creating modern venues that could also provide a basis for future bids. [3] In essence, when a modern city seeks global recognition and status, the Olympic Games offer it the opportunity to present itself dynamically on the world stage. The ambitions of Athens included, among other things, improvements in transport infrastructure, urban regeneration, the promotion of tourism and a further stimulus to sport and culture through international cultural and sporting events staged in the new Olympic venues. [4] Athens did achieve the realization of some of its aspirations: others, however, await the date of their partial or full realization.

Reconstructing National Image: the Transport Infrastructure and Urban Regeneration of Athens

As already noted, the Olympic Games, the world's most prestigious sporting event, acts as a stimulus to major changes in the host city involving the renovation of both city centre and outlying districts, the creation of a modern transport infrastructure and the implementation of projects for the protection of the environment. Moreover, by exploiting the opportunities the games offer, tourism can be encouraged, leading to economic development at local and national level. [5] The 2004 Olympic Games acted as a catalyst for the urban development of Athens and accelerated changes that may otherwise have taken many years to be completed. A public opinion poll held during the period 21 February 2003 to 10 January 2004 revealed that the Greek people felt proud of the games and supported them despite the huge cost. The feelings of pride and support for the games were comparable among people of different ages and political ideologies and this strengthened the perception that there was a strong relationship between the Olympic Games and national pride. [6]

Athens had many of the common disadvantages of a large city, such as unplanned residential areas on the outskirts, obsolete infrastructure, traffic congestion and environmental pollution resulting from rapid and unregulated growth in the 1950s, 1960s and 1970s, when extensive internal immigration to the city took place. Making use of the experience gained by large cities which hosted the Olympic Games in the 1990s, Athens put into practice an ambitious regeneration plan, carried out by the Ministries of Culture and Environment, Physical Planning and Public Works, the Municipality of Athens, the Prefecture of Athens and Piraeus, the Technical Guild of Greece, the National Tourism Organization and the Unification of the Archaeological Sites of Athens SA. All of this was coordinated by the 2004 organizing committee. [7] Following the principle that construction works and innovative designs can give a new look to the host city and improve the quality of life therein, the project for the urban regeneration of Athens included construction works and the implementation of innovative designs and 'non-competitive' projects. These included building works intended to renovate the historic centre of Athens by creating a zone of walkways that would unite the archaeological sites of the city. The restoration of monuments and open spaces, the reconstruction of streets and squares in the historic city centre and the renovation of neoclassical-style buildings were included in the ambitious plan. Pioneering architectural designs of international renown were appraised as innovative, such as those submitted by the architect Santiago Calatrava. Modern designs selected by national and international competition and published architectural designs that presented new style trends were also regarded as innovative. The 'non-competitive' projects involved con-struction works for the improvement of the transport infrastructure such as new roads and junctions, new metro lines and a tram network, along with enhancement of the existing public open spaces, removal of advertising panels and billboards from building facades and facade renovation of modern buildings in the city centre. The regeneration plan for Athens was considered to be the most ambitious in the history of the city, funded by both national and European Union resources. [8]

The most important construction plan was the creation of a modern transport infrastructure so that crucial problems of traffic congestion could be eased. Athens, a congested city with approximately five million inhabitants, witnessed a speedy increase in car ownership at a rate of 350 cars per 1,000 inhabitants while only 30 per cent of the citizens made daily use of public transport. For this reason, a large number of construction projects in the 'transportation' chapter of the 2004 candidacy file aspired to improve transport infrastructure and ease traffic flow. [9] Thus the extension of the Athens Metro, the modernization of the existing public transport system, the implementation of a new tram line linking the city centre to the waterfront, the provision of motorways and slip roads to provide speedy and safe access to Athens International Airport as well as the creation of footpaths linking major attractions in the city centre were considered crucial to the improvement of the quality of life. Moreover, since thousands of athletes, team escorts, judges, referees, media and press representatives, spectators, employees and volunteers were expected to travel to the Olympic facilities on a daily basis, road and railway network improvement was regarded as crucial to the success of the games.

Of the works completed prior to the games, the Athens Metro considerably improved the quality of city life by affording Athenians the possibility of travelling faster and reducing traffic congestion and air pollution. The metro connected more than 20 municipalities of Attica with provision for new lines at a later date. Furthermore, the new suburban railway, an integral part of a wide development plan which aimed to upgrade and extend the railway network, was constructed to link Athens to districts in Attica, while a new tram line linked the centre with the southern suburbs, offering a good view of the sea.

Another ambitious construction plan completed prior to the games was Attiki Odos (Attica Road), a modern motorway of 67km passing through 30 municipalities of Attica with 32 junctions and 15 pedestrian bridges. Also much of the existing motorway was renewed or repaired and a large number of bridges and tunnels were constructed, thus reducing traffic congestion and travelling time. [10] In fact, post-Olympic Athens saw its transport infrastructure considerably improved in all sectors – road, rail and air. A total of about 140km of main road facilities were constructed to relieve traffic congestion. A modern rail system was inaugurated. The oldest railway line in Greece, 28km long and connecting Piraeus to central Athens and the northern suburb of Kifissia, was renovated with modernized stations, new security systems and additional rolling stock to increase the line capacity to 26,000 passengers per hour. [11] Second and third metro lines were extended to reach the inner suburbs of Athens. Metro trains now reach Athens Airport, located about 30km away from the city centre, in 20 minutes. In post Olympic Athens approximately 650,000 passengers use the tube every day. It has been estimated that the metro has reduced cars in the city centre by 70,000 daily. At the same time, the bus termini in the centre were reduced and new ones were created close to the metro stations, easing traffic congestion. [12] Furthermore, in May 2007 post-Olympic Athens saw the extension of metro Line 3 to 4.3km, linking Monastiraki to Egaleo with the addition of three new stations, while in September 2008 the Minister of Environment, Planning and Public Works, George Souflias, inspected the progress of the extension of metro Line 2 linking Agios Dimitrios to Helliniko, with a 5.5km underground tunnel and four new stations. 'According to the contract, the works were to be completed by December 2009 but due to archaeological finds which were excavated during the works it will not be operational until early 2010,' the Minister stated optimistically. [13] In addition, a new 32km long suburban line called Ska-Airport linked the new Athens airport to the central Greek railway interchange junction on the main Athens-Thessaloniki railway line, while a new tramway (Athens light rail system) linked the city centre to the waterfront with two tram lines of 24km, providing an attractive route along the beach. [14] Moreover, Athens International Airport, which became operational in 2001, was linked to the city centre via the new Attiki Odos motorway. The 47km Attiki Odos ring road along with the new Ymittos ring road of 13km absorbed 8 per cent of the city's daily traffic flow while the 119km long suburban railway, which commenced operation in 2004, linked the airport terminal to the Athens Metro.

More significantly, in an effort to improve environmental conditions, more than 2,000 city buses were replaced by buses running on environmentally friendly fuels. [15] However, despite its brand new highways, overpasses and modernized transport network, post-Olympic Athens returned to pre-Olympic traffic chaos within months of the conclusion of the event. The government hoped that the games might change the Athenians' habit of using their cars rather than public transport. During the games many people did make use of public transport but this habit was abandoned soon afterwards. 'The issue is how to convince Athenians to transform the occasional use of public transport into a lifelong habit,' the press reported [16] while traffic experts pointed out that there was no provision for implementation of the traffic control measures taken during the games so that post-Olympic Athens might be relieved of traffic congestion. [17] In fact, modernization of the transport system reduced air pollution to some extent, but it failed to encourage Athenians to use the modernized means of public transport instead of their cars, thus further slowing the traffic flow in the city. [18]

Apart from the improved transport infrastructure, the 2004 Athens Olympics stimulated the renovation of the city centre. Urban regeneration is one of the most important criteria that the International Olympic Committee (IOC) considers before it makes its decision on the future Olympic city. The 1960 Rome games provided the first example of the Olympics as catalyst for major urban changes when the construction of the Olympic venues as a key element in urban intervention broadened into a wide-ranging urban development programme. The main sporting facilities were clustered in three separate sites. In addition, the Tokyo Olympic Games played an important role in the urban transformation of that city on the occasion of the 1964 games, which provided the opportunity to improve infrastructure and proceed with a ten-year development plan. [19]

In the case of Athens, the Olympic Games offered a unique opportunity for regeneration of the city centre. Among other things, the unification by pedestrian paths of the archaeological sites aimed to upgrade and spotlight the historic centre, an ambitious project that was facilitated by the Ministries of the Environment, Physical Planning and Public Works and Culture. The company known as Unification of the the Archaeological Sites of Athens, established in 1997, undertook the creation of an archaeological park, the redesign of public spaces and buildings and the creation of a tramway. The works were completed in 2004. Visitors as well as Athenians now enjoy an 'open air museum' which incorporates the most important archaeological sites and monuments plus squares in the historic centre, parks, service facilities and venues intended to host cultural events – an ideal overview of the history of Greek civilization from classical antiquity to the recent past. The main feature of the archaeological park is a pedestrian zone that included Dionyssiou Areopagitou and Apostolou Pavlou roads, the ring roads of the Acropolis.

The walkway links many of the most important monuments of ancient Athens, such as the Acropolis, the ancient and Roman Agora, the Library of Adriano, the Keramikos district, the Plato Academy, Iera Odos (the Sacred Road), Thisseio, Filopappou Hill, Pnyka, the Aeropagus and the temple of the Olympian Zeus) as well as monuments of the Byzantine and post-Byzantine era, neoclassical buildings and green spaces. It also connects ancient ways and the new Acropolis museum and links residential areas to thriving business zones of small shops, recreation places and an artists' street market. Furthermore, rehabilitation and maintenance works took place on the facades of the buildings surrounding the sites. [20] Praising the impressive transformation, the foreign press reported that 'the great walk', as it is called by its architects, meanders for four kilometres past elegant neoclassical buildings to poppy-dotted knolls in the epicentre of antiquity, incorporating an arched 2,000-year-old open-air Roman theatre ringed by olive trees. Above the ruins of the Acropolis a visual feast is offered.

The Olympics provided the momentum for the project. Under the programme, called the Unification of the Archaeological Sites of Athens, hundreds of neoclassical buildings have been restored, unsightly billboards have been removed and much-needed green spaces have been planned. Downtown Athens has been aesthetically, environmentally and culturally upgraded and the residents and visitors enjoy a 'vast open museum' that includes all the archaeological sites and monuments of Athens along with the traditional neighbourhoods of its historic centre. This is one of the most tangible changes in Athens' re-vamping project that makes up, somewhat, for the city's lack of public green spaces and cycle trails so common in other European cities. [21] Additionally, squares of historic significance were re-vamped: namely Syntagma (Constitution) Square, Omonoia (Concord) Square, Monastiraki Square and Koumoudourou, which were reconstructed to facilitate movement of pedestrians in a more people-friendly manner, simultaneously showing off the cultural heritage of the city and its latter-day development. Ioannis Kalantidis, president of the Unification of the Archaeological Sites of Athens SA, pointed out that 'the unification of the historic centre has been the vision of architects, urban planners and the inhabitants of the city for many decades'. He concluded by saying that

> it is a project of great significance to the city of Athens and is expected to promote its cultural heritage and integrate history and culture in everyday life, a particularly ambitious project. The park of 4km in length and an area of 15,000 square metres in the heart of the city includes not only archaeological sites and monuments but also traditional neighbourhoods of the centre of Athens. [22]

It seemed as though Athens' ambitions for an improved transport infrastructure and an aesthetically upgraded historic centre which would attract visitors from all over the world were soon to be realized.

Tourism in Post-Olympic Athens: Realized Ambitions and Qualified Optimism

Tourism in the host city usually benefits from the worldwide publicity the Olympic Games offers. Sydney secured US$2 billion in revenue from global publicity during the 2000 games, while Barcelona experienced an annual increase in convention and business tourism at a rate of 21 per cent during the five-year period following the 1992 games. The 2004 Olympics offered Athens a great opportunity to promote itself in the global tourism market and secure an increase in visitors from all over the world and the consequent economic growth. However by the early twenty-first century tourism in Greece had suffered a decline due to the 2001 terrorist attacks in the

United States of America and the war in Iraq. There have also been unsuccessful advertising campaigns abroad, increases in hotel rates and negative comments from foreign press on the perceived inability of Greece to complete the Olympic facilities on time. The situation improved during the games when tourism increased as a result of improvement in hotel infrastructure and services.

Greece is one of the most attractive tourist destinations in the world and attracts more than 12 million tourists per year. The Olympic Games afforded the opportunity to promote new hotel businesses in Athens which gave tourism a competitive advantage in the regional and international tourism markets. In some cases host cities have turned the games to their advantage, witnessing the immediate development of tourism. Sydney set a good example of successful exploitation of the games for tourism growth as it succeeded in becoming an attractive destination for leisure and business tourists. [23] In the case of Barcelona, a strategic tourism plan was put into practice aspiring to attract an even larger number of tourists. The plan included the transformation of the Municipal Tourism Foundation into a mixed consortium for the promotion of tourism and the economy in general, the development of a hotel policy to assist hoteliers, the construction of a modern convention centre able to host international congresses and the creation of 14 large facilities capable of hosting major international events. According to statistical data released by Barcelona Economic Department, the marketing policy that was implemented contributed to an increase of visitors by 79 per cent during the period 1991–5. [24]

Following Barcelona's example, Athens developed its own infrastructure in an attempt to promote tourism in various forms such as conference, sports and environmental tourism. For this reason, big hotel chains initiated renovation programmes and developed service innovations in an effort to attract a large number of tourists. [25] Athens hoped to capitalize on the enormous publicity Greece was expected to receive during the games and to promote high-quality tourism all year round, which could be achieved by offering competitive tourist packages and developing innovative forms of tourism. [26] Some days prior to the start of the games, Dora Bakoyianni, then Mayor of Athens and Minister of Foreign Affairs, seemed to be optimistic about the growth of tourism in post-Olympic Athens. She observed that

> the image of our city during the Games will play the most important role in post-Olympic tourism development. The investment programme we are to put into practice is expected to assist our aims. Soon after the Games, the Organization for the Development and Promotion of Athens will begin operation in an effort to stimulate tourism. [27]

A few days after the games the Greek press reported, in a spirit of mixed optimism and circumspection, that 'the games are over but now what is needed is a persistent, systematic coordinated effort to make the most of the tremendous opportunity to promote Greece around the world via the Olympic Games. The government must do its best to capitalize on this unique opportunity.' [28] Moreover, in a effort to promote Athens as an attractive all-year-round tourist destination, the mayor Dora Bakoyianni proposed in February 2005 the establishment of a non-profit Tourism Development Agency. Among other comments, Bakoyianni mentioned that 'there had been a decline in tourism prior to the Olympic Games, a fact that had a negative impact on the city's economy. The Games brought Athens to the forefront of international attention and offered a unique opportunity for economic development in the short and long run.' [29] Clearly the promotion of tourism in post-Olympic Athens was a government priority. Nevertheless, the same month, *The Independent* newspaper reported that 'the Athens Hoteliers Union informed us that despite considerable expenditure on the renovation of their hotels, bookings did not increase at the anticipated rate after the 2004 Games'. [30]

However, the results, of a survey of hotel bookings after the 2004 Olympics revealed that in 2005 Athens was able to efficiently serve a larger number of visitors than in previous years due to most of the four- and five-star hotels having undergone major renovation. Thus hotel bookings remained at a high rate all the year round and the average stay per visitor was between two and three nights. [31] In spring 2006, two years after the games, the Minister of Tourism, Fani Palli-Petralia, delivering a speech at the World Travel and Tourism Conference held at Georgetown University, Washington, DC, on the challenges and opportunities for tourism in post-Olympic Greece, pointed out that tourism had gathered momentum after the 2004 games. She remarked that tourism is a key contributor to national revenue and accounts for 18 per cent of the country's annual gross domestic product (GDP) and for more than ten per cent of overall employment. 'The Athens Olympics provided us with the opportunity to improve tourism infrastructure and develop the local and national economy. The government aspires to attract investors from abroad and to advance environmental, convention, business and sports tourism,' the Minister concluded with optimism. [32] Furthermore, when addressing the Athens municipality on the occasion of the City Break 2007 exhibition, Fani Palli-Petralia once again praised the city's modern tourism infrastructure and concluded by saying that 'Athens may walk with confidence into the future putting into practice development projects that increasingly make it the top choice of visitors from all over the world, thereby promoting economic growth'. [33]

Athens' ambitions for tourism development in the post-Olympic period seemed to have been realized. Moreover, since deeds speak louder than words, the Athens Tourism and Economic Development Company, (ATED Co) in collaboration with the Tourism Research and Study Centre of the Business Administration Department of the University of the Aegean, presented a research report in October 2008 at the Athens City Hall on the growth of tourism from the pre-to the post-Olympic period. The objectives of the report were to release statistical data on tourism in Athens from 2000 to 2007, to develop new challenges and to propose initiatives for the promotion of tourism from 2008 to 2012. According to the results, tourism in pre-Olympic Athens witnessed a decline caused by both external and internal factors. Athens tourism experienced notable growth in 2005 after the successful organization of the

Olympic Games and the improved tourism infrastructure. In 2007, full hotel bookings in the Athens municipality reached 60.3 per cent, surpassing those of previous years. [34] The results also revealed that Athens had narrowly achieved 15th place in Europe for conference tourism. Out of all the international conferences held in European cities in 2006, the majority took place in Vienna, Paris and Barcelona, followed by Berlin, Budapest, Copenhagen and Prague. Vienna was the most popular destination while Lisbon, London and Amsterdam were in eighth, ninth and tenth places respectively.

Although post-Olympic Athens had hosted a number of international conferences, the city's ambitions to achieve one of the highest rankings in conference tourism in Europe had not been realized. However, in an original research project by the University of the Aegean conducted among tour operator companies abroad which aimed to discover the extent to which the 2004 games had promoted the image of Athens in the global tourism market, the majority of those questioned answered that the Olympic Games had made a positive contribution to tourism as many of their customers had chosen to visit Athens rather than other cities in Greece. Thus, according to these results, Athens did experience tourism development between 2005 and 2007. However, the promotion of recreational activities which could attract the interest of Greek and foreign visitors was considered a prerequisite for further development. [35] The president of the Athens-Attica Hoteliers' Union, George Tsakiris, agreed that tourism had grown in Athens after the 2004 games but it had not met the expectations of the hoteliers; taking into account the fact that convention tourism usually flourishes in post-Olympic cities. He compared it with Barcelona, which witnessed a 40 per cent increase in conference tourism after the 1992 games, adding that delays in transforming the Tae-Kwon-Do Olympic Hall into an international conference centre had deprived Athens of considerable revenue. [36] Nevertheless, post-Olympic Athens saw tourism develop at a rate of 9.8 per cent in 2006; the five-star hotels witnessed a 12.5 per cent increase in customers, while four-star hotels reached 17 per cent. Furthermore, the establishment of the Athens Tourism and Economic Development Agency (ATEDA) to capitalize on the benefits gained from the Olympics and a wide advertising campaign abroad were perceived as indicative of successful tourism promotion. [37] It should be noted here that a good opportunity for tourism in post-Olympic Athens will be provided by the 13th World Summer Special Olympics scheduled to be held in Athens in 2011. More than 70,000 athletes, coaches, volunteers, sports representatives and journalists are expected to arrive in the city. [38] However, in December 2008, with Athens struggling to expand tourism in the face of the global recession, a strong blow to its efforts was dealt by the fatal shooting of a 15-year-old schoolboy by a police officer in the Exarcheia neighbourhood of central Athens. The teenager's death was the catalyst for, not the cause of, fierce rioting and violent street battles. As a result, the hotels in the city centre suffered a considerable number of cancellations during the Christmas holidays while the United States of America and Australia advised those among their citizens scheduled to visit Athens to be very careful. [39] The foreign press reported that economic stagnation, widespread corruption, a troubled education system, rising poverty and unreliable security were all thrust to the fore as thousands of Greeks spilled into the streets to protest against the government. ... Many demonstrations turned violent, led by a relatively small group of anarchists. ... In the unrest, hundreds of businesses throughout the country were destroyed, resulting in an estimated US $1.3 billion in damage. [40]

Some days after the tragic events the Prime Minister, Costas Karamanlis, unveiled a 14-step plan aimed at helping the tourism sector withstand headwinds from the global financial crisis in a scheme welcomed by industry officials. The plan included increasing funds spent on promoting Greece abroad by 50 per cent and introducing tax breaks on projects and loans. Steps also included helping companies in the tourism sector overcome the credit crunch by providing working capital and finance through the European Union's National Strategic Reference Framework (NSRF) funding programme. [41] Under the weight of the global economic crisis, however, Greek travel agencies were not optimistic about the future of tourism in post-Olympic Greece inasmuch as tourism was expected to be highly susceptible to the worsening global economic developments.

Olympic Venues: Realized and Unrealized Aspirations

Soon after the 2004 games, serious questions arose about the sustainability of the Olympic facilities. Although the four-year struggle to make effective use of the Athens post-Olympic facilities has been discussed fully elsewhere [42] a brief summary of the extent of the utilization of the venues at the time of the Beijing games is given here as a reminder of the condition of the Athens facilities four years after the games. On the occasion of the Beijing Olympics, Athens re-evaluated with retrospective regret those ambitions that had been abandoned soon after the games. On the day of the opening ceremony of the Beijing Games the *Kathimerini* newspaper reported that

as soon as the Athens Games were over, it was clear that without the International Olympic Committee's incessant carping and with the Greeks no longer needing to display their best face to the world, there was no plan for the day after. Apart from the major transportation projects that have transformed the city, the purely Olympic projects were left in limbo like the fossils of white elephants, the decaying abandoned reminders of a collective dream that we could not translate into reality. [43]

As far as the 2008 Olympics are concerned, in order to stage the 'best ever' Olympic Games, state-of-the-art venues and facilities were built in Beijing and other co-host cities. The majority of the sports facilities as well as the National Stadium,were intended to be used for public recreation and leisure after the games. [44] Unlike the Athens Olympic venues, the Beijing facilities opened to the public as soon as early October 2008 and increasing utilization has subsequently been made of them. [45] The Beijing 2008 Olympic Games Bid Committee (BOBICO) emphasized the post-games use of its sporting facilities as a priority. After the games many of the university facilities, including gymnasia at Qinghua University and the Beijing University of Science and Technology, were returned directly to their original function within the university environment. Other facilities including the National Stadium and the Wukesong Culture and Sports Centre were retained as venues for future international sports events held in Beijing. [46] Of the Olympic venues in Beijing, the National Aquatics Centre (or 'Water Cube') was to be turned into the city's largest water park with an artificial beach, aquatic recreational equipment and fitness facilities; while the Wukesong Indoor Stadium was earmarked to become the National Basketball Association's first facility in the country, hosting NBA China basketball games. The National Stadium was expected to host large sports and entertainment events such as pop concerts after being remodelled, while the 'Bird's Nest' would become home to the Beijing Guo'an Football Club. [47] Athens, on the other hand, failed to realize its hopes of fully exploiting its Olympic structures.

Following criticism from the Greek and foreign press on neglected and underused venues, Hellenic Olympic Properties SA hastened to report its progress in the utilization of the post-Olympic assets in June 2008. According to their report,

> The International Broadcasting Centre (IBC) was leased to Lamda Development SA in August 2006, with the intention of being converted into a shopping and recreation centre. The delivery protocol was signed on 30 April 2007. Moreover, the designs for the creation of the Museum of the Hellenic Olympic Games and the International Athletic Museum have been completed and the renovated Badminton Hall at Goudi is in full use.
>
> The Galatsi Olympic Centre was given to Sonae Sierra SA and Acropol SA. These two companies established Park Avenue SA, which is expected to commence further construction work on the facility. The canoe kayak slalom at Helleniko was given to J&P Avax-Gek-Bioter-Corfu Waterparks SA. The construction work licence for the creation of a water area and amusement park is expected to be issued shortly.
>
> The Agios Kosmas Sailing Centre was given to Seirios Tech SA on 2 July 2007. The construction work licence is expected to be issued shortly. The first stage of the competition for the commercial exploitation of the Faliro Tae Kwon Do Hall, intended to be transformed into an international convention centre, has been completed. At the same time, the General Secretariat of Olympic Exploitation brought to a close the competition for the selection of technical advisers to be in charge of the facility's reconstruction.
>
> In September 2006 the marina at Faliro was given to the Hellenic Sailing Federation which now makes use of the facility. The Main Press Centre (MPC) at Maroussi will house the Ministry of Health and Social Security by the end of 2008. In the meantime, the facility temporarily accommodates the Committee for the 2013 Mediterranean Games' bid while the National Centre of Health is housed in the reconstructed part of the building. As for the remainder designated to accommodate the Ministry of Health, the reconstruction work licence has already been issued.
>
> The Nikea Olympic Centre was given to Piraeus University in April 2008. A contract was signed on 10 July 2007 between Hellenic Olympic Properties SA and

the Ministry of Public Order for the utilization of the Markopoulo Olympic Shooting Centre as a police training centre and as the headquarters of the Police Special Forces. The plan for the facility's reconstruction has been completed. Its handover to the police will be effected soon. The baseball, fencing, softball and hockey facilities at the Helleniko Olympic Complex are being leased on a short-term contract and currently host conferences, commercial exhibitions and concerts. The baseball facility was given to Ethnikos Football SA for a term of three years. The Schinias Olympic Rowing Centre was turned into the FISA International Training Centre by a contract signed on 6 September 2007. The Ano Liossia Olympic Centre is earmarked to house the Arts Academy and is leased on a short-term contract until then. The Markopoulo Olympic Equestrian Centre was given to the Hellenic Equestrian Federation and now hosts international athletic events. [48]

In a positive development, the Pagritio Stadium, as was agreed, was officially assigned to the Herakleion municipality and its citizens in September 2008. [49] However, the Olympic Sports Complex remains underused and is inaccessible to the public apart from when soccer matches are held at the Olympic Stadium, while the complexes at Faliro and Helleniko await the realization of ambitious plans. [50] Nevertheless, there was at least one example of relatively rapid use of an Olympic venue: the Badminton Hall in Goudi was the single successful example of post-Olympic utilization in Athens. After renovation, it was turned into a luxurious theatre, the biggest in Greece (with seating capacity of about 2,500 spectators). It opened its doors on 31 January 2007 with a performance of Matthew Bourne's production of *Swan Lake*, a prestigious cultural event. [51] Since 2007 the Badminton Theatre has hosted the English musical production *Mamma Mia* and a concert by the English guitarist and singer-songwriter Polly Jean Harvey. It has also hosted music and dance performances including *Lord of the Dance*, *Argentina Tangos*, *Carmen Dances Flamenco*, *Romeo and Juliet* by the ballet company of the National Theatre of Prague, the international dance performance *Solo for Three* and the production *Rain* by the Cirque Eloize. [52]

The Tae-Kwon-Do Indoor Hall at Faliro has hosted occasional international music and dance performances: a concert by the guitarist Gary Moore, the Todo Latino Salsa Festival and a three-day international Salsa dance festival were among the most important. [53] In the Olympic Sports Complex at Maroussi, which was redesigned by the Spanish architect Santiago Calatrava, national and international sporting and cultural events have been held, among them the 2007 UEFA Euro league, the Rally Acropolis Tournament, the 2005 Eurovision Song Contest and a 2008 concert by the singer Madonna. [54]

Athens 2004 and the Environment: Ambitious Projects; Post-Games Disillusionment

The United Nations Environment Programme (UNEP) and the International Olympic Committee (IOC) have been working together since 1994, when they signed an agreement of cooperation to incorporate environmental issues in the planning and organization of Olympic Games. The IOC subsequently established the Sport and Environment Commission to provide advice to its executive board on environmental issues closely related to the Olympics. In 1999, UNEP collaborated with the IOC in developing the project Agenda 21 for Sport and the Environment. According to this, the cities that bid for the games are obliged to present a precise environmental programme which should be followed during the preparation for the games.

The environment is recognized as the third most important aspect of the Olympics, after sport and culture. For this purpose the Olympic Charter was amended, stipulating that the Olympic Games should be held in conditions conducive to the protection of the environment. At the same time, a special Athletic and Environment Committee was created to promote environmental policy programmes. [55] In the case of the Athens Olympics the city received many negative comments about its environmental policy. A few days before the 2004 Olympics, Greenpeace reported that

> when Athens was a candidate city, the official position of the Greek authorities was that the Olympic Games were a challenge and an opportunity for the implemen-tation of programmes of action which are environmentally friendly and in accordance with the principles of sustainable development. However, with the exception of the improvement of the public transport system due to the Games and the decision by some sponsors, such as Coca Cola, McDonald's and Unilever to use cooling equipment based on natural refrigerants that do not damage the earth's climate, the environmental record of Athens was very low. Exploitation of green energy methods is the most striking failure of Olympic and post-Olympic Athens.
>
> The Athens Olympic Committee had promised that during the Games the electric lights used in the venues would be produced by renewable sources of energy. However, no green energy was used in the Olympic facilities during the Games. [56]

More importantly the Greek branch of the World Wide Fund for Nature (WWF) issued a report criticizing Athens for falling short of its environmental commitments and gave the city a score of 0.77 points on a scale of zero to four. The WWF remarked that 'the authorities failed to incorporate into their plans green energy and water-saving and recycling programmes while natural areas like the mountains of Parnitha, Hymettus and Pendeli have been "trapped" within Olympic constructions and road networks'. According to the same report, the gains of Athens were evident in the fields of public transport, the renovation of the city centre and the promotion of environmental awareness.

The ecologists also remarked that in the contract between Athens and the IOC there was only a general reference to the environment according to which

> the city of Athens and the Hellenic Olympic Committee recognize and agree that respect for the environment is an important issue and undertake to fulfil their obligations with regard to the adoption of the principles of sustainable

development, observance of relevant environmental legislation and promotion of environmental protection wherever possible.

However, 'it was evident that the protection of the environment received little attention from the outset', the WWF observed, continuing its criticism by mentioning that

> among the missed opportunities for environmental enhancement in post-Olympic Athens were lack of green spaces, huge sports facilities with no provision for maintenance or any plan for post-Olympic use and a city expanded at the expense of the environment. Moreover, there will be no progress in the energy sector, no introduction of new water management and conservation technologies, no improvement in the waste management system and no progress in the area of environmentally friendly construction technologies. [57]

Without doubt, Athens' ambitious projects for the protection of the environment and better environmental conditions in the city after the games remain wishful thinking.

Conclusion

Post-Olympic Athens presented itself on the global stage as a modern city with new transport means (a new airport, metro, tram, suburban railway, motorway system and upgraded road network), a renovated city centre and an improved hotel infrastructure. In reality Athens failed to realize its ambitions regarding utilization of the Olympic venues. Four years after the games some of the most impressive facilities, such as the Olympic Sports Complex and the Saronic Gulf waterfront at Moschato, have still not been converted into the intended sporting, cultural and commercial venues. It is hoped that in the long term they might meet the expectations of Athenians in offering residents and tourists excellent places of recreation. [58] Of the Olympic locations, only the Badminton Hall has been successfully utilized, having been turned into a magnificent theatre which opened to the public early in 2007 and is now the venue for prestigious high-quality international shows.

Athens also failed to meet the standards for a green Olympics although the Greek authorities had promised to make the 2004 games the greenest ever. Notwithstanding all this, new means of transport like the metro, the gas-powered buses and the urban rail and tram networks have made a positive contribution to the protection of the environment. No doubt Athens could have made considerably more progress in the improvement of environmental conditions and realization of 'green' promises. In a public opinion poll held four years after the games and on the occasion of the Beijing Olympics, Greek citizens were asked to declare whether they believed their government had taken advantage of the Athens games. Eight out of ten citizens answered that they thought their government had failed to take advantage of the games' success. However, firm feelings of pride and nostalgia for the Athens games, which were regarded as a great success, were evident. According to the survey the majority of the citizens polled believed that the games had benefited the country in general and Athens in particular, but that the government had not taken advantage of the games, resulting in a missed opportunity. More importantly, the majority of respondents answered that they believed the 2004 Olympics were worthwhile despite the huge cost and failure to immediately exploit the opportunities the games had offered. [59]

In summary, Athens' aspirations in terms of modernizing transport infrastructure, regenerating and transforming the historic centre and improving hotel infrastructure to facilitate the development of tourism had been realized. The unification of the archaeological sites had unquestionably improved the image of Athens. Once notorious for its traffic chaos, the historic centre around the Acropolis was transformed by walkways that linked many of the city's monuments. In addition, main streets and squares were reconstructed while old neoclassical buildings, important tourist attractions and public facilities were renovated. Justifiably, post-Olympic Athens was described as 'a new city full of life day and night with pedestrian streets around the Acropolis, modern neighbourhoods and the best Metro in the world'. [60] Tourism developed in the first three years following the games, but there were fears that it would slow down as the result of the global economic crisis which seemed to place serious obstacles in the way of further development. In short, post-Olympic Athens saw some of its ambitions realized, thus improving its image as a modern metropolis, while hope for the realization of unfulfilled aspirations in the short or long term has not yet been extinguished. Time will tell.

Acknowledgement

I would like to thank Professor J.A. Mangan for his editorial support.

Notes

[1] Mangan, 'Prologue', 1872.
[2] Karkatsoulis et al., 'The National Identity', 582.
[3] Gold and Gold, 'Olympic Cities', 301.
[4] Synadinos, O Agonas, 133–6.
[5] Hiller. 'Post-Event Outcomes and the Post-Modern Turn', 318.
[6] Karkatsoulis et al., 'The National Identity', 583.
[7] Beriatos and Gospodini, 'Glocalising Urban Landscape', 191–3.
[8] Ibid., 193–6.
[9] Frantzeskakis and Frantzeskakis. 'Athens 2004 Olympic Games'.
[10] Tziralis et al., 'Economic Aspects'.
[11] Bovy, 'Athens 2004 Olympic Games Transport'.
[12] Attiko Metro, press release, 20 Dec. 2007.
[13] Attiko Metro, press release. 25 Sept. 2008; 24 Nov. 2008.
[14] Bovy, 'Athens 2004 Olympic Games Transport'.
[15] Tatsiopoulos and Tziralis, 'New, Post-Olympic Athens'.

[16] 'Post-Olympic Athens Returns to Traffic Anarchy', *Daily Commercial News*, 1 Dec. 2004, 4; Argyris Demerzis, 'Ten Missed Opportunities', *Eleftheros Typos*, 7 Oct. 2008, 5.

[17] Kassimi, 'Transpor', *Kathimerini*, 3 Aug. 2008.

[18] Kavaratzis, 'Marketing the City', 110.

[19] Hanwen and Pitts, 'A Brief Historical Review of Olympic Urbanization', 1238–9.

[20] Athens Olympic Committee, 'Athens 2004: The Unification'; Hellenic Ministry of Culture, 'The Unification of the Archaeological Sites of Athens', press release, 2002; Haralampidou, 'A Walkway in Athens for the Olympic Games', *To Vima*. 11 Jan. 2004, 10.

[21] Orkin, 'A Stroll through Chaotic Athens', *Associated Press*. 21 May 2004, 2.

[22] Athens Olympic Committee, 'Athens 2004: The Unification', 50; Haralampidou. 'A Walkway in Athens for the Olympic Games', *To Vima*. 11 Jan. 2004, 10.

[23] Ignatis, 'Athens 2004 Olympic Games', 1–2.

[24] Asprogerakas, 'City Competition and Urban Marketing', 12–13.

[25] Ignatis, 'Athens 2004 Olympic Games', 61.

[26] Eliopoulos, 'Post-Olympic Prospects for Greek Tourism', 46–7.

[27] Bakoyianni, 'Athens at the Centre of World Attention', 11.

[28] 'Using an Olympic Opportunity', *Kathimerini*, 31 Aug. 2004, 3.

[29] 'The City of Athens to Establish a Tourism and Economic Development Agency', Athens News Agency, 8 Feb. 2005, 1.

[30] Walker, 'Expert View: Urban Regeneration; That's the Real Olympic Ideal', *The Independent*, 20 Feb. 2005, 6.

[31] Tatsiopoulos and Tziralis, 'New Post-Olympic Athens', 82–3.

[32] Hellenic Republic, Embassy of Greece, press release, 11 April 2006.

[33] Sgartsou. 'Petralia: Post-Olympic Athens is a New Athens', *Travel Daily News*, 12 June 2007, 3.

[34] Athens Tourism and Economic Development Company, press release, 17 Nov. 2008.

[35] Ibid.

[36] Papanikolaou, 'Tourism in Athens did not increase', *Ethnos*, 10 Aug. 2008.

[37] Kavaratzis, 'Marketing the City', 113.

[38] 'The Greek Tourism Ministry Promotes 2011 Athens Special Olympics', *Olympic Times*, 30 Sept. 2008, 1.

[39] Poutetsi. 'Strong Blow to Athens Tourism', *To Vima*, 14 Dec. 2008, 11.

[40] Donadio and Carassava, 'Violence Brings Issues Plaguing Greece to the Surface', *New York Times*, 12 Dec. 2008, 1; Squires and Anast, 'Greek Riots: Banks and Cars Burned by Greek Mob', *Daily Telegraph*, 14 Dec. 2008, 33.

[41] Bouras, 'Plan Targets Vital Tourism Boost', *Kathimerini*, 19 Dec. 2008, 1.

[42] In Mangan and Dyreson, *Olympic Legacies: Intended and Unintended*.

[43] 'Life After the Games', *Kathimerini*, 8 Aug. 2008, 10.

[44] Dong and Mangan, 'Beijing Olympics Legacies', 2020–2.

[45] Tzoustas, 'The Olympic Legacy of Beijing and the 'White Elephants' of Athens', *To Vima*. 21 Sept. 2008, 56.

[46] Ong, ' New Beijing, Great Olympics', 44.

[47] Jiao, 'Olympics Venues to Leave Lasting Legacy', *China Daily*, 1 Sept. 2008, 6.

[48] Olympic Properties, press release, 16 June 2008.

[49] Olympic Properties, press release, 15 Sept. 2008.

[50] Drakos, Zaphiriadou and Kondos, 'Olympic Facilities in Dark', *Eleftheros Typos*, 10 Aug. 2008, 3; Gold and Gold, 'Olympic Cities', 309.

[51] Olympic Properties, press release, 15 May 2006; *Investor's World*, 12 Aug. 2007; Nedos. 'Olympic Assets: Seeking for Future, Private or State', *Kathimerini*, 3 Aug. 2008, 5.

[52] 'The Major Cultural Events of 2008'.

[53] Olympic Properties, press releases, 13 Sept. 2008; 28 Nov. 2008.

[54] Patoulis, 'The Contribution of Athletic Venues to the Development of Tourism Industry in the Olympic City of Amaroussion', Embassy of Greece in Beijing press release, 29 Oct. 2008.
[55] Synadinos, *O Agonas*, 131–4.
[56] Greenpeace, 'Athens Olympics Loses the Race for Environmental Excellence', press release, 5 Aug. 2004.
[57] WWF, 'Environmental Assessment of the Athens 2004 Olympic Games', press release, 16 July 2004.
[58] 'Life after the Games', *Kathimerini*, 8 Aug. 2008, 10.
[59] Kotrotsos, 'From National Pride to Regret of Missed Opportunity', *Eleftheros Typos*, 10 Aug. 2008, 3.
[60] Rigopoulos, 'The Post-Olympic Greece As Others Saw It', *Kathimerini*, 8 Aug. 2008, 11.

References

Asprogerakas E. 'City Competition and Urban Marketing: The Case of the Tourism Industry in Athens'. *Tourismos: An International Multidisciplinary Journal of Tourism* 2, no. 1 (Spring 2007): 1–26.

Athens Olympic Committee. 'Athens 2004: The Unification of Archaeological Sites'. *Olympic Review* 17, no. 40 (Aug–Sept. 2001): 49–50.

Bakoyianni, D. 'Athens at the Centre of World Attention'. *Trade with Greece* 30 (Summer 2004): 10–11.

Beriatos, E. and A. Gospodini. 'Glocalising Urban Landscape: Athens and the 2004 Olympics'. *Cities* 21, no. 3 (2004): 187–202.

Bovy, H.P. 'Athens 2004 Olympic Games Transport'. *Route et Trafic* 7–8 (Juillet–Aout 2004): 45–8.

Dong J. and J.A. Mangan. 'Beijing Olympics Legacies: Certain Intentions and Certain and Uncerrtain Outcomes'. In *Olympic Legacies: Intended and Unintended – Political, Cultural, Economic, Educational*, special issue of *The International Journal of the History of Sport* 25, no. 14 (Dec. 2008), edited by J.A. Mangan and Mark Dyreson: 2019–40.

Eliopoulos, E. 'Post-Olympic Prospects for Greek Tourism'. *Trade with Greece* 31 (Autumn 2004): 45–7.

Frantzeskakis, J. and M. Frantzeskakis. 'Athens 2004 Olympic Games: Transportation Planning, Simulation and Traffic Management. *Institute of Transportation Engineers Journal*, (Oct. 2006): 1–11.

Gold, J. and M. Gold. 'Olympic Cities: Regeneration, City Rebranding and Changing Urban Agendas'. *Geography Compass* 2, no. 1 (2008): 300–18.

Hanwen, L. and A. Pitts. 'A Brief Historical Review of Olympic Urbanization'. *The International Journal of the History of Sport* 23, no. 7 (Nov. 2006): 1232–52.

Hiller, H. 'Post-Event Outcomes and the Post-Modern Turn: The Olympics and Urban Transformations'. *European Sport Management* 6, no. 4 (Dec. 2006): 317–32.

Ignatis, C. 'Athens 2004 Olympic Games – A Challenge for the Hotel Sector of Athens and Greece'. Master's thesis, Goteborg University, School of Business, Economics and Law, 2004.

Karkatsoulis, P., N. Michalopoulos and V. Moustakatou. 'The National Identity as a Motivational Factor for Better Performance in the Public Sector: The Case of the Volunteers of the Athens 2004 Olympic Games'. *International Journal of Productivity and Performance Management* 54, no. 7 (2005): 579–94.

Kavaratzis, M. '*Marketing the City or Managing the City's Brand? The Theory of City Marketing and Three European Cases*'. Thesis, University of Groningen, 2008.

Mangan, J.A. 'Prologue: Guarantees of Global Goodwill: Post-Olympic Legacies – Too Many Limping White Elephants?' *Olympic Legacies: Intended and Unintended – Political, Cultural, Economic, Educational*, special issue of *The International Journal of the History of Sport* 25, no. 14 (Dec. 2008): 1869–83.

Mangan, J.A. and Mark Dyreson. *Olympic Legacies: Intended and Unintended – Political, Cultural, Economic, Educational*, special issue of *The International Journal of the History of Sport* 25, no. 14 (Dec. 2008).

Ong, R. 'New Beijing, Great Olympics: Beijing and its Unfolding Olympic Legacy'. *Stanford Journal of East Asian Affairs* 4, no. 2 (Summer 2004): 35–49.

Synadinos, P. *O Agonas Mias Polis* ['The Struggle of a City']. Athens: Kastaniotis: 2004.

Tatsiopoulos, E. and G. Tziralis. 'New, Post-Olympic Athens'. *About Brand Greece* (2007): 77–84.

'The Major Cultural Events of 2008'. *Trade with Greece* 39 (2008): 194–8.

Tziralis G., A. Tolis, I. Tatsiopoulos and K.G., Aravossis. 'Economic Aspects and the Sustainability Impact of the Athens 2004 Olympic Games'. *Environment Economics and Investment Assessment* 98 (2006): 21–33.

The Beijing Games, National Identity and Modernization in China

Dong Jinxia

Modern Olympics have always been about national prestige. The 2008 Olympic Games in Beijing was a good illustration. The unprecedented support level to the Beijing Games from the government to the public reflects the sense of national identity which is motivated by the memories of past grandeur and humiliation and the keenness to build a new, vigorous, modern and strong nation in the world.

Through examining Beijing's two Olympic bids, construction of infrastructural facilities, the choreography of the Games' Opening Ceremony and the widely publicized Olympic slogans, this paper explores the complicated relationship between national identity building, modernization drive and the Beijing Games. It claims that Olympic victory has been regarded as the public embodiment of national strength and symbolic of China's emerging status in the world.; the building of a new national identity has been closely linked with modernisation which is inseparable from the ongoing globalization, urbanization and migration in the country. In addition, the Games facilitated China's modernisation in industry, communication, transportation and management. The Games was not just the dream fulfilled, but a future vision.

Introduction

The 2008 Olympic Games took place in Beijing and attracted a global audience of 4.7 billion, an increase of 21 per cent over the Athens' Olympics. [1] The wide coverage of the games via media, newspaper, radio, TV and the Internet made it 'a priceless 17-day advertisement for the "Made in China" brand', [2] and a platform for China to show its modernization achievement. [3] The International Olympic Committee (IOC) president Jacques Rogge remarked in August 2008: 'I believe that history will view the 2008 Olympic Games as a significant milestone in China's remarkable transformation.' [4] Indeed, the successful staging of the games not only brought enormous pride and joy to China but also elevated Chinese confidence in their splendid culture and the future of the nation and changed China's image virtually overnight – from that of being a weak, backward 'sick man of the East Asia' to a strong, modern superpower. [5] Arguably the games might have 'far more influence than any other Games in history' [6] – on both China and the wider world.

Here some questions arise. How was the national identity of China constructed through the Beijing games? What impact did the games have on China's modernization process? What is the relationship between the Olympics, national identity and Chinese modernization? All these questions deserve serious considera-tion, especially in the twenty-first century when this relationship has become complicated and dynamic due to the influence of multinational corporations, mass migration and globalized consumerism.

It is widely accepted that national identity is a collective psychological state of identity, a sense of belonging in which all members of a nation 'identify' with one another. It is a necessary condition for the survival of the politico-legal-coercive state. [7] As an ideological construction, 'national identity needs to be constantly nurtured, reinvented and maintained'. [8]

The national identity of China has been built over time with its own characteristics. For centuries considering itself as the centre of the world because of its sophisticated and advanced culture, China was humiliated by the Western powers (including Japan) for a century after the Opium War in 1840, and gradually turned from a dynasty into a semi-colonial and semi-feudal country. After Chairman Mao announced to the world on 1 October 1949 that the 'Chinese people have stood up!' the Chinese wanted to create a new global identity – one characterized by prestige, esteem and respect.

The building of national identity has been closely linked with modernization drive in New China. Modernization is a concept of sociology, politics and culture. Due to different modernization theories over time, [9] it is held in this paper that modernization is a continuous and open-ended process of transformation from the traditional to the modern in terms of politics, economy, society, culture and civilization.

From the mid-nineteenth century onwards, the Chinese made efforts to modernize the country. However, the concept of 'modernization' did not emerge until the 'May the Fourth Movement'. [10] Since then 'modernization' became a keyword in the newspapers and journals. Due to the Japanese invasion and civil wars between the 1920s and 1940s, no significant progress was made in terms of 'modernization'. After the Communist Party came to power in 1949, the Chinese dreamed of modernizing their country. In 1958 China launched the nationwide campaign of the 'Great Leap Forward' with the intention of overtaking the West within ten years in terms of steel production and many other aspects. In 1964 China voiced publicly the goal of fulfilling the modernization of industry, agriculture, science and technology and its national defence by the turn of the century. [11] However, this modernization drive succumbed to the ten-year political movement of the Cultural Revolution between 1966 and 1976. At the Third Plenum of the 11th Central Committee in December 1978, which marked the beginning of economic reform and opening up to the outside, the 'Four Modernizations' drive was officially launched. A year later, the party paramount leader Deng Xiaoping put forward a concrete criterion for the modernizations: per capita GDP of US$1,000 by the end of the twentieth century. This goal was achieved successfully. Today, per capita GDP is over US$3,266. [12] In the twenty-first century, modernization continues to be China's overall strategic goal. The China Modernization Report 2006 envisioned that a wealthy China would provide everyone with full medical insurance and access to 17 years of education; life expectancy would rise to 80 years, and the percentage of skilled knowledge workers would rise from the current 10 per cent to 50 per cent. [13]

With the staging op the Olympic Games in Beijing, there were plenty of news and publications on this topic. However, there is little literature on the changes in relationship between the Beijing games, national identity and China's modernization prior to and after the games. Self-evidently, analysis of the Games, from its bid, infrastructure construction, the Opening Ceremony to athletic preparation and people's attitude towards the Games, is a rich source of discourse of the relationships between national identity, modernization and sport. Based on governmental documents, media reports, literature review and interviews to volunteers and staff of the Beijing Games, this paper will attempt to examine this complicated relationship.

Sport has always been used as an effective political instrument in China. After the People's Republic of China was founded in 1949, Chinese athletes achieved remarkable accomplishments in international competitions in the four decades from 1950 to 1990, which had brought national pride and glory to the nation. [14] However, the Chinese were not completely satisfied with what they had achieved. They wanted more: to host sports mega-events – an effective means to raise Chinese standings in the world and to facilitate the social, economic and cultural development of the world's most populated country. Thus, in 1990, just a year after the Tiananmen Student Movement which resulted in immediate Western economic sanction and consequent sudden reduction of foreign investment (from US$2 billion in the fourth quarter of 1988 to $900 million in the first quarter of 1990), Beijing successfully staged the Asian Games. This encouraged the Chinese to bid to host an even larger international sports event: the Olympic Games. In 1991 Beijing submitted its application to the IOC for the 2000 Olympic Games. The event was expected to help break the post-1989 political deadlock and build a new positive national image with a collective consciousness of national identity. To help it win the bid, Beijing built a number of infrastructures including an expressway from the airport to the city and a large railway station. [15] The capital soon possessed 76 per cent of stadia and gymnasia that would be necessary for the staging of the Olympic Games and various sport-related activities were organized to help support the bid. In the meantime, with the introduction of market-oriented economy in 1992, Chinese economic exchanges with the West were recovered and accelerated. The number of projects with direct foreign investment increased from 12,978 in 1991 to 83,437 in 1993 and the value of those projects from US$11.98 billions to US$111.44 billions accordingly. [16] Self-evidently, the bid itself promoted Beijing's modernization process to a certain extent.

Despite all the efforts and investment involved, unfortunately, Beijing lost its bid by two votes to Sydney (Australia). [17] This failure, largely circumscribed by the social and economic situation of the post-Tiananmen student movement and the accompanied huge international criticism over China's human rights, plunged the whole nation into depression, but at the same time aroused and reinforced a strong nationalism in all Chinese, which reached its pinnacle in 1996 with the publication of a book, *China Can Say No and China Can Still Say No*. The 1999 American bombing of the Chinese embassy in Belgrade further fuelled the rising nationalism, which saw the anti-US demonstrations and the resultant harsh criticism of 'Western values'. Clearly, 'China's new nationalism is a reaction to a changing international environment'. [18]

Against this backdrop, in 1999 Beijing made its second bid this time for the 2008 Olympic Games and won pledged all-out support from the government to its citizens. People from all walks of life volunteered to contribute to the bid. Celebrities, including the Sydney games' champion Liu Xuan and the film stars Gong Li and Jack Cheng, were officially appointed as promoters of the Beijing games to help sway IOC voters; some 1,100 non-governmental groups from various fields including hi-tech, commerce, construction, sports, education, sanitation and environment, wrote a letter to the IOC president Juan Samaranch in support of Beijing's bid. [19] A public poll conducted by the Gallup Organization in Beijing in November 2000 showed that 94.9 per cent of residents in Beijing strongly supported the city's bid to host the 2008 Olympics and 62.4 per cent were fairly confident that Beijing would win. [20]

As in its first bid, China was again confronted with Western opposition for the reasons of its human-rights record. [21] This opposition somehow strengthened Chinese determination to fight and win. The incident of 2001 spy plane collision over the South China Sea [22] between China and America further fuelled the already strong nationalism.

As well as the concerted efforts stirred up by the heated nationalism, the bid was also strengthened by China's rising influence in the world since its previous bid. In the eight years between the first bid in 1993 and the second in 2001, China accomplished great achievements in many respects, from improved living standards and modernized communication to expanded higher education. Between 1993 and 2001, per capita annual disposable income for urban households was boosted from 2,577 yuan (US$296.2) to 6,860 yuan (US$829.5). Net income for rural households rosefrom 921.6 yuan (US$ 105.9) to 2,366.4 yuan (US$286.5); the number of civil motor vehicles owned increased from some 817.58 for every 10,000 people to 1,802.04. During the same period, the number of mobile phone users from 639,300 to 116 million. After the Internet emerged in 1995, its subscribers numbered 33,700,000 by 2001. There were also more university graduates, from 57.1 out of 10,000 people in 1993 to 103.6 in 2001, and students studying abroad rose significantly, from 10,742 in 1993 to 83,973 in 2001. [23] All this reflected China's rapid advancement in the process of modernization.

Progress in Beijing, the host city, was more evident with its gross domestic product surging to 284.565 billion yuan (US$34.45 billion) in 2001 from 86.353 billion yuan (US$15.5 billion) in 1993, registering a per capita GDP of over 26,998 yuan (US$3269) compared to 8006 yuan (US$ 1404.5) in 1993. [24] In 2001 Beijing was one of the five provinces or municipalities that had achieved the first modernization – transformation from the Agriculture Age to the Industrial Age – and entered the second phase of modernization, from the Industrial Age to the Knowledge Age. [25] Thus Beijing confidently voiced its wish to the world of hosting the 2008 Olympic Games.

By the end of twentieth century, the world's economic frontiers had changed greatly from industrialization to post-industrialization, from industrialized, standardized techniques to information and greening techniques, and from industry to the knowledge and information industry, from agriculture and industry to services and other new industry. Thus the strategic focus of China's modernization in the twenty-first century, advocated by China's modernization study group, endorsed the 'new four modernizations': knowledge, information, urbanization and democratization'. [26] Clearly, the focus had changed from an exclusively economic emphasis to broader social and cultural spheres involving socio-political institutions, value systems and life and behaviour modes. Holding the games 'will surely advance the city's modernization by a big margin', claimed Tang Long, spokesman for the Beijing Municipal Government after the successful bid in 2001. [27]

In a nutshell, the rapid development of modernization in the 1990s laid a foundation for Beijing to successfully launch the Olympic bid in 2001, which in turn would speed up the modernization process. When the former IOC president Samaranch announced on 13 July 2001 that Beijing would be the host city of the 2008 Olympic Games, the Chinese at home and abroad burst into thunderous cheers and applause. National pride was demonstrated publicly on a scale unprecedented in Chinese history. National identity assumed by an 'imagined community' is moulded by specific historical circumstances at a particular point in a time. Hosting the Olympic Games for the first time would be a symbol of China's power and place in the world. The games would mark the history of China's modernization.

Modern Infrastructural Facilities – Materialized National Identity and Modernization

The Olympics was an eye-opener to foreigners visiting China or watching China via the media. 'New Beijing, Great Olympics', the self-assured bid slogan, first materialized through its physical outlook that projected to the world a new, vigorous image of an open, modernized, civilized and well-developed nation. After wining the bid in 2001 a vast investment and construction programme was immediately put in place. Virtually everything, from sports facilities and venues, communications networks, traffic systems, hotels and an irport terminal, talent recruitment and environmental protection to athletic performance, media and cultural activities, Olympic marketing, Olympic education and much else, was taken into account.

To enable China to host the Games 36 stadia and 66 training venues and other specialised facilities were required. Thus, direct investment in the construction of Olympic venues and facilities amounted to about 19.5 billion yuan (US$2.72 billion), most of which came from local Government funding. [28] The National Stadium, known as "Bird's Nest" because of its giant lattice-work structure of irregularly angled metal girders with 91,000-seat and cost about 3.5 billion yuan (about US$488 million), less than the originally planned 4 billion yuan (about US$506 million). It became symbolic of the Games, a new landmark and the most attractive tourist attraction of Beijing after the Games. It topped the list of the 60 Beijing scenic spots voted by Internet users in 2009, overtaking the globally well-known Great Wall and the Forbidden City. From October 2008 when it was opened to public to May 2009, its revenue reached 0.364 billion yuan (US$53.4 million). [29] Nevertheless, the process of constructing the stadium was not without any problems. The budget for the "Bird's Nest" was cut due to the pressure from the IOC's 'scaling down plan', and resulted in the halting of the stadium's construction for five months. It was not completed until April 2008. [30] In addition, the problem of how to rebuild the 'modern' city while maintaining it's historical and cultural uniqueness was a difficult task, for which government officials were frequently criticised.

Guided by the 'Hi-tech Olympics' (*ke ji ao yun*), one of the games' three ideas (the other two were 'Humanitarian Olympics' and 'Green Olympics'), the latest technological innovations were used in construction, communications, transportation, food supply and competition management. The construction of information technology alone, from a digital communication system, a software and intelligent management system for competition to a fibre-optic network for journalists or officials to obtain a video pictures of what was happening at any site, cost some 30 billion yuan (US$3.797 billion). To provide a satisfactory transport service during the games, Beijing invested 90 billion yuan (about US$11.25 billion) to construct subways, light railways, expressways and airports. Eight new subway lines were constructed in the urban area and the number of public transit lines had increased to over 650 by 2008. It was expected that by adopting 3S-based core technology a highly effective intelligent traffic network system would be created and the capacity and efficiency of Beijing's passenger and freight transport would catch up with the rest of the world. [31] In total, more than 290 billion yuan (about US$40 billion) was used to modernize Beijing's airport and other city infrastructures, build the required competition venues and tackle pollution and environmental hazards. [32] Although the Beijing Olympic Organizing Committee (BOCOG) claimed in 2009 that the games had a surplus of 1.16 billion yuan (US$170 million) – 20.5 billion yuan (US$3 billion) income and 19.3 billion yuan (US$ 2.84 billion) expenditure [33] some questioned whether it was worth spending so much money on the Beijing Games. [34] It is argued here that infrastructural facilities that consumed the majority of the budget will survive after the Beijing games and provide a solid base for modernization of the country. Therefore the games were far beyond an athletic event. They were a mega-event with great social, political and economic implications. The country made an 'effort to give shape to an emerging national identity'. [35]

The eye-catching stadia, the state-of-the-art airport terminal, hundreds of star hotels and modern subway lines, among other things, have changed the outlook of China, Beijing in particular. These new infrastructures, from the highways, airports and rails that transport people and the streets that divide private property through to the sewerage and water systems and the electrical and communication networks that sustain the limitless activities of daily life, provided the physical framework for people's settlement, urbanization and social life. Undoubtedly the preparation for the games facilitated the pace of China's modernization in industry, communication, transportation and management.

Billions of dollars of direct investment in the building of infrastructure and related activities possibly boosted China's annual GDP by about 0.3 per cent. [36] Some industries benefited more from the games. For example, the construction industry increased its gross production from 593,167 million yuan (US$71,812 million) in 2001 to 1,401.410 billion yuan (US$201.9 billion) in 2008. Chinese tourism overseas also increased from 3.69 million in 2001 to 28.55 million in 2008 and the countries and regions visited have expanded from 18 to 132. [37] Foreign exchange earnings through Tourism jumped from US$2.95 billion in 2001 to US$4.58 billion in 2007, while the number of international tourists rose from 2.858 million (person-time) in 2001 to 4.355 million in 2007. [38] However, in 2008, the total number of inbound travellers to China was, at 130 million, down from 132 million in 2007. [39] There were many reasons for this decline. The global economic downturn and the tight control on visa entry during the months prior to the Olympics were two of them. For example, only 389,000 foreign tourists visited Beijing in August, 2008, far below the expected 500,000 visitors. [40]

Beijing, the host city of the games, benefited more than any other city in the country. It has kept two-digit growth for nine years in terms of GDP. [41] By 2006 Beijing had fulfilled the goal of US$6,000 per capita GDP two years earlier than planed, and well above the country's average per capita GDP of US$1,740. [42] In 2008 Beijing's GDP rose to US$146.2 billion per capita, over US$8,000. Beijing's annual GDP growth from 2005 to 2008 reached about 11.8 per cent on average, 0.8 percentage points higher than the 2001–5 period. [43] One of the reasons for the growth was the huge investments in the Olympics. Some estimated that economic activities related to the games might have generated a combined GDP of 105.5 billion yuan (US$13.6 billion) for Beijing during 2004–8. [44] As a result, the capital city has become as vibrant and dynamic as any capital city in the world.

The games injected tremendous vitality into Beijing's real-estate market. In 2001 investment in real estate surged remarkably with a 50.12 per cent increase. [45] By 2006 the investment in real-estate market reached 171.99 billion yuan (US$22 billion), 51 per cent of total investment in fixed capital. [46] However, the price of land, housing and renting in Beijing, as happened when Sydney staged the 2000 Games, were also pushed up. In 2001 and 2004 house prices in Beijing increased 3per cent and 6.7per cent respectively, but by 20005 it jumped to 20 per cent. [47] The soaring prices of land and property in Beijing and other cities raised great concern about their impact on inflation, employment and social stability.

Coupled with the Games preparation, the nature of Chinese industries has changed over time. Tourism, service, insurance and sports industries are the major beneficiaries of the Beijing Games. The 'third industry' value increased from 4.44 trillion yuan (US$0.53 trillion) in 2001 to 12.05 trillion yuan (US$1.59 trillion) in 2007 and its employees increased by 15.9 per cent. [48] With the changes to consumer-oriented service industries, the Games boosted the pace of Beijing's becoming a modern service-centred city. During the Olympic Games, 4,000 Olympic standards for three major categories, including food safety, environmental protection, transport management, public security, public hygiene and other matters were released and implemented. All this has become a part of the long-term mechanism for Beijing municipal management and operation after the games. [49]

It is evident from the above analysis that the Olympic Games advanced modernization in Beijing and in China as a whole. During the decade following Beijing's announcement of its intention to host the 2008 Olympic Games in 1999 to the actual holding of the Games in 2008 China underwent dramatic changes. In 2002, China realized 82 per cent of its first modernization, ranking it 60th among the 108 countries in the world. The second modernization index was 32, ranking China 56th in the world. [50] Though such indexes for most recent years are not available, they have surely moved forward significantly. Chinese GDP rose from 1,096,551.7 billion yuan (US$132,754.4 billion) in 2001 to 3,006,700 billion yuan (US$433,242.1 billion) in 2008 and per capita GDP increased from US$1,042 to US$3,266.8 [51] during the same period. China is expected to be the world's leading economic power by 2025. [52]

China's modernization drive cannot be separated from globalization, urbaniza-tion and migration. China has integrated with the world more closely after it was admitted into the World Trade Organization in 2001. In 2002 the total inflow of Foreign Direct Investment (FDI) into China reached US$400 billion, making it the world's largest recipient of FDI. [53] Non-financial FDI inflows increased from US$46.9 billion in 2001 to US$92.4 billion in 2008. [54] The total value of imports and exports in 2008 reached US$2,561.6 billion, of which the value of exports was US$1,428.5 billion, and the value of imports was US$1,133.1 billion. [55] Now virtually all the World Top 500 enterprises have investment in China that has been the largest purchaser of US Treasury Bonds in recent years years. China and the world have become intimately intertwined. To some extent the Games helped raise Chinese awareness of the interaction or relationships between itself and other countries in realising its modernization target. A strategic framework of realising modernization in China called 'Doves of Peace' was put forward in the '2008 China's Modernization Report'. More attention than before was given to the international environment in which China exists. [56] China's modernization is intimately linked with globalization.

It should be noted that preparations for the games took place against a background of rapid urbanization of China. The urban population was only 30.1 per cent of China's total population in 1999; by 2008, it had reached 45.68 per cent. [57] The process of urbanization was accompanied by an inward migration of the rural population. In the pre-reform era, due to the existence of household registration (*hu kou*) there was little geographic mobility for Chinese people. Since the 1980s control on geographic mobility has been gradually relaxed. Domestic migration reached about 150 million in number in 2008.

In sum, the billions of dollars investment in infrastructure, a remarkable Olympic village and venues, along with hotels and modern shopping centres for the Games, provided material foundation for consolidating the national identity of China and propelled the process of its modernization. [58]

Opening Ceremony – Overt Display of National Identity and Modernization

The Opening ceremony of the Olympic Games was the most attractive event. The Beijing Opening Ceremony alone attracted leaders from over 80 countries, [59] nearly 850 million Chinese [60] and a global audience of billions. It won applause and admiration from both foreigners and Chinese alike.

'Although the ceremony ostensibly celebrates all member nations, in practice both compulsory and interpretative elements mirror the values and experiences of the host nation.' [61] Recognizing the unique local appeal and global significance of the opening ceremony, BOCOG put the ceremony at the top of its agenda after the Athens games in 2004. Proposals for the Opening (and Closing) Ceremonies were solicited from March 1 to July 31, 2005, with 409 proposals being forthcoming. After careful reviewing, thirteen excellent proposals were selected and publicly presented and questioned, [62] based on which the opening ceremony choreography was designed by a choreographic team that was established in April 2006. This team was directed by the internationally well-known film director Zhang Yimou. [63] Parallel to the choreographic team were the technical and management teams, each of which had its sub-divisions. For example, under the choreographic team were different design offices for firework, lighting, musical, stage art, costume and props. All available human, material and financial resources were utilized in accordance with a centralized plan. Experts, specialists, technicians, artists, students and soldiers were all mobilized from home and abroad to work for the opening ceremony. [64] The operation centre under the management team alone had over 700 staff. [65] About 14,000 performers, including 9,000 People's Liberation Army (PLA) soldiers, actually participated in the performance of the ceremony. They spent a whole year in exercise and rehearsal. Take the group of martial arts students who participated in the opening ceremony display as an example. In total, there were 2,008 students from three different martial arts schools situated in Henan and Shangdong provinces. The students came to Beijing to practise the exercises for a whole year until the opening ceremony. [66] This illustrates China's superb governing capacity and exceptional organizational skills.

As Jackie Hogan has rightly pointed out, 'the consciously universalist rituals of the ceremonies are in a sense domesticated by the host nations and imbued with national meanings', [67] the opening ceremony of the Beijing games was full of national meanings. First, China's 5,000 years of history was encapsulated in the impressive and loudly applauded one-hour choreographic display. Three of the 'four great inventions' (*si da fa ming*) of the pre-modern era were presented in the first act,

'Brilliant Civilization' (*can lan wen ming*). The trade and exchange between China and the West on the Silk Road, five long scrolls of paintings representing the five major dynasties of Tang, Song, Yuan, Ming and Qing in Imperial China, and the Chinese philosophy of harmony between human and nature were all vividly presented through various kinds of arts. [68] Second, the entry of participating nations, for the first time in Olympic history followed the order of Chinese Pinying instead of the Roman alphabet. This proves that 'national identity has been actively reconstructed and endowed with indigenous meanings that are specific to China'. [69]

It is noticeable that throughout the performances, high technology went hand in hand with traditional Chinese culture Performance of movable type printing, one of the four great inventions of ancient China, took an image of both an ancient Chinese character and a modern computer keyboard; fairies fell from the sky, costumes glowing with light, to represent 'Apsaras', an image in the mural paintings of the Mogao Grottoes of Dunhuang in north-west China's Gansu Province. The impressive countdown drum display also combined Chinese ancient history with modern high technology. The drums themselves were an imaginative interpretation of the ancient *fou*, a vessel or instrument originally made from earthenware or in some cases bronze.

The climax of the opening ceremony was the entrance of the Olympic torch and the lighting of the Olympic cauldron by Chinese gymnast Li Ning, which perfectly combined technology, traditional arts and personal effort.

It is beyond doubt that China achieved its goal of a high-tech Olympics by incorporating the latest domestic and international scientific and technological achievements into the Ceremony. The control centre of the opening ceremony was equipped with the 'Shenzhou 4000' control system that was used during space missions. Cellular materials designed for the space sector were used to make paper in the painting scroll. Light-emitting diodes (LEDs) were installed across the 20,000-square-metre 'Bird's Nest' to create an ideal multimedia environment with storage cells backing up electricity supplies. Tiny LED beads were also embedded in the costumes of performers, who ran out to create a falling starry sky and a brightly-lit Bird's Nest. A technical monitoring system was also employed to control more than 18,000 performers through their identification codes.

The fireworks with the image of 29 footsteps along Beijing's axis to the Bird's Nest were the most dazzling show, behind which were sophisticated new technologies – compressed air launches, chamber pressure launches and computerized ignition technologies. The use of a digital ignition control system minimized the time difference of the fireworks display to a few milliseconds at more than 30 locations across Beijing. Despite a rare eruption of more than 40,000 shots, Beijing used smokeless powder to reduce pollution to a record low. [70]

To ensure a good weather for the opening ceremony on 8 August 2008, Beijing mobilized all its science and engineering capability, including satellite monitoring and cloud seeding, to prevent rain. This had a 41 per cent chance of success based on historical data. The weather engineering office wove a defensive web from adjacent provinces to the Beijing suburbs, and 26 control stations were deployed to fend off clouds or delay their movement. The office hired 32,000 people and recruited light aircraft, rockets and shells to spread silver iodide crystals or dry ice in clouds 50 km upwind of Beijing. Result estimates could be reported from control stations to the headquarters within ten minutes. [71]

It is clear from the above description that the Beijing games helped promote the modernization of science and technology in China. This is especially true given that the most complicated technologies employed in the Beijing Olympics opening ceremony were independently developed by domestic companies. The Beijing Olympic Games served as an engine for modernizing the country, and also a window to showcase the country's hi-tech achievements and its innovative strength. One Chinese academic claimed:

> The rise of the Chinese nation cannot be hidden from the audience who watched the opening ceremony. For long we had been quietly working hard to be successful. This time, it seems that the ambition to be a great nation was demonstrated ... sending a clear signal to the world: the revival of Chinese nation has started. [72]

The revival was a product, in large measure, of three decades of economic reform and the 'opening up' to the world. For the past 30 years China's economy has grown at an average of 9.6 per cent annually, making it the world's second-largest economy. [73] Economic strength and the determination to link up with the world, among other thingstouched on earlier, paved the way for the successful Games. There can be no equivocation. The success of the Beijing Games is the reflection of China's risen power in the world. Through its Games, China wanted to show the world that not only it was an economic power that had buried a humiliated past, but that it was also a nascent important global political power that will play a crucial part in shaping the new world order. China used the Games not only as a stage on which to display its staggering economic progress, but also as a launch pad to propel itself into the international diplomatic stratosphere. [74]

In short, the compulsory rituals of the opening ceremony in Beijing were incorporated into China's own narratives of nation, refiguring these universalist moments as displays of national character, pride, power and progress. The blending of tradition with cutting-edge technology helped create a special moment for Chinese people to restore their national grandeur, erase past memories of defeat and ensure present memories of success.

'Go, China' and 'One World, One Dream' – New National Identity and Cultural Modernization

During the Beijing Games, *zhong gou, jia you*' ('Go, China!') was continually heard everywhere. With the Games held in their homeland, the Chinese people demonstrated unprecedented passion. They waited for hours or even though nights to buy up competition tickets. They waited for hours or even nights to buy up competition tickets. They cheered Chinese athletes tirelessly with the national flag flying and wearing shirts and hats with the national colours, red and yellow. Even when the 'odd/even number car plate' restrictions and special Olympic passes were put in place, bringing considerable inconvenience to some, few people complained or broke the rules. Instead, people expressed understanding and support. Over 1.7 million volunteers were involved in the Beijing Olympic and Paralympic Games. These volunteers were praised for their enthusiasm, friendliness and helpfulness, which resulted in a change of people's attitude towards the young generation. Prior to the Games of 2008 there were fears that the post-1980 generations were spoiled, over-indulged and self-centred as most were of single-child families. Through their actions during the Olympics they proved that they could be unselfish, helpful and reliable. It is expected that Olympic volunteers will be the vanguard of socially concerned citizens who will set new standards of civic concern in the future [75] volunteerism will spread into broader society. The Beijing municipal government predicted in the first anniversary celebration of the Beijing games that within three to five years the participation rate of public volunteer service will likely reach 20 per cent and registered volunteers are no fewer than two million. In addition, volunteerism education will be incorporated into the textbooks of primary and middle schools. [76]

Here a question can be asked: why could the Chinese sacrifice personal interests for the Olympic Games? To understand this it is necessary to be able to appreciate Chinese recent history and cultural traditions. First, the 'century of national humiliation' (*guo chi*) between the 1840s and 1940s, mentioned earlier, made the Chinese want to reclaim their 'proper' global role. Second, 'The Chinese are obsessed with appearances, what they call "face". They don't want to lose face; they want to show the absolute best.' [77] As the games were 'a festival staged with the whole nation's participation, a passionate gathering of the whole nation', [78] they could tolerate some regulations that brought inconvenience to their daily lives in order to help present a new image of China. 'Face' melded national image and pride. Third, to have a chance to serve the games was an honour that was envied greatly in society. To a large extent the Beijing games created settings in which players, supporters and the media were able to load sporting events with meanings informed by national identity. Thus, the games were closely linked to China's political image, unity and status. Of course, the state played an important part in building up the sense of national identity. Patriotic education (*ai guo zhu yi* – loving the state) was promoted and the pre-games special oath gatherings were organized at different levels for different groups.

The performance of national anthems and the raising of national flags in each medal awarding ceremony are deeply infused with national symbolism. Before the Beijing Games, American journalist Melinda Liu rightly pointed out that 'nowhere will this tilting balance of power be more pointedly symbolized than in the Olympic medal count, where China may have a better than even chance of snagging the highest number of gold medals, displacing the U.S'. [79] Indeed, China, with 51 gold medals, topped the gold medal list for the first time in history despite still being behind the United States in terms of the total medal count. Here a special note should be made concerning Chinese women. As in the past three decades, they again played a major part in ensuring the above victory in the Beijing Games. They won 27 out of the total of 51 gold medals captured by the Chinese, [80] far better than any other country in the world. [81]

This athletic success is a product of decades of centralised management and nation-wide concerted endeavours. To become an Olympic power had been the persistent and ultimate dream of China after the Olympic Strategy was issued for the first time in the mid-1980s fallowing the first ever Chinese Olympic gold medals in the 1984 Los Angeles Games. Olympic victory has been regarded as the public embodiment of national strength and symbolic of China's rising status in the world. To ensure Chinese success in 2008, 'The Programme of the Plan to Win Olympic Glory 2001–10' [*ao yun zheng guang ji hua gang yao 2001-2010*] was drafted in 2002 According to this, nine sports including shooting, judo, weight-lifting, wrestling, Taekwondo, diving, gymnastics, table-tennis, and badminton were regarded as the superior sports of China. [82] To maximize eventual Olympic performances in 2008, individual sports management centres issued a 'Project to Implement the Plan to Win Glory in the 2008 Olympics' for their own sports, and membership of the national teams expanded significantly, from 1,316 to 3,222. [83] Some 1700 athletes of fifty-five national teams for 28 sports underwent intense preparation between 2002 and the years leading to the Games, though only less than half of them could eventually participate in the Games. [84] Accordingly, the sports budgets soared dramatically over time, from 1.5 billion yuan (over US$181 million) in 2003 to 2.1 billion yuan (US$253.7 million) in 2006. [85] Clearly, considerable resources were poured into elite sport. It was disclosed for the first time in September 2008 by Liu Peng, Director of the National Sports Administration, that the state invested 800 million yuan (US$116.79 million) each year into sport. Based on this figure and the fact that China won 51 gold medals at the Games, investment for each gold medal was about 15.7 million yuan (US$2.29 million), and about 8 million yuan (US$1.17 million) per medal of any kind (dividing by 100 medals). [86] Apart from the state budget, lottery money was also used to support the elite athletes. In 2007 the Olympic Glory Programme was allotted 362.50 million yuan (US$52.92 million) and more than the 331.52 million yuan (US$48.4 million) went to the National Fitness Programme through the income of the sports lottery in 2006. [87] Obviously, Olympic performance took precedence over mass sport. To prepare for the 2008 games, a special budget from the state reached over 4 billion yuan (US$583.94 million). [88]

In addition to the rising budget from the State, various measures were taken to ensure athletes committed to the Olympics. For example, an athletes' insurance system was established and their incomes rose significantly after the income distribution system for athletes was reformed. and 'Athletes', as an independent occupational category in the sports field, was first listed in the national occupational management system. [89]

It is noticeable that while 'Go, China' was shouted in virtually every competition venue, the games' slogan 'one world, one dream' was seen virtually everywhere. Although the Chinese wanted to see Chinese athletes winning medals and went to stadia to cheer them enthusiastically, they became more tolerate and sympathetic towards home athletes even if they did not meet their expectations. This is shown in Liu Xiang's case. When the most popular hurdler gave up his race in the last minute due to his ankle injury, the Bird's Nest Stadium was stunned silence and the Chinese in front of televisions across the nation were desolate. Sport possesses a capacity to impact on the public mood in such a powerful way! Though Liu's withdrawal disappointed millions, with some accusing him of being afraid to lose, most Chinese expressed their concern over his injury. The Chinese vice president Xi Jinping expressed the hope that Liu would fully recover and achieve great success in the future. [90] The Liu incident reflected a changed attitude towards winning and athletes. The Chinese have become more friendly and supportive not just to home athletes but also to foreign athletes. They would applaud excellent performances no matter whether by Chinese or foreign athletes. The fact that American basketball player Kobe Bryant, [91] the American swimmer Michael Phelps [92] and Jamaican sprinter Usain Bolt [93] were the most popular athletes in Beijing during the games was the best illustration of this. 'Sometimes we feel we are better supported here than back at home,' the American basketball point guard Chris Paul said. [94] Although the Chinese women's volleyball team was defeated by the American team coached by Lang Ping, formerly a famous player in China in the 1980s, the Chinese spectators still praised Lang Ping. They felt proud of her, originally from Beijing, for her intelligence, fair play and skills. This national fair-mindedness ran counter to the fear by some Chinese and foreigners that angry chauvinism would be the outcome if Chinese athletes didn't win. [95] All this illustrates that the Chinese have become more tolerant as they become more confident. [96] Nationalism and globalization coexist in today's China.

China has been assimilated more and more fully into the world scene, which was culminated in Beijing's successful Olympic bid and China's entrance into the World Trade Organization in 2001. To organise the Beijing Games successfully, a sizable number of foreign experts in design, security, environmental protection, news service, competition administration and publicity were employed as Olympic advisors, consultants and evaluators. Take the National Indoor Stadium where the gymnastics and handball competitions took place as an example. Of the197 Olympic staff eight were foreigners who worked in the Sports Presentation and Media Operation sections. In addition to this, a number of experts from companies like Omega and NBC and 20 foreign college volunteers working for the Olympic News Service were in place before and during the Games. The officials, experts and staff from the international gymnastics and handball federations numbered over 300. [97]

Apart from the foreign experts who helped organize the Beijing games, a number of foreign coaches were employed. In the Chinese delegation to the 2008 games, there were 28 foreign coaches from 16 countries including America, Canada, Germany,

France, Korea and even Japan. They worked on 17 sports including archery, canoeing, women's handball, hockey and softball, men's and women's basketball, synchronized swimming and fencing. [98] These coaches not only helped the Chinese improve their athletic performances but also provided an opportunity for the Chinese to get to know more about foreign people and their cultures. The men's sabre gold medallist Zhang Man declared: 'My French coach Christian Bauer offered tremendous help in improving my fencing skills. He is the best coach in the world. This gold medal belongs to him.' [99] Gratitude also went to the Jin Yongbo, the Korean coach of the Chinese women's hockey team that won a silver medal, the best result in its history, [100] and the Japanese coach of the Chinese synchronized swimming team that for the first time won an Olympic medal.

That the two seemingly contesting slogans, 'Go, China' and 'one world, one dream' went hand in hand is an interesting phenomenon. The years of the public moral campaign aimed at the 'civilization' of Chinese citizens prior to the games [101] and other Olympic-related promotional activities might have played their part. Lectures, seminars, TV programmes and special newspaper columns were devoted to the Olympics. Not a single day in China passed without news of Beijing 2008. Indeed for years Beijing 2008 figured prominently in Chinese minds. Photography, painting, poetry, calligraphy and foreign-language speech contests were all organized throughout China to promote an understanding of Olympism both in schools and society. Various contests for the design of sports venues, for sculpture, for the motto, for the mascots and for the theme songs were also held at national and/or international level. The most publicized and lasting event was the unprecedented Olympic Education Project that was launched throughout the nation after 2002. With the full support of educational administrators in Beijing and China, Olympic education was introduced on a hitherto unprecedented scale, involving 400 million students from 500,000 schools. [102] Nothing in the history of the Olympic movement has come close to the Chinese coverage of the nature of Olympism. As a result, hosting the Olympic Games brought about not only the infrastructural and economic changes as indicated earlier, but also changes in social values and norms.

Following such a nombardment of extensive Olympic information, Olympic ideas such as peace and friendship were gradually internalised. Before the Torch Relay was launched the majority of Chinese people were quite positive about the international community. According to a survey of the Chinese citizens of five big cities (Beijing, Shanghai, Guangzhou, Chongqin and Wuhan) in 2006, over 90% of respondents were optimistic that with the increased strength of China would help it find favour in the future international environment. [103] Thus, the Chinese designed its Olympic Torch Relay, a "journey of harmony" which would travel through the six continents of the world between April 1 and May 3, followed by a domestic relay. Altogether it lasted for four months with 21,880 torch-bearers and 5,000 escort runners involved. [104]

However, the optimistic Chinese were dealt a heavy blow by the chaotic events that affected the Torch Relay on its international route and the resultant Western condemnation that triggered a surge of nationalism in and outside China. [105] Chinese both at home and abroad took counter-protest action. Overseas Chinese in France, the United Kingdom, Germany, the United States, Australia and elsewhere reacted against the media coverage that they thought was biased and demonstrated in support of the Olympics. [106] In China there was an organized boycott of the French-owned retail chain Carrefour in major Chinese cities including Kunming, Hefei and Wuhan. The French nation was accused of pro-secessionist conspiracy and anti-Chinese racism. [107] This episode might be one of the multiple reasons for the drop of China's positive ratings from 45 per cent in early 2008 to 39 per cent in early 2009, surveyed by BBC World Service across 21 countries. [108] The protests taught the Chinese a bitter lesson: the world does not have just one dream, but many. 'One world, one dream', the slogan of the Beijing games, was exclusively a Chinese wish, but on Chinese terms, not those of the rest of the world. This episode illustrates that with rapid economic growth and modernization, the Chinese felt more confident in dealing with the outside world and required a higher level of respect from the international community. [109] However, it also indicates that Chinese should establish a more realistic and comprehensive view of the world and learn to look at China and the world from different perspectives.

Concluding Remarks

The 2008 games, through successful organization and remarkable athletic performances, helped advance the international image, esteem and dignity of China. The unprecedented support level to the Beijing games from the government to the public reflects the sense of national identity – both 'top-down' and 'bottom-up'. The Beijing games were a defining movement for 'national self-assertion'. To some extent the games were a landmark of China's modernization achievement [110] and at the same time they powered a national modernization drive. The 2008 games might be a harbinger of China's world elevation.

In terms of history the games were a festival for which the Chinese had waited for over a century. The games were not just the dream fulfilled, but a future vision. [111] If everything goes well, the world will witness in the future a modern, strong and open China. Indeed, the past year has seen China take a high-profile role in response to the global economic meltdown. According to a survey in 2008, some 86 per cent of respondents were satisfied with China's current situation and 82 per cent were optimistic about its economy, much higher than most other countries in the world. [112] However, there will be severe challenges facing China, not least to maintain the legacy of the games and use them to serve the future community, to promote the ideals of Olympism and blend green, hi-tech and humanistic values with modernization, to act on the lessons learned from the games to upgrade management skills and to promote the liberal, harmonious interaction of citizens and society. Influenced by international financial crisis, the Chinese economy slowed down significantly from late 2008. The total value of imports and exports for the first quarter of 2009 was US$428.7 billion, down by 24.9 per cent year-on-year. The total value of foreign direct investment actually utilized was US$21.8 billion, a year-on-year decrease of US$ 5.6 billion. [113] How to stabilise the national economy and fulfil the goal of eight per cent increase of GDP is a huge challenge, which will have an impact on the stability and harmony of society and the legitimacy of the party. Chinese people have to learn how to mesh Chinese custom and Western practice in order to find a place in the world without compromising its independence but at the same time becoming more acceptable to others. It is not an insurmountable problem. China has the capability – the product of history – to confront modern problems and dilemmas and overcome them. According to the 'Three step' strategy advanced by Deng Xiaoping, China will reach the level of moderately developed countries by in 2050s and the level of a developed country by the end of the Twenty-First Century. By then China will exert more impact on the global village.

Notes

[1] Lu Wenjun, 'beijing ao yun hui chuan dian shi shou shi shi xinji lu, quan qiu guan zhong da 47 yi ren' ['Beijing Olympics created record TV viewers in history, global viewers reached 4.7 billion'], available at www.xinhuanet.com, accessed 6 Sept. 2008.

[2] 'Made in China' brand reaps Olympic dividend', available at http://en.ce.cn/subject/beijing08/oe/200808/24/t20080824_16596458.shtml, accessed 24 Aug. 2008.

[3] Dong Yan, "zhong guo bao dao": aoyunhui hou de zhongguo sikao ('China Report': Post-Olympic Chinese Thinking), available at: http://www.cipg.org.cn/ywdt/qkjc/myyw/mqkzx/200809/t20080912_25575.html, accessed 12 Sept., 2008.

[4] AFP, 'History will judge Games as milestone for China, says Rogge', 5 Aug. 2008, available at http://au.news.yahoo.com/a/-/latest/4854003/history-judge-games-milestone-china-says-rogge, accessed 5 Aug. 2008

[5] 'He chuan qi: ao yun hui shi zhongguo canyu guoji shiwu di san ge li cheng bei ['He Chuanqi: the Olympic Games is the third milestone of China's involvement in the international affairs'], 23 Aug. 2008 available at http://www.chinanews.com.cn/olympic/news/2008/08-23/1358297.shtml, accessed 23 Aug. 2008.

[6] Penn, 'aoyun: rang shijie chongxin renshi "zhongguo" pingpai' [The Olympic Games Let the World Know "China" Brand', 80–81.

[7] Bostock and Smith, 'Towards measuring national identity'.

[8] Cashmore, Sports Culture: An A-Z Guide, 305.

[9] Modernization theory in the West has evolved over time. In the 1950s and 1960s it attempted to explain the diffusion of Western styles of living, technological innovations and individualist types of communication as the superiority of secular, materialist, Western, individualist culture and of individual motivation and achievement; In the 1970s and 1980s the influence of Western modernization was criticized and since the 1990s postmodernity theory has tried to be more neutral, being not in favour of or against Western modernization, to unearth the contradictions in the modernization process and to explain the consequences of modernity for individuals in contemporary society. However, the concept of postmodernity is confusing when modernization is considered as a continuous and open-ended process.

[10] Some 3,000 students from Peking University and other schools demonstrated in Beijing on 4 May 1919 to protest against the Chinese government's weak response to the Treaty of

Versailles, especially the Shandong Problem. The May the Fourth Movement takes its name from the protest. The radical intellectuals blamed traditional culture for the dramatic and rapid fall of China into a subordinate international position, and maintained that China's cultural values prevented China from matching the industrial and military development of Japan and the West.

[11] At the first meeting of the Third National People's Congress in December 1964 Zhou Enlai put forward in the Governmental Work Report that by the end of twentieth century China should become a strong socialist country with modern agriculture, industry, national defence and technology.

[12] '2008 nian zhongguo renjun GDP chao 3000 mei yuan, bao zengzhang qiao feng qi shi' ['China's per capita GDP reached over US$3000 and it is time to ensure growth'], 6 March 2009, available at china.com.cn, accessed 6 Mar. 2009.

[13] 'Zhongguo xiandaihua yanjiu xiaozu' ['Study Task Team on China's Modernization Strategy'], 6 Mar. 2009.

[14] Details can be found in Dong Jinxia, *Women, Sport and Society in Modern China*.

[15] Zhang Luya (eds.), Shiji qing – zhongguo yu aolinpike yundong [A Century of Contact – China and the Olympics], 204.

[16] Xu Yifan, *zhongguo dui wai jing ji tong ji nian jian*.

[17] After it was revealed in 1999 that Australia bribed some members of the IOC before the final vote, Chinese were furious and questioned the integrity of the bid.

[18] Yongnian Zheng, *Discovering Chinese Nationalism in China*, 159.

[19] *People's Daily*, 20 Feb. 2001

[20] Lai Hainong, 'cong zijingcheng wumen zouxiang2008' ['Moving towards 2000 from the Midday Gate of the Forbidden City'], available at http://www.chinanews.com.cn/zhonghua-wenzhai/2001-08-01/txt3/12.htm, accessed 1 Aug. 2001.

[21] Vicki Michaelis and Bill Nichols, 'Beijing Still Favored to Land 2008 Olympics', *USA Today*, 19 June 2001.

[22] Henry Chu and Paul Richter, 'US Spy Plane, Chinese Fighter Collide Over Sea', *Los Angeles Times*, 2 April 2001.

[23] *Zhongguo tongji nianjian* [Statistical Yearbook of China], 1993, 2001.

[24] State Statistics Bureau, *China Statistical Yearbook*, 1994.

[25] Chinese scholar He Chuanqi initiated the 'second modernization theory'. Based on the study of 131 countries in 2002, Chinese scholars claimed that 24 countries (18 per cent of those sampled) finished economic modernization first and 18 countries (14 per cent) entered the period of second economic modernization (for details see Study Task Team on China's Modernization Strategy, 2005).

[26] He Chuanqi, *Dong fang fu xin*.

[27] 'Olympic Games to Advance Modernization in Beijing', *People's Daily* online, 14 July 2001, available at http://peopledaily.com.cn, accessed 14 Jul. 2001.

[28] Zhonghua renmin gongheguo shenjishu bangong ting [The General Office of the National Audit Office of the People's Republic of China], zhonghua renmin gongheguo shenjishu shenji jieguo gonggao 2009 nian di 8 hao [Announcement of Audit Results by the National Audit Office of the PRC, No. 8, 2009], available at: http://www.audit.gov.cn/n1057/n1072/n1282/1831561.html, accessed on June 19, 2009.

[29] Liu Qi, 'aoyun cujin chengshi fazhan – renwen beijing, keji beijing, lvse beijing' ['The Olympics promoted city development – Humanitarian Beijing, Hi-tech Beijing and Green Beijing'], Aoyun chengshi luntan ['Olympic Host City Forum'], 8 Aug. 2009.

[30] Pan Chengqing, 'niao chao gong cheng zheng shi fu gong, she ji zhe zhong fang gu wen xi wan gong cheng shun li' ['The project of the "Bird's Nest" resumed and the Chinese designer wished it smooth'], *Jing hua shi bao* [Jing hua Daily], 28 Dec. 2004.

[31] By the year 2008, the urban railway system was expected to carry 1.8 to 2.2 billion passengers per year, the capacity of Beijing's buses and trolley buses will reach 4.5 billion passengers per year and the number of vehicles will reach 18000.

[32] Zhonggong Beijing shiwei zhuzhi bu, *xin Beijing, xin aoyun' zhishi jiangzhuo*, 60.

[33] Zhonghua renmin gongheguo shenjishu bangong ting [The General Office of the National Audit Office of the People's Republic of China], zhonghua renmin gongheguo shenjishu shenji jieguo gonggao 2009 nian di 8 hao [Announcement of Audit Results by the National Audit Office of the PRC, No. 8, 2009], available at: http://www.audit.gov.cn/n1057/n1072/n1282/1831561.html, accessed on June 19, 2009.

[34] 'Zhongguo wei choubei aoyunhui hua liao 430 yi meiyuan, ni juede qian huade zhibuzhi', 19 Aug. 2008 ['China spent US$43 billion. Do you think it worth that or not?'], Shangye diaocha – jiazhi zhongguo wang [Business Survey – value], available at China.net, available at: http://china.com.cn/overseas/txt/2008-08/14/content_16223312.htm, accessed 19 Aug. 2008.

[35] Nicolai Ouroussoff, 'In Changing Face of Beijing, a Look at the New China', *New York Times*, 13 July 2008.

[36] '1417 yi yuan aoyun touzi tisu Beijing jingji' ['141.7 billion investment speed up Beijing economy'], 24 March 2005, available at www.jingbaonet.com, accessed 24 Mar. 2005.

[37] Guojia liyou ju yinxi zhongxin [Information Centre of National Tourism Administration], 'Woguo lvyou ye zai fazhan zhong zhuangda' ['The Chinese tourist industry has developed and expanded over time'], 11 Dec. 2006, available at http://www.cnta.gov.cn/news_detail/newsshow.asp?id, accessed 21 Dec. 2006.

[38] '2007 nian Beijing lv you chang ye fa zhan shi jian da shi' ['The ten big issues in Beijing's tourism in 2007'], *Beijing ri bao* [Beijing Daily], 18 Jan. 2008.

[39] '2009 National Tourism Working Conference opens in Beijing', available at http://en.cnta.gov.cn/html/2009-1/2009-1-8-17-46-75892.html, accessed 8 Jan. 2009.

[40] 'China's Inbound Tourists Down By 1.5per cent in 2008', available at http://www.konaxis.net/index.php/20090112427/news/tourism-hotel-china/china-s-inbound-tourists-down-by-1.5-in-2008.html, accessed 12 Jan. 2009.

[41] 'Wang hailiang, renjun GDP tupo qi qian meiyuan, qunian quanshi renkou zeng 52 wan' ['Per capita GDP broke through US$7000 and the City's population increased 520,000 in number last year'], *Beijing chenbao* [Beijing Morning Post], 22 Jan. 2008.

[42] 'Beijing tiqian liangnian shixian renjun GDP liu qian meiyuan' ['Beijing realized the target of US$6000 per capita GDP two years earlier'], available at http://www.build.com.cn/hangyedongtai/ShowArticle.asp?ArticleID=1596, accessed 3 Apr. 2007; Liu yan, 'Aoyun dacan shui yu zhenggeng' ['Who will compete for the Olympic Market'], *Beijingxiandai shangbao* [Beijing Modern Commerce Post], 4 April 2003.

[43] Beijing shi tong ji ju, *2009 beijing jing ji she hui tong ji bao gao*.

[44] 'Official: Beijing's GDP to break 1-trillion-yuan mark in 2008', Xinhuanet.com, 3 Aug. 2008, available at http://xinhuanet.com, accessed 3 Aug. 2008.

[45] Zhonggong Beijing shiwei zhuzhi bu, *xin Beijing, xin aoyun' zhishi jiangzhuo*, 69.

[46] 'Ying lijuan, beijing fangdi chang kaifa touzi zhan guding zichan youzi guoban' ['The development investment of Beijing's Real Estate accounted for over half of the fixed assets investment'], xinhuanet.com, 25 Jan. 2007, available at: http://xinhuanet.com, accessed 25 Jan. 2007.

[47] 'Baogao cheng quanguo fangjia jiang changqi shangzhang, beijing qunian shangchang jin 20per cent' ['Report claims that the house price at national level will grow for long and the growth rate in Beijing was nearly 20per cent last year'], 25 April 2006, available at http://www.sina.com.cn, accessed 25 Apr. 2006.

[48] Feng Huiling, 'Beijing aoyunhui jingji jiazhi fenxi' ['Analysis of the economic value of the Beijing Olympic Games]', Aoyun chengshi luntan [Olympic Host City Forum], 8 Aug. 2009.

[49] Liu Qi, 'aoyun cujin chengshi fazhan – renwen beijing, keji beijing, lvse beijing' ['The Olympics promoted city development – Humanitarian Beijing, Hi-tech Beijing and Green Beijing'], Aoyun chengshi luntan ['Olympic Host City Forum'], 8 Aug. 2009.

[50] China Modernization Report 2005. The first modernization means the transformation from a traditional agricultural economy to a modern industrial economy and from an agrarian to an industrial society. The second economic modernization refers to the change from industrial time and society to knowledge time and society.

[51] 'Zhongguo xiandaihua yanjiu xiaozu' ['Study Task Team on China's Modernization Strategy']

[52] Hawksworth and Cookson, 'The World in 2050 Beyond the BRIC Economies, 13.

[53] Guthrie, *China and Globalization*, 291.

[54] On Foreign Direct Investment in China, see http://www.uschina.org/statistics/fdi_cumulative.html, accessed 28 Dec. 2009.

[55] National Bureau of Statistics of China, 26 Feb. 2009, available at http://data.acmr.com.cn, accessed 26 Feb. 2009.

[56] 'Zhongguo xiandai hua baogao shou chang guoji xiandaihua "heping ge" zhanlue' ['China's Modernization Report advocates for the first time the "peace pigeon" strategy of international modeernization', 29 Jan. 2008, available at http://www.sina.com.cn, accessed 29 Jan. 2008.

[57] 'Shen yubiao, tongji ju: zhongguo chengzhen renkou chao 6 yi renkou chengzhen hua sudu jianhuan' ['Statistics Bureau: China's urban population surpasses 600 million and the pace of urbanization slows down'], available at http://www.chinanews.com.cn/gn/news/2009/02-15/1563938.shtml, accessed 25 Feb. 2009.

[58] 'He Chuanqi: ao yun hui shi zhongguo canyu guoji shiwu di san ge li cheng bei' ['He Chuanqi: The Olympic Games is the third milestone of China's involvement in the international affairs'], 23 Aug. 2008, available at http://www.chinanews.com.cn/olympic/news/2008/08-23/1358297.shtml, accessed 23 Aug. 2008.

[59] David Crary, 'China strides onto Olympic stage', 8 Aug. 2008, available at http://sports.yahoo.com/olympics/news?slug=ap-openingceremony&prov=ap&type=lgns, accessed 8 Aug. 2008.

[60] Yan Tao, Chen Weihua, 'Jin 8.5 yi zhong guo guan zhong shou kan Beijing ao yun hui kai mu zhuan bo' ['Nearly 850 million Chinese viewers watched the live broadcast of the Opening Ceremony of the Beijing Games'], 9 Sept. 2008, available at www.xinhuanet.com, accessed 9 Sept. 2008.

[61] Hogan, *Gender, Race and National Identity*, .96

[62] 'Beijing Seeks Olympic Ceremony Proposals', 1 March 2005, available at crienglish.com, accessed 1 Mar. 2005.

[63] Ibid.

[64] For example, the chief designer of virtual effects, Cai Guoqiang, and the chief music designer of the opening ceremony, Chen Qigang, were overseas Chinese from USA and France respectively.

[65] 'Zhuti qingxi, chuangyi xinying, zhizuo jingliang, guoji shiye – cong Beijing ao yun hui kai mu shi kan d axing huo dong de zu zhi yun ying' ['Clear topic, novel idea, delicate making, international vision – analysis of the mega-event organization and operation from the Openning and Closing Ceremonies of Beijing Olympic Games'], *Guang Ming Ribao* [Guang Ming Daily], 20 Sept. 2008

[66] Data from interview with a Martial arts judge at the games.

[67] Hogan, *Gender, Race and National Identity*, 98.

[68] Li Huan, 'ao yun kai mu shi zhongguo yuan su jie du' ['Analysis of the Chinese Elements of the Olympic Opening Ceremony], *Hua xi du shi bao* [West China City Daily], 9 Aug. 2008.

[69] Hogan, *Gender, Race and National Identity*, 3.

[70] 'Feature: Beijing conjures Olympic opening epic with high technology', 9 Aug. 2008, available at www.chinaview.cn, accessed 9 Aug. 2008.

[71] 'Beijing uses high-tech to prevent rain from dampening Olympic opening', 28 July 2008, available at xinhuanet.com, accessed 28 Jul. 2008.

[72] Fang Ning, 'Zhe yang de ao yun hui zhi neng chu xian zai zhong guo' ['Such an Olympics can only occur in China'], *Zhong guo qing nian bao* [China Youth Daily], 26 Aug. 2008.

[73] Chen Shaoguo, 'zhongguo yi chaoyue riben chengwei shijie di er da jingji ti' [China has surpassed Japan to become the world second-largest economy], available at: http://content.caixun.com/NE/02/4r/NE024ruo.shtm, accessed 30 July 2010.

[74] Ren Zhongping, 'Beijing xin zheng tu de you yi ge qi dian – xie zai di 29 jie ao yun hui bi mu zhi ji' ['Beijing, another starting point of new journey – writing on the moment of the close if the 29th Olympiad'], *Beijing cheng bao* [Beijing Morning Post], 26 Aug. 2008.

[75] Deng Shengguo, 'Ao yun qi ji yu zhong guo zhi yuan fu wu de fa zhan' ['Olympics and the development of volunteer service in China], *Beijing xing zheng xue yuan xue bao* [Journal of Beijing Administrative College] 2 (2007).

[76] He Chuanqi, *Dong fang fu xin*.

[77] Simon Dingley, 'Final impressions of a Great Olympics, CBC News, 25 Aug. 2008.

[78] Yao Jian, ' Mei you zui hao, zhi you geng hao' ['There is not the best, but the better'], *Beijing Wan Bao* [Beijing Evening Post], 26 Aug. 2008.

[79] Melinda Liu, 'The Opening Ceremony and China's Past', 8 Aug. 2008, accessed 8 Aug. 2008.

[80] On women athletes and national identity in China, see Dong Jinxia, 'National Identity, Olympic Victory and Chinese Sportswomen'.

[81] Regarding women athletes and national identity see ibid.

[82] 'Juzhang dahui dianmin nvpai xu nuli, nvwang ticao tupo cheng kaimo' ['The Women's Volleyball Team, named by the Director of the SSA Liu Peng at a meeting, needs to make great effort, Women's tennis and gymnastics become role models for making breakthrough in performance'], 18 Jan., 2007, available at http://sports.sina.com.cn. accessed 18 Jan. 2007.

[83] 'Yi kuai jin pai de cheng ben gu suan: 3000–8000 wan' [the cost evaluation of an Olympic god medalist: 30 to 80 million], *Quan qiu chai jing guan cha* [Global Financial Observer], 21 Aug. 21, 2004.

[84] Yang Ming, Wang Jinyu and Li Li, 'Zhong guo ao yun jun tuan cheng li shi shi, can sai gui mo jug e tuan zhi shou' ['Formation and Oath of Chinese Olympic Delegation with the largest participants in the world'], 25 July 2008, available at www.xinhua.net.cn, accessed 25 Jul. 2008.

[85] Data from the Department of Economics of the State Sports Administration.

[86] Chen Weisheng, 'Ti yu zong ju fu ju zhang: guo jia jian li jin pai xuan shou mei ren 35 wan' ['Deputy Director of the National Sports Administration: The state will award each gold medallist 350,000 yuan], *Beijing Qingnian Bao* [Beijing Youth Dialy], 24 Aug. 2008.

[87] Guo jia ti yu zong ju [The National Sports Administration], '2007 nian di guo jia ti yu zong ju cai piao gong yi jin shi yong qing kuang gong gao' ['Report on the use of the national sports administration's sports lottery commonweal money in 2007'], available at http://www.sports.cn/ 2008-08-25, accessed 25 Aug. 2008.

[88] 'Yi kuai aoyun jinpai de chengben gusuan: 3000–8000 wang' ['The estimated cost of an Olympic gold medal: 30–80 million yuan'], *Quan qiu cai jing guan cha* [Global Financial Observer], 21 Aug. 2004.

[89] Mutual Funding Insurance for Elite Athletes' Injuries and Disability [*youxiu yundongyuan shanchang huzhu baoxian shixing banfa*] renti zi (2002l), no. 137, 15 April 2002, available at http://www.sport.gov.cn/show_info.php?n_id=691, accessed 15 Apr. 2002.

[90] 'Xi Jinping zhi dian wei wen gu li Liu Xiang' ['Xi Jinping made a call to sympathize and encourage Liu Xiang'], 18 Aug. 2008, available at http://www.xinhuanet.cn, accessed 18 Aug. 2008.

[91] Kobe is an NBA All-Star shooting guard for the Los Angeles Lakers. Most Chinese young people wanted to go to the basketball stadium because of him. Therefore, it was extremely difficult to get a ticket for the matches between the US and other teams.

[92] He became the most successful and popular athlete in Beijing 2008 where he won eight gold medals in swimming.

[93] Bolt not only won three gold medals in athletics, but also became the first sprinter to set three world records in the same Olympics.

[94] Dan Wetzel, 'China offers warm embrace for Team USA', 10 Aug. 2008, available at www.yahoo.com, accessed 10 Aug. 2008.

[95] Dong Jinxia, 'Women, Nationalism and the Beijing Olympics'

[96] Chao Huanrong, Hu Guo and Wang Xiaodong, 'Xu xie geng jia mei hao de "zhong guo huai juan" – wei bei jing ao yun hui chenggongbi mu er zuo' ['To continue to paint a more beautiful "Chinese picture"—for the successful closing of the Beijing Olympic Games'], *Ren Min Ri Bao [People's Daily]*, 26 August 2008.

[97] The author worked in the National Indoor Stadium. The data are either from the information provided by the venue management team or observation and interview.

[98] Yang Ming, Wang Jinyu and Li Li, 'Zhong guo ao yun jun tuan cheng li shi shi'.

[99] Zhou Yan, 'Chinese fall hard for sportsmanship, heroism at Olympics', 21 Aug. 2008, available at http://www.cctv.com/english/20080821/108950.shtml, accessed 21 Aug. 2008.

[100] Yu Jian and Li Li, 'Ao lin pi ke zhi dian' ['The summit of the Olympics'], *Beijing Wan bao [Beijing Evening Daily]*, 26 Aug. 2008.

[101] On this, see Brady, 'The Beijing Olympics as a Campaign of Mass Distraction'.

[102] Huang Yong, 'Zhongguo jiang zai gengduo de xuexiao zhong kaizhan aolinpike jiaoyu' ['China will promote Olympic education in more schools'], 18 Sept. 2007, available at http://www.xinhuanet.com, accessed 18 Sept. 2007.

[103] 'Quan guo wu da cheng shi nian zhong min yi diao cha: zhongguo ren ru he kan hi jie' ['Poll of the nation's five big cities at the end of the year: how Chinese think about the world'], *huan qiu ri bao [Global Daily]*, 31 Dec. 2006.

[104] 'Beijing 2008: BOCOG Launches Torchbearer Selection Programme', 26 June 2007, available at http://www.webwire.com/ViewPressRel.asp?aId=40575, accessed 26 June 2007.

[105] 'Why China's Burning Mad', *Time*, 24 April 2008.

[106] 'Overseas Chinese rally against biased media coverage, for Olympics', *People's Daily*, 20 April 2008; *People's Daily*, 21 April 2008.

[107] 'Kun ming wang you fa qi fan di zhi xing dong, jia le fu qian: guo qi du men shui ping za ren' ['Internet users in Kunming launched anti-boycott action, doors were stifled by national flags the and people were smashed by water bottles'], www.sina.com, 17 April 2008; 'Angry Chinese burn French flag outside Carrefour', 18 April 2008, available at http://www.reuters.com/article/topNews/idUSPEK30252620080418?feedType=RSS&feedName=topNews, accessed 18 Apr. 2008.

[108] 'Views of China and Russia Decline in Global Poll', 5 Feb. 2009, available at http://www.worldpublicopinion.org/pipa/pdf/feb09/BBCEvals_Feb09_rpt.pdf, accessed 5 Feb. 2009.

[109] Yongnian Zheng, *Discovering Chinese Nationalism in China*, 19.

[110] Dong yan, 'Ao yun hui hou de zhongguo si kao: dui hua Beijing da xue li shi xi qian cheng dan jiao shou' ['Post-Olympic thinking: dialogue with professor Qian Chengdan from the History Department of Peking University'], *zhongguo bao dao [China report]* 9 (12 Sept. 2008).

[111] Ren Zhongping, 'Beijing xin zheng tu de you yi ge qi dian – xie zai di 29 jie ao yun hui bi mu zhi ji' ['Beijing, another starting point of new journey – writing on the moment of the close if the 29th Olympiad'], *Beijing cheng bao [Beijing Morning Post]*, 26 Aug. 2008.

[112] Pew Research Center, 'Global Economic Gloom – China and India Notable Exceptions: Some Positive Signs for US Image', 12 June 20008, available at http://pewglobal.org/reports/display.php?ReportID=260, accessed 5 Feb. 2009.

[113] National Bureau of Statistics of China, 15 April 2009, available at http://data.acmr.com.cn, accessed 12 Jun. 2008.

References

Beijing shi tong ji ju [The Beijing Statistics Bureau]. *2009 beijing jing ji she hui tong ji bao gao* [2009 Social and Economic Statistics Report of Beijing]. Beijing: tong xin chu ban she [Tong Xin Press], 2009

Bostock, William W. and Gregg W. Smith. '*Towards Measuring Identity*'. *Social Science Paper Publisher*, 4, no. 1 (June 2001).

Brady, Anne-Marie. 'The Beijing Olympics as a Campaign of Mass Distraction'. *The China Quarterly*, special section on the Beijing 2008 Olympics, 2009: 1–24.

Brownell, Susan. *Beijing's Games: What the Olympics mean to China*. New York: Roman & Littlefield Publishers, 2008.

Cashmore, Ellis. *Sports Culture: An A–Z Guide*. London & New York: Routledge, 2002.

Dong Jinxia. *Women, Sport and Society in Modern China*. London: Frank Cass, 2003.

Dong Jinxia. 'Women, Nationalism and the Beijing Olympics: Preparing for Glory'. In *Modern Sport: The Global Obsession – Politics, Religion, Class, Gender: Essays in Honour of J.A. Mangan,* edited by Boria Majumdar and Fan Hong. London and New York: Routledge, 2007

Dong Jinxia. 'National Identity, Olympic Victory and Chinese Sportswomen in the Global Era'. In *The Olympics in East Asia: The Crucible of Localism, Nationalism, Regionalism, and Globalism,* edited by Bill Kelly and Susan Brownell. New Haven: Yale University Press, forthcoming.

Guthrie, Doug. *China and Globalization: The Social, Economic and Political Transformation of Chinese Society,* revised edn. New York and London: Routledge, 2009.

Hawksworth, John and Gordon Cookson. *The World in 2050 Beyond the BRIC Economies: Broader Look at Emerging Market Growth Prospects*. London: PricewaterhouseCoopers LLP, 2008

He Chuanqi. *Dong fang fu xin: xian dai hua de san tiao dao lu* ['Orient Renaissance: Three Roads to Modernization']. Beijing: Shang wu yin shua guan [Commercial Press], 2003.

Hogan, Jackie. *Gender, Race and National Identity: Nations of Flesh and Blood*. London: Routledge, 2009.

Majumdar, Boria and Fan Hong, eds. *Modern Sport: The Global Obsession – Politics, Religion, Class, Gender: Essays in Honour of J.A. Mangan,* Lodon and New York: Routledge , 2007.

Penn, 'aoyun: rang shinjie chongxin renshi "zhongguo" pingpai' [The Olympic Games let the World Know "China" Brand]. *Fortune China*, no.1, 2008, 80–81.

State Statistics Bureau. *China Statistical Yearbook*, Beijing: Zhong guo tong ji chu ban she [China Statistics Press], 1994.

Study Task Team on China's Modernization Strategy, China Center for Modernization Research, Chinese Academy of Sciences. *China Modernization Report 2005 – A Study on the Eonomic Modernization, Summary*. Beiging: Beijing University Press, 2005.

Xu Yifan, ed. *Zhongguo dui wai jing ji tong ji nian jian* ['China External Economic Statistical Yearbook']. Beijing: Zhongguo tong ji chu ban she [China Statistics Press], 1994.

Yongnian Zheng. *Discovering Chinese Nationalism in China: Modernization, Identity and International Relations*. Cambridge: Cambridge University Press, 1999.

Zhang Luya (eds.), Shiji qing – zhongguo yu aolinpike yundong [A Century of Contact – China and the Olympics]. Renmin tiyu chuban she, 1993, p.204.

Zhonggong Beijing shiwei zhuzhi bu, Beijing shi renshi ju, Beijing shi kexue jishu weiyuan hui, eds. *Xin Beijing , xin aoyun' zhishi jiangzhuo* ['Lectures on New Beijing, Great Olympics']. Beijing: Beijing Chuban she [Beijiing Publishing Press], 2006.

Zhongguo tongji nianjian [Statistical Yearbook of China], Beijing: Zhong guo tong ji chu ban she [China Statistics Press], 1993, 2001.

Olympic Aspirations: Reconstructed Images, National Identity and International Integration

Ying Yu

The 2008 Olympic Games is so significant in reconstructing Chinese nationalism as well as reshaping the state-society relationship because in the single year of 2008 most of the political mobilization and social movements were driven by the games; most of the focusing events (e.g. accidents and disasters) are redirected or reinterpreted due to the games; most of the contradictions and conflicts are concealed or exposed under the name of the games. Both the authorities and the public faced more opportunities, challenges and pressures from the domestic and international community because of the games. The reconstruction of Olympic-mobilized nationalism then lies in such dynamic official and popular responses and also reflects transforming state-society relationships.

Introduction

The Olympic Games always bring many opportunities as well as challenges to its host and to the rest of the world, while the 2008 Games in Beijing were even more spectacular and controversial at the same time. The 2008 Olympic Games will be regarded as a momentous turning point in China's reconstruction of national identity. [1] Besides presenting the stunning opening and closing ceremonies, successfully organizing such a global mega-event and becoming the top gold-medal winner, China made more efforts in urban makeover, courtesy re-establishment, cultural regeneration, environmental protection, policy reformation, technological innovation and media liberation during the pre-Olympic preparations. Motivated by such mega-catalysts, substantial and comprehensive transformations have taken place at a high speed not only materially but also psychologically. Chinese nationalism is under reconstruction by the party state and involves a more globalized, modernized, civilized and harmonized conceptualization. However, this government-led and

Olympic-initiated nationalism has faced great pressures exerted by Tibet unrest, protests around the Olympic torch relay and criticisms from Chinese dissidents on China's human rights violations and authoritarian rules as well as increasing domestic appeals by eviction victims, underpaid migrants and environmental activists. All of these have raised the question: how does the party state and the public respond differently to Western criticism and domestic crises in relation to the 2008 Olympic Games? How is this Olympic-initiated nationalism being reconstructed? How is the state-society relationship reflected during the process?

This paper believes that the initiation and re-construction of nationalism before and during the Olympic Games not only displays a new China to the world and boosts its international prestige, but more significantly, about balancing the official and popular ways in participation and in response of the transforming process. Notably, the dynamics of official and popular nationalism is the co-existence of different facets. Firstly, the nationalist and patriotic conceptualization of a great China in the light of hosting the 2008 Olympics is merged with a party-state-centred and -sponsored project, while the popular expressions of this mainstream articulation and responses to international criticism are diverse. Secondly, the Olympic re-development has exacerbated pre-existing polarisation, further projected the problems of pollution, corruption and other social injustice, which reinforced social unrest and contradictions. The interpretations of national identity are then contested between the Party-state, the disadvantaged groups, and various dissident groups who propose more radical solutions and demand more public hearings in the wake of the historic moment of the Olympic Games in Beijing. However, because these voices are conflicting, deviated and controversial, most of them are marginalized from the general public discussion as being devastating to social stability, to the national image and to the Games. Thirdly, the official and popular forces working to re-establish the national identity have been brought together most remarkably from the time of the Wenchuan Earthquake up to the Games with mutual trust arising between the state and society with a development of the use of cyberspace. However, as tested by continual state-society negotiation and conflicts of interest, such collaboration is still unstable, non-institutionalised and fluctuant. This paper will demonstrate these three aspects respectively and conclude that state-society relations are being dynamically re-structured, connected with the nationalism re-construction in the pre-, mid- and post-Olympic era, with an enlarging private and civic sphere promoting individual and group rights, diversification and creativity and transforming the Party-state responses.

Converged but Diverse

National identity, which is an introversive counterpart of its extroversive national image, is politically, socially and psychologically established. In China since the epoch of reform and opening up, the establishment of national identity has mainly been dominated by the Party-state behaviour in tandem with China's increased economic power and enhanced national prestige. Nationalism (*minzuzhuyi* in Chinese) has then been promoted by the Chinese Communist Party (CCP) as an assertive and patriotic ideology to legitimise its power. [2] As for hosting the Olympics, promoting a new national image internationally was one of China's key strategic goals. [3] The new image aimed to allay international fears about China's increasing political, economic and military power, while at the same time projecting international awareness and acceptance of its renewed strength and prosperity. [4] Meanwhile the popular establishment has been basically in compliance with this Olympic-oriented official ideology.

The official voice of the party state described China as a 'peacefully rising' great power [5] that was working for a 'harmonious world' within the international system, based on the domestically promoted theory of 'harmonious society'. [6] This Chinese foreign policy narrative of a 'harmonious world' was then co-opted into the 2008 Olympics slogan 'One World, One Dream'. [7] The domestic masses were also mobilized with soft propaganda messages aiming at gaining social and political stability such as the two-year 'Welcome the Beijing Olympics campaign'. [8] The Party state has taken conscious actions for national convergence such as in its economic, political, ethnic and religious policies during the preparation for the Games. Nation-building and stability maintenance has thus been prioritised in this stand and has guided a series of nationalist movements in response to the waves of domestic and international protests in the run-up to the Beijing Olympics.

Tibetan protestors were the most violent and radical as Buddhist monks and other ethnic Tibetans erupted in March 2008 following the 49th anniversary of the Tibetan Uprising of 1959 and reached a climax in their clash with Chinese security forces in Lhasa, the Tibetan capital. The 2008 Olympic Torch relay was another uneasy period. When the torch was lit on Mount Olympia in Greece on 24 March 2008, the ceremony was disrupted by members of 'Reporters without Borders' and 'Free Tibet' activists. Clashes occurred along the route of the torch in London, Paris, San Francisco and India and even in Hong Kong. There was fierce official condemnation of the 'Dali clique', 'splittist forces', 'international reactionary forces' and 'biased foreign media' and a call to congregate all Chinese people in preventing the subversion and sabotage of the Olympic Games. The CCP government explicitly linked support for the Olympics to patriotism, so for anyone to oppose or in any way criticise the Olympics was to be unpatriotic or, for foreigners, anti-China. [9] The general public has responded to the call actively and empowered nationalism against the unpleasant international environment, as people were claiming to have even greater pride and responsibility of the nation when facing threats towards the Olympics. The official guidance of 'Olympics put first' and the maxim of non-interference worked especially well with the majority of the younger generation and urban middle class in China, who had a strong self-identity and identitified with the nation-state while employing a more radical means of expression.

The Games has thus witnessed the continuity of the Party-state's efforts to reconstruct a harmonious national identity and an Olympic-driven nationalism, but has also revealed new trends among the public. There were diverse presentations of pro-active and re-active nationalism. In essence pride in the nation and resentment against those perceived as attacking or harming its interests. The most prominent trend was the 'internet nationalism', which has become popular since the 2005 anti-Japanese protests. [10] Chinese netizens [11] showed their support for Chinese sovereignty and administration of Tibet by collecting and spreading evidence of the true face of Western media in the Tibet riot [12] to disprove and criticise Western perceived and biased coverage of Tibet. The whole campaign began with an individual effort initiated by a 20 year-old Canadian Chinese young man who first created the video 'Tibet was, is and always will be a part of China', [13] to 'tell the world a real Tibet'. After two weeks this had received over 2 million clicks and tens of thousands of comments. It was reported on CCTV, forwarded by bloggers and major Chinese portal sites, followed by a spontaneous establishment of particular forums/websites such as www.anti-cnn.com and a series of further analyses by Chinese scholars on Western media agenda.

Chinese people overseas, mainly students, also organised and called for demonstrations against Tibet independence and Western media distortion as they managed to support and protect the Olympic torch relay. They had fierce fights physically against the pro-Tibet protesters and other anti-Chinese government forces in major cities of Canada, Australia, USA, UK, France, and Germany and discursively through online websites, forums, instant messaging and emailing mobilisation, which were widely reported by Chinese domestic media but largely ignored by Western counterparts. [14] The post-1980s and post-1990s Chinese students studying abroad were also portrayed as a generation of loyal and fervent followers of the party-state line on nationalism, who echoed the government's anti-Western and nationalist propaganda in a series of debates over human rights in Taiwan, Tibet and Falun Gong.

From another angle, the divergence of nationalist sentiments lay in the informal, casual, vivid and radical way of communicating rather than completely complying with official channels both online and offline. Creative strategies by netizens have emerged for nationalist expressions and protests inside and outside China. The 'I (Heart) China' movement spread like wildfire over MSN to millions of Chinese netizens in two days. [15] 'Don't be too CNN' – a retort in the form of musical ditty to western media outlets such as CNN and the BBC also caught the imagination of Chinese blogs and chat-rooms and were disseminated throughout online communities. [16] Offline activities also quickly converged with the online information flow. For example, Olympic protests in Paris during the torch relay had drawn particular indignation in China and led to calls for a boycott of French goods, resulting in a large-scale Carrefour boycott in Beijing, Wuhan and other major cities. [17] With nationalist sentiments heating up, printed T-shirts with creative nationalist slogans, which in Chinese were called *wenhua shan* (cultural T-shirts), suddenly became very popular in the free markets of Beijing in the few months before the Olympics. There were even anti-CNN T-shirts and a line of related products released immediately after the CNN host's insulting words shocked and infuriated Chinese at home and abroad; proving that in certain situations in China, politics quickly becomes fashion. [18]

Human flesh search engines [19], which mobilised a large number of young and well-educated citizens to participate in searching for and punishing individual perpetrators of morality crimes [20] were also politicized and widely used during the waves of nationalist explosions. Grace Wang, a Chinese student at Duke University in the USA, was one of the most famous targets. On the day of the Olympic torch relay in San Francisco, Wang encountered a handful of students gathered for a pro-Tibet vigil facing off with a much larger pro-China counter-demonstration. She had written 'Free Tibet' on a protester's back and later defended her action in the *Washington Post*, saying that 'I did this at his request, and only after making him promise that he would talk to the Chinese group.' Having been spotted by other overseas Chinese and identified as having betrayed her country, some angry Chinese students immediately launched a human flesh search engine witch hunt on the Chinese language online portal Tianya. They found personal information about Wang and her family and began the torrents of horrid abuse. Grace Wang said her parents had to go into hiding in China, with no help from the police. [21] It is argued that as the Chinese continued to over-react to international criticisms and unpatriotic behaviours with hypersensitivity and rage, China indeed disseminated a carnivorous nationalism, wherein love of one's own nation was intertwined with hatred of and aggression towards other groups. [22]

The Olympics-related contentions about the Tibet turmoil and the Olympic Torch Relay had driven the nationalist movement to a climax, which took the form of public demonstrations, newspaper editorials, online petitions, and other internet activism. Such nationalist reaction and re-construction involved both official and popular forces. Notably the Party-state had taken a leading role in converging all attributions while popular expression and participation became increasingly diverse within the enlarging cyberspace activity, as shown in the large-scale nationalist campaigns on the internet.

The internet has given nationalists more power to vent their anger and these above mentioned incidents have clearly illustrated the huge influence of the Chinese in Southeast Asia, Europe, and North America and their close contact with mainland residents through the internet. Undoubtedly the pro-China, anti-Tibet separatist and anti-Western biased media sentiments in Chinese cyberspace became a landmark of 'internet nationalism' in China. It has also proved, similar to the anti-Japan campaign in 2005, that nationalism has reshaped the crucial elements underlying most popular political communication in cyberspace, and the offline nationalist movements have become more connected and intertwined with online activism. [23] The Chinese government could further employ the internet to develop what has been begun by its citizens through the medium of the internet to advance its national interests in the international arena. [24]

As for state-society dynamics, firstly, the converged and officialdom-led nationalism still dominates Chinese society. No matter how diverse the expressions and responses towards international criticisms, the popular mindset was still non-interference: the domestic problems could be discussed domestically, but foreign criticism was hardly accepted or admitted.

Secondly, the popular diversity has challenged the official boundaries especially on media openness and tolerance. When the Chinese authorities first removed the BBC ban after the Tibet riot and opened domestic access to other foreign media, there was a great deal of negative online comment in China against the BBC and others that was unexpectedly antagonistic to the habitual thinking and one-sided coverage by Westerners. [25] The government quickly learned from this and its practice was becoming 'let people judge'. The authorities also realised that China needed strategic and genuine communication with outside world. After the Tibet riot, during the interrupted Olympic torch relay and the global human rights protests related to Olympic Games, the authorities have further lifted restrictions on the domestic media including the internet and tried to guide the public nationalist sentiments in debates to support the Beijing Olympics and against the Western critics.

Thirdly, it also proved that the survivability of a diverse range of public opinion and popular nationalist participation could only be guaranteed when it was aligned with the interest of the state. This fact strongly demonstrated that the internet could also function as a state activation apparatus in domestic as well as international online political communication. [26]

Conflictive but Marginalized

It is well known that tensions over the widening income gap, official corruption, power abuse, falling social services, and self-serving alliances between Party leaders and businessmen have increased during China's modernising progresses. However, Olympic re-development has exacerbated such pre-existing polarisation, further projected the problems of pollution and corruption, reinforced social unrest and increased appeals by under-paid migrants, eviction victims and human rights activists. These domestic contradictions have become even more conflictive when domestic problems have become 'internationalised' through the reports of human rights organisations or foreign news media as a consequence of increased global attention on the Olympic Games.

According to Amnesty, [27] China promised an improvement in human rights, media freedom and better provision in health and education. Instead, it said, 'Beijing has locked up, put under house arrest and forcibly removed individuals they believed may threaten the image of stability and harmony they wanted to present to the world during Olympic Games'. The Games have indeed made life more difficult for many of the poor in China. One of the heaviest sufferers were the migrant workers. As Beijing moved into the midst of the biggest makeover in its history, with over 10,000 building sites and huge construction projects all over the city, about one million migrants formed 90 per cent of Beijing's vast army of construction workers. However, many of them suffered a range of abusive conditions and discriminatory treatment from their employers and the government and often lacked basic health care and protection, as reported by Human Rights Watch. [28] In the approach to the Beijing Olympic Games those migrant workers were further blamed for overcrowded communities, deteriorating public security, environment and hygiene problems. According to Beijing's pre-Olympic clean-up campaign, which involved regulations restricting registration, halting construction in the city, shutting factories and limiting the number of cars on the road to help combat chronic pollution and a security crackdown, many migrant workers had to go home or seek jobs in other cities. [29] However, the voice of this disadvantaged and deprived group could hardly reach domestic public discussion or gain a strong public hearing.

Land-related disputes have remained another chief cause of social disturbances in China, since a growing awareness that much new wealth and corruption arose from real-estate development and speculation – often at the direct expense of the poor – has sparked demands for a modicum of distributive justice. [30] Evictions have undoubtedly affected and seriously victimized the urban poor, especially laid-off workers, [31] who were sometimes violently forced out of their houses with little compensation. Such violence often involved a combination of public security forces and mafia forces hired by the developers. These confrontations between evictees, urban planners, estate developers and security forces were also intensified by the overall makeover of the urban landscape in the pre-Olympics time. Anger stemmed not just from the loss of residence and livelihood, but also from the violation of fundamental citizenship rights. However, the highest emphasis was placed by the authorities on control and stability behind the Olympics spectacles and the 'laobaixing' (common people) were urged to sacrifice compliantly or be punished. For example, there were protesters who persisted in raising the issue of inadequate compensation for housing demolished as part of the Olympic preparations who were sentenced to a year's 're-education through labour'. [32]

It is also noticeable that Chinese dissidents, who still had deep affections, attachments and national identities, were more likely to develop nationalism in a cosmopolitan sense and work to integrate it with universal values of human rights and democracy to transform China. These dissident movements and cyberspace activists were mainly established in Western developed countries, taking advantage of the environment for intellectual and other freedoms , and access to information. They regarded themselves as more objective, precise and critical of what happened in China and in the outside world, and as both actors and outsiders in the patriotic movement. The internet was chosen as their main battlefield on which to reveal the existing problems of an authoritarian China, to circulate their viewpoints and ideals, and to influence overseas Chinese students. The pressure on democratisation and the improvement of China's human rights record from Chinese communities abroad was growing in pre-Olympic period. There were also numerous offline demonstrations and rallies and other international appeals along with on-line websites, forums and publications.

The contentions of dissidents have shown an increasing union with with those of domestic human rights defenders, disadvantaged groups and victims of brutal land grabbing, forced eviction, exploitation of labour, and arbitrary detention. This has been shown in the list of demands presented in a typical open letter published online to Chinese leaders before the 2008 Olympic Games:

1. Declare amnesty for all prisoners of conscience so that they can enjoy the Olympic Games in freedom;
2. Open China's borders to all Chinese citizens who have been forced into exile for their beliefs, expression or faith, so that they can reunite with their loved ones and celebrate the glory of the Olympics in their motherland;
3. Implement the government ordinance to allow foreign journalists to conduct interviews and reporting without pre-approval by authorities before 17 October 2008, granting Chinese journalists the same access and independence;
4. Provide fair compensation to the victims of forced evictions and land appropriations that have been done in order to construct Olympic facilities, and release people who have been detained or imprisoned (often violently) for protesting or resisting such actions;
5. Protect the rights of workers on all Olympic construction sites, including their right to organize independent labour unions; end discrimination against rural migrant labourers and give them fair compensation;
6. End police operations intended to intercept, detain or send home petitioners who try to travel to Beijing to complain about local officials' misconduct; abolish illegal facilities used for incarcerating, interrogating and terrorizing petitioners; end the 'clean up' operations aimed at migrants that demolish their temporary housing and close down schools for their children;
7. Establish a system of citizen oversight over Olympics spending and provide public accounting and independent auditing of Olympics-related expenditures; make the process of awarding contracts to businesses transparent; and hold legally accountable any official who embezzles or wastes public funds. [33]

While nationalism and patriotism have been deeply rooted in overseas Chinese intellectual communities and have motivated them to be involved in the continuous pro-democracy movements outside China, it was still a nationalist sentiment advanced by the Chinese party state to disclaim them as anti-China plotters in association with foreign hostile forces. The creed of liberal democracy was no longer the common faith of domestic intellectuals; it was further questioned as representing no more than the imposition of Western values and standards on developing nations such as China. For some domestic scholars, the promotion by Western countries of democracy and human rights in China was designed both to defame, divide and weaken Chinese competitive ability. [34] Therefore, for decades the influence of Chinese dissidents overseas seemed to be limited to a small circle of intellectuals and it was difficult to break through the mainland's information block and reach a wide audience. They were usually accused of lacking patriotic sentiment or of worshipping the Western system and powers. This was partly because most exiles were seen as people who were prepared to do anything – including asylum-seeking – to get a green card abroad.

In the light of preparing for the Olympic Games with a more prestigious international status for China, the public were more concerned about issues such as the speed, pace and scale of modernization, national sovereignty and international status as showcased in the Olympic Games than which political form the government should take – liberal democratic or authoritarian. It was also part of the strategy of the authorities to blur the differences, to justify the status quo, maintain national cultural identity and dignity and to marginalize liberal democracy. The justification for accelerating the process of modernization with a nationalist call has largely outweighed cultural criticism and opposition thinking, and shown an intentional avoidance of sensitive socio-political issues. [35] On the other hand, a propaganda campaign of mass distraction described by Dr Ann-Marie Brady was designed to mobilize the population around a common goal, and distract them from more troubling issues such as inflation, unemployment, corruption or environmental degradation. [36]

For the party state, and indeed for many Chinese citizens, hosting the Olympics was always more about international image and domestic prestige [37] than a time to expose inner problems. Though there were numberless appellants and petitioners waiting and queuing at the national petition office every day with various grievances, no matter how conflicting or peaceful they were, they were largely restricted and marginalized – or popularly speaking – 'harmonized'. The party state has focused rather on a top-down construction of a harmonious society and scientific thinking on development by initiating new policies to solve rising social problems [38] than facing bottom-up challenges. The term 'harmonious society' became a party mantra and a classical notion of social order in which people do not challenge their role in life and treat each other kindly. Traditional cultures have also been revived, not only in the party's propaganda efforts but also during the Olympic ceremonies, as a way of giving China more cohesion in its state of rapid economic and social flux. Confucius has been restored as a moral exemplar emblematic of service to the state and respect for hierarchical authority and hence lending traditional weight to the party state's watchword of social stability. [39]

This idea of bringing opposites into harmony, as a traditional Chinese value, has been relevant today. [40] Indeed, China's national image claimed to harmonize opposites, even though these 'opposites' were not admitted into an equal dialogue. The power between party-state nationalist discourse and other interpretations was largely unbalanced and deeply unequal. The authorities still dominated the nationalist tune and rule-making. As part of the policy adaptation required in order to adhere to Olympic traditions such as free expression outside sporting venues, China innovatively announced before the games that it had set up zones in three Beijing parks where demonstrators could legally stage protests during the Olympic

Games. [41] Though there was hardly any approval, it was claimed that this legally provided measure would help reduce the risk that unexpected large-scale demonstrations would harm the public interest. The motive of protecting the majority interest became the official rhetoric of democracy during the politically sensitive period of the Olympic Games, while stability became the basic human right. The time when the games were in progress seemed not a good time to vent any private or public grievance that contradicted the official Chinese interpretation of democracy and human rights.

As might be concluded, the response to varied Olympic-related problems revealed different social groups – especially disadvantaged and dissident groups – striving to make sense of their own situations, assert their own influences and seek feasible solutions to their problems in an effort to interact effectively with the authorities in the wake of the Olympic Games; their petitions were regarded as conflictive and disruptive by the authorities as well as the majority of the populace. Their efforts to connect nationalism and the Olympics with democracy and human rights as alternative perspectives basically failed to challenge the officially monopolized narrative or change the unequal power structure.

Collaborative but Fluctuant

During the transformation of nationalism in the run-up to the games, there also appeared to be collaboration between the state and society. The authorities cooperated to different extents with associated actors and organizations in order to guide the pace of the action and therefore achieve their intended goal. Such collaboration was still fluctuant because although the party state was attempting to have equal dialogue with society it was also sometimes authoritarian and repressive. Notably the natural catastrophe of the Wenchuan earthquake on 12 May both initiated and tested such collaboration in national identity reconstruction.

When this devastating earthquake happened, the presence of highly-developed communications including the Internet, live broadcasts and other forms of mobile communication greatly facilitated and affected the way people received and spread information. In a very short time the destruction caused by the earthquake was well-known and became the focus of global broadcasts covering topics related to the disaster. The awareness and power of citizens and netizens can be shown in their response to appeals and participation in charitable contributions and appeals, along with their voicing of suspicions, critiques and revelations of the truth. There was a spontaneous organizing of a range of activities to search for those missing, disseminate touching stories, give blood, raise funds, transport materials, and provide medical support as well as psychological counselling.

The eroded social ethos, value vacuum, worship of money and materialism was transformed into empathy, mercy, selflessness, caring, mutual trust and help through a volunteer ethos. Moreover, when the nationalist youth of the time experienced the catastrophe of the earthquake and acutely felt the pain, they also began to develop an understanding of catastrophes that had happened in other countries. The grave experience melted away the public rage, cruelty, and violence generated in response to the Tibet turmoil and the disturbances associated with the Olympic torch relay, and made young people more tolerant to different voices in the international community. As for the cohesion and maturation of Chinese nationality, it found the pivot of revitalization for rationality, tolerance, democracy and civilization through great sufferings and struggles.

It is remarkable that on 18 May the State Council decided that the whole country would mourn for the tens of thousands earthquake victims for three days from 19 to 21 May. During the mourning period, all national flags at home and at Chinese missions abroad were flown at half-mast, and public recreational activities were cancelled. The public, including professors and experts, actively expressed approval for such governmental action. This was an extremely rare experience in China, and it was seen as precious and meaningful that for the first time the CCP had established a period of national mourning on behalf of ordinary people. Internally the government showed more concern about people's livelihood, embodied in the concept that 'your pain is my pain' (the government is also suffering the pain of people). [42] Externally, it was also in line with international practice, which showed that China had learned from international experiences and sought to be more easily acceptable to the world. The three-day pause in the torch relay was also an acknowledgement that the Olympic Games should give way to the tragic loss of life. When this regime, often regarded as ignoring and violating human rights by the West, paid great respect to every life under the ruined town, China's image as a nation was gradually seen to be both enlightened and humanistic.

Apart from spontaneous individual and collective contributions, hundreds of NGOs were also active in varied ways to provide help and support during the Wenchuan earthquake. Aided by the proliferation of online bulletin boards, blogs and on-the-ground coordination centres, unregistered grass-roots organizations, considered to be weak due to their lack of a supportive environment, were essentially functioning as legitimate earthquake-relief NGOs and helped to manage the crisis. [43] Some organizations mobilized teams of volunteers in the quake zone almost as quickly as the People's Liberation Army, which showed effective organizing capabilities in terms of the rescue work and also proved itself to be a healthy and positive force in society. In fact in terms of both disaster relief and reconstruction after the earthquake, over three million Chinese volunteers and over 300 NGOs played an unprecedented active role. This massive collective participation has created waves of voluntary movements within civil society. [44] The central authority then realized the strength of these civil forces in spheres that governmental hands found it difficult to reach. It also promoted current government thinking on the need to build a (managed) civil society in China. [45] So some of the restrictions on the registration of social organizations were eased after the earthquake, and some of the restrictive policies became ones of encouragement, guidance and cooperation. Local officials have also been increasingly open-minded towards local non-governmental organizations and have been more efficient in dealing with registration procedures. 2008 could be marked as the first year of an NGO era or a volunteers' era. The disasters have recharged collective values and nationalist sentiments among Chinese people, who have also regained some social consciousness and seen an easing of tension in the state-society relationship.

There was a continuity from the time of the Wenchuan earthquake through to the Beijing Olympics in building up a national identity of collectivity, morality and volunteerism based on the collaboration between state and society. A more equal interaction between state and society and the recognition of people's power has also been a theme from the time of China's bidding for the Olympic Games. On 8 August 2008, it was hoped that the opening ceremony would present the world with a vision of China as a modern, open and humanist society that 'put the people first' and 'makes people the focus'. [46] The director Zhang Yimou and his colleagues concentrated much on the fulfilment of a humanity that acted for the collective good, which was a neat interpretation of the transforming party line. [47] The attempt was to bring together and orchestrate various social sections behind this initiative to build up to a 'High Level Olympics with Distinguishing Features' [48] and with an emphasis on participation and state-managed volunteerism. During the Olympic period, nationalist sentiments had been institutionalized as a vital input in domestic mobilization, a source of legitimation, a tool for consensus building between the state and the society and for bridging the divide among the different sections of society. [49]

A case in point is the Olympic education [50] action plan. There was not only a 'top down' effort imposed by the party state but also a subterranean, non-official 'people's' or civil effort that was supported by the eight legally-recognized non-Communist parties through consultation. [51] This effort included organizing academic and professional conferences, public lectures, museum exhibitions and teacher training classes, inventing textbooks and courses for schools and universities, producing educational television and radio shows, magazine and newspaper essays, websites and more. At the point where 'state' met 'society', collaboration lay in the de-politicization of Olympics-branded patriotic education that linked national identity with sports heroes rather than political systems, and re-shaped old nationalist symbols by new associations with symbols of internationalism, the global community and world peace. [52] The success of non-political Olympic education brought new dynamics into existing socialist moral education and proved more acceptable, attractive, effective and inclusive for students, teachers, parents and the public in general. Such reconciliation between nationalism and internationalism has also indicated that China's 'soft power' was associated with a growing awareness and significance of its position on the international stage while the Olympics was used to tell China's story to the world. [53]

As for state-media relations, 2008 was a momentous year which challenged the coverage, circulation and impact of the Chinese state and mass media, as well as Western media from the time of the Tibet riot, the Olympic torch relay and the

Sichuan earthquake, right up to the Olympic Games. Especially on such huge events and vital moments, the government response gradually changed from an initial old instinctive blocking of sensitive information to a proactive approach to a liberalization of the state and mass media. As a result, the party state has tasted the sweetness of a positive image construction at both domestic and international levels, with public sentiment being supportive of the government and dismissive of Western media. As Chinese netizens were communicating daily beyond national borders on numerous issues concerning China's politics, international relationships and the prospects for Chinese civilization as well as local administration, judicatory and personal morality, the government has increasingly been forced to take critical public opinion into account because of its inherent mobilizing potential. The scope of a more obvious dialogue between state and society has significantly widened [54] and it is true that constructive and creative negotiation has gradually replaced direct confrontations. China has been trying to show to the world a true, real China, with its high efficiency, collective strength, openness, transparency and harmony between state and society.

However, such collaboration is unstable, selective and fluctuant. In terms of its relationship with NGOs, even when the government *was* showing a more welcome face to professional, executive and business-oriented charity foundations, it still insisted upon high compulsory requirements for registration that excluded most active environmental NGOs, health or legal consultancy organizations and most human-rights advocates. As for the defending of individual and collective rights, initial toleration of protests by parents whose children had been killed by the collapse of school buildings had given way, by the end of the year, to a clampdown on continued expressions of discontent on this issue. As for media control, in the period just before and during the Beijing Olympics, news was suppressed of a breaking scandal over the contamination of powdered milk with a chemical designed to boost its apparent protein content. Central government stipulations that only 'positive' news be reported during the Olympics appeared to have prevented or deterred both local officials from taking action and the Chinese media from publicizing this issue earlier. It was only after the Olympics that news of the scandal surfaced and action was taken to withdraw tainted products from circulation. By then however, a number of children had died and several hundred more were taken ill. [55]

With reference to the Internet in particular, cyberspace has provided an officially co-opted and tolerated outlet for nationalistic sentiments as long as the postings were not directed against the Chinese government and did not challenge state policies. [56] Otherwise cyberspace was not always a free environment where people could experiment with various identities without fear of social, political or legal repercussions – especially at the time when the Olympics were regarded as a sensitive topic. There were government regulations, censorship and occasional clampdowns on Internet use and it was easy for censors to delete comments deemed offensive or dangerous to the 'discursive environment' of the games. Supervision and control mechanisms, preventive regulations and repressive actions were implemented at central, local, institutional and individual levels. It is argued that the Internet has actually reinforced surveillance and social control and strengthened the apparatus of the ideological state. [57]

Therefore complete transformation is still a long way off. To avoid going backwards, this process of state-society collaboration should be institutionalized: a system should be built for NGOs and public media so they can participate in an orderly way. [58] Those NGOs currently tolerated should not be forced underground again; those existing reporting media and Internet forums should not be blocked again; citizens who defend their own, or others', rights should not be arrested or accused of subverting state power. All the setbacks should be seen as bigger challenges for a reconstruction of nationalism and reshaping of the state-society relationships in manner beneficial to both the nation and the people.

Reflections

Chinese people did have, to different degrees, an emotional attachment to the nation; a sense of duty to the nation; a sense of the precedence of national over individual and regional interests and a desire for China to be a more powerful nation. The 2008 Beijing games were seen as an excellent opportunity for the Chinese to mobilize and reconstruct such nationalist sentiments, to show the world a new China and to help the Chinese demonstrate their 'can-do' spirit and thus become confident in themselves and their nation. [59]

The convergent facet of nationalism was to use the Olympics as a symbol for China's unity and rising power in global affairs. [60] Hosting the Olympics was intended to improve China's international profile by reshaping its international image as well as increasing public approval and domestic support for the government. The pride of being Chinese was getting reinforced during the preparation for the event and further augmented during the actual games. The splendour of the Olympics shone through the two-week spectacle with multiple connections developed between state and society towards producing Olympic civilization, modernization and champions. From the Chinese viewpoint, the Olympic dictum of 'faster, higher and longer' resonated across its society, culture, politics and the economy. [61] As a result, the 2008 Olympic Games in China were deemed a sporting and public relations triumph and a major source of national pride for both the Chinese government and the Chinese people. However, this rosy depiction was only part of the picture.

The above-mentioned three aspects of nationalism reconstruction – diverse convergence, marginal conflict and fluctuant collaboration – also demonstrated the characteristics of the state-society relationship. Even though the party state was still taking a leading role, popular diversity and self-consciousness grew to an extent that the state had to acknowledge such transformations and be responsive and cooperative. While official nationalism was trying to include all social classes in a common national goal under the party's leadership at the special moment of the

Olympic Games, there was a non-governmental multiculturalism and divergence re-emerging outside the reach of the party state's controlling hand; conflicting with it or negotiating with it. In fact different groups had varied degrees and ways in which to express nationalism. They were attached to different versions of nationalism, which can be emotional, cultural, liberal and pragmatic. There has been an attempt to both 'self-build' and re-build Chinese national identity during self-reflections between the party state and society.

Firstly, the converging nationalism and nationalist movements attached to the Tibet unrest and the torch relay were under constant reflection within both authority and intellectual circles. The party state was fully aware that nationalism was clearly a double-edged sword. [62]. On the one hand, with pro-China demonstrations spreading, Chinese Foreign Ministry spokeswoman Jiang Yu said that Chinese protesters were determined to safeguard China's national interests. She said she believed the patriotic enthusiasm displayed by Chinese people was 'encouraging' and 'touching'. [63] On the other hand, while many *fen qing* (angry youth), [64] displaying the most heated patriotic enthusiasm for the nation, became the most radical and active vanguards in pro-China and defending-Olympics activities against 'international reactionary forces', the party state also realized that an excessive encouragement of patriotic feelings also had dangerous and negative aspects. The important risks lay in the potential for public discontent and nationalist anger that, once unleashed, could be difficult to contain. [65] So the coopting of and support for nationalist movements was also combined with tight surveillance and occasional repression. The authorities were also aware that they should be particularly careful if this impacted upon their most important strategic relationships, e.g. with the USA or Europe. Chinese leaders also feared that any potential nationalism could be used not just for conferring legitimacy on the government but also for taking it away, [66] since it could turn against them in the form of criticism if they failed to deliver on their nationalistic promises.

Certain aspects of popular nationalist behaviour were also under the scrutiny of the public, of intellectuals and of students themselves. The utilization of the 'human flesh search engine' referred to previously was criticized as having bordered on a lynch-mob mentality. [67] Such moral judgements and consequent implementation, with an assumption of moral superiority or nationalist justification, were based on a form of collective violence, which gave birth to new terms such as 'Internet punk' or 'Internet mob'. Therefore some rational and reflective netizens opposed the use of such nationalist contentions as an outlet for indignation. They called for more complete Internet laws, a cessation of cyber-violence, [68] a collective expression of netizen rationality for social conscience and for nationalism. These reflections and efforts have been regarded as opportunities to rebuild a Chinese national value system, since it is argued that the simple-minded, ignorant nationalism of angry youth should be transformed into rational calls for a democratic and legal system. There are also intellectuals now trying to adopt a broad sense of nationalism, not negatively exclusive, revengeful or arrogant; but a positive, inclusive and comprehensive nationalism – a self-renewing nationalism that will learn from other countries and cultures, rediscover and preserve its own national merits and reconstruct Chinese national identity. [69]

Secondly, the party state could tolerate diversified expression and participation of its converged nationalist goal towards the Olympics. However, there were certain premises and boundaries that could not be compromised by the party state. China has always fought hard against cultists, splittists, human-rights activists and all other dissidents with little tolerance for deviant voices of whatever persuasion, and other contentious disadvantaged groups who have also been at the boundaries of toleration. There has still been a heavy use of controlling measures, which seek to intimidate potential protesters and encourage self-policing. On the other hand, the atmosphere created by intensive Olympic propaganda also saw nationalistic responses and support from the majority of the general public, particularly urban youth. Many citizens felt the government had been more open, adaptive and positive in dealing with problems, and they believed that it was necessary for the government to take action to suppress social instabilities at the time of the Olympic Games. Within this intellectual ethos, where nationalism also outweighed democratism, pro-democracy and rights-defending sentiments were marginalized for the general public as contrary to nationalism and social stability. However, the dissident voices were concurrently driven underground or outside China, and even became the seeds for the mobilization of new secret societies or the basis for miscommunications between Chinese and international society. Not surprisingly, popular protests and contentious activities, including the most challenging and confrontational examples, still occurred frequently, despite tight control by the party state.

Thirdly, the party state realized the power and strength of people in the period following the Wenchuan earthquake, and in the process of preparing and holding the games. The party was both adept and sophisticated at moulding its ideology to be 'people-oriented' to fit practical reality [70] with great flexibility and adaptability. The nationalist and moral re-establishment motivated by the earthquake relief could be a massive lesson for the authorities in realizing the importance of collaboration between the people and social organizations. Urban makeover, cultural regeneration, environmental protection, policy reformation, technological innovation and the mobilization of resources during the Olympics all required collaboration between people and society. Inclusiveness and cooperation were also required to overcome critical situations, showcase achievements and to solve problems. While the party state was learning how to cooperate and engage with society, such liaison was also fluctuant. However, one of the most engaging ways was to acknowledge the power of the Internet.

Characterized by publicity, openness, interactivity, diversity and instantaneity, network media have changed the logic of the public agenda. [71] Although the Internet has not dramatically disrupted the basic structure of power relations among state, society and individuals, because of its porous nature it has fundamentally reinvented grass-roots social and political activism by breathing new life into cyberspace networks and by devolving power into the hands of individuals and marginal groups in different ways. [72] The Internet could facilitate the formation of public opinion, the orchestration of popular political movements and the production of a trans-boundary public sphere. Gradually maturing public opinion and the collective civic wisdom of netizens have also promoted a willingness on the part of the Chinese government to frequently take action to address issues of concern to Chinese netizens. [73] There has been the possibility of mutual dialogue between leaders and citizens rather than the previous strictly 'top-down' communications. Though there has still been strict Internet censorship, due to the vast size of China, the spread and influence of information has often been beyond the controlling capacity of state hands. Freedom of expression has expanded considerably and the boundaries of the arbitrarily set 'limited zones of freedom' have constantly been tested and renegotiated.

In general the Olympics-mobilized reconstruction of nationalism is optimistic and gives hope for further positive transformations. It is also admitted that the relationship between state and society contains missing links and implies unequal power structures. An old Chinese proverb says that 'to lose is sometimes to gain'. Chinese authorities should learn how to wisely lose control of society, give up power to the people, build up mutual negotiation and dialogue and explore mechanisms to provide more social spaces and institutions for these to take place. Only after this can they gain genuine authority, legitimacy, popular support, social stability and harmony.

Notes

[1] Xu, *Olympic Dreams*.

[2] Wei and Liu, *Chinese Nationalism in Perspective*.

[3] Xinhua News, 'BOCOG adviser: The Olympics is a turning point for the strategy of promoting the national image', available at http://news.xinhuanet.com/politics/2008-08/04/content_8934954.htm, accessed 11 Oct. 2008.

[4] Brady, 'The Beijing Olympics as a Campaign of Mass Distraction'.

[5] Zheng, 'China's "Peaceful Rise" to Great-Power Status'.

[6] Zheng and Sow, 'Harmonious Society and Harmonious World'.

[7] Callahan, 'Patriotic Cosmopolitanism'.

[8] Brady, 'The Beijing Olympics as a Campaign of Mass Distraction'.

[9] Ibid.

[10] During the 2005 anti-Japan protests, the Internet played an essential role in organizing public demonstrations and parades in major cities regarding the time, venue, route, slogans and other instructions. Online messages about real-time protest pictures and information were circulated via Internet forums, BBS, emails, SMS and texts, and called for ongoing recruitment (J. Yardley, 'A Hundred Cellphones Bloom, and Chinese Take to the Streets', *New York Times*, 25 April 2005, avilable at http://www.nytimes.com/2005/04/25/international/asia/25china.html, accessed 2 Oct. 2008.

[11] 'Netizen', a portmanteau of Internet and citizen, was coined by Michael Hauben in 1992 (Hauben and Hauben, *Netizens*) and refers to people who use Internet resources and engage in online communities through participation, contribution, creation and other responsible actions.

[12] Youtube, 'Tibet, True face of western media', available at http://www.youtube.com/watch?v= hX280NmYrWs, accessed 5 Oct. 2008.

[13] Youtube, 'Tibet was, is and always will be a part of China', available at http://www.youtube. com/watch?v=x9QNKB34cJo&feature=related, accessed 5 Oct. 2008.

[14] 'Olympic media coverage: China vs West', BBC News, 10 April 2008, available at http:// news.bbc.co.uk/1/hi/world/asia-pacific/7340832.stm, accessed 5 Oct. 2008.

[15] '(L) China: Nationalist netizens on MSN Messenger "heart" China', Shanghaiist Web-blog, 25 May 2008, available at http://www.chinasupertrends.com/chinas-human-flesh-search-engine- not-what-you-might-think-it-is/, accessed 10 Oct. 2008.

[16] 'Chinese netizens flight against the CNN and other Western media', Sina BBS [bulletin board system], 28 Mar. 2008, available at http://bbs.sina.com.cn/zt/w/08/attackcnn/index.shtml, accessed 10 Oct. 2008.

[17] 'Chinese netizen discussion of "boycott on French goods"', People's Daily Online, 15 April 2008, available at http://english.peopledaily.com.cn/90001/90780/91342/6392966.html, ac- cessed 10 Oct. 2008.

[18] J. Goldkorn, 'Souvenir of nationalism 2008', Danwei Web-blog http://www.danwei.org/ fashion/too_cnn_tshirts.php, accessed 10 Oct. 2008.

[19] An Internet term: netizens searched out all the private details of leading roles in the cases, and publicized their private information and contacts while calling upon the public to participate in the attacks on individuals, not limited only to discursive abuse but also expanding to insults, disturbance and harassment in real everyday life.

[20] H. Fletcher, 'Human flesh search engines: Chinese vigilantes that hunt victims on the web', The Times, 25 June 2008, available at http://technology.timesonline.co.uk/tol/news/tech_- and_web/article4213681.ece, accessed 31 Aug. 2008.

[21] S. Dewan, 'Chinese Student in US Is Caught in Confrontation', New York Times, 17 April 2008, available at http://www.nytimes.com/2008/04/17/us/17student.html?_r=1&oref=slogin; X. Eberlein, 'Human Flesh Search: Vigilantes of the Chinese Internet', New America Media, 30 April 2008, available at http://news.newamericamedia.org/news/view_article.html?article_id= 964203448cbf700c9640912bf9012e05; 'China online: Tibet and torch reaction', BBC News, 17 April 2008, available at http://news.bbc.co.uk/1/hi/world/asia-pacific/7347821.stm, all ac- cessed 15 Oct. 2008.

[22] M. Chang, 'The Two Faces of Chinese Nationalism', China Briefing, Aug. 2008, 9–11, available at http://fundamentaloption.blogspot.com/2008/07/two-faces-of-chinese-nationalism.html, accessed 10 Oct. 2008.

[23] Liu, 'Boomerang Effect of Chinese Internet Nationalism'.

[24] Chow, 'Internet Activism'.

[25] 'BBC website "unblocked in China"', BBC News, 25 March 2008, available at http:// news.bbc.co.uk/1/hi/world/asia-pacific/7312240.stm, accessed 11 Oct. 2008.

[26] Chow, 'Internet Activism'.

[27] Amnesty International, 'People's Republic of China: The Olympics countdown – broken promises', available at http://www.amnesty.org/en/library/asset/ASA17/089/2008/en/8249b304- 5724-11dd-90eb-ff4596860802/asa170892008eng.pdf, accessed 11 Oct. 2008.

[28] G. York, 'Migrant workers feel like "slaves" to Beijing's Olympic projects'. The Globe and Mail, 17 Mar. 2008, available at http://www.david-kilgour.com/2008/Mar_17_2008_09.htm, accessed 11 Oct. 2008.

[29] K. Bu, 'Beijing Olympic clean up sweeps out migrant workers', Reuters, 21 July 2008, available at http://www.reuters.com/article/GCA-Olympics/idUSSP26521520080721, accessed 1 Oct. 2008.

[30] Broudehoux, 'Spectacular Beijing'.

[31] Because many of them lived in the old welfare houses provided by their former work-units and now faced either sale or reconstruction of the factory/dormitory sites, they could become

direct sufferers under the power-money exchange between urban planners and estate developers and with SOE managers sometimes.

[32] N. Venter, 'China – Orwell's dream come true', *The Dominion Post*, 25 Aug. 2008.

[33] 'Beijing 2008: Intellectuals and activists publish letter on Olympic Games and human rights', *Asia News*, 8 September 2007, available at http://www.asianews.it/index.php?l=en&art=10047, accessed 15 Oct. 2008.

[34] Zhang, 'China's National Interests'.

[35] Xu, *Olympic Dreams*, 1-3.

[36] Brady, 'The Beijing Olympics as a Campaign of Mass Distraction'.

[37] Ibid.

[38] Zheng, *Globalisation and State Transformation in China*: 87.

[39] Makeham, *Lost Soul*, 316–30.

[40] Ramo, *Brand China*.

[41] 'Spokesperson: Beijing authorities receive 77 demonstration applications since Aug. 1', Xinhua News, 18 August 2008, available at http://news.xinhuanet.com/english/2008-08/18/content_9468325.htm, accessed 15 Oct. 2008.

[42] 'Attention paid to the national mourning day', Sina News, 18 May 2008, available at http://news.sina.com.cn/c/2008-05-18/233515566932.shtml, accessed 15 Oct. 2008.

[43] M. Fan, '"Citizens" groups step up in China; wary rulers allow role in quake aid', *Washington Post*, 29 May 2008, available at http://en.chinaelections.org/newsinfo.asp?newsid=17714, accessed 12 Oct 2008.

[44] Zhu *et al.*, *Responsibility, Action and Cooperation*.

[45] Gao, 'New Developments in Civil Society'.

[46] Cai, 'Use the Olympic Games'.

[47] Barmé, 'China's Flat Earth'.

[48] Pramod, 'The Spectacle of the Beijing Olympics'.

[49] Ibid.; Owen, 'The Sydney 2000 Olympics'.

[50] The label for educational curricula and activities about the Olympic Games.

[51] Brownell, 'Beijing's Olympic Education Programme'.

[52] Ibid.

[53] Zhang, 'Using an International Language'.

[54] Fewsmith, *China since Tiananmen*, 161.

[55] Vickers, 'Selling "Socialism with Chinese Characteristics"'.

[56] Wacker, *China and the Internet*, 70; Hughes, 'Nationalism in Chinese Cyberspace'.

[57] Mengin, *Cyber China*, 7.

[58] Fan, Fan, 'Citizens' groups step up in China'.

[59] Xu, *Olympic Dreams*.

[60] Yu *et al.*, 'Governing Security at the 2008 Beijing Olympics'.

[61] Pramod, 'The Spectacle of the Beijing Olympics'.

[62] Fewsmith, *China since Tiananmen*, 13.

[63] S. Ho, 'Chinese Nationalism May Tarnish Beijing Olympics', Voice of America. 24 April 2008, available at http://www.voanews.com/english/archive/2008-04/2008-04-24-voa21.cfm?CFID=228578772&CFTOKEN=19523434&jsessionid=66307b65f9c6943402a6782e7d76575641d3, accessed 5 May 2009.

[64] They are usually defined as nationalistic to a certain extreme, even fanatical, with the mood of indignation and radicalism.

[65] Hvistendahl, 'Hooking Up'.

[66] J. Bajoria, 'Nationalism in China', Council on Foreign Relations Web-blog, http://www.cfr.org/publication/16079/nationalism_in_china.html, accessed 10 Oct. 2008.

[67] Shirky, *Here Comes Everybody*.

[68] Eberlein, 'Human Flesh Search'.
[69] Y. Liang, 'The moral foundation of anti-corruption in China', *China Weekly*, 16 February 2005, available at http://www.china-week.com/html/2417.htm, accessed 10 Sept. 2008.
[70] Chang, *The Coming Collapse of China*, 67.
[71] Wang, 'Changing Models'.
[72] Tai, *The Internet in China*, 259.
[73] Ibid., xiii.

References

Barmé, G. 'China's Flat Earth: History and 8 August 2008'. *The China Quarterly*, 197, no. 1 (2009): 64–86.

Broudehoux, A. 'Spectacular Beijing: The Conspicuous Construction of an Olympic Metropolis'. *Journal of Urban Affairs* 29, no. 4 (2007): 383–99.

Brady, A. 'The Beijing Olympics as a Campaign of Mass Distraction'. *The China Quarterly* 197, no. 1 (2009): 1–24.

Brownell, S. 'Beijing's Olympic Education Programme: Re-Thinking Suzhi Education, Re-Imagining an International China'. *The China Quarterly* 197, no. 1 (2009): 44–63.

Cai, F. 'Use the Olympic Games as an Opportunity to Create a New Vista for Media Propaganda Work in the Capital'. *Seeking the Truth* 485 (2008): 23.

Callahan, W. 'Patriotic Cosmopolitanism: China's Non-official Intellectuals Dream of the Future'. Paper presented at 'New China at 60' Forum, Centre for Contemporary Chinese Studies, University of Durham, UK, 2009.

Gao, Y. 'New Developments in Civil Society and Political Thought Work'. *Political Cadre Forum* 9 (2007): 28–30.

Chang, G. *The Coming Collapse of China*. New York: Random House, 2001.

Chow, P. 'Internet Activism, Trans-National Public Sphere, and State Activation Apparatus: A Case Study of Anti-Japanese Protest'. Paper presented at the annual meeting of the International Communication Association, San Francisco, CA, 2007.

Fewsmith, J. *China since Tiananmen: The Politics of Transition*. Cambridge: Cambridge University Press, 2001.

Hauben, M. and R. Hauben. *Netizens: On the History and Impact of Usenet and the Internet*. Los Alamitos, CA: IEEE Computer Society Press, 1997.

Hughes, C. 'Nationalism in Chinese Cyberspace'. *Cambridge Review of International Affairs* 13, no. 2 (2000): 195–209.

Hvistenda, M. 'Hooking Up and the Rise of Chinese Nationalism'. *New Republic* 238, no. 4832 (2008): 16–17.

Liu, L. 'Boomerang Effect of Chinese Internet Nationalism: A Case Study of an Anti-Japan Incident in China'. Paper presented at the annual meeting of the Midwest Political Science Association, Palmer House Hilton, Chicago, 2005.

Makeham, J. *Lost Soul: 'Confucianism' in Contemporary Chinese Discourse*. Cambridge, MA: Harvard University Asia Centre, 2008.

Mengin, F., ed. *Cyber China: Reshaping National Identities in the Ages of Information*. New York: Palgrave Macmillan, 2004.

Owen, K. 'The Sydney 2000 Olympics and Urban Entrepreneurialism: Local Variations in Urban Governance', *Australian Geographical Studies* 40, no. 3 (2002): 323–36.

Pramod, C. 'The Spectacle of the Beijing Olympics and the Dynamics of State Society Relationship in PRC'. *China Report* 44, no. 2 (2008): 111–37.

Ramo, J. *Brand China*. London: Foreign Policy Centre, 2007.

Shirky, C. *Here Comes Everybody: The Power of Organizing Without Organizations.* New York: Penguin Press, 2008.

Tai, Z. *The Internet in China: Cyberspace and Civil Society.* New York: Routledge, 2006.

Wacker, G. and Hughes, C., eds. *China and the Internet: Politics of the Digital Leap Forward.* London: Routledge Curzon, 2003.

Wang, S. 'Changing Models of China's Policy Agenda Setting'. *Modern China* 34, no. 1 (2008): 56–87.

Wei, C. and X. Liu, eds. *Chinese Nationalism in Perspective: Historical and Recent Cases.* Westport, CT: Greenwood Press, 2001.

Vickers, E. 'Selling "Socialism with Chinese Characteristics" "Thought and Politics" and the Legitimisation of China's Developmental Strategy'. *International Journal of Educational Development* 29, no. 5 (2009): 523–31.

Xu, G. *Olympic Dreams: China and Sports, 1895–2008.* Cambridge, MA: Harvard University Press, 2008.

Yu, Y., F. Klauser and G. Chan. 'Governing Security at the 2008 Beijing Olympics'. *The International Journal of the History of Sport* 26, no. 3 (2009): 390–405.

Zhang, H. 'Using an International Language to Tell China's Story'. *Sanlian Life Weekly* 492 (2008): 68–71.

Zhang, W. 'China's National Interests in the Process of Globalisation'. *Strategy and Management* 1 (2002): 52–64.

Zheng, B. 'China's "Peaceful Rise" to Great-Power Status'. *Foreign Affairs* 84, no. 5 (2005): 18–24.

Zheng, Y. *Globalisation and State Transformation in China.* New York: Cambridge University Press, 2004.

Zheng, Y. and K. Sow. 'Harmonious Society and Harmonious World: China's Policy Discourse under Hu Jintao'. China Policy Institute Briefing Series 26. Nottingham University, 2007.

Zhu, J., J. Chen, Q. Zhang, H. Zhang, Y. Zhou and C. Wang. eds. 2008. *Responsibility, Action and Cooperation – Case Studies on NGO's Participation in Wenchuan Earthquake.* Beijing: Peking University Press, 2008.

Beijing 2008: Volunteerism in Chinese Culture and its Olympic Interpretation and Influence

Juan Zhuang

Research on volunteerism is dominated by Western analyses and there is a paucity for studies concerning Chinese society. Volunteerism has in fact a strong cultural base in Chinese society, with a history stretching back several thousand years. This paper therefore reviews the evolution of volunteerism in Chinese culture at three historic periods, including the main schools of thought from Confucian benevolence, Mohist universal fraternity, Daoist philanthropy and Buddhist leniency to 'Lei Feng Spirit'. Overall, it is conceptualized as 'dedication, fraternity, mutuality and progress' and that is the key concept of volunteerism for the Beijing 2008 Olympic Games. The paper also examines the interpretation of the long tradition of volunteerism in specific policies for the Beijing 2008 Olympic Games and the influence of Beijing 2008 volunteerism within Chinese society after the Olympic Games.

Introduction

Volunteers are an essential element of the organization of events. Their contributions of time, enthusiasm and professionalism, in particular to Mega Sports events such as the Olympic Games, help to ensure that the events will be successful. In fact, it is an Olympic tradition for organizing committees to use volunteers; partly for budgetary reasons, but more importantly to allow people within the host community to feel that they are participating in and contributing to the games. [1] In the Athens 2004 Olympic Games, volunteers were described as the heart and soul of the games, [2] and Juan Antonio Samaranch, honorary life president of the International Olympic Committee (IOC), further addressed the importance of volunteering by stating 'the Olympic Movement thrives on volunteerism'. [3] Moreover, the activities of volunteers are considered to be the fundamental social and cultural base of the Olympic Movement. [4]

At the 120th IOC Session on 24 August 2008, Dr Jacques Rogge, president of the IOC, highly praised the tremendous support and contribution of Chinese volunteers to the success of the Beijing 2008 Olympic Games:

> To hundreds of thousands of enthusiastic volunteers, we have heard you say it many times, now it is my turn to say: Thank you for your cooperation! We will leave China with warm memories of your smiles, your enthusiasm and your eager willingness to help. You are the future of China. We wish you the best....
>
> The Games have been a dream fulfilled and a source of inspiration for a generation of young Chinese people. Some of the friendly volunteers we have met over the past two weeks will be tomorrow's leaders. They have emerged from this experience with new confidence and a better understanding of Olympic values. That may ultimately the greatest legacy of these Games. [5]

On the same day, Rogge made another formal expression of appreciation to the volunteers at the closing ceremony of the Beijing 2008 Olympic Games.

In Chinese society, volunteerism has a strong cultural base, with a history stretching back several thousand years, mostly from Confucian benevolence, Mohist universal fraternity, Daoist philanthropy and Buddhist leniency. Overall, it can be conceptualized as 'dedication, fraternity, mutuality and progress' [6] and that was also the key concept of volunteerism for the Beijing 2008 Olympic Games. However, organized volunteering services in China did not start until 1989, when the first volunteer association was set up in Shenzhen, southern China. [7] Research into the work of this society has also yet to mature [8] and a review of research on Chinese society by Western academics shows that some appear to lack sufficient understanding of the long traditions of Chinese culture and their profound influence on Chinese society today.

This paper therefore aims to provide a historical framework of the evolution of volunteerism in Chinese society, its ideology and the cultural meaning of volunteerism, and how it was interpreted in the volunteer programme for the Beijing 2008 Olympic Games. In order to establish the historical context in which volunteerism was conceived and developed, several thousand years of Chinese history is reviewed in three eras: the ancient era, including slavery and feudal society up to the Opium War of 1840; the modern era, including semi-feudal and semi-colonial society from 1840 to 1949; and the establishment of the People's Republic of China in 1949, which marks the opening of the contemporary era. Lastly, this paper discusses preliminary findings on the influence of Beijing 2008 volunteerism within post-Olympic Chinese society and is a part of continuing doctoral research.

Volunteerism in Ancient China

Of the three historical stages, ancient China is the longest period. At this stage, China experienced many dynastic changes, as a result of which there were many different cultures and beliefs existing at same time. [9] Out of all the differences, however, there were some general moral principles in Chinese tradition. [10] For example, 'respect elders of our own and of others, love our children as well as those of others', and 'we are all brothers and sisters from the five continents'. [11] These are also considered to be the fundamental basis of volunteerism in Chinese society, and volunteerism is recognized firstly by the development of fraternity and mutuality among neighbourhoods as well as friendship. [12] This section analyses four main traditional elements of philanthropic culture: Confucian benevolence, [13] Mohist universal fraternity, [14] Daoist accumulating merits and practising philanthropy, [15] and Buddhist leniency. [16] In addition to these cultural origins of volunteerism in Chinese society, it also discusses other key philanthropic ideals that have contributed to the development of volunteerism.

Confucian Benevolence – The Cultural Origin of Chinese Philanthropy

Confucianism is regarded as the origin of Chinese culture and the single most influential school of thought in Chinese society. [17] This might possibly explain the popularity of Confucian research in Chinese and non-Chinese academia. Most research on Confucianism focuses on understanding Chinese culture and Chinese history. [18] Few have discussed this school of thought in specific relation to volunteerism in Chinese society. To be precise, the benevolence value of Confucianism is regarded as the cultural origin of volunteerism in China [19] and can in fact be analysed on two levels – individual and family circles; and the state.

At an individual level, Confucian benevolence advocates filial piety that begins with being kind-hearted to people as individuals, then to their family members and others in more distant relationships. [20] This kindness differs between blood relations and the more distantly related, as it is addressed in *Moderation*. [21] Benevolence is owed to all humanity, but blood relationship takes precedence. Zhang argues that this is different from today's volunteerism in Chinese society, in which people should love others from both inside and outside of their families, and in particular, to love and take care of those people who are vulnerable. [22] Moreover, Confucian benevolence advocates individuals to extend their kindness to the state. For example, Mencius called for the virtue that, in obscurity, scholars should maintain their own integrity; in times of success, they should make perfect the whole empire, [23] which advocates that, for the well-being of the state, successful people should share their good fortune with those in need. The ideal of this benevolence was also close to the core of the political system at that time – 'one family, one country'. It was therefore relied heavily upon by the state, both to educate people and so solidify the dominion of the ruler [24] and is believed to have been the means by which Confucianism was passed from generation to generation. Accordingly, Confucianism has had a huge impact on the development of philanthropy in China, and its benevolence represents 'dedication' and 'fraternity'. They all contribute to the development of volunteerism in Chinese society. [25]

Mohist Universal Love – Fraternity and Mutuality

The philanthropic promoted by the concept of Mohist universal love is different from Confucian benevolence in the sense that Mohism argues that all people are equal. [26] The three main concepts of this philanthropism are: (a) 'benevolence loves benevolence', which means that benevolent people should regard society's rewards as their duty, which in time will be reciprocated; (b) 'loyalty' is regarded as the standard by which one should love people, and is determined by morality and justice, not by blood relationship; (c) this love also includes the love of oneself. [27] Consequently, Mohist universal fraternity has greater impact on volunteerism today than Confucian benevolence. It encourages people to volunteer and love others in terms of their 'loyalty', as well as improving themselves through helping others. [28] Thus fraternity and mutuality are the two elements that Mohist universal love contributes to volunteerism in Chinese society today.

Daoism – Accumulating Merits and Practising Philanthropy

In Daoism, the supreme state of a Daoist is to become a supernatural being. *The Classic of Great Peace* also states that the only way to the supreme state is through accumulating merits and practising philanthropy. [29] Daoists often used a 'Merits and Demerits Note' to mark their contributions and blunders and so motivate themselves to practise further philanthropy. [30] This approach is actually applied to the current volunteering services in China to motivate and manage volunteers. [31] For example, in most well-developed volunteer organizations, every volunteer receives a personal record card to keep track of all their activities. [32] In addition, the contribution of this philosophy to volunteerism includes encouraging more people to devote their love to helping others, especially those who themselves have been helped, and in doing so to spread volunteerism. Dedication and progress are the two elements that Daoism has contributed to developing volunteerism in China.

Buddhist Leniency – Donation and Dedication

In a similar vein to Confucian and Mohist philosophies, the 'leniency of Buddhism' means to love people. [33] This 'leniency' involves mercy and sympathy. In Buddhism, mercy means to bring happiness to people and so be with pleasure, while sympathy is to help people eradicate their afflictions and therefore reduce their suffering. Indeed, the embodiment of this 'lenient Buddhism' is to donate money and/or payment in kind to free captive animals. The rigour of Buddhist leniency expands and fulfils the traditional philanthropy of Chinese culture, to the extent that the leniency extends love from people to animals, which is more comprehensive than the other three philosophies. [34] However, Shen and Fu [35] argue that this kind of 'volunteering activity' is based on the concept of 'retribution of sins'. This is essentially different from the current motivation for volunteerism, which is selfless dedication and progress with free choice, not the fear of retribution afterwards.

Guan Zhong's Nine Compassions and Legalists' Laws for the Poor

Besides the above four main schools of thought, Zhou and Zeng [36] suggest that there are other philosophies, among hundreds of schools of thought, that have also contributed to the development of volunteerism in Chinese society, such as Guan Zhong [37] and Legalism. [38] In terms of philanthropy, both of these philosophies focused on the well-being of the state.

Guan Zhong's philanthropic thoughts are mainly embodied in his 'nine compassions'. [39] The nine compassions are all aspects of philanthropic policies including: (a) honouring the elderly, (b) caring for the young, (c) pitying the orphaned, (d) providing for the disabled, (e) bringing together those who are alone, (f) inquiring after the sick, (g) keeping track of the destitute, (h) providing relief for those in distress, (i) continuing the sacrifices for a family line that has been broken. [40] These nine compassions are one of the few early documented sets of philanthropic policies in Chinese society, [41] and their comprehensive nature has been highlighted as contributing to the hegemony of the Kingdom of Qi during the period of warring states (c.476–221 BCE). [42] The literature also recommends that this should be utilized in constructing the current social and volunteering services. [43] From a long-term point of view, however, Yue criticizes the nine compassions as passive philanthropic policies, which did not educate or train people to work with their capabilities, thus adding an extra burden to the nation and eventually damaging its stability.

In fact, the Legalists also promoted their philanthropic philosophies through policies. Shang Yang, one of the major Legalists, advocated legal reforms in the Kingdom of Qin on the grounds that the best way to govern a country well is to make the poor richer and the rich poorer; when this happens, the country becomes a powerful nation. [44] This new law was designed to bridge the divide between the rich and poor as a means of attaining the sustainability of society and ultimately to achieve a greater standing for the kingdom. However, his follower Han Fei disagreed with this action, stating that penalizing the rich to help the poor might prevent people from working hard and promote the idleness of the poor. He did not deem this to be effective in motivating people to work and save harder. [45] This opinion is actually in line with Yue's critique of Guan Zhong's nine compassions, that the possible long-term burden to a nation would negate the original intention. Zhou and Zeng further explain that this is why Chinese philanthropic activities in the modern era began to emphasize helping and training those people in need. Nevertheless, the nine compassions left a legacy of comprehensive practices to future philanthropy, which, as the Legalists advocated, could be implemented through governmental policies. [46]

In the ancient era, volunteerism was developed on the basis of philanthropy and cultural values. These included Confucian benevolence, Mohist universal love, Daoist accumulation of merits and practising philanthropy, Buddhist leniency, Guan Zhong's nine compassions and Legalistic laws to aid the poor. Influenced by Guan Zhong's nine compassions and Legalistic law reform, rulers in feudal societies gave food and goods to people who suffered due to natural disasters and chaos caused by wars, as a means of showing their benevolence and of consolidating their regime. Buddhist karma and Daoism's 'going to heaven' theories stimulated local communities and individuals to help people in need by setting up philanthropic organizations. Confucian benevolence and Mohist universal love were the main influence in inspiring people to help each other in neighbourhood and circles of families and friends in traditional Chinese societies.

Volunteerism in Modern China

As a result of the Opium War of 1840, Chinese feudal society was gradually replaced by a semi-feudal and semi-colonial society in which Western religious and philosophical ideas were slowly injected into traditional Chinese society. [47] The literature also points out that China was troubled by a great deal of natural disasters and national and international wars in this era, which explains why philanthropy at the time concentrated on saving society and social relief. [48] Hence, the combination of Western philanthropy, the nationalism of Chinese people with lofty ideals and traditional philanthropic ideologies caused Chinese philanthropy to move from the traditional to the modern. [49] This section therefore explores modern philanthropy in Chinese society from 1840 to 1949 with regard to the influence of western philanthropy, Chinese nationalism and philanthropic activities.

Western Philanthropic Ideologies

The influence of Western philanthropic ideologies on the development of Chinese philanthropy, especially though Christianity, is generally acknowledged in Chinese literature. [50] Moreover, Zhou and Zeng point to three channels through which Western philanthropic ideologies were promoted in Chinese society: Christian churches and missionaries, Western newspapers and periodicals, and the overseas knowledge of Chinese travellers. In fact, the details of such influence are only found in the work of Zhou and Zeng. They indicate that Christian missionaries practised philanthropy by setting up facilities to provide Western medicine, care and education for both Western and Chinese people in need, as well as fundraising to relieve people in disasters. These exclusive approaches exerted subtle influences on the Chinese people and were soon adopted by Chinese philanthropists, especially in the regions that had more contact with Western ideologies. [51] Zhou and Zeng believe this advanced the modernization of Chinese traditional philanthropic ideologies.

Western philanthropic practices were also promoted in Western newspapers and periodicals when they established their semi-colonial regime in China. [52] The humanitarian spirit of the Red Cross, such as in the saving of wounded soldiers regardless of their allegiance, became widely accepted by Chinese people. [53] In addition, Chinese travellers brought back Western philanthropic ideologies and practices to China, specifically regarding charitable fundraising, along with their own experiences, which convinced the Chinese people and accelerated the influence of Western philanthropic ideologies into traditional Chinese philanthropy. [54] Although Chinese literature criticizes the promotion of Western ideologies as one of many methods of constraining the education of Chinese people, [55] they also acknowledge the positive influences of those ideologies on the development of Chinese philanthropy at the individual level.

Nationalism of Chinese Idealists

The fact that traditional Chinese society came to an end as a result of the Opium War of 1840 and that Westerners to some extent colonized part of China, stimulated a great deal of nationalism among Chinese people that focused on saving and relieving society. [56] Literature identifies the most influential philanthropic ideals of three main progressive Chinese thinkers of the modern era: Hong Ren-Gan, Kang You-Wei and Sun Yat-Sen. [57] As their intentions were to save the country from colonization, their philanthropic ideals were focused at the level of the state.

Hong Ren-Gan (1822–1864) was a cousin of Hong Xiu-Quan, the King of the 'Heavenly Kingdom of Great Peace' (*Tai Ping Tian Guo*). Hong Ren-Gan was a military adviser and the prime minister of the kingdom, and was later honoured as Gan King. [58] His ideal of philanthropy was embedded in the *New Compilation of Political Advice*. [59] Hong Ren-Gan introduced ideas that include modern Chinese philanthropy imitating that of Western countries, raising philanthropic funds from society, and strengthening the supervision and inspection of philanthropic organizations by setting up citizens' guilds. [60] Zhou and Zeng explain that these thoughts show the interest of powerful groups in promoting philanthropy at the time, but they were never put into practice. It was the same for Kang You-Wei's philanthropic ideals. By integrating the Confucian ideal of 'great harmony' with Western ideals of democratic and human rights, Kang You-Wei (1858–1927) addressed his philanthropic ideologies in *An Ideal World*. [61] He was one of the leaders of the Hundred Days Reform during the Qing Dynasty in 1898 and his ideal philanthropy was that the public should be responsible for the care, funding and education of people in need, in order to build up a society of great harmony. [62] Although these ideas carried a great deal of idealism, they did reflect the activities of some progressive Chinese people: saving the nation and promoting philanthropy by using the experiences of Western countries for reference. [63]

Sun Yat-Sen (1866–1925) was the leader of the Chinese democratic revolution that successfully overthrew the Qing Dynasty in 1911. In fact, his philanthropic assertions are similar to those of Kang You-Wei and are primarily embodied in the principle of people's livelihood in his *Old and New Three People's Principles*, [64] which comprised several philanthropic ideologies including, the Confucian great harmony ideal, Marxist equality and western philanthropic ideals. [65] Because Sun Yat-Sen was the first president of the Republic of China and was honoured as the father of the republic, his philanthropic ideals were carried out and treated as the principles of the government, encouraging it to act philanthropically. [66] Although such nationalistic ideals did not fully covert into philanthropic activities, they did make an important breakthrough in traditional Chinese philanthropy in that they were devoted to saving the nation from colonization rather than the stability of a kingdom or a dynasty. [67] This has encouraged the development of Chinese philanthropy in the modern era. [68]

Philanthropic activities in modern China relied heavily on international aid. Although mutual help and fraternity were still strong in communities, history indicates that Christian church missionaries practised philanthropy by setting up hospitals and offering free Western medicines and treatment to both Western and Chinese people. It could not however solve the large scale of dysfunction that resulted from constant warfare and natural disasters.

Volunteerism in Contemporary China

Upon prevailing over the Nationalists in the Second Civil War, the Chinese Communist Party led by Chairman Mao Zedong founded the People's Republic of China on 1 October 1949. China entered its contemporary era as a socialist country, and 'Lei Feng Spirit' (based on the life of Lei Feng – see below) was adopted as the model of Chinese traditional virtue and the Communist system. It was promoted by the Communist Party for the development of the spiritual civilization of the nation as a whole from the 1960s. [69] In fact, learning about Lei Feng's activities is regarded as the inspiration for volunteerism in contemporary Chinese society. [70]

Lei Feng Spirit

Lei Feng was a soldier in the Chinese army in the 1950s. He became well-known in China, and remains well-known today, for devoting his life to helping others and society any time and anywhere. [71] 'Lei Feng Spirit' mainly includes the 'spirit of the nail', the 'spirit of a blockhead' and the 'spirit of the screw'. [72] The 'spirit of the nail' means to make the best use of one's time and to work persistently to achieve one's purpose; the 'spirit of a blockhead' means to dedicate oneself to helping others for the good of society without the desire to receive any kind of reward; and the 'spirit of the screw' means to work hard in any position as an individual in society, just like a screw in a machine. [73] The stories of Lei Feng inspired Chinese people to help each other whenever and wherever they could.

Moreover, the leaders of the country, including Chairman Mao, wrote commendations for this selflessness and called on the whole country to 'learn from comrade Lei Feng' (epigraph by Mao Zedong in 1963), [74] because 'Lei Feng Spirit' embodies the principles of Communism. [75] Consequently, Lei Feng's teachings were spread throughout the nation, and 'Lei Feng Spirit' became the influential moral model of Chinese traditional virtue and Communist principles. [76]

Since 1978, the 'reform and opening up' policy has been applied to the whole nation. The Chinese Communist system has embraced an element of a market economy and that has brought capitalism into the society. Volunteerism, as a new form of Lei Feng Spirit, has been developed to promote spiritual civilization in the context of a market economy. [77] Therefore governmental input is now an important element in the development of volunteerism in Chinese society. However, Wang and Lin [78] argue that there are certain differences between the Lei Feng Spirit and volunteerism. Lei Feng Spirit is the spirit of 'utter devotion to others without any thought of self', meaning to 'devote all of finite life into infinite service of people', which is entirely altruistic and top at the supreme moral level.

The introduction of formal volunteerism in China began in 1989 when the first volunteer association was set up in Shenzhen, southern China. [79] The Shenzhen Volunteer Association was set up by the Shenzhen Committee of the Chinese Communist Youth League and registered as a non-governmental organization. It runs independently from the Shenzhen Committee of the Chinese Communist Youth League or other bureaus. [80] However, the association, like many others later set up in other cities of China, is supervised by government offices and receives financial support from the government. [81] Since the end of the 1980s, volunteerism has developed significantly and is recognized as 'a noble project in current Communist society'. [82] Generally it can be conceptualized as 'dedication, fraternity, mutuality and progress'. [83]

Volunteerism for the Beijing 2008 Olympic Games

'In 2008, the smiles of the volunteers will be the best name-card of Beijing.' [84] According to the Beijing Organizing Committee for the Olympic Games (BOCOG), there were 70,000 games-time volunteers for the Beijing 2008 Olympic Games. The majority were recruited from university students in Beijing, but the administrative divisions of China, including 23 provinces, five autonomous regions, three munici-palities [85] and two special administrative regions, each recruited 80 volunteers for the games. [86] In addition, BOCOG claims that the Beijing Olympic volunteers also included 400,000 city volunteers, 1,000,000 societal volunteers and 200,000 cheering squad volunteers. On the basis of its long cultural history, this section discusses the interpretation of volunteerism in the Beijing Olympic volunteer programme and the visions of the Chinese state and the BOCOG.

Staging the Event

The use of volunteers to help in staging the games is an Olympic tradition and therefore the first and foremost goal for BOCOG was to recruit more than one million volunteers to help in doing so. As the Beijing Olympic Volunteer Programme Action Plan clearly indicated:

> Providing unique, high-standard volunteer services for the 2008 Olympic and Paralympic Games is the most direct and most important goal of the Beijing Olympic Volunteer Programme. While a large, wide-range, highly representative and competent volunteer force will be formed, volunteer spirit will be advocated, service forms will be innovated, service contents will be expanded and service quality will be improved so that they can provide friendly, personalized and specialized services for the Beijing Olympic and Paralympic Games. Efforts will be made to establish a volunteer service system in line with the Olympic rules, Chinese styles and international standards so as to add a Chinese touch to the Olympic Movement and leave an indelible impression of Beijing. [87]

This statement somehow also indicates that BOCOG intended to achieve the premier goal by integrating Chinese traditions of volunteerism into implementing the action plan. However, Guan and Tan [88] argue that it is against the long tradition of volunteerism if they are simply used as a free means of obtaining organizational improvement. It is immaterial whether they might be used to help the economy, for propaganda or for their efficiency or efficacy, as the goal of volunteerism is for the common good and is altruistic. While the BOCOG's great ambition of using volunteers to stage the Olympics promoted the tradition of volunteerism within Chinese society, the Beijing Olympic Volunteer Programme might have also violated the traditional value of volunteerism as dedication, fraternity, mutuality and progress. The Olympic Volunteer Action plan further pointed out that

> Beijing Olympic volunteers will be people-oriented and will guide their actions with the concept of 'Service First, Harmony First'. Advocating service spirit, stimulating service enthusiasm and upgrading service abilities, the volunteers will provide unique and high-standard voluntary service for the Olympic and Paralympic Games, with their innovative courage, spirit and methods. In one sentence, the quality of games-time volunteers directly affects a spectator's impression on the delivery of Beijing 2008 Olympic Games as a whole. [89]

The last sentence explains why 90 per cent of volunteers were recruited among university students in Beijing. One of the officials of the Volunteer Group at BOCOG revealed BOCOG's vision for this decision:

> First of all, we have a big pool of university students who are well educated with excellent skills and basic knowledge. Language is the most important capability. If we recruited volunteers among retirees, as at previous Olympics, it is very likely that Chinese retirees could not speak a full sentence in a foreign language. Then communication would be jeopardized. This was the most important reason. Secondly, university students in Beijing were very enthusiastic about becoming a

volunteer for the Beijing 2008 Olympic Games. That's why we chose them as the main volunteer force. I think the fact that all the university student organizations in Beijing are supervised under the Communist Youth League of Beijing Committee was another very important factor for BOCOG. This is different from other Olympics. The clear architecture enabled and guaranteed effective and efficient organization of such a massive volunteer operation during the Olympic Games.

Strengthening the Image and Power of the State

'China's Olympics – A Century-old Dream Comes True'. [90] From its bid to the successful delivery, the Beijing 2008 Olympic Games have been seen as a century-old Chinese dream coming true. Being honoured as the host city for the 29th Olympiad in 2001 was seen as indicating that the economic strength and social development of China was finally recognized by the whole world. Staging the games successfully had also become a governmental initiative. As Dong and Mangan state, 'The *most* important legacy of the Beijing games, as stated assertively by He Zhenliang, chairman of the IOC Commission for Culture of Olympic Education, is "the elevation of our Chinese people's self-confidence and sense of pride".' [91]

The Olympic Volunteer Programme was visualized as a unique opportunity to promote civilization and harmony in Chinese society, which would implement the ideology of the president of China, Hu Jintao, that of building a harmonious society. This had been passed as a motion at the Sixth Plenum of the 16th Communist Party of China (CPC) Central Committee in 2006. [92] This vision was also stated explicitly in the Beijing Olympic Volunteer Action Plan: 'Emphasizing harmony and respecting diversity, they will promote mutual respect and understanding among the people of different races, regions and cultures, promote harmonious coexistence between man and nature, and promote coordinated development between man and society.' [93]

That is to say that the Beijing Olympic Volunteer Programme was one that China hoped to present as a showcase to the rest of world. In China, the development of volunteerism is considered as important for accelerating the system of a Communist market economy, developing and setting up a Chinese social welfare system, and shaping social fashion in order to generate positive impacts on developing the society. [94] Some of the volunteer services meet some important aspects of building a harmonious society and for those aspects of social security in the current transitional society that the Chinese government has not been able to cover. [95]

The fact that 90 per cent of Beijing Olympic volunteers were university students in Beijing illustrates that volunteerism for the Beijing 2008 Olympic Games was seen as a platform to nurture China's younger generations. As Rogge stated in the Olympic session: 'We will leave China with warm memories of your smiles, your enthusiasm and your eager willingness to help. You are the future of China.' It summarized the vision of the Chinese government of the Beijing Olympic Volunteer Programme presenting a showcase to the world about its bright and capable future – the young generation of Chinese people.

Influences of Beijing 2008 Volunteering on Chinese Society

The data used to measure the influence of volunteerism at Beijing 2008 on the post-Games Society after the games were primarily generated through nine focus-group interviews with university students in Beijing. This included those who volunteered for the games and those who did not. Readers are reminded that the findings here are a part of an ongoing analysis in continuing PhD research.

Increasing Social Networking

During their time as volunteers, university students worked together with other Olympic volunteers from different universities in Beijing, as well as those from elsewhere in China and other countries. Many research participants stated that they developed such a strong sense of friendship, almost like that between soldiers who fight shoulder-to-shoulder in a war. After the Olympics, however, student volunteers pointed out that their liaisons with other volunteers from outside Beijing now mainly rely on the exchange of emails and telephone calls. Geographical distance is the main cause of the limited contact, even though their organizations (e.g. universities and volunteer associations in other Chinese cities) do organize formal activities to help maintain such friendships. Future contact seems harder to maintain, as some student volunteers in Beijing indicated:

> I met and made friends with a lot of volunteers during my volunteering duty. Some of them were from other Chinese cities, others were from other countries. After the Olympics, they have returned back home. We are still in contact with each other, but not much. Some foreign volunteers sent me Christmas cards before the New Year. We have not been able to stay in touch as much as we do with volunteers from other universities in Beijing.
>
> It is difficult to organize group activities with volunteers from outside of Beijing. Funding is a big issue. I don't think that we will have opportunity to volunteer together again. Though we are sending text messages and emails to each other, the quantity has gradually reduced since they went back home. In future? I don't know.

Olympic volunteers based in Beijing maintain much more frequent contact with each other. The most regular form is gathering together for a meal and most of time it is organized by the group leader or volunteer managers of a specific volunteer group or Olympic stadium. One of the student volunteers indicates that:

> Participating in Olympic volunteering really can help you make a lot of friends. No matter whether they were your colleagues or subordinates, your social network will definitely be increased. Especially with those who have similar personalities, moreover, we have been going out a lot, for example, gathering together for a meal, celebrating a birthday for one of us, organizing outdoor activities etc. As a matter of fact, we have gone travelling together. Anyway, the 'revolutionary gang' have

good fun together after the Olympics. We all agree that if it were not for the Olympic volunteering, we would never have made such good friends with each other.

Evidence indicates that contacts are most frequent among volunteers who are from the same universities. In some cases, these Olympic volunteers have been involved in other voluntary activities since the Beijing 2008 Olympic Games. They also indicated that relationships formed through volunteering for the Olympic Games could last their whole lives.

Enhancing Graduate Employability

There is a clear consensus that by volunteering for the Beijing 2008 Olympic Games, student volunteers have increased their understanding and apprehension of the world – the differences between countries and cultures; different working styles and ways of handling issues. Their English-language capability has also generally improved. Depending on their particular experiences, volunteers have increased their knowledge in business etiquette, skills and methods of dealing with emergency scenarios, and their communication skills, especially the use of body language with disabled spectators or those who spoke a language that the volunteers did not. Their self-esteem and self-confidence have also increased as a result of their experience.

Informants also pointed out that the Beijing Municipal Government Office organized a special graduate recruitment fair for Olympic volunteers. Many of them were offered jobs at the fair and some even found a job simply because of their experience as volunteers at the games, irrespective of their academic specialities. Olympic volunteering experiences have had a major influence on enhancing graduate employability. The question of whether this influence could be prolonged will of course be subject to further review at different stages after the event.

Future Participation

It is evident that the student volunteers widened their social circle and developed a series of skills through their participation in the Beijing games. However, will they continue to volunteer? Research findings indicate that most of those who were involved in volunteering activities before the games expressed willingness to participate again. Of those who had not volunteered prior to their involvement, some showed interest in future participation. They did explain that the nature of the volunteering itself would be a major factor in determining the likelihood of their participation. For example, they would consider whether the work could help people in need, whether it is relevant to their interests and whether they could learn new knowledge and skills. Otherwise, the possibility of future participation is low.

Widening Understanding of Volunteerism in Chinese Society

In general, all the participants indicated that the series of training and actual volunteering experiences accumulated at the Beijing Olympics had increased their understanding of being a volunteer and volunteering. More specifically, volunteering for the Olympic Games has stimulated them to think on how to be an eligible volunteer. In addition to increasing their own understanding of volunteerism and Olympism, participation has subsequently widened such understanding among people in their social circles. For example, one of volunteers explained:

> The Beijing Olympics affected every Chinese heart. For my family, as an example, my mum and dad paid extensive attention to Olympic-related programmes during the Olympics, especially at the times of my volunteering shifts. They were trying to identify me from the millions of people on the TV (a lot of laughs and nodding head among the group) and of course, they never could! My cousins also phoned up my dad and asked him whether it was me who showed on the TV in Olympic volunteering uniform just now. They were all proud of me being an Olympic volunteer. I think the fact that we volunteered for the games, to some degree, has widened our families' and friends' understanding of the Olympic Games, of Olympism and surely of what volunteering means.

Most university students in Beijing come from different parts of China. These volunteers pointed out that their friends from home expressed interests in carrying out volunteering activities at similar platforms in future, or participating in some generic volunteering that can help people in need. Though the younger generation of Chinese people seem keen on future participation, the older generation (i.e. the generation of the volunteers' parents) are limited by their professions and the lack of free time to contribute in such a way.

Boosting Field Research

It should also be noted that the success of the Beijing 2008 Olympic Volunteer Programme has boosted research on volunteerism in Chinese society. To take the Beijing Volunteers Association as an example, the association established and published a series of books and articles including *Volunteer Magazine*, which is a serial magazine specially focussed on volunteering at the Beijing 2008 Olympic Games. Since the Olympics, the association has also set up a volunteer research group that aims to conduct research on volunteerism from both a practical point of view and for academic purposes.

Conclusion

In conclusion, volunteerism has a strong cultural base in China that can be traced back several thousand years. Volunteerism is rooted in the philanthropic ideals of many of the hundreds of schools of thought in Chinese traditional culture, including

Confucianism, Mohism, Daoism, Buddhism, Guan Zhong's nine compassions and the Legalists' law to aid the poor. Added to these are Western philanthropic ideals, the progressive nationalism of modern China and the contemporary manifestation of Lei Feng Spirit that embodies Chinese Communist ideology. Volunteerism in Chinese society is conceptualized as 'dedication, fraternity, mutuality and progress'.

Inspired by the idea that philanthropy contributes to consolidation of their regime, and faced with many dynamic changes, government bodies have played a key role in promoting volunteerism to the extent that they allocated funds and made policies to encourage people to practise formal and informal volunteerism. Following this tradition, the Beijing Olympic Volunteer Programme was intended to help stage the Beijing 2008 Olympic Games and at the same time to strengthen the image and power of China as a whole – both domestically and on the world stage. In post-Olympic society, volunteerism for Beijing 2008 has been seen to be most influential on university student volunteers with regard to increasing social networks and enhancing graduate employability. Moreover, the massive participation promoted and widened the understanding of volunteerism in Chinese society and as a result, future participation seems promising and research on volunteerism is increasing.

This paper therefore makes a contribution to exploring the Chinese understanding of volunteerism, its cultural meaning, its philanthropic practices, its Olympic interpretation and its post-Olympic influence on society. Ultimately, this paper adds valuable information about volunteerism in Chinese society into a body of literature that is currently Western-dominated.

Acknowledgements

The author would like to express her gratitude to her director of study, Dr Vassil Girginov of Brunel University, for his valuable advice and support in the completion of this paper.

Notes

[1] Sydney Organising Committee for the Olympic Games, *Official Report*, vol. 1.
[2] Athens 2004 Olympic Committee, Athens 2004 Volunteers, available at http://www.athens 2004.com/en/Athens2004Volunteers, accessed 10 Oct. 2005.
[3] Walker and Gleeson, *The Volunteers*, ix.
[4] Jin, '100,000 Volunteers, One "Name-card"'; MacAloon, 'Volunteers, Global Society and the Olympic Movement'; Pound, 'Volunteers and the Olympic Movement'.
[5] International Olympic Committee, 'IOC President's Remarks to the 120th IOC session', 2008. Available at http://www.olympic.org/uk/news/olympic_news/full_story_uk.asp?id=2772, accessed 20 June 2009.
[6] Zhao, 'Volunteerism'; Zheng, 'The Spirit of Volunteers and Harmony Society'; Hou, 'A Discussion of the Development and Concept'.
[7] Tian, 'Several Issues on Developing Volunteering Service'; Tan, 'Chinese Volunteer Service'; Ding, 'Measuring Volunteering in China'.
[8] Girginov and Zhuang, 'The Framing of the Idea of Volunteering', 42–3.
[9] Zhang, 'Chinese Ancient Philanthropy Culture'; Zhou and Zeng, *A Brief History of Chinese Philanthropy*.

[10] Zhao, 'Volunteerism'; Hou, 'A Discussion of the Development and Concept'.

[11] 'Mencius' here refers to the book written by Mencius or Meng Ke (*c*.385 BCE–*c*.304 BCE), who was one of the most famous Confucian representatives during the Warring States period.

[12] Zhao, 'Volunteerism'; Hou, 'A Discussion of the Development and Concept'.

[13] Confucianism is a Chinese traditional philosophy founded by Confucius (551–479 BCE).

[14] Mohism is another popular philosophy in Chinese society; the founder was Mo Zi (479–221 BCE).

[15] Daoism is the only native-born religion in China, and may be traced to the second century of the Christian era.

[16] Buddhism originates in India, and had come to China by the fourth or fifth century of the Christian era.

[17] Shen and Fu, Volunteerism'; Zhou and Zeng, *A Brief History of Chinese Philanthropy*; Shun and Wong, 'Introduction'.

[18] Wilkinson, *Chinese History*; Cotterell, *China: A History*; Hao and Wang, 'Changing Chinese Views'; Cotterell and Morgan, *China: An Integrated Study*.

[19] Zhang, 'Chinese Ancient Philanthropy Cultures'.

[20] Ibid.

[21] 'Moderation' is *zhong yong* in Chinese, and here refers to the book written by Confucius's grandson Zi Si.

[22] Zhang, 'Chinese Ancient Philanthropy Cultures'.

[23] This is the translation of 'qiong ze du shan qi shen, da ze jian ji tian xia'.

[24] Zhang, 'Chinese Ancient Philanthropy Cultures'; Shen and Fu, 'Volunteerism'.

[25] Ibid.

[26] Ibid.; Xu, 'Analysing the Basis of Volunteering Spirit'.

[27] Zhang, 'Chinese Ancient Philanthropy Cultures'.

[28] Ibid.

[29] Wang, *The Classic of Great Peace* is one of the main scriptures of Daoism, and is also called *Taiping Jing* in Chinese.

[30] Zhang, 'Chinese Ancient Philanthropy Culture', 40.

[31] Tan, 'Organizing and Encouraging the Community Volunteering Service'.

[32] Tan, 'Chinese Volunteer Service'.

[33] Ibid.

[34] Ibid.

[35] Shen and Fu. 'Volunteerism'.

[36] Zhou and Zeng, *A Brief History of Chinese Philanthropy*.

[37] Guan Zhong (d. 645 BCE) was the famous Chinese minister of state of the Kingdom of Qi during the Warring States era.

[38] 'Legalism' is *fa jia* in Chinese, and its well-known representatives include Shang Yang and Han Fei.

[39] Anhui China Jiuhuashan Travel Gateway Network, 'The Philosophical Foundations'; Yue, 'The Idea Transformation'; Zhou and Zeng, *A Brief History of Chinese Philanthropy*; Chang, 'Guan Zhong's "Nine Compassions"'; Zhang, Pre-Qin Social Security Philosophies'.

[40] The nine compassions, in Guanzi, are: '(1) *lao lao*, (2) *ci you*, (3) *xue gu*, (4) *yang ji*, (5) *he du*, (6) *wen bing*, (7) *tong qiong*, (8) *zhen kun*, (9) *jie jue*' (Guan *et al.*, 'Entering the Country', 218). See Guanzi and Rickett, *Guanzi*, 227–8.

[41] Chang, 'Guan Zhong's "Nine Compassions"'; Guan and Rickett, *Guanzi*.

[42] See Appendix A for the chronology of dynasties in Chinese History.

[43] Anhui China Jiuhuashan Travel Gateway Network, 'The Philosophical Foundations'.

[44] Shang Yang (390 BC–338 BCE) was a major Legalist. He carried out the Reforms of Shang Yang in the Kingdom of Qin during the Warring States period, which is believed to have reformed the Qin to create the powerful nation that led to the union of the other six kingdoms and the formation of the Qin Dynasty. The ideology was originally written in the Book of Shang Yang

(*Shang Jun Shu*): 'zhi guo zhi ju, gui ling pin zhe fu, fu zhe pin. Pin zhe fu, fu zhe pin, guo qiang', 13.

[45] Han Fei (280–233 BCE) was another major Legalist. *Han Fei Zi* is one of his major writings. These are originally written in Han Fei, 'Xian Xue': 'jin shang zheng lian yu fu ren yi bu shi yu pin jia, shi duo li jian er yu yi duo ye, er yu suo min zhi ji zuo er jie yong, bu ke de ye',222.

[46] Zhou and Zeng, *A Brief History of Chinese Philanthropy*.

[47] Zhou and Zeng, *A Brief History of Chinese Philanthropy*; Wilkinson, *Chinese History*; Cotterell, *China: A History*; Hao and Wang, 'Changing Chinese Views'; Cotterell and Morgan, *China: An Integrated Study*. Purcell, *The Rise of Modern China*.

[48] Sun, *The Chinese Reassessment of Socialism*.

[49] Ibid.

[50] Ibid.; Hao and Wang, 'Changing Chinese views of Western Relations'.

[51] Zheng, 'The Sprit of Volunteers'; Zhou and Zeng, *A Brief History of Chinese Philanthropy*.

[52] Ibid.

[53] Ibid.

[54] Ibid.

[55] Ibid.

[56] Ibid.

[57] Ibid.

[58] Ibid.

[59] *New Compilation of Political Advice* is *Zi Zhen Xin Bian* in Chinese. It was Hong Ren-Gan who proposed it to the King of the Heavenly Kingdom of Great Peace in order to advocate political reforms by learning from the successful experiences of western countries (Zhou and Zeng, *A Brief History of Chinese Philanthropy*).

[60] Zhou and Zeng, *A Brief History of Chinese Philanthropy*.

[61] *An Ideal World* is *Da Tong Shu* in Chinese.

[62] Zhou and Zeng, A Brief History of Chinese Philanthropy.

[63] Ibid.

[64] The principle of people's livelihood, of his 'Old and New Three People's Principles', in Chinese, is *Xin jiu san min zhu yi de min sheng zhu yi*.

[65] Zheng, 'The Spirit of Volunteers'; Zhou and Zeng, *A Brief History of Chinese Philanthropy*.

[66] Zhou and Zeng, *A Brief History of Chinese Philanthropy*.

[67] Zheng, 'The Spirit of Volunteers'.

[68] Zhou and Zeng, *A Brief History of Chinese Philanthropy*.

[69] Peng, 'Before the Volunteering Service'.

[70] Ibid.; Zheng, 'The Spirit of Volunteers'; Zhou and Zeng, *A Brief History of Chinese Philanthropy*.

[71] Ibid.; Hong, 'Learning from Leifeng'; Zhu, 'The Sublimation of Chinese National Spirit'.

[72] Peng, 'Before the Volunteering Service'; Zhou and Zeng, *A Brief History of Chinese Philanthropy*.

[73] Peng, 'Before the Volunteering Service'; Hong, *Learning from Lei Feng is Not a Bask, Vol. 3A*. Zhu, 'The Sublimation of Chinese National Spirit'.

[74] Cheng, 'The Value of Lei Feng's Spirit', 104.

[75] Ibid.; He, 'Youth Ethic Education'.

[76] Peng, 'Before the Volunteering Service'; Shen and Fu, 'Volunteerism'.

[77] Peng, 'Before the Volunteering Service'; Cheng, 'The Value of Lei Feng's Spirit in This Epoch'; Liao, 'The Communist Youth League'.

[78] Wang and Lin, 'Youth Volunteering Activities'.

[79] Tian, 'Several Issues on Developing Volunteering Service'; Tan 'Organizing and Encouraging the Community Volunteering Service in China'. Ding, 'Fostering Volunteering Service for Civil Society'.

[80] Tan, 'Chinese Volunteer Service'.
[81] Wang, 'Discussing Building up the System'.
[82] Tian, 'Several Issues on Developing Volunteering Service'.
[83] Ibid.
[84] Beijing Olympic Volunteer Programme Action Plan, preface.
[85] Beijing is one of the four municipalities.
[86] Li, 'Recruiting Volunteers from Outside Beijing Regions for the Beijing Olympics and Paralympics', 36.
[87] Beijing Olympic Volunteer Programme Action Plan, I: General Principles.
[88] Guan, 'Analyse the Value, Principles and Function System'; Tan, 'Chinese Volunteer Service'.
[89] Beijing 2008, 'Li Binghua uses five "yeses" to explain the work of Beijing 2008 Olympic Volunteer Programme', 28 August 2006. Available at: http://www.beijing2008.cn/62/83/article212038362.shtml, accessed 15 Mar. 2007.
[90] Beijing Olympic Volunteer Programme Action Plan, preface.
[91] Dong and Mangan, 'Beijing Olympic Legacies', 2026.
[92] 'The Communist Party's Decision on Building a Harmonious Society', Xinhua News, 18 Oct. 2006.
[93] Beijing Olympic Volunteer Programme Action Plan, preface.
[94] Ibid.
[95] Ibid.

References

Anhui China Jiuhuashan Travel Gateway Network. 'The Philosophical Foundations of Chinese Ancient Philanthropy' ['Lun zhong guo gu dai ci shan shi ye de si xiang ji chu'], 2008. Available at http://www.jiuhuashan.cc/marketing/Content.do?topid=2101, accessed 30 Dec. 2008.

Athens 2004 Olympic Committee. 'Athens 2004 Volunteers', 2004. Available at http://www.athens2004.com/en/Athens2004Volunteers, accessed 21 Oct. 2005.

Beijing Olympic Organizing Committee. 'Beijing Olympic Volunteers' Action Plan' ['Beijing ao yun hui zhi yuan zhe xing dong ji hua'], 2005. Available at http://www.beijing2008.com/83/99/article211989983.shtml, accessed 8 Nov. 2005.

Beijing Olympic Organizing Committee. 'Who Could Be Smiley Volunteers for the Beijing Olympics?' ['Shui jiang chen wei Beijing ao yun hui de "wei xiao" zhi yuan zhe'], 2005. Available at http://www.beijing2008.com/25/60/article211716025.shtml, accessed 8 Nov. 2005.

Chang, C. 'Guan Zhong's "Nine Compassions"' ['Guan zhong de "jiu hui zhi jiao"'], 2005. Available at http://dzrb.dzwww.com/dazk/ws/200503/t20050330_1013501.htm, accessed 30 Dec. 2008.

Cheng, J. 'The Value of Lei Feng's Spirit in This Epoch' ['Lun lei feng jing shen de dang dai jia zhi']. Postgraduate Seminar [Yan jiu sheng lun tan] 3 (May 2003): 104–7.

Cotterell, A. China: A History. London: Pimlico, 1995.

Cotterell, A. and D. Morgan. China: An Integrated Study. London: George G. Harrap and Co. Ltd., 1975.

Ding, Y. 'Measuring Volunteering in China'. Volunteer Service Journal 1, no. 5 (2003): 8–20.

Ding, Y. 'Fostering Volunteering Service for Civil Society: Volunteering Service in China and Policy Evaluation'. 2003. Available at: http://civa.org.cn/magazine.htm, accessed 25 Mar. 2006.

Dong, J.X. and J.A. Mangan. 'Beijing Olympic Legacies: Certain Intentions and Certain and Uncertain Outcomes'. The International Journal of the History of Sport 25, no. 14 (2008): 2019–40.

Girginov, V. and J. Zhuang. 'The Framing of the Idea of Volunteering in Olympic and Chinese Discourses'. *Proceedings of the 2008 International Convention on Science, Education and Medicine in Sport* 1, 1–4 Aug. 2008, Guangzhou, China: 42–3.

Guan, X. 'Analyse the Value, Principles and Function System of Volunteering Services' ['Lun zhi yuan fu wu de jia zhi, yuan ze yu yun xing ji zhi'], 2006. Available at http://www.cnvolunteer.org/2006/3-7/16483.shtml, accessed 22 March 2006.

Guan, Z., B. Fang and C. Gu. 'Entering the Country' ['Ru guo']. In *Guanzi*, edited by Z. Guan, B. Fang and C. Gu. China: China Art Net, 1929: 218.

Guan, Z. and A. Rickett *Guanzi: Political, Economic, and Philosophical Essays from Early China (A Study and Translation)*, vol. 2. Princeton, NJ: Princeton University Press, 1998.

Han Fei. 'Xian xue'. In *Han Fei Zi*. Available at: http://ctext.org/hanfeizi/xian-xue/zh, accessed 17 Jan. 2008.

Hao, Y.P. and E.M. Wang. 'Changing Chinese views of Western relations, 1840–95'. In *The Cambridge History of China*, vol. II: *Late Ch'ing 1800–1911, part 2*, edited by D.Twitchett and J. Fairbank. Cambridge: Cambridge University Press, 1980: 142–201.

He, X.Y. 'Youth Ethic Education Through Social Activities' ['Zai she hui shi jian zhong dui qing nian yi wu ren yuan jin xing yi de jiao yu de yan jiu']. *Chinese Medical Ethics [zhong guo yi xue lun li xue]* 27 (5) (2004): 57–8.

Hong, X. 'Learning from Leifeng is not Basking in the Sun' ['Xue lei feng, bu shi jiao ni 'shai tai yang']. *Jiangsu Education [Jian su jiao yu]*, 3A (2005).

Hou, J. 'A Discussion of the Development and Concept of Volunteerism' ['Qian yi zhi yuan zhe jing shen de fa zhan yu ji bei nei han'], 2005. Available at http://www.bjyouth.gov.cn/gzyj/qcbb/73113.shtml, accessed 13 June 2006.

Jenner, W.J.F. *The Tyranny of History: The Roots of China's Crisis*. London: Penguin Books, 1994.

Jin, Y. '100,000 Volunteers, One "Name-card": The Value and Meaning of Olympic Volunteering Activities'. The International Forum on Voluntary Services and People's Olympics, 2005. Available at http://www.bjyouth.gov.cn/special/bov/fyg/43698.shtml, accessed 4 April 2006.

Liao, G. 'The Communist Youth League in the Transitional Society' ['She hui hua bian ju zhong de gong qing tuan']. *Southern Youth Research [Nan fang qin shao nian jiao yan jiu]* 1 (2002): 20–2.

Li, B.H. 'Recruiting volunteers from outside Beijing regions for the Beijing Olympics and Paralympics'. Beijing Olympic Volunteer Work Coordination Group 2007 Bulletins Compilation, compiled by the Beijing Olympic Volunteer Work Coordination Group, 2007, 36.

MacAloon, J. 'Volunteers, Global Society and the Olympic Movement'. Paper presented at the *Volunteers, Global Society and the Olympic Movement, Volunteers as a Social Phenomenon*. Lausanne, 24–25 November 1999. Available at http://olympicstudies.uab.es/volunteers/macaloon.html, accessed 27 March 2006.

Peng, X. 'Before the Volunteering Service' ['Zhi yuan fu wu zai wo guo xing qi de qian zou']. In *Approaching Volunteering Service [Zou jin zhi yuan fu wu]*, edited by Beijing Volunteer Association, 2007.

Pound, R. 'Volunteers and the Olympic Movement: past, present and future'. Paper presented at the *Volunteers, Global Society and the Olympic Movement: Olympic Volunteers*. Lausanne, 24–25 November 1999. Available at http://olympicstudies.uab.es/volunteers/pound.html, accessed 27 March 2006.

Purcell, V. *The Rise of Modern China*. London: The Historical Association, 1962.

Ren, H. 'The Beijing Olympics: Chance for Developing Chinese Volunteering Sector' ['Beijing ao yun: wo guo zhi yuan zhe shi ye fu wu de ji zhi']. Paper presented at the *The International Forum on Voluntary Services and People's Olympic*, Beijing, 5–6 June 2005. Available at http://www.bjyouth.gov.cn/special/bov/fyg/43679.shtml, accessed 4 April 2006.

Shang Jun Shu. *Book of Shang Yang* [Shang Jun Shu]. Available at: http://guji.artx.cn/article/8218.html, accessed 2 Feb. 2008.

Shen, J.L. and Z.D. Fu. 'Volunteerism – The Model of Advanced Culture' ['zhi yuan jing sheng: xian jin wen hua de dian fan']. *Journal of Beijing Youth Politics College* 13, no. 2 (2004): 19–24.

Shun, K.L. and D.B. Wong. 'Introduction'. In *Confucian Ethics: A Comparative Study of Self, Autonomy, and Community,* edited by K.L. Shun and D.B. Wong. Cambridge: Cambridge University Press, 2004: 1–7.

Sun, Y. *The Chinese Reassessment of Socialism, 1976–1992.* Princeton, NJ: Princeton University Press, 1995.

Sydney Organising Committee for the Olympic Games. *Official Report of XXVII Games.* Sydney: Sydney Organising Committee for the Olympic Games, 2001.

Tan, J. 'Chinese Volunteer Service in Social Transformation', 2005. Available at http://www.cnvolunteer.org/2005/9-14/232332.shtml, accessed 22 March 2006.

Tan, J. 'Organizing and Encouraging the Community Volunteering Service in China' ['Zhong guo she qu fu wu de zu zhi yu ji li'], 2006. Available at http://www.cnvolunteer.org/2006/3-7/162616.shtml, accessed 22 March 2006.

Tian, K. 'Several Issues on Developing Volunteering Service' ['Guan yu shen hua zhi yuan zhe fu wu de ji ge wen ti'], 2005. Available at http://www.cnvolunteer.org/2005/9-14/233136.shtml, accessed 22 March 2006.

Walker, M. and G. Gleeson. *The Volunteers: How Ordinary Australians Brought About the Extraordinary Success of the Sydney 2000 Games.* Crows Nest: Allen & Unwin, 2001.

Wang, M. *The Classic of Great Peace (Taiping Jing).* Beijing. Zhonghua Publishing House, C. Ming Dynasty. Available at: http://www.daoism.cn/up/data/093tpjh.HTM, accessed 20 Feb. 2008.

Wang, S. 'Discussing Building Up the System of Chinese Community Volunteering Service' ['Lu lun wo guo she qu zhi yuan fu wu de zhi du jian she'], 2006. Available at http://www.cnvolunteer.org/2006/2-21/155933.shtml, accessed 22 March 2006.

Wang, S.K. and H. Lin. 'Youth Volunteering Activities and Learning Lei Feng Activities' ['Qing nian zhi yuan zhi xin dong yu xue lei feng xing dong'], *Youth and Juvenile Study* 39, no. 1 (2003): 3–5.

Wilkinson, E. *Chinese History: A Manual,* revised and enlarged. Cambridge, MA: Harvard University Asia Center, 2000.

Xu, Y.L. 'Analysing the Basis of Volunteering Spirit Developing in China'. *Journal of Tangshan Teachers College* 26, no. 6 (2004): 51–3.

Yue, Z.F. 'The Idea Transformation of Modern Chinese Social Relief and Legislation Demands' ['Jin dai zhong guo she hui jiu ji de li nian shan bian yu li fa su qiu']. *Journal of Zhejiang University (Humanities and Social Sciences)* 3, (2007). Available at http://qkzz.net/magazine/1008-942X/2007/03/1457623.htm, accessed 30 Dec. 2009.

Zhang, R.X. 'Pre-Qin Social Security Philosophies in Shang Dong' ['Qi lu xian qin zhu zi de she hui bao zhang si xiang'], 2004. Available at http://www.lm.gov.cn/gb/insurance/2004-06/18/content_36651.htm, accessed 30 Dec. 2008.

Zhang, Y. 'Chinese Ancient Philanthropy Culture' ['wo guo gu dai de chuan tong ci shan wen hua']. In *Approaching volunteering service [Zou jin zhi yuan fu wu],* edited by Beijing Volunteer Association, 2007.

Zhao, F. 'Volunteerism' ['Shuo shuo zhi yuan zhe jing shen'], 2006. Available at http://www.westwomen.org/modules/contents_7/front/leaf_info.asp?leaf_id=105, accessed 13 June 2006.

Zhao, Y. 'Promoting Volunteerism for Social Development'. *Volunteer Service Journal* 1 (2003): 4.

Zheng, H. 'The Spirit of Volunteers and Harmony Society: A Sociology Perspective' ['Zhi yuan zhe jing shen yu he xie she hui—yi zhong she hui xue shi ye'], 2006. Available at http://www.cnvolunteer.org/2006/2-21/144859.shtml, accessed 22 March 2006.

Zhou, Q.G. and G.L. Zeng. *A Brief History of Chinese Philanthropy.* Beijing: Renmin Publications, 2006.

Zhu, X. 'The Sublimation of Chinese National Spirit – on Lei Feng and Lei Feng Spirit'. *Journal of NUC (Social Sciences)* 21, no. 2 (2005).

Zi, Si. *Moderation*. Available at: http://cn.netor.com/know/hist/book24.htm, accessed 25 Feb. 2008.

Appendix A

Table A1 A brief history of Chinese Chronology

Xia Dynasty			c.2100–c.1600 BC
Shang Dynasty			c.1600–c.1100 BC
Zhou Dynasty	Western Zhou Dynasty		1100–771 BC
	Eastern Zhou Dynasty	Spring and Autumn	770–476 BC
		Warring States	770–221 BC
Qin Dynasty			221–206 BC
Han Dynasty	Western Han		206 BC–24 AD
	Eastern Han		25–220 AD
Three Kingdoms	Wei		220–265
	Shu Han		221–280
	Wu		222–280
Western Jin Dynasty			265–316
Eastern Jin Dynasty			317–420
Northern and Southern Dynasties	Southern Dynasties	Song	420–479
		Qi	479–502
		Liang	502–557
		Chen	557–589
	Northern Dynasties	Northern Wei	386–534
		Eastern Wei	534–550
		Northern Qi	550–577
		Western Wei	535–556
		Northern Zhou	557–581
Sui Dynasty			581–618
Tang Dynasty			618–907
Five Dynasties	Hou Liang		907–923
	Hou Tang		923–936
	Hou Jin		936–946
	Hou Han		947–950
	Hou Zhou		951–960
Song Dynasty	Northern Song Dynasty		960–1127
	Southern Song Dynasty		1127–1279
Liao Dynasty			916–1125
Jin Dynasty			1115–1234
Yuan Dynasty			1271–1368
Ming Dynasty			1368–1644
Qing Dynasty			1644–1911
Republic of China			1912–1949
People's Republic of China			1949–

Source: Department of Xinhua Dictionary, 2001: 1281.

The Effect of Beijing 2008 on China's Image in the United States: A Study of US Media and Polls

Nafees A. Syed

The 2008 Beijing Olympics were widely regarded as China's 'coming out party', a belief strengthened by the extravagance and efficiency of the games. China was open about the image it wished to convey to the world, dubbing its games as the 'humanistic Olympics', 'green Olympics' and 'technological Olympics'. Now, one year after the 2008 Olympics, this paper wishes to examine the extent to which China's Olympics were successful as a public-relations campaign in the United States by focusing on the images of China portrayed in the American media before, during and after the Olympics to detect any significant trends. The analysis focuses on editorial boards of widely circulated newspapers, representing the nine major divisions of the United States, and the three largest cable news networks: Fox News, CNN and MSNBC. Finally, there is an assessment of public opinion polls gauging amity towards China. The results indicate that overall, US media images of China became increasingly negative directly before, during and after the Olympics. US public opinion of China correspondingly became more negative. To conclude, there is a reflection upon the implications of these findings on US-Sino relations and the image China wishes to impart to the American media and public.

1. Introduction

The reason why China, or any other country, wishes to host the Olympics goes beyond its appreciation for physical sports. In *Beyond the Final Score* Victor Cha refutes 'sports purism', the idea that sports have no relevance beyond the physical importance of the game to its players and fans, through three main arguments. [1] The first is that sports create diplomatic breakthroughs, such as the way ping-pong assisted in strengthening United States-China relations. The second is that sports are an 'unmistakable prism through which nation-states project their image to the world

205

and to their own people', [2] while the third is that sports can cause change within a country itself. So, although the original Olympic Charter declares that the use of sports for political goals is against the spirit of the Olympics, in reality the Beijing Olympics has immense political significance.

This may offer an explanation as to why China worked diligently to host the Olympics in Beijing, in the face of intense opposition from other countries and human-rights organizations, and in fierce competition with other candidate countries. In response to criticism, the Chinese worked diligently for the bid in three areas that were also retained as goals during the games: the environment, political campaigns and order/security.

China was very explicit about the image it wished to impart to its own nation and the international community via the themes of a 'humanistic Olympics', 'green Olympics' and 'technological Olympics'. Sinologists use this as a springboard for their own analyses of the games. Karen Christensen sees these three modern themes as China's way of including Western Olympic ideals within traditional Chinese philosophies. [3] Susan Brownell contends that the theme of 'humanistic Olympics', focusing on Chinese culture and image of unity, was the Chinese response to Western criticism of Chinese human rights. [4] Other scholars also affirm that China was trying to impart this message before and during the Olympics. Paul Close, David Askew and Xu Xin argue that China implemented an amendment to its constitution in 2004 stating that it 'respects and safeguards human rights'. This is the first mention of the concept of human rights in the Chinese Constitution: as a result of being chosen an Olympic host country. [5] Close *et al.* also assert that the Olympics were China's 'coming out party'. This was the opportunity for China to present an image of itself as a unified, successful nation on a par with the Western countries that traditionally host the Olympics. [6]

The Official History of the Olympic Games and the IOC hails the 2008 Beijing Games as 'the heralding of a broadening relationship between China and the world in which it is an increasingly significant nation'. This is one of the few references the International Olympic Committee (IOC) makes to a political topic, and it also refers to media coverage with a message from the chairman of NBC Sports and Olympics that NBC would be announcing coverage of the Beijing Olympics for an unprecedented 2,000 hours, [7] which indicates that Americans would have greater opportunity than ever before to be influenced by the Olympics.

Many scholars also emphasize that China's success hinges on media coverage. Grant Jarvie, Dong-Jhy Hwang and Mel Brennan assert that supporters of China's 2008 bid believed that media coverage would emphasize that China was a part of the international community. [8] Xin Xu believed the Olympics would make or break China's legitimacy, based on international perceptions of the 2008 Olympics (he does not specifically mention the US). [9] Nicholas Cull also asserts that the Olympics was China's opportunity to fix its image problem, but its two-pronged message of emphasizing its culture while proving it is also a modern country can only be successful as 'public diplomacy' if foreign media are similarly impressed. [10]

So, after the Olympics, the obvious question is: what were the effects of the Olympics on China's image? As the aforementioned authors argue, the 2008 Beijing Olympics was a tool of soft power in Chinese foreign policy. Three main sources of tension in Sino-US relations include the environment, human rights and the economy. The US media have been critical of what they regard as poor standards in these three areas and the Olympics were significant in that it served as China's public-relations response to negative images in the international media, especially in the US, its most important partner in the international community. China undoubtedly realizes that engaging American media and public opinion is important in strengthening US-Sino relations, especially in an American democracy. Assessing the effect of the Beijing games on China's image not only tells us how successful the Olympics were in raising US media and public amity towards China, an important prerequisite to strengthening US-Sino relations, but also indicates whether the Chinese government's soft-power approach to foreign policy is working.

The answer to the question of the effect of the Beijing Olympics on US images of China will be provided through a detailed analysis of US media and polling. Initially, this involves an analysis of the positions of the editorial boards of widely circulated newspapers in each of the nine divisions of the United States recognized by the US Census Bureau from 2000 to 2006 (to note any secular trends), 2007 (before the Olympics), 2008 (during the Olympics) and 2009 (after the Olympics). This will provide a representative indication of American print media images of China.

The respective publications of these regions (and their circulations) include:

New England: *New York Times* (876,638);
Middle Atlantic: *USA Today* (1,830,594);
East North Central States: *Cleveland Plain Dealer* (252,608);
West North Central States: *Star Tribune of Minneapolis-St Paul* (297,478);
Pacific States: *San Francisco Chronicle* (223,549); [11]
Mountain States: *Salt Lake Tribune* (109,703); [12]
West South Central States: *Houston Chronicle* (343,952); [13]
East South Central States: *St Louis Post Dispatch* (207,145); [14]
South Atlantic States: *Atlanta Journal-Constitution* (181,504). [15]

It is important to note that the positions of the editorial board of a paper published in editorials are distinct from the opinions published in 'op-eds' – often written by people who are not part of the editorial board of a newspaper. The editorials reflect the collective, institutional position of the newspaper and impart this view to their readership.

TV images of China will be analysed using the 'big three' cable news networks: Fox News, CNN and MSNBC. Next to local news broadcasts, these are the most viewed, and their larger audiences receive the same message. [16] Coverage from 2000 to 2006 will be examined (to note any secular trends), 2007 coverage (before the Olympics), 2008 coverage (during the Olympics) and, finally, 2009 coverage (after the Olympics) using transcripts from Fox News, MSNBC and CNN on LexisNexis

News (Transcripts). Focus will specifically be on headlines that relate to China across these time periods. Of course, it is not impossible to make a thorough examination of all of the news broadcasts made by these sources but an assessment of the headlines and transcripts across various news shows will hopefully provide a fairly representative assessment of the broad news coverage and a more thorough analysis of Chinese media images than existing studies. It is also important to note that there are variations in terms of news 'talk shows' and news 'reports', with the former having individual editorial orientations that are generally more critical of China. So the trends noted are more reflective of news reports whose functions do not include opinionated commentary.

Finally, an analysis of American public opinion polls will attempt to gauge amity towards China; asking questions pertaining to China and the Olympics, China's influence as positive or negative and China as a threat, adversary or serious problem. These polls will span the same time ranges: 2000–6 (to note any secular trends), 2007 (before the Olympics), 2008 (during the Olympics) and finally 2009 (after the Olympics). For all three aspects of this research, simultaneous events that may have had an effect on media or public opinion, and which may affect results, will be noted.

2. Literature Review

There is a surprising dearth of literature dealing in any detail with the effects of the 2008 Beijing Olympics on American media and public images of China. Anne-Marie Brady claims that the Olympics were a phenomenal success, with the largest-ever estimated television audience of 2 billion people watching the 8 August opening ceremony. However, she backs up this assessment with little more than that particular statistic and the almost-perfect organization and extravagance of the games. [17] The IOC and countries around the world were amazed by the organization and grandeur of the 2008 Olympics. However, did a positive impression reach America? As America is China's main trading partner and the most powerful nation in the world, this is undoubtedly the most important country at which China would want to direct this Olympic message.

While there is extensive scholarly research into the message that the Chinese government was trying to impart through the Olympics, there have been a few attempts to find what impact of the games have had on images of China produced in the American media. Sonja Foss and Barbara Walkosz, who argue that the media interpret and classify the world for others, have analysed how the American media covered China before and during the Olympics. However, they have used only the *New York Times* and the *Wall Street Journal*, which is a small, unrepresentative sample size from which to analyse American media reactions, and have ignored television media, which are far more popular than print media. Furthermore, they assert that the media covered China in multiple contradicting ways without any analysis of which form of coverage was more prevalent. For example, they write that media themes were as follows: 'China as Western', 'China as Unique' (Asian), 'China as a Violator of Human Rights', 'China as an Upholder of Human Rights', 'China as Abundant Resources', 'China as Limited Resources', 'China as a Powerful Economic Partner' and 'China as an Unreliable Economic Partner'. Their analysis was helpful, however, in identifying different areas of coverage: modernity, human rights and economic power. [18]

John Kamm's 'A Marathon Challenge to Improve China's Image' was the only article discovered that explicitly discussed the effect of the Olympics on China's image using empirical data; although it only examines a short period prior to the Olympics, not during or afterwards. From 2005 to 2007, favourable worldwide opinion of China dropped, coinciding with reports of China's own human-rights violations and affiliations with other repressive countries, in a slogan called the 'Genocide Olympics'. Professor Steve Kull, of the University of Maryland commented: 'Recent stories of a tightening of state controls appear to have hurt China's image in the world.' The percentage of Americans with a favourable opinion of China was 52 per cent in 2006 but only 43 per-cent in 2007. The annual Harris Poll found that the percentage of Americans who considered China an ally or friend dropped from 46 in 2006 to 30 in 2007. Only 37 per cent of Americans trusted China to act responsibly in the world, according to a Chicago Council on Global Affairs poll, and according to a UPI/Zogby poll less than 4 per cent of Americans believed that human-rights reforms introduced in China before the Olympics would be long-lasting. According to an NBC poll in July 2007, two-thirds of Americans had little or no interest in visiting China to see the Olympics. However, almost 80 per cent of Americans opposed a boycott of the Olympics. There was no doubt that China wished to use the Olympics to attempt to counter its tainted reputation, with Chairman Hu Jintao telling a group of party propagandists that 'We should work hard on overseas propaganda to further display and improve a positive state image'. [19]

Interestingly, Daniel Bell, along with Grant Jarvie, Dong-Jhy Hwang and Mel Brennan, were the only authors discovered who predicted that China's image agenda, including telling its citizens how to behave with 'Olympic civility', might fail because 'To Western ears, all this might sound like yet another example of an authoritarian state telling its subjects what to think and do'. [20]

In short, there is no literature specifically dealing with the impact of the Olympics on American public opinion after the event. This paper is intended to fill this gap. Most scholarship focused on explaining the image China wished to present. There was some speculation about what effect this would have on the international community, but little empirical analysis. There was even less scholarship on the effect this would have on American media or public opinion, but even this was limited to before or during the Olympics, not afterwards. The analysis of the effect of the Olympics on American media was also inadequate in its scope and explanation; and again did not assess the coverage of China after the Olympics. In short, the literature is not particularly helpful in answering the question of whether China was successful in using the Olympics to affect the American media and the public image of China.

3. The Argument

The hypothesis will be tested that the 2008 Olympics, which were the most lavish to date, had the effect of increasing media and public amity towards China. The prediction will therefore be examined that during and after the games, American news media would convey the image of a modern China capable of joining the US and other developed countries on the world stage. If this prediction is correct, then American public opinion of China will also improve during and after the games and Americans will view China more positively, as a modern, rising power. The united image imparted by China throughout the games, along with the image of technological and economic advancement, will have countered the negative image of China as a human-rights violator, polluter and economically inefficient country.

4. Findings

4.1. Print Media Sources

From 2000 to 2006, the *New York Times* published differing views on China and its policies. The editorial board notably did not have a favourable view of China and focused on human rights criticisms, with occasional foreboding references to China's rising power. In 2007, the editorial board referenced 'China's spectacular growth' and other positive views of China's economy. [21] In fact, the editorials were often sympathetic to China at the expense of the US government. For example, the board spoke disparagingly of the protectionist policies of the US Congress, calling them 'blame China bills'. [22] One editorial described US complaints about China's trade as 'misunderstandings – intensified by growing anti-China sentiment in this country'. [23] At the same time, there were frequent references to China as a 'puzzle' economically, alluding to the contradiction of China's open-market economy but closed, repressive policy with regard to human rights. [24]

In contrast, the editorial board was very sceptical about China's environmental policies. There was demand for 'China's full participation' if greenhouse gases were to be reduced, as well as repeated mention that China 'should soon surpass the United States as the world's leading emitter of carbon dioxide'. [25] The articles were not sympathetic to China as a source of the emissions; but instead focused on criticizing the Chinese government for not using enough of its economic surplus to help the environment. [26]

The harshest criticism was directed at China's human-rights policies. It was censured for its role as Sudan's main trading partner and its lack of effort to address the situation in Darfur. It was also criticized for supporting other repressive regimes in Africa and Burma. [27] The board also frequently referenced China when citing examples of repressive regimes. In the months preceding the Olympics, this criticism became much harsher. Even before August 2008, China was reprimanded for not keeping its Olympic promise. [28] Two editorials were published in the *New York*

Times in March 2008 alone about China 'terrorizing Tibet' [29] and several more on Chinese suppression of freedom – from the jailing of dissidents to the restrictions for overseas visitors to China. [30] This negative image persisted during the Olympics in an editorial position summed up in the paper's final Olympic editorial: 'The final gold medal – for authoritarian image management – can already be safely awarded to China's Communist Party leadership.' [31] Interestingly, there have been only a couple of editorials since the Olympics criticizing China's human rights violations (both regarding Tibet).

USA Today also wrote from a negative viewpoint on China between 2000 and 2006, mainly on the lack of democracy, although it was much less prolific on the subject than the *Times*. [32] The negative image of China intensified in 2007 and the editorial board condemned China on various human-rights fronts, including the detention of journalists and trying to trade with Sudan. It remained sceptical of what it called China's empty promise to improve human rights conditions in order to become host of the 2008 Olympics. [33] The Olympics also served only to strengthen the board's conviction that while China 'wanted to come in with a bang, and they succeeded', the games also highlighted China's repression. The Olympics was even likened to a 'Sputnik moment', hinting at an imminent Cold War. The chilling conclusion: 'In Beijing, China served notice it will be a formidable competitor, and not just in the athletic arena. It's a challenge that the US dare not avoid.' [34] Interestingly, following that harsh editorial, the tenor of the *USA Today* board became much less aggressive. Although subsequent editorials emphasize China's rising power at the expense of the US, they do not allude to Cold War-like rivalry. For example, the board raised fears that the Chinese had lent one trillion dollars to the US, giving Chinese Premier Wen Jiabao leverage to actually scold the US in March 2009. However, the article also criticized the American government more than China's for its financial irresponsibility. [35]

Although the *Cleveland Plain Dealer* was critical of China's human-rights policies, its views were more neutral than those of its counterparts. It even acknowledged that China had a right to be confused about America's ambivalent policy towards Taiwan. [36] In 2007 the paper continued condemning China for not doing more regarding Darfur. [37] In the months before the Olympics, the *Plain Dealer* shifted its attention to Tibet and the Chinese crackdown on peaceful protesters. [38] It also criticized China's unfair trading practices. [39] During the Olympics, coverage of China increased in negativity. The editorial board published a series called 'Let the Games Begin' which published polls indicating that Chinese citizens were dissatisfied with their government. [40] Subsequent 2008 Olympic articles centred on US gold-medal wins and not on China or the extravagance of its ceremonies. Thereafter, there was little mention of China in any editorials from the 2008 Olympics to 1 May 2009.

The *Star Tribune of Minneapolis-St Paul* also portrayed a neutral image of China, leaning towards strong US-China relations instead of harsh criticism of China, and cited the need for Americans to learn Chinese in order to strengthen US-Sino relations. [41] Before August 2008, there were suggestions that the Olympics could signal a change, bringing more freedom into the Communist nation. [42] There was surprisingly little coverage of China during and after the games.

The San Francisco Chronicle editorial board was steadily disparaging of China from 2000 to 2006. The newspaper sceptically questioned US deals with China. [43] Most articles made some allusion to China's growing power in the world, especially its economic power. The editorial board also frowned upon America's growing dependence on China to buy its debt. [44] In the months leading up to the Olympics, the coverage of China became more negative. Chinese products were denounced for being low-quality and China was reprimanded for having poor production and inspection standards. [45] Like the articles from 2000 to 2006, editorials were more critical of China as an unfair economic player than as a human-rights violator. This might have to do with the fact that California has a larger economy that any other US state and therefore economic relations with China would be of interest at a state level.

In 2008, the same paper's editorial board began condemning China for already ruining the spirit of the Olympics. China was accused of 'banking on the popularity of the Olympics to outshine its problems', throwing journalists into prison and hoping few would notice and being complicit in the destruction in Darfur. [46] Attention shifted from China's economic power to its violation of human rights, especially 'Tyranny in Tibet'. [47] During the Olympics, editorials did not mention the slick organization and extravagance of the Beijing Olympics, instead conferring upon China 'a gold medal for smog'. [48] Following some angry 'Letters to the Editor' demanding that the paper offer less biased coverage of the Olympics, the editorial board wrote its least critical article on China, which highlighted its Olympic glory and hoped that in the future China would value liberty as much as it values the economy. [49] Post-Olympic editorials on China were more favourable, one even asserting that the US had much to learn from China's $586 billion-stimulus plan. [50]

The *Salt Lake Tribune* followed the same pattern of portraying negative views of China from 2000 to 2006. This negative image, however, was shaped on economic terms; China was viewed as a rising economic power that was increasingly financing American debt. [51] On an environmental front, China was accused of pressuring scientists to mitigate their findings on the seriousness of global warming. [52] During the Olympics, there was only one *Tribune* editorial on China, which both criticized China for repressing protesters while acknowledging its need for intense security, using the example of Salt Lake City's tight security during the 2002 Winter Olympic Games. [53] There has been little mention of China in its editorials since then.

The *Houston Chronicle* also emphasized a negative economic view of China between 2000 and 2006. [54] In 2007, there was criticism of poor food and drug regulation [55] but it was not until 2008 that the emphasis shifted to China's human-rights performance. The editorial board pushed for the US government to use the Olympics as leverage to persuade China to loosen its restrictions on human rights. [56] This criticism intensified during March and April 2008, when world media attention focused on the plight of Tibetans and Uighurs and protesters lined the route of the Olympic flame relay. [57] During the Olympics, China was portrayed as a strong and rising economic power, hosting a lavish and spectacular Olympic Games. However, the editorial board was equally strong in denouncing China's suppression of dissent during the games and failure to uphold its promise of 2000 to improve human rights before, during and after the Olympics. [58] Since then, however, the *Chronicle* has refrained from publishing editorials on China.

The *St Louis Post Dispatch*, like most of the print media sources researched, also portrayed a negative view of China. Its editorials were also unique in that they were well researched and distinctly different from those of other newspaper sources, which mainly condemned Chinese censorship, relationship with other authoritarian regimes and the quelling of dissent. For example, the *Dispatch* ran editorials on China's removing organs from executed prisoners, adherents to the beliefs and practices of Falun Gong and others as a gruesome example of Chinese violations of human rights. Besides the few editorials attacking China's poor human rights record, there was little attention paid to it until March 2007, when there were several editorials on China, most of which were negative. The board described China's growing economic power compared to that of the the the US, arguing that China's rise was worrisome. [59] The 2008 Olympics were linked to genocide, referring to China's relationship with Sudan [60] and during the games the board published a scathing editorial on the Beijing Olympics, likening it to the coming-out party of Hitler's Nationalist Socialist Party during the 1936 Berlin Olympics. The editorial made it clear that while China was flaunting its money and economic clout, the world was not fooled and knew of its human rights violations. [61] Since the Olympics, the board has not produced any editorials specifically on China.

The *Atlanta Journal-Constitution* portrayed a negative view of China, as an economic adversary annihilating US industries such as its textile industry. [62] In a somewhat contradictory stance, the paper has also refuted claims that China is responsible for America's economic problems, claiming that such a viewpoint merely diverts politicians from any domestic causes of economic downturns. [63] However, beyond criticism of Chinese Internet censorship, there was little attention paid to Chinese human rights before 2007. [64] During that year, there were several editorials deploring China's poor safety standards and warning American consumers of toxic Chinese products. [65] The newspaper differed from other print sources in that it argued that America needs to maintain healthy relations with China for economic reasons rather than censuring it, because China is a rising power. It further maintained that by being a strong economic partner, the US could subsequently pressurize China to adhere to human rights. [66] Surprisingly, there were no editorials on China after the Olympics until 1 May 2009.

Of course, every newspaper has its editorial board with it own collective views, but equally, most share similar ideological values with their readerships. It is important to keep in mind, however, that the states within each region can vary somewhat in their views even though they can often be aligned on political or ideological views.

However, the following results assume that each publication selected (for the wide circulation in their region) is a representative sample for an entire division of the US.

The *New York Times* editorial board was most comprehensive and vehement in its criticism of China before 2007. It was the harshest critic of China's human rights and environmental policies. The only other publication to portray a negative image of China's human rights was the *St Louis Post Dispatch* and, to a lesser degree, *USA Today*. The *Salt Lake Tribune* was the only publication that portrayed China as a giant guzzler, unconcerned about the environment. The fact that only New England and Middle Atlantic states were concerned about human rights between 2000 and 2006 might suggest that liberal states were more cognizant of this issue, but the notable exception was the East South Central states, which are Republican and were similarly critical of human rights. The Pacific states however, which are liberal, focused on the economy instead of human rights. The *San Francisco Chronicle*, the *Atlanta Journal-Constitution*, the *Houston Chronicle* and the *Salt Lake Tribune* all focused on portraying China negatively as an economic rival instead. In fact, only New England had a positive economic image of China, and only the *Cleveland Plain Dealer* and the *Star Tribune of Minneapolis-St Paul* portrayed an overall positive or neutral image of China.

While coverage before 2007 covered a wide but largely negative spectrum of images of China, between 2007 and the Olympics, the portrayed image changed almost uniformly to focus on China as a human-rights abuser. The notable exception was the *Salt Lake Tribune*, whose negative image was of China economically, not in terms of human rights. Only the *Star Tribune of Minneapolis-St Paul* and the *The Atlanta Journal-Constitution* offered a positive image of China.

During the Olympics, these two publications made little mention of China, while those of almost every other region intensified the image of China as a human-rights abuser. The *Salt Lake Tribune* and the *Houston Chronicle* changed from its pre-Olympic negative image to a mixed portrayal of China, sometimes offering a positive image and sometimes a negative one. The change following the Olympics was most drastic. All publications, with the exception of the *New York Times*, paid less attention to China and when they did, were fairly neutral. The *New York Times*, however, continued its negative image of China as a human-rights abuser although it no longer portray China as an environmental danger.

Prior to the Olympics, all but two of the publications examined portrayed a negative image of China. All of them strengthened this viewpoint between 2007 and the staging of the games, except for the *Star Tribune* and the *AJC*, which improved their images of China, and all but one of these publications lessened their negative portrayal of China towards the end of the Olympics and afterwards. One possible explanation is that these print sources had focused extensively on China during early 2008 and sought to cover other areas after the Olympics in order to sustain the interest of their readership. It is possible that this decreased negative focus on China was due to the success of China's 'coming out party' in proving its economic modernity, its environmental advances and its ability to bring its people together to create what was hailed by many as the best Olympics thus far. As Table 1 indicates, acknowledgement of this success was limited in New England, where environmental criticism of China had decreased but human-rights criticisms continued. During this period , another major Chinese event covered by the media was the baby-formula scandal, which centred on the discovery that Chinese milk and infant formula had been contaminated by the toxic chemical melamine. This was however a reflection of China as an unsafe country beset with corruption issues rather than as an abuser of human rights.

There is one noteworthy and confounding variable that may explain a positive effect on China's image: the 30 August 2008 Panzhihua earthquake. It is possible that this tragedy, so soon after the destructive Sichuan earthquake in May of that year, may have evoked sympathy and improved China's image. It occurred only a few days after the Olympics, so it is difficult to isolate the effect of either event in terms of an enhanced image of China. However, the Sichuan earthquake had not reduced negative images of China, so it is unlikely the August earthquake did the same. Some publications also showed a decline in negative portrayals during the Olympics, even before the earthquake. In comparison the earthquake coverage was minimal compared to the extensive Olympic coverage.

4.2 TV Media Sources

Of the 'Big Three' cable networks, CNN was the most prolific on China between 2000 and 2006, followed by Fox and then MSNBC, which is probably due to CNN's greater international focus (see Figure 1). During that period of time, MSNBC was fairly neutral towards China. For example, in 2001 it called the US reconnaissance aircraft a 'spy plane' and instead of reprimanding China for its actions reported more on the US and China reaching a compromise on the issue. [67] This favourable, sympathetic view of China was noticeable across news segments, even with regard to human rights. For example, when a human rights protester interrupted President Hu Jintao and President Bush, MSNBC questioned why the protester was allowed to get a media pass since she was a journalist from a Falun Gong newspaper. [68]

MSNBC's image of China became more critical in 2007 after it had destroyed a space satellite with a ballistic missile. This was portrayed as China 'flexing its military muscle' and 'fuelling fears of an arms race'. [69] References to the Chinese Olympics were fairly positive, probably because NBC and its networks won the rights to air the Olympics in 2008. [70] Certain shows were far more critical, including *Tucker*, in which Tucker Carlson called China a 'freaky place'. [71] In 2008, prior to the Olympics, except for negative references on Chris Matthews's *Hardball*, there were rare references to Tibet and China's crackdown on reporters and protesters before the Olympics. [72] Chris Matthews also criticized President Bush for not taking a tougher stance towards the Chinese government. For example, when President Bush planned on visiting members of an underground church, the Chinese government

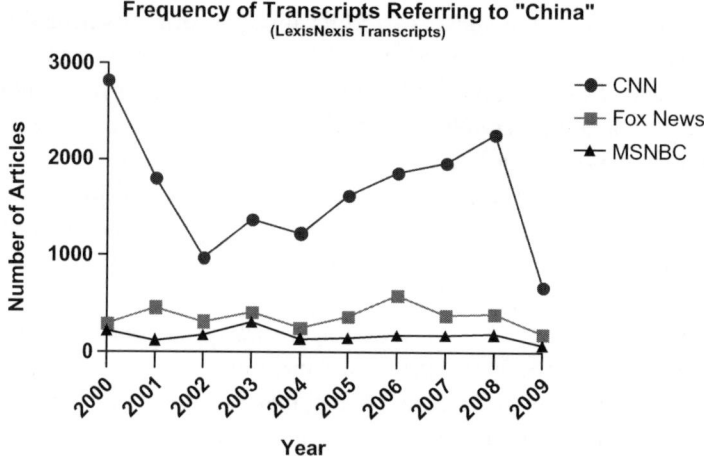

Figure 1 Frequency of cable news transcripts referring to China over time

ordered its members to leave during the president's visit and President Bush did not pursue the subject. [73]

Initially, the Olympics were described as 'an all-American moment in terms of the rooting for American teams'. [74] However, when news leaked that a Chinese girl was lip-synching the national anthem, MSNBC began portraying the hi-tech 'perfectionist' Olympics as fake. [75] The theme of a 'fake' Olympics continued along with suggestions that certain Chinese athletes were younger than the required age, and whenever the splendour of the Olympics was mentioned, it was usually alongside a negative comment that parts of the Olympics were staged, that the fireworks displays were digitally enhanced, or equally negative comments. [76]

After the Olympics, China was portrayed as a rival to the US, especially in terms of what was portrayed as its growing economic clout as that of the US was waning. [77] There were a few instances in which it was suggested that America learn from China's stimulus package and other economic measures, which implies a positive image of China as an economic superpower. [78] There were few broadcasts that highlighted human rights in China or China as a military threat.

Fox News was highly critical of China between 2000 and 2006. Bill O'Reilly, for example, likened China to Nazi Germany and the USSR for 'killing babies', referring to China's one-child policy and consequent abortions. [79] In 2001, Fox covered the fall of the US reconnaissance aircraft rather differently from MSNBC, blaming the Chinese for not turning the Americans over. There were even accusations that China had tried to influence the outcome of a US presidential election by donating money to President Bill Clinton's campaign. [80] There were also fears of nuclear war with China, especially over Taiwan [81] There was also debate over China's involvement in the 'war on terror', with general agreement that China is repressive towards its Tibetan and Muslim minorities, but also that America still needs it as an ally in the war on terror. [82]

In 2007 Fox was highly critical of China's missile destruction of its space satellite, portraying this as a test of China's military prowess. It predicted that this would hinder US-China relations and urged the Bush administration to take action to ensure that China did not do this again. [83] Furthermore, Fox was critical of Chinese relations with Iran, portraying the country negatively as an arms dealer. [84] There was little portrayal of China as a human-rights abuser, although Fox did criticize its Internet censorship. [85]

In 2008, Fox began to sharply condemn Chinese repression of Tibetan protesters. There was a negative portrayal of China as a police state, which made it dangerous for journalists to enter the country and cover the plight of dissidents and protesters. [86] Furthermore, there was intense criticism of NBC for using Beijing as a 'backdrop for NBC'. CNN argued that NBC did less than it might have to cover the repression of protesters during the Olympics. A Fox guest, Jim Pinkerton, said: 'I think NBC spent a billion dollars on the Olympics and they weren't about to have the Chinese pull the visa of Tom Brokaw or Brian Williams by coverage they didn't want.' [87] At the start of the Olympics, Fox portrayed China positively while covering President Bush's presence there as the first sitting American president to attend a foreign Olympics. Bush stated that he believed that the Olympics were a time of cooperation. Fox was also sympathetic to Chinese security efforts during the games. [88] There was also positive coverage of the Chinese people as friendly and hospitable, even though coverage of the attack on the US couple during the games rather questioned this. [89]

Towards the end of the Olympics, as it became evident that China was leading the gold-medal count, it received much more negative coverage. Fox revealed that the Chinese were winning because they trained children from an early age, giving them little time to visit their families and forcing them to practise for several hours a day. In making these children into world champions, the Chinese authorities often lied about their age in order to make them eligible for competition. China's authoritarianism was described as even being evident in its sports. [90]

Like CNN, after the Olympics Fox's portrayed image of China was negative and indicated a US-China rivalry. When five Chinese vessels surrounded a US ship in what the Pentagon contended were international waters, it was described as a 'face-to-face showdown at sea'. [91] Fox also portrayed China negatively for taking advantage of US economic weakness and trying to gain advantage by means of its hold on US debt. [92] As MSNBC had also suggested, there were fears of Chinese cyber-spies. [93] In general terms, the image of China was negative, although more focused on portraying China as a rival than a human-rights abuser, as had largely been the case before the Olympics.

CNN's reported image of China between 2000 and 2006 was similar to that of MSNBC. The coverage of the fall of the US reconnaissance aircraft was fairly neutral and CNN used the phrase 'spy plane' when Fox preferred the more favourable (for the US) 'reconnaissance aircraft'. [94] There was moderate human-rights criticism, but like the other two major cable networks, negative reporting of Chinese human rights was not as strong as in the print media. [95] With regard to China as a potential rival, however, its reported image was highly negative. China was portrayed as an economic threat for bidding to buy Maytag [an electrical goods manufacturer], for example. The threat of a top Chinese general to make nuclear strikes against the US also raised alarm bells, and heightened fears that China would soon be a military as well as economic rival to the US [96]

In 2007, CNN was more prolific with China-related broadcasts than its MSNBC and Fox counterparts – and also more critical than it was from 2000 to 2006. The term 'Communist' was sometimes mentioned before 'China'. There were also allegations of China refusing to obey international trade rules and implications that it should not be part of the World Trade Organization. This further raised fears that the US was losing jobs to China because the latter was not adhering to fair standards. [97] Furthermore, there were broadcasts on safety concerns, reprimanding 'Communist China' for its poor safety standards and warning the American consumer that because China does not follow international trade rules, its products might be dangerous. [98] On pollution, CNN was equally harsh towards China and the US, recognizing that it was not fair of the US to demand that only China as a developing country should work to reduce greenhouse gas emissions. [99] Although there was praise for Chinese progress towards the games, already believed to be better planned than the Athens games, towards the end of 2007, 'human rights' were frequently mentioned alongside 'Olympics' in interviews, including those with Hollywood stars such as Richard Gere who were vocal about Chinese repression of Tibetans and others.

During 2008, there was a marked increase in CNN broadcasts referring to China: 2263, up from 1963 in 2007. CNN portrayed a positive image of China's economy, discussing its economic boom and how the Chinese could now enjoy the same luxuries that many Americans had, such as cars. [100] However, this coverage was tempered by criticism of Chinese regulations, including poor safety standards and the image of China as a cyber- and economic threat – an image especially evident in the *Lou Dobbs Show*. [101] Again, the use of 'Communist China' was popular. Criticism of Chinese repression of human rights became harsher in March, when CNN sympathized with Tibetan protesters and again interviewed the frequent CNN interviewee, actor Richard Gere. [102] CNN's image of China became more and more negative as it covered the protests during the Olympic torch relay and ongoing Chinese restrictions of its minorities, protesters and journalists. CNN even questioned whether President Bush should attend the Olympics after House Speaker Nancy Pelosi recommended that he should not attend the opening ceremonies (although she thought he should attend the games to support American athletes). [103] Immediately before the Olympics, the image of China was positive. The Chinese were commended for their security measures, even though those were criticized elsewhere for being an excuse to crack down on protesters. [104] China was also commended for its efforts to reduce pollution in Beijing. [105] There was relatively less coverage of human rights situations in China, including in Tibet, Xinjiang and so on.

During the Olympics, CNN praised the splendour of the Opening Ceremonies highly, but became highly critical of the pollution in Beijing and the Chinese government's efforts to ignore the seriousness of the problem by calling the pollution 'mist' and the natural result of evaporation. [106] They also reported extensively on the American tourists attacked and killed in Beijing. At the end, there was acknowledgement that China had hosted an amazing, expensive Olympics and that London 'will have a tough act to follow' when hosting the 2012 Olympics. [107]

After the games, focus was shifted to the presidential elections and fears that the US was sinking behind economic giants like China. [108] CNN continued to refer to China as 'Communist China' and even made attempts to align China with communist North Korea. [109] There were also heightened fears of China's military capabilities. The 2009 Pentagon report on China was highly publicized, along with fears that its navy had already caught up with that of the US. [110] In March there were several reports on China as a cyber-spy, hacking into the computers of its citizens and those of international governments. [111] Interestingly, there was a positive view of China's economy and consumers, and it was portrayed as an economically modern, successful country. [112] Subsequently, this perception of China was mostly portrayed as a symbol of America's decline, especially with reports that China owned much of the US debt. Generally, the image of China was just as negative, if not more so, as it was before the Olympics. [113]

TV coverage of China was generally speaking much more positive than print media coverage from 2000 to 2006. Only Fox, the notably conservative news source, was highly critical of China, followed by CNN, which was fairly neutral but portrayed a negative image of China as a human-rights abuser, and MSNBC, which had a fairly positive image of China. MSNBC may have had such a positive view because it had won the rights to air the 2008 Olympics and may have been afraid of offending China and losing those rights, which would have had huge financial implications. Up until the Olympics, MSNBC continued this positive image while that portrayed by Fox and CNN became more negative. All networks covered China's destruction of the satellite in a negative manner, but Fox and CNN continued, showing China as a military threat. Both also showed China as a human-rights violator and as a manufacturer of unsafe goods, from dangerous baby formula to toys. CNN further criticized China's pollution. During the Olympics, all three news networks aired negative images of China – even MSNBC. The theme was China as a 'fake' country, which was only able to stage such a spectacular Olympics by using authoritarian measures such as making children compete, and using a little girl to lip-synch for the national anthem because she was more attractive than the real singer. MSNBC's image of China then became much more negative than the one it had presented from 2000 to 2006. Fox and CNN also continued to present an image of China as a rival to the US, rather than as a human-rights abuser. This suggests that the Olympics were successful in positioning China as an economically modern nation but in general terms China continued to be reported negatively by US cable networks. The 'economically modern' image came at a time when America's own economic image was declining, and the cable news networks highlighted to this change by portraying China as a rising power that the US would have to contend with in the future. This could be interpreted as a successful measure to distract TV media from the image of China as a human rights and environmental violator, but the image of China among cable news networks remained a negative one.

4.3 Public Opinion Polls

There were several polls on China that attempted to gauge different aspects of its image among Americans. The most consistent was a Gallup Poll asking the question 'What is your overall opinion of ... China? Is it very favourable, mostly favourable, mostly unfavourable, or very unfavourable?' This was in an annual survey that questioned Americans' overall opinion on several different countries (see Figure 2). Between 2000 and 2006, the trend was for Americans to have increasingly favourable views of China, until a decade high in 2006, but this trend reversed in 2007 with an all-time high (55 per cent) number of Americans who had an unfavourable view of China in 2008. This suggests that there was a noticeable increase in the number of Americans holding a negative image of China in the latter part of the decade. This trend began in 2007, the year before the Olympics, when media coverage of China became intense. [114]

Several polls asked some variation of the question 'Is China a threat?', although these were not consistently asked, and questions that were phrased differently generated different responses. For example, the question 'Do you think that ... China's emergence as a world power is a major threat, a minor threat or not a threat to the well being of the United States?' produced more negative responses than the question 'All things considered, which of these descriptions comes closest to your view of China today. ... Do you think China is ... an adversary, a serious problem,

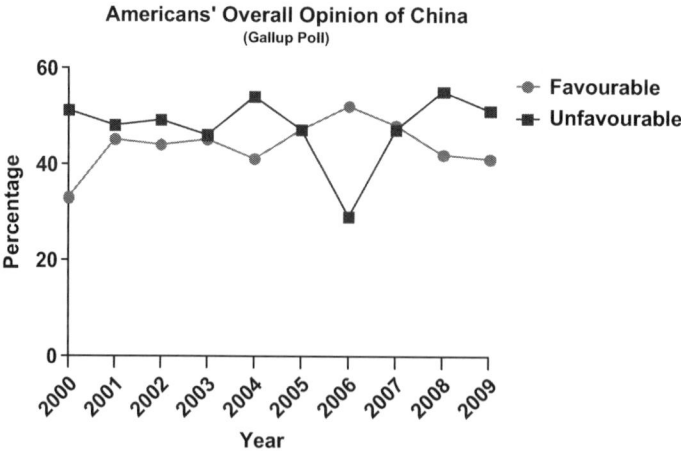

Figure 2 Americans' favourable/unfavourable opinion of China over time

but not an adversary, or, not much of a problem?' The only question for which the poll from 2008 could be compared with polls of several previous years was the Pew Research Centre for the People and the Press Political Survey's asking 'Do you think that. ... China's emergence as a world power is a major threat, a minor threat or not a threat to the well being of the United States?' (see Figure 3). Although the question was not asked annually, it was asked in 2000, then 2002, 2003, several times in 2008 and in 2009. The results showed a marked increase in the percentage of Americans who viewed China as a threat as opposed to those who did not. Before 2008, the percentage of Americans who viewed China as a threat was in the 70s, ranging from 70 to 79 per cent, but in the three 2008 polls and the one in 2009, the percentage was consistently in the 80s. There was also a steady decrease in the percentage of Americans who did not see China as a threat. [115]

Since the word 'threat' is rather vague, there has been an attempt to identify just what type of threat Americans thought was posed by China. Between 2005 and 2008, there were a few differently worded polls that asked Americans whether China was a military threat. An NBC News/*Wall Street Journal* poll asked Americans 'Do you consider China to be a military threat to the United States, or not?'; 50 per cent thought China was a military threat while 48 per cent did not. [116] A CNN/Opinion Research Corporation Poll asked the same question in 2008 before the Olympics, and the opinion was 51 per cent 'Yes' and 49 per cent 'No'. [117] A 2009 Gallup Poll found that 91 per cent of Americans were concerned about China's military power, 74 per cent of whom were 'moderately to very concerned'. [118] This exact question had not been asked before, so there is no way to gauge just when the percentage of Americans concerned increased so dramatically. However, if this poll is compared to the closest question, 'Do you consider China to be a military threat to the United States, or not?', the percentage of Americans who do seems to have increased, even if

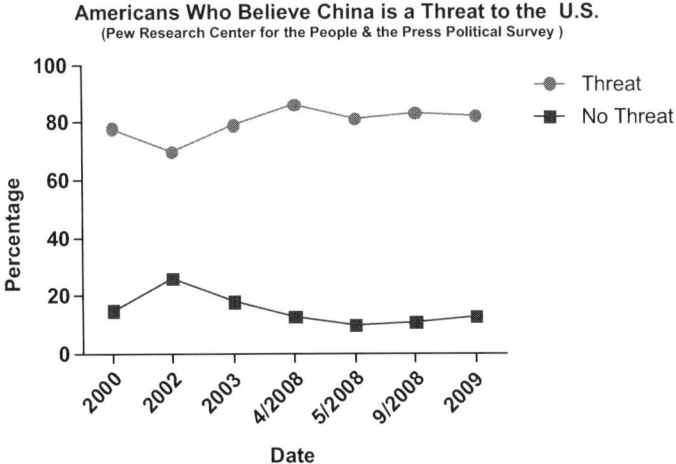

Figure 3 American opinion of China as a threat over time

we regard only the 'moderately and very concerned' Americans as those who view China as a military threat.

The wording of questions asking whether Americans view China as an economic threat has also been inconsistent across time. A Gallup/CNN/USA Today Poll in 2005 and 2008 (in July, before the Olympics) asked, 'Do you consider China to be an economic threat to the United States, or not?': in 2005 64 per cent thought 'Yes' it was a threat, as opposed to 33 per cent who did not think so. A much larger 70 per cent answered 'Yes' in 2008 as opposed to 30 per cent who did not consider China a threat. [119] In 2007, World Public Opinion found that 60 per cent of Americans thought China's economy will grow as large as that of the US and only 35 per cent thought America's economy would be larger. Nine per cent saw this as positive, 52 per cent as equally positive or negative and 33 per cent saw this as mostly negative. [120] Also in 2007, A Pew Global Attitudes Project, 'Global Unease With Major World Powers', found that 41 per cent of Americans viewed China's growing economy as 'good' as opposed to 45 per cent who saw it as a bad development. In 2005 a much larger 49 per cent thought it was good. [121] A July 2008 Chicago Council on Global Affairs poll found that 76 per cent of Americans thought the Chinese economy would become as large as that of the US and among this same group 43 per cent saw China's rising global power as a 'critical threat' to vital US interests. [122] It is possible that news coverage of China's economic investment in the $40 billion Olympics may have contributed to this increase, although it is difficult to tell if the percentage would have been higher if it had not been for the Olympics. The only comparable poll after the Olympics asked: 'China's emergence as a world power is a major threat, a minor threat or not a threat to the well being of the United States?' If we assume 'economic power' correlates with 'global power' (and as we see above the Chicago Council and other organizations often combined these concepts), then this indicates that the percentage of Americans who think China is an economic threat has increased to 83 per cent compared to the 11 per cent who do not think so. [123] In 2009 this figure remained steady at 82 per cent. [124] It is more than likely that China's 'threat' is seen in both military *and* economic terms, as in China's case the two are often conflated by the media.

When the question was asked in terms of whether or not China was an adversary, the issue of the 'threat' was specifically placed in foreign policy terms: 'All things considered, which of these descriptions comes closest to your view of China today. Do you think China is an adversary; a serious problem but not an adversary; or not much of a problem?' Between 2000 and 2004, there was a slightly decreasing percentage of Americans who saw China as an adversary and a serious problem and an increasing percentage who thought that China was not a big problem (See Figure 4). Between 2005 and 2008 the trend was reversed to 2000 levels, so the Olympics seemed to have a minimal effect on how Americans viewed their relationship with China – the possible effect of this being that slightly more Americans viewed China as a problem or adversary than would be expected from the secular, slightly decreasing trend. [125] BBC polls producing similar results found

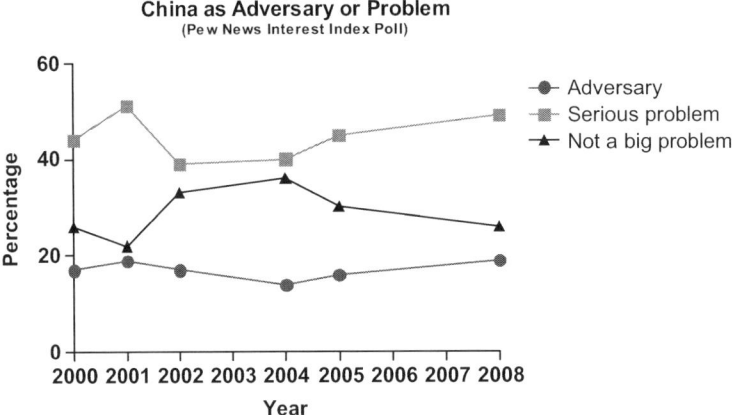

Figure 4 Americans who see China as an adversary or serious problem, over time

that those younger than 35 were less likely to see China as a threat, but as not all of the poll datasets were available it is difficult to make a generalization. However, this certainly indicates that views on China are split along age lines. [126]

The percentage of Americans who saw China as a threat and an adversary to the US increased. Interestingly, before the war in Iraq in 2001 and 2002, Fox polls asked Americans 'Which country in the world do you think is the greatest military threat to the US (United States) today?' The number one country mentioned was China, with more responses than Iraq, with Afghanistan not even accumulating the one per cent needed to make it onto the list. [127] This explanation is supported by the fact that in July 2008, the Chicago Council on Global Affairs found that 43 per cent saw China's rising global power as a 'critical threat' to vital US interests but 64 per cent opposed active efforts to limit China's rise. [128]

Although these trends seem to correlate with those of TV Cable News – China was increasingly portrayed as an economic and military threat to the US, and American opinion seemed to follow this trend – an important question is: how many Americans were actually paying attention to media reports? In early 2008, 65 per cent of Americans said they were following news reports on Tibetan protests against the Chinese government. [129] In April of the same year, 54 per cent of Americans were already watching news of the 2008 Olympics, a percentage that increased to 72 per cent in July, [130] and after the Olympics 85 per cent of Americans said they had followed the Olympics. [131] In a Pew Research Center Political Knowledge Update Survey for the People and the Press Opinion Research Corporation testing Americans' knowledge based on what they had seen in the news, 71 per cent correctly stated that China holds most US government debt, which was repeatedly mentioned in the media after the Olympics. [132] In 2007, 73 per cent of Americans said they got much of their news about China from English TV and 50 per cent said they also got their news from English newspapers. This suggests that Americans were following the news and specifically watching TV news and reading newspapers as their primary sources of knowledge. All of this also suggests that the media did have an influence on public opinion polls, although it is important to note that other factors, such as party affiliation, may have also been influential.

There were also several polls that were specific to the Olympics. An NBC News/ Wall Street Journal Poll in July 2008 found that 63 per cent of Americans thought that President Bush should attend the opening ceremonies and 25 per cent thought he should not at a time when Nancy Pelosi and others were asking him to make a statement about Chinese human rights instead. [133] A CNN/Opinion Research Corporation Poll from April 2008, asking 'Do you feel the US (United States) should participate in the Beijing Olympic Games or boycott them?' found that 72 per cent of Americans believed the US should participate while 22 per cent thought that the US should boycott the games. [134] The fact that 22 per cent (a large percentage considering the extremity of the answer) of Americans felt antagonistic enough towards China to argue that the US should not attend the games suggests that the American media were successful in promoting the negative image of China's human rights. In the same month, a CNN/Opinion Research Corporation poll found that 73 per cent of Americans rated 'the job the government of China does in respecting the human rights of its citizens' as 'mostly' or 'very' bad. [135] The same survey enquired: 'Regardless of your views on whether the US should boycott the Olympic Games, do you think it is a good thing or a bad thing that the Summer Olympic Games are being held in China this year?' Only 48 per cent thought it was a good thing and 45 per cent saw it as a bad thing. [136] After the games, an Associated Press/Ipsos-Public Affairs poll found that 55 per cent of Americans thought the International Olympic Committee made the right decision to hold the games in China [137] and a Pew Weekly News Interest Index Poll similarly found that 52 per cent of Americans thought it was a good decision. 19 per cent of Americans said the Olympics had given them a more favourable impression of China, but 20 per cent said they now had a less favourable impression. [138] This seems to contradict the aforementioned polls that indicate a growing negative image of China.

There were two major media events in addition to the Olympics (although not covered nearly as much as the games), which could have affected the results. One was the earthquake in China, which 86 per cent of Americans said they followed on the news, [139] and the other was the story about contaminated milk powder, which was followed by 68 per cent of Americans. [140] The earthquake story would probably have decreased Americans' negative perceptions of China, especially since coverage was generally sympathetic. This does not explain the increasingly unfavourable view of China and belief that China is a threat, unless Americans had perceived China's handling of the disaster negatively. Far fewer Americans followed the contaminated milk powder report, and it was covered for rather less time than the Olympics. It is unlikely to have had a larger effect than the Olympics, but it is a possible, minor confounding influence.

5. Conclusion

There are a few findings that support the hypothesis proposed in this paper. First of all, the editorial boards representing the print sources, with the exception of the *New York Times*, which represented the New England region, ran very few editorials on China towards the end of the Olympics and afterwards. This might be due to their focusing on other topics after heavy coverage of China before and during the Olympics in order to engage readers. On the other hand, the results can be interpreted as a less negative image of China being reported after the Olympics, leaving it to become gradually less important in readers' minds. Although the criticism of China peaked in the period before and during the Olympics, as the games progressed, criticism on human rights, the environment and the economy decreased noticeably. Since this trend mirrored the course of the Olympics, the Beijing games were most likely the determining factor. The other China-related events covered by the media – the earthquakes in China and the baby-formula scare – were too brief to have been likely to have had as much of an effect. The other finding that would seem to support the hypothesis is that Americans increasingly viewed the decision to hold the Olympics in Beijing as a positive move; even though there were concerns about China as a human rights violator being allowed to host the event.

While the success of the Beijing Olympics as an exercise in logistics may have had a positive effect on China's image, as this hypothesis contends, the positive effect seems to have had minimal impact on Americans' image of China. Polls indicated increasingly unfavourable attitudes towards China, growing opinions that China was a threat or potential threat to the US and increasingly negative views of China's rising economic and military power. This trend more closely follows TV media images of China, as predicted by Daniel Bell along with Grant Jarvie, Dong-Jhy Hwang and Mel Brennan. Again, since this TV media trend followed the course of the Olympics and, like print sources, the earthquake in China and the baby-formula scare were the only other major, if brief, possible confounding factors, the Beijing games were probably the determining factor for these results. This suggests that in general terms, the image of China held by Americans became more negative because of the Olympics, in direct contradiction to what China had anticipated and much of the secondary literature had predicted.

Therefore, the analyses of the print sources, TV sources and polls suggest that the hypothesis that Americans' image of China would improve as a result of the 2008 summer Olympics coverage seems to be incorrect. It improved in some ways. For example, the presentation of China as an accomplished, advancing nation was successful. The months before the games saw an increase in human-rights criticisms, but during and after the Olympics attention was diverted from Chinese human-rights abuses and environmental criticisms and towards the Chinese economy. However, this image of an economically strong and collected China is correlated with increasing TV images of China as more formidable, which is perhaps why more Americans view China as a threat.

Table 1 Summary of print source editorial board findings

	2000–6	2007–Olympics	Olympics	Olympics–2009
New England: *New York Times*	Extremely negative image of human rights, environment. Positive image of economy	Focus almost exclusively on negative image of human rights – stronger than before	Strongest negative image of human rights – even stronger than before	Extremely negative image of human rights, little mention of environment or economy. Few editorials on China
Middle Atlantic: *USA Today*	Moderately negative image of human rights	More intense negative image of human rights	Strongest negative image of human rights – allusion to Cold War	Slightly negative image of Chinese economic rivalry. Few editorials on China
East North Central States: *Cleveland Plain Dealer*	Neutral image of China. Balanced coverage of Taiwan.	Moderately negative image of human rights	Extremely negative image of human rights	Few editorials on China
West North Central States: *Star Tribune of Minneapolis-St Paul*	Positive image of China as a partner in U.S. foreign relations	Positive image of China as a partner in U.S. foreign relations	Few editorials on China	Few editorials on China
Pacific States: *San Francisco Chronicle*	Extremely negative image of economic rivalry	Focus almost exclusively on negative image of human rights	Strongest negative image of human rights and environment	Few editorials on China and more favorable
Mountain States: *Salt Lake Tribune*	Extremely negative image of economic rivalry, environment	Extremely negative image of economic rivalry, environment	Mixed favourable and unfavourable, weak view of China	Few editorials on China
West South Central States: *Houston Chronicle*	Extremely negative image of economic rivalry	Focus almost exclusively on negative image of human rights	Mixed favourable and unfavourable view of China – both strong	Few editorials on China
East South Central States: *St Louis Post Dispatch*	Extremely negative image of human rights	More intense negative image of human rights, economy	Strong negative image of human rights	Few editorials on China
South Atlantic States: *Atlanta Journal-Constitution*	Extremely negative image of economic rivalry	Positive view on China's future	Few editorials on China	Few editorials on China

Table 2 Summary of cable news source findings

	2000–6	2007–Olympics	Olympics	Olympics–2009
MSNBC	Neutral/positive Image of China	Less coverage of China (except for the 'satellite' event). Positive coverage of Olympics	Negative image of China as 'fake'	Mixed positive/negative image of China
Fox News	Extremely critical of human rights and lack of military responsibility	Negative image of China as a military threat (especially with 'satellite' event). Intensifying criticism of human rights	Negative image of Chinese authoritarianism in sports	Negative focus on an image of China as a rival instead of China as a human rights abuser
CNN	Neutral/slightly negative view of human rights, potential rivalry with US	Extremely critical of China on multiple fronts: environment, human rights, economic rivalry, unsafe/poorly regulated country	Positive image of China's economy and role in the games. Negative image of China as unsafe and as an environmental danger	Negative image of China as a dangerous rival, rising as America is falling

This means that China should consider reassessing its soft diplomacy if it wishes to improve its image in the US, strengthen American amity and therefore potentially improve Sino-US relations. While China invested $40 billion in this endeavour and many secondary sources had lauded its public relations campaign, China needs to do more than show it can throw a great 'coming-out party' if it wishes to address major American concerns that China is a threat. Polls and the media suggest that Americans are afraid of an economically and militarily powerful China – perhaps the Olympics exacerbated that fear – and believe that China has an unfair advantage via its poor safety and economic regulations. The solution of course is not for China to curb its economic growth at the expense of improving American amity. China needs instead to assure Americans that its increasing economic power does not take away but rather contributes to America through the benefits of mutual trade. China must also avoid displays of military power that can upset Americans, such its use of an anti-satellite weapon in 2007 to destroy one of its own satellites.

China should not view the decreasing human-rights coverage in American media as a sign that the Olympics have worked as an instrument of soft diplomacy. It is quite possible that the human-rights criticism has decreased as economic criticism has increased. Furthermore, China's image as a repressive state may be a reason why so many Americans view its rising power as a threat.

To address these concerns, China must take tangible measures to improve its treatment of minorities in Tibet, Xinjiang and elsewhere and allow more freedom for foreign journalists. Obviously, China will have to make concession in terms of its own form of government if it wishes to strengthen Sino-US relations. The Chinese government was, however, far too wishful in believing that one extravagant Olympics could combat a deeply ingrained belief that its system of government is seen as repressive and a threat to US interests. Finally, China should continue the environmental measures that were so highly publicized during the Olympics, including using advanced technology and reducing congestion in Beijing. Those measures seem to have been at least partially successful in countering environmental criticism.

Notes

[1] Cha, *Beyond the Final Score*.
[2] Ibid., 2.
[3] Fan Hong *et al.*, *China Gold*.
[4] Brownell, 'The Strategy for Dealing with the International Criticism'.
[5] Close *et al.*, *The Beijing Olympiad*, 109.
[6] Ibid., 121–44.
[7] Miller, *The Official History of the Olympic Games*.
[8] Jarvie *et al.*, *Sport, Revolution and the Beijing Olympics*, 117–27.
[9] Xin Xu, 'Modernizing China in the Olympic Spotlight'.
[10] Cull, 'The Public Diplomacy of the Modern Olympic Games'.

[11] Audit Bureau of Circulations, 'Circulation Averages', 30 September 2010, available at http:// abcas3.accessabc.com/ecirc/newstitlesearchus.asp, accessed 5 Nov. 2010.

[12] Audit Bureau of Circulations, 'Circulation Averages', 30 September 2010, available at http:// abcas3.accessabc.com/ecirc/newstitlesearchus.asp, accessed 5 Nov. 2010.

[13] Audit Bureau of Circulations, 'Circulation Averages', 30 September 2010, available at http:// abcas3.accessabc.com/ecirc/newstitlesearchus.asp, accessed 5 Nov. 2010.

[14] Audit Bureau of Circulations, 'Circulation Averages', 30 September 2010, available at http:// abcas3.accessabc.com/ecirc/newstitlesearchus.asp, accessed 5 Nov. 2010.

[15] Audit Bureau of Circulations, 'Circulation Averages', 30 September 2010, available at http:// abcas3.accessabc.com/ecirc/newstitlesearchus.asp, accessed 5 Nov. 2010.

[16] Pew, 'News Audiences Increasingly Politicized', 8 June 2004, available at http://people-press. org/report/?pageid=834, accessed 7 May 2009.

[17] Brady, 'The Beijing Olympics as a Campaign of Mass Distraction'.

[18] Foss and Walkosz, 'Definition, Equivocation, Accumulation, and Anticipation'.

[19] Kamm, 'A Marathon Challenge'.

[20] Bell, *China's New Confucianism*, 102–3.

[21] 'The Autoworkers' Pain', *New York Times*, 16 Feb. 2007.

[22] 'China and the Chest Thumpers', *New York Times*, 20 June 2007.

[23] 'Global Harming: Politicians and Scientists Don't Mix', *New York Times*, 10 April 2007.

[24] 'China's Economic Puzzle', *New York Times*, 19 Oct. 2007.

[25] Colleen McEdwards and Brian Nelson, 'US/China Relations: What to Expect from Wednesday's Meeting', *New York Times*, 16 April 2001.

[26] 'China's Signals on Warming', *New York Times*, 16 April 2007.

[27] 'Patron of African Misgovernment', *New York Times*, 19 Feb. 2007.

[28] 'Empty Olympic Promises', *New York Times*, 4 Feb. 2008.

[29] 'China Terrorizes Tibet', *New York Times*, 18 March 2008.

[30] 'China's List of Olympic Don'ts', *New York Times*, 11 June 2008.

[31] 'Beijing's Bad Faith Olympics', *New York Times*, 22 Aug. 2008.

[32] 'US Firms Help China Censor fr**dom, d*mocr*cy', *USA Today*, 19 June 2005.

[33] 'China Retreats on Free Press', *USA Today*, 11 Dec. 2007.

[34] 'Beyond Beijing: Games Show Two Faces of China', *USA Today*, 22 Aug. 2008.

[35] 'China's Wake-Up Call for US', *USA Today*, 18 March 2009.

[36] 'Wise Clarity on Taiwan', *Cleveland Plain Dealer*, 10 Dec. 2003.

[37] 'Backsliding in Darfur', *Cleveland Plain Dealer*, 28 Nov. 2006.

[38] 'Assault on Tibet Hurts China, Too', *Cleveland Plain Dealer*, 21 March 2008.

[39] 'A Trade Lesson for China', *Cleveland Plain Dealer*, 3 July 2008.

[40] 'Let the (Olympic) Games Begin', *Cleveland Plain Dealer*, 6 Aug. 2008.

[41] Opinion Exchange, 'Learning a Language to Welcome the Future; Two Decades Hence, Americans should be Speaking Chinese', *Star Tribune of Minneapolis-St Paul*, 10 Sept. 2006.

[42] Opinion Exchange (Nancy Barnes), 'Get Ready for the Swirl of the Olympics; In our Pages, You'll Find the Local Tales You can't Get Elsewhere, but also the Overarching Narrative: China', *Star Tribune of Minneapolis-St Paul*, 3 Aug. 2008.

[43] 'China Deal Tests Free-Trade Tenets', *San Francisco Chronicle*, 10 July 2005.

[44] 'A Rising Power Comes Calling', *San Francisco Chronicle*, 20 April 2006.

[45] 'Made in China, Badly', *San Francisco Chronicle*, 5 July 2007.

[46] 'China's Games; Beijing Resists Global Pressure to Change', *San Francisco Chronicle*, 25 Feb. 2008.

[47] 'Tyranny in Tibet', *San Francisco Chronicle*, 18 March 2008.

[48] 'A Gold Medal for Smog', *San Francisco Chronicle*, 23 July 2008.

[49] 'China's Next Act', *San Francisco Chronicle*, 26 Aug. 2008.

[50] 'Lessons from the Chinese', *San Francisco Chronicle*, 13 Nov. 2008.

[51] 'Conflicted on China; OIL COMPANY DEAL Dark Side of Free Trade Goes Well Beyond Oil', *Salt Lake Tribune*, 4 Aug. 2005.

[52] 'Global Harming: Politicians and Scientists Don't Mix', *Salt Lake Tribune*, 10 April 2007.

[53] 'China's Games: Utahns Understand what the Olympics Mean to the Host', *Salt Lake Tribune*, 7 Aug. 2008.

[54] 'China Shop; Government should Not Hamper China; Unocal Deal Unless, Improbably, it would Harm National Security', *Houston Chronicle*, 5 July 2005.

[55] 'China Syndrome; Recent Infractions Abroad Highlight Need for Better Safety System for Global Food and Drug Supply', *Houston Chronicle*, May 24, 2007.

[56] 'Olympic Leverage; with China in the Spotlight, this is the Year to Press Beijing to Free its Muzzled Media', *Houston Chronicle*, 4 Feb. 2008.

[57] 'Tibet's Agony; Developments in China and Taiwan Illustrate a Tale of Two Systems', *Houston Chronicle*, 21 March 2008.

[58] 'Power show; Beijing Olympics showcased the rising might of China', *Houston Chronicle*, 25 Aug. 2008.

[59] 'The Shanghai Flu', *St Louis Post-Dispatch*, 1 March 2007.

[60] 'Genocide and Games', *St Louis Post-Dispatch*, 1 June 2007.

[61] 'China Comes Out', *St Louis Post-Dispatch*, 7 Aug. 2008.

[62] 'Chinese New Year; 2005 Ushers in the End of Trade Barriers on Textiles, Positioning China to Conquer what US Long Ruled', *Atlanta Journal-Constitution*, 3 Jan. 2005.

[63] 'US Economic Challenges Aren't China's Fault', *Atlanta Journal-Constitution*, 20 April 2005.

[64] 'Free Speech Not the Bottom Line', *Atlanta Journal-Constitution*, 12 Jan. 2006.

[65] 'Tainted Food Won't do: When Americans Read "made in China," Safety should be a Guarantee; Congress must See to it', *Atlanta Journal-Constitution*, 22 June 2007.

[66] 'Playing "Good Cop" to China', *Atlanta Journal-Constitution*, 25 April 2008.

[67] Brian Williams *et al.*, 'China Still Refusing to Release US Air Crew, but Sides may be Moving Toward Compromise', MSNBC, 5 April 2001.

[68] Keith Olbermann *et al.*, '*Countdown* for April 20, 2006', MSNBC, 20 April 2006.

[69] Keith Olbermann, David Shuster and Michelle Kosinski, '*Countdown* for January 19, 2007', MSNBC, 19 Jan. 2007.

[70] Keith Olbermann *et al.*, '*Countdown* for February 15, 2007', MSNBC, 15 Feb. 2007.

[71] Tucker Carlson, Bill Wolff and Mike Viqueira, 'From July 13, 2007', MSNBC, 13 July 2007.

[72] Chris Matthews *et al.*, '*Hardball* for April 24, 2008', MSNBC, 24 April 2008.

[73] Heidi Collins *et al.*, 'Security Measure Taken for the Beijing Olympics', 5 Aug. 2008.

[74] Chris Matthews, Andrea Mitchell and Howard Fineman, '*Hardball* for August 11, 2008', MSNBC, 11 Aug. 2008.

[75] Chris Matthews *et al.*, '*Hardball* for August 12, 2008,' MSNBC, 12 Aug. 2008.

[76] Dan Abrams, Lee Cowan and Tom Costello, '*The Verdict* for August 14, 2008', MSNBC, 14 Aug. 2008.

[77] David Shuster and Chuck Todd, '*1600 Pennsylvania Avenue* for April 1, 2009', MSNBC, 1 April 2009.

[78] Ed Schultz and Jim Miklaszewski, 'For April 24, 2009', MSNBC, 24 April 2009.

[79] Bill O'Reilly, and John Gibson. 'Debate Over the Born Alive Infant Protection Act', Fox News, 28 Dec. 2000.

[80] Sean Hannity, and Alan Colmes, 'China Refusing to Release US Air Crew, US Refusing to Apologize for Collision', Fox News, 4 April 2001.

[81] John Gibson, 'China Threatens Nuke use', Fox News, 15 July 2005.

[82] Bill O'Reilly, 'Unresolved Problem: Finding Allies in the War on Terrorism', Fox News, 19 Sept. 2001.

[83]   Brit Hume *et al.*, 'Political Headlines', Fox News, 31 Jan. 2007.

[84]   Brit Hume *et al.*, 'Political Headlines,' Fox News, 11 April 2007.

[85]   Brit Hume *et al.*, 'Political Headlines', Fox News, 19 Nov. 2007.

[86]   Bret Baier *et al.*, 'China Suppresses Tibet Protests,' Fox News, 21 March 2008.

[87]   John Scott, and Kirsten Powers, 'Olympic Messages', Fox News, 23 Aug. 2008.

[88]   Bret Baier, Mike Emanuel and Dana Lewis, 'President Bush Meets US Olympians; Security in Beijing', Fox News, 8 Aug. 2008.

[89]   Bret Baier *et al.*, 'Political Headlines', Fox News, 13 Aug. 2008.

[90]   Bret Baier, Major Garrett and Carl Cameron, 'China's Olympic Success', Fox News, 22 Aug. 2008.

[91]   Greta Van Susteren, 'Chinese, Russian Cyber Spies Penetrate US Electrical Grid', Fox News, 7 April 2009.

[92]   Greta Van Susteren, 'What Happens if China Stops Buying US Debt?', Fox News, 27 March 2009.

[93]   Greta Van Susteren, 'Chinese, Russian Cyber Spies Penetrate US Electrical Grid', Fox News, 7 April 2009.

[94]   Colleen McEdwards and Brian Nelson, 'US/China Relations: What to Expect from Wednesday's Meeting', CNN, 16 April 2001.

[95]   Betty Nguyen *et al.*, 'Bush in Asia', CNN, 15 Nov. 2005.

[96]   Lou Dobbs *et al.*, 'China's Threat', CNN, 18 July 2005.

[97]   Christine Romans *et al.*, 'China and the WTO', CNN, 7 Dec. 2007.

[98]   Kitty Pilgrim *et al.*, 'Toxic Toys Still on Shelves', CNN, 23 Dec. 2007.

[99]   Fredricka Whitfield *et al.*, 'Climate Change Summit', CNN, 15 Dec. 2007.

[100] Frank Sesno, 'Encore Presentation – we were Warned: Out of Gas', CNN, 22 June 2008.

[101] Lou Dobbs *et al.*, 'China's Cyber Threat', CNN, 24 June 2008.

[102] Wolf Blitzer *et al.*, 'Trouble in Tibet', CNN, 14 March 2008.

[103] Candy Crowley *et al.*, 'Bush is Advised to Boycott Olympic Opening Ceremonies', CNN, 1 April 2008.

[104] Heidi Collins *et al.*, 'Security Measure Taken for the Beijing Olympics', CNN, 5 Aug. 2008.

[105] Dr Sanjay Gupta *et al.*, 'China Struggles to Lessen Pollution for Olympics', CNN, 6 Aug. 2008.

[106] Don Lemon *et al.*, 'China and the Games', CNN, 8 Aug. 2008.

[107] Betty Nguyen *et al.*, 'Beijing Olympics Close, London Prepares', CNN, 24 Aug. 2008.

[108] Joe Scarborough *et al.*, 'For August 26, 2008', CNN, 26 Aug. 2008.

[109] David Horowitz *et al.*, 'Changing the Tone; Geithner Under Fire; China and North Korea Standoff', CNN, 12 March 2009.

[110] Wolf Blitzer *et al.*, 'Pentagon Worries about China again', CNN, 25 March 2009.

[111] John Roberts *et al.*, 'China Denies Spying on Computer Globally', CNN, 31 March 2009.

[112] Tony Harris *et al.*, 'Retailers Moving to China to make Up Lost US Business', CNN, 23 April 2009.

[113] Kiran Chetry *et al.*, 'The China Factor: How Much do we Owe?', CNN, 30 April 2009.

[114] Survey by Gallup Organization, 25–26 Jan. 2000;urvey by Gallup Organization, 1–4 Feb. 2001; survey by Gallup Organization, 4–6 Feb. 2002; survey by Gallup Organization, 3–6 Feb. 2003; survey by Gallup Organization, 9–12 Feb. 2004; survey by Gallup Organization, 7–10 Feb. 2005; survey by Pew Global Attitudes Project and Princeton Survey Research Associates International, 2–14 May 2006; survey by Gallup Organization, 1–4 Feb. 2007; survey by *USA Today* and Gallup Organization, 11–14 Feb. 2008; survey by Gallup Organization, 9–12 Feb. 2009. All at iPOLL Databank, The Roper Center for Public Opinion Research, University of Connecticut, available at http://www.ropercenter.uconn.edu.ezp-prod1.hul.harvard.edu/ipoll.html, accessed 7 May 2009.

[115] Survey by *Time*, Cable News Network and Yankelovich Partners, 14–15 June 2000; survey by *Time*, Cable News Network and Harris Interactive, 22–23 May 2002; survey by *Time*, Cable News Network and Harris Interactive, 15–16 Jan. 2003. All at iPOLL Databank, The Roper Center for Public Opinion Research, University of Connecticut, available at http://www.ropercenter.uconn.edu.ezp-prod1.hul.harvard.edu/ipoll.html, accessed 7 May 2009.

[116] Survey by Cable News Network, *USA Today* and Gallup Organization, 9–11 Dec. 2005. iPOLL Databank, The Roper Center for Public Opinion Research, University of Connecticut, available at http://www.ropercenter.uconn.edu.ezp-prod1.hul.harvard.edu/ipoll.html, accessed 7 May 2009.

[117] Survey by Cable News Network and Opinion Research Corporation, 27–29 July 2008. iPOLL Databank, The Roper Center for Public Opinion Research, University of Connecticut, available at http://www.ropercenter.uconn.edu.ezp-prod1.hul.harvard.edu/ipoll.html, accessed 7 May 2009.

[118] Survey by Gallup Organization, 1–2 April 2009. iPOLL Databank, The Roper Center for Public Opinion Research, University of Connecticut, available at http://www.ropercenter.-uconn.edu.ezp-prod1.hul.harvard.edu/ipoll.html, accessed 9 April 2009.

[119] Survey by Cable News Network, *USA Today* and Gallup Organization, 9–11 Dec. 2005; survey by Cable News Network and Opinion Research Corporation, 27–29 July 2008. Both at iPOLL Databank, The Roper Center for Public Opinion Research, University of Connecticut, available at http://www.ropercenter.uconn.edu.ezp-prod1.hul.harvard.edu/ipoll.html, accessed 7 May 2009.

[120] 'World Public Think China Will Catch Up With the US – and That's Okay', World Public Opinion: Global Public Opinion on International Affairs, 25 May 2007. Available at http://www.worldpublicopinion.org/pipa/articles/views_on_countriesregins_bt/366.php?lb=btvoc&pnt=366&nid=&id=, accessed 7 May 2009.

[121] 'Global Unease With Major World Powers', Pew Global Attitudes Project, 27 June 2007. Available at http://pewglobal.org/reports/display.php?ReportID=256, accessed 7 May 2009.

[122] Chicago Council on Global Affairs, 'Aware of China's Rise: Worried Americans Still Prefer to Engage', available at http://www.thechicagocouncil.org/UserFiles/File/POS_Topline%20Reports/PO%202008/2008%20POS_Chinas%20Rise.pdf, accessed 7 May 2009.

[123] Survey by Pew Research Center for the People & the Press, Council on Foreign Relations and Princeton Survey Research Associates International, Abt SRBI, 9–14 Sept. 2008. iPOLL Databank, The Roper Center for Public Opinion Research, University of Connecticut, available at http://www.ropercenter.uconn.edu.ezp-prod1.hul.harvard.edu/ipoll.html, accessed 7 May 2009.

[124] Survey by Pew Research Center for the People & the Press and Princeton Survey Research Associates International, 7–11 Jan. 2009iPOLL Databank, The Roper Center for Public Opinion Research, University of Connecticut, available at http://www.ropercenter.uconn.edu.ezp-prod1.hul.harvard.edu/ipoll.html, accessed 9 April 2009.

[125] Survey by Pew Research Center for the People & the Press, Council on Foreign Relations and Princeton Survey Research Associates International, Abt SRBI, 9–14 Sept. 2008; survey by Pew Research Center for the People & the Press, Council on Foreign Relations and Princeton Survey Research Associates International, 12–24 Oct. 2005; survey by Pew Research Center for the People & the Press, Council on Foreign Relations and Princeton Survey Research Associates International, 8–18 July 2004; survey by Pew Research Center for the People & the Press and Princeton Survey Research Associates, 12–18 Feb. 2002; survey by Pew Research Center for the People & the Press, Council on Foreign Relations and Princeton Survey Research Associates, 15–28 May 2001; survey by Pew Research Center for the People & the Press and Princeton Survey Research Associates, 15–19 March 2000. All at iPOLL Databank, The Roper Center for Public Opinion Research, University of Connecticut, available at

http://www.ropercenter.uconn.edu.ezp-prod1.hul.harvard.edu/ipoll.html, accessed 7 May 2009.

[126] BBC World Service Poll, 'Views of China and Russia Decline in Global Poll,' available at http://www.worldpublicopinion.org/pipa/pdf/feb09/BBCEvals_Feb09_rpt.pdf.

[127] Survey by Fox News and Opinion Dynamics, 12–13 Feb. 2002; survey by Fox News and Opinion Dynamics, 21–22 Feb. 2001. Both at iPOLL Databank, The Roper Center for Public Opinion Research, University of Connecticut, available at http://www.ropercenter.uconn.edu.ezp-prod1.hul.harvard.edu/ipoll.html, accessed 7 May 2009.

[128] Chicago Council on Global Affairs, 'Aware of China's Rise: Worried Americans Still Prefer to Engage'.

[129] Survey by Pew Research Center for the People & the Press and Opinion Research Corporation, 20–24 March 2008. iPOLL Databank, The Roper Center for Public Opinion Research, University of Connecticut, available at http://www.ropercenter.uconn.edu.ezp-prod1.hul.harvard.edu/ipoll.html, accessed 7 May 2009.

[130] Survey by Pew Research Center for the People & the Press and Opinion Research Corporation, 25–28 July 2008. iPOLL Databank, The Roper Center for Public Opinion Research, University of Connecticut, available at http://www.ropercenter.uconn.edu.ezp-prod1.hul.harvard.edu/ipoll.html, accessed 7 May 2009.

[131] Survey by Pew Research Center for the People & the Press and Opinion Research Corporation, 22–25 Aug. 2008. iPOLL Databank, The Roper Center for Public Opinion Research, University of Connecticut, available at http://www.ropercenter.uconn.edu.ezp-prod1.hul.harvard.edu/ipoll.html, accessed 9 April 2009.

[132] Survey by Pew Research Center for the People & the Press and Opinion Research Corporation, 26–29 March 2009. iPOLL Databank, The Roper Center for Public Opinion Research, University of Connecticut, available at http://www.ropercenter.uconn.edu.ezp-prod1.hul.harvard.edu/ipoll.html, accessed 7 May 2009.

[133] Survey by NBC News, *Wall Street Journal* and Hart and Newhouse Research Companies, 18–21 July 2008. iPOLL Databank, The Roper Center for Public Opinion Research, University of Connecticut, available at http://www.ropercenter.uconn.edu.ezp-prod1.hul.harvard.edu/ipoll.html, accessed 9 April 2009.

[134] Survey by Cable News Network and Opinion Research Corporation, 28–30 April 2008. iPOLL Databank, The Roper Center for Public Opinion Research, University of Connecticut, available at http://www.ropercenter.uconn.edu.ezp-prod1.hul.harvard.edu/ipoll.html, accessed 9 April 2009.

[135] Ibid.

[136] Ibid.

[137] Survey by Associated Press and Ipsos-Public Affairs, 7–11 Aug. 2008. iPOLL Databank, The Roper Center for Public Opinion Research, University of Connecticut, available at http://www.ropercenter.uconn.edu.ezp-prod1.hul.harvard.edu/ipoll.html, accessed 9 April 2009.

[138] Survey by NBC News, *Wall Street Journal* and Hart and Newhouse Research Companies, 15–18 Aug. 2008. iPOLL Databank, The Roper Center for Public Opinion Research, University of Connecticut, available at http://www.ropercenter.uconn.edu.ezp-prod1.hul.harvard.edu/ipoll.html, accessed 9 April 2009.

[139] Survey by Pew Research Center for the People & the Press and Opinion Research Corporation, 30 May–2 June 2008. iPOLL Databank, The Roper Center for Public Opinion Research, University of Connecticut, available at http://www.ropercenter.uconn.edu.ezp-prod1.hul.harvard.edu/ipoll.html, accessed 7 May 2009.

[140] Survey by Pew Research Center for the People & the Press and Opinion Research Corporation, 26–29 Sept. 2008. iPOLL Databank, The Roper Center for Public Opinion Research, University of Connecticut, available at http://www.ropercenter.uconn.edu.ezp-prod1.hul.harvard.edu/ipoll.html, accessed 7 May 2009.

References

Bell, Daniel. *China's New Confucianism: Politics and Everyday Life in a Changing Society.* Princeton, NJ: Princeton University Press, 2008.

Black, David R. and Shona Bezanson. 'The Olympic Games, Human Rights and Democratisation: Lessons from Seoul and Implications for Beijing'. *Third World Quarterly* 25 (7) (2004): 1245–61.

Black, David R. and Janis van der Westhuizen. 'The Neglected Allure of Global Games?' *Third World Quarterly* 25 (7) (2004): 1191–4.

Brady, Anne-Marie. 'The Beijing Olympics as a Campaign of Mass Distraction.' In *Owning the Olympics: Narratives of the New China,* edited by Monroe E. Price and Daniel Dayan. Ann Arbor, MI: University of Michigan Press, 2008: 1–24.

Brownell, Susan. 'The Strategy for Dealing with the International Criticism on Human Rights'. Paper given at conference, 'The 2008 Beijing Olympic Games: Public Diplomacy Triumph or Public Relations Spectacle?', 30 January 2009, organized by Center on Public Diplomacy, US-China Institute and Center for International Studies at the University of Southern California.

Cha, Victor. *Beyond the Final Score: The Politics of Sport in Asia.* New York: Columbia University Press, 2008.

Close, Paul, David Askew and Xu Xin. *The Beijing Olympiad: The Political Economy of a Sporting Mega-event.* New York: Routledge, 2007.

Collins, Heidi, et al. "Security Measure Taken for the Beijing Olympics." August 5, 2008. LexisNexis News (Transcripts).

Committee of 100. '2005 National Survey: American Attitudes Toward China'. Available at http://www.committee100.org/publications/survey/survey_uschina05.htm, accessed 7 May 2009.

Committee of 100. 'Hope and Fear: a Summary of Key Findings of C-100's Survey on American and Chinese Attitudes Towards Each Other'. Available at http://www.survey.committee100.org/2007/files/C100SurveyKeyFindingsReport.pdf, accessed 7 May 2009.

Foss, Sonja K. and Barbara J. Walkosz. 'Definition, Equivocation, Accumulation, and Anticipation: American Media's Ideological Reading of China's Olympic Games'. In *Owning the Olympics: Narratives of the New China,* edited by E. Monroe and Daniel Dayan. Ann Arbor, MI: University of Michigan Press, 2008: 346–74.

Fan Hong, Ping Wu and Huan Xiong. 'Beijing Ambitions: An Analysis of the Chinese Elite Sports System and its Olympic Strategy for the 2008 Olympic Games'. *The International Journal of the History of Sport* 22 (4) (2005): 510–29.

Fan Hong, Duncan Mackay and Karen Christensen. *China Gold.* Great Barrington, MA: Berkshire Pub. Group, 2008.

Jarvie, Grant, Dong-Jhy Hwang and Mel Brennan. *Sport, Revolution and the Beijing Olympics.* New York: Berg, 2008.

Kamm, John. 'A Marathon Challenge to Improve China's Image'. In *China's Great Leap: The Beijing Games and Olympian Human Rights Challenges,* edited by Minky Worden. New York: Seven Stories Press, 2008: 223–234.

Miller, David. *The Official History of the Olympic Games and the IOC: Athens to Beijing, 1894–2008.* Edinburgh: Mainstream, 2008.

Stokstad, Erik, Adrian Cho, Andrea Lu, Greg Miller and Martin Enserink. 'Will Beijing's Dirty Air Hurt Performance'. *Science,* new series, 321 (5889) (2008): 624–27.

Stone, Richard, 'Beijing's Marathon Run to Clean Foul Air Nears Finish Line'. *Science,* new series, 321 (5889) (2008): 636–7.

Xu, Xin. 'Modernizing China in the Olympic Spotlight: China's National Identity and the 2008 Beijing Olympiad'. In *Sports Mega-events: Social Scientific Analyses of a Global Phenomenon,* edited by John Horne and Wolfram Manzenreiter. Malden, MA: Blackwell Publishing, 2006.

The 'Black Auxiliaries' in American Memories: Sport, Race and Politics in the Construction of Modern Legacies

John Gleaves and Mark Dyreson

At the 1936 Olympics a contingent of African American track and field athletes garnered eight gold, three silver, and two bronze medals to highlight an otherwise disappointing performance by the American team. Dubbed the 'black auxiliaries' by the German press, they were led by the luminous Jesse Owens who through his four-gold medal performance built an enduring global legacy as an Olympic icon. Lost in Owens' long shadow were the other 'black auxiliaries', David Albritton, James LuValle, Ralph Metcalfe, Fritz Pollard, Jr., Mack Robinson, Archie Williams, and John Woodruff. Owens' teammates, however, slowly built their own legacies at the local, regional, and national levels. In many respects they excelled Owens in their post-athletic careers, personifying the admonitions of African American leaders in that era. The ways in which this less famous group of Olympians were forgotten and then remembered illuminates the changing complexities of American relations during the twentieth century.

Memories and Milliseconds

In a 1972 study sponsored by the Ralph Nader Congress Project that provided biographical sketches and political analyses of members of the US House of Representatives, the authors began one entry with the following vignette:

> Thirty-six years ago, a young black man found immortality by winning the 100-meter dash in the Olympic games at Berlin. Films preserve what many call the most dramatic moment in Olympic history: an indignant Adolf Hitler leaving the stadium as the American flag is hoisted and the strains of the national anthem begin. Everyone knows that the black man was Jesse Owens, but except for a few milliseconds it would have been someone else. [1]

The vignette illuminates a profound national memory which, if inaccurate in some details, has been a celebrated moment in American history since 1936. [2] Owens remains an icon in American visions of national identity, a vision of speed and an emblem of the complexities of segregation and racism. [3]

Owens's enormous shadow obscures the other African Americans who before Owens ran and jumped to four gold medals in Berlin comprised with their now more famous teammate what the German press labelled the 'black auxiliaries' to a white-dominated American civilization, serfs in their racial overlords' designs. [4] The other African American members of the Olympic team in Berlin, nine fellow members of the men's track and field squad, five boxers and two female track and field athletes, have been eclipsed by Owens's bright star, even though in men's track and field they added four more gold medals, three more silver medals and two more bronze medals to Owens's impressive harvest. [5]

Indeed, as the authors of Ralph Nader Congress Project study observed in their opening lines, but for a few milliseconds it would have been someone else breasting the 100-metre tape in Berlin, earning everlasting fame both as the world's fastest man and as an African American demonstrating kinetic proof of the falsehoods of Nazi racial ideology – and the racial beliefs of many of their fellow Americans. That someone else in 1936 ironically also finished just milliseconds behind the winner in 1932 Olympics at Los Angeles. His name was Ralph Metcalfe. In 1970 Metcalfe won election to the US House of Representatives. [6] Though Metcalfe had reigned before Owens in the 1930s as the world's dominant sprinter, and though he went on to serve four terms in Congress, he remained in many ways an 'auxiliary' to Owens's commanding presence in American memories of sport, politics and race relations during the twentieth century.

The Superstar and his Supporting Cast

In the eight decades since the dramatic 'Nazi Olympics', an extensive collection of biographies have documented the life and legacies of Owens. [7] Scholars have devoted almost no attention to the legacies of the other 'black auxiliary' medallists – Ralph Metcalfe, Mack Robinson, Archie Williams, James LuValle, Fritz Pollard, Jr., John Woodruff, David Albritton and Cornelius Johnson. [8] Owens's rise to luminous stardom after the Berlin games and his eclipse of his fellow 'auxiliaries' obscures a more complex set of narratives that initially developed around the African American track and field athletes. Before he ran by a few milliseconds and jumped by a little more than seven inches to four gold medals, Owens was one of an ensemble of African American heroes bound for Germany to battle the globe's athletes and global racial stereotypes. [9]

The African American stars bound for Berlin provided a key template through which the US media interpreted the 1936 games. Race took centre stage in many American narratives as reporters revelled in the possibilities of the US contingent of black stars defeating a Nazi army of Aryan athletes. In what otherwise proved a lacklustre performance by the American track team, the 'black auxiliaries', led by

Owens's unprecedented four victories, produced eight gold medals and a total of 13 medals, accounting for 83 of the 167 total points the US garnered in winning the men's track and field competitions. [10]

Owens's stellar feats pushed the other victories scored by African American athletes into the background, particularly in the mainstream white media accounts of the Berlin Olympics, altering a tradition that had developed in American Olympic interpretations of treating African American medals as representations of the collective triumphs of an entire 'race'. For white Americans, Berlin came to represent the triumph of a transcendent black individual, Jesse Owens, rather than the victory of a team, the 'black auxiliaries'. [11]

The black press in the US, though enchanted by Owens's medals, took a more complex perspective. In a 1936 account in an African American journal, the *Southern Workman*, Charles Williams contended that Berlin should be remembered not merely as Jesse Owens's showcase but as the stage on 'which Negro athletes from the United States came to the front and showed superiority over the best athletes of all races from every quarter of the globe'. In his contemporary account he certainly devoted a great deal of attention to Owens, but Williams was careful to detail the feats of the other African American Olympians, including even long jumper John Brooks, who failed to medal. [12] Sixty years later, Arthur R. Ashe, Jr., the African American tennis star, offered a similar corporate history in his chronicle of African American struggles to integrate sport. While Ashe also paid significant attention to Owens, he reminded readers that the Berlin Olympic triumphs had been a team effort. 'The victories of black Americans at Berlin served as a beacon for all Americans of African descent', Ashe concluded. [13]

Patterns of Remembering and Forgetting

The processes of remembering and forgetting sporting stars, teams and moments reveal much about a culture and how it views its history. As the cultural historian Daniel Nathan has contended, a variety of historical and social factors shape the process through which 'storytellers come to understand and represent the past differently'. [14] The ways in which the 'black auxiliaries' have been remembered and forgotten illuminate modern American racial and cultural dynamics. Clearly, the white and black communities in the US have remembered and forgotten the 'black auxiliaries' in different ways, as one of the leading historians of African American experiences in sport, David K. Wiggins, has documented. White interpretations of their feats framed the 'black auxiliaries' almost exclusively as athletes, examining little beyond the physical dimensions of their performances. Indeed, the accomplishments of the 'black auxiliaries' fuelled the growth of a pernicious and popular strain of American racism which credited black triumphs to mere biology and discounted any intellectual or moral properties in their endeavours. [15]

Conversely, Wiggins contends that the black community interpreted the triumphs of Owens and the 'black auxiliaries' as one of the most significant events in American history. Wiggins also reveals that at the same time the black press celebrated their athletic feats, it implored the black community to produce stars in realms beyond American playing fields, in law and medicine, in art and literature, in science and engineering, in education and entrepreneurship, and in government and politics. [16]

The black press demanded a legacy that transcended athletic genius, counselling African Americans to rise to leadership in every avenue of civic endeavour. Columnists and editors warned that success in sport alone, while rewarding a select few, would not solve the complex maladies of racism and segregation. In the wake of the homecoming of the 'black auxiliaries', the black press warned its readership that a narrowing of focus on athletic genius would ultimately maintain rather than diminish white racism. [17] Nearly three-quarters of a century later, the African American social critic William Rhoden contends in *$40 Million Dollar Slaves* (2006) that the black media's 1936 warning has become a twenty-first-century cultural reality. [18] Indeed, historians have noted that Owens, though he achieved some limited successes in business, entertainment and public service, was himself forever stereotyped mainly as just an athlete, a sporting prodigy who failed to finish his college education or fully grasp the reins on his entrepreneurial and civic opportunities and was reduced to a racial caricature, the once-upon-a-time world's fastest man running carnival races against horses for the amusement of white audiences and the perpetuation of white stereotypes. [19]

Though Owens ultimately left a more complex legacy, the stereotype of the athletic savant who never achieved greatness in any other realm certainly comprises a major component of white national memories of the greatest American star of the 'Nazi Olympics'. The post-Olympic lives of the eight other African American Olympic medallists in track and field reveal very different legacies and alternative memories. Though hardly as famous as Owens, each has been commemorated over the course of the decades that followed their 1936 triumphs by a variety of local, regional and national organizations. In places throughout the US, the names of the rest of the 'black auxiliaries' dot the rosters of halls of fames, grace public buildings and popularize local running events. The biographies of the 'black auxiliaries' also reveal that they took to heart the urgings of the black press in the post-Olympic euphoria and built impressive careers beyond the realms of sport. If Owens's legacy was ultimately bounded by his athletic imprint on the national consciousness, the legacies his teammates forged frequently transcended their stellar moments in Berlin's Olympic stadium.

A Prosopography of the 'Black Auxiliaries'

The 'black auxiliaries' who laboured in Owens's shadow were all born within a six-year span: the eldest, Ralph Metcalfe, in 1910; the youngest of the group, Archie Williams, John Woodruff and Frederick Douglass 'Fritz' Pollard, Jr., in 1915. Four were born, like Owens, in the segregated former Confederacy. David Albritton was born in the same year as Owens, 1913, and nearly in the same place. Owens's Oakville, Alabama, birthplace was just two-and-a-half miles away from Albritton's birthplace in Danville. Metcalfe was born in Atlanta, Georgia; Matthew 'Mack' Robinson in Cairo, Georgia; and James LuValle in San Antonio, Texas. Like Owens, each of these Southern-born 'auxiliaries' joined during their childhoods the 'great migration' out of the Jim Crow South to new homes in the North or West. Albritton, like his Alabama neighbour Owens, moved to Cleveland. Metcalfe's family migrated to Chicago. James LuValle and Mack Robinson's families took them to southern California, to Los Angeles and Pasadena, respectively. The other 'auxiliaries' were born in the North or West. Archie Williams was born in Oakland and grew up there and in Berkeley, California. Cornelius Johnson was born and grew up in Los Angeles. John Woodruff was born and grew up in Connellsville, Pennsylvania, a steel-mill town on the outskirts of Pittsburgh. Fritz Pollard, Jr., the son and namesake of a pioneering African American football star, was born in Springfield, Massachusetts, where his father was prepping to attend Brown University. The younger Pollard grew up in Chicago where his father played for and coached the Bears in the early National Football League. [20]

Each of the 'black auxiliaries' spent their formative years in 'integrated' urban or suburban neighbourhoods in a major metropolitan area – Cleveland, Chicago, Los Angeles, Oakland or Pittsburgh. Segregation and racism certainly existed in these locales during their childhoods, but it took the de facto form of custom and practice rather than the legalized *de jure* segregation of the Jim Crow South where several of them had been born. They each recalled the erratic nature of the racial exclusion that plagued their childhoods, the specific swimming pools, restaurants, movie theatres or amusement parks that sometimes refused to admit them based on their skin colour, while remembering in general that most public venues were open to them. They remembered also the slurs and social exclusions that sometimes came from classmates, teammates and neighbours. They all attended integrated public schools, though as was common practice in that era, many of them were channelled to 'technical' high schools designed to provide them with working-class job skills. Albritton attended East Technical with Owens in Cleveland. James LuValle, a stellar student, was nevertheless relegated to Los Angeles Polytechnic. Ralph Metcalfe went to Tilden Technical in Chicago. Mack Robinson matriculated at Muir Technical in Pasadena. [21]

They each became accomplished track and field athletes in high school and several starred in other sports as well. They each generated interest from major athletic programmes at northern and western universities. They were all intercollegiate stars or very recent graduates when they made the 1936 US Olympic team. LuValle had just graduated from UCLA and Metcalfe had just graduated from Marquette University. Williams was a student at the University of California, Berkeley. Woodruff was at the University of Pittsburgh. Albritton attended Ohio State with Owens. Pollard was at the University of North Dakota after having spent a freshman year at Brown University, his father's alma mater. Mack Robinson was a student at Pasadena Junior College and Cornelius Johnson attended Compton Junior College, both in the greater Los Angeles area. [22]

Their academic accomplishments exceeded those of their more famous teammate. Jesse Owens attended but never graduated from Ohio State. The rest of the 'auxiliaries', with the exception of Cornelius Johnson, who after a stint at Compton Junior College took a job with the US postal system in 1937, earned baccalaureate degrees, and several earned graduate degrees. Though later accounts claimed that Mack Robinson dropped out of the University of Oregon in 1938 to support his family during the Great Depression, the university's records indicate he earned a bachelor's degree in physical education in 1941. Ralph Metcalfe earned a PhB from Marquette in 1936 and then a master's degree in physical education from USC in 1939. David Albritton graduated in 1938 from Ohio State with a teaching degree in industrial arts and a minor in physical education. Fritz Pollard, Jr., completed his degree at the University of North Dakota that same year. Archie Williams earned a BS in mechanical engineering in 1939 from the University of California. John Woodruff earned a BA in sociology from the University of Pittsburgh in 1939 and an MA in sociology from New York University in 1941. James LuValle, the most distinguished academic among the group, graduated Phi Beta Kappa from UCLA in chemistry in 1936, earned his MS in chemistry and physics from UCLA in 1937 and then in 1940 earned his PhD in chemistry and mathematics from the prestigious California Institute of Technology under the tutelage of Nobel Laureate Linus Pauling. [23]

Several members of the 'black auxiliaries' achieved leadership positions at their institutions, in spite of the fact that African American students represented a tiny percentage of the population at the schools they attended. Archie Williams ran for the office of secretary of student government after returning to the University of California from Berlin and came within 80 votes of victory. Before he went to Berlin James LuValle won the Jake Kimball Award as the outstanding senior man at UCLA and earned a nomination as a Rhodes Scholar. On his return LuValle enrolled in graduate school and became the founding president of the UCLA Graduate Student Association. In 1934 the track team at Marquette University elected Ralph Metcalfe as their captain, making him one of the first African American athletes to hold that position in the history of intercollegiate sport. Metcalfe also won election as senior class president in 1936 – before he went to Berlin and medalled. [24]

In the aftermath of the Olympics, Metcalfe, LuValle and Williams retired from active athletic competition. The others continued competing and would have been Olympic medal contenders again in 1940, and perhaps even in 1944, had the Second World War not cancelled those games. Fritz Pollard, Jr., went back to North Dakota and continued to excel in the hurdles as well as earning Little All-American (the award for small colleges) honours as running-back on the football squad. Woodruff and Robinson dominated intercollegiate and AAU track meets into the 1940s. Johnson won another AAU high jump title in 1937 and then turned his attention to his postal career. David Albritton then took his turn as the dominant high jumper in the US for more than a dozen years. He won the 1937 and 1938 NCAA high jump titles and was AAU national champion in the event in 1937 and 1938, from 1944 to 1947, and, amazingly, in 1950 – 14 years after his silver medal in Berlin. [25]

Heeding the counsel of the African American press, the 'black auxiliaries' excelled even more outside athletic arenas than they did inside them. Silver medallist Albritton took a position teaching and coaching in a Dayton, Ohio, high school, leading the track team to several state titles. He joined the US Department of State during the 1950s and helped, with his old friend Owens, to organize goodwill tours of American athletes and set up sports programmes in Iran, Iraq, Pakistan and Turkey. He returned to Dayton in the late 1950s and ran a successful insurance business. He won a seat in the Ohio House of Representatives in 1960 and served several terms in office, becoming the first black to chair a committee in the state legislature. Albritton's fellow high-jumper, gold medallist Cornelius Johnson, worked for the US Post Office from 1937 until 1945. At the end of the Second World War he joined the US Merchant Marine. On a 1946 voyage he contracted pneumonia and became, the first of the 'black auxiliaries' to perish, at the tender age – particularly for that group – of 32. [26]

Silver medallist Mack Robinson returned to Pasadena after his college career in Oregon. For several years he could only find work as a menial labourer, sweeping the streets of his home town clad in his US Olympic team sweatshirt. He later became a community activist and sought to rebuild the increasingly impoverished and racially segregated neighbourhoods in his city. Fritz Pollard, Jr., came back to Chicago after his college football career in North Dakota. He taught physical education in the Chicago school system and worked for the parks and recreations department. Mayor Richard Daley appointed him the director of the Human Relations Commission in the late 1950s. He joined the US Department of State as a Foreign Service officer during the administration of President Lyndon B. Johnson in the 1960s. He retired in 1981, having risen to a position as the director of the State Department's overseas schools for US citizens. [27]

The 400-metre gold medallist Archie Williams could not find an engineering position in spite of his University of California degree so he took a menial job in aviation shortly after his 1939 graduation. He also learned how to fly, and became first a civilian instructor and then an enlisted military instructor for the famed 'Tuskegee Airmen' during the Second World War. He also earned meteorology and aeronautical engineering degrees while in the military. After the war he continued a career in the US Air Force, rising to the rank of lieutenant colonel before retiring in 1966. He returned home to California and became a high-school mathematics and computer science teacher for two more decades while also owning a flying service in Sonoma County. The 800-metre gold medallist John Woodruff also joined the military during the Second World War. Woodruff rose to the rank of captain when he was discharged in 1945. He re-entered the army in 1950 during the Korean conflict and finished his career in 1957 as a lieutenant colonel after serving as a battalion commander. He then coached and taught in New York City, worked for the New York Department of Welfare and the New York City Police Athletic League, and moved on to positions as a parole officer for the state of New York and as an assistant to the director of a federal job corps centre in New Jersey. [28]

The 400-metre bronze medallist James LuValle became the academic champion of the 'black auxiliaries'. He earned an MS at UCLA and a PhD at Cal Tech. He taught for a year at Fisk University, a historically black college in Nashville, Tennessee, and then began a career as a research scientist at Eastman Kodak and several other major corporations. During the Second World War LuValle worked for the federal Office of Scientific and Research Development in Chicago on chemical and biological warfare projects. After the war he went back to Kodak. He joined the chemistry department at Stanford in the 1970s, retiring in 1984. [29]

Ralph Metcalfe, the perennial Olympic bridesmaid, enjoyed perhaps the most successful post-athletic career of all of the 'black auxiliaries'. Immediately after the Berlin Olympics Metcalfe became the track coach and a faculty member at Xavier University, a historically black college in New Orleans, Louisiana. He led Xavier to a national reputation in track and field before leaving in 1942 to serve as a first lieutenant in the US army during the Second World War. After the war he returned to Chicago to serve as the director of the division of civil rights in the city's Commission on Human Relations. In 1949 he was appointed as an Illinois athletic commissioner. In 1952 he joined the Third Ward Democratic Committee and in 1955 he won election as Third Ward Alderman as a loyal soldier in Mayor Richard J. Daley's new political machine's climb to power. In 1970, Metcalfe won election to the US House of Representatives. He became a powerful member of the Congressional Black Caucus and a significant player in national politics, winning three consecutive landslide re-elections. [30]

Black Memories

The 'black auxiliaries', with a few exceptions, enjoyed long lives filled with accomplishments beyond the world of sport. They left a variety of imprints on national and local memories. In the immediate aftermath of Berlin, the 'black auxiliaries' remained powerful icons in the African American community. Writing in the *Southern Workman* just a few months after the 1936 Olympics, Charles Williams proclaimed that the 'brilliant performances of these athletes, their tact and diplomacy, their impeccable manners and "unimpeachable demeanor" all con-tributed toward making them ambassadors of good will and racial understanding'. Williams insisted that not just Owens but all the black medallists from Berlin had contributed mightily to racial understanding both in the US and around the world. 'Their achievements in the games showed to an unsuspecting world great racial talents and possibilities', he declared, noting that white as well as black Americans cheered their contributions to the nation. The African American community, in particular, could profit from their examples, Williams contended. 'Certainly the race needs such examples as were given by these young men who met the best the world could offer; and yet, by training, grit, perseverance and a fighting heart, they excelled and brought honour to themselves, their race and their country', he concluded. [31]

In the decades after Williams penned his homage to the 'black auxiliaries', they became icons in the national African American community. Though Owens certainly got the lion's share of attention, as he had even in Williams's 1936 essay, Albritton, Johnson, LuValle, Metcalfe, Pollard, Robinson, Williams and Woodruff remained heroic figures. Edwin Bancroft Henderson, a pioneering African American scholar of sport at Howard University, a historically black college in Washington, DC, kept them alive almost single-handedly in a series of books and articles. [32] Henderson revelled in pointing out that James LuValle, the bronze medallist in the 400 metres, was the only Phi Beta Kappa honours graduate on the American track team – black or white. [33] Henderson made the 'auxiliaries' heroes in the twentieth century struggle for racial equality. 'If evidence were needed to convince skeptics or Hitlers that the Negro has the brawn, the brain and the competitive urge to win in contests of skill, speed, endurance and strength, the record made by colored boys in modern Olympic Games should supply the data desired', he declared. [34] Other champions of the 'black auxiliaries' in the black sporting press such as Andrew S. 'Doc' Young and Arna Bontemps made similar claims. [35]

The 'black auxiliaries' also crossed over during the period from the 1930s to the 1960s into the realm of supporting figures in tales of Jesse Owens and Jackie Robinson that filled the celebratory volumes aimed at juvenile audiences by black authors, including Ben Brawley's *Negro Builders and Heroes* (1937); Langston Hughes's *Famous American Negroes* (1954) and Ben Richardson's *Great American Negroes* (1956). [36] While never the focus of these discourses, Albritton, Johnson, LuValle, Metcalfe, Pollard, Robinson, Williams and Woodruff stayed alive in black consciousness through the 1960s and into the 1970s.

White Memories

The 'black auxiliaries' remained in white as well as black memories of Berlin, though they were certainly fuzzier in the minds of the white chroniclers of American Olympic fables. John Kieran and Arthur Daly's *The Story of the Olympic Games*, published in the wake of the Berlin games, mentioned each of the 'black auxiliaries' who medalled but clearly made Owens the overwhelming star of the narrative. The authors, both prominent *New York Times* sports writers who had been in Berlin to cover the Olympics, portrayed the African American track stars as heroes who dismantled Hitler's racial theories and spun rhetorical highlights of the 'Charge of the Black Brigade'. [37] They focused intently on the blackness of the 'black auxiliaries', turning Metcalfe into 'just as much a Negro as Owens and much darker in shade'. [38] In Bill Henry's *An Approved History of the Olympic Games* (1948), another popular American history, Cornelius Johnson and David Albritton appeared briefly and accurately as the gold and silver medallists that Adolf Hitler might have snubbed, but Jesse Owens again dominated the narrative. 'The name of Jesse Owens is hammered deep in bronze, embedded in the stone Marathon Gate of the Berlin stadium, and appears there more often, even than that of Hitler', Henry declared.

'The feats of Jesse Owens were almost without parallel in Olympic history', Henry concluded. [39]

Memories of the 'black auxiliaries' not only appeared in occasional histories but also shaped the practices of the United States Olympic Committee (USOC). In a 1948 official report, veteran USOC leader Gustavus T. Kirby insisted that in all future opening parades of nations at the Olympics the US flag-bearer should be accompanied by a 'Negro' to showcase African American contributions to the Olympic cause. [40] As African Americans after the Second World War continued to win copious numbers of Olympic medals in track and field, the legacies of Owens and the rest of the 'black auxiliaries' in defeating Hitler in Berlin were transformed by the white press into a new legacy of American blacks supporting their nation's Cold War struggle to defeat the Communists. [41] In 1960, at the height of the Cold War, the USOC extended Gus Kirby's admonition about featuring African American athletes in the parade pageant and made black decathlete Rafer Johnson the first African American flag-bearer. [42]

Making Local Memories of the 'Black Auxiliaries'

While tales of Owens and his four gold medals have for decades filled white and black national memories of the 'Nazi Olympics', Albritton, Johnson, LuValle, Metcalfe, Pollard, Robinson, Williams and Woodruff became footnotes in national reminiscences. In one such footnote, when in 1960 the NBC television programme *This Is Your Life* turned to the Olympics for a storyline it featured Jesse Owens in the lead role as the subject of the programme while casting Ralph Metcalfe and David Albritton in minor roles. [43] Forty-seven years later, in another footnote, an ESPN reporter in a 2007 television story on the last surviving member of the 'black auxiliaries' observed that 'while Owens plays a leading role in American sports lore, John Woodruff has slipped into anonymity'. [44] ESPN's assessment fit not just Woodruff but all the rest of the 'black auxiliaries', none of whom received any sustained national attention, with the exception of Ralph Metcalfe. Metcalfe's post-Olympic moments in the national imagination, however, owed mainly to his service in the US Congress from 1970 to 1978 rather than to his silver-medal finishes in Olympic 100-metre dashes – though Metcalfe's athletic stardom certainly played a role in his political popularity. The lack of national attention did not mean that the remaining 'black auxiliaries' were entirely forgotten in American memories. At the local level, especially in their home towns and at their alma maters, they were periodically commemorated, particularly from the late 1960s on as the changing racial sensibilities of the post-Civil Rights era increasing popularized African American contributions to American history. [45]

Induction into Halls of Fame marked one measure of the local rediscovery of the 'black auxiliaries' after the 1960s. With the exception of Johnson, who did not matriculate beyond Compton Junior College, all of the 'auxiliaries' made their university athletic halls of fame. Some also made county or state halls of fame.

Woodruff earned membership in the Fayette County Sports Hall of Fame and the Penn Relays Wall of Fame. Robinson was inducted into the Oregon Sports Hall of Fame. Metcalfe, though he spent just the first five years of his life there, made the Georgia Sports Hall of Fame. [46] In 1994 Johnson made the United States Track and Field Hall of Fame, alongside Owens and Metcalfe, who in 1975 were charter members, Woodruff (1978), Albritton (1980) and Williams (1992). [47]

The 'black auxiliaries' have left behind a variety of local legacies and monuments. James LuValle, the 400-metre bronze medallist, had a graduate dormitory named after him at UCLA, joining four other distinguished black alumni from that institution – Ralph Bunche, Tom Bradley, Arthur Ashe, Jr. and Jackie Robinson – to be so honoured by the university. [48] The 400-metre gold medallist, Archie Williams, received a 1988 special citation for his Olympic service from the California State Senate. [49] Both Williams and LuValle were rediscovered in the 1980s and 1990s by local historians in California who collected oral histories from them. Their own personal memories of their experiences as 'black auxiliaries' reveal that they were quickly forgotten when they returned home. Both experienced intense discrimination in spite of their starring roles in helping their nation win the track and field contests at the 1936 games. Williams, a mechanical engineering graduate of the University of California, was barred from the campus honorary society in his field and after graduation could not find a job. LuValle, a Phi Beta Kappa graduate of UCLA who went on to earn a doctorate at the prestigious California Institute of Technology, could only find an academic job at Fisk University, a segregated college for blacks. Following the call of the black press to excel in realms beyond athletics, both men fought to overcome discrimination and completed distinguished careers. LuValle became a prominent research scientist who ended up on the chemistry faculty at Stanford University. Williams was a pioneering black aviator who served a distinguished career in the US Air Force, and then completed a distinguished second career in teaching. Both recalled that in the post-Civil Rights era they began to be 'rediscovered' every four years by local reporters who began to celebrate their old athletic feats every time an Olympic Games rolled around. [50]

The Complexities of Local Memories: John Woodruff and Mack Robinson

Two members of the 'black auxiliaries', John Woodruff and Mack Robinson, illuminate the complexities of local memories of Olympic heroism. From the moment they both returned to their home towns from Berlin, their lives and the local memories of their service to their communities diverged in significant ways. John Woodruff came home to Connellsville, a steel-mill town outside Pittsburgh, to an enthusiastic welcome. A crowd of 10,000 gathered for a parade celebrating Woodruff's triumphant homecoming. Connellsville's leaders gave Woodruff a gold watch and he presented them with an oak sapling, a gift from the German government to all gold medallists. Proud townsfolk planted the tree at the local high school where Woodruff had attended. Ironically, when he had tried to drop out of high school to go to work in the local mills to help his family during the Great Depression his race made him impossible to hire. Woodruff stayed in school and went on to college. The tree grew and stayed at the school as well, relocated once during a construction project to spread its shade over the new high school football stadium. [51]

Woodruff won his gold medal after completing his freshman year at the University of Pittsburgh. After Berlin he spent three more years at Pitt and became the dominant middle-distance runner of his era in intercollegiate and AAU meets. During his stellar post-Olympic career, Woodruff never lost a single race. At the Penn Relays, Woodruff won eight races in his three appearances. [52] In his final competitive race, the 1940 Compton Invitational, Woodruff won the 800 metres, setting a US record that lasted until 1952. Had the 1940 Olympics not been cancelled, Woodruff surely would have been the favourite in the 800 metres. [53]

Woodruff's career as a 'black auxiliary' continued as well. In 1937 the United States Naval Academy requested that Woodruff be left home when the University of Pittsburgh competed in segregated Annapolis, Maryland. Pitt officials complied with the request, a decision that deeply troubled Woodruff. [54] 'Now here I am, an Olympic champion, and they told the coach that I couldn't run. I couldn't come,' recalled Woodruff. 'So I had to stay home, because of discrimination. That let me know just what the situation was. Things hadn't changed.' [55] That same year, Woodruff and his fellow African American teammates at the Pan American 'Olympics' in Dallas had were barred from the athletes' 'Olympic village' at segregated Southern Methodist University and consigned to a black YMCA. [56] In spite of his international victories for his nation, Woodruff found that his race still limited his opportunities.

After graduating from Pitt, Woodruff relocated to New York City. He earned a master's degree in sociology from New York University in 1941 and then served in the military during the Second World War and the Korean conflict. He spent the rest of his professional career in the New York City metropolitan area, and then retired to Arizona. Outside the greater Pittsburgh area, Woodruff only very occasionally appeared in the public memory, such as the 2007 ESPN report or a short feature in a 2008 issue of a children's magazine, *Highlights*, or when comedian Bill Cosby, a former participant in the Penn Relays who ran track for Temple University, lamented that Woodruff had unfortunately been overshadowed by the accomplishments of Owens. [57]

Back in Pennsylvania, however, Woodruff's home town and alma mater redis-covered him in the 1980s and began to honour him with a series of awards. In Connellsville, Woodruff's Olympic tree stood as a reminder of his contributions. He donated his Olympic sweater and medals from various track meets including the prestigious Penn Relays to his high school, where they remain on prominent display. Since 1983, Connellsville hosts an annual John Woodruff Day that includes a five-kilometre race honouring the track legend and raises money for college scholarships to further Woodruff's legacy in higher education. [58]

His alma mater began remembering John Woodruff once again beginning in the 1990s. In 1990, the University of Pittsburgh established a tribute to Woodruff in the Hillman Library, displaying Woodruff's gold medal. In the years that followed the university transformed Woodruff into a symbol of racial reconciliation and racial change. Woodruff had not forgotten his exclusion from the 1937 track meet at the US Naval Academy. 'John was angry about the incident and how it was handled and rightfully so', recalled 1948 Olympian and fellow Pitt alum Herbert Douglas. 'Here is this kid who is an Olympic gold medallist and he's being told he can't compete for his own team in his own country, at the Naval Academy, no less', Douglas recalled. In 2006, for a celebration of the 70th anniversary of Woodruff's 1936 gold medal, Pitt chancellor Mark Nordenberg took advantage of an opportunity to apologize for the university's abandonment of Woodruff to the segregationists in Annapolis. The university made Woodruff the guest of honour at its homecoming festivities. Despite declining health and the loss of both of his legs from a circulatory condition, Woodruff returned to his alma mater and received recognition from both Pitt's African American Alumni Council and its Varsity Letter Club. Pitt also recognized Woodruff's contributions during a half time ceremony at their 2006 homecoming football game. In summarizing the university's new-found appreciation of Woodruff, at the Varsity Club dinner Chancellor Nordenberg turned to the aged Olympian and in front of a large crowd announced, 'both personally and for the University of Pittsburgh, I want to apologize to you – and I feel certain that, if those responsible for leading our University 70 years ago were here today, they would stand with me and join me in this expression of regret'. [59]

Following Woodruff's death in 2007, Pitt put together a commemorative video documenting his gold medal performance in Berlin and regularly displays the brief film at home sports events. [60] Woodruff's alma mater and home town transformed his legacy in the post-Civil Rights era, remembering his challenges to racial segregation at home and abroad while at the same time heralding him as an icon of racial reconciliation in a new era that they insisted now fostered racial harmony. Woodruff became in the last decades of his long life a symbol of how far American culture had progressed in race relations since the 1930s.

The home-town legacy of another member of the 'black auxiliaries', Mack Robinson, offers a different history of the complexities of local memories and race relations. Robinson came home to Pasadena, California, without the fanfare that John Woodruff found in Connellsville. Robinson later remembered that no parade nor public ceremony of any kind greeted him on his return, even though the *Los Angeles Times* reported that both he and Cornelius Johnson attended a downtown Los Angeles parade hosted by the mayor for returning American Olympians. [61] 'If anybody in Pasadena was proud for me, other than my family and close friends, they never showed it. I was totally ignored,' Robinson later complained, perhaps referring specifically to his suburban home town rather than Los Angeles. [62] 'I felt they should've honoured me in some way, such as a hero should have been', Robinson recalled. Robinson bitterly contended that 'the only time I was noticed was when somebody asked me during an assembly at school if I'd race against a horse' – something Owens had done after the Olympics. [63]

Robinson returned to Pasadena Junior College where his younger brother, Jackie, joined him in the winter of 1937. [64] Still dissatisfied, however, he left Southern California in 1938 behind for what he hoped were greener pastures at the University of Oregon. Like Woodruff, he became a post-Olympic intercollegiate and AAU track star, winning the 1938 National Collegiate Athletic Association (NCAA) 220-yard dash and 1938 Amateur Athletic Union (AAU) 200-metre sprint. Had Tokyo staged its 1940 Olympics, Robinson would no doubt have been a serious contender for an Olympic crown in his speciality. [65] Though later accounts often claimed that Robinson dropped out of the University of Oregon to return home to help his family survive during the Great Depression, [66] the University of Oregon's records indicate Robinson completed his degree in physical education in 1941. [67]

After his sojourn in Oregon, Robinson went to Pasadena where he found only menial jobs. In fact, Robinson would never find the same level of work as most of his fellow 'auxiliaries' enjoyed. Despite his track success and his training as a physical educator (if the Oregon sources are accurate), Robinson was not offered employment as a teacher or coach. The other 'black auxiliaries' found that their Olympic medals combined with their college degrees helped them earn respectable middle-class jobs as coaches, teachers, military officers, civil servants and entrepreneurs. Some even won election to public office. Robinson's Olympic notoriety only earned him a spot on a crew sweeping streets, cleaning sewers and digging ditches for the city of Pasadena. He often wore his US Olympic team sweater on chilly winter mornings while he laboured, a wardrobe choice that displeased some Pasadenans who felt he was intentionally trying to embarrass the city. [68] After decades as a city worker, Robinson also earned a reputation as a community activist and civil-rights leader. He helped to integrate the municipal pool where he and other African Americans were allowed during his childhood to swim only one day a week. He fought against racism, organized youth programmes, and sought to revitalize the declining neighbourhood in north-west Pasadena where he spent most of his life. [69]

Robinson faced another burden the rest of the 'black auxiliaries' did not share – with, perhaps, the exception of Fritz Pollard, Jr., whose father and namesake was a far more famous and successful athlete than junior. [70] Not only did Robinson labour in the shadow of Jesse Owens but he was also eclipsed by the fame of his younger brother, Jackie Robinson, who in 1946 led the integration of American baseball and became a key figure in the struggle against racial segregation in the United States. Jackie Robinson has become a towering figure in American national memories, rivalling and in many cases surpassing even Jesse Owens as a sign of the contributions African American athletes have made to the nation's history. [71] Indeed, when Mack Robinson passed away in 2000, *Sports Illustrated* ran a brief notice of his life entitled 'Ahead of Jackie, Behind Jesse', a fitting epitaph for his public life. [72] Memories of Mack Robinson always placed him between the gigantic poles of his superstar brother and his Olympic teammate, such as the 1997 commemoration in an African

American newspaper, the *Philadelphia Tribune*, that explained Mack Robinson's claim to fame as 'Besides being Jackie's older brother, ... he was nipped by Jesse Owens in the 1936 200 meters'. [73]

In 1984, after both his brother and Jesse Owens had passed away, Mack Robinson received some attention at the opening ceremony of the Los Angeles Olympics when organizers selected him as a member of the team of former Olympians who carried the Olympic flag into Los Angeles Memorial Coliseum. Jesse Owens's granddaughter, however, served in an even more prominent role as the torch-bearer who brought the Olympic flame into the Los Angeles Coliseum. [74] Even after his brief return to the international spotlight in 1984, Robinson remained frustrated by the lack of recognition he felt he received from his home town. [75] He was also frustrated by Pasadena's faltering efforts to memorialize his brother, and fought tirelessly after Jackie's 1972 death to have the city develop a memorial to baseball's civil-rights trailblazer. [76] In the late 1990s, Pasadena finally recognized Mack Robinson, albeit still in conjunction with his more famous sibling. The Robinson brothers share several monuments including a stadium at Pasadena City College, a local park and a pair of bronze sculptures at city hall in downtown Pasadena. [77]

Ironically, even as Pasadena rediscovered Mack Robinson, the details of his career grew fuzzy. In 1997 when the city unveiled the bronze busts of the brothers outside Pasadena's city hall, the reporter covering the event for the *Los Angeles Sentinel*, the major African American newspaper in southern California, misreported a basic detail, asserting that Mack Robinson had won a silver medal in the 100-metre dash, not the 200-metre dash in which he actually medalled. [78] While Jackie Robinson and Jesse Owens found their faces on postage stamps, symbolic of their national legacies, Mack Robinson's commemorations remained more parochial. The United States Postal Service dedicated a Pasadena post office to Mack Robinson – for once a memorial that he did not have to share with his brother. [79]

Robinson found warmer receptions honouring his legacy north of his home town, far up the Pacific coast in Oregon. During the lead-up to the 1984 Los Angeles Olympics, the Oregon Sports Hall of Fame inducted Robinson. Still under the Olympic spell, his alma mater, the University of Oregon, awarded Robinson their 'Webfoot' award in 1984, an honour that 'recognizes a graduate who exemplifies the best the university has to offer'. [80] In the year prior to the 1996 Atlanta Olympics, his alma mater enshrined Robinson in the University of Oregon Sports Hall of Fame. [81] Robinson expressed great appreciation for his Oregon recognitions. His wife, Delano Robinson, recalled that when she and her husband drove up to Oregon they visited the university and Mack Robinson reminisced 'about all the happy times he had there'. [82]

The local memories that communities built around Mack Robinson and John Woodruff illuminate the continuing power of the black auxiliaries' narratives in the post-Civil Rights era. Though long gone from Connellsville and the University of Pittsburgh, local groups resurrected Woodruff's gold-medal performance and life story and used it to present images of their region as a progressive culture that was evolving towards a more harmonious racial climate. In contrast, Robinson spent most of his life in his home town of Pasadena, and while some groups sought to claim him as a racial pioneer who helped lead southern California towards a more integrated and equitable society, he remained throughout his life a lightning-rod for dissent, reminding Pasadenans of their long history of mistreatment of their African American neighbours. Whereas Woodruff served his community as a symbol of racial progress, Robinson on many levels served his community as a reminder of the stubbornness of racial divisions.

A National Legacy after Decades in the Shadows: Memories of Ralph Metcalfe

Racial division and racial reconciliation marked the monuments erected to the man who lost the 1936 Olympic 100-metre dash and the crown as the 'world's fastest man' to Owens by milliseconds. Ralph Metcalfe was the only member of the 'black auxiliaries' besides Owens to garner sustained national attention. Metcalfe, who for four decades after the Berlin Olympics built a reputation mainly at the local level, fully re-emerged in for the first time since the conclusion of his athletic career on the national stage when in 1970 he won a seat in Congress.

Before his ascension to the House of Representatives, Metcalfe earned fame as the track coach and a faculty member at segregated Xavier University in New Orleans. He built Xavier into a regional track powerhouse and authored a text on sprinting techniques with the famous University of Southern California and Olympic track coach Dean Cromwell. [83] He left Xavier during the Second World War and after a stint in the US armed services he returned to Chicago and began a distinguished career in public service. In 1945 he became the director of Chicago's Department of Civil Rights, an agency that tried to deal with Chicago's volatile race relations. Metcalfe built power bases in both the black and white communities. [84] The most influential politician in mid-twentieth century Chicago, Richard J. Daley, became Metcalfe's patron. When Daley swept into the mayor's office in 1955, Metcalfe rode his coat-tails to a seat as a city alderman. For the next 25 years Metcalfe served as a Daley loyalist. [85]

Metcalfe's athletic background helped to shape his political career. Metcalfe's athletic legacy proved useful in the world of politics. In 1949, while Metcalfe laboured for the Department of Civil Rights, he also became the first African American to serve on the state athletic commission when Illinois Governor Adlai Stevenson appointed him to the office. [86] Metcalfe also served as the co-chair of the organizing committee for the third Pan American Games organizing committee, held in Chicago in 1959. He made a diplomatic tour of 15 Latin American countries promoting the Chicago spectacle. He also served on Chicago's failed bids to land the 1964 or 1968 Olympic Games. [87] In 1962, Metcalfe started the Ralph H. Metcalfe Youth Foundation, which supported young athletes from Chicago's Third Ward. [88]

Right up to the middle of the 1960s, Ralph Metcalfe, like many of his fellow 'black auxiliaries', built a powerful local legacy. On the national stage however, his place in public memory had faded. *Sports Illustrated* observed in a 1961 article entitled 'Olympic Bridesmaid', that Metcalfe was once the 'world's fastest human', a sprinter who owned or shared every world record from 40 to 220 yards. He never won an Olympic gold, however, and 'his name is remembered by few people other than track enthusiasts'. [89]

Outside Chicago, or Milwaukee where he starred for Marquette University, very few Americans by the 1960s still remembered Ralph Metcalfe. His local legacy, however, continued to flourish. Like Woodruff, Robinson and many of his other teammates, Metcalfe earned honours from both his home town of Chicago and from his alma mater. Marquette enrolled him in its athletic hall of fame in the 1970s. [90] Marquette's library designed exhibits to memorialize Metcalfe's athletic feats. [91] The Milwaukee Public Museum featured several of Metcalfe's Olympic medals and a pair of his running shoes along with a life-size bronze statue of the 'Marquette Meteor'. [92] The city of Milwaukee dedicated the Ralph Metcalfe Elementary School. [93] Chicago also dedicated an elementary school and a park to Metcalfe. [94]

Metcalfe's legacies, however, eventually transcended local memories. From the mid-1960s to his death in 1978, Metcalfe once again rose to national prominence. Though his former athletic deeds certainly aided his return to the national spotlight, race relations and politics served as the primary vehicles for his re-emergence in a larger American arena. During the mid-1960s Metcalfe became embroiled in the racial controversies that swirled through Chicago and the nation. When Martin Luther King, Jr., came to Chicago in 1967 to fight against racism in the North, Mayor Daley and the political establishment used Metcalfe and other African American loyalists to counter King's claims that blacks were systematically disenfranchised in the nation's second largest metropolitan area. Metcalfe led a group of black leaders who painted King as an outside agitator who did not speak for Chicago's black community. [95] At the same time, Metcalfe sided with Owens in the very public feud between older and younger generations of black leaders over the Olympic Project for Human Rights' (OPHR) campaign to persuade African American athletes to boycott the 1968 Olympics to protest against the continuing scourge of racism in American society. [96] Metcalfe, who had been depicted as a stooge of the white power structure for supporting Mayor Daley during Martin Luther King's travails in Chicago, earned even more enmity from the 'black power' faction by joining his old teammate Jesse Owens in a very vocal opposition to OPHR's boycott plans. [97]

Metcalfe's connections to both sport and politics increasingly pushed him into the national discourse on civil-rights issues. His Olympic heritage and his new political connections both contributed to his rising national profile. During the 1960s US Vice President Hubert Humphrey appointed Metcalfe to the National AAU and NCAA Sports Arbitration Board, where he sought to act as a peacemaker between the two warring factions in American amateur athletics. [98] Metcalfe also won a term on the executive board of the United States Olympic Committee. In the 1970s President Gerald Ford appointed Metcalfe to the President's Commission on Olympic Sports. [99]

The forces that lubricated Metcalfe's ascension to national prominence – race, politics and sport – converged in 1969 when William Dawson, just the second African American in US history to win election to the US House of Representatives in the post-Reconstruction era, announced his retirement. The 83-year old Dawson represented Chicago's First Congressional District, the sprawling Southside neighbourhoods where Metcalfe had grown up and where he had been re-elected for decades to the Chicago Board of Aldermen. The district with the largest population of African Americans in the US struggled in the late 1960s with widespread poverty, the loss of significant economic infrastructure, high unemployment rates and escalating crime rates. Metcalfe, a loyal lieutenant in the Daley machine, was dubbed the heir apparent by the Chicago power structure. His opponent in the Democratic primary, community activist A.A. Rayner, labelled Metcalfe an 'Uncle Tom' who worked for the white oppressors. 'Right On' Rayner, as his supporters and his bumper stickers dubbed him, earned the support of the Black Panthers and other radical groups, as well as activists such as Mayor Richard Hatcher of Gary, Indiana, comedian Dick Gregory and Julian Bond, founder of Georgia's Legislative Black Caucus. Rayner promised to lead the charge to overthrow the Daley machine and drum white reactionaries out of the Democratic Party. Metcalfe, however, trounced Rayner in the primary, earning 70 per cent of the vote. He then won 90 per cent of the vote against his white Republican opponent in the general election. His campaign pamphlets recounted 'The Ralph Metcalfe Story', asserting to voters that

> children raised in slum areas are unusually aware of the rights of people, if only because they have been denied so many themselves. At an early period, this street-taught awareness became a part of Metcalfe's personality. When Olympic fame and college degrees were attached to this knowledge, Metcalfe the leader developed. [100]

Metcalfe the congressional leader quickly proved an enigma. The Daley machine had brought him to power but in the volatile local and national political climate of the era in which Mayor Daley increasingly became a national symbol of obstructionism and power-mongering for his handling of the 1968 Democratic National Convention riots and his iron-fisted grip over the police force in squelching dissent in Chicago, Congressman Metcalfe quickly and publicly broke with his patron. His startled campaign rival, A.A. Rayner, suddenly discovered a 'black and beautiful' Ralph Metcalfe who by threats of congressional investigations forced the issue of police brutality against African Americans into the national consciousness and helped to spark a major reform of law enforcement in Chicago. [101]

Metcalfe won three more terms in office from the voters of the First Congressional district. His stature as a leader grew in Chicago as he broke with the Daley machine. He developed a reputation as a force to be reckoned with in Chicago's rough-and-tumble political culture and on the national stage. [102] The *Chicago Tribune's* editorials painted Metcalfe in an increasingly positive light. [103] Indeed, by the 1976 election, the *Tribune* fully endorsed Metcalfe: 'Ralph Metcalfe has gained not only experience in his three terms in congress, but honorable battle scars at home in his fight to loosen Democratic machine control over his district.' Chicago's most powerful newspaper urged voters to select Metcalfe over his old rival, A.A. Rayner, the old Black Panther ally who had amazingly become a Republican convert. [104]

Metcalfe trounced Rayner again and returned to Washington. During his Congressional career Metcalfe worked on both racial and athletic causes. He joined the newly formed Congressional Black Caucus, introduced the congressional resolution that officially established Black History Month, and co-sponsored the 1978 Amateur Athletic Act, a legislative edict that dramatically transformed Olympic sport in the United States and provided expanded opportunities for minorities, women and disabled Americans to participate in a wide variety of sports. [105] Once milliseconds behind in an Olympic race that would have won him everlasting fame in the national spotlight, Ralph Metcalfe had returned to centre stage.

In Memoriam

In October 1978, with his own re-election seemingly assured, Ralph Metcalfe returned to Chicago to help his son, Ralph Jr., campaign for his old seat as Third Ward alderman. A heart attack struck him down at the age of 68. His sudden death, while still a vibrant member of Congress, drew national coverage. Obituaries remembered Metcalfe as 'an Olympic track star' who rose through Chicago's political ranks to become, in the words of the president of Chicago's urban league, 'a valiant soldier in the battle to ensure human rights'. [106] Members of the US House and Senate held memorial services in the national capitol, singing Metcalfe's praises. [107] Back home in Chicago more than two thousand people, including Jesse Owens and numerous public officials, attended Metcalfe's funeral. [108]

Metcalfe's passing offered Chicagoans and the nation a chance to reflect on the achievements of one of the key members of the 'black auxiliaries'. The 1936 Olympics certainly played a large role in memorializing Metcalfe. Directly underneath the front-page *Chicago Tribune* article on Metcalfe's death ran an article entitled 'Owens Recalls Beloved Teammate', which devoted more ink to Owens's four gold medals than to any of his memories of Metcalfe. [109] Even in death Metcalfe could not entirely escape Owens's shadow. Metcalfe's obituaries, however, offered a portrait that extended beyond Owens and the 1936 Olympics, showcasing a life of public service and distinguished accomplishments in education and politics that personified the admonition of black press in the wake of the 'Nazi Olympics' to extend African American achievement beyond stadiums to new horizons. In 1991, after a heated debate in Congress that reignited some of the racial and political animus in Chicago that always swirled about Metcalfe's career in public life, the federal government added to the local schools and parks that memorialized the former Olympic hero and put his name on a national monument, a massive new federal building in downtown

Chicago. [110] Metcalfe had found a permanent place, however small in comparison to Owens's fame, in the national imagination.

In death the other 'black auxiliaries' returned for a moment to the national spotlight. With the exception of Cornelius Johnson, who died of pneumonia on board a merchant ship in 1946 at the age of 32, the 'black auxiliaries' were remarkably long-lived. Metcalfe was just the second member of the group to pass away. Two years later in 1980, the most famous black medallist from Berlin, Jesse Owens, died at 68. Archie Williams lived to 78, passing away in 1993. James LuValle, who also died in 1993, and David Albritton, who died in 1994, lived to 81. Mack Robinson, who died in 2000, and Fritz Pollard, Jr., who died in 2003, lived to 87. John Woodruff, who died in 2007, lived to the age of 92. [111]

Johnson's tragic early death made the national newspaper of record, the *New York Times*, as well as his home-town *Los Angeles Times*. The *New York Times* remembered Johnson as 'one of several Negro victors for the United States', whose success 'was reviled by the Nazis'. The *Los Angeles Times* remembered his wartime service to the nation in the merchant marine corps. [112] As each of the 'black auxiliaries' passed away, newspapers across the nation returned to the same themes first evoked in the 1946 memories of Johnson, and later amplified in the 1978 accolades to Metcalfe. Their death notices chronicled the athletic feats that startled the Nazis and challenged racial attitudes in the United States. Their epitaphs also recalled their dedication to public service in a myriad of realms beyond sport. [113]

Here and there across the nation, monuments to the 'black auxiliaries' have sprouted. The Ralph Metcalfe Federal Building stands in Chicago. The Mack Robinson Post Office processes mail in Pasadena. The James LuValle Commons houses students at UCLA. The sapling John Woodruff received for his gold medal run has grown into a gigantic oak that spreads its limbs over the high-school football stadium in a declining Pennsylvania steel town. [114] Halls of fame in far-flung locations briefly mention that once upon a time the 'black auxiliaries' shocked the world in the political blast furnace of the Berlin Olympics. Newspaper stories recalling their feats appear as anniversaries of the 'Nazi Olympics' roll by. In these snippets the rest of the 'black auxiliaries' remain tied forever to Jesse Owens, though in their post-athletic professional careers they surpassed their more famous teammate on many levels.

In death, the majority of the 'black auxiliary' medallists revealed legacies and memories that far outpaced their Olympic feats. Though never as prominent as their teammate Owens, they often found subtle recognition at local, regional and national levels. Yet their lives, marked by accomplishments that extend beyond the cinder tracks and into the realm of civic service, reflect a significantly altered trajectory from that of Owens. In American memories a few milliseconds made Owens the unforgettable star of the 1936 Olympics. Decades of perseverance made the rest of the 'black auxiliaries' into symbols of the complicated legacies of racial and civil rights in their nation's history. The African American press in the 1930s had demanded a legacy that transcended athletic genius and the 'black auxiliaries' provided numerous triumphs in academics, politics and civics. They heeded their generation's call to pursue greatness beyond the realms of sport, and by doing so these Olympic medallists continued to pen their legacies long after the books closed on the Berlin games.

Notes

[1] Cornfield and Baker, *Ralph H. Metcalfe*, 1.
[2] Adolf Hitler's 'snub' of Jesse Owens generated intense media coverage in the United States. The US press reported that the German leader pointedly refused to congratulate Owens and the other 'black auxiliaries' after their victories. *Time* magazine alleged that Hitler 'conspicuously neglected to invite Negro winners up to shake hands with him in his box': 'Olympic Games (Cont'd)', *Time*, August 1936. For similar reactions see Arthur J. Daley, 'Owens Captures Olympic Title', *New York Times*, 4 Aug. 1936, 1 and 23; John Kieran, 'Sports of the Times: There He Goes Again!', *New York Times*, 5 Aug. 1936, 26; 'Non-Aryan Victors in Nazi Olympics', *The Literary Digest*, 29 Aug. 1936. In fact, the 'snub' was more complex than the American press revealed. Hitler participated in public congratulations of winners on the opening day of the track and field competitions, clasping hands in front of the world press corps with German and Finnish athletes who won early events. As rain and darkness descended on the opening day's afternoon session, Hitler left the stadium before African American high jumper Cornelius Johnson won gold. Whether Hitler would have saluted Johnson remains uncertain. After Hitler's opening-day performance, IOC President Henri Baillet-Latour reproached the *Führer* for his breach of Olympic protocol by engaging in public celebrations with some victors. Baillet-Latour warned Hitler that as host he was not allowed to demonstrate any favouritism through public congratulations of winners. Bowing to the IOC dictum, Hitler congratulated future German winners in private. He directly snubbed neither Owens nor any other Olympic champion in public. Indeed, during the Berlin games Owens denied to a sceptical American press that Hitler had in fact snubbed him. Eventually, as the tale became American folklore, Owens made the alleged snub a standard highlight in his many retellings of his Olympic experiences: Baker, *Jesse Owens*, 89–91; Guttmann, *The Games Must Go On*, 78–9; Mandell, *The Nazi Olympics*, 227–9.
[3] Baker, *Jesse Owens*; Dyreson, 'Jesse Owens: Leading Man'.
[4] On the German media's usage of 'black auxiliaries' see 'Topics of the Times: Some Olympic Performers', *New York Times*, 14 July 1936, sec. 1, 18; 'Trials & Tryouts', *Time*, 20 July 1936; 'Olympics: Record-Holders and Champions Too Slow to Qualify', *News-Week*, 18 July 1936; 'Olympic Trials', *The Nation*, 18 July 1936.
[5] In addition to Owens, the African American athletes who made the 1936 Olympic team included high jumpers David Albritton and Cornelius Johnson; sprinters Ralph Metcalfe, Matthew 'Mack' Robinson, Archie Williams and James LuValle; middle-distance runner John Woodruff; hurdler Frederick Douglass 'Fritz' Pollard, Jr.; long jumper John Brooks; women's hurdler Tidye Pickett and women's 400-metre runner Louis Stokes; boxers Arthur Oliver, Willis Johnson, James Atkinson, Howell King and Jack Wilson; and weightlifter John Terry. The African American medallists in track and field were a gold by Cornelius Johnson and a silver by David Albritton in the high jump, a gold by Archie Williams and a bronze by James LuValle in the 400-metres, a gold by John Woodruff in the 800-metres, a bronze by Fritz Pollard, Jr., in the 110-metre hurdles, a silver (behind Owens) by Mack Robinson in the 200 metres and a silver (behind Owens) by Ralph Metcalfe in the 100 metres as well as a gold (with Owens) by Metcalfe in the 4x100 metres relay. In addition, Jack Wilson earned a silver medal

in boxing, which his coaches insisted should have been a gold medal but for nefarious judging. American Olympic Committee, *Report of the American Olympic Committee*, 111–50, 151–3, 173–6, 289–90.

[6] Cornfield and Baker, *Ralph H. Metcalfe.*

[7] The essential biography of Owens is Baker, *Jesse Owens*. See also Dyreson, 'Jesse Owens: Leading Man'. Publishers flocked to Owens. He wrote at least five autobiographies: *The Jesse Owens Story*; *Blackthink*; *I Have Changed*; *Jesse: A Spiritual Autobiography*; *Jesse, The Man Who Outran Hitler*. He has been the subject of several biographies by large volume trade publishers such as McRae, *Heroes without a Country*; Schapp, *Triumph*. Owens has found a place in standard US history texts and in several films and documentaries. For texts see Boyer *et al.*, *The Enduring Vision*. For films see *100 Years of Olympic Glory*; *The Journey of the African-American Athlete*; 'To Be Somebody'; *The Jesse Owens Story*; *The Black Athlete*; and *Jesse Owens Returns to Berlin*. He has also made his way into African American literature: Lewis, *Freedom Like Sunlight*; Hammer, *African America*. Owens has also been the subject of several juvenile biographies, including McKissack, *Jesse Owens*; Coffey, *Jesse Owens*; Adler, *A Picture Book of Jesse Owens*; Sanford and Green, *Jesse Owens*; Sabin, *Jesse Owens*; Kaufman, *Jesse Owens*.

[8] Beyond Owens, only Metcalfe has been the subject of book-length biography, an obscure monograph in the Ralph Nader Congress Project series: Cornfield and Baker, *Ralph H. Metcalfe*. Metcalfe and the rest of the 'auxiliaries' have not been entirely forgotten, as each has his own Wikipedia page, one measure of American 'collective memory' in the twenty-first century. Of course, Owens has a more extensive Wikipedia page than any of 'auxiliaries'. See http://en.wikipedia.org/wiki/Jesse_Owens; http://en.wikipedia.org/wiki/Archie_Williams; http://en.wikipedia.org/wiki/David_Albritton; http://en.wikipedia.org/wiki/John_Woodruff; http://en.wikipedia.org/wiki/Cornelius_Cooper_Johnson; http://en.wikipedia.org/wiki/James_LuValle; http://en.wikipedia.org/wiki/Ralph_Metcalfe; http://en.wikipedia.org/wiki/Matthew_Robinson_(athlete); http://en.wikipedia.org/wiki/Frederick_Pollard,_Jr., all sites accessed 1 March 2010.

[9] 'Topics of the Times: Some Olympic Performers', *New York Times*, 14 July 1936; 'Trials & Tryouts', *Time*, 20 July 1936.

[10] Wiggins, 'The 1936 Olympic Games in Berlin', 286.

[11] Dyreson, *Making the American Team*; Dyreson, *Crafting Patriotism for Global Domination*; Dyreson, 'Return to the Melting'; Dyreson, 'Selling American Civilization'; Dyreson, 'Scripting the American Olympic Story-Telling Formula'; Dyreson, 'Marketing National Identity'; Dinces, 'Padres on Mount Olympus'; Welky, 'Vikings, Mermaids, and Little Brown Men'; White, 'The Los Angeles Way of Doing Things'.

[12] Williams, 'Negro Athletes in the Eleventh Olympiad'. Williams devotes the most space, three pages, to Owens, but includes a page or two on all of the other black Olympians, including the boxers, the weightlifters and the women's track athletes, as well as chronicling the participation of athletes of African descent from other nations.

[13] Ashe, *A Hard Road to Glory*, 88.

[14] Nathan, *Saying It's So*, 13. For readings of the intersections of memory, sport and race, see Schultz, '"Stuff from Which Legends Are Made"'.

[15] Wiggins, 'The 1936 Olympic Games in Berlin', 290. On the rise of scientific racism and the mythology of 'athletic genes' see Wiggins, '"Great Speed But Little Stamina"'; Miller, 'The Anatomy of Scientific Racism'; Dyreson, 'American Ideas About Race and Olympic Races'; Hoberman, *Darwin's Athletes*.

[16] Wiggins, 'The 1936 Olympic Games', 290.

[17] Ibid., 278–9.

[18] Rhoden, *$40 Million Slaves*.

[19] Baker, *Jesse Owens*; Dyreson, 'Jesse Owens: Leading Man'.

[20] In constructing this prosopography of the 'black auxiliaries' we have consulted a wide variety of sources in an effort to trace their lives. Newspaper and magazine stories from the black and white press, including articles on their athletic careers and their obituaries have provided numerous bits and pieces for composite. The *Philadelphia Tribune, Pittsburgh Courier, Chicago Defender* and *Los Angeles Sentinel* have been most helpful from the black press, while the *New York Times, Chicago Tribune, Los Angeles Times, Los Angeles Daily News, Washington Post, Milwaukee Journal Sentinel, Pittsburgh Post-Gazette, Dallas Morning News, San Francisco Chronicle, San Jose Mercury News, Oakland Tribune, Sports Illustrated* and *Time* have provided useful details from mainstream white perspectives.

Journal articles with information on the 'black auxiliaries' include Williams, 'Negro Athletes in the Tenth Olympiad'; Carter, 'The Negro in College Athletics'; Allen, 'Breaking World's Records'; Henderson, 'The Negro in the Olympic Games'; Williams, 'Negro Athletes in the Eleventh Olympiad'; Meade, 'The Negro in Track Athletics'; Bush, 'The Grandest Olympian'; Wiggins, 'The 1936 Olympic Games'. For monographs see Henderson, *The Negro in Sports*; Young, *Negro Firsts in Sports*; Bontemps, *Famous Negro Athletes*; Henderson, *The Black Athlete*; Carlson and Fogarty, *Tales of Gold*; Wiggins, *Glory Bound*; Ashe, *A Hard Road to Glory*; Wiggins and Miller, *The Unlevel Playing Field*. The following reference works contain bits and pieces: *The Black Olympians, 1904–1984*; *Compton's Gift to the Olympic Games*; Page, *Black Olympian Medalists*; Porter, *African-American Sports Greats*; Wiggins, *African Americans in Sports*. On specific members of the 'auxiliary', we have consulted a variety of websites from halls of fame, university alma maters and various commemorations and memorials. Specific citations can be found in appropriate sections of the paper.

Other relevant oral histories, government documents, and special websites on individual members include the following:

David Albritton: 'Albritton, David, in the *Encyclopedia of Cleveland History* (Cleveland: Case Western Reserve University, 1997), available at http://ech.case.edu/ech-cgi/article. pl?id=AD1, accessed 11 Jan. 2010.

James LuValle: Interview with Dr James E. LuValle, interviewed by 1936 Olympic Track & Field, interviewed by George A. Hodak, June 1988, Palo Alto, CA, An Olympian's Oral History Collection, Amateur Athletic Foundation of Los Angeles (now the LA84 Foundation), Los Angeles, California; Oral History with James E. LuValle, Founding President of UCLA's Graduate Students Association, interview conducted by Ranford B. Hopkins in 1987; Oral History Collection, Department of Special Collections, University Library, University of California, Los Angeles; 'LuValle Biography', available at http://www.spotlight.ucla.edu/alumni/james-luvalle_biography/, accessed 15 Jan. 2010.

Ralph Metcalfe: The University of Marquette Website, 'Ralph Metcalfe, The Olympic Years', available at http://www.marquette.edu/library/information/news/2008/Metcalfe. html, accessed 22 Dec. 2009; 'Memorial Services held in the House of Representatives and Senate of the Unites States, together with remarks presented in eulogy of Ralph H. Metcalfe', 'Ralph H. Metcalfe Federal Building', Report of the US House of Representatives, 168, 102nd Congress, 1st Session, 26 July 1991 (Washington, DC: US Government Printing Office, 1991); Cornfield and Baker, *Ralph H. Metcalfe*; *The Metcalfe Report on the Misuse of Police Authority in Chicago*; Ralph Harold Metcalfe, 'A Study of the Effects of Alcohol and Tobacco on Athletic Performance', M.Ed. thesis, University of Southern California, 1939; 'Ralph H. Metcalfe', The Biographical Directory of the United States Congress Website, available at http://bioguide.congress.gov/scripts/biodisplay.pl? index=m000675, accessed 20 Nov. 2008; 'Ralph Harold Metcalfe', The Black Americans in Congress Website, available at http://baic.house.gov/member-profiles/profile.html?int ID=62, accessed 10 Nov. 2008.

Fritz Pollard, Jr.: Carroll, *Fritz Pollard*.

Mack Robinson: 'The Early Years', available at http://sportshistory.uoregon.edu/details/show/8; accessed 20 Nov. 2008; 'Remembering Matthew 'Mack' Robinson', *Affinity*, available at http://www.affinityonline.org/Departments/ALookBack/MatthewMackRobin-son/tabid/179/Default.aspx, accessed 15 March 2010; University of Oregon, available at http://www.uoregon.edu/~uadvance/awards/descriptions.html#WebfootSociety, accessed 11 Nov.2008.

Archie Williams: Archie F. Williams, 'The Joy of Flying: Olympic Gold, Air Force Colonel, and Teacher', an oral history conducted in 1992 by Gabrielle Morris, Regional Oral History Office, The Bancroft Library, University of California, Berkeley, Berkeley, CA; Interview with Archie F. Williams, 1936 Olympic Track & Field, interviewed by George A. Hodak, June 1988, Santa Rosa, CA, An Olympian's Oral History Collection, Amateur Athletic Foundation of Los Angeles (now the LA84 Foundation), Los Angeles, California.

John Woodruff: John Woodruff Recognition Video, available at http://pittsburgh panthers.cstv.com/sports/m-track/spec-rel/110207aac.html; http://www.visionaryproject. org/woodruffjohn, accessed 23 Nov. 2008; George Tanber, 'Woodruff's Forgotten Run to Olympic Glory', ESPN.com, available at http://sports.espn.go.com/espn/blackhistory2007/ news/story?id=2780877, accessed 15 Jan. 2009); John Woodruff interview, available at http://www.visionaryproject.org/woodruffjohn, accessed 10 Sept. 2009; http://sports.espn. go.com/espn/blackhistory2007/news/story?id=2780877, accessed 23 July 2009; http:// www.chronicle.pitt.edu/?p=987, accessed 23 July 2009; Sharon Blake, 'Woodruff High-lighted in Exhibition at Holocaust Museum', *The Pitt Chronicles*, 12 May 2008, available at http://www.chronicle.pitt.edu/wp-content/uploads/2008/05/chronicle5-12-08.pdf, accessed 20 Nov.2008.

[21] Ibid.
[22] Ibid.
[23] Ibid.
[24] Ibid.
[25] Ibid.
[26] Ibid.
[27] Ibid.
[28] Ibid.
[29] Ibid.
[30] Ibid.
[31] Williams, 'Negro Athletes in the Eleventh Olympiad', 58–59.
[32] Henderson penned four editions of *The Negro in Sports* (1939, 1949, 1975, 1979) and two editions of the *The Black Athlete* (1968, 1978). He also penned a journal article: Henderson, 'The Negro in the Olympic Games'. For a biography of Henderson, see Wiggins, 'Edwin Bancroft Henderson, African American Athletes, and the Writing of Sport History', in *Glory Bound*, 221–40.
[33] Henderson, 'The Negro in the Olympic Games', 43; Henderson, *The Negro in Sports*, 71.
[34] Henderson, 'The Negro in the Olympic Games', 43.
[35] Young, *Negro Firsts in Sports*; Bontemps, *Famous Negro Athletes*.
[36] Brawley and Richardson penned chapters on Owens with the 'black auxiliaries' swirling about him while Hughes focused on Jackie Robinson while briefly mentioning connections to Mack Robinson and Jesse Owens. Brawley, *Negro Builders and Heroes*; Hughes, *Famous American Negroes*; Richardson, *Great American Negroes*.
[37] Kieran and Daley, *The Story of the Olympic Games*, 239–51.
[38] Ibid.
[39] Henry, *An Approved History of the Olympic Games*, 238.

[40] Kirby, 'Report of the Chef de Mission', in American Olympic Committee, *Report of the United States Olympic Committee: Games of the XIVth Olympiad*, 247.

[41] Meade, 'The Negro in Track Athletics'; Jesse Owens, 'My Great Olympic Prize', *Reader's Digest*, October 1960; Lincoln Barnett, 'The Modern Heroes', *Sports Illustrated*, 19 Nov. 1956; 'The Negro in American Sport', special issue, *Sport*, March 1960.

[42] 'Russia Follows US in Not Dipping the Flag', *New York Times*, 26 Aug. 1960; 'Rousing Acclaim Greets US Team', *Washington Post*, 26 Aug. 1960; Oscar Fraley, 'US, Russia Favored to Grab To Honors', *Times Recorder* [Zanesville, OH], 26 Aug. 1960; 'US Gets Top Ovation at Opening of Olympic Games', *Daily News* [Galveston, TX], 26 Aug. 1960; 'US Flag Erect', *Chicago Tribune*, 26 Aug. 1960. Interestingly, the US did not select another African American flag bearer until women's basketball player Dawn Staley carried the Stars and Stripes at Athens in 2004, followed by another African American, track star Lopez Lomong at Beijing in 2008.

[43] *This Is Your Life*, NBC Television, 27 April 1960.

[44] Tanber, 'Woodruff's Forgotten Run to Olympic Glory'.

[45] Norrell, *The House I Live In*; Sugrue, *Sweet Land of Liberty*; Tuck, 'We Ain't What We Ought to Be'.

[46] David Albritton, 1979 inductee of the Ohio State University Varsity 'O' Hall of Fame, available at http://www.ohiostatebuckeyes.com/ViewArticle.dbml?DB_OEM_ID=17300&ATCLID=92523; Ralph Metcalfe, 1980 inductee of the Georgia Sports Hall of Fame, available at http://gshf.org/pdf_files/inductees/track_and_field/ralph_metcalfe.pdf; and a 1972 inductee of the Marquette University 'M' Club Hall of Fame, http://www.gomarquet-te.com/hallfame/marq-hallfame.html; Mack Robinson, a 1995 inductee of the University of Oregon Hall of Fame, available at http://www.goducks.com/ViewArticle.dbml?DB_OEM_ID=500&ATCLID=246730, and inductee of the Oregon Sports Hall of Fame, http://www.oregonsportshall.org/inductee-members.html; Fritz Pollard, Jr., a 1975 inductee of the University of North Dakota Letterwinners Hall of Fame, available at https://admin.xosn.com/ViewArticle.dbml?DB_OEM_ID=13500&ATCLID=750087; Archie Williams, a 1986 inductee of the University of California Athletic Hall of Fame, available at http://www.calbears.com/trads/cal-halloffame.html, and John Woodruff, a 2009 inductee of the Fayette County Sports Hall of Fame, available at http://fayettecountysportshalloffame.com/woodruff.html; and a 1994 inductee of the Penn Relays Wall of Fame, http://news.pennrelaysonline.com/event-history/the-stars-of-the-relays/relays-wall-of-fame/; James LuValle, a 1986 inductee of the UCLA Athletic Hall of Fame, available at http://www.uclabruins.com/ot/hof-inductees.html. All websites accessed 10 March 2010.

[47] http://www.usatf.org/HallOfFame/TF/index.asp?mode=alphabetical, accessed 1 April 2010.

[48] http://www.spotlight.ucla.edu/alumni/james-luvalle_biography/, accessed 10 March 2010.

[49] Williams, 'The Joy of Flying'.

[50] Interview with James LuValle; Oral History with James E. LuValle; Williams, 'The Joy of Flying'; Interview with Archie F. Williams.

[51] John Woodruff interview, http://www.visionaryproject.org/woodruffjohn; David Fleming, 'Living Legacies', *Sports Illustrated*, 20 Feb. 1995; Chuck Finder, '70 Years Ago Today, Connellsville Native John Woodruff Sprinted from Last to First to Win Gold at Berlin Olympics', *Pittsburgh Post-Gazette*, 4 Aug. 2006; Carlson and Fogarty, *Tales of Gold*, 177–85.

[52] http://sports.espn.go.com/espn/blackhistory2007/news/story?id=2780877, accessed 23 July 2009.

[53] http://www.chronicle.pitt.edu/?p=987, accessed 23 July 2009.

[54] Paul Zeise, 'Obituary: John Woodruff/Pitt Gold Medalist Ran Against Racism'. *Pittsburgh Post-Gazette*, 2 Nov. 2007.

[55] Sharon Blake, 'Woodruff Highlighted in Exhibition at Holocaust Museum', *The Pitt Chronicles*, 12 May 2008, available at http://www.chronicle.pitt.edu/wp-content/uploads/2008/05/chronicle5-12-08.pdf, accessed 20 Nov. 2008.

[56] 'Two Visiting Athletes Are Y House Guests', *Dallas Express*, 17 July 1937, 3.

[57] James Ragland, 'Race is on to Solve a '37 Math Problem', *Dallas Morning News*, 19 Oct. 2006. In a preview of 1996 Atlanta Olympics, the *Philadelphia Tribune* portrayed Woodruff simply as a teammate of 'the legendary Jesse Owens'. Samuel Davis, 'Black Athletes Ready for Olympic Glory: They Hope to Follow in Heroes Footsteps', *The Philadelphia Tribune*, 7 June 1996.

[58] Finder, '70 Years Ago Today, Connellsville Native John Woodruff Sprinted'; Judy Kroeger, '*Highlights Magazine* Showcases Olympian Woodruff', *Pittsburgh Tribune-Review*, 17 Feb. 2008; Angie Kay Dilmore, 'Stopping for Olympic Gold', *Highlights Magazine*, Feb. 2008; Deepak Karamcheti, 'Pitt's "Greatest Athlete" Honored: NCAA Program Recognizes Olympic Gold Medalist John Woodruff and Others'. *The New Pittsburgh Courier*, Pittsburgh, 21 Nov. 1998; http://www.visionaryproject.org/woodruffjohn.

[59] Karamcheti, 'Pitt's "Greatest Athlete" Honored'; Frank Litsky, 'John Woodruff, An Olympian, Dies at 92', *The New York Times*, 1 Nov. 2007.

[60] John Woodruff Recognition Video, available at: http://pittsburghpanthers.cstv.com/sports/m-track/spec-rel/110207aac.html; http://www.visionaryproject.org/woodruffjohn, accessed 23 Nov. 2008.

[61] 'Los Angeles Fetes Athletes', *Los Angeles Times*, 23 Sept. 1936.

[62] Litsky, 'Mack Robinson, 85, Second to Owens in Berlin'.

[63] Michael Rosenthal, 'Hometown Hero? Robinson's Brother, Mack, Felt Shunned by Pasadena', *Los Angeles Daily News*, 8 April 1997; Lanning, 'Remembering Matthew "Mack" Robinson', available at: http://www.affinityonline.org/Departments/ALookBack/MatthewMackRobinson/tabid/179/Default.aspx, accessed 10 Nov. 2009.

[64] 'Robinson in School', *Los Angeles Times*, 3 Feb. 1937.

[65] Robinson so soundly dominated the 100 metres, 200 metres, 1100metre hurdles and long jump that his University of Oregon team did not lose a single dual meet in 1938: 'The Early Years'.

[66] 'Mack Robinson, 1914–2000: Ahead of Jackie, Behind Jesse', *Sports Illustrated*, 27 March 2000.

[67] 'The Early Years'.

[68] Bert Mann, 'From Olympic Silver to Sewer', *Los Angeles Times*, 8 June 1980; Gary Libman, 'Pioneer Olympian Gold Medalist Helped Set Pace for Black Athletes', *Los Angeles Times*, 15 July 1984; Shav Glick, 'For Mack Robinson, Memories of Silver Medal Aren't Glittering', *Los Angeles Times*, 22 July 1984. Ken Wheeler, 'Another Robinson Legacy', *The Oregonian*, 17 May 1997; Rosenthal, 'Hometown Hero?'

[69] Jack Birkinshaw, '9 Pasadena Groups Will Meet on Improving Race Relations', *Los Angeles Times*, 3 April 1967; Bert Mann, 'Problems of Northwest Spark Pasadena Clash', *Los Angeles Times*, 15 March 1972; Mary Barber, 'Mack Robinson: Crusader Against Blight, Crime', *Los Angeles Times*, 17 July 1983; Corina Knoll, 'Pasadena Park Caught between Jackie and Mack Robinson', *Los Angeles Times*, 8 Oct. 2009; Lanning, 'Remembering Matthew "Mack" Robinson'.

[70] Carroll, *Fritz Pollard*.

[71] Tygiel, *Baseball's Great Experiment*.

[72] 'Mack Robinson, 1914–2000'.

[73] Todd Burroughs, 'Tribute to Jackie: Robinson brothers were Great Track Stars', *The Philadelphia Tribune*, 25 April 1997. See also, Dwight Chapin, 'Mack Robinson: More Than 'Jackie's Brother', *Los Angeles Times*, 12 June 1968; 'The Other Robinson', *Los Angeles Times*, 22 June 1978.

[74] Earl Gustkey, 'Jesse Owens Loved by All', *Los Angeles Times*, 22 July 1984; Randy Harvey, 'Old Glory Stars in a Parade', *Los Angeles Times*, 29 July 1984; Kenny Moore, 'Hey Russia, It's a Heck of a Party', *Sports Illustrated*, 6 Aug. 1984.

[75] 'Jackie Robinson's Brother: Mack Robinson Dies at 85', *The Los Angeles Sentinel*, 22 March 2000.

[76] Bert Mann, 'Pasadena Petitioned for Memorial to Robinson', *Los Angeles Times*, 23 May 1973; Bert Mann, 'Plan for Memorial Irks Jackie Robinson's Kin', *Los Angeles Times*, 5 July 1973; Mary Barber, 'Jackie Robinson', *Los Angeles Times*, 19 Aug. 1984; Mary Barber, 'Jackie Robinson Statue Is His Brother's Dream', *Los Angeles Times*, 23 Aug. 1984.

[77] Knoll, 'Pasadena Park Caught between Jackie and Mack Robinson'; Lanning, 'Remembering Matthew "Mack" Robinson'; Robinson Stadium at Pasadena City College, available at http://www.pasadena.edu/foundation/FundedProjects/stadium.cfm; Mack Robinson Post Office, Pasadena, available at http://www.waymarking.com/waymarks/WM5REQ_Matthew_Mack_Robinson_Post_Office__Pasadena_CA; Robinson Memorial in Pasadena, available at http://ww2.cityofpasadena.net/landmarks/memorialhome.asp, all accessed 2 April 2010; 'Jackie Robinson's Brother'; 'City of Pasadena Honors Jackie and Mack Robinson', *Los Angeles Sentinel*, 28 May 1997.

[78] 'City of Pasadena Honors Jackie and Mack Robinson'.

[79] Matthew 'Mack' Robinson Post Office, available at http://www.waymarking.com/waymarks/WM5REQ_Matthew_Mack_Robinson_Post_Office__Pasadena_CA,, accessed 10 Dec. 2009.

[80] Robinson found himself in good company as his fellow inductees for the award included famed writer Ken Kesey, Olympic track coach and Nike co-founder Bill Bowerman and Olympic marathoner and author Kenny Moore: University of Oregon, WebfootSociety.

[81] Ibid.

[82] Wheeler, 'Another Robinson Legacy'.

[83] Cromwell and Metcalfe, *The Sprint Races*.

[84] Martin, 'Incident at Fernwood'; '4 Great Negro Athletes Guide South Side Boys; Jesse Owens Directs Program of 400', *Chicago Tribune*, 2 Nov. 1950; 'Metcalfe Will Address Banquet for Y Champs', *Chicago Tribune*, 24 April 1951; *Memorial Services held in the House of Representatives and Senate of the Unites States ... Ralph Metcalfe*.

[85] Cornfield and Baker, *Ralph H. Metcalfe*; Robert Wiedrich, 'Ald. Metcalfe Is a Man with Lots of Dash; Readily Admits His Tieup to Rep. Dawson', *Chicago Tribune*, 26 May 1956; 'Negro Leaders Protest Police District Shifts', *Chicago Tribune*, 4 May 1963; Edward Schreiber, '4 Aldermen, School Board Leader Meet; Discuss Grievances of Negro Groups', *Chicago Tribune*, 21 Aug. 1963; John Handlet, 'Metcalfe Takes Control as Zoning Chairman', *Chicago Tribune*, 1 April 1965.

[86] Frank Mastro, 'Metcalfle Gets Boxing Board Post, Report', *Chicago Tribune*, 11 March 1949; 'Rumor Radzienda, Triner, and Metcalfe as Sport Commission', *Chicago Tribune*, 12 March 1949; Frank Mastro, 'No Racketeers in Boxing Here, Says Metcalfe', *Chicago Tribune*, 24 May 1952.

[87] 'Council Urges Fund Group for Pan-Am Games', *Chicago Tribune*, 8 June 1957; 'Pan-Am Games Group to Hear Chicago Bid', *Chicago Tribune*, 1 Aug. 1957; 'Award Pan-American Games to Chicago; Group Votes 13 to 6 Over Brazil Site 2,000 Athletes to Meet in '59 Chicago Is Awarded '59 Pan Games', *Chicago Tribune*, 4 Aug. 1957; 'Chicagoans Out to Land Olympics; Seeks Games of 1964 or '68', *Chicago Tribune*, 27 March 1957; Ralph Metcalfe Reflects on Olympic Legacy, http://www.chicago2016.org/our-plan/news/chicago-news/ralph-metcalfe-jr-reflects-on-an-olympic-legacy.aspx, accessed 23 July 2009.

[88] 'Youth Corps Will Provide Summer Work for 3,000; Special Program to Operate Only Thru August', *Chicago Tribune*, 18 July 1965.

[89] 'Olympic Bridesmaid', *Sports Illustrated*, 24 July 1961.

[90] He was inducted in 1972. See http://www.gomarquette.com/hallfame/marq-hallfame.html, accessed 12 Jan. 2010.

[91] The University of Marquette Website, 'Ralph Metcalfe, The Olympic Years', available at: http://www.marquette.edu/library/information/news/2008/Metcalfe.htm, accessed 22 Dec. 2009.

[92] Jackie Loohauis, 'The Marquette Student and Future Congressman Who Took Gold in 1936', *Milwaukee Journal Sentinel*, 27 September 1998.

[93] The Ralph Metcalfe Elementary School, 3400 W North Avenue, Milwaukee, Wisconsin, 53208.

[94] The Ralph Metcalfe Elementary School Website, http://www.metcalfe.cps.k12.il.us/, accessed 20 Nov.r 2008; The Chicago Parks District Website, 'Metcalfe Park', http://www.chicagoparkdistrict.com/index.cfm/fuseaction/parks.detail/object_id/05573de4-0773-4f25-a026-52cdb5593fe3.cfm, accessed 20 Nov. 2008.

[95] 'Cancel Rights Marches; Pact Provides Equal Access to Housing, Loans, It's Great Day for Chicago, Daley Says', *Chicago Tribune*, 27 Aug. 1966; David Halvorsen, 'Aspirations of City's Negroes Revealed; Survey Shows Leaders More Interested', *Chicago Tribune*, 11 Sept. 1966; Ralph, *Northern Protest*; Cornfield and Baker, *Ralph H. Metcalfe*.

[96] Two recent studies provide excellent analysis of the controversies and protests surrounding the Mexico City games. Bass, *Not the Triumph But the Struggle*; Hartmann, *Race, Culture and the Revolt of the Black Athlete*.

[97] 'Negro Athletes Express Olympic Boycott Views; Negroes Tell Views about Boycott Idea', *Chicago Tribune*, 25 Nov. 1967; 'Voice of the People; Negro Athletes', *Chicago Tribune*, 30 Nov. 1967.

[98] 'Name Group to End AAU, NCAA Fight', *Chicago Tribune*, 15 Dec. 1965; Biographical Directory of the United States Congress Website, 'Ralph H Metcalfe'.

[99] 'Ralph H. Metcalfe', Biographical Directory of the United States Congress Website.

[100] Cornfield and Baker, *Ralph H. Metcalfe*, 1.

[101] *The Metcalfe Report on the Misuse of Police Authority in Chicago*; Cornfield and Baker, *Ralph H. Metcalfe*.

[102] Michael Kilian, 'Daley Choices Win Key Tests; Metcalfe Overwhelms Rayner in 1st', Party Men Win Bids for House Races', *Chicago Tribune*, 18 March 1970; Frank Blatchford, 'Metcalfe Will Start Own Police Review', *Chicago Tribune*, 1 June 1972; David Young, 'Metcalfe Asks Probe of FBI File on Blacks', *Chicago Tribune*, 23 March 1974; Barbara Reynolds, 'Metcalfe Now Blacks' Man in Middle', *Chicago Tribune*, 11 Nov. 1974; James Strong, 'Labor Backs Daley's Slate – and Metcalfe', *Chicago Tribune* 16 Jan. 1976; Eleanor Randolph, 'Adlai Endorses Metcalfe; Rebuffs Daley's Candidate', *Chicago Tribune*, 2 Feb. 1976; Neil Mehler, 'The Real Winner: Daley; Metcalfe', *Chicago Tribune*, 18 March 1976; Robert Davis, 'Metcalfe Wins Committee Race', *Chicago Tribune*, 27 March 1976.

[103] 'Improving the Police', *Chicago Tribune*, 21 May 1972; 'A Black Speaks Out', *Chicago Tribune*, 1 June 1972; 'The King's Crown Tilts', *Chicago Tribune*, 12 July 1972; 'The Bar and the Police', *Chicago Tribune*, 14 Dec. 1972; 'Wild Talk by Jesse Jackson', *Chicago Tribune*, 26 March 1974.

[104] 'Our Choices for Congress', *Chicago Tribune*, 14 Oct. 1976.

[105] 'Ralph Harold Metcalfe, 'The Black Americans in Congress Website'.

[106] 'Ralph Metcalfe Dead', *Chicago Tribune*, 11 Oct. 1978, 'Obituaries: Ralph Metcalfe', *New York Times*, 6 Nov. 1978.

[107] *Memorial Services held in the House of Representatives and Senate of the Unites States ā Î Ralph Metcalfe*.

[108] Monroe Anderson, '2,000 Mourn Metcalfe at Funeral', *Chicago Tribune*, 15 Oct. 1978.

[109] Dorothy Callin, 'Jesse Owens Recalls a Beloved Teammate', *Chicago Tribune*, 11 Oct. 1978.

[110] 'Why Not the Metcalfe Building', *Chicago Tribune*, 24 May 1991; Edward T. Hean, 'Savage Rips House Panel, *Chicago Tribune*, 22 May 1991; Mitchell Locin, 'Metcalfe is Likely Name for Building', *Chicago Tribune*, 26 July 1991; 'New US Building Honors Metcalfe, *Chicago Tribune*, 1 Aug. 1991; Teresa Wiltz, 'Scars Haven't Healed on Metcalfe Building', *Chicago Tribune*, 11 Oct. 1991; 'Ralph H. Metcalfe Federal Building', Report of the US House of Representatives, 168, 102nd Congress, 1st Session, 26 July 1991.

[111] See the following obituaries: '"Corny" Johnson Dies; Negro Olympic Star', *New York Times*, 17 Feb. 1946; 'Johnson, Former Star Athlete, Dies on Ship', *Los Angeles Times*, 17 Feb. 1946; 'Ralph Metcalfe Dead', *Chicago Tribune*, 11 Oct. 1978; Dorothy Callin, 'Jesse Owens Recalls a Beloved Teammate', *Chicago Tribune*, 11 Oct. 1978; Monroe Anderson, '2,000 Mourn Metcalfe at Funeral', *Chicago Tribune*, 15 Oct. 1978; 'Obituaries: Ralph Metcalfe', *New York Times*, 6 Nov. 1978; *Memorial Services held in the House of Representatives and Senate of the Unites States ã Î Ralph Metcalfe*; 'Chemist James Lu Valle Dies at 80', *Stanford University News Service*, 16 Feb. 1993; 'Archie Williams Is Dead at 78; Won a Gold at Berlin Olympics', *New York Times*, 26 June 1993; 'Archie Williams', *San Francisco Chronicle*, 25 June 1993; 'Archie Williams, 1936 Gold Medal Olympian', *San Jose Mercury News*, 26 June 1993; 'Dave Albritton', *New York Times*, 16 May 1994, 'Miscellany; Dave Albritton Buried', *Los Angeles Times*, 19 May 1994; 'Frederick Douglas "Fritz" Pollard, Jr.', *Washington Post*, 22 Feb. 2003; 'Passings: Frederick Pollard, Jr.', *Los Angeles Times*, 8 March 2003; Frank Litsky, 'Mack Robinson, 85, Second to Owens in Berlin', *New York Times*, 14 March 2000; Shav Glick, 'Olympian Mack Robinson Dead at 88', 13 March 2000; 'Jackie Robinson's Brother: Mack Robinson Dies at 85', *Los Angeles Sentinel*, 22 March 2000; 'Mack Robinson, 1914–2000: Ahead of Jackie, Behind Jesse', *Sports Illustrated*, 27 March 2000; Frank Litsky, 'Obituary: John Woodruff, 92, US Runner in 1936 Berlin Olympics', *New York Times*, 1 Nov. 2007; 'Obituaries; John Woodruff, 92; 1st Black Athlete to Win Gold at 1936 Olympics in Berlin', *Los Angeles Times*; 2 Nov. 2007; 'Connellsville's Olympian John Woodruff Dead at 92', *Pittsburgh Tribune Review*, 2 Nov. 2007; Paul Zeise, 'Obituary: John Woodruff/Pitt Gold Medalist Ran Against Racism'. *Pittsburgh Post-Gazette*, 2 Nov. 2007.

[112] '"Corny" Johnson Dies; Negro Olympic Star', *New York Times*, 17 Feb. 1946.

[113] See note 111 for a list of their obituaries.

[114] Judy Kroeger, 'Sapling Marks Spot for Woodruff's Memorial Service', *Pittsburgh Tribune Review*, 17 Nov. 2007.

References

100 Years of Olympic Glory. Atlanta: Turner Home Entertainment, 1996.

Adler, David. *A Picture Book of Jesse Owens*. New York: Holiday House, 1992.

Allen, Frederick. 'Breaking World's Records'. *Harper's* 173 (Aug. 1936): 302–10.

American Olympic Committee. *Report of the American Olympic Committee: The Games of the XIth Olympiad, Berlin Germany, IVth Olympic Winter Games, Garmisch-Partenkirchen, Germany, 1936*. New York: American Olympic Committee, 1936.

American Olympic Committee. *Report of the United States Olympic Committee: Games of the XIVth Olympiad, London, England, Vth Olympic Winter Games, St. Moritz, Switzerland*. New York: United States Olympic Association, 1948.

Ashe, Arthur, Jr. *A Hard Road to Glory: A History of the African American Athlete, 1919–1945*. New York: Warner Books, 1998.

Baker, William J. *Jesse Owens: An American Life*. New York: Free Press, 1986.

Bass, Amy. *Not the Triumph but the Struggle: The 1968 Olympics and the Making of the Black Athlete.* Minneapolis, MN: University of Minnesota Press, 2002.

The Black Athlete. Santa Monica, CA: Pyramid Film & Video, 1980.

The Black Olympians, 1904–1984. Los Angeles: Afro-American Museum, 1984.

Bontemps, Arna W. *Famous Negro Athletes.* New York: Dodd, Mead, 1964.

Boyer, Paul S., Clifford E. Clark, Jr., Joseph Kett, Neal Salisbury, Harvard Sitkoff and Nancy Woloch. *The Enduring Vision,* 2nd edn. Lexington, MA: DC Heath, 1993.

Brawley, Benjamin. *Negro Builders and Heroes.* Chapel Hill, NC: University of North Carolina Press, 1937.

Bush, Joseph Bevans. 'The Grandest Olympian: James Cleveland "Jesse" Owens'. *Journal of Negro History* 25 (May 1962): 191–3.

Carlson, Lewis H. and John J. Fogarty. *Tales of Gold.* Chicago: Contemporary Books, 1987.

Carroll, John M. *Fritz Pollard: Pioneer in Racial Advancement.* Urbana, IL: University of Illinois Press, 1992.

Carter, Elmer A. 'The Negro in College Athletics'. *Journal of Negro Life* 11 (July 1933): 208–10; 219.

Coffey, Wayne. *Jesse Owens.* Woodbridge, CT: Blackbirch Press, 1992.

Compton's Gift to the Olympic Games. Compton, CA: Robinsons' Research, 1984.

Cornfield, Michael and Susan Baker. *Ralph H. Metcalfe, Democratic Representative from Illinois* (Ralph Nader Congress Project: Citizens Look at Congress). Washington, DC: Grossman Publishers, 1972.

Cromwell, Dean B. and Ralph H. Metcalfe, *The Sprint Races.* Indianapolis, IN: International Sports, Inc., 1939.

Dinces, Sean. 'Padres on Mount Olympus: Los Angeles and the Production of the 1932 Olympic Mega-Event'. *Journal of Sport History* 32 (Summer 2005): 137–66.

Dyreson, Mark. 'Marketing National Identity: The Olympic Games of 1932 and American Culture'. *Olympika: The International Journal of Olympic Studies* 4 (1995): 23–48.

Dyreson, Mark. 'Scripting the American Olympic Story-Telling Formula: The 1924 Paris Olympic Games and the American Media'. *Olympika: The International Journal of Olympic Studies* 5 (1996): 45–80.

Dyreson, Mark. *Making the American Team: Sport, Culture and the Olympic Experience.* Urbana: University of Illinois Press, 1998.

Dyreson, Mark. 'Selling American Civilization: The Olympic Games of 1920 and American Culture'. *Olympika: The International Journal of Olympic Studies* 8 (1999): 1–41.

Dyreson, Mark. 'American Ideas About Race and Olympic Races from the 1890s to the 1950s: Shattering Myths or Reinforcing Scientific Racism?' *Journal of Sport History* 28 (Summer 2001): 173–215.

Dyreson, Mark. 'Return to the Melting Pot: An Old American Olympic Story'. *Olympika: The International Journal of Olympic Studies* 12 (2003): 1–22.

Dyreson, Mark. 'Jesse Owens: Leading Man in Modern American Tales of Racial Progress and Limits'. In *Out of the Shadows: A Biographical History of the African American Athlete,* edited by David W. Wiggins. Fayetteville, AK: University of Arkansas Press, 2006: 111–32.

Dyreson, Mark. *Crafting Patriotism for Global Domination: America at the Olympics.* London: Routledge, 2009.

Guttmann, Allen. *The Games Must Go On: Avery Brundage and the Olympic Movement.* New York: Columbia University Press, 1984.

Hammer, Roger A. *African America: Heralding a Heritage.* Golden Valley, MN: The Place in the Woods, 1992.

Hartmann, Douglas. *Race, Culture and the Revolt of the Black Athlete: The 1968 Olympic Protests and Their Aftermath.* Chicago: University of Chicago Press, 2003.

Henderson, Edwin Bancroft. 'The Negro in the Olympic Games'. *Negro History Bulletin* 15 (December 1951): 43–44.

Henderson, Edwin Bancroft. *The Negro in Sports*. Washington, DC: Associated Publishers, 1939.

Henderson, Edwin Bancroft. *The Negro in Sports,* rev. edn. Washington, DC: Associated Publishers, 1949.

Henderson, Edwin Bancroft. *The Negro in Sports,* rev. edn. Washington, DC: Associated Publishers, 1975.

Henderson, Edwin Bancroft. *The Negro in Sports,* rev. edn. Washington, DC: Associated Publishers, 1979.

Henderson, Edwin Bancroft and the Editors of *Sport. The Black Athlete: Emergence and Arrival.* New York: Association for the Study of Negro Life and History and Publishers Agency, 1968.

Henderson, Edwin Bancroft and the Editors of *Sport. The Black Athlete: Emergence and Arrival.* Cornwells Heights, PA: Association for the Study of Afro-American Life and History and Publishers Agency, 1978.

Henry, William Mellors. *An Approved History of the Olympic Games.* New York: G. P. Putnam's Sons.

Hoberman, John. *Darwin's Athletes: How Sport Has Damaged Black America and Preserved the Myth of Race.* Boston, MA: Houghton Mifflin, 1997.

Hughes, Langston. *Famous American Negroes.* New York: Dodd, Mead, 1954.

Jesse Owens Returns to Berlin. Toronto: CTV Television, 1965.

The Jesse Owens Story. Los Angeles: Paramount, 1984.

The Journey of the African-American Athlete. New York: HBO Home Video, 1996.

Kaufman, Mervyn. *Jesse Owens.* New York: Crowell, 1973.

Kieran, John and Arthur Daley. *The Story of the Olympic Games, 776 B.C. – 1936 A.D.* New York: Frederick A. Stokes, 1936.

Lewis, J. Patrick. *Freedom like Sunlight: Praisesongs for Black Americans.* Mankato, MN: Creative Editions, 2000.

McRae, Donald. *Heroes Without a Country: America's Betrayal of Joe Louis and Jesse Owens.* New York: Harper Collins, 2002.

McKissack, Patricia and Fredrick. *Jesse Owens: Olympic Star, rev. edn.* Berkeley Heights, NJ: Enslow Publishers, 2001.

Mandell, Richard D. *The Nazi Olympics.* New York: Macmillan, 1971.

Martin, John Bartlow. 'Incident at Fernwood'. *Harper's* 199 (Oct. 1949): 86–98.

Meade, George P. 'The Negro in Track Athletics'. *Scientific Monthly* 75 (Dec. 1952): 366–71.

Memorial Services held in the House of Representatives and Senate of the Unites States, together with remarks presented in eulogy of Ralph H. Metcalfe. Ninety-Fifth Congress, Second Session. Washington, DC: US Government Printing Office, 1978.

The Metcalfe Report on the Misuse of Police Authority in Chicago. Blue Ribbon Panel convened by the Honorable Ralph H. Metcalfe. Chicago: Chicago Defender, 1973.

Miller, Patrick B. 'The Anatomy of Scientific Racism: Racialist Responses to Black Athletic Achievement'. *Journal of Sport History* 25 (Spring 1998): 119–51.

Nathan, Daniel. *Saying It's So: A Cultural History of the Black Sox Scandal.* Urbana, IL: University of Illinois Press, 2003.

Norrell, Robert J. *The House I Live In: Race in the American Century.* New York: Oxford University Press, 2005.

Owens, Jesse. *I Have Changed.* New York: William Morrow, 1972.

Owens, Jesse. *Jesse: A Spiritual Autobiography.* Plainfield, N.J.: Logos International, 1978.

Owens, Jesse, and Paul Neimark. *Blackthink: My Life as Black Man and White Man.* New York: William Morrow, 1970.

Owens, Jesse, and Paul Neimark. *The Jesse Owens Story.* New York: Putnam's, 1970.

Owens, Jesse, with Paul Neimark. *Jesse, The Man Who Outran Hitler*. New York: Ballantine Books, 1983.

Page, James. *Black Olympian Medalists*. Englewood, CO: Libraries Unlimited, 1991.

Porter, David L. *African-American Sports Greats: A Biographical Dictionary*. Westport, CT: Greenwood, 1995.

Ralph, James R., Jr. *Northern Protest: Martin Luther King, Jr., Chicago, and the Civil Rights Movement*. Cambridge, MA: Harvard University Press, 1993.

Rhoden, William C. *$40 Million Slaves: The Rise, Fall, and Redemption of the Black Athlete*. New York: Crown, 2006.

Richardson, Ben. *Great American Negroes*. New York: Crowell, 1956.

Sabin, Francene. *Jesse Owens: Olympic Hero*. Mahwah, NJ: Troll Associates, 1986.

Sanford, William R. and Carl R. Green. *Jesse Owens*. New York: Crestwood House, 1992.

Schapp, Jeremy. *Triumph: The Untold Story of Jesse Owens and Hitler's Olympics*. New York: Houghton Mifflin, 2007.

Schultz, Jaime. "'Stuff from Which Legends Are Made": Jack Trice Stadium and the Politics of Memory'. *The International Journal of the History of Sport* 24 (June 2007): 715–48.

Sugrue, Thomas J. *Sweet Land of Liberty: The Forgotten Struggle for Civil Rights in the North*. New York: Random House, 2008.

'To Be Somebody'. Part 6 of *The Great Depression*, produced by WGBH-TV (Boston, MA). Alexandria, VA: PBS Video, 1993.

Tuck, Stephen G.N. *'We Ain't What We Ought to Be': The Black Freedom Struggle, From Emancipation to Obama*. Cambridge, MA: Belknap Press of Harvard University Press, 2010.

Tygiel, Jules. *Baseball's Great Experiment: Jack Robinson and His Legacy, rev. edn*. New York: Oxford University Press, 1997.

Welky, David. 'Vikings, Mermaids, and Little Brown Men: US Journalism and the 1932 Olympics'. *Journal of Sport History* 24 (Spring 1997): 24–49.

White, Jeremy. 'The Los Angeles Way of Doing Things: The Olympic Village and the Practice of Boosterism'. *Olympika: The International Journal of Olympic Studies* 11 (2000): 79–116.

Wiggins, David K. *African Americans in Sports*. Armonk, NY: Sharpe Reference, 2004.

Wiggins, David K. *Glory Bound: Black Athletes in a White America*. Syracuse, NY: Syracuse University Press, 1997.

Wiggins, David K. "'Great Speed but Little Stamina": The Historical Debate over Black Athletic Superiority'. *Journal of Sport History* 16 (Summer 1989): 158–85.

Wiggins, David K. 'The 1936 Olympic Games in Berlin: The Response of America's Black Press'. *Research Quarterly for Exercise and Sport* 54 (Sept. 1983): 278–292.

Wiggins, David K., and Patrick B. Miller. *The Unlevel Playing Field: A Documentary History of the African American Experience in Sport*. Urbana, IL: University of Illinois Press, 2003.

Williams, Charles, H. 'Negro Athletes in the Eleventh Olympiad'. *Southern Workman* 66 (Feb. 1937): 45–59.

Williams, Charles, H. 'Negro Athletes in the Tenth Olympiad'. *The Southern Workman* 61 (Nov. 1932): 449–60.

Young, Andrew S. 'Doc'. *Negro Firsts in Sports*. Chicago: Johnson, 1963.

Outsiders: Muslim Women and Olympic Games – Barriers and Opportunities

Gertrud Pfister

In this article I explore the opportunities that women from Islamic countries have of participating in the Olympic Games and the barriers which they face when taking part in elite sport. Here, it must be taken into account that women's personal situations vary greatly according to - among many other things - the country they live in, their place of residence, their social background and their religious orientation. After giving an overview of participation rates of women and of athletes from Islamic countries at the Olympic Games, I will undertake a more in-depth analysis of the Muslim women taking part in the Beijing Olympics. In addition, trends and participation patterns will be discussed and influential female athletes will be presented.

In the second part of the article I will focus on the reasons for the small number of female athletes in Islamic countries, focusing on conditions of life as well as on culture and religion.

Introduction

Since their very beginnings and until quite recently, sports and sporting competitions, the Olympic Games in particular, have been men's domains – in spite of the claim that equal conditions and equal access are provided for all. Today, all discrimination with regard to gender, race, religion and politics is considered incompatible with the principles of the Olympic movement. [1] Nonetheless, the demand for equality and the claim that this demand has been enforced within the 'Olympic family' raises a number of questions (and doubts). Do all national Olympic committees (NOCs) really have the same opportunity of sending delegations to the games? Does gender have an impact on an athlete's chance of participating in the Olympics? How do religion and culture interact with gender and how do these intersecting categories influence the sporting careers of women (and men)?

Here, it must be remembered that sports and Olympism emerged in Western countries and are rooted in Western culture. The quantification and comparison of performance, the focus on competition and records are not only the rationale of modern sport but also the precondition as well as the product of modern society, in which achievement in principle determines the position and status of a person irrespective of provenance or world view. Competitive sport and a competitive society need – and also nurture – people who are willing to submit to notions of cost-effectiveness and to pressures of acting rationally, regardless of religious or political orientation. In Western countries to an increasing degree this also applies to women, who participate today in all areas of sport and society.

It can be assumed that non-Western societies are based on different paradigms, which do not focus on achievement and competition. Modern sport, with its record orientation, may not be in accordance with their values, beliefs and mentalities. This may be particularly true of women since for various reasons taking up sport is scarcely reconcilable with women's roles in many traditional societies, especially in Islamic cultures.

In this paper I wish to explore the opportunities that women from Islamic countries have of participating in the Olympic Games and the barriers which they face when taking part in elite sport. [2] Here, it must be taken into account that women's personal situations vary greatly according to – among many other things – the country they live in, their place of residence, their social background and their religious orientation. After giving an overview of participation rates of women and of athletes from Islamic countries at the Olympic Games, I will undertake a more in-depth analysis of the role of female athletes from Islamic countries at the Beijing Olympics in 2008.

In the second part of the article I will present reasons for the small number of female athletes in Islamic countries, focusing on conditions of life, culture and religion.

Women at the Olympic Games – from Exclusion to Sexualization

The participation of women in the Olympic Games mirrors the development of women's sports (and women's roles in society) in general. In 1896, women were excluded from the games, which were considered to be a male preserve, as they had been in ancient Greece. Throughout his life, the founder of the modern Olympics, Pierre de Coubertin, was convinced that the event should celebrate the athletic prowess of men whereas women should merely admire the athletes and crown the victors. [3] However, de Coubertin and his followers in the IOC succeeded only once in totally excluding women, namely in 1896. In 1900, the Olympics were held as part of the World Fair in Paris, and de Coubertin did not have any influence on the programme. The organizers of the *Concours Internationaux d'Exercices Physiques et de Sports* (as the games were officially called) arranged competitions for women in two sports, tennis and golf. In addition, women participated in a wide range of events ranging from sailing and ballooning to equestrian dressage.

(There is disagreement, however, as to which contests can be regarded as Olympic disciplines.) According to Drevon, [4] 58 women took part in ten events during this sports festival in Paris.

At the next games in St Louis in 1904, likewise held as part of a World Fair, the only women to take part were six American archers, although again there is disagreement as to whether it was a genuine contest or merely a demonstration of archery. In the 1908 games in London, the percentage of female athletes was 2 per cent. Since then, the proportion of women rose slowly but steadily to 8 per cent in 1936, 11 per cent in 1960, 21 per cent in 1980 to 38 per cent in 2000. At the Beijing games in 2008 more than 42 per cent of the athletes were women. In the Chinese delegation there were 327 men and 312 women – the first time since 1988 that men outnumbered women in the team. [5]

As the number of participants grew, so also did the number of sports and events open to women. [6] In 1908, when the Olympic Games were held in England, the birthplace of modern sport, women competed in four disciplines: tennis, sailing, ice-skating and archery – all of them sports with high social prestige. Swimming was introduced into the women's programme in 1912 by the 'feminist' Swedes (according to the minutes of the IOC assembly in 1911), and this was the first event in which women could compare performance quantitatively. However, up to 1928 women were excluded from sports that involved visible exertion, physical strength or bodily contact. [7] After a lengthy struggle between the IAAF and the IOC on the one side and the International Women's Sports Federation on the other, women were first allowed to compete for metres and seconds in the Olympic stadium in 1928. Out of the disciplines that were included in the programme (high jump, discus, the 100 metres, the 4 x 100 metres relay and the 800 metres) it was the 800 metres that caused by far the most controversy. Because some of the runners appeared exhausted at the finishing line, this event was removed from the Olympic programme (until 1960). [8] The first team sport in which women were allowed to take part at the Olympic Games was volleyball in 1964. Team handball and basketball followed in 1976, football in 1996 and ice hockey in 1998. In 1984 cycling and the marathon were included in the women's programme, in addition to rhythmic gymnastics and synchronized swimming, events in which exclusively women compete. Since then nearly all sports and disciplines, even those considered male domains such as wrestling, weightlifting, pole vaulting and hammer throwing have been opened to women.

In Beijing men competed in 28 sports, women in 27. Two sports (baseball and boxing) were reserved for men, while in one sport (softball) and in two disciplines (rhythmic gymnastics and synchronized swimming) only women competed. Of the 302 events, 127 were open to women, 165 to men, and ten were mixed events. [9]

In the 2012 Olympic Games boxing will be included in the women's programme, and baseball and softball will be removed from the Olympic schedule. This means that the only step to be taken in order to achieve gender equality (at least with regard to the programme) is to admit men to rhythmic gymnastics and synchronized swimming.

This short overview reveals an enormous increase in the number of female competitors and a huge expansion of the women's programme. This development must be considered against the backdrop of the constant disputes over the admission of sports to the Olympic canon or their removal from it. In view of the current number of around 11,000 participants, a further expansion of the programme would seem impossible. The inclusion of new sports, therefore, means a reduction in the number of existing (mostly men's) events, e.g. a reduction of weight classes in boxing in 2012, when women's boxing will become an Olympic discipline.

Hence the continual increase in sports and events for women can be viewed not only as a success for the organizations and groups that have actively supported women's sports but also as a result of the IOC's equality politics. However, it must also be taken into account that the people and groups who advocated gender equality in Olympic sports (not so much in the IOC) were also undoubtedly pursuing their own interests. Being able to send many (and above all successful) athletes to the games, for example, has a positive effect on the status and the resources of sports federations. Especially in sports that have long been men's domains, the number of women participants is relatively small and the chance of success relatively high, so that it is not really surprising that federations promote 'their' female athletes.

The admission of women to sports that a decade ago were quite out of the question for them points to the change in women's roles and ideals of womanhood that has taken place in Western countries. As already mentioned, women are increasingly taking over responsibilities in sport, as well as in other areas of society, that a few years ago they would never have been either trusted or burdened with – and areas to which they were not admitted anyway. The 'feminization' of sport is multi-faceted, and also ambivalent. On the one hand, top performance requires the utmost exertion of women without any regard for their gender; on the other, the commercialization of sport has led to an increasing sexualization of media sports, as well as to the willingness of many sportswomen to the sell themselves profitably with the help of their femininity and erotic attractiveness.

The gradual increase in the number of female Olympians, as well as of sports and events for women, obscures the reality that women's chances of participating and competing in elite sports depend to a large extent on their cultural and religious backgrounds. Traditionally, Islamic cultures have not attached any importance to 'modern sport' [10] and thus the number of male – and above all female – athletes from Islamic countries who compete in the Olympic Games continues to be relatively low. [11]

The question arises whether – and, if so, how – the developments described above, i.e. the expansion of women's roles not only in sport but elsewhere, the inclusion of women in formerly male domains and the presentation of erotic images, have had an impact on women and women's sport in Islamic countries.

Outsiders at the Olympic Games – Women from Islamic Countries

The first athlete from an Islamic country [12] participated at the Olympic Games as early as 1900, when when the Iranian prince Freydoun Khan Malkom took part in the fencing competitions. [13] In 1908 one Turk competed in gymnastics; in 1912 two men from Turkey and one from Egypt attended the games. [14] The number of athletes from Islamic countries attending the games increased gradually to 565 (11 per cent of the 5,263 male athletes) in 1984.

However, the chances that sportsmen from Islamic countries had of competing in the Olympics depended, at least to some degree, on the location of the event. The rates of their participation decreased in the games in Melbourne, Tokyo, Mexico and Montreal, cities which required long and expensive travel. [15]

There are various reasons for the relatively low numbers of athletes from an Islamic background competing at the Olympics, among them the roots of modern sport in Western cultures, the lack of sporting traditions and the dearth of sporting infrastructure in Islamic countries, which is partly due to the economic situation. In areas of the world where the majority of the population struggles to survive, there is no surplus of resources to be 'invested' in sport.

Whereas male athletes were more or less socially accepted in most Islamic countries, women participating in sports competitions were a contradiction in terms for most of their rulers and (religious) leaders, as well as for the largest part of the population. Up to 1980, only women from secular countries, i.e. Turkey, Indonesia and pre-revolutionary Iran, were given the opportunity to compete in elite sports and the Olympics. The first female Olympians from an Islamic country were two fencers from Turkey who participated in Berlin in 1936. [16] The Turkish NOC also sent a woman to the next games in 1948. Uner Teoman, a 100m runner, was the only woman in the Turkish Olympic team and the only woman from an Islamic country at these games. She was already eliminated in the heats. [17]

In the following decades Muslim women were tiny minorities at the Olympics – if they were present at all. In 1952 and in 1968 no female athlete from an Islamic country participated in Olympic events. [18] In 1956 there were two, in 1960 five and in 1964 four female Olympians from Turkey and Indonesia. In addition, three female track-and-field athletes and one gymnast from (pre-revolutionary) Iran competed at the 1964 games.

In 1972, besides one Turkish and three Indonesian athletes, two Moroccan women attended the games for the first time. One of them was Fatima El Faquir, who gained many African and Arab records in running (100m, 200m, 400m and hurdles) and subsequently made a career as a coach, administrator, manager and activist for women's sport. [19] In addition, Syria sent a female 800m runner, but she did not finish her race. [20] Two Indonesian and one Turkish women and four female fencers from Iran took part in the 1976 Olympics. [21]

The number of female Muslim Olympians increased only slowly at the following games: five competed in Moscow in 1980, including for the first time athletes from

Algeria and Libya; and 13 participated in the 1984 games, for the first time with women from Jordan (one) and Egypt (six).

Three Egyptian women had already qualified for the Olympic Games as early as 1960, but for unclear reasons they did not participate. In 1984, six female athletes represented Egypt in diving, swimming and synchronized swimming. [22]

The number of male athletes reached approximately 400 in the 1980s and has stagnated since then; the number of female athletes was under 5 per cent until 1988, since then it increased continuously from 8 per cent in 1992, to 11 per cent in 1996, 17 per cent in 2000, 19 per cent in 2004 and 25 per cent (125 female athletes) in 2008.

In recent decades, an increasing number of NOCs have included women in their Olympic teams. Whereas in 1988 26 per cent of the 160 NOCs (half of them NOCs from Islamic countries) sent only male athletes to the Seoul Olympics, the number of all-male teams dropped to 33 in Barcelona (1992), 28 in Atlanta (1996) and nine in Sydney (2000).

In 2008, 380 men and 127 women from Islamic countries competed in Beijing, representing respectively 6 per cent of all male and 3 per cent of all female athletes. These figures are very low considering the large population of these countries. As already mentioned above, the overall percentage of female athletes at the 2008 Olympic Games was 42 per cent; the percentage of women among the athletes from Islamic countries, by contrast, was only 25 per cent.

Three delegations (Saudi Arabia, Qatar and Kuwait) consisted of 'men only' teams at the Beijing games in 2008. Jordan's delegation consisted of three men and four women; and the North African nations included a considerable number of female athletes, even a women's volleyball team. [23] The Beijing games were the first games to which Oman and the United Arab Emirates (UAE) sent women to compete.

Nevertheless, in most delegations women were a tiny minority. Iran, for example, sent only three women among 53 athletes to Beijing.

Sports, Participants and Performances

Until the 1980s, women from Islamic countries competed in relatively few sports, among which were swimming, gymnastics, athletics and fencing. These physical activities had already been introduced to some countries such as Egypt or Iran in the first half of the twentieth century, when progressive rulers and governments established physical education (at least in some schools in big cities) and PE teacher training followed the European model. [24]

In 1988, women from Islamic countries participated in ten sports, most of them in archery (nine), athletics (eight), Judo (seven), table tennis (six) taekwondo (six) and badminton (six). [25]

For Iranian women athletes (after the revolution) there was still another rationale behind their choice of sport: they had – and still have – to compete in the *hijab*. In 1996, 2000 and 2004 they competed in shooting, and in 2008 in archery, rowing and taekwondo. [26] Nassim Hassanpour, the only woman in the Iranian team in

2004, took part in shooting even though her favourite sport was gymnastics. But gymnastics cannot be done in a *hijab*. [27] As the Muslim women's choices of sports in 2008 show, body contact, combat and the demonstration of strength do not appear to be considered unfeminine in Islamic cultures. A fair number of women athletes from Islamic countries participated in sports – even in the *hijab* – that are looked upon as men's sports in Western countries such as judo, taekwondo, weightlifting and wrestling. [28] Women from Islamic countries not only participated in these sports in the years of their introduction but also gained medals. In Afghanistan, Iran and other Islamic countries women and girls (wearing the *hijab*) are already training for the boxing competitions at the 2012 games. [29] Until the turn of the century, the female delegations from Islamic countries were very small, and the few women who participated competed in individual sports. In 2008, for the very first time, a women's team from an Islamic country competed at the Olympic Games, namely the Algerian volleyball team. Although some of the women in the team played professionally in Europe, the Algerians were eliminated in the preliminary round. [30]

The first female Olympians from Islamic countries seem to have found their way to the Olympics more or less by chance. It can be assumed that they came from middle- and upper-class families because doing sport per se and training in sports such as fencing or swimming was (and still is in many countries) restricted to a small minority of girls and women who had the necessary resources and the backing of their families. Several of the Olympians of the 1970s and 1980s, among them Fatima El Faquir or Nawal El Moutawakel, studied in Western countries.

The recruitment procedures changed decisively in the 1980s, at least for the North African female track athletes who received systematic training and support in their countries. In Morocco, Fatima El Faquir, a successful runner, became the coach of some of the track stars of the next generation. She and other female athletes from the Maghreb enjoyed the support of their families and popularity among their fellow citizens. [31] In some cases, as in that of the Jordanian table tennis player, Zeina Shaban, who had started her international career at the age of ten and participated in the 2004 and 2008 games, the families 'invested' in their daughters and provided resources for travelling and training: 'Zeina's parents even hired a private coach to train her at their home in the garage-turned-training hall together with her then seven-year-old brother Zeid.' [32]

Zeina Shaban's career illustrates the diversity of the biographies, lifestyles, opportunities and challenges of female athletes in Islamic countries. Whereas Zeina participated in the games as an adolescent, backed by her obviously affluent parents, other Muslim sportswomen were (or are) married, not infrequently with fellow athletes or their coaches, who encourage and support them. The birth of a child does not necessarily mean the end of their athletic careers. Examples are the Moroccan hurdle specialist Nouzha Bidouane, the Algerian 1500m gold medallist in 2000 Nouria Benida-Merah, as well as Hamide Bıkçın Tosun from Turkey, who as a young mother won a bronze medal in taekwondo in Sydney. [33]

Before the start of the new millennium most women from Islamic countries were eliminated in the preliminary rounds. For them, just to have taken part in the games was a huge success, and they never competed in contests for the better places, let alone for medals. This changed with the participation of North African women – at least as far as the foot races were concerned. In 1984, the Moroccan hurdler Nawal El Moutawakel was the first Muslim woman to win a gold medal at the Olympic Games. [34] In 1992, the Algerian runner Hassiba Boulmerka won the 1500m race. They were followed by further excellent women athletes from North Africa: for example, Nouzha Bidouane from Morocco with a bronze medal in the 400m hurdles and the Algerian 1500m gold medallist in Sydney, Nouria Benida-Merah. Ghada Shouaa, a member of the small Christian minority in Syria, [35] participated in the games in 1992, 1996 and 2000, and won gold in 1996 in the pentathlon, becoming the first Syrian Olympic champion. After finishing first in the heptathlon at the 26th Olympic Games in Atlanta, Ghada received a heroine's welcome in Damascus. According to El-Houda Karfoul,

> she is one of the greatest Arab female athletes of all time. ... Successful female athletes, as the Syrian Ghada Shouaa are treated as heroines. ...She attained celebrity status in Syria and became the inspiration for many boys as well as girls to train as athletes. Postage stamps were issued bearing her picture and she became a figure of immense national pride in Syria. [36]

Since the 1990s Muslim women have become successful in a variety of sports: in 1992 the judoka Hülya Şenyurt was the first Turkish woman to win a medal (bronze) in the Barcelona games. As mentioned earlier, Hamide Bıkçın Tosun won a bronze medal in taekwondo in Sydney in 2000. At the same games, three Indonesian women gained medals in weightlifting, a discipline newly introduced for women at these games. [37] In 2004, the weightlifter Nurcan Taylan became the first Turkish female athlete to win a gold medal; and in 2008, an Algerian athlete won the bronze medal in judo.

This overview shows that women from an Islamic background were successful not only in athletics but also in strength and combat sports /martial arts, possibly because these sports were long frowned upon in Western countries as physical activities for women.

Since 2000 the image of Muslim women as outsiders has changed, although only slightly. They compete in more and new sports, for instance in physically demanding disciplines such as the modern pentathlon, weightlifting and wrestling. Some of them have learned their sports quite recently or trained only sporadically. The Iranian rower Homa Hosseini, for example, was a former basketball player who had been recruited for rowing together with other tall women only two years before the Beijing games; it is no wonder, then, that she finished last in this event. [38] However, the performance level of Muslim athletes is increasing, some of them achieving top performances, and not only in track and field events. The Iranian Sara Khoshjamal qualified for Beijing in taekwondo, and the Egyptian Aya Medani counts among the world's best in the modern pentathlon, taking eighth place in Beijing.

When evaluating the success of teams from Islamic countries, it must be taken into account that few nations at the Olympics have any realistic chance of gaining medals. In 2008, six out of the 204 teams competing won 53 per cent of the gold medals. Five delegations came from Western countries, of the rest only China had a place among the top-ranking teams. [39] Another 118 countries did not gain any medals.

In Beijing, Turkey was the most successful Islamic country, winning eight medals, four of which were gained by the 19 female athletes in the team (48 men). Two silver medals, in the 10,000m and 5,000m races, were won by Elvan Abeylegesse, the long-distance runner of Ethiopian origin. Further, Sibel Ozkan won a silver medal in weightlifting, a sport with a long Turkish tradition; and another silver medal was won by Azize Tanrikulu in taekwondo. In addition, there were two further female medal winners from Islamic countries: an Algerian judoka, who won bronze, and the Moroccan 800m runner Hassna Benassi, who won silver.

The low level of participation and low success rate (only six out of 381 medals for women were won by women from Islamic countries) clearly points to the marginalization of this group in elite sport, which remains a hitherto under-researched and neglected issue. [40]

In order to evaluate the success chances of athletes from non-Western countries, one must bear in mind that some female Olympians from Islamic countries do not meet the required performance standards and compete in the games because of specific regulations for countries with few athletes. NOCs from those countries have 'the possibility of requesting invitation places for their best athletes' although they do not pass the trials. [41] In most cases these athletes do not have any chance at all of reaching even the second round of the competition. They come in order to gain the experience of taking part in international competitions.

As shown below, women from Islamic countries do not fail because they are less talented or possess less will power and commitment but because they have to struggle with obstacles and limitations, ranging from the lack of training facilities and financial support to conflicts with families or attacks from Islamists. Although women's participation in the Olympics is a contested issue among traditional Muslims, women from Islamic countries are extremely proud to represent their nations, and their compatriots join their female athletes in the celebration of national and Muslim identity.

Backgrounds and Developments

The Role of Sport and the Struggle for Prestige in Islamic Countries

The opportunities that women in Islamic countries have of practising sport and taking part in competitions are dependent on numerous interrelated factors which can only be touched upon briefly here. Orientation towards the West and being a secular society have always created favourable conditions for sport in general and women's sport in particular. This is made clear, for example, by the medal count of Islamic countries at the Olympic Games. Turkey, a secular state, is – in terms of sport – the most successful country with a majority Muslim population. Winning 82 medals, most of them gained by men, Turkey occupies 36th place in the medals list of the summer games out of more than 200 countries. The second strongest 'sports power' among Islamic countries is Iran with 48 medals, the majority of them won between 1948 and 1976. [42] Indonesia and Egypt are also to be found among the 50 most successful nations.

Countries that have adopted Islam as the ideological foundation of the state have achieved relatively little success at the Olympic Games, although it must be pointed out that not only religious orientation has played a role here but also culture and economic conditions. In the 'all-time Olympic Games medal table' Saudi Arabia (two medals), Afghanistan, Kuwait and Iraq (with one medal each) and Bahrain (without a medal) occupy bottom places. [43]

Only where sport is generally accepted and supported do women have a chance of taking part in sporting activities and participating in competitions. Furthermore, the roles, situation and rights of women, i.e. the extent of gender equality generally, have a crucial influence on the development of women's sport. The Social Institutions and Gender Index (SIGI), a measure of gender discrimination based on social institutions, enables us to compare and rank 13 Middle East and North African countries and Indonesia. [44] The first places are occupied by Tunisia, Morocco, Indonesia and Syria, the last places by Yemen, Iran, Iraq and Saudi Arabia. Even though this index tells us little about the actual situation of individual women and women's groups, we can at least measure the general level of gender equality in the various countries, especially as it draws on numerous sources in the country profiles.

In Western-oriented countries such as Iran before the revolution or Turkey (which is not included in the SIGI), but also in several Gulf states in recent years, sport – and to a certain extent women's sport, too – is considered a symbol of modernity and the will to achieve. On the role of sport in Turkey Koca and Hacisoftaoglu comment: 'In the early Republican Period, as a part of the modernization project the state supported sport and physical exercise by providing opportunities and enforcing participation for young people, particularly young men.' [45]

In some countries European gymnastic systems and/or sport along Anglo-American lines have a relatively long tradition. At the turn of the twentieth century German *Turnen* and Swedish gymnastics had already been introduced at schools in Iran. During the Pahlavi dynasty from 1926 onwards, physical education and sport were seen as part of the modernizing agenda. In the 1960s and 1970s there were close contacts e.g. with the German Sport University in Cologne, with Iranian students, both male and female, being educated and trained in Germany. There were even plans to build a sports university on the German model. The 'Western orientation' produced results: Iranian women appeared internationally in the Asian Games as early as 1958 (track-and-field athletics), 1962 (volleyball), 1974 and 1976 (fencing). [46]

In the Middle East enthusiasm for sport emerged in the early days of colonization. According to Lopez,

> many of the most famous soccer clubs in the region trace their origins to the period of European imperial control. The history of clubs (and leagues) such as Egypt's Al-Ahli (founded 1907), Turkey's Besiktas (1903) and the Tehran Football Association (1907) are all intertwined with the rise of nationalism in their respective countries. [47]

Some of these clubs, for instance Al-Ahly in Cairo, brought together many young men still at high school who were football enthusiasts. These were also the main forces in the struggle against British occupation. Here the occupiers' game was used by the colonized populace as a means of resistance. [48] As early as the 1920s, Egypt's and Turkey's football teams participated in international competitions, and an Egyptian football team competed in the Olympics in 1924 and 1928. However, the popularity of football and the enactment of the game as a demonstration of masculinity may have led to the identification of sport as a men's affair. Nevertheless, some sport clubs also accepted girls and women, in particular, the members of the men's families. [49]

According to Ebid, Egyptian women were allowed to practise and play sports in the Al-Ahly club in the 1930s. They participated in basketball, athletics, hockey, tennis, lacrosse and gymnastics. But participation in sport was restricted to a small group of upper-class women. Physical education was introduced in some girls' high schools already at the turn to the twentieth century. However, only very few girls could attend such schools. In the 1930s, the first PE teachers were educated in Cairo and later also in Alexandria. Later, PE teacher training was extended from three to four years and, in the 1970s, integrated into universities. [50]

In the case of track and field disciplines, the success of male athletes seems to have a positive influence on the development of women's sport, at least in Maghreb countries. Men such as Mohammed Gammoudi from Tunisia, Nourredine Morceli from Algeria or the Moroccan Said Aouita were pioneers of African long-distance running and role models for young people. El Faquir remembers: 'The fame of the sport stars motivated teenagers, male and female, to emulate such role models.' [51] Male and female athletes, however, are not only role models; some of them act as advisers and/or coaches, thus helping to construct an effective competitive sport system with possibilities of support for both male and female athletes. A good example of this is Morocco, where Fatima El Faquir was closely involved in developing a first-rate training centre.

In a number of countries the development has been due to dynamic and assertive women who as coaches or officials have contributed to the advancement of women's sport. For example, the synchronized swimmers in Egypt owed their Olympic participation to Safeya (Sofi) Tharwat, a former athlete and influential woman in the Egyptian Swimming Federation. [52] In an interview, one of the swimmers gives much of the credit for the development of synchronized swimming to Safeya (Sofi) Tharwat: 'Sofi fought for synchronized swimming to be recognized. ... She was always defending us, protecting us and making sure that we were getting our rights. ... Maybe other girls in other sports do not have Sofi Tharwat. ... If it wasn't for Sofi, synchronized swimming wouldn't be here.'

Progress for women and women's sport always depended, and still depends today, to a high degree on the support of governments and rulers. The successes of athletes in Morocco, for example, are due to the support of Moroccan royal family. Fatima El Faquir, athlete and later coach and sports manager, reports: 'First steps to a professionalization of sport and the emergence of new systems and ideas for training found approval and support of Royalty, for example the late King Hassan II. His particular love of track-and-field athletics ensured particular interest and support.' [53] In Syria, too, the government finances special training centres for talented young people and supports top male and female athletes: 'Since 1981 a series of legislative decrees enacted by the then President of the Republic, Hafez Al Assad, has ensured social and financial security for Syrian sporting champions.' [54] A further example is the active support of the ruler and members of the Al-Maktoum family in the development of equestrian sports in Dubai.

Structural and Economic Conditions

The development of sport and especially the creation of an effective competitive sport system depend to a large degree on economic resources. Countries with a low GDP, often termed 'developing countries', are not able to invest large funds in non-essential areas such as sport; neither do they possess the infrastructure necessary for the development of elite athletes. This is also true of many Islamic countries. Furthermore, in these countries there is a lack of well-established and firmly anchored sport structures, and, in addition, there is no appreciation of 'sport for all', through which sport and its values and benefits might be instilled in the consciousness of the people.

For the largest part of the population, living in a 'developing' Islamic country means difficult living conditions, and, for women, as already mentioned, legal prohibitions and discrimination which may prevent them – with few exceptions – from even dreaming of doing sport or participating in sporting competitions. [55] Alsharif reports, for example, on the situation of sportswomen in Egypt, a country that allows Western clothes and lifestyles:

> But while there's been some record-breaking, women in this country continue to face challenges above and beyond the race to the finish line. They report unequal treatment and fewer privileges within sports federations, and face a nation that has long held a less than positive perception of their involvement in sport. [56]

The few resources that are available are then mostly invested in men's sport. Like many other female athletes, Hayat Farag, an Egyptian wrestler, criticizes the lack of support: 'Male athletes are given better trainers than women and are sent to camps to compete abroad more often than women are. The subsequent lack of training women receive broadens the competency gap between Egyptian female athletes and their foreign counterparts.' [57] In spite of her religious orientation, Hayat trains with men simply because there are no female sparring partners who come up to her standards. For many women, this would not be an option on account of their religion or culture. Added to the limited opportunity for practice and training is the little chance women have of gaining experience in contests since in most countries few competitions are held for female athletes.

Sporting careers begin in the kindergarten or at least at school. In many countries, women's sport suffers from the absence or low quality of girls' physical education, which leads, among other problems, to difficulties in recruiting girls for sporting activities.

Even in countries with ample resources and the will to modernize, girls and women face major obstacles at the regional and local levels. Benn and Al-Sinani characterize the situation in Oman as follows: 'Main challenges remain in working with communities to educate men and women about the values of physical activity. Also resources are needed to provide culturally appropriate facilities for women's participation in schools and communities.' [58]

Women's Sport – Awareness and Visibility

Browsing the websites of NOCs in Islamic countries reveals that women's sport is indeed an issue. The Jordanian website, for instance, reports on measures of support for women and includes portraits of female elite athletes.

A short investigation of the NOC websites of the three countries that sent a 'male only' delegation to Beijing showed at least some hope for the future. In Qatar, as a 'major milestone in the women's sports movement', a Women's Sports Committee (QWSC) was established in 2001 'by HH Sheikh Tamim Bin Hamad Al-Thani, the Heir Apparent of Qatar, President of the Qatar Olympic Committee (the QOC) and Member of the International Olympic Committee'. The aim of this body is to support girls and women all along their way to sporting excellence. [59] The Kuwaiti and Saudi Arabian NOCs' websites were not accessible, but the *Jordanian Post* reports on a private initiative of the young female basketball player, Lina Al Maeena, which can be regarded as one of the first women's sports projects in Saudi Arabia. She and her husband have founded the Jeddah United Sports Company (JUSC), which aims to promote girls' and women's sport. The *Jordan Times* quoted her as saying: 'The idea of Saudi women playing sports is socially unacceptable to some people. That's the barrier we're trying to break.' In March 2010 the JUSC team played in Amman, and the team members hope that Saudi women will compete in the Olympic Games in 2012. However, there is a long way to go in a country where 'women's sport is banned in public schools and where there are no federations that organize women's sport'. [60]

'Political correctness' with regard to gender equality is demonstrated by those NOCs that have chosen women as flag bearers at Olympic opening ceremonies. The growing number of women who carry the flags of their countries signals the acceptance and recognition of female Olympians and women's sport as a whole. Even some Islamic delegations have followed this trend. The first Muslim woman to carry the flag of her country at the Olympic Games 1996 was the Iranian Lida Fariman, a markswoman, who wore the *hijab*. In 2000, Princess Haya of Jordan, the sister of King Abdullah and later the wife of Sheikh Muhammed, the ruler of Dubai, became the first female Arab flag bearer at the Olympic Games. She wore Western clothes and took part in the show jumping events.

In 2008 again a woman, the rower Homa Hosseini, carried the Iranian flag during the opening ceremony, causing controversial reactions and discussions. Although she was dressed 'correctly', strict Islamists were infuriated: 'To make this woman march means to openly declare war to our religious values. Whoever is responsible for this unforgivable act, he should know that this gesture constitutes an obstacle for the appearance of Mahdi,' stated an influential religious leader. [61] Others interpreted the role of Hosseini as a symbol of Muslim womanhood and proof of the high social status of women in Iran.

In Beijing, runner Roqaya Al-Gassra, covered from head to foot by a long and wide red robe, represented Bahrain as its flag bearer, demonstrating Islamic values at the same time. The 2008 games were the second Olympics for Al-Gassra as she had already participated in the 2004 Olympics, the first-ever female competitor from Bahrain.

The Jordanian flag was carried by a young student, table tennis player Zeina Shaban, one of the most popular athletes in the country. She also wore a long red robe and had her long hair open. The flag-bearer of the UAE was Sheika Maitha als Maktoum, a taekwondo athlete who wears Western clothes in everyday life. During the opening ceremony, she represented her country in a black *hijab*.

The symbolic importance of the representation of a nation during the opening ceremony is also evident in the entrance of the 'men only' delegation from Saudi Arabia, during which the Saudis did not even allow 'women of the host nation to carry the placard bearing the name of the Kingdom of Saudi Arabia'. [62]

Athletes gain visibility, social recognition and prestige not only through the mass media but also through public receptions and prize-giving and award ceremonies. As mentioned earlier, successful Muslim sportswomen have received numerous honours and medals. Some of them have even become 'Sportswoman of the Year', such as Zeina Shaban, who was named Jordan's top athlete of 2003 after a nationwide poll organized by Sport Up Jordan. The popularity of Zeina can be seen in the fact that she gained 44 per cent of the votes, compared with 34 per cent for a male taekwondo athlete and 15 per cent for a footballer player. [63] The Emirates' karate star, Sheikha Maitha Al Maktoum, was voted best Arab female athlete for the year 2006 by the largest Arab online community (Maktoob.com), the only woman among a host of male idols.

The best example of the fact that, for women too, sporting achievements (may) bring with them high esteem and public recognition is the career of Nawal El Moutawakel, who captured gold in the inaugural 400m hurdle race in 1984. Spontaneously, people in her home town of Casablanca poured into the streets to celebrate her victory. She received numerous awards and medals, among them the Flo Hyman Memorial Award of the Women's Sport Foundation in remembrance of her studies in the United States. She has had an extremely successful professional career as Secretary of State to the Minister of Social Affairs, responsible for youth and sport in 1997–8 and Moroccan Minister of Youth and Sports in 2007–9. In addition, El Moutawakel plays an important role in the IOC, acting as chairperson or member of various commissions and since 2008 a member of the executive committee. [64]

El Moutawakel used her fame and her positions to work for changes in women's roles and women's lives in a male-dominated society, organizing for example a women's run in Casablanca, an event that has been held since 1993 and attracts each time more than 20,000 participants. [65]

Princesses, Migrant Sport Stars and Happy Losers

Since the beginning of the new millennium the growing significance of sport as a symbol of achievement and progress has led to new developments in women's Olympic sports. This can be seen from a variety of indicators and illustrated by a variety of stories – stories that bear witness to transformations and adaptations, and demonstrate overlapping and intertwined discourses on nationality, religion and gender.

Participation in sport, and especially in the Olympic Games, has gained increasing prestige, at least in some countries and in some circles of society, especially when the sport signals conspicuous consumption. This is particularly true of horse riding, not least because the breeding and ownership of thoroughbred horses enjoys a high degree of prestige, above all in Arabian countries. Princess Haya, the daughter of King Hussein of Jordan, became the first Arab woman to compete in equestrian events at the Olympic Games in 2000. [66] As already mentioned, she was the Jordanian flag-bearer at the opening ceremony. She also qualified for the Athens Olympics, but in the end did not compete.

Haya, who graduated from Oxford University and wears elegant Western-style clothes, is an excellent horse rider, owning only the best horses. She began riding as a child and gained her first sporting successes at the age of 13. In the years that followed she competed in numerous national and international tournaments with remarkable success. She won a bronze medal at the Pan Arab Equestrian Games in 1992, the first woman ever to have done so; and, riding her father's outstanding horses, she took part in an average of 39 international competitions in show jumping per year between 1995 and 2002. In recent years she has additionally competed in endurance riding, qualifying for the 2005 World Endurance Championship in Dubai. She holds many honorary offices in international sport and has been a member of the IOC since 2007.

In 2004 she married Sheik Muhammed Al-Maktoum, the ruler of Dubai and Prime Minister of the UAE. A sportsman and a poet, and also allegedly a billionaire, he combines Eastern and Western lifestyles and has a talent for self-promotion. He is a major figure in both international horse racing and the breeding business, and has also won numerous international competitions as an endurance rider. [67] Quite a number of his many sons and daughters are also sports enthusiasts, for the most part active in horse riding. His daughter Maitha is an internationally successful taekwondo athlete, who competed, as already mentioned, in the 2008 Olympics.

In 2008 Maitha and Latifa Al-Maktoum were the first women from the UAE to take part in the Olympic Games, Maitha in takwondo, Latifa in show jumping. Neither of them were 'wild card' athletes: Maitha had won the silver medal at the Women's over-60kg karate event at the 2006 Asian Games.

Dubai's ruling family seems to bring forth Olympic competitors: besides Maitha and Latifa, two 'Al-Maktoum Sheikhs' competed in shooting events at the 2008 Olympics. Saeed Al-Maktoum, a billionaire and sport enthusiast, even competed three times, in the 2000, 2004 and 2008 games. Ahmad Al Maktoum, a hunter, is also a successful squash player. He won a gold medal in the double trap event in 2004 but competed without success in 2008. [68]

Other countries that are strongly rooted in religious tradition, for example Bahrain and Qatar, prefer to rely on 'migrant athletes', especially track-and-field athletes from Ethiopia or Kenya, in order to gain prestige through sport. The general issue of such 'buying in' cannot be gone into here. In connection with women's sport, the question arises as to the effects which the 'hiring' of such 'legionnaires' has on the girls and women of the 'host' country.

Bahrain's 'showcase athlete' is Maryam Yusuf Jamal, whose former name was Zenebech Tola when she lived in Ethiopia. [69] Several times world champion over 1500m, she belongs to an ethnic minority but left her home country because of political and/or economic problems. In 2004 she lived with her husband/coach in Lausanne and asked for asylum in Switzerland. At the same time she applied to various countries for citizenship. Bahrain obviously offered the best conditions for her and her husband. They had to change their names, but were able to keep their religion. She still seems to live and train in Lausanne, but competes for Bahrain.

Maryam Yusuf Jamal fulfilled all expectations, achieving great sporting success. This, however, attracted international attention, which was received in Bahrain with mixed feelings. When pictures of her appeared in the press wearing shorts and a top revealing a bare midriff, many conservative Bahrainis responded with criticism and rejection. Her idol is Al-Gassra, the 100m and 200m runner who competed in the 2004 and 2008 games wearing long trousers and with her hair covered.

Another migrant athlete is Elvan Abeylegesse, an Ethiopian middle- and long-distance runner, who moved to Turkey because she had a better chance of support there than in her home country. [70] She married (and later divorced) a Turk, gaining Turkish citizenship in 1999. Since then she has competed for Turkey, her latest Olympic achievements being two silver medals in Beijing. Despite her outstanding results, Elvan is not without controversy. In secular Turkey it is not her scanty clothing that causes feelings to run high, as in Bahrain, but rather the runner's nationality. In Turkey 'Turkishness', a person's commitment to and identification with the nation, is of extreme importance. However, nationalism is not a homogeneous concept but a series of discourses and an area of struggle for the power of definition. Traditionally, it is a person's 'blood' that defines Turkish ethnicity. In the case of Elvan, she definitely does not have Turkish 'blood', and her lack of Turkishness, very visible in her language and appearance, greatly detracts from the joy of certain groups of the population at her victories, which Elvan seems to have achieved for herself rather than for Turkey.

Nevertheless, there is also a liberal nationalism in Turkey which focuses on the achievements of the country in and through modernization. For the proponents of this discourse, Elvan's medals are an indication of the country's modernity and ability to perform. Elvan herself has commented: 'I am Turkish as much as other Turkish girls. I wasn't born in this land but I love its people. Now, I am glad I became Turkish. I dedicate this medal to both my family and all Turkish people.' [71]

Taking Part is Important, Not Winning

'Athletes of fortune' who achieve success in the service of Islamic states have so far been the exception at the Olympic Games, the majority of Muslim sportswomen competing for their own country, albeit without any prospects of winning a medal. It would be wrong, however, to commiserate with these athletes; on the contrary, for them it is a huge success to be able to take part. The chance of participating in world-class competitions by means of a 'wild card' system is only granted them at the Olympics. The IOC's aim in introducing this system is to demonstrate solidarity, an aim also pursued by the Olympic Solidarity programme, which has been set up to support national Olympic committees.

A relatively large number of the women from small or troubled countries who have taken part in the games thanks to this system have competed in running events, i.e. disciplines which do not need any special facilities or equipment.

One of them was Robina Muqimyar, in 2004 one of the two first women in the Afghan Olympic team. During the Taliban regime she could not play any sport at all. Since 2001 she has trained under very poor conditions in dilapidated Kabul. But she is an optimist, remarking: 'I hope I can open the way for Afghan women.' At the 2004 Olympics, after finishing the 100m in 14.14 seconds, she commented: 'At least I was ahead of one person. ... I will never, ever forget this moment. ... I'm sure if I get the facilities [in Afghanistan], I will win at least one medal in the Olympic Games in 2008.' Her dream did not come true; she participated again in 2008, but finished last in a field of 85 runners. However, she competed in the same heat as the American, Gail Devers. 'That,' she said, 'was a great moment for me.'

Alaa Jassim, from Iraq, lives and trains in Baghdad under similar, or even worse, conditions than Muqimyar in Afghanistan. At the Athens games she finished with a time of 12.70 seconds and did not get beyond the preliminary rounds. She had only started to prepare for the games in March 2000, but often could not train because of bombs and explosions. Given these circumstances, she was satisfied with her performance and proud to represent her country: 'I feel I am representing all of the Iraqi people, not just the women.'

Jassim's successor in 2008 was Dana Hussein Abdul-Razzaq, a successful athlete at pan-Arabic competitions, who comes from a sport-loving family. An American journalist describes her as follows: 'She had withstood the handicaps of being a female athlete in a Muslim culture, the continuing threat of violence (she had told of fainting after having to sprint through sniper fire) and abominable training conditions.' Abdul-Razzaq finished sixth in her heat, 'not good enough to advance, but not last, and surely not enough to dampen her spirits ... It's not important to be the best,' she said afterwards. 'It's important to represent your heart.' [72]

Cultural and Political Issues

The Case of Hassiba Boulmerka

Women's sport was, and still is, a symbol of secularism and modernity, and this explains why the participation of women in sport sparks off disputes over influence and the power of interpreting right and wrong. Not all women athletes have become actively involved in these disputes, but several of them have taken a firm political stance on the issue. The best-known 'women's rights activist' among Muslim sportswomen is Hassiba Boulmerka, who in the 1990s was one of the world's best middle-distance runners. [73] 'Boulmerka's story contains a subtext that involves the imagination of Algeria as a nation and, especially, the role of Islam and gender in Algerian society.' [74]

Sport and women's sport had been developed and promoted in postcolonial Algeria as a part of a nation-building process and the construction of national identity. Especially in the Boumediène era (1965–78) and the following regime of the National Liberation Front (FLN), sport was both a project of the state and a source of empowerment for women. Boulmerka grew up in this relatively liberal period when Algeria was a pluralist society with considerable opportunities for girls and women. This allowed her to develop her talent, to focus on running and to embark on an athletic career. In addition, she was fortunate enough to come from a family which gave her full support in her plans and activities. Her father was lorry driver who had worked in France for many years, her mother a housewife who had never attended school. Both were determined that her daughter should be allowed to follow her dreams.

Among other things, the political significance of sporting success was manifested in awards for Nouredine Morceli and Boulmerka after their victories in the Athletics World Championships in 1991. They were greeted at the airport by the president and swarms of enthusiastic supporters: 'It took the National Service to control the crowds.' [75] Both athletes were awarded the prestigious Medal of Merit and politicians praised Boulmerka's achievement for the unification of the country. In an interview she reported: 'Several leaders of political parties told me, "You did what we haven't been able to do for years. You brought us together."' Boulmerka internalized this role, describing the moment of victory in an interview with *Sports Illustrated* in the following terms: 'I screamed for joy and of shock, and for much more ... I was screaming for Algeria's pride and Algeria's history, and still more. ... I screamed finally for every Algerian woman, every Arabic woman.' [76] In the 1992 Olympics she won the first gold medal for Algeria. After a dramatic race she knelt on the track, wrapped in the Algerian flag. [77] Boulmerka hit the headlines again in 1995. After a pause in her career following an injury, she unexpectedly won the 1500m at the world championships in Stuttgart. Her sporting career ended in 1999.

Boulmerka's success did not go unchallenged. She increasingly became the target of criticism and attacks by Islamists. [78] Not only her appearance in public and her political leanings but also (and especially) her sportswear caused outrage among religious fundamentalists, who denounced Boulmerka as 'un-Muslim' for 'running with naked legs in front of thousands of men'. [79]

With the outbreak of civil war at the end of 1991 and the growing power of the Islamic Salvation Front (FIS), the attacks on Boulmerka increased while at the same time the opportunities and rights of Algerian women became more and more restricted. In 1990, 'one-third of the Algerian National Assembly voted to abolish organized sport for females as "immodest". She dashed to the rescue just as the Islamic Salvation Front swept to victory in dozens of city elections and began disbanding women's teams.' [80] Due to harassments and death threats Boulmerka had to train in Europe.

Boulmerka was an open and active supporter of the secular government, dedicating her Olympic gold medal, for example, to the president, Mohamed Boudiaf, who was assassinated in June 1992. In an interview with *Sports Illustrated* in 1992 she declared her interest in politics and her willingness to be politically active in her country in terms of wishing to fight for justice and the distribution of power. This wish has been fulfilled in her commitment to l'*association algérienne de solidarité avec le peuple sahraoui* (Algerian Association of Solidarity with the Sahrawi People), with which she wishes to draw attention to social problems, fundamentalism and violence against women. [81]

Boulmerka is a confessed adherent of Islam and thinks of herself as a good Muslim. At the same time, she has repeatedly spoken out against extremism and has especially condemned restrictions placed upon women in and outside sport. With her achievements Boulmerka wanted to prove that 'women don't have to hide behind their chadors'. [82] For many girls and women she was an idol and role model: 'I've become a representative of all Algeria, and of young women in particular. I've gotten so many letters wishing me courage,' she told an American journalist in 1992. [83]

According to El Faquir, secular women and women's associations considered Boulmerka's success a victory in the fight against men's domination and against the sharia-based Family Law, introduced in 1984, which prescribes women's subordinate position. [84]

In 1995 Boulmerka was appointed to the IOC's Women and Sports Commission; and, shortly before the end of her sporting career in 1996, she was elected a member of the IOC's Athletic Commission. She drew attention to her work in the summer of 1999 when she appealed to the IOC to actively contribute to putting an end to, as she called it, terrorism against women, pointing to Pakistan and Mexico, countries which she declared were discriminating against women in sport. [85]

In the meantime the IOC's Reform Commission has taken up its work. The harshest criticism of both the IOC's composition and its conduct had come from athletes, above all Hassiba Boulmerka, who remarked: 'We do not need an organization of old men. Athletes must play the main role in the IOC. We are elected, and we should have the power.' [86]

When, following the reforms, places were reserved for athletes in the IOC, she was elected a member of the IOC at the end of 1999. [87] As early as 2000, however, her term of office in the Athletic Commission was over, and thus her role in the IOC as well. [88] At the end of her term she left this body dismayed and disappointed: 'Enormous sums were available to promote women in sport, but nothing happened.' [89]

After this Boulmerka appeared less frequently in the news; she lived partly in Miami, but then settled in Algeria, where she built up a small firm named HBI (Hassiba Boulmerka Internationale), which distributes and sells medicines. In addition, she acts as the general representative of Diadora, an Algerian company. She continues to be actively involved in international sports organizations, including the International Athletics Federation, and numerous sports associations in Algeria, as well as in the *Association Algérienne de Solidarité*. In an interview conducted in 2009 she admitted that she would like to do more for sport, but that the Ministry for Youth and Sport did not make any use of her experience and competence. [90] Boulmerka was again in the limelight in 2008, when she was admitted to the International Women's Sports Hall of Fame in New York.

There is no doubt that Boulmerka paved the way for women's sport in Algeria. She soon had a worthy successor in Nouria Merah-Benida, who won the gold medal over 1500m in the year 2000, reportedly inspired by Boulmerka's legacy and her presence at the Olympic Games. [91]

Hargreaves describes Boulmerka as a 'spokeswoman and an ideologue ... for Muslim women throughout the world. But her position is untypical and controversial ... arguing that it is possible to take the best from Islam and Western philosophies and still be a good Muslim.' [92] However, her position seems to be typical for many Muslim athletes who argue from a faith-based perspective and summon a re-appraisal of the Hadiths that the rules on moderate clothing are a matter of interpretation and that they are good Muslims, even if they wear 'normal' sportswear.

Islam and Women's Sport – Empowerment and Restrictions

Participation in sports by girls and women from Islamic countries is influenced by religion in various complex and ambiguous ways. There is not a general prohibition of sports in Islam, a rule that is also applicable to girls and women. [93] Like other Islamic sport scientists, Leila Sfeir emphasizes that

> Islamic religion in no way tries to depreciate, much less deny sport for women. On the contrary, it attributes great significance and function to physical strength and sport activities. Islam has a constant concern with one's body, cleanliness, purification and force, with segregation of the sexes. But certain religious elements, such as Islamic fatalism ... have been dominant factors in controlling general access to sport. [94]

These arguments are supported by Islamic feminists, who continue to fight for the rights of girls and women to participate in sporting activities. However, there are principles inherent in Islamic cultures that are not readily reconcilable with a career in elite sport.

Gender Roles and Relations in Islam Countries

Statements of athletes and sport officials show that Muslim women often live in a double bind since it is difficult to combine being a good woman and a good athlete. The Egyptian wrestler Hayat Farag knows very well, for example, 'that society expects women to do no more than finish school, marry and start a family'. 'I wanted to break that rule,' she told the magazine *Egypt Today*. On the other hand, she does not want to abandon her faith and destroy her future. For her, it is not the physical contact of the sport but the wrestling outfit that is a violation of the religious rules, and she has decided to give up her sport after the Olympic Games in order to live as what she believes to be a good Muslim woman.

Mohamed Ibrahim, president of the Egyptian Weightlifting Federation, mentioned in an interview 'that women's sports careers are short-lived due to Arab and Egyptian culture. Athletes may be forbidden to continue weightlifting by their fiancés or parents.' Hence, it does not make any sense for sports federations to make great investments in female athletes since one cannot be sure whether they will have a long career. [95]

Both quotes refer to the gender hierarchy and the role of women in the family as well as in society at large, both of which in Islamic cultures are regulated by the Sharia, a legal system based on religious rules.

Age and sex determine one's position, duties and privileges within the family. [96] According to the Sharia, the husband is the head of the family and decides on all major issues. He is obliged to maintain his wife/wives who, in return, is/are committed to obedience. The husband has the right and the duty to control and 'protect' the family members, especially the women and girls, whose modesty and – in Islamist contexts – 'covered' bodies signalize and guarantee gender differences and hierarchies. [97] However, despite its claim to be universal, the Sharia is used in different ways in the various countries with a majority Muslim population.

Gender hierarchies, as well as the social and cultural superiority of men, are based on the concept of honour and the regulation of sexuality. [98] Sexual relations outside marriage are strictly forbidden; and it is the obligation of women to protect their chastity and prevent any sexual assaults. Sexuality is controlled by gender segregation, meaning that women should either not appear in public or must be dressed in 'decent' clothes that fully cover their bodies. However, it must be remembered that gender roles and rules are complex and contested and that there are various translations of the Koran, as well as interpretations of and debates about Islamic laws and traditions.

According to Islamic tradition, family respectability and the honour of male family members depend on the moral integrity of their wives and the virginity of their daughters. Men must have control over the female family members, prevent any actions that might dishonour them and punish transgressions. In traditional Muslim communities, the main strategy is to control women and to prevent them from having contact with the other gender. [99] Sports may affect the respectability of women and the honour of their families in many ways. Women's participation in sports leaves them uncontrolled by the family, but the family's reputation may also be endangered if its female members engage in activities that are seen as unfeminine, immoral, against Islamic laws or harmful to the female body. [100]

Covering the Body – the *Hijab*

Meanings and Practices

For Muslim women integrity is indispensable; it means following Islamic rules about the body and its presentation in public. For traditional Muslims, women's covered bodies have become symbols of Islam. 'Women's bodies are pivotal in the mix of religion, politics and culture ... [they] are central in the construction of a diasporic, truly global "Muslim society"'. [101] However, 'covering' has various forms and meanings, depending on religious affiliation, the environment, culture and tradition. In many Islamic countries the *hijab* covers the entire body with the exception of the face and the hands, in others women can decide if and how they want to cover their hair.

Women have various and often intertwined motives for dressing according to Islamic precepts. A woman may be forced to wear a veil, but she may also wear a veil of her own free will. For religious women, 'modesty' signals submission to god. Some women wear a veil as protection against the male gaze. The veil may also be a fashion or simply a habit. Women may also choose to wear the *hijab* not on religious grounds but because to 'unveil' could be interpreted as an action against Islam. Thus the veil signals solidarity with Islamic traditions and resistance against Westernization. [102] In recent years a growing number of girls and women even in secular countries such as Turkey have started to (re-)discover religion, to re-interpret Islam and to use the veil as an instrument of individual identity politics and policies.

Benn, Dagkas and Jawad draw our attention to the fact that 'religion is enacted with the body, is felt and "done" with, through and in the body'. [103] According to these authors, 'faith is embodied in the sense that presentation of the body, appearance, physicality, social interaction and behaviour are integral to religious identity, to lived reality of the daily embodiment of religious belief. Embodied faith reflects outward manifestations inseparably connected to internalized belief.'

But women who believe in Islam and follow its rules may decide not to cover their heads. Some Muslim feminists even claim that neither the Koran nor the *hadiths* demand that women be 'covered' (or excluded from public life). According to these women, the rules about covering the body are to be attributed to a mixture of Islam and patriarchal traditions rather than to religion. [104]

The Hijab and Sporting Activities

Because of the contested field of women's bodies, sports attire is a highly controversial topic in Islamic and Western gender discourses. In countries where traditional Islamic beliefs prevail, e.g. Iran and Saudi Arabia, women must wear the *hijab* in public – and thus also when they participate in sport in a mixed-gender environment.

Sports feminists with a 'faith-based' approach operate within an Islamic framework, citing the Koran to support their demand of equal opportunity for women in sports and demanding the acceptance of the *hijab* in and outside sport. In contrast to secular feminists, they believe that equal opportunity in sports is compatible with the traditional Islamic rules in respect of 'modest clothes' and/or the segregation of the sexes. Secular (sports) feminists – a minority in Islamic countries – demand a separation of state and religion; they advocate freedom of choice with regard to religion, dress and lifestyle and demand that women be given the same access as men to all parts of society, including sports.

There is, however, a third view of women, sport and religion. There are Islamic feminists who deny that the necessity of wearing the veil is prescribed in the Koran. They argue that there are no religious rules which prohibit participation in sports and/or the wearing of Western-style clothes.

Nevertheless, in some countries and/or groups, women's participation in sports with or without a *hijab* remains irreconcilable with Islamic values, the culturally rooted concept of femininity and the gender roles that restrict women's actions to the home and family. In some countries growing re-Islamization tendencies are to be observed. According to Safeya (Sofi) Tharwat, a board member of the Egyptian Swimming Union, Egyptians have become more conservative in their attitudes towards the *hijab* since the 1950s. She reports that 'sports like fencing and horseback riding are less criticized because the outfits do not reveal much of the woman's body, but diving and swimming cause challenges. ... So we fight for the girls' right to swim.' [105]

Wearing the Hijab at the Olympic Games

Until recently, for Muslim women, participation in international competitions meant adopting the dress codes of the international sports federations, which are oriented first and foremost to functionality but – at least in the case of beach volleyball – also to erotic attractiveness.

Therefore sports attire is one of the issues constraining participation in the Olympics by women from Islamic countries. The official dress codes in competitive sport do not conform to Islamic standards of modesty, but most Muslim athletes opt to wear the official dress, claiming that this does not conflict with their faith. This was also (and still is) the conviction of Hassiba Boulmerka, who according to Hargreaves is a symbol of 'the potential for Muslim women to develop their interests in the modern world without rejecting their Muslim faith'. [106] However, dress codes that require a bathing suit or a bikini (as in beach volleyball) not only conflict with the rules of many Islamic countries but may also offend the sensibilities of practising Muslims.

At Olympic Games Iranian women have always been 'covered', but in their main sport, shooting, this is not a problem. Running, too, is possible with covered hair and body; three athletes, among them the Bahraini Roqaya Al-Gassra, competed in the Olympic Games in Athens in long trousers, a shirt with long sleeves and a headscarf in the 100m race.

The question of clothing became a highly contested issue at the Olympic Games in Beijing when a number of female athletes insisted on their right to compete in the *hijab*. At the same time, the discourses (including practices) regarding the public appearance of Muslim sportswomen and their duty or right to dress according to their faith have changed considerably.

On the website 'famous faces', which profiles 'influential Muslim women who wear the hijab', 12 athletes are presented who competed in Beijing properly veiled. They were from Afghanistan, Yemen, Iran, Bahrain and Egypt, and participated in rowing, fencing, table tennis, shooting, archery, taekwondo and running. The portraits of some of them depict proud and confident women who seem to manage to combine the love of their sport with their religion.

One of them is the Egyptian fencer Shaimaa El Gammal, who has participated three times in the Olympics, the third time wearing the *hijab*, which according to her comments in an interview gives her confidence and inner strength: 'When I fence I'm proud that I'm a Muslim,' she told the interviewer. 'It's very symbolic for women in my country.' [107]

Whereas the Turkish athlete Hamide Bıkçın Tosun was not allowed to cover her hair in the 2000 Olympic taekwondo competition, the World Taekwondo Federation accepted the decision of women to wear the *hijab* during the 2008 Olympics and changed its dress code permanently in 2009. This decision also served the sport's political aims, indicating 'that taekwondo is one of the few sports that treat women and men equally in the Muslim world. We believe that our respect for others' cultures and beliefs will allow taekwondo to enhance its status as an Olympic sport.' [108] There are also other federations, among them the table tennis federation, which allow Muslim women 'officially' to wear the *hijab* during competitions.

While some federations accept a free choice of sport clothes, others seem to administer a strict dress code. Currently, the Modern Pentathlon Federation seems to forbid the so called 'burqini', a suit which covers the whole body, in swimming events. This decision raised discussion among Muslim athletes, among them, the Egyptian world-class athlete Aya Medany, who has threatened to end her career if she is not allowed to dress 'properly'. [109]

The 'burqini' discussion, as well as the outfit worn by Al-Gassra, indicates a new trend: the production and marketing of sports clothes that are adapted to Islamic requirements. Aheda Zanetti, an Australian-Lebanese Muslim business-woman, claims to have invented the burqini, a swimsuit that covers the whole body, and the 'hijood', sports attire which includes a close-fitting hood. [110]

Al-Gassra, one of the few world-class Muslim athletes, wears the 'hijood'. She belongs to the top performers at the Asian Games and reached the semi-final in the 100m event in Beijing. [111] She comments on her outfit as follows:

> It's great to finally have a high-performance outfit that allows me to continue my need for modesty with a design made from fabric that allows freedom of movement and flexibility. ... I hope that wearing this type of sports top will inspire other women to see that modesty or religious beliefs don't have to be a barrier to participating in competitive sports. [112]

She and several other athletes affirm their Islamic identity through their attire and gain approval and praise not only from enthusiastic compatriots but also from traditional Muslims. [113] However, even the burqini and the hijood fail to find the approval of conservative groups, who consider not particularly the clothes but rather the sporting activities and the public appearance of women to be un-Islamic. On the other hand, it is argued that the opportunity of wearing the *hijab* could be used by religious groups and leaders to exert pressure on athletes and require them to wear clothing which they regard as 'correct'.

Hargreaves concludes that the greatest barrier for participation in sports by women from Islamic countries is

> the opposition that continues to face them from Islamist leaders who wield power in their local communities. All forms of participation attract critical religious commentary from conservative Muslim clerics. ... They encourage feelings of guilt and sometimes fear in young Muslim sportswomen who are ignorant of alternative Qu'ranic definitions of womanhood. [114]

One of the numerous examples of the type of problems that Muslim athletes face despite wearing 'modest' sporting attire is the case of the Afghani runner Mehbooba Andyar, who was so terrified by threats from Muslim fundamentalists that she decided not to participate in the Beijing Olympic Games. According to newspaper reports, she sought asylum in Norway. [115]

Perspectives

There have been a number of initiatives aimed at improving the opportunities of Muslim women to participate in sport, some of them sparked off by Western feminists. They include the Atlanta+ initiative, which asked the International Olympic Committee (IOC) to exclude all NOCs from the games which did not include women in their delegations. [116] The IOC rejected these demands, primarily on the grounds that they interfered in the internal affairs of sovereign countries.

In contrast to Atlanta+, Islamic feminists are striving for changes in an Islamic framework. The most spectacular events that placed Muslim sportswomen on the international agenda were the Muslim Women's Games, conducted in 1993, 1997, 2001 and 2005 in Tehran. [117] The Muslim Women's Games were welcomed in Iran as an opportunity for women's sports and as an alternative to the Olympic Games. Many Iranian participants described the contact and the competition with foreign women as a wonderful experience. However, many athletes (and also feminists interested in sports) pointed out that events of this kind would confirm and legitimize the exclusion of women from the 'real' world of sports. In addition, athletes complained that the participants from Western countries were not top-level athletes and that the events at the Muslim Women's Games were neither serious nor high-ranking competitions. [118] A further important problem for many athletes competing in these games is the lack of an audience and media coverage.

As shown above, there are many causes of the marginalization of Muslim women in the world of sport. These include the rigid rules of modern sports on the one hand and the interpretation of Islamic laws and restrictions because of cultural traditions on the other.

A workshop in Oman, sponsored by the Sultan Quaboos University and supported by IAPESGW, [119] provided the opportunity for a cross-cultural discussion with and about Muslim women engaged in physical education and/or sport. The participants, one man and 15 women (including the author) from 14 countries across Europe as well as the Middle and Far East, came together to exchange knowledge, opinions and best practices based on openness and the willingness to learn from and understand each other. Some women were atheists while many were religious and had different ways of practising their faith. Some wore Western clothes and hairstyles; others observed Islamic dress codes. [120] The purpose of the gathering was to identify means of improving opportunities for Muslim women and girls in and through sport and physical education.

The question remained to what extent it was possible to achieve a balance between global values and cultural diversity. In order to avoid this difficult issue, the Oman workshop participants chose to focus on freedom of choice. We did this on the advice of Islamic feminists who shared with us their considerations about framing empowerment for Muslim women from within the religion:

> Islamic feminism has been helpful in showing ways in which space can be created and negotiated for positive change. This knowledge, and the opportunity it created for women's participation in physical activity, was important in understanding the positions of those Muslim women whose most essential layer of identity was religion and for whom the display of this identity through adherence to modest dress codes was integral to sustaining that. [121]

However, choice should also be possible for those women who re-interpret Islam, adapt its rules to modern life and combine their religion with Western attire and elite sports. This is an option in most Islamic countries, as the case of female athletes from countries such as Indonesia, Morocco, Algeria, Jordan, the UAE and Turkey in the 2008 Olympics has demonstrated.

It must be mentioned that the workshop participants' focus on 'freedom of choice' is not unproblematic because it inherently includes the structure/agency dilemma. In this particular case, one can question whether women (and men) are really free to make decisions about their lives or whether their choices are determined by their families, environments, culture and society. It took one exciting week to come to a consensus and to draft the declaration 'Accept and Respect'. The declaration supports Islam as an enabling religion that endorses women's participation in physical activity: 'We recommend that people working in the sport and education systems accept and respect the diverse ways in which Muslim women and girls practise their religion and participate in sport and physical activity, for example choices of activity, dress and gender grouping.' [122]

This declaration is directed to Islamic and Western countries, as well as to religious and sports leaders, encouraging them to accept the choices of women (and men) and to respect their cultural backgrounds. The essence of this declaration can be applied to other areas, groups and cultures. The text is recognized by a number of international sports bodies that lobby for a broad acceptance of the declaration and its principles.

Notes

[1] The Olympic Charter, available at http://en.beijing2008.cn/spirit/symbols/charter/index. shtml, accessed 29 March 2010.

[2] This article deals with women from Islamic countries (see footnote 6). 'Muslim' refers here to the home country and culture of the women and does not indicate religion or religiosity.

[3] Pfister, 'Women and the Olympic Games'; Wamsley and Pfister, 'Olympic Men and Women'.

[4] Drevon, *Les Jeux olympiques oubliés*, 178.

[5] Jinxia Dong, a Chinese sport historian, in an email of 1 Feb. 2010 to the author.

[6] On the literature of the Olympic Games see Veal and Toohey, 'The Olympic Games: A Bibliography'.

[7] Pfister, 'Women and the Olympic Games'.

[8] Ibid.

[9] See the website of the Beijing Olympics: http://en.beijing2008.cn/, accessed 29 March 2010.

[10] The definition of the term sport varies widely depending on language and culture. 'Modern' sport with a focus on quantitative performances, competition and record orientation emerged in the nineteenth century.

[11] See the numbers of Muslim athletes, p. 2929.

[12] All states have non-Muslim minorities and we do not know whether female athletes are recruited from non-Muslim groups. However, we can assume that they are influenced by culture and society. I have included Islamic states that have adopted Islam as the ideological foundation of their political institutions or have had Islam officially endorsed. In addition, secular states with a population of more than 85 per cent Muslims: Afghanistan, Algeria, Bahrain, Bangladesh, Egypt, Indonesia, Iran, Iraq, Kuwait, Libya, Maldives, Mauritania, Morocco, Oman, Qatar, Pakistan, Turkey, Tunisia, United Arab Emirates, Yemen, Saudi Arabia. Because of the considerable cultural differences, the 'black' African countries and countries of the former Soviet bloc are not included in this analysis.

[13] http://www.sports-reference.com/olympics/athletes/ma/freydoun-malkom-1.html, accessed 29 March 2010.

[14] Sfeir, 'The Status of Muslim Women'.

[15] See the statistics provided by the IOC Research and Reference Service. See also the information at http://www.sports-reference.com/olympics/countries/, accessed 29 March 2010. I thank Bill Mallon and Nuria Puig for their support.

[16] http://www.metu.edu.tr/~settar/hp4.htm, accessed 29 March 2010; see also Sfeir, 'The Status of Muslim Women' with data on Muslim elite sport until 1984.

[17] http://www.gsgm.gov.tr/sayfalar/olimpiyatlar/1948.htm, accessed 29 March 2010.

[18] I refer here and in the following to statistics provided by the Reference Service [reference@ olympic.org] and http://www.sports-reference.com/olympics/, accessed 29 March 2010. I thank Bill Malon and Nuria Puig for their support.

[19] El Faquir, 'Sport in North Africa'; see also http://www.gbrathletics.com/ic/magc.htm, accessed 29 March 2010.

[20] Die Spiele *The Official Report of the Organizing Committee for the Games of the XXth Olympiad*.

[21] http://en.wikipedia.org/wiki/Iran_at_the_1976_Summer_Olympics#Fencing, accessed 29 March 2010.

[22] A. Alsharif, 'Ladies at the Forefront', *Egypt Today*, July 2008, available at http://www. egypttoday.com/article.aspx?ArticleIDx=8092, accessed 29 March 2010.

[23] A. Bannayan, 'Muslim Sportswomen Gain Standing in Beijing', Womensenews, 2008, available at http://www.womensenews.org/article.cfm?aidx=3696, accessed 29 March 2010.

[24] Ebid, 'Femmes et sport'.

[25] See the statistics provided by the IOC Research and Reference Service. See also the information provided by http://www.sports-reference.com/olympics/countries/, accessed 29 March 2010.

[26] Koushki Jahromi, 'Physical Activities and Sport'.

[27] http://news.bbc.co.uk/2/hi/middle_east/3570040.stm., accessed 29 March 2010.

[28] Muslim athletes have competed in these sports since their inclusion in the Olympic Games: in judo since 1992, taekwondo and weightlifting since 2000 and wrestling since 2004.

[29] The International Boxing Association (IBA) accepts that women fight in the hijab, as long as their faces are uncovered. See *Sunday Times* (London), 4 Oct. 2009, available at http://www.timesonline.co.uk/tol/news/politics/article6860256.ece, accessed 29 March 2010.

[30] http://www.fivb.org/EN/Volleyball/Competitions/Olympics/2008/W/Teams/Team_Roster.asp?TEAM=ALG&TRN=WOG2008, accessed 29 March 2010.

[31] El Faquir, 'Sport in North Africa'.

[32] http://www.angelfire.com/ak5/zeina/profile.htm, accessed 29 March 2010.

[33] Moroccan runner Hasna Benhassi, who won the last indoor championships over 1500m, is expecting a baby for the end of the year. She is married to athlete Mouhcine Chahbi. See http://www.africathle.com/gb/perso/news/news01.html accessed 29 March 2010.

[34] See El Faquir, 'Sport in North Africa'.

[35] *Washington Post*, 2 Aug. 1996.

[36] El-Houda Karfoul, ' Women and Sport in Syria'.

[37] See http://en.wikipedia.org/wiki/Indonesia_at_the_Olympics

[38] See http://www.khaleejtimes.com/DisplayArticleNew.asp?xfile=data/sports/2008/July/sports_July558.xml&section=sports., accessed 29 March 2010.

[39] See the Overall Medal Standings, http://results.beijing2008.cn/WRM/ENG/INF/GL/95A/GL0000000.shtml., accessed 29 March 2010.

[40] See also many webpages, among them http://muslimahmediawatch.org/2008/08/14/muslimahs-at-the-beijing-olympics/, accessed 29 March 2010.

[41] Email from Olympic Reference Service about the regulation in 2008: reference@olympic.org, sent 23 March 2010.

[42] http://en.wikipedia.org/wiki/Iran_at_the_Olympics#Medals_by_Summer_Games, accessed 29 March 2010.

[43] http://en.wikipedia.org/wiki/All-time_Olympic_Games_medal_table, accessed 29 March 2010.

[44] http://genderindex.org/. Inequality is measured in five areas – family code, physical integrity, son preference, civil liberties and ownership rights – in 102 non-OECD countries. The index was developed by the OECD Development Centre in collaboration with Göttingen University and the Erasmus University Rotterdam.

[45] Koca and Hacisoftaoglu, 'Religion, the State and Sport'.

[46] Pfister, 'Women and sport in Iran.

[47] Lopez, 'Sport and Society in the Middle East', 256.

[48] http://www2.sis.gov.eg/En/Society/Sport/HFegypt/090703000000000001.htm, accessed 29 March 2010.

[49] For Egypt, I am indebted for email from Marc Ran Oppenheim, author of 'Twilight of Colonial Ethos'.

[50] Ebid, 'Femmes et sport'.

[51] El Faquir, 'Sport in North Africa'.

[52] A. Alsharif, 'Ladies at the Forefront'

[53] El Faquir, 'Sport in North Africa.

[54] El Houda Karfoul, 'Women and Sport in Syria'.

[55] Pfister, 'Frauen und Sport in der Türkei'; 'Women and Sport in Iran'. See the Social Institutions and Gender Index, available at http://genderindex.org/, accessed 29 March 2010.

[56] A. Alsharif, 'Ladies at the Forefront'.

[57] http://www.egypttoday.com/article.aspx?ArticleID=8092, accessed 29 March 2010.

[58] Benn and Al-Sinani, 'The Sultanate of Oman'.

[59] http://www.qatarolympics.org/topics/index.asp?g=C6153A81-F4B1-41E3-A9F4-58750A7C1421, accessed 29 March 2010; the webpages of the NOCs of Saudi Arabia and Kuwait were not accessible.

[60] http://www.jordantimes.com/, accessed 29 Mar. 2010.

[61] http://www.jihadwatch.org/2008/08/iran-clerics-say-female-flag-bearer-at-olympics-constitutes-an-obstacle-for-the-appearance-of-the-ma.html, accessed 29 March 2010.

[62] http://www.huffingtonpost.com/david-wallechinsky/should-saudi-arabia-be-ba_b_115736.html, accessed 29 March 2010.

[63] http://www.maktoobgroup.com/Press-1-151-Sheikha_Maitha_tops_Arab_.htm, accessed 29 March 2010.

[64] http://www.olympic.org/en/content/The-IOC/Members/Ms-Nawal-EL-MOUTAWAKEL-/, accessed 29 March 2010.

[65] http://encyclopedia.jrank.org/articles/pages/5668/El-Moutawakel-Nawal-1962.html#ixzz0iXQT8oxh, accessed 29 March 2010.

[66] http://www.princesshaya.net/, accessed 29 March 2010.

[67] Ibid.

[68] http://en.wikipedia.org/wiki/United_Arab_Emirates_at_the_2008_Summer_Olympics#Shooting, accessed 29 March 2010.

[69] http://www.bloomberg.com/apps/news?pid=20601079&sid=aQmlNj6rdOGs&refer=home, accessed 29 March 2010.

[70] http://www.sports-reference.com/olympics/athletes/ab/elvan-abeylegesse-1.html, accessed 29 March 2010.

[71] Quoted 17 Aug. 2008, available at www.hurriyet.com.tr, accessed 29 March 2010.

[72] *New York Times*, 31 Dec. 2008, available at http://www.nytimes.com/2008/12/31/sports/olympics/31araton.html, accessed 29 March 2010.

[73] Essential information on Boulmerka is to be found on the webpages http://www.lesdebats.com/editionsdebats/110309/nation.htm; http://www.algerie-femme.com/, accessed 29 March 2010; K. Moore, 'A Scream And A Prayer. Politics and Religion are Inseparable from Sport in the Lives of Algeria's World-champion Runners, Noureddine Morceli and Hassiba Boulmerka,' *Sports Illustrated*, 3 Aug. 1992, available at http://sportsillustrated.cnn.com/vault/article/magazine/MAG1004061/index.htm, accessed 29 March 2010.

[74] http://encyclopedia.jrank.org/articles/pages/5619/Boulmerka-Hassiba-1968.html, accessed 29 March 2010.

[75] Moore, 'A Scream And A Prayer'.

[76] Ibid.

[77] http://www2.iaaf.org/News/EventReports/getnews.asp?Event=WCH99&Code=3100; *St Petersburg Times* (Florida), 10 Aug. 1992.

[78] Moore, 'A Scream And A Prayer'.

[79] Ibid.

[80] *Daily Mail* (London), 5 Aug. 1992.

[81] *Neue Züricher Zeitung*, quoted in Fembio, 4 August 2002, available at http://www.fembio.org/biographie.php, accessed 29 Sept. 2010.

[82] Quoted in Hargreaves, *Heroines of Sport*, 62.

[83] Moore, 'A Scream And A Prayer'.

[84] El Faquir, Sport in North Africa'.

[85] *Daily Telegraph* (Sydney, Australia), 13 Dec. 1999.

[86] *Die Welt*, 3 June 1999.

[87] See http://sports.espn.go.com/oly/summer08/fanguide/athlete?athlete=1521, accessed 29 March 2010.

[88] Email from Reference Service of the IOC dated 13 March 2010: 'In the case of members of the IOC Athletes' Commission elected as IOC members upon the occasion of the 110th IOC Session, their terms shall end immediately following the closing ceremony of the Games of the Olympiad or Olympic Winter Games four years after they were elected as members of the IOC Athletes' Commission.' (Bye-Law to Rule 20, 37).

[89] *Neue Züricher Zeitung*, quoted in Fembio, 4 August 2002, available at http://www.fembio. org/biographie.php, accessed 29 Sept. 2010.

[90] http://www.lesdebats.com/editionsdebats/110309/nation.htm, accessed 29 March 2010.

[91] http://encyclopedia.jrank.org/articles/pages/5619/Boulmerka-Hassiba-1968.html, accessed 29 March 2010.

[92] Hargreaves, *Heroines of Sport*, 68.

[93] On women's sport in Islam, see, for example, Lindsay *et al.*, 'Islamic Principles'; Sfeir, 'The Status of Muslim Women'; Daiman, 'Women in Sport in Islam'; Walseth, 'Young Muslim Women and Sport'; Dahl, 'Zum Verständnis von Körper'; Pfister, 'Muslim Women'.

[94] Sfeir, 'The Status of Muslim Women'; Daiman, 'Women in Sport in Islam'.

[95] Alsharif, 'Ladies at the Forefront'.

[96] See also, among others, Delaney, *The Seed and the Soil*.

[97] Nakamura, 'Beyond the Hijab'; Schirrmacher and Spuler-Stegemann, *Frauen und die Scharia*.

[98] Schiffauer, *Die Gewalt der Ehre*; Khader, *Ære og skam*. See also http://www.spsrasd.info/fr/ infos/2007/11/sps-041107.html 2006, accessed 29 March 2010.

[99] Khader, *Aere og skam*.

[100] Nakamura, *Beyond the Hijab*.

[101] Hargreaves, 'Sport, Exercise, and the Female Muslim Body', 76.

[102] Ibid., 75.

[103] Benn *et al.*, *Embodied Faith*.

[104] On the literature regarding the veil see Hargreaves, 'Sport, Exercise, and the Female Muslim Body'.

[105] Alsharif, 'Ladies at the Forefront'.

[106] Hargreaves, 'Sport, Exercise, and the Female Muslim Body', 83.

[107] See http://www.islamonline.net/servlet/Satellite?c=Article_C&cid=1218386145199&page name=Zone-English-News/NWELayout#ixzz0eDLxAxrO, accessed 29 March 2010.

[108] http://www.aroundtherings.com/articles/view.aspx?id=33197, accessed 29 March 2010.

[109] http://pentathloncircuit.blogspot.com/2009/11/2009-seasons-best-women-swimming.html, accessed 29 March 2010.

[110] www.asianewsnet.net/epaper/pdf/AsiaNews_May22-28_2009.pdf, accessed 29 March 2010.

[111] http://globalsportstars.wordpress.com/2008/08/20/roqaya-al-gassra/, accessed 29 March 2010.

[112] http://bahraini.tv/2008/08/22/she-did-it-wearing-hijab-head-covering/, accessed 29 March 2010.

[113] Hargreaves, 'Sport, Exercise, and the Female Muslim Body', 87.

[114] Ibid., 88.

[115] *The Times* (London), 10 July 2008, available at http://www.timesonline.co.uk/tol/sport/ more_sport/article4304884.ece, accessed 29 March 2010.

[116] Nakamura, 'Beyond the Hijab'.

[117] Pfister, 'Islamic Countries'.

[118] Quoted in J. Steel, 'Sport and the Scarf', BBC News, 9. Dec. 2005, available at http://news.bbc.co.uk/2/hi/middle_east/4511680.stm; see also http://www.taipeitimes.com/News/editorials/archives/2005/09/27/2003273432, both accessed 29 March 2010

[119] International Association of Physical Education and Sport for Girls and Women.

[120] The participants came from Bahrain, Bosnia and Herzegovina, Denmark, Egypt, Iran, Iraq, Malaysia, Morocco, Oman, South Africa, Syria, Turkey, the United Arab Emirates and the United Kingdom.

[121] Benn and Koushki Jahromi, 'Evidence and Influence'.

[122] See the declaration on the webpage of IAPESGW: http://www.vagacms.co.uk/vagacms/iapesgw/ianews.aspx, accessed 29 March 2010.

References

Benn, T., S. Dagkas and H. Jawad: *Embodied Faith: Islam, Religious Freedom and Educational Practices in Physical Education, Sport, Education and Society* (in press).

Benn T. and M. Koushki Jahromi. 'Evidence and Influence: Making a difference for girls and women in physical education and sport'. Paper presented at the IAPESGW Symposium during the International Convention on Science, Education and Medicine in Sport, Guangzhou, 2008.

Benn, T. and Y. Al-Sinani. 'The Sultanate of Oman: Modrnization Processes and the Participation of Girls and Women in Physical Education and Sport'. In *Muslim Women and Sport*, edited by T. Benn, G. Pfister and H. Jawad. London: Routledge, 2010 (in press).

Benn, T., G. Pfister and H. Jawad, eds. *Muslim Women and Sport*. London: Routledge, 2010 (in press).

Dagkas, S., M. Koushki Jahromi and M. Talbot. 'The Values of Physical Activity, Sport and Physical Education in the Lives of Young Women'. In *Muslim Women and Sport*, edited by T. Benn, G. Pfister and H. Jawad. London: Routledge, 2010 (in press).

Dahl, D. 'Zum Verständnis von Körper, Bewegung und Sport in Christentum, Islam und Buddhismus – Impulse zum interreligiösen Ethikdiskurs im Spitzensport'. PhD thesis, Sport University Oslo, 2007.

Daiman, S. 'Women in Sport in Islam'. *ICHPER-SD Journal* 32, no. 1 (1995): 18–21.

Delaney, C., *The Seed and the Soil. Gender and Cosmology in Turkish Village Society*. Berkeley, CA, Los Angeles and Oxford: University of California Press, 1991.

Die Spiele. *The official report of the Organizing Committee for the Games of the XXth Olympiad.* Munich: Pro Sport, 1972.

Drevon, A. *Les Jeux olympiques oubliés: Paris 1900*. Paris: CNRS, 2000.

Ebid, M. 'Femmes et sport dans les pays mediterraneens'. Paper presented at the Euromediterranean Conference on Women and Sport, 23–25 Nov. 2000, Nice, France.

El Faquir, F. Sport in North Africa: Voices of Moroccan Female Athletes. In *Muslim Women and Sport*, edited by T. Benn, G. Pfister and H. Jawad. London: Routledge, 2010 (in press).

El-Houda Karfoul, N. Women and Sport in Syria. In *Muslim Women and Sport*, edited by T. Benn, G. Pfister and H. Jawad. London: Routledge, 2010 (in press).

Hacisoftaoglu, I. 'Newspaper Coverage of Naturalized Athletes in Turkey: The Case of Elvan Abeylegesse'. Unpublished paper, 2009.

Hargreaves, J., *Sporting Females: Critical Issues in the History and Sociology of Women's Sports.* London: Routledge, 1994.

Hargreaves, J. *Heroines of Sport: The Politics of difference and Identity*. London: Routledge. 2000.

Hargreaves, J. 'Sport, Exercise, and the Female Muslim Body: Negotiating Islam, Politics and Male Power'. In *Physical Culture, Power, and the Body*, edited by J. Hargreaves and P. Vertinsky. London: Routledge, 2007: 74–100.

Khader N. *Ære og skam*. København: Borgens Forlag, 2006.

Koca, C. and I. Hacisoftaoglu. 'Struggling for Empowerment – Sport Participation of Women and Girls in Turkey'. In *Muslim Women and Sport,* edited by T. Benn, G. Pfister and H. Jawad. London: Routledge, 2010 (in press).

Koca, C. and I. Hacisoftaoglu. 'Religion, the State and Sport: The Story of a Turkish Elite Athlete'. In *Muslim Women and Sport,* edited by T. Benn, G. Pfister and H. Jawad. London: Routledge, 2010 (in press).

Koushki Jahromi, M. 'Physical Activities and Sport of Women in Iran'. In *Muslim Women and Sport,* edited by T. Benn, G. Pfister and H. Jawad. London: Routledge, 2010 (in press).

Lindsay, K., S. McEwan and J. Knight. 'Islamic Principles and Physical Education'. *Unicorn* 13, no. 2 (1986): 75–8.

Lopez, S. 'Sport and Society in the Middle East: An Alternate Narrative of Middle Eastern History for the American College Classroom'. *Middle East Critique* 18, no. 3 (2009): 251–60.

Nakamura Y. 'Beyond the Hijab: Female Muslims and Physical Activity'. *Women in Sport & Physical Activity Journal* 11 (2002): 21–48.

Pfister, G. 'Frauen und Sport in der Türkei'. In *Ethnisch-Kulturelle Konflikte im Sport,* edited by M. Klein and J. Kothy. Hamburg: Czwalina 1997: 127–45.

Pfister G. 'Doing Sport in a Headscarf? German Sport and Turkish Females'. *Journal of Sport History* 27, no. 3 (2000): 497–525.

Pfister, G., 'Women and the Olympic Games'. In *Women in Sport,* edited by B. Drinkwater. Oxford: Blackwell, 2000: 3–19.

Pfister, G., 'Women and Sport in Iran: Keeping Goal in the Hijab'. In: Hartmann- Tews I. and G. Pfister eds. *Sport and Women. Social Issues in International Perspective.* London: Routledge, 2003, 207–223.

Pfister, G. 'Islamic Countries' Women's Sport Solidarity Games'. In *Berkshire Encyclopedia of World Sport,* Vol. 2, edited by D. Levinson and K. Christensen, 844–7. Great Barrington, MA: Berkshire Publishing Group, 2005.

Pfister, G. 'Women and Sport in Islamic Countries'. Forum for Idræt, Historie og Samfund, 2010, 35–49.

Pfister, G. 'Muslim Women in the Diaspora: Sport related Theories, Discourses and Practices – Analysing the Situation in Denmark'. In *Muslim Women and Sport,* edited by T. Benn, G. Pfister and H. Jawad. London: Routledge, 2010 (in press).

Ran Oppenheim, Marc. 'Twilight of Colonial Ethos: The Alexandria Sporting Club , 1890–1956'. PhD thesis, Columbia University, 1991.

Schiffauer, W. *Die Gewalt der Ehre.* Frankfurt: Suhrkamp 1983.

Schirrmacher, C. and U. Spuler-Stegemann. *Frauen und die Scharia.* München: Goldmann, 2006.

Spuler-Stegemann, U. *Muslime in Deutschland.* Freiburg: Herder, 1998.

Veal, A.J. and K. Toohey. 'The Olympic Games: A Bibliography'. Sydney: Australian Centre for Olympic Studies, University of Technology, Sydney, available at www.business.uts.edu.au/lst/research/research_papers.html, accessed 29 March 2010.

Walseth, K. 'Young Muslim Women and Sport: The Impact of Identity Work'. *Leisure Studies* 25, no. 1 (2006): 75–94.

Wamsley, K. and G. Pfister. 'Olympic Men and Women: The Politics of Gender in the Modern Games'. In *Global Olympics: Historical and Sociological Studies of the Modern Games,* edited by Kevin Young, Kevin and Kevin B. Wamsley (Research in the Sociology of Sport, vol. 3). Amsterdam: Elsevier JAI, 2005.

'Team GB' and London 2012: The Paradox of National and Global Identities

Iain MacRury and Gavin Poynter

This article explores the problems associated with 'national identity' in the UK and examines the tensions arising between the international and local dimensions of the games through examples of domestic (UK) and international (Brazil, Chicago) media coverage of the key debates relating to London's period of preparation. The chapter proposes a conception of London 2012 as exemplar of an event poised to generate insights and experiences connected to a new politics of 'cosmopolitan' identity; insights central to grasping the cultural politics of contemporary urban development – and the paradoxes of national identity in current discourses of Olympism.

> Properly speaking, cosmopolitanism suits those people who have no country, while internationalism should be the state of mind of those who love their country above all, who seek to draw to it the friendship of foreigners by professing for the countries of those foreigners an intelligent and enlightened sympathy. [1]

Introduction

According to Tessa Jowell, the UK's Olympics minister, the inclusive character of Britain's cultural identity was an essential ingredient of London's bid to host the 2012 Olympics:

> [O]ur success as a nation has in no small part been based on the fact that we have been willing to embrace new people, new ideas and new influences. Individual differences have never diminished the concept of Britishness; in fact, I'd go as far to say that our differences have always enhanced us, as a nation,

and helped to make us who we are ... we define ourselves increasingly in terms of our common values – fairness, openness and tolerance. ... And it was this spirit of inclusive British cultural identity that won us the right to host the Olympics. [2]

The bid stressed the nurturing of 'grass-roots' involvement in sport and the value of hosting the event in multicultural east London, a relatively deprived area of the city. The young people, from the London borough of Newham, who accompanied the bid team to their presentation of London's pitch in Singapore, symbolized the bid's aspirations and its projected legacy. London's bid captured the imagination of the International Olympic Committee (IOC) members, providing, perhaps, a timely contrast to China's confident re-assertion of its international standing and national identity as host of the 2008 games.

London's success occurred in the wake of Britain's participation in a war in Iraq that had attracted considerable international condemnation. There were also rising domestic concerns about citizenship and what is meant by being 'British', concerns prompted in part by responses to the perceived threats arising in the wake of terrorist attacks in London and recent patterns of immigration within the enlarged European Union. The hosting of the 2012 games provided an opportunity for the UK government and the organizers of London 2012 to appropriate the event, and sport more generally, to engage in the redefining of Britain's national identity both domestically and in relation to the perceptions of the rest of the world. The claim to social inclusiveness rested easily with the bid's ambition to utilize the 2012 games as a catalyst of urban renewal in a multi-ethnic and socially deprived area of East London – one where recent successes for the far-right British National Party in European Elections point to a resurgence, expressed at the fringe of the political sphere, of a deep-seated set of tensions around identity, belonging and ethnicity.

This contribution provides a preliminary assessment of the attempt to use the London 2012 Olympics, and sport more generally, as a vehicle for redefining Britain's national identity, in the domestic sphere and within the international community, during a period of significant turmoil in the global economy and in the relationships between the 'advanced' and 'emerging' nations in the world. The first section identifies the problems of national identity facing 'Team GB'; how these have surfaced in the preparations for 2012 and in the domestic social and political debates concerning devolution, citizenship and 'Britishness'. The second section examines how two other cities and nations, each located in different continents, have perceived and reported London's preparations for 2012, comparing and contrasting their aspirations to host the summer Olympics in 2016 with those of the UK. The final section provides some initial conclusions concerning the utilization of the world's leading sporting event to assist Britain's political and social leaders in achieving a 'new' politics of identity in the UK and in presenting a new image to the rest of the world.

'Team GB' and the National Identity Problem

'I am determined to work with the football associations and the Olympic Committee to ensure that when we come to 2012 we have a men's football team and we have a women's football team playing,' Mr Brown said.

The SNP's sport spokesman in Westminster Pete Wishart said: 'This is a spectacular own goal for Brown. He is out of touch with the overwhelming views of football supporters throughout the UK.

'All the national supporters groups oppose this move and see it as a threat to the status of their nations to field independent football squads.' [3]

Scottish opposition to Prime Minister Brown's wish to see a 'Team GB' playing football in the 2012 Olympics reflects the paradox of identity that contemporary Britain faces when it comes to participation in international sporting events. Britain consists of England, Wales, Northern Ireland and Scotland. Each of these have national teams who compete in a wide range of sports, but for the Olympics these 'nations' come together, as in the 2008 games, as the brand 'Team GB'.

Since the inception of the modern Olympics in 1896, Britain has consisted of one team drawn from the nations that created the Union of Great Britain and Ireland in 1801 (modified to the Union of Great Britain and Northern Ireland following the formation of the Irish Free State in 1921). While England has historically been the dominant nation in this alliance, English and British national identities have been typically considered as synonymous. In the nineteenth century, at the peak of the British Empire, the English/British bourgeoisie created a 'model' for several sports and their organization, exporting this to many other parts of the world, and used sporting activities to enhance social integration and the class order that underpinned the power relations of the empire. The British 'model' contained several complex dimensions that constituted the 'foundation for modern sports', not least of which was the conception that it was through participation in sporting activities that a person could learn how to be a gentleman. [4] As Kidd makes clear in his attempt to historicize and demystify imputed continuities between ancient Olympic traditions and de Coubertin's modern Olympic Games, [5] there were numerous cross-overs tying the development of precepts central to early modern Olympism directly to debates around culture, sport, national character and the English gentleman in the middle and later decades of the Victorian nineteenth century. Smith and Porter argue convincingly that 'It is impossible to overlook the role of British teams, associations, and models in the formal development of the Olympic Games'. [6]

In the long process of the British Empire's unravelling, some nations, including the United States and Ireland, sought to escape historic ties and this form of cultural imperialism by developing their own sporting activities and associations. [7] Echoes of this historical resistance may be found in the Scottish response to Prime Minister Gordon Brown's aspiration to field British football teams in the 2012 Olympic Games. The model of inclusivity that rested with an imperial past was clearly outdated by the end of the twentieth century; the Scottish Football Association's opposition to a 'Team GB' being only one of many challenges to the integrity and inclusivity of British national identity.

Inclusivity is an elusive concept. Its role and meaning has changed over time for Britain's political and social elites. At the height of the British Empire, British imperial consciousness overcame the parochial interests of the specific nations of the British Isles. [8] The British industrial revolution and the expansion of the empire across the world helped to forge a British ruling class and an imperial service that was staffed by Scots, Welsh, Irish and English. As Kumar has argued, empire builders are reticent in promoting their specific national identity, but this is not born of modesty – 'indeed the opposite. This missionary, or imperial, nationalism engaged with a civilizational project of world-historic-importance'. [9] Identity with Britain and 'Britishness' was less important to the creators of the empire than it was to those whom it conquered. Inclusiveness rested with the acceptance by the conquered of being part of a much greater civilizational project and knowing their social position within it.

In the wake of the demise of the empire in the second half of the twentieth century, the question of national identity within the British Isles has surfaced in various ways. In the political sphere, for example, with the re-emergence of nationalist movements in Northern Ireland, Scotland and Wales, a Scottish parliament and Welsh assembly have been established to address demands for greater independence, while the 'peace process' in Northern Ireland has witnessed the restoration of its assembly. In their response to demands for devolution and the modernization of the constitution and growing social concerns, especially about the younger generation's attachment to Britain, government spokespersons have replaced the 'old' paternal inclusivity of empire with a 'new' egalitarian vision of 'social inclusivity' as a defining characteristic of Britishness. . As Smith and Porter [10] underline, the Commonwealth Games – previously called the British Empire and Commonwealth Games – have permitted, in the twentieth century, an ongoing and active articulation of national sporting identities and differences within the UK, under the (formal and latent) umbrella of 'empire', while also articulating increasingly attenuated (post)colonial links.

Inclusivity, in this social context, acknowledges that citizens may hold dual identities as, for example, Welsh/British or Asian/British, though this duality may also reflect different degrees of the feeling of belonging to Britain, especially for the younger generation of ethnic-minority citizens. [11] This vision of inclusivity was reflected in the values that informed the government's support for hosting the 2012 games: 'We want to harness the power of sport to help address some of the key issues our nation faces – health, social inclusion, educational motivation and fighting crime.' [12] Inclusion has been re-defined with the emergence of multiculturalism as a central characteristic of a new British identity. This new approach seeks to integrate different cultures and traditions into a 'creative' society that has distanced itself from its imperial past and the rigid social hierarchies that were intimately associated with it.

Successive Labour governments, since their return to political power in 1997, have been concerned to foster this sense of belonging or attachment to Britain, especially among young people and in particular those from lower social class and income backgrounds. [13] The preparations for London 2012 have reflected this concern in several ways, including in the commitment to achieve a lasting social legacy in east London, in the promotion of sports participation and volunteering across the UK and even in the choice of design of the 2012 logo, a dynamic brand aimed specifically to be attractive to young people: 'The new emblem is dynamic, modern and flexible reflecting a brand savvy world where people, especially young people, no longer relate to static logos but respond to a dynamic brand that works with new technology and across traditional and new media networks.' [14] Noticeably the 2012 Olympic logo, unlike the imagery surrounding the pre-2005 city candidacy and the 'back-the-bid' marketing campaigns, has largely eschewed the patriotic, flag-waving colour palette (red, white and blue), in favour of vivid, jarring greens and pinks. One marketing expert interprets this refusal of the 'obvious' colour choices in terms of London as a diverse metropolis: 'The colours reflect the diversity of the city which is absolutely right. It would have been an obvious move if we had seen a variation on the nationalistic red, white and blue, or simply adopted the Olympic colours.' [15]

This re-presentation of British national identity around London 2012 attempts to achieve a difficult balance between a domestic agenda informed by sport serving the needs of a wider social policy and the international promotion of London as a 'global city' and Britain as a leading nation in the world with a heritage that is reflected in some of the iconic venues chosen to host specific events in London for the games. The dual, and perhaps conflicting, themes of heritage and an inclusive, youthful modernity were reflected in London's handover ceremony conducted at the end of the Beijing games. A classic London red bus delivered a multicultural troop of young dancers whose 'hip hop' routines were designed to reflect the modern face of a 'creative' capital city – although the perhaps inadvertent cultural reference to Cliff Richard in *Summer Holiday* (1962) may have undermined the success of this gesture towards urban-contemporary cultures.

The international promotion of London is equally complex and potentially contentious when considered from the perspective of the relations between city, state and nation. London may be seen as a cosmopolitan zone, an important hub in a new international social order that is focused upon the role of great 'city states'. [16] The networks or relationships between these cities are the dominant feature of the social organization of this new order. The nation state is in decline. Such a perspective complements the principles of Olympism in so far as the latter seeks to rise above the narrow interests and outlook of nationalism and promote universal humanistic values. London's cosmopolitan character and its identity as an international hub or metropole may sit well with the aspirations of Olympism and the interests of an IOC familiar with the hazards of the host city using the games to aggressively promote nationhood but it may also serve, domestically, to (further) distance London from the rest of the UK. The value of London 2012 as a vehicle for establishing a new

'British' identity is at once diminished; hence the concern of its organizers to stress the value of the games to all parts of Britain. The institution of a regions-based structure for delivering the Cultural Olympiad and the emphasis given to the geographic distribution of events (notably soccer, in stadiums nationwide) has not so far, or convincingly, offset the institutionally metropolitan character of 2012, as the *London* games.

In summary, the Olympic Games provide the host nation with an opportunity to re-present itself to its own population and to the wider world. For the Labour government and the organizers of 2012, the key themes of the games and its legacy were associated with achieving an ambitious domestic agenda that stressed the regeneration of a multi-ethnic and relatively poor part of London and the achievement of a wider social and cultural renewal founded upon a new politics of identity, the egalitarian inclusivity of multiculturalism. [17] This new form of British identity has been promoted in a variety of ways, including via the branding of 'Cool Britannia' in the late 1990s, but perhaps its clearest exposition has been in the sporting context, and in particular in the public discussions concerning the preparations for London 2012. As has been noted, this process is fraught with duality and perhaps contradiction. The extent to which this re-defining of British national identity has been successful may be examined by looking at how other cities and nations who are also engaged in bidding for the summer games have reported and been influenced by London's preparations for 2012.

Chicago 2016

An IOC evaluation team, visiting Chicago in March 2009, considered the city's bid for the 2016 games to be strong. The bid was supported by President Obama (a long-time resident of the city) and other sporting and media celebrities, including Oprah Winfrey, who hosted a dinner for the IOC team. In a reference to the London 2012 bid team's deployment of the Queen to host a similar event in the lead-up to the decision concerning the 2012 bids, one city daily reported that Oprah was the nearest 'we' had to a Queen [18] The Chicago bid contained other features comparable to London's, in particular, with its emphasis on Chicago being a dynamic and multicultural city, 'a city of immigrants' [19] and one in which there is a strong commitment to involving urban youth in sport participation. Like a number of candidate cites in recent rounds, and like London and Barcelona perhaps in particular, Chicago faces some of the challenges peculiar to post-industrial reconstruction, with the games heralded as part of an address to a nexus of social policy problems that links employment, education, patterns of leisure and consumption, social cohesion, land use and environmental concerns.

The Chicago bid aspired to delivering a 'blue/green' games; blue representing the fresh water lakeside location of the city and the green its extensive parklands; and together these themes were designed to reflect the city's commitment to the environment and the achievement of a sustainable games. The Olympic event sites were mainly focused upon the city's lakeside area creating a compact games location that would not, unlike London, require significant investment in infrastructure, except in transportation, an area of concern noted by the IOC when it announced that Chicago was one of the four international finalists in June 2008. This was reflected in the bid's projected overall cost of $4.8 billion, approximately a third of the projected total cost of the London games. The bid also stressed the opportunity to redevelop Chicago's south and west sides, leaving a lasting urban renewal legacy. [20]

The Chicago plan envisaged four venue clusters located within a 15km radius of the Olympic village with the main Olympic stadium constructed in the Southside's Washington Park. The funding for the games was primarily focused upon securing private-sector support with the city providing a guarantee of $500 million to meet contingencies and a further $125 million from the sale of public assets (owned by the Metropolitan Pier and Exposition Authority – McPier) that would go directly toward meeting Olympic construction costs. Chicago's design for the Olympics drew upon Barcelona's experience of keeping the games venues in close proximity and integral to the city's centre while also opening up the waterfront for development and after-games leisure use.

In the year following the announcement of Chicago achieving the status of a finalist in the race to be awarded the games by the IOC, the city's plans had evolved in several ways, particularly in response to IOC evaluations. The IOC, in addition to expressing concerns about transportation, also expressed doubts about the low level of the construction budgets for the four main Olympic venues and that the wording of Chicago's financial guarantees did not comply fully with the Olympic Charter. [21] In response to these concerns, the Chicago organizers refined construction plans, focusing upon costs and sustainability, and developed more specific proposals for the post-games use of games facilities. The main stadium, an 80,000-seat facility, was projected to be reduced to a smaller athletics facility post-games while other plans, which increasingly emphasized a community legacy, included the possibility of providing a new pool for a local high school and the conversion of an armory, to be used during the games as a staging area for athletes and performers, to become an indoor recreation centre for community use.

There was some evidence that Chicago's increased commitment to 'legacy' had arisen, in part, from a dialogue with the organizers of London 2012, alongside the heightened signalling around 'legacy' from the IOC over recent years. [22] In May 2008 it was announced that Chicago was considering reusing parts of London's Olympic stadium by importing 55,000 seats at the end of the 2012 games. This proposal, designed to address concerns about Olympic cities being left with white elephants post-games, was complemented by the adjustment of legacy plans which emphasized the positive benefits of urban renewal and a post-games legacy designed to benefit young people and encourage them to engage in sports activities. In autumn 2008, leading figures in Chicago's bid, acknowledged that they had held several meetings with Lord Coe, the chair of London's Olympic Organising Committee, and that these meetings had focused on sharing experiences and identifying 'things to do and not to do'. Through these exchanges, it was recognized that the Chicago strategy had similarities to that of London 2012:

> Ryan said that Chicago's bid contained a similar strategy to London by planning to leave a regenerated urban area once the games are over. 'London also did a great job selling the legacy as a benefit to the youth of the world..We are not copying them but it is a natural thing to do.' [23]

At first sight, therefore, it seems that the Chicago bid was influenced by London's experience in perhaps three main ways. First, the bid had taken heed of the negative debates concerning the escalating costs of the London games. The Chicago budget included a $500 million city guarantee and a separate tranche of public funds arising from the sale of public assets by the Metropolitan Pier and Exposition Authority, a government agency, which would have contributed about $125 million to the Chicago games. The balance of funding, however, was clearly 'tilted toward' wealthy individuals and corporations, [24] in contrast to the London games, which rely heavily upon public funding, especially in the wake of the credit crunch and subsequent economic recession. Second, the Chicago bid had been informed of the favourable response that the IOC gave to the aspirations of London 2012 which stressed the multicultural nature of east London and the significance of increasing young people's participation in sport. This is reflected in the Chicago team's development of legacy plans, including the specific commitments given to providing community facilities on the Olympic Park site after the games. Finally, the proposed legacy arising from the 2016 games included a programme of urban renewal, though the scope of the Chicago 2016 committee's commitment had been criticized as rather narrow. [25] In this sense, as the Chicago bid had been refined and developed so a legacy discourse had emerged that had drawn upon London's experience. The language and approach shared a common concern of many major cosmopolitan cities in the West, to sustain social integration in circumstances where there are significant disparities in income, wealth and social status, particularly for ethnic minority groups and their younger generations. While the patterns of inequality arise from the specific histories of cities such as London and Chicago, the social and political elites within these cosmopolitan centres have recognized the value of sport and the hosting of major sporting events as a means of enhancing social integration and legitimizing schemes for urban development and renewal.

Underpinning Chicago's bid, however, was the recognition that the city was seeking international status, a designation that London already enjoys. Patrick Ryan, the founder and chief executive of Aon Corporation, a leading international insurance broker company based in Chicago and, alongside Chicago's mayor, Richard Daley, a major figure in the Chicago bid, stressed this point on hearing of Chicago's success in beating Los Angeles and San Francisco to become the US Olympic Committee's candidate for the 2016 games: 'I think what's at stake is an opportunity for Chicago to really be exposed broadly to the world for all its beauty, charm, its attributes, its culture, its welcoming people. Big international acceptance – that's at stake here.' [26]

Rio de Janeiro 2016 [27]

At a meeting of IOC members in March 2009, Carlos Nuzman, President of Brazil's Olympic bid committee, outlined the strengths of the Rio bid to his audience:

> We can offer a new country and a new continent experiencing the Games. A nation with 65 million people under the age of 18 and a continent of 180 million young people. We can offer a very favorable time zone for broadcasters, new markets for sponsors and a stage like no other to host the Games. We can build a bridge from London 2012 to Rio 2016, passing the baton to pursue the mission of inspiring young people all around the world. [28]

Rio's candidature for the 2016 games followed the country's hosting of the Pan American Games in 2007 and its success in securing the FIFA World Cup soccer finals taking place in 2014. The city was considered to be an early front-runner in the competition to host the 2016 Olympics, though the IOC's Candidature Acceptance Working Group report, published in March 2008, placed the city fourth (behind Tokyo, Madrid and Chicago) in its comparative evaluation of the seven cities that sought to host the games. [29]

Rio's bid, titled 'Show your Passion', focused upon the unique qualities of the festive city of Rio de Janeiro and emphasized that a successful bid would ensure that the games would take place on the South American continent for the first time. The candidature file had several key themes. First, and most importantly, reflecting its demographic profile, the bid was oriented to an engagement with Brazil's young. It expressed clearly how sport may be 'a transformation tool for social inclusion and education'. [30] Second, the catalytic effect of hosting the games on the city's infrastructure and, in particular, improving its deprived areas was stressed. Third, the bid highlighted the growing importance of Brazil as the seventh largest economy in the world and how hosting the games would affirm the country's rising global status. Fourth, Brazil's regional role in sports development was underlined by a commitment to further develop training and support facilities for the continent's athletes. The facilities that were first established for the 2007 Pan American Games would be upgraded to provide a regional 'sports hub' incorporating a National Olympic Training Centre for around 20 sports post-Games and an 'X-Park' for high performance training and community involvement. [31] Finally, the bid underlined the environmental improvements that hosting the games would bring, including improvements to waterways, air quality, waste management and land encroachment. [32]

In the IOC Working Party report, Rio scored highly in the governance category, reflecting that the application was presented jointly by the National Olympic

Committee and all three levels of government – federal, state and city. Financial guarantees for the games were underwritten by the national government, with the games' related costs being estimated at $2.8 billion and infrastructure developments estimated at $14.4 billion. The proposed games venues divide into four zones – the Barra (the Rio Olympic Park precinct), Deodoro, Maracana and Copacabana Beach – with 12 new sports venues being built in the period up to 2015. The IOC Working Party's assessment of the Rio bid identified relative weaknesses in security, a concern arising from high levels of crime in the city, and accommodation: the shortage of three-, four- and five-star hotel rooms and the proposed use of cruise ships to meet demand. Rio's bid achieved a similar score to Chicago's while the technical quality of Madrid and, in particular, Tokyo, placed these two cities in the leading positions.

Necessarily, the candidate files address a pre-defined IOC template and, therefore, focus upon common themes. In the period since its short listing, however, the Rio bid team and its government partners at city, regional and national levels focused in particular upon legacy and the role of mega events in catalysing improvements in the socio-economic and cultural life of a city. [33] This discourse reflects the emergence of Rio de Janeiro as a global city in the last decade for whom the process of urbanization, population growth and economic expansion, including the expansion of a significant informal economy, has exacerbated the long-standing problems of social segregation, street crime and violence and the trend towards a middle class that establishes itself in relatively secure and gated enclaves within the city and its suburbs. There is, however, strong evidence of the city's political, intellectual and business leadership's commitment to strategic planning to address these issues.

The first strategic plan was implemented between 1993 and 1996 and this was followed by a second version in 2001–4, 'As cidades da Cidade', that involved the specification of 12 regional strategic plans for different parts of the city which recognize their specific historic patterns of socio-economic development and engages with local communities in creating public/private partnerships for local development projects. The innovative nature of this plan includes the monitoring of its implementation by independent university research teams and community-based institutions, the promotion of the cultural industries and scientific and technological research facilities to support the development of new industries and sectors of employment and the engagement of local communities in the financial and budgetary processes required for the delivery of local projects. [34] Complementing these local projects, other projects, reflective of the city's ambitions for enhancing its international status, were devised for constructing a Guggenheim Museum in Rio and developing the waterfront, with the latter project drawing inspiration from the successful developments undertaken in Barcelona in preparation for its hosting of the Olympic and Paralympic Games in 1992. The Guggenheim proposal, in particular, met with significant criticism from within Brazil, with critics arguing that the financial support that such an iconic project would demand would divert much needed investment away from more pressing social needs such as housing, infrastructure and education and would threaten the future of existing, smaller, cultural institutions already located in the city. [35]

Perhaps Rio's bid to host the 2016 games reflects the city, regional and national governments intentions to address such concerns, to reconcile the desire to utilize iconic events to promote the city's global status with the urgent need to address its underlying social, economic and environmental problems. In this context, London 2012 is a useful exemplar. The Brazilian authorities have over recent years drawn upon the experiences of major international cities when developing strategic plans for urban development. The hosting of the 2007 Pan American Games reflected the city and nation's recognition of the value of sport, and sports mega-events, as a potential catalyst for urban renewal and the promotion of social integration. The bid to host the Olympics in 2016 was consistent with this outlook and London's success in securing the 2012 games based upon its emphasis on the 'soft' legacies of youth participation in sport, social inclusivity and the celebration of multi-culturalism has influenced public discussion and clearly informed the 'legacy debate' within Brazil. [36]

Part 3: London 2012 and its Cosmopolitan' Legacy

> London's not just about crime, you don't just look at London and see crime … it's a good city. … It's about people from different countries, you know; being one, and you know, being united … yeah, being united. [37]
>
> The mood and cityscape of the early twenty-first century that … we see as we move through London's public and private spaces, could not have been imagined by the social scientists fifty years ago … one thing this domestic visceral cosmopolitanism may offer is a new image in the world, a new way of being modern, a supranational national identity, a means by which to counter Britain's old and new imperial projects. [38]

In conclusion, there is evidence that London 2012 has generated a new dimension to the discussion of 'legacy' through its expression of a reformulated national identity that is based upon programmes designed to enhance social inclusivity and cohesion in the cosmopolitan city. In their specific historic contexts, a brief review of the Chicago and Rio de Janeiro proposals for 2016 suggests that London's 'cosmopolitan' legacy discourse has found some resonance in cities seeking to host future summer games and achieve recognition of a global status in the twenty-first century. Such cities are currently confronted by multiple challenges, multi-ethnic urban conflicts, an attenuation of national state government authority and a fracturing of confidence in national identity as a substantial resource for attachment and orientation; London 2012 seeks to address these issues. [39] This concluding section develops this perspective through returning to a brief consideration of the promises made in contemporary bid presentations and to the foundational principles and debates concerning the 'international mission' of de Coubertin's Olympic movement.

One argument is that the Olympics merely provide governments, and adjacent power-brokers, with a proxy vehicle for governance and urban renewal, serving as a mask to legitimate 'big' government interventions in city planning; a means of bypassing enfeebled and moribund public systems of local and municipal governance and accountability. [40] In this reading the Olympics serve not to bolster living, complex communities, but to resuscitate the categorical clichés of modern state government in the face of crisis and exhaustion. The Olympics perform a propping-up job, on behalf of a failing modernity.

In such a conception it is easy to dismissively identify London's leaders' Olympic appeals to grass-roots multiculturalism as a cynical indulgence in classic liberal rhetoric, empty justifications broadcast to legitimate grandiose policy decisions and massive expenditures – likewise in Rio and Chicago. There may be some substance in such critiques. However, to accept too readily that city-wide and national expressions of optimistic enthusiasm for hosting the Olympics are simply derived from the manipulation of public sentiment is to succumb to an all too familiar dismissal of popular sensibility. The 'national' love of sport – and of Olympic sport in particular – is neither simple nor simplistic; we would argue that it points to a contemporary recognition of the unique power of sport to adumbrate and articulate everyday complexities and intensities attaching to contemporary local, national and personal identities.

A hint that a cynical dismissal of Olympic boosterism may not provide an exhaustive address to a complex topic lies, for instance, in a growing sense of a genuine popular engagement with the London Olympics. [41] There is evidence of popular support, in anticipation at least, for an optimistic sense of the games as a credible vehicle for positive change in the city. It should be noted however, that when asked about a key cultural benefit of the games, 'bringing people together through sport', only 3 per cent of Londoners felt this was the most important outcome of 2012. [42]

A further recent small and exploratory study [43] has examined the extent to which the 'grass-roots' populations invoked by politicians engage with and are engaged by the promises made about change and London's 'multicultural' Olympic legacy. The evidence base is small, but there is, in respondents' testimonies, a sense of a detailed, reflexive engagement with some of the issues raised by politicians regarding community building, explored in this chapter. Notably such issues link to questions of identity and belonging in the (changing) city.

It is clear from a preliminary review of these focus group discussions that populations in east London are highly alert to the significance of the games in relation to a deep-seated local experience – living in a multicultural, multi-ethnic city. Their reflections provide insights into the ways local people anticipate the impact of the Olympics in articulating the paradoxes of identity: reframing and reconstructing identities – at a personal level, across the city and its various areas, and in terms of English, UK and the global conceptions of 'London' in 2012. In among some considered scepticism, the Olympic Games serve as an object of hope and aspiration, enabling respondents to project optimistic future scenarios for the city. In many instances there is an appeal to the idea that the Olympics will mobilize 'unity'; as that goodwill emergent around the excitement of the events will induce a broader effect, one that will reduce the sense of unease that contributes to an ongoing characterization of east London localities as 'dangerous', and where gang violence is a threatening reality. What might this have to do with Olympism, not to say any re-figuring of Olympic ideas?

The Olympics, Cosmopolitanism and New Urbanities

> Olympism emerged as a mixture of aristocratic, modern, cosmopolitan and nationalistic ideas. [44]

As Kidd points out, the de Coubertin Olympic games are 'an important part of world culture' reaching media audiences across the globe and drawing attention to the 'knotty' problems of division and belonging:

> The question of whether the Olympic Games unite men, as Coubertin thought, or divide them, as Maurras insisted, has been from the very first that they do both (MacAloon 1981: 269). Amongst other things, it is the emergent function of the Olympics (as London should witness in 2012) to help refigure, traverse and rehearse knotty paradoxes of identity and identification – an unfolding and refolding of the 'Modern' categories of inter- and intra-national identities. [45]

It is important to remember that while sport is political, sport is not directly politics. There is a means, perhaps distinctive to sporting cultural events, which enables peculiar and widespread modes and means of engagement. Smith and Porter argue that

> the physical, competitive, supra-linguistic, and populist nature of most sports have made them perfect media for the expression of group identities. Sports are places in which groups can find peaceful physical fora for the beliefs they hold about themselves as entities, a feature that much sports historiography has linked to Benedict Anderson's model of the 'imagined community'. [46]

It may be that an extension of the valuable conception of 'imagined community' can be found in Nava's conception of a 'visceral' cosmopolitanism. While for Nava, sports seem not to feature as a resource for the affirmation of the affective connectedness she highlights within her conception of an embodied cosmopolitan, there is no reason not to see sport as a highly fertile site for affective engagement and informal, developmentally rich, cultural connectivity.

The 2012 Olympics offers a unique opportunity to refresh, restore and reframe 'London' in the national and global imagination. Likewise London can refigure Olympism, asserting the increasing presence and puissance of cosmopolitan urbanities/urbanites as a twenty-first-century counterpart to de Coubertin's 'modernist ideal' – the English gentleman. Nava offers a personal account of her engagement with London:

> London, my city, is much more comfortable with its cultural and racial mixing, with merger, hybridity and conviviality, with its acknowledgement of differ-ence ... its multiple connections to elsewhere, with its everyday ordinary visceral cosmopolitanism (despite the persistence and sometimes escalation of divisions) than is any other city in the Western world ... cultural texts and rituals are required in order to sustain these social worlds ... expressive work of acknowl-edging others and performing mutuality. [47]

As Carrington has argued, the Olympics offer a grand-scale opportunity for the performative expressivity Nava has associated with 'visceral cosmopolitanism'. He argues that the Olympics offer 'opportunities to realize a sense of global, post-national belonging that is grounded in the politics of the local, the city, the regional'. These temporary moments of intensive reciprocal engagement, mediated by sports, allow for the expression and exploration of 'wider solidarities' and for 'new senses of self to be formed'. Carrington concludes that 'the fact that such a politics remains indeterminate is all the more reason to see Olympism as a possible site for progressive forms of intervention'. [48]

In London 2012's adoption, delivery and performance of this informal, Olympic-cultural function there is evidence of an experiential affirmation of cosmopolitan insight and affection: in a space which will necessarily, also, provide and provoke telling articulations of conflict and controversy. The 2012 games' capacity to contain such conflicts, centred on and within 'global' cosmopolitan London, and east London in particular, and creatively nourish the national imagination depends upon an active alertness to the tensions and paradoxes that constitute the city in the twenty-first century. The explicit commitments made to grass-roots 'multicultural' London announced in the bid presentation in Singapore in 2005 may be fulfilled through the re-evaluation and practical acknowledgement of London as a resource of cosmo-politan cultural capital, a kind of developmental crossroads for national and post-national life. Such an achievement would take its place as a major 'intangible' legacy, whose discourse has, we suggest, already influenced presentations by other candidate cities such as Rio and Chicago. This component of London's Olympic legacy is a necessary complement to the tangible culturally-developmental outcomes claimed for London's games. Positive urban development may be founded upon a cosmopolitan east side that is emerging via a process of urban regeneration in one of the world's global cities. Such a development is an important aspect of any genuinely regenerative and lasting legacy for London that may arise from hosting the 2012 games.

Acknowledgements

The authors wish to acknowledge and thank Fabiana Rodrigues de Souza for her research into and translation of source materials on Rio de Janeiro's 2016 bid.

Notes

[1] de Coubertin, 'Does Cosmopolitan Life Lead to International Friendliness?', cited in Carrington, 'Cosmopolitan Olympism'.

[2] Olympics Minister Tessa Jowell, 'Capturing the Value of Heritage', speech to the Royal Geographical Society, January 2006, available at http://www.culture.gov.uk/reference_library/minister_speeches/2063.aspx, accessed 23 April 2009.

[3] 'Brown Wants British Football eam at 2012 Olympics', *The Scotsman*, 23 August 2008, available at http://thescotsman.scotsman.com/latestnews/Brown-wants-British-football-team.4421659.jp, accessed 17 April 2009.

[4] Scambler, *Sport and Society*, 36–42; Kumar, 1–17.

[5] Kidd, 'Recapturing Alternative Olympic Histories', 144–7.

[6] Smith and Porter, *Sport and National Identity*, 13.

[7] Bairner, *Sport and the Irish. Histories, Identities, Issues*.

[8] Kumar, *The Making of English National Identity*, 174.

[9] Ibid.

[10] Smith and Porter, *Sport and National Identity*, 13.

[11] Heath and Roberts, 'British Identity'.

[12] Tessa Jowell, 'London 2012 Olympics Statement to the House of Commons', 15 May 2003, available at http://www.culture.gov.uk/reference_library/minister_speeches/2103.aspx, accessed 1 May 2009.

[13] Heath and Roberts, 'British Identity'.

[14] LOCOG, 'New Brand and Vision revealed for London 2012 Olympic and Paralympic Games', 4 June 2007, available to http://www.london2012.com/news/media-releases/2007/2007-06/new-brand-and-vision-revealed-for-london-2012-olympic-ga.php, accessed 2 May 2009.

[15] T. Geoghegan, 'Oh no logo', BBC News Magazine, 5 June 2007, available at http://news.bbc.co.uk/1/hi/6719805.stm, accessed 28 July 2009.

[16] Castells, *The Network Society*; Roche, *Mega-Events and Modernity*, 232–3.

[17] Kumar, *The Making of English National Identity*, 234–5.

[18] See Gamesbids.com, 'Olympic Digest – Vancouver 2010, Chicago 2016', 3 April 2009, available at http://www.gamesbids.com/eng/other_news/1216134259.html, accessed 4 June 2009.

[19] It is important to note, however, that the historical conditions and circumstances that created Chicago's attachment to multiculturalism are fundamentally different from that of London's. Historically, Chicago's immigrants included those seeking freedom from the British Empire, the turbulence of the European mainland and the exploitative plantations of America's southern states.

[20] Chicago 2016 Candidate File, 9.

[21] P. Hersch, 'Chicago Third of Four Finalists for 2016 Olympics', *Chicago Tribune*, 4 June 2008, available at www.chicagotribune.com/sports/chi-chicago-2016-olympics-finalist,0,6779343.story, accessed 5 June 2009.

[22] MacAloon, '"Legacy" as Managerial/Magical Discourse'.

[23] Robert Booth, 'Chicago Turns to Coe in Bid for 2016 Olympics', *The Guardian*, 3 Oct. 2008, available at http://www.guardian.co.uk/sport/2008/oct/03/1, accessed 7 June 2009.

[24] Bennett *et al.*, 'Why Host the Games?', 18.

[25] Ibid. Along with the official documentation published by the Chicago 2016 Olympic Organizing Committee and other reports (see References), 58 articles from the *Chicago Tribune* were accessed for the period 30 November 2008–31 May 2009. Of these, 12 referred to London's bid and subsequent preparations. The main focus of the articles were as follows: the Chicago bid, 9; Chicago logo, 1; Park design/architecture, 7; Finance, 9; Obama election impact upon bid, 4; Creation of Chicago Olympic Committee, 1; Chicago and other competing cities, 13; Corruption, 1; IOC Visit to Chicago, 6; Community support, 5; Environment, 1; Security, 1. See http://www.chicagotribune.com/news/local/chi-chicago-olympic-bid, accessed 2–5 June 2009.

[26] Source: K. Bergen, '2016 or Bust – Chicago's Quest for the Games is an All-or-nothing Bid to Make the City a Clayer on the World Stage', *Chicago Tribune*, 14 April 2007, available at chicagotribune.com, accessed 6 June 2009.

[27] Along with the official documentation published by the Rio 2016 Olympic Organizing Committee and reports (see References), 40 articles from the newspaper *O Globo* were accessed for the period 26 September 2008–28 June 2009. Of these, two referred to London 2012. The main focus of the articles were: The Rio 2016 bid and IOC's assessment, 12; Support for the bid, 6; Rio 2016 and the hosting of other mega-events, 5; Finance and the Brazilian economy, 5; Transport, 3; Environment, 3; Security, 2; Other, 4. See http://oglobo.globo.com/, accessed 27–29 June 2009.

[28] Reuters, 'Rio 2016 Bid Committee Presents Games Vision at Sport Accord 2009', 26 March 2009, available at http://www.reuters.com/article/pressRelease/idUS14715+27-Mar-2009+ PRN20, accessed 7 Jun. 2007.

[29] IOC. Rio de Janeiro came third behind Tokyo and Madrid; it was, in fact, placed behind Doha in the final evaluation but Doha, despite the technical quality of the bid, was considered too small as a nation to host such a major sporting event and was, therefore, dropped from the final short list of four competitor cities.

[30] Rio, Brazilian Olympic Committee (2009) Rio de Janeiro 2016 Candidate File, Lausanne, IOC, 11

[31] IOC, *Games of the XXXI Olympiad*, 43.

[32] Ibid., 110.

[33] Ministerio do Esporte, *Legados De Megeventos Esportivos*; 'Projeto do Dossie Rio 2016, revitalizacao do porto transforrma area historica da citade', *O Globo*, 23 June 2009, available at http://oglobo.globo.com/rio/mat/2009/06/14/projecto-de-revitalizacao-da-zona-portuaria-sera-apresentado-no-proximo-sabado-756336065.asp, accessed 10 July 2009.

[34] Duarte, 'Large Scale Urban Projects and Dual City'.

[35] Ibid., 32.

[36] Ministerio do Esporte, *Legados De Megeventos Esportivos*, 21.

[37] Focus Group Respondent, F 14 (Walthamstow).

[38] Nava, 'Visceral Cosmopolitanism', 15.

[39] Rivenburgh, 'The Olympic Games', 46.

[40] Burbank *et al.*, *Olympic Dreams*.

[41] GLA, 'Annual London Survey 2009', 11–12.

[42] Ibid. See Table 1 for questionnaire results.

[43] 15 focus groups were recorded between January 2009 and August 2009. These groups, usually involving about six respondents, invariably reflecting the complex ethic, cultural and hybrid identities characteristic of their boroughs' population were sampled from various age groups, especially young people in local schools, representing each of the five Olympic boroughs. The groups lasted between 45 minutes and one hour, and were video-recorded for inclusion in the 'East London Lives' 2012 digital archive. The participants were invited to discuss and consider an array of topics, with an emphasis on 'legacy' – and to explore thoughts and ideas about the

2012 Games – a mega event on their doorstep. Questions of identity and nation often emerged spontaneously. The cited excerpts refer to groups conducted in schools in Newham and in Waltham Forest.

[44] Damkjær, 'Post-Olympism and the Aestheticisation of Sport', 213.
[45] Kidd, 'Recapturing Alternative Olympic Histories'. MacAloon, *This Great Symbol*.
[46] Smith and Porter, *Sport and National Identity*, 13.
[47] Nava, 'Visceral Cosmopolitanism', 164.
[48] Carrington, 'Cosmopolitan Olympism', 97.

References

Bairner, A., ed. *Sport and the Irish. Histories, Identities, Issues.* Dublin: University College Dublin Press, 2005.

Bale, J. and M.K. Christensen, eds. *Post-Olympism? Questioning Sport in the Twenty-First Century.* Oxford: Berg, 2004.

Bennett L., M. Bennett and S. Alexander. 'Why Host the Games? Chicago and the 2016 Olympics' (Egan Urban Center, DePaul University). Chicago: De Paul University, November 2008, available at http://www.chicago2016.com/2016/files/reports/BennettBennettAlexanderRev4.pdf, accessed 20 May 2009.

Burbank, M.J., G. Andranovitch and C. H. Heying. *Olympic Dreams: The Impact of Mega events on Local Politics.* Boulder, CO: Lynne Rienner, 2001.

Carrington, B. 'Cosmopolitan Olympism, Humanism and the Spectacle of "Race" Post-Olympism?' In *Questioning Sport in the Twenty-First Century,* edited by J. Bale and M. Christensen. Oxford: Berg, 2004.

Coubertin, P. de. 'Does Cosmopolitan Life Lead to International Friendliness?' *Review of Reviews* 17 (1898): 29–34,

Castells, M. *The Network Society.* Oxford: Blackwell, 1996.

Chicago 2016 Candidate File, 2008. Available at http://www.chicago2016.org/our-plan/bid-book/bid-book.aspx, accessed 21 May 2009.

Damkjær, S. 'Post-Olympism and the Aestheticisation of Sport'. In *Questioning Sport in the Twenty-First Century,* edited by J. Bale and M. Christensen. Oxford: Berg, 2004.

Duarte N. *'Large Scale Urban Projects and Dual City: The cases of Rio de Janeiro and Bogota'.* Dissertation report submitted in part fulfilment of requirements for MSc in development and Planning, Bartlett Development Planning Unit, University College, London, 3 Sept. 2007.

GLA (Greater London Authoruty). *'Annual London Survey 2009 Top line results February 2009'.* Available at http://www.london.gov.uk/mayor/annual_survey/index.jsp, accessed 10 June 2009.

Heath, A. and J. Roberts *'British Identity: Its Sources and Possible Implications for Civic Attitudes and Behaviour'.* Research Report for Lord Goldsmith's Citizenship Review, 2008, available at www.justice.govuk/docs/british-identitypdf, accessed 12 April 2009.

IOC (International Olympic Committee). *Games of the XXXI Olympiad, Working Group Report.* IOC: Lausanne, March 2008. Available at http://multimedia.olympic.org/pdf/en_report_1317.pdf, accessed 20 July 2009.

Kidd, B. 'Recapturing Alternative Olympic Histories'. In *Global Olympics: Historical and Sociological Studies of the Modern Games,* edited by K. Young and K. Walmsley. London: Elsevier, 2005.

Kumar K. *The Making of English National Identity.* Cambridge: Cambridge University Press, 2003.

MacAloon, J. *This Great Symbol: Pierre de Coubertin and the Origins of the Modern Olympic Games.* Chicago, University of Chicago Press, 1981.

MacAloon, J. '"Legacy" as Managerial/Magical Discourse in Contemporary Olympic Affairs'. *The International Journal of the History of Sport* 25, no. 14 (Dec. 2008): 2060–71.

Ministerio do Esporto, L. DaCosta D. Correa, E. Rizzuti, B. Villano and A. Miragaya, eds. *Legados De Megeventos Esportivos.* Brasilia: Ministerio do Esporto, 2008.

Nava, M. *Visceral Cosmopolitanism: Gender, Culture and the Normalisation of Difference.* London: Sage, 2007.

Rivenburgh, N. 'The Olympic Games: Twenty-First Century Challenges as a Global Media Event'. In *Sport, Media, Culture: Global and Local Dimensions,* edited by A. Bernstein and N. Blain. London: Frank Cass, 2005.

Roche, M. *Mega-Events and Modernity.* London: Routledge, 2000.

Scambler G. *Sport and Society, History, Power and Culture.* Maidenhead: Open University Press, 2005.

Smith, A. and D. Porter, eds. *Sport and National Identity in the Post-War World.* London: Routledge, 2004.

Olympiads as Mega-events and the Pace of Globalization: Beijing 2008 in Context

Paul Close

This article is about the relationship between the 2008 Beijing Olympic Games and 2004-8 Beijing Olympiad as mega-events and the processes of globalisation, on the one hand, and the progress of the post-Cold War new world order, on the other. The article outlines the globalisational approach *to conceptualising, analysing and making sense of mega-events in general and the Beijing Olympiad in particular; and suggests that the Beijing Olympiad was the greatest mega-event of all time, and is likely to remain the greatest mega-event for the foreseeable future, over-shadowing for instance the London Olympiad. The author argues that the 2008 Games were awarded (by the West) to Beijing as a reward for the PRC both coming outside and coming onside as a capitalist social formation; for the PRC having embraced mainstays of the* Western cultural *account and, above all, of Western-style capitalism (albeit with Chinese characteristics); for the PRC having peacefully abandoned its ideological struggle against capitalism and its Cold War stand-off with the West; and for the PRC having in effect sealed the fate of* historical materialism, *the* old world order, *and the second phase of globalisation. The Beijing Games and Olympiad are likely to remain extra special in that they were a* coming-out party *not just for the PRC, but also for the world as a whole; for the* international community; *and for the emerging* global community. *They were a celebration of the transitions to the new world order in conjunction the current third stage of globalisation, marked by a major advance in the Western-led drive towards a single global social space.*

Introduction

It is widely recognized and broadly agreed that the clearest example of a mega-event, sporting or otherwise, is provided by the modern Olympic Games, with another sporting spectacle, the FIFA World Cup coming in second. [1] There is nothing like the same consensus over what else, if anything, qualifies as a mega-event, how to identify mega-events or how to basically characterize, distinguish and define 'mega-event'.

Still, the agreement that does exist provides a benchmark for categorizing all events as 'mega' or otherwise, for deciding on the basic, or defining, characteristics of mega-events, and so for conceptualizing 'mega-event' in general, or abstract, terms. The Olympic Games are an appropriate starting-point for coming up with the most useful notion of 'mega-event' for sociological, analytical and explanatory purposes. While, of course, there cannot be a correct definition of 'mega-event' (just as there cannot be a correct definition of anything), there may be a most useful one. There may be a most helpful, beneficial and productive way of defining 'mega-event' for the purpose of distinguishing and identifying mega-events, the first step in the process of studying, analysing and making sense of any particular example and of the phenomenon in general.

The Globalizational Approach

Well before the start of the twenty-first century, Olympic Games were mega-events, or more precisely mega-*social* events. As with social events broadly speaking, Olympic Games display three principal, or fundamental, dimensions: the economic, the political and the cultural; and as befits an event that warrants the label 'mega', Olympic Games have assumed for several decades a big, great or *abnormally large* economic, political and cultural presence. [2] What is more, and crucially, Olympic Games have not only been big, but also assumed the mantle of the biggest, perhaps the biggest possible, [3] and perhaps even the biggest conceivable of all social events anywhere in the world.

Olympic Games as mega-events will display certain basic defining characteristics which they share with not only all other mega-*events*, but also all other mega-*social phenomena*, such as mega-cities, the significance of which has been indicated in one study as follows:

> This paper examines the transformation of urban space in the peri-urban areas of Latin American mega-cities, further exacerbating the multi-jurisdictional political divisions that cover a single urban entity. ... It argues that previous approaches have failed to recognize that globally and nationally-derived economic development processes are often vested in these meta-urban peripheries. .... Much of the contemporary vibrancy and dynamics of Mexico City's metropolitan development are occurring in 'hot-spots' in the extended periphery, which, to date, have rarely been considered an integral part of the mega-city. Yet these areas are also some of the principal loci of contemporary globalization processes. [4]

According to this, mega-cities, and especially 'hot-spots' within the extended periphery of them, are *some of the principal loci of globalization processes*.

Globalization has been defined, of course, in many ways, some of the most cited and influential of which lend themselves, it seems to me, to the following distillation:

> Globalization is the set of processes, whereby – facilitated by enhanced global flows of such things as industry, investment, individuals and information [5] – the world is becoming structurally (economically and politically) more integrated [6] and

culturally (ideationally) more homogenized. [7] The world is becoming, in other words, a 'borderless' [8] 'single place'. [9]

For me, globalization is the process, or set of processes, through which the world is becoming a single global social (economic, political and cultural) place, or *space*. [10]

The origins of globalization lie in the West (or, more specifically, in Europe); the evolving globalized world is highly Westernized around (economic) market capitalism, (political) liberal democracy, and (cultural) individualism; [11] and the resulting single global social space is likely to be dominated by these features and their affiliated Western traits, albeit not necessarily in an unqualified manner:

> Ideationally, globalization is the vehicle whereby the 'Western cultural account' [12] is being globally diffused, if somewhat unevenly and erratically. Western cultural forms, expressions and items are being adopted, albeit at different speeds, more or less everywhere including throughout East Asia. ... The growing popularity of football (otherwise known as *soccer*) in East Asia matches what is occurring elsewhere in the world, and provides a highly instructive example of how the Western cultural account is being presented, or purveyed, to and acquired by a significant non-Western *Other*. ... In East Asia as elsewhere, the Western cultural account is interacting with local cultures. ... The results are syntheses of the global and the local. [13]

Globalization, market capitalism, liberal democracy, the Western cultural account, individualism and much else associated with the West, and especially with what some regard as continuing Western hegemony, imperialism and decadence (including such Western offerings as 'excessive individualism', consumerism, 'the commodification of everything', the Olympic Games, the Olympic Movement and Olympism) are enjoying a far from completely smooth, wholly uniform or universally endearing progress.

While globalization is probably inevitable and unstoppable, in the sense of a process that is leading to a single global social space, the content of globalization is unsettled, as is therefore the economic, political and cultural character of the eventual single global social space. Economic globalization appears to be proceeding at a faster rate than its political and cultural counterparts, notwithstanding any setbacks due to the global financial crisis which sprung up in 2008 and the fact that globalization, overall or in part, is facing widespread resentment, rejection and resistance. Globalization is being constantly impeded and amended, not least because of the shifting, or declining, economic, political and cultural weight of the West relative to the rest, and especially in comparison with those parts of the world centred on the 'BRIC Economies' – those of Brazil, Russia, India and China. [14]

Globalization entails and depends upon acceptance, compliance and conformity at the local level, but the content of globalization is in flux, and is being constantly shaped and reshaped in interaction with the local – under the influence, impact and weight of local economics, politics and culture. Of course, not all local economics, politics and cultures have equal weight, and so equal influence and impact on the content of globalization. None the less, the West is not the only player involved, and its relative weight after all is declining. The content of globalization is not singularly 'Western', and it is likely to become less and less so. Globalization is being modified, revised and transformed at the local level – through accommodation, adaptation and 'localization', 'global localization' or 'glocalization' – and at the global level itself through playback, feedback or interference from the local level. This is perhaps especially applicable to East Asia, and is perhaps especially apparent in matters surrounding mega-events.

The statement above by Close and Askew about cultural globalization, East Asia and football (the origins of which, of course, lie in the West, and more specifically in England) was made with regard to the 2002 FIFA World Cup finals, which were held in Japan and South Korea. But it might have been made about globalization overall, China and the Olympic Games vis-à-vis the 2008 Beijing event. It is to be expected that the distinctive 'local' culture, or cultures, of China will be far from simply swept aside and away by globalization and the Western cultural account with the assistance of the Beijing games. Instead, the 'local' will have made an appearance at, will have made its presence felt during and will have imposed itself upon this sporting extravaganza; will have ensure that the Western cultural account content of globalization is somewhat localized; and will to some extent be played back on, influencing globalization through the process of *glocalization*.

Still, this does not detract from the view of globalization, as alluded to by Aguilar *et al.*, [15] as the *exemplar par excellence* for illustrating and identifying mega-social phenomena in particular cases and in general, of whatever type or sub-type, due to its status as the supreme manifestation of the *mega-social* genre and, connectedly, its association with other major examples, including such mega-events as the FIFA World Cup, such mega-organizations as FIFA and the International Association of Athletics Associations (IAAA) and mega-cities. Not only mega-cities such as Mexico City, but also mega-events such as Olympic Games and the FIFA World Cup may act as *principal loci of globalization processes*. [16]

It may be that globalization and Olympic Games as mega-social phenomena not only share certain basic, defining characteristics but also share a close mega-social (economic, political and cultural) relationship, whereby each shapes and sustains, feeds into and feeds off the other; and whereby Olympic Games as *principal loci of globalization processes* can be used to investigate and illuminate globalization. This seems to be what John Short has in mind when he says:

> The existence, extent, meaning and measurement of economic, political and cultural globalization have provided a rich and argumentative agenda for contemporary social theorizing [see Short, 2001]. A discussion of the Games provides an opportunity to consider a very concrete example of globalization. The Games not only actualize some of the forces and many of the paradoxes of globalization, they also exemplify the complex intersections of cultural and political, as well as the more commonly studied, economic globalization. [17]

Globalization, the Olympic Games and the social relationship, or interaction, between globalization and the games are mega-social phenomena, each of which is built around the three principal intersecting dimensions of social life. The economic, political and cultural dimensions of Olympic Games intersect in a complex manner, especially so due to the way in which the games 'are embodied in at least three scales: global, national and local', while having become since 'their inauguration in 1896, ... increasingly global'. [18] Short is primarily interested in how the 'modern Summer Olympic Games are global spectacles, national campaigns and city enterprises', at one and the same time; and thereby in how the games are loci, or sites, of 'connections between the global and the local' in *an era of globalization*. [19] The challenge for anyone trying to study, analyse and make sense of Olympic Games will be to clarify the *complex intersections* of their economic, political and cultural dimensions at and between the different levels of their *embodiment*, while taking into account how – reflecting the progress of globalization – they have become and are becoming more globalized.

Guided by Short, Olympic Games as social events occur, or are embodied, not only at the local level (of the city, the nation state or whatever), but also at the global level, and as such are sites not only *from which* the local interacts with the global, but also *at which* this interaction takes place. Olympic Games are not only local social events, they are also global social events, or spectacles, and so entail an interaction between *the local* and *the global* at the local level itself. Olympic Games facilitate the presence of the global at the local level, the interaction of the global and the local at the local level, and consequently the direct, immediate influence and impact of the global – and so of globalization – on the local at the local level (which is not to ignore how Olympic Games may also facilitate the influence and impact of the local on the global, and so on globalization – see below).

From this, certain questions arise. While Olympic Games are necessarily local events, are they necessarily global events? While currently, Olympic Games are global events, and under globalization are assuming a greater and greater global presence, have they always been global events – even in this *era of globalization*? And, what are the substantive, empirical and conceptual relationships between Olympic Games as global events, on the one hand, and the games as mega-events, on the other? While currently Olympic Games are global spectacles, it does not necessarily follow that they have always qualified as such. Olympic Games may have only become global spectacles under globalization, and perhaps only relatively recently under this process. Of course, while some Olympic Games may not qualify as 'global', they may none the less qualify as 'mega', depending on the meaning attached to the latter.

However, it seems to me that if and when Olympic Games are global spectacles, then they might usefully – for sociological, analytical and explanatory purposes – be distinguished as 'mega-events'; while, on the other hand, if and when Olympic Games are not global spectacles, then they might usefully be regarded as falling short of 'mega-event' definitional requirements. That is, it may be analytically useful to define 'mega-social event' in global terms; to distinguish a 'mega-social event' as one which is (by definition) necessarily global; to identify mega-social events with reference to their global presence, spread, or reach.

This approach would be consistent both with viewing globalization in particular as the primary example of a mega-social phenomenon, and with accounting for mega-social phenomena in general in terms of the advent and subsequent advance of globalization. Thus, what I will call the *globalizational approach* to mega-social events hinges upon defining and distinguishing these occasions as global, global reach or globalized economic, political and cultural phenomena; upon recognizing the way in which they are principal loci, or sites, of globalization, with which they have a close, intimate and mutually-shaping social relationship; and upon acknowledging the way in which they are major vehicles for the progress of globalization, as well as (methodologically) for studying, analysing and making sense of globalization.

The globalizational approach to mega-events in general and to Olympic Games in particular can be compared and contrasted with the alternative approaches of a range of prominent contributors to the study of the games, some of whom nonetheless have hinted at the globalizational approach. Among the most notable writers in this regard is Maurice Roche. [20] In *Mega-events and Modernity*, Roche 'explores the social history and politics of "mega-events"' from the late nineteenth century to 'the current crisis of the Olympic movement in world politics and culture' by examining, for instance, 'the ways in which these kinds of events have contributed to the meaning and development of "public culture", "cultural citizenship" and "cultural inclusion/exclusion" in society, at both the national and the international levels'. [21] For Roche,

> The concept of 'mega-events' refers to specially to constructed and staged international cultural and sports events such as the Olympic Games and World's Fairs (hereafter Expos). Mega-events are short-lived collective cultural actions ('ephemeral vistas' ...) which nonetheless have long-lived pre- and post-event social dimensions. They are publicly perceived as having an 'extra-ordinary' status, among other things, by virtue of their very large scale, the time cycles in which they occur, and their impacts. [22]

While Roche's definition of 'mega-event' is a useful starting point for studying the phenomenon in general and Olympic Games in particular, it presents considerable operational difficulties given the issue of measuring 'very large', or for that matter 'large', and an event's *publicly perceived extra-ordinary status*. Because of this, Roche's definition is not readily amenable to distinguishing and identifying mega-events in practice, and therefore to studying, analysing and making sense of them.

Still, Roche alludes to a way of obviating this impasse when he tells us that mega-event 'genres have had an enduring mass popularity in modernity since their creation in the late 19th century and continue to do so in a period of globalization'. Roche draws attention to the relationship between mega-events and globalization, including by way of both the temporal aspect and the *functional* character, relevance and importance of mega-events. For Roche, 'the mega-event phenomenon' pre-dates globalization, while subsequently enduring under globalization, in relation to which – along with such accompanying phenomena as 'contemporary society' and 'modernity', and in particular 'late modernity' – it is *functional*. [23]

Roche argues that mega-events, due to especially, 'but not exclusively, their temporal characteristics and what can be called their "dramaturgical" features and appeal', constitute 'resources for sustaining personal time structure in contemporary conditions that threaten this'. For Roche, 'the main structures of meaning that continue to be associated with mega-events in modernity' are *functional* in relation to personal and interpersonal 'identity'. Roche claims that these *structures* are highly 'relevant to the understanding of mega-events' in that they help account for how mega-events functionally relate to, facilitate and support the 'microsocial' processes of 'what phenomenological sociology refers to as the "life world"' on the one hand and the '"macrosocial" systems' that entail, for instance, globalization processes on the other. Mega-events have become *functional* in relation to both, and so bridge the microsocial and macrosocial spheres from within the intermediary '"mesosocial" sphere in contemporary society'. [24]

Roche tells us:

> Mega-event genres were born in the late 19th century during a period of national building and empire building in the industrializing capitalist societies of the USA and Western Europe. This period has been ... portrayed by Eric Hobsbawm [Hobsbawm and Ranger, 1992] as being characterized by a wave of 'inventions of tradition', and he refers to sports and expositions as leading examples of such cultural invention. ... [The] enduring popularity and institutionalization of mega-event genres in national societies and in international and global society since that 'early modern' period derives from their social functions for elites and mass publics. ... [The] periodic production of particular mega-events can be usefully understood as the production of intermediate 'meso-sphere' processes, involving socio-temporal 'hubs' and 'exchanges' in the economic, cultural and [other] 'flows' and 'networks' which can be said to contribute to the current development ... of culture and society at the global level. It is on this basis that ... mega-event movements such as the Olympic [movement] can be usefully understood as [having] important ... roles in the cultural aspects of contemporary global-level governance and institution building [see Roche, 2000, Chapter 7]. [25]

The '"mesosocial" sphere in contemporary society' is 'the intermediary sphere through which the life world, and its "microsocial" processes, is connected with "macrosocial" systems ... and change', where the 'life world' is the sphere of in particular 'personal identity formation'; [26] and the macrosocial sphere includes the activities and processes of 'global-level governance and institution building' as befits 'global society'. Within the mesosocial sphere, mega-events constitute *exchange hubs* in the economic, political and cultural networks and flows of social life within and between the microsocial sphere and the macrosocial sphere.

However, in so far as mega-events will not be the only exchange hubs within the mesosocial sphere, the question arises of how to distinguish them from the rest. Guided by Roche, mega-events can be identified by their *very large scale* and *publicly perceived 'extraordinary' status.* [27] But, if only because these two indicators, or measures, are difficult to operationally interpret and apply, what about instead taking mega-events to be *the largest events*, or to be *extraordinarily large events*, or to be *events that are so large as to have a global presence, spread or reach*? If mega-events are defined, distinguished and identified as being those events that have global reach – have been globalized – then they will be the only mesosocial sphere events that will also have a presence within the macrosocial sphere. Mega-events defined in accordance with this approach – the *globalizational approach* – will link the microsocial sphere and the macrosocial sphere by being present in both, and therefore will do so directly and immediately. Moreover, mega-events will not merely accompany globalization, but will be instead integral features of this process.

The globalizational approach to mega-events has been inferred by a few recent writers, including John Horne and Wolfram Manzenreiter in their assessment of the impact of the 2002 FIFA World Cup finals on the host countries, Japan and Korea, [28] and Alan Tomlinson and Christopher Young in their account of the relationship between politics, culture and national identity, on the one hand, and what they refer to as *global sports events*, in particular the Olympics and the World Cup, on the other. [29] Horne and Manzenreiter focus on 'the specific regional political economy of the 2002 World Cup; the role of sports mega-events in identity construction and promotion; and how such events are both constituted by and constitutive of globalization'. [30] Presumably, if a mega-event is *constitutive* of globalization, then it will be a *global-reach event*, that is a 'global event'. [31] A mega-event will have simultaneously both a global and a local embodiment; and, while being a mesosocial sphere phenomenon in the first instance, a mega-event will have concurrently both a microsocial and a macrosocial presence.

However, adopting the globalizational approach to mega-events may result in some of the events that Roche takes to be mega-events being left out of the frame. It may mean excluding all expos as well as some FIFA World Cup finals, and even some Olympic Games. It cannot be assumed that a particular event will qualify as a mega-event merely because of its *very large scale* and *publicly perceived 'extraordinary' status*; [32] because of aspirations for it to qualify; or because its predecessors or successors qualify. From the globalizational standpoint, the earliest Olympic Games were not mega-events in that they did not attain the required global social reach. Indeed, even when judged with reference to Roche's operational criteria, the earliest games will not qualify as mega-events.

Thus, for John Short, it was only at the 2000 Sydney Games, when there were athletes from *199 countries* – or *countries and territories* [33] – and so 'most countries of the world competed', that the Olympic Games had become 'truly global'. [28] Although the first modern Olympic Games 'was an important national event', it 'had limited international impact'. In the early years, the games were not 'a global phenomenon', an 'early limiting factor to the global diffusion of the Olympic Games [being] the cost and difficulty of international travel'. According to Short, it 'took a long while for the Games to become global spectacles and the process is intertwined with [the] development of mass media, particularly television'. For Short, the 'increasing globalization' of the games is closely connected with expanding television coverage. In 1960, when the games were held in Rome, 'CBS paid $660,000 for the right to fly film from Rome to New York, while Eurovision transmitted the first live coverage of the Games'. A total of 21 countries and territories received television coverage, a figure which increased tenfold to 214 for the 1996 event held in Atlanta. In 2000, when they were held in Sydney, over 3.7 billion people watched the games in 220 countries and territories. The 'typical viewer' watched the games on eleven occasions, 'resulting in a combined viewing audience estimated at 36 billion'. In 1972, when the games were held in Munich, 'less than 10% of the revenue of the Games came from television companies, but by Atlanta in 1996 this had increased to almost 40%'. Television coverage revenues have increased by an average of 30 per cent between events, 'from $40 million in 1972 to $556 million in Atlanta. In a package deal, NBC paid $3.5 billion to cover the Sydney Olympics, Athens, and Beijing as well as the winter games of 2002 and 2006.' By the 2000 Games, television revenues constituted 55 per cent of the total marketing revenue of the International Olympic Committee (IOC), with US television companies accounting for 60 per cent of all worldwide rights. In effect, the 'Summer Games are now thoroughly corporatized, providing a huge global audience of consumers and a global opportunity to sell goods and services around the world'. [35]

The Olympic Games have acquired a huge global audience, which provides an attractive opportunity for corporations to increase their sales of goods and services and so profits. This provides in turn an incentive for corporations to invest – to become (highly influential, or indeed *powerful*) stakeholders – in the games and the Olympic movement. The huge global audience now provided by the games has meant a boost not only for the marketing revenues of the IOC, but also for the global economic presence, weight and clout of the games and the Olympic movement; while the same audience provides an attractive opportunity not only for economic players of various kinds and at various levels (such as at the nation-state level), but also for political players, perhaps especially at the nation-state level – and for political regimes, governments and so on at this 'local' level. Consequently, the games' huge global audience and corporate and political appeal have been rounded out by the games' global political presence, relevance and importance.

If the early modern Olympic Games fell short of qualifying as mega-events, then this may reflect how globalization either had still to get under way (as inferred by Roche) or was still in its early stages. It may be argued that globalization has a long, centuries-old history, but nonetheless took off and rapidly progressed on a significantly higher plane during the 1960s, which therefore mark the start of the distinctive *era of globalization*. If so, then the earliest mega-events, sporting or otherwise, will have occurred at around the same time, during the 1960s. The first mega-event of any type may have been the 1964 Tokyo Olympics, the first games to be staged in Asia; and the second mega-event may have been the 1966 FIFA World Cup finals, which were staged in England. Moreover, it could be that Olympic Games and the FIFA World Cup finals remain the only events that can be categorized as 'mega-events'. While Olympic Games are probably the biggest (multi-sport) mega-events, World Cup finals are undoubtedly the biggest single-sport mega-events. Indeed, there is a good chance that the 2008 Beijing Games will be the greatest mega-event of all time, perhaps not only for now, but also for a long time to come (see below).

Having said this, however, there is another contender for 'the greatest mega-even of all time' accolade. It is *the Beijing Olympiad*, depending on whether the socio-temporal [36] boundaries around *the Olympics* are re-drawn by looking beyond the spectacle and glare of the games themselves to the pre-games build-up, in and in particular to the period following the close of the previous games, given the social (economic, political and cultural) intimacy and integration entailed.

According to Roche, *mega-events are short-lived but have long-lived pre-event and post-event social dimensions.* [37] But this presumes too much, and perhaps imposes artificially exaggerated stages within what might otherwise, and more appropriately and usefully, be regarded as relatively long-lived mega-events. It precludes the possibility of mega-events being long-lived by covering more than the short-lived spectacles, extravaganzas and the like upon which they may well be centred. This possibility has been indicated in the case of Olympic Games:

> A mega-event strategy unfolds over a considerable period of time; typically there is a decade between launching a bid and the closing ceremonies and, of course, the legacy of the event can last for many more years. To facilitate comparison ... we divide the Olympic mega-events into three periods: the bid process, the organization period, and the legacy of the Olympics. [38]

An Olympiad is the four-year period between the close of one modern summer Olympic Games and the close of the next, as exemplified by the interval between the closing ceremony of the 2004 Athens games and the closing ceremony of the 2008 Beijing games. If Olympiads rather than just the games of Olympiads are regarded as mega-events, then this will mean of course that *Olympic mega-events* will follow on from each other in tandem, as an unbroken chain of abutting sporting mega-events, at least in so far as and for as long as (in accordance with the globalizational approach to mega-events) Olympiads remain global in stature. This is not to ignore how Olympiads do not follow on from each other in a neatly demarcated fashion, but instead flow into each other in various ways, in particular via the economic, political and cultural dimensions of social life through which they are intermeshed.

Following John Short (above), an indication, or measure, of the mega-event status of any Olympic Games or its encompassing Olympiad will be the number of competing countries and territories involved, there being 199 at the 2000 Sydney games. [39] Since 2000, there has been a significant increase in number that are eligible to send teams of competitors to Olympic Games through the IOC membership of their national Olympic committees (NOCs), the result being that as of 2009 all the member states of the United Nations had become eligible. Consequently, every UN-recognized (independent, sovereign) nation state except for the Holy See has acquired the (albeit still conditional) right to send a team to the games. There are 205 NOC members of the IOC, covering all 192 UN member states plus 13 other territories: Taiwan, or the Republic of China (ROC), which the IOC calls *Chinese Taipei*; the Palestinian territories, which the IOC calls *Palestine*; four US overseas territories (American Samoa, Guam, Puerto Rico, and United States Virgin

Islands); three UK overseas territories (Bermuda, British Virgin Islands, and Cayman Islands); two Netherlands constituent territories (Aruba and Netherlands Antilles); Hong Kong, a Special Administrative Region (SAR) of the People's Republic of China (PRC); and Cook Islands, an associated state of New Zealand. Three NOCs joined the IOC during the 2004–8 Beijing Olympiad, these being from Marshall Islands (2006), Montenegro (2007) and Tuvalu (2007). Through the 205 NOCs, almost every (geo-politically defined) nation state, country and territory and every (ethnically defined) *nation* was at least formally represented by a team of competitors at the 2008 Beijing games. On these grounds, it is reasonable to claim that the IOC, the Olympic Games and the Olympic movement have reached global saturation point. [40]

The clear signs are that the Beijing games and Olympiad are mega-events; are the greatest mega-events of all time; and will remain the greatest mega-events for the foreseeable future. In particular, they are likely to be far greater mega-events than the follow-on 2008–12 London Olympiad and games, although not so much because of the number and global coverage of the competing teams as of another consideration – that of the *coming-out* character of the Beijing Olympiad and games.

The *Asian discourse on the Olympics*, as discussed in *The Beijing Olympiad: The Political Economy of a Sporting Mega-Event* [41] focuses on the three games that have been hosted by Asian cities – Tokyo (1964), Seoul (1988) and Beijing (2008) – and their three encompassing Olympiads, distinguishing these events from all others given the way in which they have certain similar and special features. The three Asian Olympic Games have been viewed as *coming-out parties*, [42] and with some justification. [43] For me, each of the Asian Olympic Games and Olympiads can be regarded as a coming-out party in the sense of a *coming-of-age celebration* and *rite de passage*, whereas all other Olympic events, including the subsequent London ones (Olympiad and games), for example, cannot. What is more, the Beijing Olympiad and Olympics as coming-out celebrations assumed far greater proportions than the earlier Asian Olympic events, in particular because of their global ramifications. The Beijing Olympiad and games constitute a mega-event, a global event and a coming-out party which was unprecedented, and which is unlikely to be matched, never mind superseded, for the foreseeable future, if not forever.

The Tokyo and Seoul games were about celebrating, showcasing and augmenting Japan's and then South Korea's economic development and *maturation*. The Beijing Olympiad and games were about doing the same things vis-à-vis the surge of the People's Republic of China (PRC), but in a more inclusive and more globally pertinent way than applies to either Tokyo or Seoul. As Jörn-Carsten Gottwald and Niall Duggan have put it:

> the Beijing Olympics are a political spectacle which intends to create a facade of sustainable and equal economic growth in China which has created a new world power. However, looking beyond the smokescreen of 'China's coming out party' you will see that many of the institutional structures needed to maintain this impressive growth such as a strong and independent media and legal system are

absent or at best very weak. Beijing 2008 was an excellent opportunity to create or strengthen these much needed institutions. Unfortunately, this opportunity looks destined to be a missed opportunity. [44]

The Beijing Olympiad and games were about celebrating, showcasing and augmenting the PRC's emergence as a *new world super-power*, to paraphrase Gottwald and Duggan, or – to put it yet another way – as a *new world order* super-power. [45] The Beijing events were a celebration of the PRC's coming out – or emergence – from its rigid socialist (Marxist-Leninist-cum-Maoist) shell, and of its re-emergence, rebirth or metamorphosis as a capitalist social formation and (political-economy) superpower within the post-Cold War *new world order*.

One way of looking at the 2008 games is that they were awarded (by the West) to Beijing as a reward for the PRC both *coming outside* and *coming onside* as a capitalist social formation; for the PRC having embraced mainstays of the *Western cultural account* and, above all, of Western-style capitalism (albeit with Chinese characteristics); for the PRC having peacefully, even meekly, given up its ideological struggle against capitalism and Cold War stand-off with the (victorious and vindicated) West; and for the PRC having more or less sealed the historical fate of *historical materialism*, the *old world order*, and the second phase of globalization.

The first phase of globalization began with the imperialist expansion of the West (or, more accurately, of Europe) including into east Asia. The first phase gave way at around the time of the 1960–4 Tokyo Olympiad to the second phase, during which globalization took off while, however, being constrained by the Cold War *old world order*. This second phase was a bridging stage, which gradually led during the 1984–92 Seoul to Barcelona Olympiads into the current third stage. The second phase of globalization is perhaps most notable for the concluding, 1991, collapse of the Soviet Union. However, it also entailed the PRC's *Era of Reconstruction* (1976–89), the PRC's *Dengist reforms* (around the four modernizations), and Beijing's decision to make its first bid to host an Olympic Games. The advent of the third phase of globalization coincided with Beijing's 1993 loss to Sydney to host the 2000 games. Beijing lost to Sydney by just two votes (out of a total of 88) in the final round of voting, after having won in the previous three rounds. [46] Eight years later, in July 2001 in Moscow, Beijing became the clear winner to host the 2008 games, securing 44 of the 102 votes in the first round and 56 in the second and final round (when Toronto attracted 22 votes, Paris 18 and Istanbul nine).

As inferred, what makes the 2004–8 Beijing Olympiad so extra special and such an extraordinarily huge mega-event is that it was a coming-out party not just for the PRC, but also for the world as a whole; for the so-called *international community*; and for the emerging *global community*. It was a celebration of the peaceful transition to the (if not completely peaceful and *orderly*) *new world order* in conjunction with that to the third stage of globalization – the current stage. This third stage is marked by the way in which the Western-led drive towards a *single global social (economic, political and cultural) space* has been greatly assisted and far more firmly secured by the Eastern-socialist bloc's – including the PRC's – embrace in varying degrees of market capitalism, liberal democracy and the *Western cultural account* centred on individualism, the doctrine that underpins the global human rights regime (GHRR), for instance. [47]

Everyone was invited to join in the 2004–8 *global community coming-out party*, and to enjoy especially this mega-event's climax, the 2008 games spectacular. Of course, far from everyone took up the invitation. Apart from the fact that there was still a large number of people who were unable to participate in the extravaganza even via mass media, there were many people who refused, resisted, or tried to spoil the party. In the run-up to the games, the Olympiad was used as an opportunity to draw attention to and protest about a range of internally oriented issues, including the PRC's human-rights record, treatment of minorities, lack of (liberal) democracy, suppression of separatist movements and 'occupation' of Tibet. Of course, the prospective party-poopers did not stand a chance:

> It may be the world's premier sporting extravaganza, but China is turning the Beijing Olympics into the biggest security operation in history. There will be 100,000 police on duty in Beijing during the 17 days of the Games, backed by 100,000 members of China's armed forces, 300 specialists in nuclear, biological and chemical warfare, fleets of airplanes, helicopters and warships, and 600,000 'security volunteers', including retirees, students and neighbourhood committees. Surface-to-air missile launchers are already positioned around prime Olympic sites, such as the 'Bird's Nest' stadium and the 'water cube' aquatics centre. Unmanned security drones will patrol the skies above Olympic sailors near the naval port of Qingdao. Access to Olympic Games sites will be monitored with security checks, X-ray machines, metal detectors, full-body scanners, electronic passes and biometric keys, such as fingerprint and iris scanning. ... 'After a hiatus of 150 or more years, China is preparing once again to play on the world stage a role proportional to the importance of its size, history and geography', said Frank Ching, a Hong Kong-based journalist and columnist. 'The Games are now seen as the "coming out" of China, serving as a rebirth, as it were, after generations of foreign dominance and domestic oppression'. And China's authoritarian leaders are not about to let anyone spoil their party.' [48]

But the PRC was far from being alone in its determination to prevent its celebration from being exploited by dissidents. Lined up alongside the PRC's state apparatus were the full gamut, weight and influence of all the other state apparatuses around the world, in unison with the world's 205 NOCs, not to mention of course the IOC, and the whole of the Olympic movement. In turn, the alliance of the Olympic movement and state apparatuses enjoyed the support of the *business community*, both within the PRC and everywhere else. In turn again, this global-reach, political-economy *social compact* was able to bask in the tacit, if not active, support of the bulk of the world's population. The spoilers put in an appearance, and perhaps added to the spectacle, but any *free-Tibeters* and the like were far from able to compete with the global-reach popularity of Olympic Games in general and appeal of the 2008 Beijing event in particular. The popularity of Olympic Games is simply too strong, perhaps especially so in the post-Cold War *new world order*. After all, where else can *small* (the least powerful) countries and territories, nation states and nations, NOCs and governments so spectacularly challenge, defeat and humiliate the *big* (the most powerful) ones?

According to John Short, while the games 'have broadened in participation', both 'athletic success and the hosting of the Games reflect the global inequalities in wealth'. Quite simply, 'richer countries can send more athletes and can afford the necessary expenditure in sports development and training that ensures success', [49] the outcome being their disproportionate success at the games when judged in terms of their medals tally. Of the 927 medals won at the 2000 Sydney games, 357 were won by just five countries: 96 by the USA, 88 by Russia, 59 by the PRC, 58 by Australia and 56 by Germany. Fifty per cent (463) of the medals were won by competitors from Europe and North America; while just over two per cent (50) were won by those from sub-Saharan African teams. A contributing factor, of course, is hosting the games, as reflected in the final medal table of the Beijing games, when the PRC came out top with 51 gold medals and 101 medals in all, beating the USA with 36 gold medals and 110 overall, followed by Russia, Great Britain, Germany, Australia, Korea, and Japan (which won just nine gold medals and 25 medals overall). [50]

In effect,

> Success at the Olympic Games reflects wealth and national spending on sports. Countries with few resources and little spending are less successful. ... Even as participation in the Games becomes more global, success at the Games becomes more uneven. In effect, the Games reinforce the unequal distribution of resources in the world by the unequal participation of different countries and their unequal success in standing on the medal podium. [51]

Perhaps, but measuring an NOC's, country's or territory's success at a games with reference to its medals tally without taking into consideration other factors is, for some commentators, misleading. For instance, the Australian Bureau of Statistics (ABS) has claimed that 'the traditional measure of medals as a "raw score" [does] not take into account the population of the competing country, a possible factor in the ability of nations to field medal winning athletes'. [52] The ABS has published 'an alternative view of the traditional Olympic medal tally to take into account the populations of competing nations', and at the 2004 Athens games the result was a remarkable turn around in favour of the *smaller countries*. Whereas in the raw score final medal table the USA came out top with 36 gold medals and 102 medals overall, followed by China, Russia, Australia, Japan, Germany, France, Italy, South Korea, Great Britain and Cuba (with nine gold medals and 27 medals overall), in the ABS's *medal table by world population*, the Bahamas, Norway, Australia, Hungary and Cuba occupy the top five places. There is probably nowhere else but at the Olympic Games where Cuba (itself in the process of jumping on the bandwagon of giving way to globalization and capitalism), with its population of just 11,323,000, can so spectacularly beat the USA, which – despite its population of 297,031,000 – achieved only 34th place in the ABS table.

The Cuban NOC, state apparatus, government and people will have eagerly grasped the next opportunity, that provided by the Beijing mega-event, but would have been disappointed with their relatively poor showing of only two gold medals, 24 medals overall, and 28th place in the raw medal table. There is no doubt that Cuba is now looking forward to and preparing hard for the 2012 London games, just like all the other 204 territories with NOC membership of the IOC.

All the signs are that the 2012 games will be a mega-event in the globalizational sense, while not being anything like as great an occasion as the 2008 Beijing games, which were a coming-out party when the London games will not be, at least not in anything like the same sense. The London games will be a party of sorts, but will be a relatively sober, less heady affair. The Beijing Olympiad and games constitute a mega-event, global event and coming-out party of unprecedented and unlikely-to-be-repeated proportions, at least for a long time to come. The Beijing event was and is likely to remain extra special in that it was a coming-out party not just for China, but also for the world as a whole; for the *international community*; and for the emerging *global community*. It was a celebration of the transition to the *new world order* in conjunction with that to the current third stage of globalization, marked by a major advance in the Western-led drive towards a single global social (economic, political and cultural) space.

While the 2008–12 Olympiad will be a mega-event in the globalizational sense, it will be conducted in the shadow of the greatest mega-event, sporting or otherwise, so far and perhaps for a very long time to come: the 2004–8 Beijing Olympiad and games. This is not to ignore or to diminish the way in which the London mega-event will continue the work, so to speak, of the Beijing extravaganza by variously promoting globalization towards a single global social space primarily around the Western-based doctrines as capitalism, liberal democracy and individualism, closely articulated as these are, have become and are increasingly becoming with the Olympics – the games and Olympiads themselves, the Olympic movement and that other Western-based doctrine, Olympism.

The Regional Legacy of the Beijing Games and Olympiad

One way of summing up the decision to award the 2008 games to Beijing is to say that it reflects how, more generally, 'awarding Games to facilitate or reward reintegration into the world community has been an IOC objective'. [53]

In the particular case of China, however, *reintegration into the world community* has been accompanied by the withering of the *old world order* around the bi-polar division and *Cold War* conflict between a Western capitalist camp on the one hand and an Eastern communist bloc on the other. The 2008 games were awarded to Beijing as a reward for China being especially instrumental in bringing about the transition to the *new world order*, and concomitantly in facilitating the current, third stage of globalization process towards a *single global social space* primarily around (Western-style) market capitalism. The transition has been marked, perhaps above all, by the emergence, or re-emergence, of China as a major, pivotal political-economy player on both the regional and the global planes, replacing Japan regionally and rivalling the USA globally. As India's *Business Standard* has put it:

> As advertisements go, [the Beijing Games were] a barely concealed attempt to send out an unequivocal message that the Olympics are really the trumpets that herald the arrival of a new power on the global stage. China has used the occasion entirely to its advantage. There were an unprecedented 79 heads of state and governments [*sic*] who attended. They were there to cheer their teams, but also for China's formal coming-out party. [54]

In my view, all those who attended, watched or otherwise celebrated the 2008 games, the greatest mega-event of all time, were variously participating in *the world's* coming-out party – *the world's* emergence from the stifling *old world order* stand-off.

The *Business Standard* draws a comparison between the 2008 games and both the 1936 Berlin games, 'which performed a similar role for Nazi Germany (which was raising its head after the bankruptcy that followed World War I)', and the 1964 Tokyo games, a celebration of Japan's rise 'from the ashes of World War II'. Of note is how like China presently, Germany and Japan 'had crossed into the category of upper-middle-income countries, with per capita incomes of $3,000 or more'; how similarly 'the Soviet Union (Moscow 1980) and South Korea (Seoul 1988) were also typical upper-middle-income countries when they hosted the Olympics'; and how, furthermore, 'Europe's per capita income when the modern Olympic Games were born in 1896 was also about $3,000'. The *Business Standard* concludes: 'Clearly, there is a level of development at which countries acquire the capabilities needed to join the club of modern industrial nations, and also the ambition to show off.' [55]

This argument has been taken up by Suman Bery, for whom the 'Beijing Olympics commemorate China's arrival as a near-developed country'. Thus:

> A glance at the World Bank's [1 July 2008] estimates of 2007 per capita Gross National Income (GNI) ... shows China at 132nd position at $2360, while India at $950 holds a lowly 160th rank. By way of comparison, per capita GNI at purchasing power parity exchange rates from the same source reveals a figure for China of $5370 (rank 119) while that of India is $2740 (rank 152). [China] today is at roughly the same level of per capita income as other past 'emerging' hosts [of 'coming out' party games] such as Mexico, Japan, South Korea and even Italy. [56]

According to Bery, the *real* per capita GDP of Germany at the time of the 1936 Berlin games was $4,451; of Italy during the 1960 Rome games was $5,916; of Japan in 1964 (Tokyo games) was $5,668; of Mexico in 1968 (Mexico City games) was $4,073; and of South Korea in 1988 (Seoul games) was $7,621. Bery tells us that by 2007, the 'Chinese [*real*] per capita income ... would have been around $5375, placing it almost exactly where Japan and Italy were in the 1960s'. [57]

Referring to, in particular, 'the four-hour opening ceremony of the Beijing Olympics', the *Business Standard* suggests that while it would have 'left no one in

[Asia in] any doubt ... as to what modern China is capable of, ... most of [the USA] would have been asleep'. [58] However, this assumption about television audiences beyond Asia appears to be misguided. According to estimates by Nielsen (the marketing and media information company), the Beijing games attracted a television a total audience of 4.7 billion (70 per cent of the world's population) over the 17 days from 8 to 24 August 2008, 'setting a new viewing record for an Olympic Games'. [59] The audience for the whole of the 2004 Athens games was 3.9 billion, and that for the 2000 Sydney games was 3.6 billion. Of China's 1.3 billion people, around 94 per cent watched some of the television coverage, as did 94 per cent of people in South Korea and (on the other side of the Pacific) 93 per cent in Mexico. In total, more than 2 billion people, or almost a third of the world's population, watched the opening ceremony. The 'highest audience ... for the opening ceremony was in the Asia-Pacific, where more than five in 10 people tuned in, followed by Europe, where 30 per cent of the population watched, and North America, at 24 per cent. [60]

Of note is how in this account the region to which the term 'Asia-Pacific' refers is that region that is otherwise frequently labelled either 'Pacific-Asia' or 'East Asia', [61] and so which constitutes the Asian (or western) section of the Asia-Pacific as more inclusively demarcated by a range of alternative sources, including the Asia-Pacific Economic Cooperation (APEC) forum. [62] East Asia is widely regarded as having two sub-regions, South East Asia and North East Asia. [63] South East Asia covers the ten member states (countries) of the Association of Southeast Asian Nations (ASEAN) plus East Timor (Timor-Leste), while North East Asia covers China, [64] Japan, North Korea, South Korea and perhaps one or both of Mongolia and Russia, or at least Siberia. [65] The 21 *member economies* (or countries and territories) of APEC include seven from South East Asia (Brunei Darussalam, Indonesia, Malaysia, Philippines, Singapore, Thailand and Vietnam); five from North East Asia (Hong Kong, Japan, the People's Republic of China, the Russian Federation, South Korea and Chinese Taipei (Taiwan); five from the Americas, or eastern Pacific Rim (Canada, Chile, Mexico, Peru and the USA); and three from Oceania, or southern Pacific Rim (Australia, New Zealand and Papua New Guinea). [66] In my view, the most appropriate and useful approach to defining 'Asia-Pacific' is that guided by APEC's membership, while including the whole of East Asia. [67]

In East Asia, not surprisingly, 'China had the highest percentage of people tuning into the opening ceremony' of the 2008 games, while 44 per cent of people in South Korea, 43 per cent of people in Greece and a similarly high percentage of people in Australia watched. Nielsen claims that 'Viewing levels were also impressive in the US, where ... 65 million people watched the opening ceremony'. [68]

According to Nielsen, the variation in viewing levels 'across regions and markets' was affected by 'time zone and broadcast time differences'. [69] However, the way in which similar proportions to the 94 per cent of Chinese that watched some of the 2008 games in South Korea and Mexico, together with how in the USA 'the Summer Games ranked as the most-viewed TV event ever, with a total audience of 211 million and an average daily audience of 27 million people', and how Australia registered a similarly high percentage of viewers for the 17 days overall, [70] indicates that on both the western side and the eastern side of the Asia-Pacific region there was comparable interest in the event.

Conceivably, television viewing figures may be taken as the single best indicator of the status and stature of 2008 Beijing games as a mega-event, and indeed as the greatest mega-event and biggest coming-out party of all time. But also conceivably, a measure of the 2008 games as a mega-event lies in its legacy; that is, the event's post-games (social) consequences and (sociological) significance. According to William Kelly,

> All Games continue to exist after the fire is extinguished through the required work of completing and publishing official and unofficial records of the Olympiad (reports, documentaries, etc.), fashioning a retrospective theme and narrative, protecting and burnishing the public memories, and engaging broadly in the culminating project of legacy-making. A legacy may be a retrospective refashioning, but the end game of a Games era is a clash of competing legacies as well as a contentious accounting of the multiple after-effects. [71]

As if to concur, Cindy Sui, writing for *New Kerela*, the India-based Internet news portal, suggests that whether the 2008 games have 'left a good or [a] bad impression depends on who you talk to', [72] adding:

> In a year or two, what people will remember might be little more than the star athletes. The vast majority of people worldwide watch the Games more for the sports than to learn about the host country or the political, human rights and other issues. ... China, however, feels the Olympics [have] been a huge boost the country. 'The Beijing Olympic Games are a milestone in the course of the great reinvigoration of the Chinese nation', said a commentary Saturday in the government's Xinhua news agency. 'The success of the Beijing Olympic Games has also reflected the great achievements China has scored after three decades of reform and opening up'. ... 'Through the Beijing Olympic Games, the world has had a better knowledge of what China is like – a country that makes constant progress, emphasizes friendship and harmony, keeps its promises, and respects all international rules', said the Xinhua commentary. [73]

Echoing Xinhua's optimism, Gustaaf Geeraerts (professor of international relations and vice-dean of the Faculty of Economic, Social and Political Sciences, Vrije Universiteit Brussel) is reported to have suggested that the 'success of the Beijing Olympic Games has showcased China's strong capabilities, boosted mutual understanding between the Chinese and foreign citizens, and will surely stimulate its further opening up'. [74] Similarly, Asia One, Singapore is reported to have claimed that 'the Olympics have helped to open up Chinese society despite reported human rights abuses linked to the games'. [75]

In contrast, the *Los Angeles Times* has been less sanguine: the 'Beijing Games are over, declared a resounding success. The question now is whether China will finally loosen up or justify its authoritarianism'; [76] and Jaquelin Magnay, writing in the *Sydney Morning Herald*, has said:

> These were the Coming Out Games for a prospective world power that was supposed to open up to the rest of the world. But … China was exposed to international scrutiny of its social interactions at levels that upset the ruling Communist Party. … Throughout all of August, the organisers were battling a Western media that was not focusing on the sport, but rather the country's political regime, its human rights record, oppression of protesters, restrictions on reporting, brutality of photographers. … From its initial enthusiasm of giving the Games to China to become an instrument of great social change, the [IOC] was forced to the sidelines and became a bit-part player. … Time will tell if these Games are remembered more for … China's pretence of giving its citizens a voice. [77]

Interest in the legacy of the 2008 Beijing games has concentrated on two dimensions of *social change* – one internally oriented and the other externally oriented. Internally, the focus of attention has been on China's authoritarianism, *citizenship* and human rights. Externally, the focus has been on China's 'opening up' through its relations with the rest of the world at various levels, including the individual (with *foreigners*), the international (or *inter-nation-state*), the regional (especially within East Asia) and the global.

In the area of human rights, which drew considerable attention before and during the games, there is broad agreement among observers at least outside China that the games have had little or no effect. [78] The consensus is that the games themselves have not had much of an impact on China's human-rights profile, nor consequently on that of East Asia or on *the global human rights regime* [79] Of course, this does not mean that there are no signs whatsoever of a shift in China's human-rights record, only that the Beijing games and Olympiad have made little difference. After all, as of 16 November 2009, of the 18 UN human-rights instruments that are available for ratification by member states, the PRC had ratified eight – the International Convention on the Elimination of All Forms of Racial Discrimination (CERD); the International Covenant on Economic, Social and Cultural Rights (CESCR); the Convention against Torture and Other Cruel, Inhuman or Degrading Treatment or Punishment (CAT); the Convention on the Elimination of All Forms of Discrimination against Women (CEDAW); the Convention on the Rights of the Child (CRC); the optional protocol to the Convention on the Rights of the Child on the involvement of children in armed conflict (CRC-OPAC); the optional protocol to the Convention on the Rights of the Child on the sale of children, child prostitution and child pornography (CRC-OPSC); and the Convention on the Rights of Persons with Disabilities (CRPD). This number compares with only five ratifications by the USA, which is just one more than North Korea's tally, the same number as Somalia's, one fewer than Iran's, four fewer than Japan's and eight fewer than South Korea's. [80]

Still, while the citizens of China may have scarcely benefited from the 2008 games in terms of their human rights, they may have benefited in another way, in that

'Beijing Olympic organizers say they made a profit out of hosting [the] Games'. According to figures released 'by the government audit bureau, $2.8 billion was spent on organizing and staging the Games, including the Paralympic Summer Games that followed', whereas as of almost a year later the games had generated an income of $3 billion, 'leaving a profit of $176 million'. [81] At the same time, however, some both inside and outside China will have benefited far more than others in economic terms: 'Sponsors of the Beijing Olympics have spent hundreds of millions of dollars for 16 days in the spotlight and they reckon it was money well spent to get a foothold in the huge Chinese market.' [82]

Nonetheless, there appears to be broad agreement that, apart from what might be called short-term revenue gains, there will be little or no 'long-term economic impact of the games on Beijing and China overall': [83]

> Virtually every country that has hosted an Olympics since World War II saw its GDP growth drop – in some cases, sharply – in the year following their respective Olympics. ... Most economists, however, argue China will avert the Olympics curse. 'Fears of a post-Olympics slump are overblown', says HSBC economist Frederic Neumann. 'China is a $4 trillion economy, and in the larger context, the games aren't terribly important for the economy as a whole. We don't foresee a slump by any means'. Beijing's contribution to national GDP, and its population as a proportion of national population are insignificant, particularly when compared with other Olympic host cities in recent decades, ... points out UBS economist Jonathan Anderson. [84]

As Dinah Gardner has put it, the Olympic Games were 'only a small blip in China's grand scheme – now it is simply back to business as normal'. [85] That is, argues Xiao Gongqin, a Shanghai Normal University professor of history, the games were 'a driving force to push China forward but it is still within the scope of [the] existing development system'. [86]

Economics aside, however, the people of China were 'enthused with a vibrant sense of national pride', and consequently Xu Wu (a professor of journalism at Arizona State University) has prophesied, 'Post-Olympics China, at least in the first one or two years, will be marked with triumphant glory and renewed ambition'. [87] Accordingly, on 'the political front there is a general consensus with both Chinese and foreign observers that the success of the Olympics has significantly bolstered domestic support for the Chinese Communist Party (CCP)', as a result of which, Xiao Gonqin suggests, 'the Chinese government's credibility, prestige and authority will reach the highest point ever'. [88]

China's *Olympic fever* is assumed to help account for how a Pew Research Centre survey a few weeks before the 8 August 2008 opening of the Beijing games found that 86 per cent of Chinese people had 'a positive view of their country and the economy (and thus the government) – ranking China the most satisfied out of 24 nations'. [89] Gardner reports how in the survey, 93 per cent of Chinese people believed the Olympics would 'improve China's international image', and how Xu Wu has argued that 'Through the Olympic mirror China certainly saw a strong, proud, and magnificent image of itself'; and that 'This image will bury a long-endured painful memory. [The] collective sentiment of post-Olympics Chinese will be more redeemed, more relaxed, and thus more "normal"' [90] For Xu Wu, the games provided 'a confidence boost that may help China open up further'.

In Gardner's view, China successfully used 'the sports extravaganza' as 'a gateway to gaining international recognition':

> 'We used to have a very sad nationalism because we struggled through a lot of humiliation and setbacks during the last 100 years', says Xiao [Gonqin]. 'And that is not healthy because it has made us unconfident and overly sensitive. The Olympic games shows that China has already been accepted and acknowledged internationally. ... Chinese people's confidence is boosted and our nationalism has become more optimistic, healthy and mature'. On a global scale, the Olympics have also fuelled the government's world power aspirations, says Professor Edward Friedman, a China expert at the University of Wisconsin. 'The goal of the CCP internationally is to establish China as a great power at least the equal of the US', he says. 'So far, the [party] should feel that the Beijing games, from the facilities to the Chinese team's performance, have succeeded in moving China ahead in its preferred direction'. [91]

The boost provided by the 2008 games to China's national pride, confidence and assertiveness appears to have had not only internal but also external ramifications. Externally, it has had an impact at both the regional and global levels, in particular through its spill-over effect on the Olympic movement itself. As William Kelly has put it,

> the Olympic Movement is a global formation of governance, events, and political economy. ... The Olympic Movement is really a crucible of localism, nationalism, regionalism, and globalism. Struggles to define and direct Olympic aims, events, properties, and agendas take place within and among cities and national sports federations, among nation-states of world regions, and across the IOC member-ship. In the case of Japan, the support for its bid has been shored up by a national anxiety about the political and economic challenge of its rival East Asian superpower, China. [92]

The legacy of the Beijing games has included the impact of this mega-event on Tokyo's bid for the right to host the 2016 games. [93] In the run-up to the IOC's decision in October 2009 on the 2016 games, William Kelly examined the circumstances surrounding and background to the Tokyo bid. [94] He emphasized the bid's 'embeddedness' both in the 'jockeying for global city preeminence' and in 'East Asian regional politics', and claimed that in the build-up to the result of the bid the Japanese people were 'feeling anxious about the balance of power and prestige in both spheres' – in, that is, both the global sphere and the regional sphere.

For Kelly, any applicant or candidate city must be attuned 'to ongoing Games cycles', which in the case of Tokyo's 2016 bid 'required a triangulation between' the 'long and fraught Sino-Japanese relationship' and the competitive London-Tokyo relationship over each city's global financial centre ambitions. He argues that Japan viewed the 2008 Beijing Olympics 'with one eye towards the upcoming Games in London and the other towards its own bid to return the 2016 Summer Games to Tokyo'. Japan's reactions to the games were 'decidedly mixed', ranging 'from admiration to anxiety'. This was in part 'based on the deeply ambivalent Sino-Japanese relationship, which some Japanese leaders feel is replacing the US-Japan relationship as the country's most problematic bilateral relation'.

The Beijing games, precisely because of their success and impact on China's self-confidence in relation to the rest of the world, caused concern in the East Asian region, and perhaps above all in Japan. The Japanese people responded ambivalently to the Beijing spectacle:

> Forty-four years after the first Asian Olympic Games in Tokyo, Japan still feels that the region is less than fully acknowledged by the IOC and the Olympic Movement, and the country took satisfaction in a third Asian nation [following Japan in 1964 and South Korea in 1988] joining the host list. Japanese popular and press coverage of the Opening and Closing Ceremonies was glowing, and the architecture and organization of the Games were generally well-reviewed. But the massive economic resources and the oppressive political coordination of the Chinese government drew harsh criticism and stirred deep nervousness about Japan's ability to contend with China's growing clout in the region. [95]

On the one hand, Japanese people tend to share an *Asian identity* with China in relation to the rest of the world, as a result of which they were well disposed towards Beijing hosting the 2008 games, and were then highly impressed with the event itself. Thus, 'the statements by Japanese officials and the coverage by the Japanese media [indicate] a genuine admiration for the smooth logistical efficiencies of the overall production of the Games and the beauty of architecture and performances that foreground Chinese but more generally East Asian competencies and aesthetics'. [96]

On the other hand, the award of the 2008 games to Beijing followed by the August 2008 extravaganza itself served to sharply emphasize China's growing presence and power on the world stage, and associated power within (East) Asia, in particular in relation to Japan. Consequently, the Japanese people's admiration for China and the Beijing games was tempered by their sense of nervousness over China's growing political-economy weight and military might: [97]

> Japanese public opinion and media commentary ... understood the subtext of China's sloganeering of a 'one hundred year dream' to mount the Olympics. To many Japanese, the phrase was a thinly veiled code for an end to 'one hundred years of national humiliation' and a clear reference to the Western and Japanese aggressions that proceeded the PRC era. At the same time, the implied belligerence stirred deep anxieties in Japan about its ability to respond to the growing economic and [political] power of China. [98]

According to Kelly, *in any Games timeline*, or *stages through which all Olympics pass*, 'there is interplay of at least four levels of political and economic interests and ideologies that shape the direction and eventual outcome of bidding and hosting':

There are local agendas, nationalist sentiments, regional rivalries, and global ambitions. All [were] on display in the case of Tokyo's efforts to secure the 2016 Games [...]. At the local level, the bid [was] deeply enmeshed in the political economy of metropolitan development and in the populist bravado of [Tokyo's mayor Ishihara Shintarō]. [99]

Thus the Tokyo bid was 'shaped by – and buffeted by – the local politics of metropolitan development', while also there was 'an effort to create an Olympic narrative with strong nationalist undertones'. [100] Kelly explains:

The current malaise in Japan is wide and deep. It is felt by the most fanatical rightwing militants who rue Japan's pacifism and weak patriotism, by the broad mainstream population who are losing confidence in government competence and are facing massive retrenchment in secure employment, and by progressives on the left, who are gravely concerned about the spectrum of social problems, rising militarism eroding the Constitution's peace provision, and lack of national political vision. [In the wake of] the collapse of the speculative bubble in [1991, the] 1990s were tagged the 'lost decade' but [this] decade ... is reaching twenty years in duration, and the country has yet to find its way out of its collective angst. [101]

Kelly notes that the 1964 Tokyo Olympic Games stand out 'in national memory as a peak moment of collective accomplishment'. They are a poignant reminder of Japan as a 'nation rising from the material and moral devastation of wartime defeat and mobilizing to produce a mega-event that symbolized domestic resolve, national recovery, and international acceptance'. In the case of Tokyo's bid for the 2016 games, there was a 'very pointed deployment of a rhetoric of "reviving the 1964 Olympic spirit" in order to resuscitate national confidence and redress the widespread pessimism of the present moment'. At the time of the bid, there was a 'sense of decline', which moreover was 'aggravated by fear of China's dynamism, on the one hand, and a frustration with lingering subordination' to the USA on the other. While many Japanese found the 'strident neo-nationalism of mayor Ishihara ... repugnant', most harked 'back nostalgically to the legacy of 1964 as impetus for a renewal of the same national spirit and international acclaim'.

Kelly argues that the supporters of Tokyo's bid for the 2016 games were 'gambling that the potential gains at the local and global levels [would] justify the enormous costs to the national government and the risks of aggravating East Asian regional tensions by an "Ishihara" Tokyo Games'. These tensions are far from being confined to the relationship between Japan and China:

much of the nationalist sentiment that fuels Japanese supporters of Tokyo's bid is embedded in the long-term and contemporary rivalries in East Asia – vis-à-vis China, but also in response to the serious tensions on the Korean peninsula. At least since the 1950s, when the IOC confronted the two-China issue, the politics of East Asia have been played out in the Olympic Movement. Although it is often said that the East Asian countries have only recently been given proper standing and importance in the Olympic Movement, it has long been the world region that most directly confronts the IOC with the fundamentally political nature of its mission.

As national entities, as national sports federations, and as host cities, Japan, South Korea, North Korea, China, and Taiwan have been locked in a wary embrace, allies in their quest for Olympic parity, but often bitter rivals in their competition for Olympic acknowledgement and prestige. Thus, the Tokyo Bid Committee [was] at pains to distinguish its application from the [2008] Games even as it [appealed] to the growing significance of East Asia as a region, economically and ideologically, in the IOC's vision of the Olympic future. [102]

It is the tension, conflict or contradiction between, on the one hand, Japan, China and the rest of East Asia increasingly sharing a distinct identity and sense of common, collective destiny in relation to the rest of the world and, on the other hand, the way in which the same political-economy players are locked in deeply rooted rivalries and antagonisms that provides the key to understanding much about decisions and developments within East Asia and the Asia-Pacific, including much about Olympic bids and prevailing levels of regional coherence and cohesion, regionalization and regional integration.

William Kelly suggests that from the 'perspective of IOC geopolitics, the sequence of Sydney 2000, Athens 2004, Beijing 2008, and London 2012 leads prevailing wisdom to assume that the 2016 must be in the Americas – either Chicago in the north or Rio de Janeiro in the south'. Indeed, Tokyo was unsuccessful in its bid to host the 2016 Olympic Games. This honour went to Rio de Janeiro. It went for the first time to a South American city, and for first time to a country in the southern hemisphere other than Australia, but nonetheless to yet another (like China) *rapidly emerging market* in yet another (like East Asia) *rapidly emerging region* within the global political economy.

The choice of Rio fits into a pattern also in so far as, to paraphrase William Kelly, *awarding games to reward or facilitate integration into the world community, or global political economy, is an IOC objective*, a result of which is that games become *coming-out parties*. The 2012 London games aside, it is as if the Olympic torch has been passed from one coming-out party (the 2008 Beijing games) for one *BRIC economy* (the PRC) to another (the 2016 Rio games) for a second *BRIC economy* (Brazil). [103]

In the mean time, in 2010, South Africa hosted the biggest *single-sport* mega-event, the FIFA World Cup finals, awarded to South Africa as if in recognition of the country's rapid development among the BRICSAM nation-states (Brazil, Russia, India, China, South Africa, ASEAN and Mexico). [104] Perhaps, in effect, the way is being prepared for South Africa to host the Olympic Games, even as early as 2020:

organizers of South Africa's 2010 World Cup think a successful tournament could lead to a bid for the 2020 Summer Olympic Games. ... Organizing committee chief executive officer Danny Jordaan [has said] 'the IOC decided to give South America its first Olympics, so the only continent now without an Olympics is the African continent and therefore I think it's something that the IOC certainly will have to begin to think about'. Jordaan said he could envision Johannesburg, Cape Town or Durban bidding along with Egypt for the 2020 Games. [105]

As well as a bid from a South African city for the 2020 games, a bid has been signalled on behalf of Tokyo. [106] However, Tokyo may well be disappointed again if Danny Jordaan has his way, and in so far as a South African games would have the lure of a further *coming-out party*, a further reward for – as well as to further facilitate – South Africa's *integration into the global political economy*, and doing so as if lighting the way for the rest of Africa.

Conclusion

Whatever motivates and shapes any bid by Tokyo for the 2020 Olympics, Tokyo's bid for the 2016 games was affected by (if William Kelly is to be believed) Japan's anxiety about China, fuelled as this was by the 2008 games. Still, it is likely that neither the Beijing games nor any subsequent Olympics-related event will have much influence in the long term on the course of Sino-Japanese relations, largely dependent as these are on what are regarded on both sides of the East China Sea as more important considerations.

It is these considerations that lie behind how China and Japan in concert with most other East Asian political economy players – including the Association of Southeast Asian Nations (ASEAN) – appear to be increasingly engrossed in strengthening their network of intra-regional bilateral and multilateral ties, including through both *de facto* and *de jure* regionalization and regional integration, processes that in the view of many policy-makers and others in East Asia are inexorably leading to the creation of an East Asian Community (EAC), perhaps somewhat akin to the European Union (EU). [107]

In the midst of these processes and what is driving them, any Olympic-related matters are likely to have little influence on Sino-Japanese, East Asian or Asia-Pacific relations, while any influence had is likely to be affirmative vis-à-vis regionalization towards an East Asian Community, in particular through their boost to the formation of a distinct East Asian regional identity in relation to the rest of the world.

Perhaps, above all, the value of hosting an Olympic Games in East Asia, the Asia-Pacific or any other region, such as South America or southern Africa, lies in how the games put all competition, rivalries and anxieties in perspective – in their place – in particular in comparison with and in relation to each another. Any Olympics-related competition, rivalry and anxiety will pale relative to what will stand out as far more important, fundamental and vital considerations, concerns and interests. What will appear more important in East Asia and the Asia-Pacific is the prevailing and rapidly growing competition from political economy players in other regions, including India in South Asia, Brazil in South America and South Africa in southern Africa, and the advantages of confronting this competition in a collective, organized manner. What will appear more important is how external nation states are increasingly turning for competitive purposes to regional integration and organizations, exemplified not only by the European Union (EU) and the North American Free Trade Agreement (NAFTA) but also by the South Asian Association for Regional

Cooperation (SAARC), the Union of South American Nations (UNASUR) and the Southern Africa Development Community (SADC).

The part played by and relative importance of the Olympics in East Asia and the Asia-Pacific in the future will depend largely on the degree to which the games (wherever they are held) will help enhance regional identity and robustness in confronting external challenges in the interregnum prior to the construction under globalization of a *single global social space*. On these grounds, it might be anticipated that the appeal of the Olympics in East Asia and the Asia-Pacific will remain strong, and indeed will become stronger.

Notes

[1] FIFA, the *Fédération Internationale de Football Association* (or the International Federation of Association Football) is the international governing body of association football. It is responsible for organizing football's major international tournaments, above all the FIFA World Cup. It has 208 member associations, 16 more members than the UN and three more than the IOC, but five fewer than the International Association of Athletics Federations (IAAF).

[2] The prefix 'mega-' comes from the Greek word *megas*, meaning *great* (Peasall, *Concise Oxford Dictionary*, 886). It means 'abnormally large' ('mega-', MedicineNet.com. available online at http://www.medterms.com/, accessed 21 Jan. 2009), or denotes 'surpassing other examples of its kind' ('mega-', Answers.com. available online at http://www.answers.com/topic/mega, accessed 5 Dec. 2008).

[3] What comes to mind is the word 'elephantine', meaning *of extraordinary size and power* (Answers.com, available online at http://www.answers.com/topic/elephantine, accessed 5 Feb. 2009).

[4] Aguilar *et al.*, 'Globalization, Regional Development, and Mega-city Expansion'.

[5] Ohmae, *The Borderless World*; Ohmae,*The End of the Nation State*.

[6] See Baylis and Smith, *The Globalization of World Politics*.

[7] Cf. Berger and Huntington, *Many Globalizations*.

[8] Ohmae, *The Borderless World*.

[9] Robertson, *Globalization*; Scholte, *Globalization*; Close *et al.*, *The Beijing Olympiad*, 34.

[10] Close, 'Regional Integration the East Asian Way'.

[11] Ibid.

[12] Axford, *The Global System*; Meyer *et al.*, 'Ontology and Rationalization'.

[13] Close and Askew, *Asia Pacific and Human Rights*, 243–4; Close *et al.*, *The Beijing Olympiad*, 35.

[14] See Wilson and Purushothaman, 'Dreaming with BRICs'; Jain, *Emerging Economies*.

[15] Aguilar *et al.*, 'Globalization, Regional Development, and Mega-city Expansion'.

[16] See also Andranovich *et al.*, 'Olympic Cities'.

[17] Short, 'Going for Gold'; see also Axford, *The Global System*; Baylis and Smith, *The Globalization of World Politics*; Held *et al.*, *Global Transformations*.

[18] Short, 'Going for Gold'.

[19] Ibid.

[20] Roche, *Mega-Events and Modernity*; 'Mega-events, Time and Modernity'; 'Mega-events and Modernity Revisited'.

[21] Roche, *Mega-Events and Modernity*, 1.

[22] Roche, 'Mega-events, Time and Modernity', 99.

[23] Ibid., 99–101.

[24] Ibid., 100–1.

[25] Ibid.

[26] Ibid., 100.

[27] Ibid., 99.

[28] Horne and Manzenreiter, *Japan, Korea and the 2002 World Cup*.

[29] Tomlinson and Young, *National Identity and Global Sports Events*.

[30] Horne and Manzenreiter, *Japan, Korea and the 2002 World Cup*, 187.

[31] Short, 'Going for Gold'.

[32] Roche, 'Mega-events, Time and Modernity', 99.

[33] John Short refers to *199 countries* (Short, 'Going for Gold'), but he might have referred to *199 countries and territories*.

[34] Short, 'Going for Gold'.

[35] Ibid.

[36] Roche, 'Mega-events, Time and Modernity', 100–1.

[37] Ibid., 99.

[38] Andranovich *et al.*, 'Olympic Cities', 118.

[39] Short, 'Going for Gold'.

[40] All NOCs apart from one, that of Brunei, participated in the 2008 summer Olympic Games.

[41] Close *et al.*, *The Beijing Olympiad*.

[42] Ibid., 21–44.

[43] On the coming-out view of Asian Olympic Games, see Black and Bezanson, 'The Olympic Games, Human Rights and Democratisation'; Gottwald and Duggan, 'China's Economic Development'; Levine, 'A Golden Opportunity'; Manheim, 'Rites of Passage'.

[44] Gottwald and Duggan, 'China's Economic Development', 339.

[45] See Close and Ohki-Close, *Supranationalism in the New World Order*.

[46] See 'Past Results', GamesBids.com, available online at http://www.gamesbids.com/english/archives/past.shtml, accessed 6 Feb. 2009.

[47] See Close and Askew, *Asia Pacific and Human Rights*.

[48] 'China Leaves Nothing to Chance', *National Post* (Canada), 11 July 2008, available online at http://www.nationalpost.com/news/story.html?id=648855, accessed 23 Sept. 2010.

[49] Short, 'Going for Gold'.

[50] See Sky Sports, 'Medals Table', 24 Aug. 2008, available online at http://msnsport.skysports.com, accessed 23 Sept. 2010.

[51] Short, 'Going for Gold'.

[52] Australian Bureau of Statistics, 'Australia Finishes Third'. ABS, 30 Aug. 2004, available online at http://abs.gov.au/, accessed 23 Sept. 2010.

[53] Kelly, 'Asia Pride, China Fear'.

[54] 'Upper-middle Income Magic', *Business Standard* (New Delhi), 10 Aug. 2008, available online at http://www.business-standard.com/india/news/editorial-upper-middle-income-magic/330930/, accessed 23 Sept. 2010.

[55] Ibid.

[56] S. Bery, 'The Next Twenty Years', *Business Standard* (New Delhi), 13 Aug. 2008, available online at http://www.ncaer.org/downloads/MediaClips/Press/sumanbery-nexttwentyyears.pdf, accessed 23 Sept. 2010.

[57] Ibid.; see also Maddison, *The World Economy*.

[58] 'Upper-middle Income Magic'.

[59] R. Dhoot, 'Beijing Olympics Draws 4.7 Billion Television Viewers', *Top News*, 5 Sept. 2008, available online at http://www.topnews.in/sports/beijing-olympics-draws-4-7-billion-television-viewers-24445, accessed 23 Sept. 2010

[60] Ibid. See also BOCOG, 'Global TV Viewing of Athens 2004 Olympic Games Breaks Records', 12 Oct. 2004, available online at http://en.beijing2008.cn/16/87/article211928716.shtml, accessed 23 Sept. 2010; '4.7 Billion Saw Olympics: Nielsen'. *Japan Times*, 7 Sept. 2008, available online at http://search.japantimes.co.jp/cgi-bin/so20080907a1.html, accessed 23 Sept. 2010; Nielsen Company, 'The Most Viewed Olympics Ever', 24 Aug. 2008, available online at http://en-us.nielsen.com/main/news/news_releases/2008/august/the_most_viewed_olympics; Nielsen Company, 'Beijing Olympics Draw Largest Ever Global TV Audience', 5 Sept. 2008, available online at http://blog.nielsen.com/nielsenwire/media_entertainment/beijing-olympics-draw-largest-ever-global-tv-audience/, accessed 23 Sept. 2010.

[61] On 'Pacific Asia, see Mark Borthwick, *Pacific Century*; Fu-chen Lo, *Emerging World Cities in Pacific Asia*; Xiaoming Huang, *Politics in Pacific Asia*; Yumei Zhang, *Pacific Asia*. On 'East Asia', see EASG, *Final Report*; Shiraishi, 'Regional Cooperation in East Asia'; Temple University, 'East Asia'; Terada, Constructing an "East Asian" Concept'.

[62] See Asia-Pacific Economic Cooperation (APEC), 'About Us', available online at http://www.apec.org/, accessed 4 Dec. 2009; see also Connors *et al.*, *The New Global Politics*; Eccleston *et al.*, *The Asia-Pacific Profile*.

[63] See ERINA, 'Maps of Northeast Asia'.

[64] For the sake of convenience, by 'China' is meant the People's Republic of China (PRC) plus the Special Administrative Region (SAR) of Hong Kong, the SAR of Macau and the Republic of China (otherwise known as Taiwan or Chinese Taipei).

[65] ERINA, 'Maps of Northeast Asia', 2009.

[66] See APEC, 'About Us'; see also UNSD (United Nations Statistics Division), 'Composition of Macro Geographical (Continental) Regions, Geographical Sub-regions, and Selected Economic and Other Groupings', 15 April 2009, available online at http://millenniumindicators.un.org/unsd/methods/m49/m49regin.htm#oceania, accessed 23 Sept. 2010..

[67] See Close and Askew, *Asia Pacific and Human Rights*; Close and Askew, 'Globalisation and Football in East Asia'; Close *et al.*, *The Beijing Olympiad*.

[68] Nielsen Company, 'Opening Ceremony Draws 2 Billion Global Viewers', 14 Aug. 2008, available online at http://blog.nielsen.com/nielsenwire/media_entertainment/beijing-opening-ceremonys-global-tv-audience-hit-2-billion/, accessed 23 Sept. 2010.

[69] K. Sharma, 'Nearly One in Three Worldwide Watched Olympics Opener', *Top News*, 14 Aug. 2008, available online at http://www.topnews.in/sports/nearly-one-three-worldwide-watched-olympics-opener-survey-23186, accessed 23 Sept. 2010.

[70] Nielsen Company, 'Beijing Olympics Draw Largest Ever Global Audience'.

[71] Kelly, 'Asia Pride, China Fear'; see also Mangan and Dyreson., *Olympic Legacies*.

[72] Cindy Sui, 'What Will China's Olympic Legacy Be?'. NewKerela.com, 25 Aug. 2008, available online at http://www.newkerala.com/topstory-fullnews-14612.html">http://www.newkerala.com/topstory-fullnews-14612.html, accessed 23 Sept. 2010.

[73] Ibid.; see also 'China After the Olympics', *All About China*, Aug. 2008, available online at http://www.radio86.co.uk/china-insight/, accessed 23 Sept. 2010.

[74] G. Geeraerts, 'After the Games: China's Olympic Legacy', *All About China*, Aug. 2008, available online at http://www.radio86.co.uk/china-insight/world-viewpoints/9348/top-events-of-2008-after-the-games-chinas-olympic-legacy, accessed 23 Sept. 2010.

[75] Asia One (Singapore), 'Olympics Helped to Open Chinese Society', *All About China*, Aug. 2008, available online at http://www.radio86.co.uk/china-insight/, accessed 23 Sept. 2010.

[76] *Los Angeles Times*, '"The Best Olympics Ever" – Now What?', *All About China*, Aug. 2008, available online at http://www.radio86.co.uk/china-insight/world-viewpoints/9348/top-events-of-2008-after-the-games-chinas-olympic-legacy, accessed 23 Sept. 2010.

[77] Jaquelin Magnay, 'Beijing Gloss Fades After Going Through the Wringer', *Sydney Morning Herald*, 28 Aug. 2008, available online at http://www.radio86.co.uk/china-insight/

world-viewpoints/9348/top-events-of-2008-after-the-games-chinas-olympic-legacy, accessed 23 Sept. 2010.

[78] See Amnesty International, 'China: Legacy of the Beijing Olympics', 26 Feb. 2008; Amnesty International, 'China: Free Thwarted Olympics PetitionerJi Sizun', 5 May 2009, both available online at http://www.amnesty.org/, accessed 23 Sept. 2010; also 'China: Beyond the Games', *Financial Times*, 4 Aug. 2008, available online at http://www.ft.com/, accessed 23 Sept. 2010.

[79] Close and Askew, *Asia Pacific and Human Rights*.

[80] Office of the United Nations High Commissioner for Human Rights (OHCHR), 'Status of Ratification', 16 Nov. 2009, available online at http://www2.ohchr.org/english/law/docs/ HRChart.xls, accessed 23 Sept. 2010; see also OHCHR, 'International Law', 2007.

[81] 'Beijing Claims Profit on 2008 Olympics', *Japan Times*, 20 June 2009, available online at http://search.japantimes.co.jp/cgi-bin/so20090620a2.html, accessed 23 Sept. 2010.

[82] Reuters, 'For Sponsors, Games Were Money Well Spent', 25 Aug. 2008, available online at http://www.reuters.com/article/GCA-Olympics/idUSSP1708120080825, accessed 23 Sept. 2010. In 2010, 'Shanghai will host the 2010 World Expo, replacing the Olympic "One World, One Dream" motto for the Expo's catchphrase of "Better City, Better Life"' (D. Gardner, 'China's Olympic Legacy', Aljazeera.net, 25 Aug. 2008, available online at http:// english. aljazeera.net/focus/beijing08/2008/08/20088255274440438.html, accessed 23 Sept. 2010).

[83] A. Naidu, 'China May Avert the "Olympics Curse"', *Outlook Business*, 6 Sept. 2008, available online at http://business.outlookindia.com/printarticle.aspx?101450, accessed 23 Sept. 2010.

[84] Ibid.

[85] Gardner, 'China's Olympic Legacy', *Al Jazeera*, 25 August 2008. Available online at http:// english.aljazeera.net/focus/beijing08/2008/08/20088255274440438.html, accessed 23 Sept. 2010.

[86] Ibid.

[87] Ibid.

[88] Ibid.

[89] Ibid.; see also Pew Research Center, 'The Chinese Celebrate'.

[90] Gardner, 'China's Olympic Legacy', *Al Jazeera*, 25 August 2008. Available online at http:// english.aljazeera.net/focus/beijing08/2008/08/20088255274440438.html, accessed 23 Sept. 2010.

[91] Ibid.

[92] Kelly, 'Asia Pride, China Fear', 2009.

[93] 'Competition among Japanese cities for the right to mount a 2016 bid began in 2004, and the Japan IOC settled on Tokyo on August 30, 2006': Kelly, 'Asia Pride, China Fear'.

[94] Ibid.

[95] Ibid.

[96] Ibid.; see also Farrer, 'One Bed, Different Dreams', 2008.

[97] See 'Japan Eager for U.S. to Keep Nuke Deterrence', *Japan Times*, 24 Nov. 2009, available online at http://search.japantimes.co.jp/cgi-bin/nn20091124a1.html, accessed 23 Sept. 2010: 'The shift in political power in September [in Japan following the parliamentary general election], Japan aggressively lobbied a US congressional nuclear task force to maintain the credibility of the US "nuclear umbrella" to deter possible attacks by China and North Korea, sources said Monday.'

[98] Kelly, 'Asia Pride, China Fear'.

[99] Ibid.; see also Nathan, *Japan Unbound*; Sherif, 'The Aesthetics of Speed'.

[100] Kelly, 'Asia Pride, China Fear'.

[101] Ibid.; see also Leheny, *Think Global*; Harootunian, *Japan After Japan*.

[102] Kelly, 'Asia Pride, China Fear'.

[103] 'Over the next 50 years, Brazil, Russia, India and China – the BRIC economies – could become a much larger force in the world economy. … If things go right, in less than 40 years, the BRIC economies together could be larger than the G6 in US dollar terms. By 2025 they could account for over half the size of the G6. Currently they are worth less than 15%. Of the current G6, only the US and Japan may be among the six largest economies in US dollar terms in 2050' (Wilson and Purushothaman, 'Dreaming with BRICs').

[104] 'The BRICSAM countries are a group of large developing economies whose elevated economic growth and growing regional and international influence will have ripple effects on the world. Not only will these countries experience significant changes as a result of their economic and political rise, but the BRICSAM countries are also likely to be the beneficiaries of this change as the global economic balance of power shifts away from the industrialized countries' (CIGI, 'BRICSAM'). Brazil has been selected by FIFA to host the 2014 World Cup, and in December 2009 the Japanese government decided to support a bid by Japan to host either the 2018 or the 2022 event (see J. Hongo, 'Cabinet OKs Move to Pursue World Cup', *Japan Times*, 10 Dec. 2009, available online at http://search.japantimes.co.jp/mail/nn20091209a4.html, accessed 23 Sept. 2010.

[105] Games Bids, 'South Africa Considers 2002 Bid', available online at http://www.gamesbids.com/eng/olympic_bids/future_bids_2016/1216134798.html, accessed 22 Oct. 2009.

[106] Games Bids, 'Tokyo to Bid for 2020 Summer Games', available online at http://www.gamesbids.com/eng/olympic_bids/future_bids_2016/1216134834.html, accessed 7 Nov. 2009.

[107] See Close, 'Regional Integration the East Asian Way' (Nov. 2008); Close, 'Regional Integration the East Asian Way' (Dec. 2008); EAVG, 'Towards an East Asian Community'; Kim, 'Regionalization and Regionalism'.

References

Aguilar, Adrián, Peter Ward and C. B. Smith. 'Globalization, Regional Development, and Mega-city Expansion in Latin America: Analyzing Mexico City's Peri-urban Hinterland'. *Cities* 20, no. 1 (2003): 3–21.

Andranovich, G., M. Burbank and C. Heying. 'Olympic Cities: Lessons Learned from Mega-event Politics'. *Journal of Urban Affairs* 23, no. 2 (2001): 113–31.

Axford, B. *The Global System: Economics, Politics and Culture.* Cambridge: Polity Press, 1995.

Baylis, J. and S. Smith. *The Globalization of World Politics,* 3rd edn. Oxford: Oxford University Press, 2004.

Berger, P. and S. Huntington. *Many Globalizations.* Oxford: Oxford University Press, 2002.

Black, D. and S. Bezanson. 'The Olympic Games, Human Rights and Democratisation: Lessons from Seoul and Implications for Beijing'. *Third World Quarterly* 25, no. 7 (2004): 1245–61.

Borthwick, M. *Pacific Century: the Emergence of Pacific Asia,* 3rd edn. Boulder, CO: Westview Press, 2006.

CIGI (Centre for International Governance Innovation). 'BRICSAM'. Available online at http://www.cigionline.org/project/bricsam/, accessed 7 Dec. 2009.

Close, P. 'Regional Integration the East Asian Way: Towards an Analytical Framework'. Paper presented at conference on EU and East Asia within an Evolving Global Order, EU-NESCA (Network of European Studies Centres in Asia), l'Institut d'Etudes Européennes (IEE), Université Libre de Bruxelles (ULB), Nov. 2008.

Close, P. 'Regional Integration the East Asian Way'. *Newsletter of the Center for Southeast Asian Studies (CSEAS), Kyoto University* 59 (Dec. 2008): 16–17.

Close, P. and D. Askew. *Asia Pacific and Human Rights: A Global Political Economy Perspective.* Aldershot: Ashgate, 2004.

Close, P. and D. Askew. 'Globalisation and Football in East Asia'. In *Football Goes East: Business, Culture and the People's Game in China, Japan and South Korea,* edited by W. Manzenreiter and J. Horne. London: Routledge, 2004: 243–56.

Close, P., D. Askew and Xu Xin. *The Beijing Olympiad: The Political Economy of a Sporting Mega-Event.* London: Routledge, 2007.

Close, P. and E. Ohki-Close. *Supranationalism in the New World Order.* Basingstoke: Macmillan, 1999.

Connors, M.R. Davison, and J. Dosch. *The New Global Politics of the Asia-Pacific.* London: Routledge, 2004.

EASG (East Asian Study Group). *Final Report of the East Asian Study Group.* Jakarta: ASEAN Secretariat, 2002. Available online at http://www.aseansec.org, accessed 23 Sept. 2010.

EAVG (East Asia Vision Group (EAVG). *Towards and East Asian Community.* Jakarta: ASEAN Secretariat, 2001. Available online at http://www.aseansec.org, accessed 23 Sept. 2010.

Eccleston, B., M. Dawson and D. McNamara, eds. *The Asia-Pacific Profile.* London and New York: Rouldege and Open University, 1998.

ERINA (Economic Research Institute for Northeast Asia). 'Maps of Northeast Asia', *ERINA.* 2009, available online at http://www.erina.or.jp/, accessed 23 Sept. 2010.

Farrer, J. 'One Bed, Different Dreams: The Beijing Olympics as Seen in Tokyo'. *Policy Innovations,* Aug. 2008, available online at http://www.policyinnovations.org/ideas/commentary/data/000079, accessed 23 Sept. 2010.

Fu-chen Lo. *Emerging World Cities in Pacific Asia.* New York: United Nations University Press, 1997.

Gottwald, Jörn-Carsten and Niall Duggan, Niall. 'China's Economic Development and the Beijing Olympics'. *International Journal of the History of Sport* Vol. 25, no. 3 (2008): 339–54.

Harootunian, Harry. *Japan After Japan.* Durham NC: Duke University Press, 2006.

Held, D., A. McGrew, D. Goldblatt and J. Perraton. *Global Transformations: Politics, Economic and Culture.* Cambridge: Polity Press, 1999.

Hobsbawm, E. and T. Ranger. *The Invention of Tradition.* Cambridge: Cambridge University Press, 1992.

Horne, J. and W. Manzenreiter eds. *Japan, Korea and the 2002 World Cup.* London: Routledge, 2002.

Jain, S.C.. *Emerging Economies and the Transformation of International Business: Brazil, Russia, India and China.* Cheltenham: Edward Elgar Publishing, 2007.

Kelly, W. W. 'Asia Pride, China Fear, Tokyo Anxiety: Japan Looks Back at 2008 Beijing and Forward to 2012 London and 2016 Tokyo'. *Asia-Pacific Journal* 23 (June 2009). Available online at http://www.japanfocus.org/-William_W_-Kelly/3167, accessed 23 Sept. 2010.

Kim, S. 'Regionalization and Regionalism in East Asia'. *Journal of East Asian Studies* 4 (2004): 39–67.

Leheny, D. *Think Global, Fear Local: Sex, Violence, and Anxiety in Contemporary Japan.* Ithaca, NY and London: Cornell University Press, 2006.

Levine, J.F. 'A Golden Opportunity for Global Acceptance? How Hosting the Olympic Games Impacts a Nation's Economy and Intellectual Property Rights with a Focus on the Right of Publicity'. *Sports Lawyers Journal* 15 (2008): 245.

Maddison, A. *The World Economy:Historical Statistics.* Paris: OECD, 2003.

Mangan, J.A. and M. Dyreson eds. *Olympic Legacies: Intended and Unintended – Political, Cultural, Economic, Educational.* London: Routledge, 2008.

Manheim, J. B. 'Rites of Passage: the 1988 Seoul Olympics as Public Diplomacy'. *Western Political Quarterly* 43, no. 2 (1990): 279–95.

Meyer, J.F. Ramirez and J. Boli. 'Ontology and Rationalization in the Western Cultural Account'. In *Institutional Structure: Constituting State, Society and the Individual*, edited by G. Thomas, J. Meyer, F. Ramirez and J. Boli. Beverley Hills, CA: Sage, 1987.

Nathan, J. *Japan Unbound: A Volatile Nation's Quest for Pride and Purpose*. Boston, MA and New York: Houghton Mifflin Company, 2004.

Ohmae, K. *The Borderless World*. New York: HarperCollins, 1990.

Ohmae, K. *The End of the Nation State*. New York: HarperCollins, 1995.

Peasall, Judy ed. *The Concise Oxford Dictionary*. 10th edn. Oxford: Oxford University Press, 2001.

Pew Research Center. 'The Chinese Celebrate their Roaring Economy'. *Pew Global Attitudes Project*, 22 July 2008, available online at http://pewglobal.org/reports/display.php?ReportID=261, accessed 23 Sept. 2010.

Robertson, R. *Globalization: Social Theory and Global Culture*. London: Sage, 1992.

Roche, M. *Mega-Events and Modernity: Olympics and Expos in the Growth of Global Culture*. London: Routledge, 2000.

Roche, M. 'Mega-events, Time and Modernity: on Time Structures in Global Society'. *Time and Society*. Vol. 12, no. 1 (2003): 99–126.

Roche, M. 'Mega-events and Modernity Revisited: Globalization and the Case of the Olympics'. *Sociological Review* 54, suppt. 2 (2006): 25–40.

Scholte, J. A. *Globalization: A Critical Introduction*. Basingstoke: Macmillan, 2000.

Sherif, A. 'The Aesthetics of Speed and the Illogicality of Politics: Ishihara Shintarō as a Cold War Youth'. In *Japan's Cold War: Media, Literature, and the Law*. New York: Columbia University Press, 2009: 173–202.

Shiraishi, Takashi. 'Regional Cooperation in East Asia and the Role of Public Intellectuals'. *Asian Public Intellectuals Quarterly Newsletter* 18 (Jan. 2009): 1–4.

Short J. *Global Dimensions: Space, Place, and the Contemporary World*. London: Reaktion, 2001.

Short, J. 'Going for Gold: Globalizing the Olympics, Localizing the Games'. *Globalization and World Cities Research Bulletin* 10 (2003). Available online at http://www.lboro.ac.uk/gawc/rb/rb100.html

Temple University. 'East Asia'. Available online at http://astro.temple.edu/~bstavis/courses/east_asia_map.jpg, accessed 6 Dec. 2009.

Terada, Takashi. 'Constructing an "East Asian" Concept and Growing Regional Identity: from EAEC to ASEAN + 3'. *Pacific Review* 16, no. 2 (2003): 252–77.

Tomlinson, A. and C. Young. *National Identity and Global Sports Events*. Albany, NY: State University of New York Press, 2005.

Wilson, D. and R. Purushothaman. 'Dreaming with BRICs: the Path to 2050'. *Goldman Sachs, Global Economics* 99 (2003). Available online at http://www2.goldmansachs.com, accessed 23 Sept. 2010.

Xiaoming Huang. *Politics in Pacific Asia: An Introduction*. Basingstoke: Palgrave Macmillan, 2009.

Yoda, Tomiko and H.D. Harootunian, eds. *Japan after Japan: Social and Cultural Life from the Recessionary 1990s to the Present*. Durham, NC and London: Duke University Press, 2006.

Yumei Zhang. *Pacific Asia: The Politics of Development*. London: Routledge, 2003.

The Geopolitics of Global Aspiration: Sport Mega-events and Emerging Powers

Scarlett Cornelissen

What is the significance of the fact that several recent or upcoming sport mega-events are hosted by emerging powers such as China (the 2008 Beijing Games), India (2010 Commonwealth Games), South Africa (2010 FIFA World Cup), Russia (2014 Winter Olympics in Sochi) or Brazil (2014 FIFA World Cup)? This paper analyses events hosted by three states of the emerging power (or so-called BRICSA) axis. These are the 2008 Olympics, the 2010 FIFA World Cup and the 2010 New Delhi Commonwealth Games. It suggests that the hosting of such events by today's emerging powers occurs through a common agenda: to showcase economic achievements, to signal diplomatic stature or to project, in the absence of other forms of international influence, soft power. Furthermore, emerging powers can reshape the way in which events are viewed, planned for and commercialized, and by which they impact upon stakeholders. In all, sport mega-events constitute a key part of the political imagineering of emerging powers, serving as a focal point both for the type of society and state these authorities try to create, as well as for the position in the international order these rulers attempt to craft. While this strategy has some success, it also tends to come at some material and symbolic costs for these states.

Introduction

The decision by the International Olympic Committee (IOC) to select the city of Beijing as host of the games for the twenty-ninth Olympiad inaugurated a new era of relations between this body and the People's Republic of China (PRC). As one of the larger non-Western powers in the Olympic movement, China's ties with the IOC during the twentieth century, and particularly during the period of the Cold War, was more often than not shaped by the politics of the time. This often meant that events in the wider political environment affected not only China's relations with the IOC, but also the country's placing in the general movement. [1] The selection of Beijing as host for the 2008 Olympic Games served to invert this history in a number of related ways: by positioning China more centrally in the movement, at least for the duration of the Olympiad; by providing opportunity for the PRC to demonstrate to the outside world the extent of its recent economic expansion and modernization; by inviting discourse (sometimes quite acrimonious) about the universality of Olympism; and through China's attempt to leave a particular organizational legacy which could be replicated in subsequent games.

But the 2008 Beijing games – and in particular its size, success and aftermath – is also important for the kind of path it marks for the hosting of mega-events by other states, and the overarching tale about the greater significance of such events in today's context. In particular, the 2008 games inducted a series of future mega-events held by a number of hosts who, in the wider history of sport mega-events, are rather unorthodox. In 2010 South Africa played host to the nineteenth World Cup of the Fédération Internationale de Football Association (FIFA), the first African country to do so. In the same year New Delhi was to be the location for the Commonwealth Games. While the Commonwealth Games has always had a strong regional home in Asia, the Indian authorities were seeking to signal India's own recent economic emergence through the 2010 event. According to the organizers of the 2010 Commonwealth Games, the event was also intended to foster 'democracy, progress and peace' in India. [2] Also, in 2014, the Russian city of Sochi will host the Winter Olympics. In addition, in 2012 the Ukraine and Poland will co-host the championships of the influential European football federation, i.e. the Union of European Football Associations' (UEFA's) Euro tournament. Both members of the former Communist bloc, these countries' hosting of the Euro 2012 tournament at the least disrupts the geographical pattern set thus far in the European championship's history. With the exception of Yugoslavia's hosting of the 1976 finals, all prior tournaments were hosted in west European centres. Finally, in 2014 Brazil will host the next FIFA World Cup after South Africa.

Given this, it could be said that the 2008 Beijing Games inaugurates an important new direction in sport mega-events, where many future or aspirant hosts are based in the developing world. More than that: states such as Brazil, Russia, India, China and South Africa (or in the parlance of geopolitics scholars, the BRICSA grouping) all fall in the class of what has been termed 'emerging powers'. These are states which in the contemporary era have seen rapid rates of industrialization and growth and which by virtue of their industrial output, economic size and influence in certain international sectors – such as commodities – are important players in the contemporary world economy. Together, Brazil, India, China and Russia for instance account for 15 per cent of global output and represent 40 per cent of the world's population. [3]

For many of these states their economic influence is matched or supported by the role they play in international politics and their resultant diplomatic stature. China and Russia – both major powers in their respective regional spheres and both permanent members of the United Nations Security Council – perhaps exemplify this best. As a member of the Group of Eight industrialized nations (G8), Russia's influence arguably derives more from the geopolitical legacy of the Cold War than its current-day economic prowess, but it remains a principal force in international diplomacy. For their part India, Brazil and South Africa not only dominate the economies and politics of their regions, but each also has a track record of seeking to act as leader of the developing world. For example, India played an initiating role in the Afro-Asian Conference, held in Bandung, Indonesia, in 1955; it is a leader in the non-aligned movement; and the country's twentieth-century diplomacy was long shaped by the politics of Third World collaboration and camaraderie. In post-apartheid South Africa the country's foreign policy built on a liberation-struggle-era tradition of solidarity among developing countries and the country sought to define itself as a leader of the African continent. [4] More recently, these three countries have sought to give greater credence to their status as leaders of the 'Global South' by establishing a trilateral alliance, the India-Brazil-South Africa (IBSA) Forum, set up to facilitate regular diplomatic exchange and to foster cohesive policies on international economic and political matters of interest for their world regions. [5]

Is it significant that many of the recently held or upcoming sport mega-events are hosted by emerging powers? This paper suggests that the hosting of such events by today's emerging powers occurs through a common agenda: events are used to showcase economic achievements, to signal diplomatic stature or to project, in the absence of other forms of international influence, soft power. Furthermore, generally informed by different (in the main, political) motives, and facing different sets of local urban, environmental, political and economic conditions from their counter-parts in the developed world, emerging powers can reshape the way in which events are viewed, planned for and commercialized and in which they impact upon stakeholders.

The paper considers these elements in analyses of the Olympics, FIFA's football finals and the Commonwealth Games. It starts off with a discussion of the relationship between sport, ideology and geopolitics by presenting a number of historical and contemporary cases. The next part of the paper explores the international and domestic politics surrounding, respectively, the 2008 Beijing games, the 2010 FIFA World Cup and the 2010 New Delhi Commonwealth Games. A concluding section highlights common themes arising from these events and discusses their implications.

Symbolic Realms: Sport Mega-events, Ideology and Geopolitics

The international Olympic Games have proved to be openly an imperialistic tool. They [are] said to have sports without politics in the Olympic Games, to have them only among nations who are not communistic, who are not against imperialism, colonialism and the IOC have excluded Indonesia from the Int. Olympic Committee because we have behaved not pleasantly to their concept. Now after that experience we Indonesians thought, let us better speak frankly. ... When they excluded Communist China, is that not politics? ... When they are not friendly to

North Korea, is this not politics? ... Now let's frankly say, *sports has something to do with politics*. Indonesia proposes to mix sports with politics and let us now establish the Games of the New Emerging Forces, the GANEFO ... against the Old Established Order. [6]

Much of the discourse that prevails today on sport mega-events centres on their economic dimensions, and the short- and long-term impacts that an event could have for hosts. Underlying this are a number of factors related to the growing economic significance of sport overall, and of sport mega-events in particular: the search for alternative developmental opportunities by public authorities in an increasingly globalized, competitive and interdependent world; and new symbolic and political values that are being attached to leisure and consumption. [7] All of these have resulted in the extended commercialization and commoditization of large-scale sport events, which in turn helped place an economic premium on the hosting of such events.

Although significant, and a central motivation for most aspiring event hosts, this emphasis on major events' economic facets tends to underplay their political and ideological contours. These are manifold and include the way in which hosting or participating in international sport events could enhance (or assuage) patriotism; the manner in which political actors such as governments could seek to attach certain ideas or messages to sport events; or how events could constitute the convergence point for competing ideologies. Indeed, the twentieth-century history of international sport competitions is suffused with examples of the interrelationship between sport and ideology. The politico-ideological conflicts of the Cold War had numerous casualties in world sport as events such as the Olympic Games presented a terrain for the continuation of doctrinal discord. The games' rocky history reminds us how many of the world's ideological issues and contests – many of them unresolved – revolve around questions of identity or challenges to domination, neo-imperial or otherwise.

For example, the annals of the Olympic Games – and the history of institutionalization and diffusion of the wider Olympic movement in the twentieth century – strongly manifest the hegemonic and counter-hegemonic struggles that were part of decolonization's early processes of state-building in the developing world. In this period many new countries from what was then termed the Third World sought membership of the Olympic movement and *de jure* recognition from the International Olympic Committee as a means to solidify their *de facto* status as states. At the same time, however, many saw the movement as a neo-imperial entity which had to be transformed.

The ideological battles that ensued reflected the major geopolitical fault lines of the Cold War era. The Afro-Asian alliance that gave rise to the establishment of the non-aligned movement and which constituted a voting lobby within the United Nations General Assembly, for instance, had its counterpart in the Olympic movement. It was this bloc – led by India and Malaysia and supported by a coalition of African states – which orchestrated the boycott of the 1968 Mexico games on the issue of the participation in the games of apartheid South Africa. This bloc also organized in November 1963 the Games of the New Emerging Forces (GANEFO), held in Djakarta, as a counter to the Olympic Games.

Instigated by the Indonesian president, Sukarno, GANEFO had the immediate purpose of avenging Indonesia's earlier exclusion from the IOC due to the country's refusal to allow participation by Israel and Taiwan in the fourth Indonesian-hosted Asian Games. Beyond that, however, GANEFO had four broader purposes: to help congeal the nascent cultural and political solidarity of the Third World; to signify the emergence of a new era in world politics; to help solidify the independence of the newly created states in the developing world; and to establish an explicit political agenda for international sport as an extension of the ideological contests between the West and the Communist bloc on the one hand, and the West and the Third World on the other in the latter's purported campaign against neocolonialism.

In the end GANEFO did not draw the widespread support that was hoped for, nor did it experience a long life as the cultural fulcrum of Third World unity. However, its hosting was sufficient to provoke alarm from the established ranks of the Olympic movement, and it sparked some changes. The then president of the IOC, Avery Brundage, decried that the organizers of GANEFO 'denounced, defied and attacked all sport authorities, and are proceeding entirely through political channels, which is completely contrary to the rules of international sport'. [8] Yet thereafter he was less reticent about the inclusion of new members from Africa and Asia into the movement, even if at one stage he remonstrated against the 'serious problem' posed 'if every tribe in Africa forms a new country, [and the IOC] will have more African members than the rest of the world put together'. [9] In addition, the ostensible assertion of sovereignty by a number of African states through their participation in GANEFO motivated Brundage to adapt a more receptive stance to African insistence that certain actions be adopted by IOC vis-à-vis apartheid South Africa. [10]

The hosting of the GANEFO and its aftermaths on the relations between developing and developed countries is one example among several of the interplay between ideology and politics in the Olympic movement. The relationship between sport and international politics was also very strong in other spheres outside the Olympic movement. For instance, the rapprochement between the PRC and the United States of America (USA) in the 1970s, while political in process and goal, could not objectively occur without the legitimizing cover of sport. Similarly, international sport federations were central actors in the ascribing of political significance and prominence to newly formed states and their political leaders. In brief, the domain of international sport has long constituted an alternative realm of state interaction. Sport has been a sphere of world engagement in which states selected to signal their interests, to follow particular courses of actions or to forge diplomatic alliances. [11]

In the contemporary era, with much of the ideological infrastructure of the Cold War period fundamentally altered and many of the world's sport organizations having been transformed or democratized, the intimate interface which had existed between sport and international politics during the twentieth century has changed. In the arena of sport mega-events, however, the symbolic dimensions and political contours of international sport still tend to be very visible. This can be observed in the degree to which the bidding contests to host mega-events such as the FIFA World Cup and the Olympics have intensified in recent years, with many cities and countries across the world seeking the prestige, profile and assumed positive economic impacts from those events. But it is particularly the political instrumentalization of sport mega-events in the contemporary era that is significant. A growing body of scholarship [12] suggests that, under a specific set of circumstances, major sport events can be deployed as political instruments by governments to which activities of signalling, legitimization or constituency-building could be aligned. Many national governments, particularly from the developing world, are also increasingly utilizing sport mega-events to defined political aims. This could be inwardly directed, to support unpopular domestic programmes, enhance the government's legitimacy or to foster nationalism. It could also be intended to serve distinct foreign policy goals.

This is not to suggest that hosting sport mega-events is a commonly used political instrument for the developing world, or one available to all states. There has been a growing complexity of sport mega-events over the years. The number of different sports involved in the Olympic Games for instance has increased significantly over the past three decades. With this, the ability of potential hosts to provide requisite infrastructure becomes all the more central to determining the decision-making of world sport governing bodies. For this reason, despite a discourse of ubiquity of events and a narrative underlying this of the expansive reach and increased 'democratization' of events – by which it is tacitly understood that a host of any size or geographical location has the opportunity to be selected in bidding competitions – there is a growing rift between the industrialized and developing worlds. There are indeed few examples of cities or countries in the developing world that have hosted the events of today's size, and with the requirements that these events have today. It is only the countries that have been able or willing to expend the resources for costly bids, or those that have understood how to present savvy and sophisticated bids to international audiences, that have had success.

Whether hosted by developing or developed countries, sport mega-events involve the representation, branding and imagineering of cities or nations for local and international consumption under the legitimation of transnational competitiveness. This involves the manipulation of material conditions and is dependent on processes of symbolic construction. In this, the meanings, values and affiliations that are attached by political actors to places in order to distinguish them can be viewed as the product of narrative assemblage. Whose narratives predominate and by which causes they prevail are generally the results of compound processes of social and political negotiation and intense if often concealed contesting.

The Hosting of Mega-events in the BRICSA States

The emerging powers of today are most distinguished by the rapidity of their industrialization and in some cases, the unique nature of their economic make-up and policies. The modernization programme launched by China's Deng Xiaoping in 1978, for instance, set in motion economic reorganization which enabled the PRC to outpace the levels of economic growth of the world's traditional major powers, to quadruple the size of its national economy in the span of 30 years, and by the time of the Beijing games, to have become the world's third largest economy in terms of industrial output. [13] Yet China's growth is the result of some idiosyncratic economic practices which combined the liberalization of the capitalist West with centrally-planned export-led expansion and moderated and well controlled deregulation. China's economic model accepts the logic of the free-market mechanism, but disciplines this logic according to pre-set visions/goals.

Similarly, over the past two decades, India's advance has been propelled by the development of niche economies, such as information and communications technology, in addition to large-scale manufacturing – sectors that the country has successfully internationalized. Like a number of other South American states, Brazil's growth in the recent past has been built on the exploitation of commodities and energy reserves. But the country has also managed to diversify its economy, making use of its demographic advantage and, in latter years, a relatively stable political order to develop into a middle-income country and the strongest economy in the South American context. Finally, South Africa has built up a colonial-era mining economy into one that is today based on industrial and tertiary production at a level that sets it apart from other African countries.

In addition to these economic attributes, emerging powers also share a number of commonalities as far as their international relations are concerned. This revolves around the political and diplomatic status which they have in their regional contexts – shaped by their economic size, and frequently by their geographical and demographic size relative to neighbouring states – as well as the way in which they fashion themselves as international leaders. In this they often try to promote alternative ideological visions about matters related to the international economy, development or political rights and justice. For example, China has lobbied both bilaterally and multilaterally for reforms to the world's institutions for economic and financial regulation (such as the World Trade Organization and the International Monetary Fund). The country's extensive trade and investment linkages with many developing countries have also more recently evoked discourse in international circles about the way in which China's form of economic engagement (termed the 'Beijing consensus') poses an alternative to Western economic orthodoxies (or the so-called Washington consensus favouring neoliberal policies). [14] For their part India, Brazil and South Africa have formed coalitions of solidarity on such issues as a more equitable international trading regime. In following these diplomatic courses, these states proclaim to represent the developing world.

Imagineering Greatness: Mega-events as Proxies for Integration and Influence

Beijing 2008

China's hosting of the 2008 Beijing Olympic Games followed a long and generally difficult twentieth-century history between the PRC and the IOC. Tentative steps towards integration into the Olympic movement at the start of the twentieth century saw the appointment of Chinese members to the IOC and Chinese athlete participation in a number of summer games in the inter-war period. China's good standing in the movement were upended at the start of the Cold War period when, as a result of political differences with the IOC over the 'two Chinas' issue, the PRC withdrew in 1958. In line with many other Communist states, the PRC's position and orientation to the Olympic Games and the wider movement was shaped by a desire to attain specific objectives informed by the ideology of the time. Indeed the PRC's debut appearance at a large-scale international sport tournament as a post-revolutionary Communist state was at the 1963 Games of the New Emerging Forces. [15]

The PRC's re-entry into the Olympic movement in 1979, through the recognition of Beijing's and not Taipei's Olympic committee by the IOC, was part of a wider process of rapprochement by the international community following the programme of modernization established under Deng Xiaoping. Even so, in many of its expressions of solidarity with the developing world and the espousal of its own political values, China adopted a position that placed it at odds with the Western bloc.

Throughout all this, even though Olympic involvement was valued by China – if mainly for political reasons – it may be said that the country stood fairly peripheral from the wider movement. This changed significantly with China's hosting of the 2008 Beijing games, which not only placed the country more centrally in the movement but also provided it with a platform to showcase its rising status in the international system. First, the games left a major organizational legacy for the movement by drawing increased television spectatorship, reversing the trend of the past two decades of dwindling international interest in the Olympics. The games consisted of some of the largest volunteer and Olympic education programmes implemented in the history of the movement. It will also produce the first complete Olympic Global Games Impact report upon which appraisals of the long-term impacts of the Olympic Games will be made. Jacques Rogge, the president of the IOC, described the games as having been 'very good for the Olympic Movement … this had strengthened the movement'. [16]

Second, through some shrewd framing, the games sparked new discourse about the proclaimed universality of Olympism and the values that underpin it, which was both of positive and negative utility for China. The games' slogan of 'One Games One World' was in part aimed to frame the event in a symbolism of harmony, humanity and common destiny, and to place China in closer contact with the world. It was in that regard intended to strengthen China's cultural integration in the international sphere. The slogan of the games was also partly an attempt to reframe much of the established discourse of Olympism to be more inclusive and tolerant. This was reinforced through the development of specific imagery for the games, which drew from Chinese cultural stock. All the 28 Olympic sports, for example, were depicted through visualizations reminiscent of Chinese characters. It is useful to view this as a form of symbolic projection on the part of China, through which Chinese culture was promoted and internationally 'naturalized' and disseminated by means of the games.

Third, and most significantly, the Beijing games were an unprecedented display of spectacle, money and scale with effects beyond the event itself. It has been estimated that the games cost in excess of US$40bn. [17] Although this figure is disputed by the Chinese authorities, it would make the 2008 Olympics the most expensive games ever held. Of note is the scale at which infrastructure was developed and upgraded. Although some development was aimed at hosting the various contingents of athletes, delegations and visitors to the games, certain mega-projects, such as the construction of the world's largest terminal at Beijing International Airport, and the world's fastest train service between Beijing and Tianjin were only tangentially related to the games. Instead they were intended to exhibit the advance which the country has made over the past decades. In this regard China's hosting of the 2008 Beijing games also came to have a political intention: to be the culmination of the country's extended but measured process of integration and internationalization which commenced in the late 1970s, and to provide a stage for presenting its variant of modernity, based on the ideologically differentiated developmental experience of the country. The magnitude at which the event was organized seems to suggest that the Chinese authorities were intent on creating an impression of greatness.

The games had both positive and negative ramifications for China's position in the international system. The successful staging of the event and the – generally – favourable international media coverage during the games were important political achievements for China, and are likely to play a positive role in some of the Asian country's future international objectives. China placed much emphasis on demonstrating prowess through athletic performance, and ending the games at the top of the medals table was an important symbolic feat. The country was also keen to illustrate charitable aspects of its society and culture, stressing inclusiveness and forbearance as primordial components of Chinese heritage. At the same time, however, belying the projection of universalism evident in much of the vocabulary and imagery used during the games, is a robust and contradictory discourse of exceptionalism to Chinese politics which has strongly coloured the country's engagement with the rest of the world. In this Chinese authorities often present the country's politico-institutional regime as stemming from a separate value system founded on Chinese norms and values. China tends to deploy a rhetoric of exceptionalism as a means of legitimation and to offset international criticism against its political system. The stand-off about human rights between China's authorities and some transnational lobby groups, as well as international criticism levelled against Chinese surveillance of foreign visitors during the games, suggest that China's hosting of the Olympics may have sharpened the country's international integration, but that it has also invited new international scrutiny and demands for openness which the emerging power will have to contend with.

FIFA 2010: The African World Cup

As the largest economy in Africa, and given the country's recent history of racial segregation and its negotiated path to majority rule, a distinct sense of exceptionalism shapes South Africa's posturing towards international politics in general and the African continent in particular. The country's authorities have tended to use the moral authority generated from the peaceful political transition to democracy to enhance its diplomatic stature. They have also sought to establish South Africa as a leader and spokesman for issues regarding African development. Sport mega-events have been one means by which South Africa pursued greater international standing and incorporation in the world economy. Hosting mega-events has also enabled the country to project an African identity in its international relations in order to fulfil certain diplomatic objectives in relation to Africa's position in the international sphere. [18]

Hence, on one level the selection of South Africa as host of the 19th FIFA World Cup may be seen as the culmination of a long-standing campaign aimed at enhancing the country's integration into the world system. From being excluded for the better part of the twentieth century from partaking in prestigious sport competitions, South Africa has become a mega-event 'crusader' since the end of apartheid, displaying a penchant for bidding for first-order events. [19] The city of Cape Town's bid – officially launched in 1992 – for the 2004 summer Olympics inaugurated a continuous and ever more aspirant sport event campaign. The city failed in its Olympic bid, but there has been speculation that another South African city, Durban, may bid for the 2020 games. In 1995 South Africa hosted the world championship of the International Rugby Board, and in 1996 the country provided the venue for the biennial continental football champion-ship, known as the Africa Cup of Nations. The national teams' serendipitous victory of the tournament trophies – and the racial unity this temporarily fostered – provided an additional rationale for South Africa's subsequent pursuits around major international sport competitions. The country hosted the All Africa Games in 1999 and two further world championships in 2003 – the International Cricket Council's World Cup and the Women's World Cup of Golf. However, securing the rights in 2004 to host the 2010 FIFA World Cup – after a failed first bid for the 2006 tournament – was a particular victory for South Africa's bid campaigners, since this presented a unique opportunity to showcase the country on the world stage. Rhetoric of the potential of the World Cup to help South Africa transcend its past racial divisions and to help foster a new nation has consistently underpinned the FIFA campaign, suggesting that the tournament was also meant to engender internal integration.

Beyond that, South Africa's authorities have sought to use the 2010 event, which has been named 'the African World Cup' to present the continent in a more favourable light. This is mostly aimed at countering the effects of Afro-pessimism on tourist arrivals and investments to the continent. The 2010 local organizing committee notably defined its aim as 'to strengthen the African and South African image, [to] promote new partnerships with the world as we stage a unique and memorable event ... [and to] be significant global players in all fields of human endeavour'. [20] Clearly, aspirations around the 2010 tournament extended well beyond the development of South Africa, but also aimed at uplifting the wider African continent. This has been a long-standing objective of South Africa's FIFA World Cup campaigns, but more recently it became more focused through the defining of an 'African legacy' programme for the 2010 World Cup. In 2007 the then minister of sport for instance stated that

> the awarding of the 2010 World Cup host to South Africa by FIFA is a legacy on its own. For South Africa and the rest of Africa, the memory of that tournament will be a lasting legacy. But we cannot end there. ... [We] believe that preparations for the 2010 World Cup must leverage the fast-tracking of some elements of our transformation agenda. ... [We] must use this opportunity to level the proverbial playing grounds, both in respect of infrastructure and otherwise. [21]

Thus defined, the 'African legacy' would stem from growth and developmental impetuses from South Africa's hosting of the World Cup. The notion of the 'African legacy' is a political programme underpinned by the leadership's desire to fashion a different international image for the African continent – one not of victimhood and disadvantage but one built on positive constructs of African agency. In this sense, the World Cup was intended to display attained levels of African modernity and the posited fertile heritage on which it has been built.

This was not an easy task, however, given the high degree of international scepticism before the tournament whether South Africa had the governance capacity and resources to complete all preparations on time and to successfully host the event. More significant was the question of what the long-term economic legacies of the World Cup would be. Even though South Africa is classified as a middle-income country, it is characterized by high levels of poverty and inequality. Shortly before the tournament, it was projected that the event would earn the country R93bn (approximately US$13.2bn) in revenue. The government invested more than six times that amount before the tournament (R600bn; US$85.7). [22] To place this in perspective, this is nearly one-tenth of South Africa's annual gross domestic product, and is much more than what was spent by the Chinese authorities for the Beijing games. It is still not clear whether these investments may translate into positive or negative economic legacies for South Africa.

Finally, South Africa's injection of a pan-African identity in its World Cup campaigns, and the country's more general claim in its diplomatic posturing to represent the plight and promise of the entire African continent have provoked some ill-feeling from African counterparts, who regard this as a display of paternalism and arrogance. Over the years feelings of resentment have manifested in continental diplomacy in various sport and non-sport related contexts. African support for South Africa's bids for the FIFA World Cup, for instance, tended to be fractious, and during crucial voting stages in FIFA for the selection of both the 2006 and 2010 hosts, several influential African states voted against South Africa. [23] South Africa has experienced similar acts of revolt by African states in wider diplomatic settings. For example, the country has faced some stiff continental challenge on its membership of emergent multilateral alliances in which South Africa often is the only African representative (such as the G20, a grouping of foreign ministers from industrialized and industrializing states, or the G5, a grouping of emerging powers which includes China, Brazil, India, Mexico and South Africa). African states have criticized South Africa for adopting positions that serve only its own economic interests. The country's politics of exceptionalism is therefore interpreted as exclusivism. As Africa's sole emerging power, therefore, the country has to overcome diplomatic resistance from other states on the continent.

Delhi 2010 Commonwealth Games

Given its comparatively larger economy and the fact that it is the second most populous country in the world, India can lay greater claim to the title of emerging power than South Africa. Indeed, evident in much of its international politics is an ambition to position itself not merely as a regional force, but as a state whose influence extends beyond a budding prominence in certain sectors of the world economy. The projection is that of a country with a long history of diplomatic proficiency, and – given its status as a nuclear power – clout in the evolving international security order. Yet India shares many features with South Africa and other emerging powers in the way in which alternative instruments of power often have to be used in the face of resource or external political constraints. India's growing military capacity, for instance, is significantly curtailed by regional politics (such as its rivalry with neighbouring Pakistan) and the longer-term effects on the country's security policy of the so-called war on terror. Furthermore, in spite of its size, the country's economy tends to be quite vulnerable to the volatilities of the global economy. [24]

In this light, the hosting of the 2010 Commonwealth Games by India's capital city, New Delhi, and the manner that the event has been framed by India's authorities is interesting. The Commonwealth Games does not equal in magnitude or economic impact football's World Cup or the Olympics. Over the years the event has also lost much of its glamour as the Commonwealth bloc has shrunk in diplomatic significance. Yet the games play an important role in sustaining the political identity of the Commonwealth; they also provide an international platform for many of the smaller states in the bloc to exhibit some prowess.

More recently attempts to raise the global prominence of the event through some more buoyant staging and media coverage seemed to have revitalized the games, raising its appeal not only for viewing audiences but also for prospective hosts. As noted by Black, [25] the conscious repositioning of the Commonwealth Games in recent years has increased the event's attraction for a number of political authorities who, in seeking to develop an international profile, pitch for world sport's smaller-scale and presumably more manageable events. It is noteworthy therefore that staging the games has become a strategy for medium-sized cities to support urban regeneration programmes (e.g. Manchester's hosting of the 2002 games) or to bolster the development of internationally competitive niche sport-tourism economies (such as the 2006 Melbourne and 2014 Glasgow games). [26]

Given this, while intended in part to raise the city's fortunes, Delhi's hosting of the 2010 Commonwealth Games is significantly different, and underpinned by a conspicuous set of wider-ranging political aims. The first involves the way the games were used as an allegory by the authorities to signal India's graduation into a league of more advanced and powerful states in the international domain, underscoring the richness and significance of the country's history and civilization for the world community. The bid document, for instance, stated that

> India is one of the world's oldest civilizations. ... The country has maintained political stability and territorial integrity with notable economic and social development. India has emerged as a nuclear power. Today it has a high standing in the development of space science and Information technology, easily being recognized as one of the most capable software developing centres in the world. Indian IT professionals are in fact at the head of the software movement of the world. [27]

Second, implied in the official narratives that frame the games, the event was also intended to bring about a realignment of India's placing within the wider Commonwealth, foreclosing perhaps a glum history of subjugation and oppositional politics that had characterized the country's integration in the Commonwealth movement. The bid document described India and 'indeed ... Delhi ... literally at the heart of the Commonwealth World'. [28] This narrative of transcendence also extended to the way in which Delhi was cast by India's authorities as a host location not of mass poverty and deprivation – a stereotypical but powerful and widely disseminated view of the city in the international media – but one that is advanced, cosmopolitan and vibrant.

The third characteristic of India's Commonwealth Games campaign, therefore, was how attention was drawn to the country's achievements in modernity through various means of projection, with the subtext being that the country had cast off its burden of underdevelopment and that it is now a world leader. Through staging the games, therefore, Delhi was meant to be transformed into a world-class capital. The authorities had spent more than US$1bn on the refurbishment of sport facilities and the development of public infrastructure. A temple constructed on the banks of the city's river aimed to showcase Indian culture and all its splendours to the world. The organizers also wanted to make the games the greenest ever, adhering to self-defined standards of ecological integrity which were intended to leave a knowledge legacy for future Commonwealth hosts. [29]

In sum, the broader political messaging of the 2010 Commonwealth Games was a blend of wider international ambition, through which the staging of the games was meant to solidify India's emerging world leadership, and developmental vision, by which the country, in part, sought to raise living standards. The Indian authorities have indicated their intention to bid for the 2020 Olympics, presumably drawing on the (somewhat chequered) experiences of the 2010 games and the Commonwealth Youth Games (that were hosted by India in 2009). As with the other BRICSA states under review in this paper, however, India displays some fragilities which could cause the strategy of using mega-events as an instrument of signalling to be both risky and uncertain.

Despite the imaging of contemporary India as sophisticated, and Delhi as the fulcrum of India's social advance, the country continues to epitomize extreme poverty; income levels are highly skewed and the benefits of the country's recent economic rise have remained largely undistributed. More worryingly, India's democratic stability is imperilled by rising insurgency in the subcontinent, a factor that has shaped internal political development but also affected the country's position in world sport. For example, insurgent attacks in 2008 on Mumbai and a terror assault on the Sri Lankan cricket team on tour in neighbouring Pakistan motivated the owners of the lucrative newly-formed cricket franchise, the Indian Premier League, to relocate for its second season in 2009 to South Africa. Important warm-up tournaments for the 2010 Commonwealth Games, such as the Commonwealth Boxing Association and World Badminton Championships, both scheduled to have been held in India in 2009, were postponed or shifted to other locations. This led some international commentators to wonder whether India could be regarded as a 'safe' location for the 2010 Commonwealth Games and whether the country's claims of world status were credible. [30]

Conclusion

The emerging powers of today not only seem predisposed to bid for very large-scale sport events, but they also seem to exploit their hosting of such events in similar ways. This frequently involves the use of an event to both place a country more centrally within the international community of states (i.e. to reinforce their international integration) and to highlight the country's distinctions. Underpinning this strategic purpose is often an ambivalent internal identity stemming from an uncertain understanding of the constitutive nature of the state and its evolving society, or of the end-point of the country's upward economic trajectory. The discourses used by the state elites and the aspirations they project for and from sport mega-events, therefore, often embody narratives that blend myth elements about their nation with visions about a realignment of the international order, and the contribution the state can play towards that. The statement by Brazil's president, Luiz Inácio Lula da Silva, the country that will host the 2014 FIFA World Cup, on Rio de Janeiro's contention to host the 2016 Olympic Games, is indicative of this duality. According to Lula,

> For the US an Olympics is just one more Olympic Games. For Europe an Olympics is just one more Olympic Games. But for us it is something that really will be the reassurance of a continent, a country and its people. Because, here in Latin America, we always feel we have to prove how to do things. [31]

In recent years emerging powers have shown a predilection for bidding for the largest and generally most expensive competitions on the world sports calendar. The politics that surround emerging powers' hosting of mega-events overlap in some significant ways with their wider external and internal politics. There are also a number of common themes to the objectives that underpin emerging powers' orientation to mega-events, and the consequences they bear. These relate to the way in which sport mega-events are frequently employed by emerging powers as a surrogate for soft power, often with the intention of boosting their integration and standing in the international system. It also involves the discourses and practices of symbolic imagineering which tend to be used by them, with there being a notable reliance on the projection of historical and political exceptionalism. Pursuing 'development' is often used as leitmotif, but in contrast to the way in which developmental objectives are set by the governments of industrialized countries, development is here framed by emerging powers in an all-encompassing fashion. This often means that such states have a 'money is no object' attitude to their hosting of events, and often these states pitch for ever larger events.

Yet the internal fragilities of emerging powers are often an obstacle to these goals. For instance, Brazil and South Africa top international rankings for income inequality; India is the world's largest democracy, but it is increasingly vulnerable in terms of its domestic and international security. China's authorities are experiencing increased difficulty in suppressing outbursts of internal dissent or in manipulating the way the country is scrutinized and presented by the outside world, and indeed in keeping its borders well controlled.

Finally, there is a close interplay between internal and external political factors in relation to the host state, and some paradoxes often arise from the hosting of mega-events as a result of domestic political volatilities or the wider external position of the state. These significantly shape the outcomes and success of the events in terms of hosts' initial political strategies.

Notes

[1] See for instance Brownell, *Beijing's Games*.

[2] 'See you in Delhi' 2010 Commonwealth Games promotional video, available at www.thecgf.com/games/intro.asp?yr_2010, accessed 17 Jun. 2009; also see Black, 'The Symbolic Politics of Sport Mega-Events'.

[3] 'Not Quite Yet a House of Brics', *Financial Times*, 17 June 2009. For analyses of emerging powers see Antkiewicz and Whalley, 'BRICSAM and the Non-WTO'; Shaw *et al.*, 'Global and/or Regional Development'; and Pattnayak, 'India as an Emerging Power'.

[4] Nel *et al.*, *South Africa's Multilateral Diplomacy*; Adebajo *et al.*, *South Africa in Africa*.

[5] See Alden and Vieira, 'The New Diplomacy of the South' for a discussion of the IBSA trilateral forum.

[6] Speech by Indonesian president, Sukarno to GANEFO Preparatory Conference, 27–29 April 1963. Cited in Pauker, 'Ganefo I', 174 (italics in original).

[7] See for instance Horne and Manzenreiter, *Sports Mega-Events* and Roche, *Mega-Events and Modernity* for reviews.

[8] Avery Brundage in correspondence to Otto Mayer, IOC Secretary-General, 14 Sept. 1963, archives of the Olympic Studies Centre, Lausanne, Switzerland.

[9] Avery Brundage in correspondence to Mayer, 5 Jan. 1963, archives of the Olympic Studies Centre, Lausanne, Switzerland.

[10] Mbaye, *The International Olympic Committee and South Africa*, 107.

[11] See for instance Allison and Monnington, 'Sport, Prestige and International Relations'; Houlihan, *Sport and International Politics* and Lowe *et al.*, *Sport and International Relations*.

[12] For instance Black, 'The Symbolic Politics of Sport Mega-Events'; Black and Van der Westhuizen, 'The Allure of Global Games'; and Cornelissen, 'Scripting the Nation'.

[13] World Bank, *World Development Indicators 2009*, 352.

[14] See for instance Taylor, *China and Africa*.

[15] This was intended to serve a number of diplomatic purposes for the country, central of which was to gesture support for the anti-Western political propaganda of Indonesia and the wider Afro-Asian bloc, but also to exhibit its own strength. The country is rumoured to have paid a substantial portion of the costs for hosting GANEFO, and it sent the largest delegation of athletes. Chinese athletes stood out for the level of their performances, winning the greatest number of medals (171 in total, 68 of those gold medals) (Pauker, 'Ganefo I'). In this China significantly outshone the Soviet Union, a key ideological rival. The country's performance also lent it symbolic prominence in the developing world which in subsequent years the PRC sought to transform into new diplomatic alliances.

[16] Rogge, interview, 'The View from the Top', *Sport Business International* 142 (2009), 26.

[17] Reuters, 'Beijing Games to be costliest, but no debt legacy', 5 Aug. 2008, available at www.reuters.com/article/GCA-Olympics/idUSPEK25823820080805, accessed 11 Mar. 2009.

[18] See Cornelissen, 'Scripting the Nation'.

[19] See Black, 'The Symbolic Politics of Sport Mega-Events'.

[20] 2010 FIFA World Cup Local Organizing Committee, media presentation, 25 May 2007.

[21] 'Opening Address by Sport and Recreation Minister M. Stofile at the International Year of African Football and 2010 World Cup Workshop, Pretoria, 7 March 2007', Government Communication and Information System, Pretoria.

[22] T. Manuel, 'Budget Speech 2007 by Minister of Finance Trevor Manuel MP'. Government Communication and Information Services, Pretoria. Grant Thornton, 'Updated Economic Impact of the 2010 FIFA World Cup'. Media Press Release, 21 April 2010.

[23] See Cornelissen, '"It's Africa's Turn!"'.

[24] Pattnyak, 'India as an Emerging Power'.

[25] Black, 'Dreaming Big'.
[26] See Smith and Fox, 'From "Event-Led" to "Event-Themed" Regeneration'; and 'People, Place, Passion', Glasgow 2014 Commonwealth Games Candidate City File.
[27] Indian Olympic Association, *Delhi 2010 Commonwealth Games*, 47.
[28] Ibid., 52.
[29] '2010 Games in Delhi to be Greenest: Dikshit', *India Today*, 13 Jan. 2009.
[30] 'Commonwealth Games has no IPL option to up sticks from Delhi', *The Guardian*, 24 March 2009.
[31] 'Lula: An Olympics would mean more to Brazil than the US', *Inside the Games*, 30 April 2009 available at www.insidethegames.com/show-news.php?id=5588, accessed 5 May 2009.

References

Adebajo, A., A. Adebayo and C. Landsberg, eds. *South Africa in Africa: The Post-Apartheid Era*. Scottsville: University of Kwazulu-Natal Press, 2007.

Alden, C. and M. Vieira. 'The New Diplomacy of the South: South Africa, Brazil, India and Trilateralism'. *Third World Quarterly* 26, no. 7 (2005): 1077–95.

Allison L. and T. Monnington, 'Sport, Prestige and International Relations'. *Government and Opposition* 37, no. 1 (2002): 106–34.

Antkiewicz, A. and J. Whalley, 'BRICSAM and the Non-WTO'. *Review of International Organizations* 1, no. 3 (2006): 237–261.

Black, D. 'The Symbolic Politics of Sport Mega-Events: 2010 in Comparative Perspective'. *Politikon* 34, no. 3 (2007): 261–76.

Black, D. 'Dreaming Big: The Pursuit of Second Order Games as a Strategic Response to Globalisation'. *Sport in Society* 11, no. 4 (2008): 467–80.

Black, D. and J. van der Westhuizen. 'The Allure of Global Games for "Semi-Peripheral" Polities and Spaces: A Research Agenda'. *Third World Quarterly* 25, no. 7 (2004): 1195–1214.

Brownell, S. *Beijing's Games: What the Olympics Mean to China*. Lanham, MD: Rowman & Littlefield, 2008.

Cornelissen, S. '"It's Africa's Turn!" The Narratives and Legitimations of the Moroccan and South African Bids for the 2006 and 2010 FIFA Finals'. *Third World Quarterly* 25, no. 7 (2004): 1293–1309.

Cornelissen, S. 'Scripting the Nation: Sport, Mega-Events, Foreign Policy and State-Building in Post-Apartheid South Africa'. *Sport in Society* 11, no. 4 (2008): 481–93.

Horne, J. and W. Manzenreiter, eds. *Sports Mega-Events: Social Scientific Analyses of a Global Phenomenon*. Oxford: Blackwell Publishing, 2006.

Houlihan, B. *Sport and International Politics*. New York: Harvester Wheatsheaf, 1994.

Indian Olympic Association. *Delhi 2010 Commonwealth Games Bid Document*. New Delhi: Indian Olympic Association, 2003.

Lowe, B., D. Kanin. and A. Strenk, eds. *Sport and International Relations*. Champaign, IL: Stiles Publishing Company, 1978.

Mbaye, K. *The Olympic Committee and South Africa: Analysis and Illustration of a Humanist Sports Policy*. Lausanne: IOC, 1995.

Nel, P., I. Taylor and J. van der Westhuizen eds. *South Africa's Multilateral Diplomacy and Global Change: The Limits of Reformism*. Aldershot: Ashgate, 2001.

Pattnayak, S. 'India as an Emerging Power'. *India Quarterly* 63, no. 1 (2007): 79–110.

Pauker, E. 'Ganefo I: Sports and Politics in Djakarta'. *Asian Survey* 5, no. 4 (1965): 171–85.

Roche, M. *Mega-events and Modernity: Olympics and Expos in the Growth of Global Culture.* London: Routledge, 2000.

Shaw, T., A. Cooper and A. Antkiewicz. 'Global and/or Regional Development at the Start of the Twenty-First Century? China, India and (South) Africa', *Third World Quarterly* 28, no. 7 (2007): 1255–70.

Smith, A and T. Fox. 'From "Event-led" to "Event-themed" Regeneration: The 2002 Commonwealth Games Legacy Programme'. *Urban Studies* 44, no. 5–6 (2007): 1125–43.

Taylor, I. *China and Africa: Engagement and Compromise.* London: Routledge, 2006.

World Bank. *World Development Indicators 2009.* Washington, DC: World Bank, 2009.

Perspectives of Sport in a Global World

Helmut Digel

Social change and sports development are related each to the other and, as with Industrial societies, the system of sports is following the idea of 'modernization'. For decades a change of paradigms has and continues to occur and as a result the system of sports is facing new challenges and increasing risks are to be mastered.

Sport has Changed

More than 40 years ago I started my active sports career. Sport was my life. For the first time I played in a youth-handball team, shot goals, was celebrated and dreamt of the national team. To me sport meant practising technique and tactics and, primarily, competition at the weekend. Athletics was almost equally important and soccer was played almost everywhere. Besides that I played in a table tennis team at position four. 'Higher, further, faster' was our maxim. Even at that time the term 'sport' was ambiguous. It could mean school sport, competitive sport, military sport or preventive sport. In comparison with today, especially in retrospect, life with sport was clear-cut and easy to grasp. At least for those who were personally active in sport it was obvious what it meant. Today it seems to be different.

To me sport is still the central purpose of life. I live for sport, write about sport, talk about it and sometimes, but too rarely, I practise sport. I play tennis, although as a juvenile, I regarded this sport as an elitist expression of an upper class and hence rejected it. I do special back and torso exercises, without pursuing any traditional sports goal. I go on cycling tours with my family, because I believe they are beneficial for our general well-being. More rarely I torment myself as a runner, since I still hope in vain that it will reduce my weight.

What sport means to me today has only little in common with what it used to mean in the past. However even today the sport of the old days still exists. The actual novelty of 'situation is primarily that the term 'sport' has received a considerably larger and still growing variety of meanings.

Today, more and more activities are described by the term sport. Furthermore, a still growing variety of functions is to be accomplished by sport. A diffuse mixture of behaviour patterns has developed from a limited number that were initially called sport. The allocation of this mixture to the total range of 'sports' depends largely on subjective value judgements. Breathing exercises, hiking, bathing, yoga or jogging, depending on the point of view, are 'real' sports or not sports at all. Codified rules, competition and performance classes are features and showpieces, if you definitely want to belong to the core of the sports family.

However, the sports family has long had its adopted children. The behaviour pattern of sport shows imperial traits. Moving bodies are sports bodies and unmoving bodies also find a place under the umbrella of sport. Sport can be everything and everywhere – with or without codified rules; with compulsory participation or without obligation; integrated into a lasting organization or informally practised; measured with externally set quality standards or informally agreed upon. State-municipal sport can be found next to private sport. New organizational structures labelled 'sport' are in great demand and make the assumption that the triumphant advance of sport – the sportification of our society – can hardly be stopped. Sport is increasingly becoming a lifetime companion of man, from kindergarten up to the sport of 90-year-olds. [1]

Changes in Society

The causes of this development can be identified. The material standard of living has been considerably rising for many social groups since the 1950s. As a result a mass consumption has developed and has already partly developed into luxury consumption. The freedom to have a share in consumption is assured by participation in the job market. Consequently the job market has not lost its importance. On the contrary – today it is more important than ever to have a job. The dynamics of the job market require mobility, which again weakens the solidity of social networks. Due to this development society has become extremely complex. In the process of increasing diversification there is more and more appeal for only functional specific items in the sub-systems of this society. We can only temporarily commit ourselves to partial relationships: as neighbour, as voter, as sportsperson, as holidaymaker. Flexibility is the watchword.

This process has been beneficial in many respects. More and more people have greater autonomy than in the old days; more and more they find scope for expression and development that was formerly denied to them; more and more they have recourse to financial means that present them with individual choice especially in their free time. In the first decade of an new century the values are promising: 'Always having free time, acting as a creative person, experiencing work and pleasure as a unity, receiving reward not only through work but also by acknowledgement and affection, being socially involved, laughing, carefree, weeping uninhibitedly, being independent philosophically, being able to love and being able to find oneself.' [2]

Who would not like to lay claim to this statement? Who does not wish creativity as a lifestyle? Who does not plead for tolerance, openness, truthfulness and a greater depth in acceptable behaviour? If sport contributes an important share in this matter, this can only be desirable.

The tendencies to individualism that are observable today can be interpreted in manifold ways. From a positive viewpoint the new individualism can be understood as a desirable global change, expressing a new understanding of work, family, culture and society. Here a turning towards a sense of life oriented by personal benefit is taking place. Also the tendency towards an expressive individualism is immense. This individualism forms a new version of a successful life, namely the desire not to be taken in and sacrificed in favour of comprehensive social goals and demands.

Considering such an understanding, it would only be logical if sport also corresponded with the tendency towards individualism, modernized and individualized its offers and hence came up to people's expectations in their freedom of choice. Looking back at the last three decades, it becomes clear that exactly this has taken place in the world of sport. However, there is doubt about whether the path sports development has taken is the only correct one. If we want to understand this critical position we have to have a closer look at the phenomenon of modernization.

Features of 'Modernization'

It is characteristic of the idea of modernization that everything that was 'modern' yesterday must be modernized today. This modernization is reflected in all parts of society but it can be especially and distinctly acknowledged in the fields of politics, economy and law, as well as in social and cultural areas.

Modernization itself is gaining acceptance primarily through specific developmental processes. Seven of these are especially worth mentioning in this context.

First there is the 'upgrading of the individual', as it has taken place in advanced industrial societies in past decades. In sociology one talks about the individualization of society. A gradual erosion of relatively firm partnerships that came down through the generations is effected by the process of individualization. Thus Ulrich Beck talks about a releasing dimension that has formed the process of individualization. [3] Furthermore this has led to a de-traditionalization of influences directing behaviour and cultural norms. Traditional fields of knowledge have become irrelevant and have been replaced by new ones; previously relevant sets of belief have become superfluous. Beck describes this as 'the dimension of losing its magic spell'. It is not particularly surprising that this release and 'loss of magic' has led to an acquisition of new forms of social integration as a reaction to disintegration tendencies. This could be described as a re-integration dimension.

A second characteristic is the more and more drastic rationalization of our thoughts and actions. Human bases of action are increasingly vehemently cleared of value-rational decision structures and replaced by purpose-rational ones. Central themes of ethical mentalities are gradually replaced by functionalistic considerations of effectivity. Life becomes increasingly an input/output calculation; sober calculation replaces faithfulness to principles.

In the course of rationalization, economic rationality is expanded and gains supremacy. Individualization and rationalization fade into a utilitarian individualism. Personal benefit and maximization of personal advantage become a rule of human action. The expectation of benefit is put in relation to the necessary effort. Cost-benefit calculations become a characteristic of everyday life. They can be observed in children, as well as in youths and adults and can be found in school, in working life and in free time. Taking advantage of privileges becomes a characteristic of today's daily practice and so it also leads to a departure from the unified community to a certain extent. Masterly cost-benefit calculations become a mark of quality for competent action. Life is completely capitalized and marketed.

A special feature of the modernization of the modern age is its increasing legalization. New hierarchy and power proportions are created among its members. Legalization touches all areas of life, especially the social and cultural sectors of our society, and the private sphere is increasingly affected by questions of civil and public law.

At the same time the influence of the media on daily life is increasing. The information technology industry is growing faster and faster while the traditional media merge into symbioses with new media. This development allows for new ways of communication and transfer in a global perspective, but it also reaches nearly every facet of life. The media define more and more decisively what is relevant and what is not.

The significance of sciences for very diverse sectors of society is increasing continuously. Science and experts as mediators for science get more and more into the role of ultimate umpire, deciding about benefits and truth. Political decisions are for example increasingly based on the recommendations of science. On the other hand, science is increasingly becoming amateur science, thus reaching people's everyday lives. This becomes particularly evident in the field of medical and psychological knowledge. Along with the growing influence of science, one can observe a process of trivialization, which is making scientific findings increasingly insignificant.

The seventh important trend is identified by the term globalization. Today the term is applied in many ways. Frequently the term integration could equally be used. It must first be stated that in spite of its incessant use it is mostly not sufficiently understood and the empirical evidence proving the process of globalization is scarce. It has to be pointed out, however, that policy-makers have started much too late in dealing with the implications of the present globalization. The latter has its origin in industrial companies and up to the present day it has been largely limited to this field. It refers to changes and an increase in cross-border activities of companies for the purpose of organizing development and production, obtaining materials, marketing and financing. At the moment these entrepreneurial behaviour patterns are going through a time of upheaval, primarily determined by new forms of flexible production. Globalization becomes evident in an empirical way in cross-border transfers of money, goods, services and know-how. Evidence for this globalization process can be found in foreign direct investment, international cooperation at company level, the changing structure of international trade and the globalization of financial markets. Increasing direct foreign investment can primarily be explained by technological change, macroeconomic structural divergence and governmental policies. It is linked up with falling communication costs which form an essential basis of the globalization process. Hence globalization is chiefly distinguished by a new labour market in which traditional influences are receding and standards of labour are undermined in advanced industrial societies. Here economy dominates everything.

The rising new world society is, politically speaking, in a kind of state of nature. Everybody is fighting in an almost anarchical way, looking for his/her individual advantage. A globalization of capitalistic production and market conditions is effected; a re-feudalization of politics comes into being. Governments, political parties and associations have to find a new identity. The most important conflicts of interest are settled by exchange and the rising costs are paid by the taxpayer. There is an almost complete lack of democratic supervision.

Change of Paradigms

Having all these changes in mind, it makes sense to talk about a change of paradigms. This change is comparable to the replacement of an agricultural society by the Industrial Revolution. The emerging change from the industrial age to a society of information, knowledge and communication will include all people: industry and all its employees, the unemployed, private life and free time. In this change of paradigms there will be some key developments that concern the whole world. Growth will not necessarily take place in areas that were important in the twentieth century. On account of the new possibilities of electronic data processing and new communication technologies, there will be new growth patterns for the national economies of the world. There will be areas where growth can be identified and there already are areas of noticeable decline. The traditional nation state loses some of its traditional power to influence questions of growth and decline. Regional economic areas come into being in a world without borders; trade is proceeding in those areas. In the twenty-first century the key to prosperity evidently lies in thinking and acting via telephone lines and via the new media of satellite communication. Those regions that are not supported by a common vision of the population will hardly have a chance in this change of paradigms. They will be swallowed up and made redundant by the rest of the global community.

Considering this development we have to consider the general question of which value systems shall mark this new world. This is closely linked with probably the most important question arising from the fact that new purposes of life have to be found when values such as work and professional success wane in importance. Which purposes of life will be important? How does man want to live in this new world? Does the metropolis, inseparably connected with traditional industry, still have justification today? And if not - in what kind of settlements do we want to live instead?

Contours of the Development and Consequences

In view of the observable changes it is already possible to assume certain contours that are likely to characterize the beginning of the new century. A continued obligation for an increased application of redistribution policies is unavoidable in the development of a globalized economy, due to rationalization processes and new technologies. If more and more sections of society cannot make their living by gainful employment, there arises the necessity to provide them with a financial income. There is no doubt about a redistribution policy being necessary to solve this issue. Redistribution is the requirement of economic reasoning. Given that companies in a globalized economy are urged to adapt quickly to the market, that they have to carry out thorough rationalization measures and hence unavoidable dismissals of employees, then it is equally obvious that such adaptations can only be enacted within an extended social system. This is true because the loss of jobs is less threatening where there is social security for those concerned. An economy can only adjust flexibly to new market conditions if redistribution in that society is implemented in favour of a broader social security.

The releasing processes cause the individual to understand himself less as a polyvalent cosmopolitan. He will be more likely to focus more on local connections. His place of residence has to cope with the tasks of integration that have to be solved urgently, considering the loss of gainful employment. For future municipal and town development this means that town and municipality structures that cultivate isolation and anonymity need to be changed in such a way that they enable individual human contact and personal perspectives. The coexistence of dwelling, free time and places of work will be especially important.

As people cannot distinguish themselves in these situations by flexible dynamics but always have to adapt to new constraints, it will be critical to provide them with a 'new' personality: one that will succeed in living a meaningful life beyond adaptation to external pressures. Virtues such as mental independence, critical distance and unconventionality will experience a new renaissance.

Education systems will also have to change. In the future it will be less important to educate people in preparation for specific job perspectives, if 'gainful employment' carries a much broader meaning. It will rather be more important to encourage a perspective of civilized behaviour and to help people discover/develop personal interests. In the universities those courses of study oriented towards a specific professional career will be given less emphasis. Focus will need to be on mediating students' curiosity and interest in substantial social matters, with universities themselves having to function in a more integral way than they currently do in order to compensate for the loss of traditional education. Study will be seen as a process of an intensive finding of self.

Considering these changes it is already foreseeable that a society without gainful employment opportunities will also create new conditions for arts and culture. Culture will serve less as a distraction for stressed members of the system of gainful employment but might rather be about inspiration; it could become a meaningful area of life. The consequences of globalization must therefore not only be seen negatively. They also offer chances that have been recognized too rarely up to now.

Sport in the Mirror of the Last Decades

In this process of social transition there now arises the question of how sport, as one of the most successful cultural phenomena of the twentieth century, is affected by these trends. A look in the mirror at sport in recent decades can help us in answering this question. General as well as specific aspects of social change can be detected.

The picture that comes into view is split. We can recognize some striking characteristics as indications of problems that could accompany and burden life in sport in the coming years. Some aspects are to be highlighted.

The ideology of the market has formed recent decades, especially in sport. The entire economization of all areas of life is marching on. This favours the already existing individualization spiral and shows a modern age dominated by the basic figure of the unattached, the single. But this also means that 'constructions of independence' have become 'prison bars of loneliness'. [4] Recent years have been characterized by the fundamental contradictions of industrial society. The contradictions directed towards private life and towards the level of the individual are aggravating.

The mirror of sport shows us that the process of de-stigmatization of behaviour patterns and life spheres is also taking place in sport. The increasing freedom of choice for the individual and the simultaneous weakening of traditional relationships will influence him/her in the future. Decision-making obligations for the individual will arise more and more. Everything has to be discussed, justified and its consequences considered. Self-evident matters become a source of conflict. De-stigmatization, increasing freedom of choice and the loss of traditional relationships become problems without an apparent solution. For many people the lifestyles produced by entertainment, consumption and the media industry become landmarks and objects of imitation. Stressing differences has a special meaning. Identity and uniformity are not in demand, but rather variety linked with very individual forms of stylization.

Also in sport a multiplication and differentiation of partial fields and hence of value patterns can be observed. Due to an increase in the number of organizations and institutions, the individual is all the more dependent on his ability to be flexible and on an exchange of roles. Rationalities of action in one area of life do not necessarily have to correspond with other areas. For many, life is somehow becoming a 'choice of menu'. Numerous combinations are possible.

The conflict of the sexes in sport has entered into a new stage. Inequality in the field of education and law has not only treated women unequally in professional life, in the family and in politics, but also in sport, clearer and more obviously than ever before. The male policy of only verbal commitment has become increasingly unsuccessful.

We can see problems that we can call crises of human experience. Ever-increasing flexibility in the field of work has brought about higher incomes for only a few, more individual free time for a few and more personal time sovereignty for a few. For most employees this has led to more night and shift work, more Saturday and Sunday work, as well as increased isolation and detachment from a commonly spent lifetime. The individual may have become richer materially but is increasingly under pressure in terms of time. Sport is especially affected. More and more people are yearning for a time organization that corresponds with their organic rhythm and the cyclic movements of nature.

We have to identify a problem of environment. The 'playground in the Alps' and 'sports facilities close to the place of residence' are the diametrically opposite poles. An increasing number of people realize the connection existing between 'plotted' and 'armoured' urban sports architecture and the escape from a world of performance into free nature. [5]

Due to a critical unimaginativeness, the mass media (especially television) are driven more than ever by the principles of the marketplace. Counting on the forgetfulness of its consumers and characterized by an ephemeral spirit of the times, television influences the perception patterns of its consumers, manipulates its messages with superficial entertainment interest and so sells questionable products. Sports coverage plays a central role in this context.

The renaissance of national values is striking. This can be observed wherever there are sporting comparisons between nations – at Olympic Games or at world or European championships. The recognizable nationalisms are however mostly nourished by images from the past that put a misleading complexion on the present and the future.

Demographically the elderly form the biggest socio-political challenge. Their importance becomes clear when we see that in many industrial societies today people above the age of 60 constitute a quarter of the total population. There is the danger that post-industrial societies will become 'selected' societies, even more than is already the case. This is not least because of the problem of an adequate old-age pension scheme, but also due to difficulties involved in integration between North, South, East and West. Inequality will increase. The selection concerns parts of the older generation and some juveniles but there is also a selection according to sex. 'New foreigners' are more frequently falling through the socio-political net of our society.

The general development of our society does not only show positive tendencies. In recent centuries the changes in working life caused traditional class loyalties to disintegrate. The individual has increasingly to look after himself and experiences his individual fate in the labour market with all its risks, chances and contradictions. The paradox is that increasing differentiation of individual situations is accompanied by an extreme standardization of life patterns. Our society is becoming more ambivalent than it already is. Paradoxes are accumulating. 'Risky chances' seems to be the epitaph of our time. [6] Processes with intensive momentum of their own are to be observed more frequently, with us seemingly ill-equipped to stop them. The constantly accelerating modernization of our society creates ever more serious consequences in terms of problems and burdens. Elevator effects have apparently brought our society towards the top. Real enhancement in prosperity, however, has shifted a physical minimizing of existence into the distance. Nevertheless, social inequality remains the central problem to the further development of our society.

Modern societies are split. The image of the one-third/two-thirds society might be exaggerated. On the tide of contemporary efforts to create a new social policy, this instance is becoming more appropriate day by day.

Let us take a closer look at those who are separated from the majority in our split society. First of all there are millions of unemployed amidst an economic boom, with, consequently, record numbers dependent on social security. In the USA and Europe millions of people are living at the fringes of subsistence. Today's poverty is the poverty of the unemployed, of old people, of those in need of care, of those in debt, of foreigners and single mothers. In terms of income distribution it is becoming ever more evident that those in the lower third of private households receive an ever-decreasing income. The middle third has 25 per cent of total income at its disposal, but the upper third more than 60 per cent. At the same time the profits of independent enterprises continue to increase, having risen four times as much as take-home salaries. The disposable income of self-employed households was four times as much as the disposable income of employee households in the 1990s. These figures make it clear that it is time to talk about social injustice in modern societies.

Yet official sports politics much too rarely takes note of this fact. Sport has come to an arrangement with the mainstream of society. It is on the side of those that follow market logic. It is not surprising, however, that critics see it as a driving force for social injustice.

Sport's Political Challenges

What could be the necessary consequences for future sports policies? To what should sport pay attention, if it also wants to be successful in socio-political terms?

The differentiation of sport systems not only changes what sport clubs offer, in the first place it produces a creeping adaptation. Therefore our thesis is: *The organizations that offer sport in our society are becoming more and more similar.* This is true in respect to their form of organization as well as to their content and offers. This becomes clear if clubs are compared with other clubs or subjected to a comparison with commercial suppliers and with municipal and federal sports organizations.

Sports associations and sports clubs were formerly characterized by offering their members a range of sports that had often grown out of different ideologies and because of contrasting sense orientations. Now these differences have been minimized and the adaptation processes in sports organizations in particular have led to an increasing convergence of policy and purpose among sports clubs and commercial suppliers and businesses. The reason for this development is, in the first place, an expansion of sports supply as well as an addition of new sportive services. The process of adaptation is a process in which the clubs primarily adopt the ideas and objects of their supposed competitors. These are partly copies of the new sport patterns that have been developed by the free sports market or in the municipal and federal field.

Conclusions

In the long term, democracies cannot flourish without the feeling of solidarity, without our willingness to put others again and again into a position that is more or less equal to our own, even though this may cost us a share of our own personal prosperity. First the perception of a common nature disappears, then – because we do not recognize ourselves in others any more – the active participation in their fate and finally the desire to be equal among equals is also diminished. Today therefore the question arises as to whether the historical compromise of capitalism and democracy could fail exactly at the moment when the alliance between capitalism and history seems to be complete.

Accordingly it is an open question as to whether modern societies increasingly lose their social and political cohesion and whether their social assets decline. The latter are distinguished by the social networks and the relationships that exist among people. These assets are an important resource for each individual and guarantee social cohesion. Various networks are to be contemplated. Family and friendship or other networks are equally part of them, as is the integration of the individual into associations and clubs. Voluntary unions especially can support the social and political integration of the community as they enable participation in social and political life. Hence the extent to which members of society can take part in social and political life by means of membership in such organizations is important for the evaluation of a society's quality.

Social networks are of central importance for the psychosocial well being of man. Sports can be considered as social networks, often providing emotional support, assisting in the growth of self-esteem and in offering practical daily help. In the future it will therefore be primarily a question of whether sports organizations are open to this experience. Bourdieu talks about our social capital in this context. A part of this will be that the sports club or venue is seen as a place like home. It has to be a place of successful communication and socialization as well as a protest against a uniform world. All this does not come by itself, but has to be worked hard for and be proven daily. There are conclusive findings showing that the availability and quality of support from our own network of relationships are decisive in how well we cope with our problems. Social networks form a kind of escort among social dangers – they can be viewed as social cushions. However, the socio-economically underprivileged and socially marginalized groups have particular deficits in the stability of their networks. They are especially not able to work on relationships in initiatives of their own. The St Matthew effect operates: 'For the man who has will be given more, till he has enough and to spare; and the man who has not will forfeit even what he has.' Those in our society who have more disposable income today and have more education will not only have more helpers, but also more contact partners. Hence those who have greater financial means and more knowledge will also have more helpers in their hour of need and more contacts in everyday life. Therefore socio-political programmes to promote networks are indispensable. Sport must be judged by whether it contributes anything to this matter. It is important to promote more tolerance, patience and readiness for sharing. In the interest of socially balanced development we have to have a particular interest in the readiness and ability of our citizens for integration and the social institutions in charge. Sport is called upon to contribute its share.

Notes

[1] Digel, 'Die Versportlichung'.
[2] Robertson, 'Szenarien für Lebensweisen und Gesundheit'.
[3] Beck, *Risikogesellschaft*.
[4] Beck, 'Jenseits von Frauen- und Männerrolle'.
[5] Digel, 'Sports in a Risk Society'.
[6] Keupp, 'Riskante Chancen'.

References

Beck, Ulrich. *Risikogesellschaft. Auf dem Weg in eine andere Moderne* ['Risk Society. On the way to a Modern Spirit]. Frankfurt am Main: Suhrkamp, 1986.

Beck, Ulrich. 'Jenseits von Frauen- und Männerrolle oder: die Zukunft der Familie' ['Beyond the role of women and men']. *Universitas* 46 (1991): n.p.

Bourdieu, Pierre. *Die Feinea Unterschiede: Kiritik der Gesellschaftlichen Urteilskraft*. Frankfurt am Main: Suhrkamp, 1982.

Digel, Helmut. 'Die Versportlichung unserer Kultur und deren Folgen für den Sport – ein Beitrag zur Uneigentlichkeit des Sports'. In *Für einen besseren Sport. Themen, Entwicklungen und Perspektiven aus Sport und Sportwissenschaft*, edited by H. Gabler and U. Göhner. Schorndorf: Hofmann, 1990: 73–96.

Digel, Helmut. 'Sports in a Risk Society'. *International Review for the Sociology of Sport* 27 (3) (1992): 257–73.

Digel, Helmut. *Sport in a Changing Society. Sociological Essays*. Schorndorf, 1995.

Keupp, Heiner. 'Riskante Chancen. Das Subjekt im gesellschaftlichen Wandel' ['Chancy risks. The subject in the change of society']. *Universitas* 45 (1990): n.p.

Robertson, J. 'Szenarien für Lebensweisen und Gesundheit' ['Scenarios for lifestyle and health']. In *Gesundheitsförderung in der Arbeitswelt. Beiträge einer internationalen Tagung in Köln vom 07. bis 10. Oktober 1985*, edited by Bundeszentrale für gesundheitliche Aufklärung. Berlin: Springer, 1989: 227–48.

Epilogue: Showcases for Global Aspirations: Meditations on the Histories of Olympic Games and World's Fairs

Mark Dyreson

In 1851, nearly half a century before the modern Olympic movement sprouted on the global stage, what was then the world's most powerful nation hosted the 'Great Exhibition of the Works of Industry of All Nations', the inaugural world's fair in modern history. At the proto-mega-event, Europe's aristocrats and techno-industrial elites mingled amidst a phantasmagoric display of the products of the Industrial Revolution, the power of the British Empire, and the signs of a high tide of global Occidentalism. Literary luminaries and scientific sages traipsed through the exhibits, including Charles Darwin and Charlotte Brontë. [1] Overwhelmed by the grand scale of the exposition Brontë marvelled at the scene: 'It is a wonderful place – vast, strange, new and impossible to describe.' [2]

Brontë's observations captured the sentiments of several generations of modern voyeurs of world's fairs, dazzling homages to Western progress that enchanted popular fancy for nearly a century following London's inaugural exposition. World's fairs challenged the imaginations of even the most intellectually gifted moderns such as Brontë with vistas so novel, so limitless, so extraordinary that they seemed impossible to capture in the language of literary convention. [3] Through the early twentieth century the global expositions stood as the featured world stages for showcasing the aspirations of individuals, corporations, collectives and nations. Then, with shocking suddenness, they dwindled into insignificance, leaving behind only memories and the palest of imitations. [4]

In 2012 Yeosu, South Korea, will hold a world's fair but few beyond the city's borders will know or care. [5] The world will ignore Yeosu's 2012 exposition as they ignored Shanghai's 2010 Chinese extravaganza. [6] Indeed, the globe has paid little heed to any of the world's fairs since the middle of the twentieth century. On the ruins of the world's fairs emerged a new global stage for exhibiting aspirations and garnering the attention of billions of spectators, every bit as vast, strange, new and difficult to describe. Significantly, this new stage first sprouted at the very expositions they replaced. [7] The seeds of the modern Olympic movement sprang to life at an educational summit in the shadow of the brand-new Eiffel Tower in Paris. Both the spire and the meeting grew up from the acreage spanned by the 1889 *Exposition Universelle*. The history of the early Olympics and the history of international expositions were firmly intertwined. [8]

In 2012, this now robust Olympian offspring of the nearly extinct world's fair movement will return to London for a third British engagement. Unlike its first London run, when the Olympics found a home alongside the 1908 Franco-British Exposition, the 2012 London Olympics will not have any direct connection to a fair. Still, Charlotte Brontë would surely recognize London's 2012 Olympics as part of the same species as London's 1851 exposition, if human lifespans would permit such observations. At the 2012 games in London the global media, the world's aristocrats and techno-post-industrial elites along with, if not literary luminaries and scientific sages then at least the transient celebrities of the postmodern moment, will traipse through the Olympic 'exhibits' captured on television and YouTube posts in cyberspace.

The Olympic movement has surpassed the world's fair movement as the premium site for the expression and advertisement of a great variety of aspirations to the globe's teeming masses. This outcome was not easily predictable. Indeed, who in the second half of the nineteenth century or the first half of the twentieth century would have imagined such a dramatic reversal of fortunes as the fall of the great exhibitions and the rise Olympian spectacles? Not even Baron Pierre de Coubertin, who cleverly pilfered structures and concepts from the exhibitions for his one-off mega-events, from the scheme to rotate spectacles around the great capitals of the world to the dream of pacific cosmopolitanism springing from mere attendance to the energetic competitive nationalism that formed the very heartbeat of both fairs and Olympics, predicted this outcome. [9] Though de Coubertin heralded the rise of the new and the athletic he did not foresee the collapse of the old and industrial and never dreamed that the Olympics would ultimately replace the fairs. Certainly no one who witnessed the brief hint of the coming power of international sport at London in 1851, the staging of one of the original America's Cup yacht races as part of the 'Great Exhibition', [10] would have imagined that in the next century fascination with the displays in grand halls of the most beautiful and fastest machines would have crumbled while fascination with the exhibits in vast stadiums of the most beautiful and fastest bodies would have triumphed.

What led to this dramatic reversal of fortunes? Curiously, the very cult of technological progress that gave birth to the fairs helped to slay them, a mechanistic Oedipal saga layered with ironies. Among many factors, a new electronic communication medium that appeared in the middle of the twentieth century, television, had a great deal to with the turnabout. Television eroded the power of the world's exhibitions by beaming Brontë's 'vast, strange, new and impossible to describe' scenes into private spheres, eroding the necessity for enormous and costly public displays at the world's fairs. At the same time, television vastly multiplied the power of the Olympics by broadcasting the 'vast, strange, new, and impossible to describe' actions of human dynamos at the outer limits of human possibilities into those very same private spheres. Indeed, television's pictures captured the spectacle with a clarity that literature had long struggled to achieve. [11]

Significantly, at the very historic moment at which the Olympics began to transcend the expositions – if one accepts the common historical interpretation that Berlin in 1936 represents the first Olympics that blossomed as a global mega-event and New York City in 1939 represents the last great fair [12] – television made its Olympic debut. Nazi Germany beamed closed-circuit television images of the Berlin games to several cities. From that point forward, after the calamity of the Second World War temporarily halted both world's fairs and Olympic Games, television simultaneously strangled the expositions and fertilized the Olympics. The location for the global display and consumption of aspirations moved dramatically from the halls teeming with cutting-edge machines to the stadiums teeming with finally-tuned athletic geniuses. [13]

One of Charlotte Brontë's American colleagues, the novelist Henry Adams, predicted in a pre-television era the shift in focus from the fabricated machine to the human mechanism after observing both an exposition and an Olympic Games. At the great 1900 exposition in *fin de siècle* Paris celebrating the beginning of the third millennium, Adams crafted his masterful essay charting the distance from the Virgin to the dynamo, the gulf between the forces that shaped the traditional world encapsulated in the Gothic edifice at Chartres Cathedral and the modern world signified by the energies generated by the humming electric dynamo at the centre of the Paris fair. If the Virgin and the dynamo marked past and present, the human dynamos sprinting and leaping at the 1900 Olympics, an adjunct of the Paris fair, represented for Adams the future. In the athletes he contemplated after his meditations on the Virgin and the dynamo, Adams speculated that he had glimpsed the next bend in the curve of the history, the control of human energies signalled by the discipline required of Olympic champions. [14]

Adams anticipated the shift in the projection of dreams on global stages from machines to flesh-and-blood dynamos, a theme *Olympic Aspirations* develops along a variety of fronts, including an insightful analysis of the links between the fairs and the games. [15] The athletes themselves have used the Olympics to promote their aspirations, especially the standard desires for global stardom epitomized by recent champions such as Michael Phelps, Usian Bolt and Shaun White. [16] Sometimes Olympic athletes manifested more profound aspirations, such as in 1936 in Berlin where the so-called 'black auxiliaries' on the US Olympic team, the African American stars led by Jesse Owens, struggled to overturn national and international stereotypes of black inferiority. As the later lives of Owens's black teammates revealed, the African American Olympians felt compelled to showcase racial abilities not only in athletics but in education, politics, business and every other field of human endeavour. The Olympics launched the 'black auxiliaries' on a lifetime of quests to highlight the aspirations of their race. [17] Likewise, Muslim women at the Olympics in a more recent epoch have challenged a variety of stereotypes that have emerged both in the Islamic world and beyond. Their aspirations have become a featured storyline in contemporary narratives of the Olympic movement's second century. [18]

Cities, regions, and nations have also played the aspiration game at the Olympics. [19] As J.A. Mangan notes in his prologue, this volume was 'born in Beijing', site in 2008 of one of most audacious efforts in Olympic history to project national dreams for inclusion as a world power of the first rank. [20] In 1851 Charles Dickens developed a sketch based on the national exhibits at the London fair of Great Britain as the world's most progressive nation and China at the globe's least progressive nation. The great English-language chronicler of *Pax Britannica* cranked out a tale of two civilizations, smugly congratulating Britain for its 'great' exhibition while dismissing China's 'little' dreams. [21] A bit more than a century and half later, the Chinese responded to Dickens and his myriad of Occidental fellow-travellers. At the 2008 Beijing Olympics the Chinese asserted that while they maintained a kinship with their ancient traditions they had arrived at the very core of progress by every 'standard' measure, from economic power to athletic prowess. [22]

How ironic that in the span of 157 years China's economic and athletic dreams, as symbolized by the Beijing games, have grown immense, while Great Britain's have become, if not 'little', then less immense than they were in the age of Dickens. In a whimsical irony of the sort that the International Olympic Committee (IOC) regularly if unconsciously bestows on the world with its scheduling decisions (recall, for example the choice of Berlin to host the 1916 games or Tokyo to host the 1940 games), the Olympics will move from China back to Britain for their 2012 episode. J.A. Mangan counsels cautious optimism about British aspirations to create a post-industrial fantasy 'island of dreams' at the 2012 London Olympics. Mangan cleverly skewers notions that an Olympic games or any other mega-event might improve the economic or social health of any nation, let alone one so concerned and so convinced that it is in grave danger of slipping from the core to the periphery of the world system. [23]

Around the former periphery of the old modern world system a broad spectrum of new cities, emboldened by China's spectacular 2008 production, has begun to cast Olympic bids to showcase their aspirations to globe's consumers. For the first time in history, the Olympics will venture to South America, as Rio de Janeiro won the battle to host the 2016 games. A global struggle to host the 2020 Olympics has now emerged with a radically different cast of cities bidding than in the past. Gone are the dark days of the 1980s when the Olympics were widely perceived as financial and social albatrosses and the number of bidders dwindled to just one, as in the case of the 1984 games when Tehran dropped out after the 1979 Islamic revolution and left Los Angeles as the only remaining candidate. [24]

At least 30 cities have launched exploratory probes to the test the waters for hosting the 2020 Olympics. In the wake of staging the 2010 World Cup football tournament, several South African cities have begun to jockey to make a bid for the 2020 Olympics. South Africa stands as the sentimental front-runner in the 2020 contest, but it is hardly the only novel capital considering a pitch. Several Muslim nations have expressed serious interest in acquiring the Olympics, including Turkey (Istanbul), Morocco (Rabat), Qatar (Doha) and the United Arab Emirates (Dubai). With the Cold War and the Iron Curtain fading memories, the re-emerging capitals of Eastern Europe also covet an Olympics as a venue for reintroducing themselves to the world. St Petersburg (Russia), Bucharest (Romania) and Budapest (Hungary) have begun preparations for 2020 bids. Like London in 2012, several once-thriving cities at the heart of the old world system, Rome, Madrid, Lisbon and Paris, are pondering 2020 Olympic quests. The Asian 'tigers' of the new world system also have Olympic dreams, including Busan, South Korea. Even New Delhi has made noises about launching a campaign to win a first Olympics for the Indian subcontinent. From the ageing 'tiger' of Japan comes news of a quixotic bid from Hiroshima. The Hiroshima bid committee has promised a 'peace'-themed Olympics scheduled to start on 6 August 2020, the 75th anniversary of world's first atomic bombing. [25]

Meanwhile, the nation that since 1945 has resided at the centre of the new world system, the United States, bides its time. The United States Olympic Committee (USOC) has expensive and extensive plans in the works to recapture the gold-medal lead from China in London as well as to extend its lead in the overall medal count. The deeply ingrained American tradition of using the Olympic games to tout American exceptionalism to the world requires spending portions of the national fortune to ensure global dominion. [26] Meanwhile, in the reigning world capital of American-style global culture, California, Shaun White continues to skateboard as well as to snowboard. The IOC continues to look for ways to 'Californicate' London 2012 by squeezing skateboarding onto the Olympic programme, providing an opportunity for the postmodern poster boy of American Olympic aspirations to cross-pollinate his 'brand' at the summer games after repeating his gold-medal performance at the 2010 Olympic Winter Games in Vancouver. [27]

From the *Los Angeles Times* Olympic blog comes word that the USOC might well sit out the bidding war for the 2020 games in an effort to avoid a repeat of the debacle surrounding the 2016 bid of Chicago for the Olympics. [28] That leak has poured blood into the American bidding waters, creating a chum that will attract the perpetually swimming sharks of southern California's never-ending campaign to host the Olympics. The veteran California Olympic boosters are no doubt planning to swallow Chicago, Dallas, Minneapolis, Tulsa and any other US pretenders by targeting a post-2020 date to bring a third Olympic spectacle to Los Angeles. [29] With London setting a precedent that a city can host thrice, shrewd bettors should wager against Los Angeles at their own peril.

As the Olympic movement's second century proceeds, there seems no chance that the global exposition movement will reclaim its former position as the most important global stage for the projection of aspirations. While the award of the 2016 Olympics to Brazil has been widely hailed as a step towards a more inclusive future, the award of the 2015 world's fair to Milan, Italy, has been greeted with widespread indifference. [30] Might the Olympics follow the same historical course as the fairs and suddenly lose their role as the global nexus for the expression of modern aspirations to some other venue? Though that seems unlikely, it is not outside the realm of possibilities. Perhaps the extreme sports that now dominate the IOC's admission of new activities to the programme will take over the Olympics and transform them into a mega-made-for-television event, a super 'X Games'. Perhaps the pseudo-sports of the new generation of computer games will switch the locus of global aspirational culture from flesh-and-blood athletes to pixillated simulacra. Until such popular fictions become realities, however, the Olympics will remain prime venues for the expression of international aspirations. Rest assured, or uneasy, however, that someone somewhere in California has new aspirations that might change the Olympic future.

Notes

[1] Auerbach, *The Great Exhibition of 1851*; Leapman, *The World for a Shilling*; Buzard et al., *Victorian Prism*; Young, *Globalization and the Great Exhibition*; Auerbach and Hoffenberg. *Britain, the Empire, and the World.*

[2] Shorter, *The Brontës:*.

[3] For a classic expression of intellectual bedazzlement at the fairs see Adams, *The Education of Henry Adams.*

[4] Allwood, *The Great Exhibitions.* Greenhalgh, *Ephemeral Vistas*; Rydell, *World of Fairs*; Findling and Pelle. *Historical Dictionary of World's Fairs and Expositions.*

[5] The website of the Yeosu fair provides a fascinating tour. See http://www.expo2012.or.kr/eng/main.asp, accessed 20 Sept. 2010.

[6] The website for the Shanghai exposition promoting 'Better City, Better Life' can be found at http://en.expo2010.cn/, accessed 20 Sept. 2010.

[7] For a fascinating analysis that tackles both the expositions and the Olympics as global 'mega-events' see Roche, *Mega-Events and Modernity.*

[8] MacAloon, *This Great Symbol.*

[9] For links between the Olympic movement and the exposition movement see Roche, *Mega-Events and Modernity* and MacAloon, *This Great Symbol.*

[10] Auerbach, *The Great Exhibition of 1851.*

[11] For a more complete development of this argument see Dyreson, '"To Construct a Better and More Peaceful World"'

[12] Mandell, *The Nazi Olympics*; Large, *Nazi Games*; Mauro, *Twilight at the World of Tomorrow*; Zim et al., *The World of Tomorrow*; Roche, *Mega-Events and Modernity.*

[13] Dyreson, '"To Construct a Better and More Peaceful World"'.

[14] Adams, 'The Dynamo and the Virgin', in *The Education of Henry Adams*, 379–90; Dyreson, *Making the American Team.*

[15] Paradis, 'Manly Displays', in this issue.

[16] Dyreson, *Crafting Patriotism for Global Domination*; Dyreson, 'Crafting Patriotism – Meditations on "Californication"'; Dyreson, 'Johnny Weissmuller and the Old Global Capitalism'; Dyreson, 'Marketing Weissmuller to the World'.

[17] Gleaves and Dyreson, 'The "Black Auxiliaries" in American Memories', in this issue.

[18] Pfister, 'Outsiders: Muslim Women and Olympic Games'.

[19] See Roult and Lefebre, 'Planning and Reconversion of Olympics' Heritages'; Brewster, 'Mexico City 1968'; Toohey, 'Post-Sydney 2000'; Kissoudi, 'Athens' Post-Olympic Aspirations and the Extent of their Realization', all in this issue.

[20] Mangan, 'Prologue', in this issue.

[21] Dickens and Horne, 'The Great Exhibition and the Little One'.

[22] Brownell, *Beijing's Games*; Xu Guoqi, *Olympic Dreams*. For additional perspectives see Dong Jinxia, 'The Beijing Games'; Ying Yu, 'Olympic Aspirations'; Juan Zhuang, 'Beijing 2008'; Syed, 'The Effect of Beijing 2008 on China's Image in the United States'; and Close, 'Olympiads as Mega-Events and the Pace of Globalization', all in this issue.

[23] Mangan, 'Prologue'; Horton and Zakus, 'How Green will my (Lea) Valley Be?'; and Macrury and Poynter, '"Team GB" and London 2012', all in this issue. For broader perspectives on the 'fall' of Great Britain from global hegemony, among the most erudite in the vast library of British decline studies is Ferguson, *The Empire*.

[24] Dyreson, 'The Endless Olympic Bid'; Dyreson and Llewellyn, 'Los Angeles Is the Olympic City.'

[25] The worldwide web has an entire site devoted solely to Olympic bid news: see http://www.gamesbids.com/eng/, accessed 23 Sept. 2010. The postmodern version of the old *Encyclopaedia Britannica*, wikipedia, has extensive information on the quest to win the 2020 Olympics: http://en.wikipedia.org/wiki/2020_Summer_Olympics, accessed 15 Sept. 2010. An excellent analysis of this trend can be found in this issue: Cornelissen, 'The Geopolitics of Global Aspiration'.

[26] Dyreson, *Crafting Patriotism for Global Domination*; Dyreson, 'Reading American Readings of the Beijing Olympics'; Dyreson, 'Preparing to Take Credit for China's Glory'.

[27] Reporting from the July 2010 meeting of the IOC in Guatemala City, Guatemala, Reuters news service revealed that the IOC wants to increase interest in the London games by 'squeezing' skateboarding onto the programme through the ruse of making it a new cycling 'discipline' since the deadline for adding new 'sports' has already passed. See http://uk.reuters.com/article/idUKMOL43678820070704, accessed 23 Sept. 2010.

[28] See http://latimesblogs.latimes.com/olympics_blog/2016-olympic-bids/, accessed 23 Sept. 2010.

[29] Helene Elliott, 'LA Olympic Leader Finds a New Purpose', *Los Angeles Times*, 13 April 2007; Bill Dwyre, 'Olympic Games', *Los Angeles Times*, 2 March 2010.

[30] For the official website of the Milan exposition see http://www.expo2015.org/?&lin=2, accessed 23 September 2010.

References

Adams, Henry. *The Education of Henry Adams*. Boston, MA: Massachusetts Historical Association, 1918.

Allwood, John. *The Great Exhibitions*. London: Studio Vista, 1977.

Auerbach, Jeffrey A. *The Great Exhibition of 1851: A Nation on Display*. New Haven, CT: Yale University Press, 1999.

Auerbach, Jeffrey A., and Peter H. Hoffenberg. *Britain, The Empire, and the World at the Great Exhibition of 1851*. Aldershot: Ashgate, 2008.

Brownell, Susan. *Beijing's Games: What the Olympics Mean to China*. Lanham, MD: Rowman & Littlefield, 2008.

Buzard, James, Joseph W Childers and Eileen Gillooly. *Victorian Prism: Refractions of the Crystal Palace*. Charlottesville, VA: University of Virginia Press, 2007.

Dyreson, Mark. *Making the American Team: Sport, Culture and the Olympic Experience*. Urbana: University of Illinois Press, 1998.

Dyreson, Mark. "'To Construct a Better and More Peaceful World" or "War Minus the Shooting"?: The Olympic Movement's Second Century'. In *Onward to the Olympics: Historical Perspectives on the Olympic Games*, edited by Gerald P. Schaus and Stephen R. Wenn. Waterloo, ON: Wilfrid Laurier University Press, 2007: 337–51.

Dyreson, Mark. *Crafting Patriotism for Global Domination: America at the Olympics*. London: Routledge, 2008.

Dyreson, Mark. 'Crafting Patriotism-Meditations on "Californication" and other Trends'. *International Journal of the History of Sport* 25 (Feb. 2008): 307–311.

Dyreson, Mark. 'Johnny Weissmuller and the Old Global Capitalism: The Origins of the Federal Blueprint for Selling American Culture to the World'. *International Journal of the History of Sport* 25 (Feb. 2008): 268–83.

Dyreson, Mark. 'Marketing Weissmuller to the World: Hollywood's Olympics and Federal Schemes for Americanization through Sport'. *International Journal of the History of Sport* 25 (Feb. 2008): 284–306.

Dyreson, Mark. 'Preparing to Take Credit for China's Glory: American Perspectives on the Beijing Olympic Games'. *International Journal of the History of Sport* 25 (June 2008): 915–34.

Dyreson, Mark. 'The Endless Olympic Bid: Los Angeles and the Advertisement of the American West'. *Journal of the West* 47 (fall 2008): 26–39.

Dyreson, Mark. 'Reading American Readings of the Beijing Olympics'. *International Journal of the History of Sport* 27 (14–15 2010): 2510–2529.

Dyreson, Mark and Matthew Llewellyn. "Los Angeles Is *the* Olympic City: Legacies of 1932 and 1984". *International Journal of the History of Sport* 25 (Dec. 2008): 1991–2018.

Ferguson, Niall. *The Empire: The Rise and Demise of the British World Order and the Lessons for Global Power*. New York: Basic Books, 2003.

Findling, John E. and Kimberly D. Pelle. *Historical Dictionary of World's Fairs and Expositions, 1851–1988*. New York: Greenwood Press, 1990.

Greenhalgh, Paul. *Ephemeral Vistas: The Expositions Universelles, Great Exhibitions and World's Fairs, 1851–1939*. Manchester: Manchester University Press, 1988.

Large, David Clay. *Nazi Games: The Olympics of 1936*. New York: W.W. Norton, 2007.

Leapman, Michael. *The World for a Shilling: How the Great Exhibition of 1851 Shaped a Nation*. London: Headline Books, 2001.

MacAloon, John J. *This Great Symbol: Pierre de Coubertin and the Origins of the Modern Olympics*. London: Routledge, 2007.

Mandell, Richard. *The Nazi Olympics*. New York: Macmillan, 1971.

Mauro, James. *Twilight at the World of Tomorrow: Genius, Madness, Murder, and the 1939 World's Fair on the Brink of War*. New York: Ballantine, 2010.

Roche, Maurice. *Mega-Events and Modernity: Olympics and Expos in the Growth of Global Culture*. London: Routledge, 2000.

Rydell, Robert. *World of Fairs: The Century-of-Progress Expositions*. Chicago: University of Chicago Press, 1993.

Shorter, Clement King, ed. *The Brontës: Life and Letters*. London: Hodder & Stoughton, 1908.

Xu, Guoqi. *Olympic Dreams: China and Sports, 1895–2008*. Cambridge, MA: Harvard University Press, 2008.

Young, Paul. *Globalization and the Great Exhibition: The Victorian New World Order*. New York: Palgrave Macmillan, 2009.

Zim, Larry, Mel Lerner and Herbert Rolfes. *The World of Tomorrow: The 1939 New York World's Fair*. New York: Harper & Row, 1988.

Index

Page numbers in *Italics* represent tables.
Page numbers in **Bold** represent figures.
Page numbers followed by n represent endnotes.